VOICES

**SIGNIFICANT SPEECHES
IN
AMERICAN HISTORY**

1640-1945

Developed under the advisory editorship of
Beverly Long University of North Carolina at Chapel Hill

AMERICAN VOICES

SIGNIFICANT SPEECHES IN AMERICAN HISTORY

1640-1945

JAMES ANDREWS
Indiana University

DAVID ZAREFSKY
Northwestern University

Longman
New York & London

American Voices: Significant Speeches in American History, 1640–1945

Longman Inc., 95 Church Street, White Plains, N.Y. 10601

Associated companies:
Longman Group Ltd., London
Longman Cheshire Pty., Melbourne
Longman Paul Pty., Auckland
Copp Clark Pitman, Toronto
Pitman Publishing Inc., New York

Executive editor: Gordon T. R. Anderson
Production editor: Dee Amir Josephson
Text design: Dee Amir Josephson
Cover design: Jill Francis Wood
Production supervisor: Kathleen Ryan

Library of Congress Cataloging in Publication Data

American voices : significant speeches in American history, 1640–1945
[edited by] James R. Andrews. David Zarefsky.
p. cm.
Bibliography: p.
ISBN 0-8013-0217-X
1. United States—History—Sources. 2. United States—Politics and government—Sources. 3. Speeches, addresses, etc., American. I. Andrews, James Robertson, 1936- . II. Zarefsky, David.
E173.A7596 1989
973—dc19

88-21010
CIP

ISBN 0-8013-0217-X

93 92 91 90 89 88 0 9 8 7 6 5 4 3 2 1

CONTENTS

ALTERNATE TABLES OF CONTENTS

The principal Table of Contents lists speeches in an approximate chronological order, grouping them according to periods in American history. Speeches may also be read and studied according to their primary purposes—the responses desired from the audience. The first alternate Table of Contents, "Speeches Listed According to Purposes," *identifies three primary purposes: speeches that attempt to influence beliefs and attitudes, speeches that are meant to inspire or to reinforce existing beliefs held by the audience, and speeches that are directly related to a specific issue or political campaign and are therefore designed to produce specific action. The purposes of these speeches will, to some extent, overlap, and some speeches may incorporate elements of all these purposes. We have tried to group the speeches according to what would seem to be the principal goal of the speaker given the audience and context.*

Speeches could also be arranged from the perspective of the setting or circumstances which brought them about. The second alternate Table of Contents, "Speeches Listed According to Settings, Circumstances," *lists courtroom speeches; sermons, commemorative and ceremonial speeches, and inaugural addresses; legislative speeches and addresses; political, campaign speeches; lectures and invited addresses; speeches at public meetings; and speeches on public policy and values addressed to a wide audience.*

Speeches Listed According to Purposes

SPEECHES TO INFLUENCE BELIEFS AND ATTITUDES

SPEECHES TO INSPIRE, REINFORCE AUDIENCE VALUES

SPEECHES TO PRODUCE SPECIFIC ACTION

SPEECHES LISTED ACCORDING TO SETTINGS, CIRCUMSTANCES

COURTROOM SPEECHES

SERMONS, COMMEMORATIVE AND CEREMONIAL SPEECHES, INAUGURAL ADDRESSES

LEGISLATIVE SPEECHES AND ADDRESSES

POLITICAL, CAMPAIGN SPEECHES

LECTURES AND INVITED ADDRESSES

SPEECHES AT PUBLIC MEETINGS

SPEECHES ON PUBLIC POLITY AND VALUES ADDRESSED TO A WIDE AUDIENCE

PREFACE

This book represents an effort to make available to students of public address and public speaking, as well as students of American history and culture, a significant sample of speeches that demonstrate the ways in which men and women have come to grips with the thorny political and social issues that have permeated our history. American voices have been raised to support or denounce causes, to implore action, to shape beliefs and values. What these speakers have said and the ways in which they have designed their messages, afford the critic, the historian of rhetoric, and the student of the American experience, as well as those who would themselves speak out on significant matters, the raw material for serious investigation of the communication process in action. "If truth were self-evident," Cicero observed, "eloquence would not be necessary." Since truth is not always evident, and in a society where the people are considered the final judges, persuasive efforts to shape perceptions of the truth will always have a profound influence on decision making and action. No one would argue that any one of the speeches in this volume can be proven to have caused measurable direct effects on a given audience; nevertheless, they do offer a panorama of our history from the point of view of those who tried, with varying degrees of success, to shape it.

Selecting speeches for a volume of this kind is always difficult. It is inevitable that there will be speeches omitted that some teachers and scholars would have unquestionably included, and some speeches will appear here that others would not have chosen. We hope, however, that our selection will give the student a fair and broad sample of important discourse on important issues by articulate spokespersons.

We have arranged the speeches in a generally chronological manner and offered alternative tables of contents for those who would like to approach the study of this material in a different way. We have not sought to prescribe a particular method of analysis or criticism, believing instead that the texts should encourage many approaches. Our introductions to the speeches are aimed at providing the reader with information, in an abbreviated form, that is essential to understanding how the speech fits into an historical and rhetorical context. The Appendix provides some specific information about each speaker and directs the reader to other useful sources.

The authors wish to acknowledge their debt to those who provided assistance in preparing this book, particularly in the tedious tasks associated with finding and verifying texts: Ann Burnette, Michelle Howard, James Kauffman, Trevor Parry-Giles, and Steven Pullum. Helen Harrell was especially helpful in typing and reproducing material and in preparing the manuscript.

James R. Andrews
David Zarefsky

Introduction: The Study of Significant Speeches

UNDERSTANDING OUR PAST

The universe in which we live is a universe of words. Much of what we know, or think we know, we have learned through the words of others. Those men and women who have attempted to lead or to prod, to inspire or to intimidate, to defend values or attack conventions, have done so by using language to shape the actions and reactions of those who would listen.

People living together in civilized communities gradually rely less and less on brute force to direct communal efforts and action. They learn instead to employ rhetoric—the process of selecting, structuring, and adapting language in order to persuade others—to promote social goals. Throughout our history, Americans have tried to discern the meaning and mission of this new world. We have tried to make sense of the events going on around us and the experiences we have shared. We interpret the past, explain the present, and envision the future through language. This language is fashioned into messages designed to shape our perceptions, alter or reinforce our beliefs, and direct our actions.

A people without a sense of their past are like a person with amnesia. They do not know where they have been or how they got where they are, and they are likely to be confused about where they are going next. The speeches selected for inclusion in this volume are but a sample of the messages that form a part of our collective past. They help to give us a sense of how our values and goals have been formed and refined. They open for us a series of windows in history that demonstrate the clashes and the compromises, the struggles to give concrete meaning to abstract ideas and ideals, the successes and failures experienced by those who would lead us.

We can see, for example, the relationships between liberty and authority as the arguments of Winthrop and Boucher are pitted against those of Williams and Samuel Adams, as Hamilton and Phillips strive for freedom of the press against arbitrary interference, or as Henry and Madison debate the nature of ordered government. Thomas Jefferson, in his Inaugural Address, lays out the foundations of democratic government, and Daniel Webster celebrates the American experience at Bunker Hill. As Sagoyewatha repudiates cultural arrogance, as Sojourner Truth and Susan B. Anthony demand equality for women and Frederick Douglass for blacks, the nation is challenged to "live out the true meaning of its creed," as Martin Luther King once put it. Efforts to preserve the great political union that had been forged through revolution while also preserving basic values may be seen in the compromising attempts of Webster and Clay and in the collision of ideas in the speeches of Calhoun, Lincoln, Douglas, and Davis. Personal and societal responsibility for the welfare of all Americans is viewed differently by Henry George and Russell Conwell, and by Eugene Debs, who proclaims his "kinship with all human beings" in declaring that "while there is a lower class, I am in it; while there is a criminal element, I am of it; while there is a soul in prison, I am not free." And the ways in which social responsibility may be translated into action are articulated by Franklin Roosevelt, Huey Long, John L. Lewis, and William Allen White. The role of the emerging American colossus on the world stage is portrayed through the views of Beveridge and Theodore Roosevelt competing with Bryan and Wilson, and finds expression again before World War II in the words of Franklin Roosevelt, Charles Lindbergh, and Wendell Willkie.

The careful study of speeches of the past teaches us that rhetorical success is usually not total, nor is it immediate, nor does it result in the ultimate and final solution to problems. Public discourse is a part of the continuous process of promoting and accommodating to change.

Understanding this process helps us to understand and judge our present values and contemplated actions in the light of our own past. Studying the process can do more, however. As we study significant speeches, we can also begin to learn and appreciate how rhetoric has been employed as ideas are sifted and sorted in the eternal search for what is best. In short, the study of speeches can enhance our own ability to respond critically to persuasion.

RESPONDING CRITICALLY

Rhetorical criticism, like any other intellectual discipline, can be approached from a variety of perspectives, and, again as with any other intellectual discipline, its practitioners develop sophistication and the appreciation for subtleties and nuances as they mature. Nevertheless, it is possible for the beginning student of public discourse to approach the study of speeches critically by cultivating a critical attitude and by learning to examine carefully and systematically those basic elements that are invariably present in a speaking situation.

What is a "critical attitude"? In common thinking, we tend to equate someone who is "critical" with one who complains, finds fault, is not satisfied with anything. That, of course, is not the kind of critical attitude to which we refer. A critical attitude is one that embraces understanding and informed judgment. In developing such an attitude, the would-be critic seeks to learn as much as can be learned about the text of the speech and the context with which that text interacts. He or she reaches judgments—judgments as to the worth of the speech, the competency of the speaker, the wisdom of recommended courses of action—only after mature reflection. Furthermore, a critical attitude disposes the critic always to be open to enlarging understanding or modifying judgments when presented with new evidence or upon viewing the evidence in a different light. The words of the 82-year-old politician and philosopher Benjamin Franklin might be as well addressed to a critic as they were to the delegates of the Constitutional Convention: ". . . having lived long, I have experienced many instances of being obliged, by better information or fuller consideration, to change opinion, even on important subject, which I once thought right, but found to be otherwise."

What factors, then, must the student investigate and understand if he or she is going to respond critically to speeches? Whatever critical method or approach one might favor, there are certain invariants in the rhetorical situation that bear scrutiny. Let us now consider those factors.

1. A Speech Is Given Within a Specific Context

Speeches are given in response to a range of events that the speaker wishes to alter or explain or influence in some way by directing the thoughts, feelings, or actions of listeners. The speech takes its meaning in the context in which it occurs, and, to understand it, one must understand that context. It is true that speeches can and do have universal appeals and implications beyond the immediate setting in which they occur. Speeches given long ago can inspire contemporary readers and can point to the values that may underlie solutions to contemporary problems. But the speakers who composed these messages found themselves faced with concrete situations, pressing problems that claimed their immediate attention. One cannot begin to appreciate how the speakers sought effectively to move audiences without understanding the situation as they viewed it, and the constraints and opportunities it presented.

It is because the situation in which rhetoric occurs is a major determinant of what will be said and how it will be said that the speeches in this volume are preceded by brief introductions that provide for the reader the broad outlines of context. How, for example, could the reader begin to understand James Otis's speech against the Writs of Assistance if he or she did not know what the Writs were, or why Boston merchants would be upset by them, or why the government would want to institute them? Relevant events surrounding the murder of Lovejoy, the content of the preceding speech, and the nature of the abolitionist movement are all contextual factors important in fostering an understanding of Wendell Phillips's message. It is essential to have some knowledge of the forces at work to divide the nation in order to understand the speeches of Clay and Webster, Socialist opposition to World War I to comprehend Debs's plea, the impact of the Great Depression to fathom Franklin Roosevelt's call to action.

In all cases, then, studying speeches in order to respond critically to them requires an understanding of the events and ideas that surround the speeches and interact with them. Ideas and events, of course, need to be made meaningful by real, living speakers who face real, living audiences to be persuaded. The questions of what motivated and influenced the speaker and what forces were at work on their audiences lead us to the next two factors that the critical reader will consider.

2. The Ethos of the Speaker Will Play a Significant Role in Determining the Effectiveness of the Speech

When an audience has trust and confidence in a speaker, when listeners respect that speaker, they are more likely to respond favorably to his or her message. Throughout the development of rhetorical theory, students of persuasion have recognized the potency of personal appeal. The classical term used to describe the force of the speaker's personality on the imagination and action of the audience is *ethos*. The early Greek and Roman theorists thought of ethos as essentially related to the character of the speaker: the proposals and policies of a good person would be likely to carry more weight with an audience than would those of one who was disreputable. As theory developed, however, scholars began to realize that the "true" nature of a man or woman might or might not be perceived by listeners. A speaker's ethical position is filtered through the screen of an audience's perception of the speaker's character or motives.

Ethos, then, is *not* synonymous with ethics. The way the audience views the character of the speaker, the audience's assessment of the speaker's intelligence, the audience's judgment of the speaker's sincerity—these are the ingredients of a speaker's ethos. It follows that ethos can be either positive or negative, depending on who is making the determination. John Brown, for example, was hated and reviled as a dangerous incendiary by many of those who heard his final words in that Virginia courtroom, but to others he was revered as a martyr whose soul went marching on. Franklin D. Roosevelt was seen as a savior by many out-of-work, desperate people suffering the agonies of poverty and hopelessness; at the same time, "that man in the White House" was bitterly resented by those who saw him as a radical demagogue, a "traitor to his class."

So, in order to understand fully the persuasive potential of any given speech, the critical student must identify the role played by the speaker's ethos, seeking to discover what assets and liabilities that speaker brings to or creates in the speaking situation. Intelligent understanding of the speech demands consideration of the extent to which and the ways in which the speaker exploits his or her ethos in the speech itself—the possible sources of influence imbedded in the speaker's identification with audiences' goals and values, and the nature of appeals made to the audence that appear to demonstrate the speaker's good judgment and sincerity.

It should be apparent—given the discussion of context and of the speaker's ethos—that an understanding of the nature of the audience is essential to an understanding of the speech: that a critical response to the speech is possible only when one has a clear comprehension of those who are the recipients of the speaker's persuasive efforts.

3. The Nature of the Audience Presents Challenges and Opportunities for the Speaker

Since the aim of any speech is to get a desired response from some audience, a knowledge of who that audience is and how the speaker takes account of the audience is basic to a full appreciation of a speech. The critic must know the specific audience to whom the speech is addressed. What do they do? Why are they gathered together? What kinds of aims do they have? People who form audiences have a variety of characteristics that are pertinent to understanding them, and the critic who wishes to reconstruct an audience for a speech needs to focus on those elements that make a difference in the rhetorical situation. When Wendell Phillips, for example addressed a public meeting in Faneuil Hall in Boston, the fact that his audience was made up of Bostonians proud of their Revolutionary heritage was a crucial factor in shaping his appeal. When Booker T. Washington spoke in Atlanta, his awareness of the reaction of the white audience members who were not used to listening to a black speaker made a difference in his message.

The audience for a speech, however, may be broader than simply those seated in front of a speaker when a speech is delivered. Even before the advent of the mass media as we know them today, the words of speakers could be widely disseminated. The speeches of many of the speakers in this volume were fully reported in the press or edited and published as pamphlets. The speeches of the 1930's and 1940's were carried by radio throughout the country. A full understanding of any speech cannot be achieved if the critic neglects the unseen listeners and readers—the sometimes nebulous, difficult to delineate audience, who, to varying degrees and in varying ways, receives, attends, acts. The Declaration on Taking up Arms in 1775, for example, had to consider the newly forming Continental Army to whom it was addressed, but it could not forget that the declaration would also be read and judged by Americans—conservative to radical—who knew the revolutionary war clouds were gathering; nor could the reactions of the British government be ignored. Theodore Roosevelt's call for a strenuous national life was not meant only for the businessmen gathered to hear him; the American people, not in agreement as to whether the United States should embrace or reject its new imperial role, were also potential targets of TR's persuasion. Charles Lindbergh did not address only the enthusiastic supporters who rallied in Madison Square Garden to declare their adherence to America First; his was clearly an effort to rally all the American people to the cause of isolationism.

As one begins to describe and understand an audience, one begins to see relationships between that audience and the speaker. The speaker hopes to direct and influence an audience; the audience, in turn, exerts a strong influence on the speaker's goals and choices. From a careful study of relationships, something of the speaker's perceptions and values, as compared and contrasted with the audience's, may begin to emerge. Who, for example, are the audience's heroes and who are their devils? To what extent are such friends and enemies shared with the speaker? In what ways do the speaker's appeals indicate a clear understanding of the audience members' ultimate goals, social or political backgrounds, special interests, fearful concerns, emotional attachments, and cherished values? A student's understanding of the audience will help that student respond critically to the speaker's efforts to move listeners.

4. The Interaction Between the Speaker and the Audience Within a Specific Context Focuses on a Particular Message

Given an understanding of the forces at work shaping the entire rhetorical situation, students, as they study the speeches themselves, should direct their critical attention to the ways in which certain features of the speech work together to promote the speaker's purpose within that situation. Particular attention should be paid to the way the speaker argues, how he or she organizes the ideas and supporting material of the speech, and the speaker's style.

Argument "Reason" is a term that has strong value qualities. Who would want to be thought of as unreasonable? Rational argument is good, irrationality is bad. But reason itself is not easily defined, nor is it always clear when one is being reasonable.

At the root of the difficulty in dealing with reason is the commonly held notion that reason is absolute, something that follows a set of immutable rules as in formal logic. Reason in rhetoric, however, is influenced and determined by at least two critical factors and relative factors: the assumptions of the audience and the foundation of argument in probability.

First consider the assumptions of the audiences. Because an audience is necessarily limited and bound by the time and place in which it exists, the historical and cultural context of a speech may influence considerations of reasonableness. In our contemporary American culture, for example, a widely held, revered assumption is that representative democracy is a good, even the best, form of government ever devised. A speaker holding this assumption, and deriving arguments from it, would be thought reasonable. One could build a logical argument against policies and leaders that sought to demonstrate that democratic principles were being subverted. A counterargument might try to prove that the speaker's evidence did not substantiate the claim that democracy was in danger, or that the speaker's conclusions did not flow logically from his or her arguments. However, it is unlikely that a counterargument would hold that the basic assumption was illogical; the strong positive cultural value of democracy is so great that few would even think to challenge it, nor would most audiences be prepared to entertain such a challenge.

Yet in 1789 such an assumption was not universally held. Much of the debate at the Constitutional Convention centered on ways to hold democracy in check. The subsequent controversy over ratification demonstrates the alarm in some quarters that the new Constitution would actually undermine democracy. In other words, the assumptions held by an audience in any given time, assumptions upon which arguments might be built with confidence at other periods, provide a firm logical foundation only to the extent that they mesh with the cultural system out of which they grow.

Much of what might be called agitative or radical rhetoric attacks basic assumptions and may shock or upset many audiences. The assumption that the Declaration of Independce was meant to include blacks or women, for example, was one that many American audiences in the past could not accept, and arguments based on such an assumption would have seemed "illogical" to them. The basic point is simply this: knowledge, perspective, and attitude shape assumptions and outlook. All these factors may cause audiences to define and perceive reason in different ways. One of the traps waiting for the critical reader of speeches is the "contemporary perspective" trap, wherein the reader acts as if he or she were the audience addressed and thus accepts as perfectly reasonable (or rejects as patently unreasonable) an argument that would have affected the actual listeners of the time quite differently.

Rhetorical logic is firmly based on the concept of probability. We rarely argue about certainties. We might disagree about the date of Woodrow Wilson's death, but we can settle that disagreement with an encyclopedia. It is a different matter when we debate the lasting values of the League of Nations experiment that Wilson supported so strongly. Such an issue raises questions dealing with the *probable* reasons for and consequences of certain international actions. Much of what occurs in public discourse is essentially prediction. When Beveridge, Theodore Roosevelt, and Bryan argued over American policy in Asia, they urged particular courses of action because of what they believed would be the consequences of such courses.

In responding critically, the student seeks to ascertain the logical relationships in the speech, uncovering assumptions in order to understand the common ground held by the speaker and his or her audience as well as the divergences that suggest potential roadblocks to successful communication. The critic will investigate the nature of the evidence used and its relationship to the generalizations made by the speaker, hoping to uncover the consistency of the reasoning and the justification for the conclusions the speaker reaches.

Organization A speech is not a random relation of information. Order is created by the speaker within the limitations imposed. Time, space, and physical setting create limitations that might influence organization. Certainly the nature of the audience and the situation may suggest relationships that call for certain organizational patterns. A speech such as the one given by Wendell Phillips, who had to deal with the attacks by the attorney general of Massachusetts on the murdered Lovejoy, or that of Sojourner Truth, who was responding to the anti-feminist arguments of hostile clergymen, would naturally be organized in a fashion imposed by the very fact that the message was a rebuttal to what had immediately preceded it. Lincoln, in accepting the nomination for the Senate, saw the need to employ a chronological pattern in his House Divided speech, since he wished to argue from events of the past to project the future.

Earlier, the essential role of purpose was discussed. Purpose, which defines the relationship between the speaker and the audience, also influences organization. Each idea that is developed may be tested by the comparison of its intent with the purpose of the speech. An idea that does not further the purpose does not belong in a speech. Ideas are, in turn, supported by material that must pass a similar test: evidence that does not make the idea more believable does not belong in a supporting position. Thus the basic pattern of a speech is determined by the intertwining relationships among purpose, ideas, and supporting material.

Responding critically to organization, the students will examine the relationships between the pattern of arrangement and the speaker's and audience's ideas and assumptions, locating and identifying the important ideas in the speech. An examination of those ideas will give additional evidence about the speaker's motives and goals. Patterning might further suggest the primacy of ideas within a given setting.

The critic then proceeds to assess the degree to which the speaker has adjusted his or her organization to the needs of the setting and the audience. Within the imposed limits, the speaker has been compelled to manage ideas; the critic attempts to understand how the speaker has done this and to judge the intellectual skill with which he or she has balanced purpose, ideas, and evidence.

Style Style is a difficult concept with which to deal. Scholars in many disciplines have long sought a definitive description of style and its distinction from content, but the issue is complex. There are, however, some basic ideas about style that are important and useful to the critical student of public speeches.

Certainly the most crucial element of style in public discourse is the use of language. Some have assumed that language "clothes" ideas—that language is a kind of decoration added to thought. It is more fruitful, however, to appreciate the nature of language as both reflective of and influencing thought. The words we choose indicate the way we perceive and feel about much that is around us. In public discourse language gives significant clues as to how the speaker sees him or herself and his or her opponents. Contrast, for example, Wendell Wilkie's depiction of the isolationists as defeatists with Lindbergh's portrayal of them as Americans who put their own country first.

Language, then, is not only means but substance as well. A speaker's style is essentially a culmination of other rhetorical factors, for it indicates much about the speaker's view of the audience and situation, about how the audience identifies with the topic, and about how the audience identifies with the speaker. All language has some emotive content that varies in intensity according to the audience and the situation. The semantic value of words, for example, could vary with experience so that mentioning a "camp" would produce different reactions in the woman who remembers with pleasure a childhood experience from the reactions produced in the Jewish refugee who spent years in a German concentration camp.

Furthermore, our culture establishes and develops certain values, and these values are reflected in the impact that language has on listeners. "Free enterprise" is probably a positive concept for most Americans, and the use of the term is likely to produce positive reactions, whereas "socialism" can have the reverse impact. The arguments of Eugene Debs, for example, were as likely as not to be dismissed out of hand because they could be labeled "socialist" or he himself a "Bolshevik."

Language may actually function in place of other evidence. For example, one can see, in the words of Theodore Roosevelt, the complete rejection of those who would argue that the United States should not control the affairs of the Philippines. TR alludes to the "difficult problems" that confront the country in the Philippines and then argues for solving them in "the proper way," arguing largely through the use of language to contrast his proposal with the ideas of the anti-imperialists: "It is cowardly to shrink from solving them in the proper way; for solved they must be, if not by us then by some stronger and more manful race; if we are too weak, too selfish, or too foolish to solve them some bolder and abler people must undertake the solution. Personally, I am too firm a believer in the greatness of my country and the power of my countrymen to admit for one moment that we shall ever be driven to the ignoble alternative." Here, clearly, is language deeply steeped in negative values that suggests the shameful, disgraceful nature of the "ignoble alternative" proposed by those who disagree with Roosevelt; the language relieves the speaker from the necessity of grappling with the specific arguments of his opponents.

The thoughtful critic can discern from a close investigation of style the speaker's values and the network of his or her ideas. From a speaker's language choice the critic, in effect, hypothesizes a whole world view that helps the critic understand the speaker's motivations and ultimate aims. Language choices that a speaker makes consistently may also indicate that speaker's belief in the efficacy of such a choice; noting these choices leads the critic to make inferences concerning the speaker's perception of the audience and its world view. Essentially, the critic searches for the forces—motivations and emotions—at work through the language.

In summary, there are three questions that the student of speeches would hope to answer by carefully considering the context of the speech, the role played by the speaker, the nature of the audiences, and the rhetorical choices exhibited in the text.

> What was the speaker trying to accomplish in the speech?
> In what ways did the speaker attempt to accomplish the task set out?
> How well did the speaker do in accomplishing this task?

These questions, although apparently simple, are complex and challenging. Ways of answering them might vary; different critical methods might be employed. Nevertheless, these questions will help the critic begin to understand how rhetoric works and will enhance the critic's appreciation of how our society has developed as he or she makes a rhetorical examination of significant issues that affected and still affect our collective lives.

SIGNIFICANT SPEECHES
IN
AMERICAN HISTORY

1640-1945

Colonial America

John Winthrop

On Liberty (1645)

England in the seventeenth century experienced a religious upheaval that, along with political crises, was to lead ultimately to Civil War. Parliament had established by law a state church, the Church of England, to which all were expected to conform. Within the Church, however, were those who found many of its religious practices and prescriptions unacceptable. Seeking, to their way of thinking, to purify the Church, various groups separated themselves from the established Church. In Scrooby, Nottinghamshire, a small congregation of these Puritan separatists formed. In an effort to escape from the jurisdiction of the state Church, the entire group emigrated to Holland and settled in Leyden in 1609. They remained there for over ten years before determining to establish their own colony in the New World. In July 1620 this little band, known subsequently as the Pilgrims, along with some indentured servants and others that they had recruited for the new colony, set out for America. In November they arrived off Cape Cod. In the years that followed, the little colony at Plymouth survived and then grew as the Pilgrims were joined by other emigrants.

By 1629 the situation in England had grown more uncomfortable for the Puritan nonconformists. The Bishop of London, William Laud, was gaining ascendancy in the Church and, indeed, was ultimately to become Archbishop of Canterbury, Primate of England. Bishop Laud was strictly devoted to conformity and did all in his power to coerce the separatists to accept the observances of the Church of England. Along with the threat of religious persecution, there was an economic depression in England, which the Puritans interpreted as a sign that the state Church had fallen into God's disfavor. With the formation of the Massachusetts Bay Company, some Puritans hoped to avoid the pressures of Bishop Laud as well as improve their economic lot by emigrating, taking with them to New England the Charter of the Company and with it the right to set up the government of the colony in Massachusetts.

The first four ships of the little fleet sailed from Southampton in March 1630, reaching Salem harbor in June. On board the *Arabella*, the first ship to reach New England, was the new governor, John Winthrop.

John Winthrop was, in many ways, typical of the English gentry of his time. He had studied first at Cambridge and then read law at Grey's Inn in London, being admitted to the bar in 1628. Convinced of the corruption spreading throughout England and seeing the opportunity to emigrate as one in which he could use "that talent which God hath bestowed upon him for public service," Winthrop joined the Puritan contingent.

The Massachusetts Bay Colony grew, attracting to it such notable clergymen as John Cotton and Thomas Hooker. The new colony, founded largely for religious motivations, based its civil government in religious belief, establishing the "Bible Commonwealth." The law, set forth in the Scriptures, was to be interpreted and administered by magistrates as God's stewards. It was not a government with any sympathy for democratic movements or with much tolerance for religious deviation. Winthrop saw no warrant in scripture for democracy and held it to be the meanest and worst of all forms of government, and it was under Winthrop's governorship that dissidents such as Roger Williams and Anne Hutchison were banished. But Winthrop never believed that his power was arbitrary and that he could do just as he wished. He held that the responsibility of a Christian magistrate for "the care of the public" should "oversway all private interests." His views, though consistent with the theocratic nature of Massachusetts government, were not unchallenged.

In the seemingly insignificant issue of whether Anthony Eames or Bozoun Allen should be captain of the Higham militia were the seeds of a major controversy. Winthrop, never one to bow to popular will, made an unpopular decision and was impeached before the General Court. Found not guilty, Winthrop addressed the assembly in the speech that follows. In it, the governor maintains that "the great questions that have troubled the country are about the authority of the magistrates and the liberty of the people." Natural—that is, corrupt—liberty, Winthrop holds to be "incompatible and inconsistent with authority," while civil liberty represents "the covenant between God and man in the moral law, and the politic covenants and constitutions amongst men themselves."

Winthrop's call for the quiet and cheerful submission to authority was capable of moving his audience and acceptable enough to sixteenth-century New Englanders to lead them to reelect him as governor and continue him in that post until his death in 1649. It was not, however, an appeal that would endure among the independent citizens of Massachusetts.

I suppose something may be expected from me upon this charge that has befallen me, which moves me to speak now to you; yet I intend not to intermeddle in the proceedings of the court or with any of the persons concerned therein. Only I bless God that I see an issue of this troublesome business. I also acknowledge the justice of the court, and for mine own part I am well satisfied. I was publicly charged, and I am publicly and legally acquitted, which is all I did expect or desire. And though this be sufficient for my justification before men, yet not so before the God who hath seen so much amiss in my dispensations (and even in this affair) as calls me to be humble.

For to be publicly and criminally charged in this court is matter of humiliation (and I desire to make a right use of it), notwithstanding I be thus acquitted. If her father had spit in her face (saith the Lord concerning Miriam), should she not have been ashamed seven days? Shame had lien upon her, whatever the occasion had been. I am unwilling to stay you from your urgent affairs, yet give me leave (upon this special occasion) to speak a little more to this assembly. It may be of some good use to inform and rectify the judgments of some of the people, and may prevent such distempers as have arisen amongst us.

The great questions that have troubled the country are about the authority of the magistrates and the liberty of the people. It is yourselves who have called us to this office, and, being called by you, we have our authority from God, in way of an ordinance, such as hath the image of God eminently stamped upon it, the contempt and violation whereof hath been vindicated with examples of divine vengeance.

I entreat you to consider that, when you choose magistrates, you take them from among yourselves, men subject to like passions as you are. Therefore, when you see infirmities in us, you should reflect upon your own, and that would make you bear the more with us, and not be severe censurers of the failings of your magistrates, when you have continual experience of the like infirmities in yourselves and others.

We account him a good servant who breaks not his covenant. The covenant between you and us is the oath you have taken of us, which is to this purpose, that we shall govern you and judge your causes by the rules of God's laws and our own, according to our best skill. When you agree with a workman to build you a ship or house, etc., he undertakes as well for his skill as for his faithfulness; for it is his profession, and you pay him for both. But when you call one to be a magistrate he doth not profess or undertake to have sufficient skill for that office, nor can you furnish him with gifts, etc., therefore you must run the hazard of his skill and ability. But if he fail in faithfulness, which by his oath he is bound unto, that he must answer for. If it fall out that the case be clear to common apprehension, and the rule clear also, if he transgresss here, the error is not in the skill, but in the evil of the will: it must be required of him. But if the case be doubtful, or the rule doubtful, to men of such understanding and parts as your magistrates are, if your magistrates should err here, yourselves must bear it.

For the other point concerning liberty, I observe a great mistake in the country about that. There is a twofold liberty, natural (I mean as our nature is now corrupt) and civil or federal. The first is common to man with beasts and other creatures. By this man, as he stands in relation to man simply, hath liberty to do what he lists: it is a liberty to evil as well as to good. This liberty is incompatible and inconsistent with authority, and cannot endure the least restraint of the most just authority. The exercise and maintaining of this liberty makes men grow more evil, and in time to be worse than brute beasts: *omnes sumus licentia deteriores*. This is that great enemy of truth and peace, that wild beast, which all the ordinances of God are bent against, to restrain and subdue it.

The other kind of liberty I call civil or federal; it may also be termed moral, in reference to the covenant between God and man in the moral law, and the politic covenants and constitutions amongst men themselves. This liberty is the proper end and object of authority, and cannot subsist without it; and it is a liberty to that only which is good, just, and honest. This liberty you are to stand for, with the hazard (not only of your goods, but) of your lives, if need be. Whatsoever crosseth this is not authority, but a distemper thereof. This liberty is maintained and exercised in a way of subjection to authority; it is of the same kind of liberty wherewith Christ hath made us free. The woman's own choice makes such a man her husband; yet, being so chosen, he is her lord, and she is to be subject to him, yet in a way of liberty, not of bondage; and a true wife accounts her subjection her honor and freedom, and would not think her condition safe and free but in her subjection to her husband's authority. Such is the liberty of the church under the authority of Christ, her king and husband; his yoke is so easy and sweet to her as a bride's ornaments; and if, through forwardness or wantonness, etc., she shake it off at any time, she is at no rest in her spirit until she take it up again; and whether her lord smiles upon her, and embraceth her in his arms, or whether he frowns, or rebukes, or smites her, she apprehends the sweetness of his love in all, and is refreshed, supported, and instructed by every such dispensation of his authority over her. On the other side, ye know who they are that complain of this yoke and say, let us break their bands, etc., we will not have this man to rule over us.

Even so, brethren, it will be between you and your magistrates. If you stand for your natural corrupt liberties, and will do what is good in your own eyes, you will not endure the least weight of authority, but will murmur, and oppose, and be always striving to shake off that yoke; but if you will be satisfied to enjoy such civil and lawful liberties, such as Christ allows you, then will you quietly and cheerfully submit unto that authority which is set over you, in all the administrations of it, for your good. Wherein, if we fail at any time, we hope we shall be willing (by God's assistance) to hearken to good advice from any of you, or in any other way to God; so shall your liberties be preserved, in upholding the honor and power of authority amongst you.

Roger Williams

Plea for Religious Liberty (1644)

Religious liberty was not easily won in America. When the Puritan colonists settled in New England, escaping from religious persecution of Old England, they brought with them the prevailing conviction that there was *a* truth, *a* right way of practicing religious beliefs. To the seventeenth-century way of thinking, error had to be combatted, rooted out of religious and civil life. From such a perspective, measures taken to silence "false" doctrine were justifiable, persecution a legitimate means of preserving God's "truth." As Cotton Mather put it in his attack on Roger Williams, "there is a vast difference between men's inventions and God's institutions; we fled from men's inventions, to which we else should be compelled; we compel none to men's inventions."

Roger Williams was unusual in his conviction that differing religious views should be tolerated and that the state did not have the right to enforce religious conformity. It was not that Williams held no strong opinions himself: throughout his life he was at the center of controversy. A Puritan minister, Williams emigrated to Massachusetts in 1631 and proceeded immediately to engage in a dispute with his new congregation in Salem because they had not separated formally from the Church of England. He challenged the right of the Massachusetts government to take land from the Indians without compensation merely on the basis of a grant from the King. The audacious, disputatious Williams went so far as to label Charles I an "anti-Christ" in a letter written to that monarch himself. It was, however, his denial of the right of civil magistrates to enforce adherence to certain of the Biblical commandments that most troubled the theocratic rulers of Massachusetts. In 1635 Williams's "new and dangerous opinions against the authority of magistrates" led to his banishment from the colony.

Williams and a few followers sought shelter with the Indians, whose culture Williams respected, and finally settled on land purchased from the natives. He named his new home Providence in gratitude for "God's merciful providence" to him in his distress. Williams eventualy obtained a charter for the colony of Rhode Island and ordered that it would be a place where "no man should be molested for his conscience" and where government would be essentially democratic. Williams was for a time a Baptist, and then he considered himself a Seeker. He disputed the tenets of Quakerism but allowed Quakers to practice their religion in Rhode Island at a time when they were liable to be hanged in other places in New England.

What follows is not a speech; it is part of a longer work, *The Bloudy Tenent of Persecution*, but it represents a mature and considered statement of views that Williams articulated in various settings at various times. In it, Williams recites twelve reasons for allowing liberty of conscience and separating civil from religious authority. Williams then creates a dialog between TRUTH on the one hand and PEACE on the other, designed to prove Williams's point that "the doctrine of persecution for cause of conscience, is most evidently and lamentably contrary to the doctrine of Christ Jesus the Prince of Peace." Williams's voice was literally a voice in the wilderness, but it spoke for principles that would ultimately become fundamental to the operation of American democracy.

First, that the blood of so many hundred thousand souls of Protestants and Papists, split in the wars of present and former ages, for their respective consciences, is not required nor accepted by Jesus Christ the Prince of Peace.

Secondly, pregnant scriptures and arguments are throughout the work proposed against the doctrine of persecution for cause of conscience.

Thirdly, satisfactory answers are given to scriptures, and objections produced by Mr. Calvin, Beza, Mr. Cotton, and the ministers of the New English churches and others former and later, tending to prove the doctrine of persecution for cause of conscience.

Fourthly, the doctrine of persecution for cause of conscience is proved guilty of all the blood of the souls crying for vengeance under the altar.

Fifthly, all civil states with their officers of justice in their respective constitutions and administrations are proved essentially civil, and therefore not judges, governors, or defenders of the spiritual or Christian state and worship.

Sixthly, it is the will and command of God that (since the coming of his Son the Lord Jesus) a permission of the most paganish, Jewish, Turkish, or antichristian consciences and worships, be granted to all men in all nations and countries; and they are only to be fought against with that sword which is only (in soul matters) able to conquer, to wit, the sword of God's Spirit, the Word of God.

Seventhly, the state of the Land of

Israel, the kings and people thereof in peace and war, is proved figurative and ceremonial, and no pattern nor precedent for any kingdom or civil state in the world to follow.

Eighthly, God requireth not a uniformity of religion to be enacted and enforced in any civil state; which enforced uniformity (sooner or later) is the greatest occasion of civil war, ravishing of conscience, persecution of Christ Jesus in his servants, and of the hypocrisy and destruction of millions of souls.

Ninthly, in holding an enforced uniformity of religion in a civil state, we must necessarily disclaim our desires and hopes of the Jew's conversion to Christ.

Tenthly, an enforced uniformity of religion throughout a nation or civil state, confounds the civil and religious, denies the principles of Christianity and civility, and that Jesus Christ is come in the flesh.

Eleventhly, the permission of other consciences and worships than a state professeth only can (according to God) procure a firm and lasting peace (good assurance being taken according to the wisdom of the civil state for uniformity of civil obedience from all forts).

Twelfthly, lastly, true civility and Christianity may both flourish in a state or kingdom, notwithstanding the permission of divers and contrary consciences, either of Jew or Gentile. . . .

TRUTH: I acknowledge that to molest any person, Jew or Gentile, for either professing doctrine, or practicing worship merely religious or spiritual, it is to persecute him, and such a person (whatever his doctrine or practice be, true or false) suffereth persecution for conscience.

But withal I desire it may be well observed that this distinction is not full and complete: for beside this that a man may be persecuted because he holds or practices what he believes in conscience to be a truth (as Daniel did, for which he was cast into the lions' den, Dan. 6), and many thousands of Christians, because they durst not cease to preach and practice what they believed was by God commanded, as the Apostles answered (Acts 4 & 5), I say besides this a man may also be persecuted, because he dares not be constrained to yield obedience to such doctrines and worships as are by men invented and appointed. . . .

Dear Truth, I have two sad complaints:

First, the most sober of the witnesses, that dare to plead thy cause, how are they charged to be mine enemies, contentious, turbulent, seditious?

Secondly, thine enemies, though they speak and rail against thee, though they outrageously pursue, imprision, banish, kill thy faithful witnesses, yet how is all vermilion'd o'er for justice against the heretics? Yea, if they kindle coals, and blow the flames of devouring wars, that leave neither spiritual nor civil state, but burn up branch and root, yet how do all pretend an holy war? He that kills, and heaven, if he bring any other faith or doctrine. . . .

PEACE: I add that a civil sword (as woeful experience in all ages has proved) is so far from bringing or helping forward an opposite in religion to repentance that magistrates sin grievously against the work of God and blood of souls by such proceedings. Because as (commonly) the sufferings of false and antichristian teachers harden their followers, who being blind, by this means are occasioned to tumble into the ditch of hell after their blind leaders, with more inflamed zeal of lying confidence. So, secondly, violence and a sword of steel begets such an impression in the sufferers that certainly they conclude (as indeed that religion cannot be true which needs such instruments of violence to uphold it so) that persecutors are far from soft and gentle commiseration of the blindness of others. . . .

For (to keep to the similitude which the Spirit useth, for instance) to batter down a stronghold, high wall, fort, tower, or castle, men bring not a first and second admonition, and after obstinacy, excommunication, which are spiritual weapons concerning them that be in the church: nor exhortation to repent and be baptized, to believe in the Lord Jesus, etc., which are proper weapons to them that be without, etc. But to take a stronghold, men bring cannons, culverins, saker, bullets, powder, muskets, swords, pikes, etc., and these to this end are weapons effectual and proportionable.

On the other side, to batter down idolatry, false worship, heresy, schism, blindness, hardness, out of the soul and spirit, it is vain, improper, and unsuitable to bring those weapons which are used by persecutors, stocks, whips, prisons, swords, gibbets, stakes, etc. (where these seem to prevail with some cities or kingdoms, a stronger force sets up again, what a weaker pull'd down), but against these spiritual strongholds in the souls of men, spiritual artillery and weapons are proper, which are mighty through God to subdue and bring under the very thought to obedience, or else to bind fast the soul with chains of darkness, and lock it up in the prison of unbelief and hardness to eternity. . . .

PEACE: I pray descend now to the second evil which you observe in the answerer's position, viz., that it would be evil to tolerate notorious evildoers, seducing teachers, etc.

TRUTH: I say the evil is that he most improperly and confusedly joins and couples seducing teachers with scandalous livers.

PEACE: But is it not true that the world is full of seducing teachers, and is it not true that seducing teachers are notorious evildoers?

TRUTH: I answer, far be it from me to deny either, and yet in two things I shall discover the great evil of this joining and coupling seducing teachers, and scandalous livers as one adequate or proper object of the magistrate's care and work to suppress and punish.

First, it is not an homogeneal (as we speak) but an hetergeneal commixture or joining together of things most different in kinds and natures, as if they were both of one consideration. . . .

TRUTH: I answer, in granting with Brentius that man hath not power to make laws to bind conscience, he overthrows such his tenent and practice as restrain men from their worship, according to their conscience and belief, and constrain them to such worships (though it be out of a pretense that they are convinced) which their own souls tell them they have no satisfaction nor faith in.

Secondly, whereas he affirms that men may make laws to see the laws of God observed.

I answer, as God needeth not the help of a material sword of steel to assist the sword of the Spirit in the affairs of conscience, to those men, those magistrates, yea that commonwealth which makes such magistrates, must needs have power and authority from Christ Jesus to fit judge and to determine in all the great controversies concerning doctrine, discipline, government, etc.

And then I ask whether upon this ground it must not evidently follow that:

Either there is no lawful commonwealth nor civil state of men in the world, which is not qualified with this spiritual discerning (and then also that the very commonwealth hath more light concerning the church of Christ than the church itself).

Or, that the commonwealth and magistrates thereof must judge and punish as they are persuaded in their own belief and conscience (be their conscience paganish, Turkish, or antichristian) what is this but to confound heaven and earth together, and not only to take away the being of Christianity out of the world, but to take away all civility, and the world out of the world, and to lay all upon heaps of confusion? . . .

PEACE: The fourth head is the proper means of both these powers to attain their ends.

First, the proper means whereby the civil power may and should attain its end are only political, and principally these five.

First, the erecting and establishing what form of civil government may seem in wisdom most meet, according to general rules of the world, and state of the people.

Secondly, the making, publishing, and establishing of wholesome civil laws, not only such as concern civil justice, but also the free passage of true religion; for outward civil peace ariseth and is maintained from them both, from the latter as well as from the former.

Civil peace cannot stand entire, where religion is corrupted (2 Chron. 15. 3. 5. 6; and Judges 8). And yet such laws, though conversant about religion, may still be counted civil laws, as, on the contrary, an oath doth still remain religious though conversant about civil matters.

Thirdly, election and appointment of civil officers to see execution to those laws.

Fourthly, civil punishments and rewards of transgressors and observers of these laws.

Fifthly, taking up arms against the enemies of civil peace.

Secondly, the means whereby the church may and should attain her ends are only ecclesiastical, which are chiefly five.

First, setting up that form of church government only of which Christ hath given them a pattern in his Word.

Secondly, acknowledging and admitting of no lawgiver in the church but Christ and the publishing of His laws.

Thirdly, electing and ordaining of such officers only, as Christ hath appointed in his Word.

Fourthly, to receive into their fellowship them that are approved and inflicting spiritual censures against them that offend.

Fifthly, prayer and patience in suffering any evil from them that be without, who disturb their peace.

So that magistrates, as magistrates, have no power of setting up the form of church government, electing church officers, punishing with church censures, but to see that the church does her duty herein. And on the other side, the churches as churches, have no power (though as members of the commonweal they may have power) of erecting or altering forms of civil government, electing of civil officers, inflicting civil punishments (no not on persons excommunicate) as by deposing magistrates from their civil authority, or withdrawing the hearts of the people against them, to their laws, no more than to discharge wives, or children, or servants, from due obedience to their husbands, parents, or masters; or by taking up arms against their magistrates, though he persecute them for conscience: for though members of churches who are public officers also of the civil state may suppress by force the violence of usurpers, as Ieholada did Athaliah, yet this they do not as members of the church but as officers of the civil state.

TRUTH: Here are divers considerable passages which I shall briefly examine, so far as concerns our controversy.

First, whereas they say that the civil power may erect and establish what form of civil government may seem in wisdom most meet, I acknowledge the proposition to be most true, both in itself and also considered with the end of it, that a civil government is an ordinance of God, to conserve the civil peace of people, so far as concerns their bodies and goods, as formerly hath been said.

But from this grant I infer (as before hath been touched) that the sovereign, original, and foundation of civil power lies in the people (whom they must needs mean by the civil power distinct from the government set up). And, if so, that a people may erect and establish what form of government seems to them most meet for their civil condition; it is evident that such governments as are by them erected and established have no more power, nor for no longer time, than the civil power or people consenting and agreeing shall betrust them with. This is clear not only in reason but in the experience of all commonweals, where the people are not deprived of their natural freedom by the power of tyrants.

And, if so, that the magistrates receive their power of governing the church from the people, undeniably it follows that a people, as a people, naturally considered (of what nature or nation soever in Europe, Asia, Africa, or America), have fundamentally and originally, as men, a power to govern the church, to see her do her duty, to correct her, to redress, reform, establish, etc. And if this be not to pull God and Christ and Spirit out of heaven, and subject them unto natural, sinful, inconstant men, and so consequently to Satan himself, by whom all peoples naturally are guided, let heaven and earth judge. . . .

PEACE: Some will here ask: Whay may the magistrate then lawfully do with his civil horn or power in matters of religion?

TRUTH: His horn not being the horn of that unicorn or rhinoceros, the power of the Lord Jesus in spiritual cases, his sword not the two-edged sword of the spirit, the word of God (hanging not about the loins or side, but at the lips, and proceeding out of the mouth of his ministers) but of an humane and civil nature and constitution, it must consequently be of a humane and civil operation, for who knows not that operation follows constitution? And therefore I shall end this passage with this consideration:

The civil magistrate either respecteth that religion and worship which his conscience is persuaded is true, and upon which he ventures his soul; or else that and those which he is persuaded are false.

Concerning the first, if that which the magistrate believeth to be true, be true, I say he owes a threefold duty unto it:

First, approbation and countenance, a reverent esteem and honorable testimony, according to Isa. 49, and Revel. 21, with a tender respect of truth, and the professors of it.

Secondly, personal submission of his own soul to the power of the Lord Jesus in that spiritual government and kingdom, according to Matt. 18 and 1 Cor. 5.

Thirdly, protection of such true professors of Christ, whether apart, or met together, as also of their estates from violence and injury, according to Rom. 13.

Now, secondly, if it be a false religion (unto which the civil magistrate dare not adjoin, yet) he owes:

First, permission (for approbation he owes not what is evil) and this according to Matthew 13.30 for public peace and quiet's sake.

Secondly, he owes protection to the persons of his subjects (though of a false worship), that no injury be offered either to the persons or goods of any. . . .

. . .The God of Peace, the God of Truth will shortly seal this truth, and confirm this witness, and make it evident to the whole world, that the doctrine of persecution for cause of conscience, is most evidently and lamentably contrary to the doctrine of Christ Jesus the Prince of Peace. Amen.

Andrew Hamilton

Defense of Zenger (1735)

In 1725 the printer William Bradford established the *New York Gazette*, one of the small but growing number of newspapers in the colonies. In this enterprise he was joined briefly by a young emigrant, John Peter Zenger. Zenger arrived in New York from his native Germany in 1710 and served as Bradford's apprentice from 1711 until 1719. The partnership did not work however, and Zenger began his own printing business in 1726.

The Royal Governor of New York in 1732, William Cosby, made himself unpopular with his high-handed and rapacious actions, even removing the chief justice of the province in order to advance a lawsuit in which he was personally involved. By this time Bradford was the official printer for the colony and his newspaper supported Governor Cosby's administration. While some attacks on the governor had been printed, sustained opposition came only with the publication in 1733 of Zenger's new periodical, the *New York Weekly Journal*. Zenger did not write the polemics against the governor; they were published anonymously. Nevertheless, Zenger, as the printer, was held responsible. His paper was publicly burned by order of the governor and his council and Zenger was arrested. When a grand jury failed to indict the printer, Governor Cosby's attorney general filed an information for seditious libel and obtained a warrant through the executive council.

Zenger's counsel, James Alexander and William Smith, questioned the right of two judges appointed by Governor Cosby to preside over the trial, only to have their names stricken from the role of attorneys in the colony for their pains. Legal talent in New York was limited, and Zenger could not look forward to a very spirited defense; certainly his new lawyer could not match the attorney general, Richard Bradley.

Finally, after languishing in jail for almost ten months, Zenger was brought to trial, and his defense was argued by Andrew Hamilton of Pennsylvania.

Hamilton was one of the most distinguished attorneys in colonial America in the early years of the eighteenth century. As a young man he had emigrated to Virginia and then settled in Philadelphia after being admitted to the bar in London in 1713. He had been attorney general of Pennsylvania and, at the time of the trial, was a member of the General Assembly; for most of the twelve years that he sat in that body, he served as its Speaker.

At almost 60 years of age, Hamilton was quite elderly by eighteenth-century standards, yet he made the uncomfortable trip from Philadelphia to New York in spite of "great infirmities of body." Hamilton, "old and weak" as he was, maintained that it was his duty "to go to the utmost part of the land" to defend the right of the people to complain "of the arbitrary attempts of men in power." Believing as he did that "a bad precedent in one government is soon set up for another," Hamilton saw as his duty, indeed, "every honest man's duty . . . to be upon our guard against power whenever we apprehend it may affect ourselves or our fellow subjects."

Consistent with libel laws of the time, the role of the jury in cases such as Zenger's was to determine whether or not the defendant had actually printed the material in question, leaving to the judge the question of whether or not the material was libelous. The chief justice had made this point clear in his charge to the jury. Nevertheless, Hamilton argued that the jury had the right to determine not only the issue of fact (Did Zenger print the material?), but also the law in the case (Was it libel?). In asserting that "the verdict is yours," Hamilton told the members of the jury that "if you should be of the opinion that there is no falsehood in Mr. Zenger's papers," they "ought to say so" and not leave the matter to the judge to determine. In bringing in a verdict of not guilty, the Zenger jury validated Hamilton's claim that the truth of statements determined libel and set a precedent for freedom of speech in America.

May it please your honors, I agree with Mr. Attorney [Richard Bradley] that government is a sacred thing, but I differ very widely from him when he would insinuate that the just complaints of a number of men, who suffer under a bad administration, is libeling that administration. Had I believed that to be law, I should not have given the court the trouble of hearing anything that I could say in this cause. I own when I read the information, I had not the art to find out (without the help of Mr. Attorney's innuendoes) that the Governor was the person meant in every period of that newspaper; and I was inclined to believe that they were written by some who, from an extraordinary zeal for liberty, had misconstrued the conduct of some persons in authority into crimes; and that Mr. Attorney, out of his too great zeal for power, had exhibited this information to correct the indiscretion of my client, and at the same time to show his superiors the great concern he had, lest they should be treated with any undue freedom. But from what Mr. Attorney had just now said, to wit, that this prosecution was directed by the Governor and council, and from the extraordinary appearance of people of all conditions which I observed in court upon this occasion, I have reason to think that those in the administration have by this prosecution something more in view, and that the people believe they have a good deal more at stake than I apprehended, and therefore, as it is become my duty to be both plain and particular in this cause, I beg leave to bespeak the patience of the court.

I was in hopes as that terrible court where those dreadful judgments were given and that law established, which Mr. Attorney has produced for authorities to support this cause, was long ago laid aside as the most dangerous court to the liberties of the people of England that ever was known in that kingdom, that Mr. Attorney, knowing this, would not have attempted to set up a Star Chamber here, nor to make their judgments a precedent to us: for it is well known that would have been judged treason in those days for a man to speak, I think, has since not only been practiced as lawful, but the contrary doctrine has been held to be law.

There is heresy in law as well as in religion, and both have changed very much; and we well know that it is not two centuries ago that a man would have been burned as a heretic for owning such opinions in matters of religion as are publicly written and printed at this day. They were fallible men, it seems, and we take the liberty, not only to differ from them in religious opinion, but to condemn them and their opinions too; and I must presume that in taking these freedoms in thinking and speaking about matters of faith or religion, we are in the right; for though it is said there are very great liberties of this kind taken in New York, yet I have heard of no information preferred by Mr. Attorney for any offenses of this sort. From which I think it is pretty clear that in New York a man may make very free with his God, but he must take special care what he says of his Governor. It is agreed upon by all men that this is a reign of liberty, and while men keep within the bounds of truth, I hope they may with safety both speak and write their sentiments of the conduct of men of power; I mean of that part of their conduct only which affects the liberty or property of the people under their administration; were this to be denied, then the next step may make them slaves. For what notions can be entertained of slavery beyond that of suffering the greatest injuries and oppressions without the liberty of complaining; or if they do, to be destroyed, body and estate, for so doing?

It is said, and insisted upon by Mr. Attorney, that government is a sacred thing; that it is to be supported and reverenced; it is government that protects our persons and estates; that prevents treasons, murders, robberies, riots, and all the train of evils that overturn kingdoms and states and ruin particular persons; and if those in the administration, especially the supreme magistrates, must have all their conduct censured by private men, government cannot subsist. This is called a licentiousness not to be tolerated. It is said that it brings the rulers of the people into contempt so that their authority is not regarded, and so that in the end the laws cannot be put in execution. These, I say, and such as these, are the general topics insisted upon by men in power and their advocates. But I wish it might be considered at the same time how often it has happened that the abuse of power has been the primary cause of these evils, and that it was the injustice and oppression of these great men which has commonly brought them into contempt with the people. The craft and art of such men are great, and who that is the least acquainted with history or with law can be ignorant of the specious pretenses which have often been made use of by men in power to introduce arbitrary rule and destroy the liberties of a free people. . . .

This is the second information for libeling of a governor that I have known in America. And the first, though it may look like a romance, yet, as it is true, I will beg leave to mention it. Governor Nicholson, who happened to be offended with one of his clergy, met him one day upon the road; and, as it was usual with him (under the protection of his commission), used the poor parson with the worst language, threatened to cut off his ears, slit his nose, and, at last, to shoot him through the head. The parson, being a reverend man, continued all this time uncovered in the heat of the sun until he found an opportunity to fly for it; and coming to a neighbor's house felt himself very ill of a fever, and immediately wrote for a doctor; and that his physician might be the better judge of his distemper he acquainted him with the usage he had received, concluding that the Governor was certainly mad, for that no man in his senses would have behaved in that manner. The doctor, unhappily, showed the parson's letter; the Governor came to hear of it, and so an information was preferred against the poor man for saying he believed the Governor was mad; and it was laid in the information to be false, scandalous, and wicked, and written with intent to move sedition among the people and bring his Excellency into contempt. But, by an order from the late Queen Anne, there was a stop put to the prosecution, with sundry others set on foot by the same Governor against gentlemen of the greatest worth and honor in that government.

And may not I be allowed, after all this, to say that, by a little countenance, almost anything which a man writes may, with the help of that useful term of art called an innuendo, be construed to be a libel, according to Mr. Attorney's definition of it; that whether the words are spoken of a person of a public character or of a private man, whether dead or living, good or bad, true or false, all make a libel; for, according to Mr. Attorney, after a man hears a writing read, or reads and repeats it, or laughs at it, they are all punishable. It is true, Mr. Attorney is so good as to allow, after the party knows it to be a libel; but he is not so kind as to take the man's word for it.

If a libel is understood in the large and unlimited sense urged by Mr. Attorney, there is scarce a writing I know that may not be called a libel, or scarce any person safe from being called to account as a libeler, for Moses, meek as he was, libeled Cain; and who is it that has not libeled the devil? For, according to Mr. Attorney, it is not justification to say one has a bad name. Eachard has libeled our good King William; Burnet has libeled, among many others, King Charles and King James; and Rapin has libeled them all. How must a man speak or write, or what must he hear, read, or sing? Or when must he laugh, so as to be secure from being taken up as a libeler? I sincerely believe that were some persons to go through the streets of New York nowadays and read a part of the Bible, if it were not known to be such, Mr. Attorney, with the help of his innuendoes, would easily turn it into a libel. As for instance: Isaiah 11:16: "The leaders of the people cause them to err, and they that are led by them are destroyed." But should Mr. Attorney go about to make this a libel, he would read it thus: "The leaders of the people" (*innuendo*, the Governor and council of New York) "cause them" (*innuendo*, the people of this province) "to err, and they" (the Governor and council meaning) "are destroyed" (*innuendo*, are deceived into the loss of their liberty), "which is the worst kind of destruction." Or if some person should publicly repeat, in a manner not pleasing to his betters, the tenth and the eleventh verses of the fifty-sixth chapter of the same book, there Mr. Attorney would have a large field to display his skill in the artful application of his inneundoes. The words are: "His watchmen are blind, they are ignorant," etc. "Yea, they are greedy dogs, they can never have enough." But to make them a libel, there is, according to Mr. Attorney's doctrine, no more wanting but the aid of his skill in the right adapting his innuendoes. As, for instance, "His watchmen" (*innuendo*, the Governor's council and assembly) "are blind, they are ignorant" (*innuendo*, will not see the dangerous designs of his Excellency). "Yea, they" (the Governor and council, meaning) "are greedy dogs, which can never have enough" (*innuendo*, enough of riches and power). Such an instance as this seems only fit to be laughed at, but I may appeal to Mr. Attorney himself whether these are not at least equally proper to be applied to his Excellency and his ministers as some of the inferences and innuendoes in his information against my client. Then, if Mr. Attorney be at liberty to come into court and file an information in the King's name without leave, who is secure whom he is pleased to prosecute as a libeler? And as the crown law is contended for in bad times, there is no remedy for the greatest oppression of this sort, even though the party prosecuted be acquitted with honor. And give me leave to say, as great men as any in Britain have boldly asserted that the mode of prosecuting by information (when a grand jury will not find *billa pera*) is a national grievance and greatly inconsistent with that freedom which the subjects of England enjoy in most other cases. But if we are so unhappy as not to be able to ward off this stroke of power directly, let us take care not to be cheated out of our liberties by forms and appearances; let us always be sure that the charge in the information is made out clearly, even beyond a doubt; for, though matters in the information may be called form upon trial, yet they may be, and often have been found to be, matters of substance upon giving judgment.

Gentlemen, the danger is great in proportion to the mischief that may happen through our too-great credulity. A proper confidence in a court is commendable, but as the verdict (whatever it is) will be yours, you ought to refer no part of your duty to the discretion of other persons. If you should be of opinion that there is no falsehood in Mr. Zenger's papers, you will, nay (pardon me for the expression), you ought to say so; because you do not know whether others (I mean the court) may be of that opinion. It is your right to do so, and there is much depending upon your resolution, as well as upon your integrity.

The loss of liberty to a generous mind is worse than death; and yet we know there have been those in all ages who, for the sake of preferment or some imaginary honor, have freely lent a helping hand to oppress, nay, to destroy, their country. This brings to my mind that saying of the immortal Brutus, when he looked upon the creatures of Caesar, who were very great men, but by no means good men: "You Romans," said Brutus, "if yet I may call you so, consider what you are doing; remember that you are assisting Caesar to forge those very chains which one day he will make yourselves wear." This is what every man that values freedom ought to consider; he should act by judgment and not by affection or self-interest; for where those prevail, no ties of either country or kindred are regarded; as, upon the other hand, the man who loves his country prefers its liberty to all other considerations, well knowing that without liberty life is a misery. . . .

Power may justly be compared to a great river; while kept within its bounds, it is both beautiful and useful, but when it overflows its banks, it is then too impetuous to be stemmed; it bears down all before it, and brings destruction and desolation wherever it comes. If, then, this be the nature of power, let us at least do our duty, and, like wise men who value freedom, use our utmost care to support liberty, the only bulwark against lawless power, which, in all ages, has sacrificed to its wild lust and boundless ambition the blood of the best men that ever lived.

I hope to be pardoned, sir, for my zeal upon this occasion. It is an old and wise caution that "when our neighbor's house is on fire, we ought to take care of our own." For though, blessed be God, I live in a government where liberty is well understood and freely enjoyed, yet experience has shown us all (I am sure it has to me) that a bad precedent in one government is soon set up for an authority in another; and therefore I cannot but think it mine and every honest man's duty that, while we pay all due obedience to men in authority, we ought at the same time, to be upon our guard against power wherever we apprehend that it may affect ourselves or our fellow subjects.

I am truly very unequal to such an undertaking, on many accounts. And you see I labor under the weight of many years and am borne down with great infirmities of body; yet old and weak as I am, I should think it my duty, if required, to go to the utmost part of the land, where my service could be of any use in assisting to quench the flame of prosecutions upon informations, set on foot by the government to deprive a people of the right of remonstrating, and complaining too, of the arbitrary attempts of men in power. Men who injure and oppress the people under their administration provoke them to cry out and complain, and then make that very complaint the foundation of new oppressions and prosecutions. I wish I could say there were no instances of this kind. But, to conclude, the question before the court, and you, gentlemen of the jury, is not of small nor private concern; it is not the cause of a poor printer, nor of New York alone, which you are now trying. No! It may, in its consequence, affect every free man that lives under a British government on the main continent of America. It is the best cause; it is the cause of liberty; and I make no doubt but your upright conduct, this day, will not only entitle you to the love and esteem of your fellow citizen, but every man who prefers freedom to a life of slavery will bless and honor you as men who have baffled the attempt of tyranny, and, by an impartial and uncorrupt verdict, have laid a noble foundation for securing to ourselves, our posterity, and our neighbors that to which nature and the laws of our country have given us a right—the liberty of both exposing and opposing arbitrary power (in these parts of the world at least) by speaking and writing truth.

Jonathan Edwards

Sinners in the Hands of an Angry God (1741)

Religion had a powerful hold on Americans in the eighteenth century, and religious questions, even more than political ones, fired the imaginations and engaged the emotional energies of the colonists. Between the late 1720's and the middle 1740's there swept across the colonies a religious movement known as the "Great Awakening," in which evangelists, most notably the English preacher George Whitfield, sought to revive religious fervor. Unquestionably the leading figure in the Awakening in New England was an evangelist of great intellectual power and fierce Calvinistic convictions, Jonathan Edwards.

Edwards was born in 1703, the son and grandson of ministers. He studied at Yale, became minister of a Presbyterian church in New York for a year, returned to Yale as a tutor, and then in 1727 began his long career in Northampton, Massachusetts. For two years he served as an assistant to his grandfather, Solomon Stoddard, and upon Stoddard's retirement in 1729 he became pastor. During his twenty years in the Northampton pulpit he preached over twelve hundred sermons.

Edward's life and work were at the heart of the religious controversies raging in his day. In direct opposition to the liberalizing influences of the enlightenment, Edwards held fast to the Calvinist doctrine of the total depravity of man. Since God was perfect, Edwards reasoned, human disobedience to God was the most terrible and heinous of crimes, worthy of the most terrible punishment. As a revivalist dedicated to the "harvesting" of souls, Edwards pictured with vividness and remarkable clarity the sinfulness of man and the vengefulness of God, fostering an intense emotionalism that was not universally admired among colonial clergy, although he might be considered relatively mild when compared with some evangelists. And, it should be acknowledge that he adhered more closely to the form of the Puritan sermon than did many preachers of his day.

"Sinners in the Hands of an Angry God," was one of Edward's best-known sermons. The vile nature of humanity—insects, hanging like spiders over the fire, worms to be crushed under the heel of God—the absolute power of God to wreak vengeance and punishment, and the will of God to do so everlastingly are vividly detailed by Edwards. His call is to be born again, to join in the great "outpouring of the Spirit" that was sweeping the land. Edwards's was not a joyous message, but rather one of fear and of submission to the absolute will of an angry but infinitely just God. He touched some of the deepest wellsprings of emotion in his audience and brought in many converts throughout the region. Yet this message was not one that, in the long run, the independent-minded Massachusetts farmers were likely to accept. By 1750 the tide of the Awakening had ebbed, and Edwards's congregation ousted him in a controversy over the place of public confession to admission to church membership. He served as a missionary to the Indians until 1757, when he went to Princeton to become president of the College of New Jersey. It was only a few months later that he died.

That Edwards could be persuasive and moving is an indication of the depth of religious intensity that existed in his audience. That his basic message was not to prevail testifies to the growing impact of the new ideas that he sought to turn back.

Deuteronomy xxxii. 35.—Their foot shall slide in due time.

In this verse is threatened the vengeance of God on the wicked unbelieving Israelites, that were God's visible people, and lived under means of grace; and that notwithstanding all God's wonderful works that he had wrought towards that people, yet remained, as is expressed verse 28, void of counsel, having no understanding in them; and that, under all the cultivations of heaven, brought forth bitter and poisonous fruit; as in the two verses next preceding the text.

The expression that I have chosen for my text, *their foot shall slide in due time*, seems to imply the following things relating to the punishment and destruction that these wicked Israelites were exposed to.

1 That they were *always* exposed to destruction; as one that stands or walks in slippery places is always exposed to fall. This is implied in the manner of their destruction's coming upon them, being represented by their foot's sliding. The same is expressed, Psalm lxxiii. 18: "Surely thou didst see them in slippery places; thou castedst them down into destruction."

2 It implies that they were always exposed to *sudden*, unexpected destruction; as he that walks in slippery places is every moment liable to fall, he can't foresee

one moment whether he shall stand or fall the next; and when he does fall, he falls at once, without warning, which is also expressed in that Psalm lxxiii. 18, 19; "Surely thou didst set them in slippery places: thou castedst them down into destruction. How are they brought into desolation, as *in a moment!*"

3 Another thing implied is, that they are liable to fall of *themselves*, without being thrown down by the hand of another; as he that stands or walks on slippery ground needs nothing but his own weight to throw him down.

4 That the reason why they are not fallen already, and don't fall now, is only that God's appointed time is not come. For it is said that when that due time, or appointed time comes, *their foot shall slide.* Then they shall be left to fall, as they are inclined by their own weight. God won't hold them up in these slippery places any longer, but will let them go; and then, at that very instant, they shall fall to destruction; as he that stands in such slippery declining ground on the edge of a pit that he can't stand alone, when he is let go he immediately falls and is lost.

The observation from the words that I would now insist upon is this,

There is nothing that keeps wicked men at any moment out of hell, but the mere pleasure of God.

By the mere pleasure of God, I mean his sovereign pleasure, his arbitrary will, restrained by no obligation, hindered by no manner of difficulty, any more than if nothing else but God's mere will had in the least degree or in any respect whatsoever any hand in the preservation of wicked men one moment.

The truth of this observation may appear by the following considerations.

1 There is no want of *power* in God to cast wicked men into hell at any moment. Men's hands can't be strong when God rises up: the strongest have no power to resist him, nor can any deliver out of his hands.

He is not only able to cast wicked men into hell, but he can most easily do it. Sometimes an earthly prince meets with a great deal of difficulty to subdue a rebel that has found means to fortify himself, and has made himself strong by the number of his followers. But it is not so with God. There is no fortress that is any defense against the power of God. Though hand join in hand, and vast multitudes of God's enemies combine and associate themselves, they are easily broken in pieces: they are as great heaps of light chaff before the whirlwind; or large quantities of dry stubble before devouring flames. We find it easy to tread on and crush a worm that we see crawling on the earth; so 'tis easy for us to cut or singe a slender thread that any thing hangs by; thus easy is it for God, when he pleases, to cast his enemies down to hell. What are we, that we should think to stand before him, at whose rebuke the earth trembles, and before whom the rocks are thrown down!

2 They *deserve* to be cast into hell; so that divine justice never stands in the way, it makes no objection against God's using his power at any moment to destroy them. Yea, on the contrary, justice calls aloud for an infinite punishment of their sins. Divine justice says of the tree that brings forth such grapes of Sodom, "Cut it down, why cumbereth it the ground?" Luke xiii, 7. The sword of divine justice is every moment brandished over their heads, and 'tis nothing but the hand of arbitrary mercy, and God's mere will, that holds it back.

3 They are *already* under a sentence of condemnation to hell. They don't only

justly deserve to be cast down thither, but the sentence of the law of God, that eternal and immutable rule of righteousness that God has fixed between him and mankind, is gone out against them, and stands against them; so that they are bound over already to hell: John iii. 18, "He that believeth not is condemned already." So that every unconverted man properly belongs to hell; that is his place; from thence he is: John viii. 23, "Ye are from beneath:" and thither he is bound; 'tis the place that justice, and God's word, and the sentence of his unchangeable law, assigns to him.

4 They are now the objects of that very *same* anger and wrath of God, that is expressed in the torments of hell: and the reason why they don't go down to hell at each moment is not because God, in whose power they are, is not then very angry with them; as angry as he is with many of those miserable creatures that he is now tormenting in hell, and do there feel and bear the fierceness of his wrath. Yea, God is a great deal more angry with great numbers that are now on earth, yea, doubtless, with many that are now in this congregation, that, it may be, are at ease and quiet, than he is with many of those that are now in the flames of hell.

So that it is not because God is unmindful of their wickedness, and don't resent it, that he don't let loose his hand and cut them off. God is not altogether such a one as themselves, though they may imagine him to be so. The wrath of God burns against them; their damnation don't slumber; the pit is prepared; the fire is made ready; the furnace is now hot, ready to receive them; the flames do now rage and glow. The glittering sword is whet, and held over them, and the pit hath opened her mouth under them.

5 The *devil* stands ready to fall upon them, and seize them as his own, at what moment God shall permit him. They belong to him; he has their souls in his possession, and under his dominion. The Scripture represents them as his *goods*, Luke xi. 21. The devils watch them; they are ever by them, at their right hand; they stand waiting for them, like greedy hungry lions that see they prey, and expect to have it, but are for the present kept back; if God should withdraw his hand by which they are restrained, they would in one moment fly upon their poor souls. The old serpent is gaping for them; hell opens its mouth wide to receive them; and if God should permit it, they would be hastily swallowed up and lost.

6 There are in the souls of wicked men those hellish *principles* reigning, that would presently kindle and flame out into hell-fire, if it were not for God's restraints. There is laid in the very nature of carnal men a foundation for the torments of hell: there are those corrupt principles, in reigning power in them, and in full possession of them, that are seeds of hell-fire. These principles are active and powerful, exceeding violent in their nature, and if it were not for the restraining hand of God upon them, they would soon break out, they would flame out after the same manner as the same corruptions, the same enmity does in the heart of damned souls, and would beget the same torments in 'em as they do in them. The souls of the wicked are in Scripture compared to the troubled sea, Isaiah lvii. 20. For the present God restrains their wickedness by his mighty power, as he does the raging waves of the troubled sea, saying, "Hitherto, shalt thou come, and no further;" but if God should withdraw that restraining power, it would soon carry all afore it. Sin is the ruin and misery of the soul; it is destructive in its nature; and if God should leave it without restraint, there would need nothing else to

make the soul perfectly miserable. The corruption of the heart of man is a thing that is immoderate and boundless in its fury; and while wicked men live here, it is like fire pent up by God's restraints, when as if it were let loose, it would set on fire by the course of nature; and as the heart is now a sink of sin, so, if sin was not restrained, it would immediately turn the soul into a fiery oven or a furnace of fire and brimstone.

7 It is no security to wicked men for one moment, that there are no *visible means of death* at hand. 'Tis no security to a natural man, that he is now in health, and that he don't see which way he should now immediately go out of the world by any accident, and that there is no visible danger in any respect in his circumstances. The manifold and continual experience of the world in all ages shows that this is no evidence that a man is not on the very brink of eternity, and that the next step won't be into another world. The unseen, unthought of ways and means of persons' going suddenly out of the world are innumerable and inconceivable. Unconverted men walk over the pit of hell on a rotten covering, and there are innumerable places in this covering so weak that they won't bear their weight, and these places are not seen. The arrows of death fly unseen at noonday; the sharpest sight can't discern them. God has so many different, unsearchable ways of taking wicked men out of the world and sending 'em to hell, that there is nothing to make it appear that God had need to be at the expense of a miracle, or go out of the ordinary course of his providence, to destroy any wicked man, at any moment. All the means that there are of sinners' going out of the world are so in God's hands, and so absolutely subject to his power and determination, that it don't depend at all less on the mere will of God, whether sinners shall at any moment go to hell, than if means were never made use of, or at all concerned in the case.

8 Natural men's *prudence* and *care* to preserve their own *lives*, or the care of others to preserve them, don't secure 'em a moment. This, divine providence and universal experience does also bear testimony to. There is this clear evidence that men's own wisdom is no security to them from death; that if it were otherwise we should see some difference between the wise and politic men of the world and others, with regard to their liableness to early and unexpected death; but how is it in fact? Eccles. ii. 16, "How dieth the wise man? As the fool."

9 All wicked men's *pains* and *contrivance* they use to escape *hell*, while they continue to reject Christ, and so remain wicked men, don't secure 'em from hell one moment. Almost every natural man that hears of hell flatters himself that he shall escape it; he depends upon himself for his own security, he flatters himself in what he has done, in what he is now doing, or what he intends to do; every one lays out matters in his own mind how he shall avoid damnation, and flatters himself that he contrives well for himself, and that his schemes won't fail. They hear indeed that there are but few saved, and that the bigger part of men that have died heretofore are gone to hell; but each one imagines that he lays out matters better for his own escape than others have done: he don't intend to come to that place of torment; he says within himself, that he intends to take care that shall be effectual, and to order matters so for himself as not to fail.

But the foolish children of men do miserably delude themselves in their own schemes, and in their confidence in their own strength and wisdom; they trust to nothing but a shadow. The bigger part of those that heretofore have lived under the same means of grace, and are now dead, are undoubtedly gone to hell; and it was not because they were not as wise as those that are now alive; it was not because they did not lay out matters as well for themselves to secure their own escape. If it were so that we could come to speak with them, and could inquire of them, one by one, whether they expected, when alive, and when they used to hear about hell, ever to be subjects of that misery, we, doubtless, should hear one and another reply, "No, I never intended to come here: I had laid out matters otherwise in my mind; I thought I should contrive well for myself: I thought my scheme good: I intended to take effectual care; but it came upon me unexpected; I did not look for it at that time, and in that manner; it came as a thief: death outwitted me: God's wrath was too quick for me. O my cursed foolishness! I was flattering myself, and pleasing myself with vain dreams of what I would do hereafter; and when I was saying peace and safety, then sudden destruction came upon me."

10 God has laid himself under *no obligation*, by any promise, to keep any natural man out of hell one moment. God certainly has made no promises either of eternal life, or of any deliverance or preservation from eternal death, but what are contained in the covenant of grace, the promises that are given in Christ, in whom all the promises are yea and amen. But surely they have no interest in the promises of the covenant of grace that are not the children of the covenant, and that do not believe in any of the promises of the covenant, and have no interest in the Mediator of the covenant.

So that, whatever some have imagined and pretended about promises made to natural men's earnest seeking and knocking, 'tis plain and manifest, that whatever pains a natural man takes in religion, whatever prayers he makes, till he believes in Christ, God is under no manner of obligation to keep him a moment from eternal destruction.

So that thus it is, that natural men are held in the hand of God over the pit of hell; they have deserved the fiery pit, and are already sentenced to it; and God is dreadfully provoked, his anger is as great towards them as to those that are actually suffering the executions of the fierceness of his wrath in hell, and they have done nothing in the least to appease or abate that anger, neither is God in the least bound by any promise to hold 'em up one moment; the devil is waiting for them, hell is gaping for them, the flames gather and flash about them, and would fain lay hold on them and swallow them up; the fire pent up in their own hearts is struggling to break out; and they have no interest in any Mediator, there are no means within reach that can be any security to them. In short they have no refuge, nothing to take hold of; all that preserves them every moment is the mere arbitrary will, and uncovenanted, unobliged forbearance of an incensed God.

APPLICATION

The use may be of *awakening* to unconverted persons in this congregation. This that you have heard is the case of every one of you that are out of Christ. That world of misery, that lake of burning brimstone, is extended abroad under you. *There* is the dreadful pit of the glowing flames of the wrath of God; there is hell's wide gaping mouth open; and you have nothing to stand upon, nor any thing to take hold of. There is nothing between you and hell but the air; 'tis only the power and mere pleasure of God that holds you up.

You probably are not sensible of this; you find you are kept out of hell, but don't see the hand of God in it, but look at other things, as the good state of your bodily constitution, your care of your own life, and the means you use for your own preservation. But indeed these things are nothing; if God should withdraw his hand, they would avail no more to keep you from falling than to thin air to hold up a person that is suspended in it.

Your wickedness makes you as it were heavy as lead, and to tend downwards with great weight and pressure towards hell; and if God should let you go, you would immediately sink and swiftly descend and plunge into the bottomless gulf; and your healthy constitution, and your own care and prudence, and best contrivance, and all your righteousness, would have no more influence to uphold you and keep you out of hell than a spider's web would have to stop a falling rock. Were it not that so is the sovereign pleasure of God, the earth would not bear you one moment; for you are a burden to it; the creation groans with you; the creature is made subject to the bondage of your corruption, not willingly; the sun don't willingly shine upon you to give you light to serve sin and Satan; the earth don't willingly yield her increase to satisfy your lusts; nor is it willingly a stage for your wickedness to be acted upon; the air don't willingly serve you for breath to maintain the flame of life in your vitals, while you spend your life in the service of God's enemies. God's creatures are good, and were made for men to serve God with, and don't willingly subserve to any other purpose, and groan when they are abused to purposes so directly contrary to their nature and end. And the world would spew you out, were it not for the sovereign hand of him who hath subjected it in hope. There are the black clouds of God's wrath now hanging directly over your heads, full of the dreadful storm, and big with thunder; and were it not for the restraining hand of God, it would immediately burst forth upon you. The sovereign pleasure of God, for the present, stays his rough wind; otherwise it would come with fury, and your destruction would come like a whirlwind, and you would be like the chaff of the summer threshing floor.

The wrath of God is like great waters that are dammed for the present; they increase more and more, and rise higher and higher, till an outlet is given; and the longer the stream is stopped, the more rapid and mighty is its course, when once it is let loose. 'Tis true, that judgment against your evil work has not been executed hitherto; the floods of God's vengeance have been withheld; but your guilt in the mean time is constantly increasing, and you are every day treasuring up more wrath; the waters are continually rising, and waxing more and more mighty; and there is nothing but the mere pleasure of God that holds the waters back, that are unwilling to be stopped, and press hard to go forward. If God should only withdraw his hand from the floodgate; it would immediately fly open, and the fiery floods of the fierceness and wrath of God would rush forth with inconceivable fury, and would come upon you with omnipotent power; and if your strength were ten thousand times greater than it is, yea, ten thousand times greater than the strength of the stoutest, sturdiest devil in hell, it would be nothing to withstand or endure it.

The bow of God's wrath is bent, and the arrow made ready on the string, and justice bends the arrow at your heart, and strains the bow, and it is nothing but the mere pleasure of God, and that of an angry

God, without any promise or obligation at all, that keeps the arrow one moment from being made drunk with your blood.

Thus are all you that never passed under a great change of heart by the mighty power of the Spirit of God upon your souls; all that were never born again, and made new creatures, and raised from being dead in sin to a state of new and before altogether unexperienced light and life, (however you may have reformed your life in many things, and may have had religious affections, and may keep up a form of religion in your families and closets, and in the house of God, and may be strict in it), you are thus in the hands of an angry God; 'tis nothing but his mere pleasure that keeps you from being this moment swallowed up in everlasting destruction.

However unconvinced you may now be of the truth of what you hear, by and by you will be fully convinced of it. Those that are gone from being in the like circumstances with you see that it was so with them; for destruction came suddenly upon most of them; when they expected nothing of it, and while they were saying, Peace and safety: now they see, that those things that they depended on for peace and safety were nothing but thin air and empty shadows.

The God that holds you over the pit of hell, much as one holds a spider or some loathsome insect over the fire, abhors you, and is dreadfully provoked; his wrath towards you burns like fire; he looks upon you as worthy of nothing else, but to be cast into the fire; he is of purer eyes than to bear to have you in his sight; you are ten thousand times so abominable in his eyes, as the most hateful and venomous serpent is in ours. You have offended him infintely more than ever a stubborn rebel did his prince: and yet it is nothing but his hand that holds you from falling into the fire every moment. 'Tis ascribed to nothing else, that you did not go to hell the last night; that you was suffered to awake again in this world after you closed your eyes to sleep; and there is no other reason to be given why you have not dropped into hell since you arose in the morning, but that God's hand has held you up. There is no other reason to be given why you han't gone to hell since you have sat here in the house of God, provoking his pure eyes by your sinful wicked manner of attending his solemn worship. Yea, there is nothing else that is to be given as a reason why you don't this very moment drop down into hell.

O sinner! consider the fearful danger you are in. 'Tis a great furnace of worth, a wide and bottomless pit, full of the fire of wrath, that you are held over in the hand of that God whose wrath is provoked and incensed as much against you as against many of the damned in hell. You hang by a slender thread, with the flames of divine wrath flashing about it, and ready every moment to singe it and burn it asunder; and you have no interest in any Mediator, and nothing to lay hold of to save yourself, nothing to keep off the flames of wrath, nothing of your own, nothing that you ever have done, nothing that you can do, to induce God to spare you one moment.

And consider here more particularly several things concerning that wrath that you are in such danger of.

1 *Whose* wrath it is. It is the wrath of the infinite God. If it were only the wrath of man, though it were of the most potent prince, it would be comparatively little to be regarded. The wrath of kings is very much dreaded, especially of absolute monarchs, that have the possessions and lives of their subjects wholly in their power, to be disposed of at their mere will. Prov. xx. 2, "The fear of a king is as the roaring of a

lion: whoso provoketh him to anger sinneth against his own soul." The subject that very much enrages an arbitrary prince is liable to suffer the most extreme torments that human art can invent, or human power can inflict. But the greatest earthly potentates, in their greatest majesty and strength, and when clothed in their greatest terrors, are but feeble, despicable worms of the dust, in comparison of the great and almighty Creator and King of heaven and earth: it is but little that they can do when most enraged, and when they have exerted the utmost of their fury. All the kings of the earth before God are as grasshoppers; they are nothing, and less than nothing: both their love and their hatred is to be despised. The wrath of the great King of kings is as much more terrible than theirs, as his majesty is greater. Luke xii. 4, 5, "And I say unto you my friends, Be not afraid of them that kill the body, and after that have no more that they can do. But I will forewarn you whom you shall fear: Fear him, which after he hath killed hath power to cast into hell; yea, I say unto you, Fear him."

2 'Tis the *fierceness* of his wrath that you are exposed to. We often read of the *fury* of God; as in Isaiah lix. 18: "According to their deeds, accordingly he will repay fury to his adversaries." So Isaiah lxvi. 16, "For, behold, the Lord will come with fire, and with his chariots like a whirlwind, to render his anger with fury, and his rebuke with flames of fire." And so in may other places. So we read of God's *fierceness*, Rev. xix. 15. There we read of "the wine-press of the fierceness and wrath of Almighty God." The words are exceeding terrible: if it had only been said, "the wrath of God," the words would have implied that which is infintely dreadful: but 'tis not only said so, but "the fierceness and wrath of God." The fury of God! The fierceness of Jehovah! Oh, how dreadful must that be! Who can utter or conceive what such expressions carry in them! But it is not only said so, but "the fierceness and wrath of Almighty God." As though there would be a very great manifestation of his almighty power in what the fierceness of his wrath should inflict, as though omnipotence should be as it were enraged, and exerted, as men are wont to exert their strength in the fierceness of their wrath. Oh! then, what will be the consequence! What will become of the poor worm that shall suffer it! Whose hands can be strong! And whose heart endure! To what a dreadful, inexpressible, inconceivable depth of misery must the poor creature be sunk who shall be the subject of this!

Consider this, you that are here present, that yet remain in an unregenerate state. That God will execute the fierceness of his anger implies that he will inflict wrath without any pity. When God beholds the ineffable extremity of your case, and sees your torment so vastly disproportioned to your strength, and sees how your poor soul is crushed, and sinks down, as it were, into an infinite gloom; he will have no compassion upon you, he will not forbear the executions of his wrath, or in the least lighten his hand; there shall be no moderation or mercy, nor will God then at all stay his rough wind; he will have no regard to your welfare, nor be at all careful lest you should suffer too much in any other sense, than only that you should not suffer beyond what strict justice requires: nothing shall be withheld because it is so hard for you to bear. Ezek. viii. 18, "Therefore will I also deal in fury: mine eye shall not spare, neither will I have pity: and though they cry in mine ears with a loud voice, yet will I not hear them." Now God stands ready to pity you; this is a day of mercy; you may cry now with some encouragement of obtaining mercy: but when once the day of mercy is past, your most lamentable and dolorous cries and shrieks will be in vain; you will be wholly lost and thrown away of God, as to any regard to your welfare; God will have no other use to put you to, but only to suffer misery; you shall be continued in being to no other end; for you will be a vessel of wrath fitted to destruction; and there will be no other use of this vessel, but only to be filled full of wrath; God will be so far from pitying you when you cry to him, that 'tis said he will only "laugh and mock," Prov. i. 25, 26, &c.

How awful are those words, Isaiah lxiii. 3, which are the words of the great God: "I will tread them in mine anger, and trample them in my fury; and their blood shall be sprinkled upon my garments, and I will stain all my raiment." 'Tis perhaps impossible to conceive of words that carry in them greater manifestations of these three things, viz., contempt and hatred and fierceness of indignation. If you cry to God to pity you, he will be so far from pitying you in your doleful case, or showing you the least regard of favor, that instead of that he'll only tread you under foot: and though he will know that you can't bear the weight of omnipotence treading upon you, yet he won't regard that, but he will crush you under his feet without mercy; he'll crash out your blood, and make it fly, and it shall be sprinkled on his garments, so as to stain all his raiment. He will not only hate you, but he will have you in the utmost contempt; no place shall be thought fit for you but under his feet, to be trodden down as the mire of the streets.

3 The misery you are exposed to is that which God will inflict to that end, that he might *show* what that *wrath* of *Jehovah* is. God hath had it on his heart to show to angels and men, both how excellent his love is, and also how terrible his wrath is. Sometimes earthly kings have a mind to show how terrible their wrath is, by the extreme punishments they would execute on those that provoke 'em. Nebuchadnezzar, that mighty and haughty monarch of the Chaldean empire, was willing to show his wrath when enraged with Shadrach, Meshech, and Abednego; and accordingly gave order that the burning fiery furnace should be heated seven times hotter than it was before; doubtless, it was raised to the utmost degree of fierceness that human art could raise it; but the great God is also willing to show his wrath, and magnify his awful Majesty and mighty power in the extreme sufferings of his enemies. Rom. ix. 22, "What if God, willing to show his wrath, and to make his power known, endured with much long-suffering the vessels of wrath fitted to destruction?" And seeing this is his design, and what he has determined, to show how terrible the unmixed, unrestrained wrath, the fury and fierceness of Jehovah is, he will do it to effect. There will be something accomplished and brought to pass that will be dreadful with a witness. When the great and angry God hath risen up and executed his awful vengeance on the poor sinner, and the wretch is actually suffering the infinite weight and power of his indignation, then will God call upon the whole universe to behold that awful majesty and mighty power that is to be seen in it. Isa. xxxiii. 12, 13, 14, "And the people shall be as the burnings of lime, as thorns cut up shall they be burnt in the fire. Hear, ye that are far off, what I have done; and ye that are near, acknowledge my might. The sinners in Zion are afraid; fearfulness hath surprised the hypocrites" &c.

Thus it will be with you that are in an unconverted state, if you continue in it; the infinite might, and majesty, and terribleness, of the Omnipotent God shall be magnified upon you in the ineffable strength of your torments. You shall be tormented in the presence of the holy angels, and in the presence of the Lamb; and when you shall be in this state of suffering, the glorious inhabitants of heaven shall go forth and look on the awful spectacle, that they may see what the wrath and fierceness of the Almighty is; and when they have seen it, they will fall down and adore that great power and majesty. Isa. lxvi. 23, 24, "And it shall come to pass, that from one new moon to another, and from one sabbath to another, shall all flesh come to worship before me, saith the Lord. And they shall go forth, and look upon the carcasses of the men that have transgressed against me: for their worm shall not die, neither shall their fire be quenched; and they shall be an abhorring unto all flesh."

4 It is *everlasting* wrath. It would be dreadful to suffer this fierceness and wrath of Almighty God one moment; but you must suffer it to all eternity: there will be no end to this exquisite, horrible misery. When you look forward, you shall see a long forever, a boundless duration before you, which will swallow up your thoughts, and amaze your soul; and you will absolutely despair of ever having any deliverance, any end, any mitigation, any rest at all: you will know certainly that you must wear out long ages, millions of millions of ages, in wrestling and conflicting with this almighty, merciless vengeance; and then when you have so done, when so many ages have actually been spent by you in this manner, you will know that all is but a point to what remains. So that your punishment will indeed be infinite. Oh, who can express what the state of a soul in such circumstances is! All that we can possibly say about it gives but a very feeble, faint representation of it; it is inexpressible and inconceivable: for "who knows the power of God's anger?"

How dreadful is the state of those that are daily and hourly in danger of this great wrath and infinite misery! But this is the dismal case of every soul in this congregation that has not been born again, however moral and strict, sober and religious, they may otherwise be. Oh, that you would consider it, whether you be young or old! There is reason to think that there are many in this congregation now hearing this discourse, that will actually be the subjects of this very misery to all eternity. We know not who they are, or in what seats they sit, or what thoughts they now have. It may be they are now at ease, and hear all these things without much disturbance, and are now flattering themselves that they are not the persons, promising themselves that they shall escape. If we knew that there was one person, and but one, in the whole congregation, that was to be the subject of this misery, what an awful thing it would be to think of! If we knew who it was, what an awful sight would it be to see such a person! How might all the rest of the congregation lift up a lamentable and bitter cry over him! But alas! instead of one, how many is it likely will remember this discourse in hell! And it would be a wonder, if some that are now present should not be in hell in a very short time, before this year is out. And it would be no wonder if some persons that now sit here in some seats of this meeting-house in health, and quiet and secure, should be there before to-morrow morning. Those of you that finally continue in a natural condition, that shall keep out of hell longest, will be there in a little time! Your damnation don't slumber; it will come swiftly and, in all probability, very suddenly upon many of you. You have reason to wonder that you are not already in hell. 'Tis doubtless the case of some that heretofore you have seen and known, that never deserved hell more than you and that heretofore appeared as likely to have been now alive as you. Their case is past all hope; they are crying in extreme misery and perfect despair. But here you are in the land of the living and in the house of God, and have an opportunity to obtain salvation. What would not those poor, damned, hopeless souls give for one day's such opportunity as you now enjoy!

And now you have an extraordinary opportunity, a day wherein Christ has flung the door of mercy wide open, and stands in the door calling and crying with a loud voice to poor sinners; a day wherein many are flocking to him and pressing into the Kingdom of God. Many are daily coming from the east, west, north and south; many that were very likely in the same miserable condition that you are in are in now a happy state, with their hearts filled with love to him that has loved them and washed them from their sins in his own blood, and rejoicing in hope of the glory of God. How awful is it to be left behind at such a day! To see so many others feasting, while you are pining and perishing! To see so many rejoicing and singing for joy of heart, while you have cause to mourn for sorrow of heart and howl for vexation of spirit! How can you rest for one moment in such a condition? Are not your souls as precious as the souls of the people at Suffield, where they are flocking from day to day to Christ?

Are there not many here that have lived long in the world that are not to this day born again, and so are aliens from the commonwealth of Israel and have done nothing ever since they have lived but treasure up wrath against the day of wrath? Oh, sirs, your case in an especial manner is extremely dangerous; your guilt and hardness of heart is extremely great. Don't you see how generally persons of your years are passed over and left in the present remarkable and wonderful dispensation of God's mercy? You had need to consider yourselves and wake thoroughly out of sleep; you cannot bear the fierceness and the wrath of the infinite God.

And you that are young men and young women, will you neglect this precious season that you now enjoy, when so many others of your age are renouncing all youthful vanities and flocking to Christ? You especially have now an extraordinary opportunity, but if you neglect it, it will soon be with you as it is with those persons that spent away all the precious days of youth in sin and are now come to such a dreadful pass in blindness and hardness.

And you children that are unconverted, don't you know that you are going down to hell to bear the dreadful wrath of that God that is now angry with you every day and every night? Will you be content to be the children of the devil, when so many other children in the land are converted and are become the holy and happy children of the King of kings?

And let every one that is yet out of Christ and hanging over the pit of hell, whether they be old men and women or middle-aged or young people or little children, now hearken to the loud calls of God's word and providence. This acceptable year of the Lord that is a day of such great favor to some will doubtless be a day of as remarkable vengeance to others. Men's hearts harden and their guilt increases apace at such a day as this, if they neglect their souls. And never was there so great danger of such persons being given up to hardness of heart and blindness of mind. God seems now to be hastily gathering in his elect in all parts of the land; and probably the bigger part of adult persons that ever shall be saved will be brought in now in a little time, and that it will be as it was on that great outpouring of the Spirit upon the Jews in the Apostles' days, the election will obtain and the rest will be blinded. If this should be the case with you,

you will eternally curse this day, and will curse the day that ever you was born to see such a season of the pouring out of God's Spirit, and will wish that you had died and gone to hell before you had seen it. Now undoubtedly it is as it was in the days of John the Baptist, the axe is in an extraordinary manner laid at the root of the trees, that every tree that bringeth not forth good fruit may be hewn down and cast into the fire.

Therefore let every one that is out of Christ now awake and fly from the wrath to come. The wrath of Almighty God is now undoubtedly hanging over great part of this congregation. Let every one fly out of Sodom. "*Haste and escape for your lives, look not behind you, escape to the mountain, lest ye be consumed.*"

Making a Revolution

James Otis

Against the Writs of Assistance (1761)

Great Britain had always asserted, and colonials generally conceded, the right to control the commerce of North America. Americans had little to complain about, since they were generally prosperous, and acts designed to control American trade, such as the Molasses Act of 1733, were not rigorously enforced. In the decade of the 1750's, however, the British fought a long and costly war with France. The Seven Years War, called the French and Indian War in America, effectively ended in the colonies with the fall of Canada in 1760. During the war, colonists had angered the British by maintaining their lucrative, but illegal, trade with the French West Indies. Smuggling was a profitable, and even respectable, practice among New England merchants; the British resolve to put an end to it and to recoup lost revenues was highly unpopular.

The problem for the British was how to get the needed evidence of smuggling when most of the population was bent on thwarting the customs officers in the performance of their duties. Authorities, who had experience with smugglers and with those who would evade excise taxes in England, had hit upon a device that made evasion more difficult. Instead of applying for a search warrant on the basis of reasonable suspicion in each individual case, the government asked the courts to issue general search warrants that allowed customs officials, with the help of the local constabulary, to search whatever premises they chose whenever they chose to do so. These "Writs of Assistance" were unpopular in England and had been attacked in the House of Commons, but they were held to be legal and they had proven effective. Writs were issued for the life of the monarch plus six months; following the death of George II in 1760, the writs had to be renewed. Accordingly, application for issuance of the Writs was made to the Superior Court of Massachusetts.

The King's Advocate General of the vice-admirality court in Boston in 1760 was a rising young attorney named James Otis. Otis was a Harvard graduate who had practiced law briefly in Plymouth before moving to Boston, where he soon achieved a reputation as an able advocate. As the King's legal officer, Otis was expected to argue for the issuance of the Writs. Rather than do so, however, he resigned his position and instead represented a group of Boston merchants opposed to the Writs. Most of Otis's four- to five-hour speech has been lost, but what remains gives good indication of his attack on the Writs as "the worst instrument of arbitrary power, the most destructive of English liberty and the fundamental principles of law, that ever was found in an English lawbook." His argument, Otis maintains, is in favor of "British liberty," fundamental to which "is the freedom of one's house." Indeed, "A man's house is his castle; and whilst he is quiet, he is as well guarded as a prince in his castle."

Otis's appeal against the misuse of power was the beginning of colonial resistance to a long series of actions by the British government that Americans claimed violated their rights as Englishmen. Otis himself, in the years that followed, wrote a series of pamphlets in which he asserted the rights of the British colonies and argued that taxation without representation was unconstitutional. But it was his speech against the Writs that John Adams was to call "the first scene of the first act of opposition to the arbitrary claims of Great Britain." In that Boston courtroom, Adams believed, "American independence was there and then born."

May it please your honors, I was desired by one of the court to look into the books, and consider the question now before them concerning Writs of Assistance. I have, accordingly, considered it, and now appear not only in obedience to your order, but likewise in behalf of the inhabitants of this town, who have presented another petition, and out of regard to the liberties of the subject. And I take this opportunity to declare that, whether under a fee or not (for in such a cause as this I despise a fee), I will to my dying day oppose with all the powers and faculties God has given me all such instruments of slavery on the one hand, and villany on the other, as this writ of assistance is.

It appears to me the worst instrument of arbitrary power, the most destructive of English liberty and the fundamental principles of law, that ever was found in an English law book. I must, therefore, beg your honors' patience and attention to the whole range of an argument, that may, perhaps, appear uncommon in many things, as well as to points of learning that are more remote and unusual: that the whole tendency of my design may the more easily be perceived, the conclusions better descend, and the force of them be better felt. I shall not think much of my pains in this cause, as I engaged in it from principle. I was solicited to argue this cause as Advocate-General; and because I would not, I have been charged with desertion from my office. To this charge I can give a very sufficient answer. I renounced that office, and I argue this cause from the same principle; and I argue it with the greater pleasure, as it is in favor of British liberty, at a time when we hear the greatest monarch upon earth declaring from his throne that he glories in the name of Briton, and that the privileges of his people are dearer to him than the most valuable prerogatives of his crown; and as it is in opposition to a king of power, the exercise of which, in former periods of history, cost one king of England his head and another his throne. I have taken more pains in this cause than I ever will take again, although my engaging in this and another popular cause has raised much resentment. But I think I can sincerely declare that I cheerfully submit myself to every odious name for conscience' sake; and from my soul I despise all those whose guilt, malice, or folly has made them my foes. Let the consequences be what they will, I am determined to proceed. The only principles of public conduct that are worthy of a gentleman or a man are to sacrifice estate, ease, health, and applause, and even life, to the sacred calls of his country.

These manly sentiments, in private life, make the good citizen; in public life, the patriot and the hero. I do not say that when brought to the test, I shall be invincible. I pray God I may never be brought to the melancholy trial; but if ever I should, it will be then known how far I can reduce to practice principles which I know to be founded in truth. In the meantime I will proceed to the subject of this writ.

Your honors will find in the old books concerning the office of a justice of the peace precedents of general warrants to search suspected houses. But in more modern books, you will find only special warrants to search such and such houses, specially named, in which the complainant has before sworn that the suspects his goods are concealed; and will find it adjudged that special warrants only are legal. In the same manner I rely on it, that the writ prayed for in this petition, being general, is illegal. It is a power that places the liberty of every man in the hands of every petty officer. I say I admit that special writs of assistance, to search special places, may be granted to certain persons on oath; but I deny that the writ now prayed for can be granted, for I beg leave to make some observations on the writ itself, before I proceed to other acts of Parliament. In the first place, the writ is universal, being directed "to all and singular justices, sheriffs, constables, and all other officers and subjects"; so, that, in short, it is directed to every subject in the king's dominions. Every one with this writ may be a tyrant; if this commission be legal, a tyrant in a legal manner, also, may control, imprison, or murder any one within the realm. In the next place, it is perpetual; there is no return. A man is accountable to no person for his doings. Every man may reign secure in his petty tyranny, and spread terror and desolation around him, until the trump of the archangel shall excite different emotions in his soul. In the third place, a person with this writ, in the daytime, may enter all houses, shops, etc., at will, and command all to assist him. Fourthly, by this writ, not only deputies, etc., but even their menial servants, are allowed to lord it over us. What is this but to have the curse of Canaan with a witness on us; to be the servant of servants, the most despicable of God's creation? Now one of the most essential branches of English liberty is the freedom of one's house. A man's house is his castle; and while he is quiet, he is as well guarded as a prince in his castle. This writ, if it should be declared legal, would totally annihilate this privilege. Custom house officers may enter our houses when they please; we are commanded to permit their entry. Their menial servants may enter, may break locks, bars, and everything in their way; and whether they break through malice or revenge, no man, no court can inquire. Bare suspicion without oath is sufficient. This wanton exercise of this power is not a chimerical suggestion of a heated brain. I will mention some facts. Mr. Pew had one of these writs, and when Mr. Ware succeeded him, he indorsed this writ over to Mr. Ware; so that these writs are negotiable from one officer to another; and so your honors have no opportunity of judging the persons to whom this vast power is delegated. Another instance is that: Mr. Justice Walley had called this same Mr. Ware before him, by a constable, to answer for a breach of the Sabbath day acts, or that of profane swearing. As soon as he had finished, Mr. Ware asked him if he had done. He replied: "Yes." "Well then," said Mr. Ware, "I will show you a little of my power. I command you to permit me to search your house for uncustomed goods"; and went on to search the house from the garret to the cellar, and then served the constable in the same manner! But to show another absurdity in this writ, if it should be established, I insist upon it that every person, by the 14th Charles II., has this power as well as the custom house officers. The words are: "It shall be lawful for any person or persons authorized," etc. What a scene does this open! Every man prompted by revenge, ill-humor, or wantonness, to inspect the inside of his neighbor's house, may get a writ of assistance. Others will ask it from self-defence; one arbitrary exertion will provoke another, until society be involved in tumult and in blood. . . . [*John Adams, after recording this first point made by Otis, summarizes the remaining three points as follows.*]

2 "He asserted that every man, merely natural, was an independent sovereign, subject to no law but the law written on his heart and revealed to him by his Maker, in the constitution of his nature, and the inspiration of his understanding and his conscience. His right to his life, his liberty, no created being could rightfully contest. Nor was his right to his property less incontestable. The club that he had snapped from a tree, for a staff or for defence, was his own. His bow and arrow were his own: if by a pebble he had killed a partridge or a squirrel, it was his own. No creature, man or beast, had a right to take it from him. If he had taken an eel, or a smelt, or a sculpin, it was his property. In short, he sported upon this topic with so much wit and humor, and at the same time with so much indisputable truth and reason, that he was not less entertaining than instructive. He asserted that these rights were inherent and inalienable; that they never could be surrendered or alienated, but by idiots or madmen, and all the acts of idiots and lunatics were void, and not obligatory, by all the laws of God and man. Nor were the poor negroes forgotten. Not a Quaker in Philadelphia, or Mr. Jefferson in Virginia, ever asserted the rights of negroes in stronger terms. Young as I was, and ignorant as I was, I shuddered at the doctrine he taught; and I have all my life shuddered, and still shudder, at the consequences that may be drawn from such premises. Shall we say that the rights of masters and servants clash, and can be decided only by force? I adore the idea of gradual abolitions! but who shall decide how fast or how slowly these abolitions shall be made?

3 "From individual independence he proceeded to association. If it was inconsistent with the dignity of human nature to say that men were gregarious animals, like wild geese, it surely could offend no deli-

cacy to say they were social animals by nature; that there were natural sympathies, and, above all, the sweet attraction of the sexes, which must soon draw them together in little groups, and by degrees in larger congregations, for mutual assistance and defense. And this must have happened before any formal covenant, by express words or signs, was concluded. When general councils and deliberations commenced, the objects could be no other than the natural defence and security of every individual for his life, his liberty and his property. To suppose them to have surrendered these in any other way than by equal rules and general consent was to suppose them idiots or madmen, whose acts were never binding. To suppose them surprised by fraud, or compelled by force into any other compact, such fraud and such force could confer no obligation. Every man had a right to trample it underfoot whenever he pleased. In short, he asserted these rights to be derived only from nature and the Author of Nature; that they were inherent, inalienable, and indefeasible by any laws, pacts, contracts, convenants, or stipulations which man could devise.

4 "These principles and these rights were wrought into the English Constitution as fundamental laws. And under this head he went back to the old Saxon laws, and to Magna Charta, and the fifty confirmations of it in Parliament, and the executions ordained against the violators of it, and the national vengeance which had been taken on them from time to time, down to the Jameses and Charleses; and to the Petition of Right and the Bill of Rights and the Revolution. He asserted that the security of these rights to life, liberty, and property had been the object of all those struggles against arbitrary power, temporal and spiritual, civil and political, military and ecclesiastical, in every age. He asserted that our ancestors, as British subjects, and we, their descendants, as British subjects, were entitled to all those rights, by the British Constitution, as well as by the law of nature and our provincial charter, as much as any inhabitant of London or Bristol, or any part of England; and were not to be cheated out of them by any phantom of 'virtual representation,' or any other fiction of law or politics, or any monkish trick of deceit and hypocrisy.

5 "He then examined the acts of trade, one by one, and demonstrated that if they were considered as revenue laws, they destroyed all our security of property, liberty, and life, every right of nature, and the English Constitution, and the charter of the province. Here he considered the distinction between 'external and internal taxes,' at that time a popular and commonplace distinction. But he asserted that there was no such distinction in theory, or upon any principle but 'necessity.' The necessity that the commerce of the empire should be under one direction was obvious. The Americans had been so sensible of this necessity, that they had connived at the distinction between external and internal taxes, and had submitted to the acts of trade as regulations of commerce, but never as taxations, or revenue laws. Nor had the British Government till now ever dared to attempt to enforce them as taxations or revenue laws. They had lain dormant in that character for a century almost. The Navigation Act he allowed to be binding upon us, because we had consented to it by our own legislature. Here he gave a history of the Navigation Act of the 1st of Charles II., a plagiarism from Oliver Cromwell. This act had lain dormant for fifteen years. In 1675, after repeated letters and orders from the king, Governor Leverett very candidly informs his Majesty that the law had not been executed, because it was thought unconstitutional, Parliament not having authority over us."

John Hancock

Boston Massacre Oration (1774)

After the Seven Years War, Great Britain was faced with a large war debt and increased taxation. The problem was compounded by the decision to keep a military establishment in the colonies to deter any future threat of French aggression. Colonial legislatures had not always been forthcoming in providing financial assistance during the war; this lack of support was highly irritating to British governments, who reasoned that Americans should be willing to pay for their own defense. In 1764 the passage of a series of Parliamentary Acts designed to raise import duties and tighten enforcement of trade restrictions coincided with an economic depression in the colonies. The Acts were bitterly resented by the colonists, who attempted to organize a boycott of British goods. The passage of the Stamp Act in 1765, imposing as it did direct taxation on the colonies, unleashed a storm of protest. Repealed under pressure from British merchants in 1766, the Stamp Act, while unsuccessful, proved to be the precursor of things yet to come. The British Parliament, having repealed the Act, immediately passed the Declaratory Act, which asserted Parliament's right to "bind the colonies in all cases whatsoever."

The next few years saw the passage by Parliament of further acts to raise revenue in America: these met with stiffened colonial resistance. Much of the impetus for American resistance came from the radicals of Massachusetts, and Boston was a hotbed of agitation. In June of 1768, Customs officials who had ordered the seizure of John Hancock's sloop, *Liberty*, were assaulted by a mob, fled the city for the protection of Castle William in Boston Harbor, and called for troops. In November two regiments of infantry were landed and stationed in the town.

Relations between the soldiers and the townspeople, consistently strained, were exacerbated by the need of the low-paid troops to seek work in off-duty hours, thus bringing them in direct competition for jobs with Boston laborers. On March 5, 1770, a fist fight on the docks soon developed into a riot and that night bands of Boston citizens, encouraged by Samuel Adams, roamed the streets. A lone sentry, surrounded by an unruly crowd, called for help and was reinforced by the guard under the command of Captain Preston. Pelted with paving stones and oyster shells, taunted with abusive epithets, and threatened by the alarming hostility of the mob, the soliders fired. Three Bostonians were killed and two later died of their wounds. In the ensuing civil trial, Captain Preston and four of his men were acquitted for murder and two soldiers found guilty only of manslaughter. They were not, however, acquitted in the popular mind. Radicals seized upon the incident to inflame opinion against the British. Samuel Adams organized an annual commemoration of the event in which a memorial oration was the centerpiece.

John Hancock, who delivered the oration in 1774, was a wealthy Boston merchant who had long been in opposition to British policy. He took part in the protest against the Stamp Act, was elected to the Massachusetts legislature in 1769, and became head of the Boston Town Committee the next year. In 1774 Hancock was elected president of the Massachusetts Provincial Congress and was subsequently to serve as president of the Continental Congress, in which capacity he was the first to sign the Declaration of Independence. His Massacre Oration marks a distinct change from the constitutional arguments prevalent in colonial rhetoric in the decade before the war and exhibits the radicals' more violent denunciation of the British and their American supporters.

Men, brethren, fathers, and fellow countrymen,—The attentive gravity, the venerable appearance of this crowded audience; the dignity which I behold in the countenances of so many in this great assembly; the solemnity of the occasion upon which we have met together, joined to a consideration of the part I am to take in the important business of this day, fill me with an awe hitherto unknown, and heighten the sense which I have ever had, of my unworthiness to fill this sacred desk. But, allured by the call of some of my respected fellow citizens, with whose request it is always my greatest pleasure to comply, I almost forgot my want of ability to perform what they required.

In this situation I find my only support in assuring myself that a generous people will not severely censure what they know was well intended, though its want of merit should prevent their being able to applaud it. And I pray that my sincere attachment to the interest of my country, and hearty detestation of every design formed against her liberties, may be admitted as some apology for my appearance in this place.

I have always, from my earliest youth,

rejoiced in the felicity of my fellow men; and have ever considered it as the indispensable duty of every member of society to promote, as far as in him lies, the prosperity of every individual, but more especially of the community to which he belongs; and also, as a faithful subject of the state, to use his utmost endeavors to detect and having detected, strenuously to oppose every traitorous plot which its enemies may devise for its destruction. Security to the persons and properties of the governed is so obviously the design and end of civil government that to attempt a logical proof of it would be like burning tapers at noonday to assist the sun in enlightening the world; and it cannot be either virtuous or honorable to attempt to support a government of which this is not the great and principal basis; and it is to the last degree vicious and infamous to attempt to support a government which manifestly tends to render the persons and properties of the governed insecure.

Some boast of being friends to government; I am a friend to righteous government, to a government founded upon the principles of reason and justice; but I glory in publicly avowing my eternal enmity to tyranny. Is the present system, which the British administration have adopted for the government of the colonies, a righteous government—or is it tyranny? Here suffer me to ask (and would to heaven there could be an answer), what tenderness, what regard, respect or consideration has Great Britain shown, in their late transactions, for the security of the persons or properties of the inhabitants of the colonies? Or rather what have they omitted doing to destory that security?

They have declared that they have ever had, and of right ought ever to have, full power to make laws of sufficient validity to bind the colonies in all cases whatever. They have exercised this pretended right by imposing a tax upon us without our consent; and lest we should show some reluctance at parting with our property, her fleets and armies are sent to enforce their mad pretensions.

The town of Boston, ever faithful to the British crown, has been invested by a British fleet; the troops of George III have crossed the wide Atlantic, not to engage an enemy, but to assist a band of traitors in trampling on the rights and liberties of his most loyal subjects in America—those rights and liberties which, as a father, he ought ever to regard, and as a king he is bound in honor to defend from violation, even at the risk of his own life.

Let not the history of the illustrious house of Brunswick inform posterity that a king descended from that glorious monarch, George II, once sent his British subjects to conquer and enslave his subjects in America. But be perpetual infamy entailed upon that villain who dared to advise his master to such execrable measures; for it was easy to foresee the consequences which so naturally followed upon sending troops into America to enforce obedience to acts of the British Parliament which neither God nor man ever empowered them to make. It was resonable to expect that troops who knew the errand they were sent upon would treat the people whom they were to subjugate with a cruelty and haughtiness which too often buries the honorable character of a soldier in the disgraceful name of an unfeeling ruffian. The troops, upon their first arrival, took possession of our senate house and pointed their cannon against the judgment hall, and even continued them there whilst the supreme court of judicature for this province was actually sitting to decide upon the lives and fortunes of the king's subjects. Our streets nightly resounded with the noise of riot and debauchery; our peaceful citizens were hourly exposed to shameful insults, and often felt the effects of their violence and outrage.

But this was not all: as though they thought it not enough to violate our civil rights, they endeavored to deprive us of the enjoyment of our religious privileges; to vitiate our morals, and thereby render us deserving of destruction. Hence the rude din of arms which broke in upon your solemn devotions in your temples on that day hallowed by heaven and set apart by God himself for his peculiar worship. Hence impious oaths and blasphemies so often tortured your unaccustomed ear. Hence all the arts which idleness and luxury could invent were used to betray our youth of one sex into extravagance and effeminacy, and of the other, to infamy and ruin; and did they not succeed but too well? Did not a reverence for religion sensibly decay? Did not our infants almost learn to lisp out curses before they knew their horrid import? Did not our youth forget they were Americans, and regardless of the admonitions of the wise and aged servilely copy from their tyrants those vices which finally must overthrow the empire of Great Britain? And must I be compelled to acknowledge that even the noblest, fairest part of the lower creation did not entirely escape the cursed snare? When virtue has once erected her throne within the female breast it is upon so solid a basis that nothing is able to expel the heavenly inhabitant. But have there not been some, few indeed, I hope, whose youth and inexperience have rendered them a prey to wretches whom, upon the least reflection, they would have despised and hated as foes to God and their country? I fear there have been some such unhappy instances, or why have I seen an honest father clothed with shame; or why a virtuous mother drowned in tears?

But I forbear, and come reluctantly to the transactions of that dismal night when in such quick succession we felt the extremes of grief, astonishment and rage; when heaven in anger, for a dreadful moment, suffered hell to take the reins; when Satan with his chosen band opened the sluices of New England's blood, and sacrilegiously polluted our land with the dead bodies of her guiltless sons!

Let this sad tale of death never be told without a tear: let not the heaving bosom cease to burn with a manly indignation at the barbarous story through the long tracts of future time: let every parent tell the shameful story to his listening children until tears of pity glisten in their eyes and boiling passions shake their tender frames; and whilst the anniversary of that ill-fated night is kept a jubilee in the grim court of pandemonium, let all America join in one common prayer to heaven, that the inhuman, unprovoked murders of the 5th of March, 1770, planned by Hillsborough and a knot of treacherous knaves in Boston, and executed by the cruel hand of Preston and his sanguinary coadjutors, may ever stand on history without a parallel.

But what, my countrymen, withheld the ready arm of vengeance from executing instant justice on the vile assassins? Perhaps you feared promiscuous carnage might ensue, and that the innocent might share the fate of those who had performed the infernal deed. But were not all guilty? Were you not too tender of the lives of those who came to fix a yoke on your necks? But I must not too severely blame a fault which great souls only can commit. May that magnificence of spirit which scorns the low pursuits of malice, may that generous compassion which often preserves from ruin even a guilty villain, forever actuate the noble bosoms of Americans!

But let not the miscreant host vainly imagine that we feared their arms. No; them we despised; we dread nothing but slavery. Death is the creature of a poltroon's brains; 'tis immortality to sacrifice ourselves for the salvation of our country. We fear not death. That gloomy night, the palefaced moon, and the affrighted stars that hurried through the sky, can witness that we fear not death. Our hearts which, at the recollection, glow with rage that four revolving years have scarcely taught us to restrain, can witness that we fear not death; and happy it is for those who dared to insult us that their naked bones are not now piled up an everlasting monument of Massachusetts' bravery.

But they retired, they fled, and in that flight they found their only safety. We then expected that the hand of public justice would soon inflict that punishment upon the murderers which by the laws of God and man they had incurred. But let the unbiassed pen of a Robertson, or perhaps of some equally famed American, conduct this trial before the great tribunal of succeeding generations. And though the murderers may escape the just resentment of an enraged people; though drowsy justice, intoxicated by the poisonous draught prepared for her cup, still nods upon her rotten seat, yet be assured such complicated crimes will meet their due reward. Tell me, ye bloody butchers! ye villains high and low! ye wretches who contrived as well as you who executed the inhuman deed! do you not feel the goads and stings of conscious guilt pierce through your savage bosoms? Though some of you may think yourselves exalted to a height that bids defiance to human justice; and others shroud yourselves beneath the mask of hypocrisy, and build your hopes of safety on the low arts of cunning, chicanery, and falsehood; yet do you not sometimes feel the gnawings of that worm which never dies? Do not the injured shades of Maverick, Gray, Caldwell, Attucks, and Carr, attend you in your solitary walks; arrest you even in the midst of your debaucheries, and fill even your dreams with terror? But if the unappeased manes of the dead should not disturb their murderers, yet surely even your obdurate hearts must shrink, and your guilty blood must chill within your rigid veins, when you behold the miserable Monk, the wretched victim of your savage cruelty. Observe his tottering knees, which scarce sustain his wasted body; look on his haggard eyes; mark well the death-like paleness on his fallen cheek, and tell me, does not the sight plant daggers in your souls? Unhappy Monk! cut off, in the gay morn of manhood, from all the joys which sweeten life, doomed to drag on a pitiful existence without even a hope to taste the pleasures of returning health! Yet Monk, thou livest not in vain; thou livest a warning to thy country, which sympathizes with thee in thy sufferings; thou livest an affecting, an alarming instance of the unbounded violence which lust of power, assisted by a standing army, can lead a traitor to commit.

For us he bled and now languishes. The wounds by which he is tortured to a lingering death were aimed at our country! Surely the meek-eyed charity can never behold such sufferings with indifference. Nor can her lenient hand forbear to pour oil and wine into these wounds, and to assuage, at least, what it cannot heal.

Patriotism is ever united with humanity and compassion. This noble affection which impels us to sacrifice everything dear, even life itself, to our country, involves in it a common sympathy and tenderness for every citizen, and must ever have a particular feeling for one who suffers in a public cause. Thoroughly persuaded of this, I need not add a word to engage your compassion and bounty towards a fellow citizen who, with long protracted anguish, falls a victim to the relentless rage of our common enemies.

Ye dark designing knaves, ye murderers, parricides! how dare you tread upon the earth which has drank in the blood of slaughtered innocents, shed by your wicked hands? How dare you breathe the air which wafted to the ear of heaven the groans of those who fell a sacrifice to your accursed ambition? But if the laboring earth doth not expand her jaws; if the air you breathe is not commissioned to be the minister of death; yet, hear it and tremble! The eye of heaven penetrates the darkest chambers of the soul, traces the leading clue through all the labyrinths which your industrious folly has devised; and you, however you may have screened yourselves from human eyes, must be arraigned, must lift your hands, red with the blood of those whose death you have procured, at the tremendous bar of God!

But I gladly quit the gloomy theme of death and leave you to improve the thought of that important day when our naked souls must stand before that Being from whom nothing can be hid. I would not dwell too long upon the horrid effects which have already followed from quartering regular troops in this town. Let our misfortunes teach posterity to guard against such evils for the future. Standing armies are sometimes (I would by no means say generally, much less universally) composed of persons who have rendered themselves unfit to live in civil society; who have no other motives of conduct than those which a desire of the present gratification of their passions suggests; who have no property in any country; men who have given up their own liberties and envy those who enjoy liberty; who are equally indifferent to the glory of a George or a Louis; who, for the addition of one penny a day to their wages would desert from the Christian cross and fight under the crescent of the Turkish sultan.

From such men as these what has not a state to fear? With such as these usurping Caesar passed the Rubicon; with such as these he humbled mighty Rome and forced the mistress of the world to own a master in a traitor. These are the men whom sceptred robbers now employ to frustrate the designs of God and render vain the bounties which his gracious hand pours indiscriminately upon his creatures. By these the miserable slaves in Turkey, Persia, and many other extensive countries are rendered truly wretched, though their air is salubrious and their soil luxuriously fertile. By these, France and Spain, though blessed by nature with all that administers to the convenience of life, have been reduced to that contemptible state in which they now appear; and by these, Britain—but if I was possessed of the gift of prophecy I dare not, except by divine command, unfold the leaves on which the destiny of that once powerful kingdom is inscribed.

But since standing armies are so hurtful to a state, perhaps my countrymen may demand some substitute, some other means of rendering us secure against the incursions of a foreign enemy. But can you be one moment at a loss? Will not a well-disciplined militia afford you ample security against foreign foes? We want not courage; it is discipline alone in which we are exceeded by the most formidable troops that ever trod the earth. Surely our hearts flutter no more at the sound of war than did those of the immortal band of Persia, the Macedonian phalanx, the invincible Roman legions, the Turkish janissaries, the gens d'armes of France, or the well-known grenadiers of Britain.

A well-disciplined militia is a safe, an honorable guard to a community like this, whose inhabitants are by nature brave, and are laudably tenacious of that freedom in which they were born. From a well-regulated militia we have nothing to fear; their interest is the same with that of the state. When a country is invaded, the militia are ready to appear in its defence; they march into the field with that fortitude which a consciousness of the justice of their cause inspires; they do not jeopard their lives for a master who considers them only as the instruments of his ambition, and whom they regard only as the daily dispenser of the scanty pittance of bread and water.

No, they fight for their houses, their lands, for their wives, their children, for all who claim the tenderest names, and are held dearest in their hearts; they fight *pro aris et focis*, for their liberty, and for themselves, and for their God. And let it not offend if I say that no militia ever appeared in more flourishing condition than that of this province now doth; and pardon me if I say, of this town in particular. I mean not to boast; I would not excite envy, but manly emulation.

We have all one common cause; let it, therefore, be our only contest who shall most contribute to the security of the liberties of America. And may the same kind Providence which has watched over this country from her infant state still enable us to defeat our enemies.

I cannot here forbear noticing the signal manner in which the designs of those who wish not well to us have been discovered. The dark deeds of a treacherous cabal have been brought to public view. You now know the serpents who, whilst cherished in your bosoms, were darting their envenomed stings into the vitals of the constitution.

But the representatives of the people have fixed a mark on these ungrateful monsters, which, though it may not make them so secure as Cain of old, yet renders them at least as infamous. Indeed, it would be affrontive to the tutelar deity of this country even to despair of saving it from all the snares which human policy can lay.

True it is that the British ministry have annexed a salary to the office of the governor of this province, to be paid out of a revenue raised in America without our consent. They have attempted to render our courts of justice the instruments of extending the authority of acts of the British Parliament over this colony, by making the judges dependent on the British administration for their support. But this people will never be enslaved with their eyes open. The moment they knew that the governor was not such a governor as the charter of the province points out, he lost his power of hurting them. They were alarmed; they suspected him, have guarded against him, and he has found that a wise and a brave people, when they know their danger, are fruitful in expedients to escape it.

The courts of judicature, also, so far lost their dignity, by being supposed to be under an undue influence, that our representatives thought it absolutely necessary to resolve that they were bound to declare that they would not receive any other salary besides that which the General Court should grant them; and if they did not make this declaration, that it would be the duty of the House to impeach them.

Great expectations were also formed from the artful scheme of allowing the East India Company to export tea to America upon their own account. This certainly, had it succeeded, would have effected the purpose of the contrivers and gratified the most sanguine wishes of our adversaries. We soon should have found our trade in the hands of foreigners, and taxes imposed on everything which we consumed; nor would it have been strange if in a few years a company in London should have purchased an exclusive right of trading to America.

But their plot was soon discovered. The peoplc soon were aware of the poison which, with so much craft and subtlety, had been concealed. Loss and disgrace ensued; and, perhaps this long-concerted masterpiece of policy may issue in the total disuse of tea in this country, which will eventually be the saving of the lives and the estates of thousands.

Yet while we rejoice that the adversary has not hitherto prevailed against us, let us by no means put off the harness. Restless malice and disappointed ambition will still suggest new measures to our inveterate enemies. Therefore let us also be ready to take the field whenever danger calls; let us be united and strengthen the hands of each other by promoting a general union among us. Much has been done by the committees of correspondence for this and the other towns of this province toward uniting the inhabitants; let them still go on and prosper. Much has been done by the committees of correspondence, for the houses of assembly, in this and our sister colonies, for uniting the inhabitants of the whole continent for the security of their common interest. May success ever attend their generous endeavors.

But permit me here to suggest a general congress of deputies from the several houses of assembly on the continent as the most effectual method of establishing such an union as the present posture of our affairs require.

At such a congress a firm foundation may be laid for the security of our rights and liberties; a system may be formed for our common safety, by a strict adherence to which we shall be able to frustrate any attempts to overthrow our constitution; restore peace and harmony to America, and secure honor and wealth to Great Britain, even against the inclinations of her ministers, whose duty it is to study her welfare; and we shall also free ourselves from those unmannerly pillagers who impudently tell us that they are licensed by an act of the British Parliament to thrust their dirty hands into the pockets of every American. But I trust the happy time will come when, with the besom of destruction, those noxious vermin will be swept forever from the streets of Boston.

Surely you never will tamely suffer this country to be a den of thieves. Remember, my friends, from whom you sprang. Let not a meanness of spirit unknown to those whom you boast of as your fathers excite a thought to the dishonor of your mothers. I conjure you, by all that is dear, by all that is honorable, by all that is sacred, not only that ye pray, but that ye act; that, if necessary, ye fight, and even die, for the prosperity of our Jerusalem. Break in sunder, with noble disdain, the bonds with which the Philistines have bound you. Suffer not yourselves to be betrayed, by the soft arts of luxury and effeminacy, into the pit digged for your destruction. Despise the glare of wealth. That people who pay greater respect to a wealth villain than to an honest, upright man in poverty, almost deserve to be enslaved; they plainly show that wealth, however it may be acquired, is, in their esteem, to be preferred to virtue.

But I thank God that America abounds in men who are superior to all temptation; whom nothing can divert from a steady pursuit of the interest of their country; who are at once its ornament and safeguard. And sure I am I should not incur your displeasure if I paid a respect, so justly due to their much honored characters, in this place. But when I name an Adams, such a numerous host of fellow patriots rush upon my mind that I fear it would take up too much of your time should I attempt to call over the illustrious roll.

But your grateful hearts will point you to the men; and their revered names in all succeeding times shall grace the annals of America. From them let us, my friends, take example; from them let us catch the divine enthusiasm; and feel, each for himself, the god-like pleasure of diffusing happiness on all around us; of delivering the oppressed from the iron grasp of tyranny; of changing the hoarse complaints and bitter moans of wretched slaves into those cheerful songs which freedom and contentment must inspire.

There is a heartfelt satisfaction in reflecting on our exertions for the public weal which all the sufferings an enraged tyrant can inflict will never take away; which the ingratitude and reproaches of those whom we have saved from ruin cannot rob us of. The virtuous asserter of the rights of mankind merits a reward which even a want of success in his endeavors to save his country, the heaviest misfortune which can befall a genuine patriot, cannot entirely prevent him from receiving.

I have the most animating confidence that the present noble struggle for liberty will terminate gloriously for America. And let us play the man for our God, and for the cities of our God; while we are using the means in our power, let us humbly commit our righteous cause to the great Lord of the universe, who loveth righteousness and hateth iniquity. And having secured the approbation of our hearts, by a faithful and unwearied discharge of our duty to our country, let us joyfully leave our concerns in the hands of him who raiseth up and putteth down the empires and kingdoms of the world as he pleases; and with cheerful submission to his sovereign will devoutly say, "Although the fig-tree shall not blossom, neither shall fruit be in the vines; the labor of the olive shall fail, and the field shall yield no meat; the flock shall be cut off from the fold, and there shall be no herd in the stalls; yet we will rejoice in the Lord, we will joy in the God of our salvation."

Jonathan Boucher

On Civil Liberty; Passive Obedience, and Nonresistance (1775)

In the war of words preceding the American Revolution, patriot writers and speakers clearly outdistanced their loyalist opponents in both number and quality. There were, however, some Tory voices raised to defend the British position. Men like the governor of Massachusetts, Thomas Hutchison, were more apt to express their sentiments in private documents than engage in public argument. Indeed, the position of Tories was a difficult one since they tended to disdain popular assemblies; as Hutchison explained to Lord Hillsboro, "in most of the public proceedings of the Town of Boston, persons of the best character and estate have little or no concern. They decline attending Town Meetings where they are sure to be outvoted by men of the lowest order." The governor, of course, did have the opportunity to address his own fractious assembly and did so in 1773 to argue that "no line" could "be drawn between the supreme authority of Parliament and the total independence of the colonies." There was the Tory lawyer, Daniel Leonard, an effective speaker and writer who, under the pen name of "Massachusettensis," argued the British cause by appeals to legal precedent and the constitution. He also clearly asserted that rebellion against legal authority was wicked—"rebellion is the most atrocious offence, that can be perpetrated by men"—as well as being unjustified by events and tending to the dissolution of the social order.

One of the most implacable foes of the patriot party in America, however, was an Anglican minister, Jonathan Boucher, rector of the parish of Queen Anne in Maryland, a noted preacher and scholar of his time.

Jonathan Boucher first arrived in the colonies from England in 1759 as a private tutor to a Virginia family. Three years later he returned to England to be ordained in the Church of England. Back in America he was rector of churches in Hanover; Caroline County, Virginia; and Annapolis, Maryland, before taking up his duties at Queen Anne's Parish, Prince Georges County, Maryland. Boucher was active in colonial affairs and served as chaplain to the Maryland House of Delegates. A friend of colonial leaders, he had once tutored George Washington's stepson. However, his absolute loyalty to the British Crown was unshakable, and he undertook to refute from his pulpit the seditious doctrine spreading throughout the colonies.

Boucher's uncompromising Toryism was far from popular with his congregation, but popularity was of little concern to Boucher, who refused to be intimidated. "For more than six months," he wrote, "I preached with a pair of loaded pistols lying on the cushions." He was finally overwhelmed, however, and forced to return to England. Years later, in 1797, he published *A View of the Causes and Consequences of the American Revolution in Thirteen Discourses*, a collection of sermons he had given in America between 1763 and 1775. "On Civil Liberty" was Discourse XIII, his last sermon. In it he stresses that "Obedience to Government is every man's duty," such obedience being "enjoined by the positive commands of God." Those who would be "refractory and rebellious subjects" are guilty of "resisting the ordinances of God." Such divine sanction for British authority was no more in tune with growing colonial resentment toward what they considered arbitrary government than was Daniel Leonard's assertion of legal sanction for obedience. Sentiment against loyalist demands for adherence to the settled order of things was strong, and Tory persuasion was not able to alter it.

Stand fast, therefore, in the liberty wherewith Christ hath made us free (Galatians 5:1).

. . . I entreat your indulgence, whilst, without too nicely scrutinizing the propriety of deducing from a text a doctrine which it clearly does not suggest, I once more adopt a plan already chalked out for me, and deliver to you what occurs to me as proper for a Christian audience to attend to on the subject of Liberty. . . .

Obedience to government is every man's duty, because it is every man's interest; but it is particularly incumbent on Christians, because (in addition to its moral fitness) it is enjoined by the positive commands of God; and, therefore, when Christians were disobedient to human ordinances, they are also disobedient to God. If the form of government under which the good providence of God has been pleased to place us be mild and free, it is our duty to enjoy it with gratitude and with thankfulness and, in particular, to be careful not to abuse it by licentiousness. If it be less indulgent and less liberal than in reason it ought to be, still it is our duty not to disturb and destroy the peace of the community by becoming refractory and rebellious subjects and *resisting the ordinances of God.*

However humiliating such acquiescence may seem to men of warm and eager minds, the wisdom of God in having made it our duty is manifest. For, as it is the natural temper and bias of the human mind to be impatient under restraint, it was wise and merciful in the blessed Author of our religion not to add any new impulse to the natural force of this prevailing propensity but, with the whole weight of his authority, altogether to discountenance every tendency to disobedience.

If it were necessary to vindicate the Scriptures for this their total unconcern about a principle which so many other writings seem to regard as the first of all human considerations, it might be observed that, avoiding the vague and declamatory manner of such writings, and avoiding also the useless and impracticable subtleties of metaphysical definitions, these Scriptures have better consulted the great general interests of mankind, by summarily recommending and enjoining a conscientious reverence for law whether human or divine. To respect the laws is to respect liberty in the only rational sense in which the term can be used, for liberty consists in a subserviency to law. "Where there is no law," says Mr. Locke, "there is no freedom." The mere man of nature (if such an one there ever was) has no freedom: *all his lifetime he is subject to bondage*. It is by being included within the pale of civil polity and government that he takes his rank in society as a free man.

Hence it follows that we are free, or otherwise, as we are governed by law, or by the mere arbitrary will, or wills, of any individual, or any number of individuals. And liberty is not the setting at nought and despising established laws—much less the making our own wills the rule of our own actions, or the actions of others—and not bearing (whilst yet we dictate to others) the being dictated to, even by the laws of the land; but it is the being governed by law and by law only. The Greeks described Eleutheria, or Liberty, as the daughter of Jupiter, the supreme fountain of power and law. And the Romans, in like manner, always drew her with the pretor's wand (the emblem of legal power and authority), as well as with the cap. Their idea, no doubt, was that liberty was the fair fruit of just authority and that it consisted in men's being subjected to law. The more carefully well-devised restraints of law are enacted, and the more rigorously they are executed in any country, the greater degree of civil liberty does that country enjoy. To pursue liberty, then, in a manner not warranted by law, whatever the pretense may be, is clearly to be hostile to liberty; and those persons who thus *promise you liberty* are themselves *the servants of corruption*.

"Civil liberty (says an excellent writer) is a severe and a restrained thing; implies, in the notion of it, authority, settled subordinations, subjection, and obedience; and is altogether as much hurt by too little of this kind, as by too much of it. And the love of liberty, when it is indeed the love of liberty, which carries us to withstand tyranny, will as much carry us to reverence authority, and to support it; for this most obvious reason, that one is as necessary to the being of liberty, as the other is destructive of it. And, therefore, the love of liberty which does not produce this effect, the love of liberty which is not a real principle of dutiful behavior toward authority, is as hypocritical as the religion which is not productive of a good life. Licentiousness is, in truth, such an excess of liberty as is of the same nature with tyranny. For, what is the difference betwixt them, but that one is lawless power exercised under pretense of authority, or by persons vested with it; the other, lawless power exercised under pretense of liberty, or without any pretense at all? A people, then, must always be less free in proportion as they are more licentious, licentiousness being not only different from liberty but directly contrary to it—a direct breach upon it."

True liberty, then, is a liberty to do everything that is right, and the being restrained from doing anything that is wrong. So far from our having a right to do everything that we please, under a notion of liberty, liberty itself is limited and confined—but limited and confined only by laws which are at the same time both its foundation and its support. It can, however, hardly be necessary to inform you that ideas and notions respecting liberty, very different from these, are daily suggested in the speeches and the writings of the times; and also that some opinions on the subject of government at large, which apear to me to be particularly loose and dangerous, are advanced in the sermon now under consideration; and that, therefore, you will acknowledge the propriety of my bestowing some farther notice on them both.

It is laid down in this sermon, as a settled maxim, that the end of government is "the common good of mankind." I am not sure that the position itself is indisputable; but, if it were, it would by no means follow that "this common good being matter of common feeling, government must therefore have been instituted by common consent." There is an appearance of logical accuracy and precision in this statement; but it is only an appearance. The position is vague and loose; and the assertion is made without an attempt to prove it. If by men's "common feelings" we are to understand that principle in the human mind called common sense, the assertion is either unmeaning and insignificant, or it is false. In no instance have mankind ever yet agreed as to what is, or is not, "the common good." A form or mode of government cannot be named, which these "common feelings" and "common consent," the sole arbiters, as it seems, of "common good," have not, at one time or another, set up and established, and again pulled down and reprobated. What one people in one age have concurred in establishing as the "common good," another in another age have voted to be mischievous and big with ruin. The premises, therefore, that "the common good is matter of common feeling," being false, the consequence drawn from it, viz., that government was instituted by "common consent," is of course equally false.

This popular notion, that government was originally formed by the consent or by a compact of the people, rests on, and is supported by, another similar notion, not less popular, nor better founded. This other notion is that the whole human race is born equal; and that no man is naturally inferior, or, in any respect, subjected to another; and that he can be made subject to another only by his own consent. The position is equally ill-founded and false both in its premises and conclusions. In hardly any sense that can be imagined is the position strictly true; but, as applied to the case under consideration, it is demonstrably not true. Man differs from man in everything that can be supposed to lead to supremacy and subjection, *as one star differs from another star in glory*. It was the purpose of the Creator that man should be social; but, without government, there can be no society; nor, without some relative inferiority and superiority, can there by any government. A musical instrument composed of chords, keys, or pipes, all perfectly equal in size and power, might as well be expected to produce harmony, as a society composed of members all perfectly equal to be productive of order and peace. If (according to the idea of the advocates of this chimerical scheme of equality) no man could rightfully *be compelled to come in* and be a member even of a government to be formed by a regular compact, but by his own individual consent, it clearly follows, from the same principles, that neither could he rightfully be made or compelled to submit to the ordinances of any government already formed, to which he has not individually or actually consented. On the principle of equality, neither his parents, nor even the vote of a majority of the society (however virtuously and honorably that vote might be obtained), can have any such authority over any man. Neither can it be mantained that acquiescence implies consent; because acquiescence may have been extorted from impotence or incapacity. Even an explicit consent can bind a man no longer than he chooses to be bound. The same principle of equality that exempts him from being governed without his own consent clearly entitles him to recall and resume that consent whenever he sees fit; and he alone has a right to judge when and for what reasons it may be resumed.

Any attempt, therefore, to introduce this fantastic system into practice would reduce the whole business of social life to the wearisome, confused, and useless task of mankind's first expressing, and then withdrawing, their consent to an endless succession of schemes of government. Governments, though always forming, would never be completely formed; for the majority today might be the minority tomorrow, and, of course, that which is now fixed might and would be soon unfixed. Mr. Locke indeed says that, "by consenting with others to make one body-politic under government, a man puts himself under an obligation to every one of that society to submit to the determination of the majority, and to be concluded by it." For the sake of the peace of society, it is undoubtedly reasonable and necessary that this should be the case; but, on the principles of the system now under consideration, before Mr. Locke or any of his followers can have authority to say that it actually is the case, it must be stated and proved that every individual man, on entering into the social compact, did first consent, and declare his consent, to be concluded and bound in all cases by the vote of the majority. In making such a declaration, he would certainly consult both his interest and his duty; but at the same time he would also completely relinquish the principle of equality, and eventually subject himself to the possibility of being governed by ignorant and corrupt tyrants. Mr. Locke himself afterward disproves his own position respecting this supposed obligation to submit to the "determination of the majority," when he argues that a right of resistance still exists in the governed; for, what is resistance but a recalling and resuming the consent heretofore supposed to have been given, and in fact refusing to submit to the "determination of the majority"? It does not clearly appear what Mr. Locke exactly meant by what he calls "the determination of the majority"; but the only rational and practical public manner of declaring "the determination of the majority" is by law: the laws, therefore, in all countries, even in those that are despotically governed, are to be regarded as the declared "determination of a majority" of the members of that community; because, in such cases, even acquiescence only must be looked upon as equivalent to a declaration. A right of resistance, therefore, for which Mr. Locke contends, is incompatible with the duty of submitting to the determination of "the majority," for which he also contends.

It is indeed impossible to carry into effect any government which, even by compact, might be framed with this reserved right of resistance. Accordingly there is no record that any such government ever was so formed. If there had, it must have carried the seeds of its decay in its very constitution. For, as those men who make a government (certain that they have the power) can have no hesitation to vote that they also have the right to unmake it, and as the people, in all circumstances, but more especially when trained to make and unmake governments, are at least as well disposed to do the latter as the fomer, it is morally impossible that there should be anything like permanency or stability in a government so formed. Such a system, therefore, can produce only perpetual dissensions and contests and bring back mankind to a supposed state of nature, arming every man's hand, like Ishmael's against every man, and rendering the world an *aceldama*, of field of blood.

Such theories of government seem to give something like plausibility to the notions of those other modern theorists who regard all governments as invasions of the natural rights of men, usurpations, and tyranny. On this principle it would follow, and could not be denied, that government was indeed fundamentally, as our people are sedulously taught it still is, an evil. Yet it is to government that mankind owe their having, after their fall and corruption, been again reclaimed, from a state of barbarity and war, to the conveniency and the safety of the social state; and it is by means of government that society is still preserved, the weak protected from the strong, and the artless and innocent from the wrongs of proud oppressors. It was not without reason, then, that Mr. Locke asserted that a greater wrong cannot be done to prince and people than is done by "propagating wrong notions concerning government."

Ashamed of this shallow device, that government originated in superior strength and violence, another party, hardly less numerous, and certainly not less confident than the former, fondly deduce it from some imaginary compact. They suppose that, in the decline perhaps of some fabulous age of old, a multitude of human beings, who, like their brother-beasts, had hitherto ranged the forests, *without guide, overseer, or ruler*—at length convinced, by experience, of the impossibility of living either alone with any degree of comfort or security, or together in society, with peace, without government, had (in some lucid interval of reason and reflection) met together in a spacious plain for the express purpose of framing a government. Their first step must have been the transferring to some individual, or individuals, some of those rights which are supposed to have been inherent in each of them: of these it is essential to government that they should be divested; yet can they not, rightfully, be deprived of them, otherwise than by their own consent. Now, admitting this whole supposed assembly to be perfectly equal as to rights, yet all agreed as to the propriety of ceding some of them, on what principles of equality is it possible to determine, either who shall relinquish such a portion of his rights, or who shall be invested with such new accessory rights? By asking another to exercise jurisdiction over me, I clearly confess that I do not think myself his equal; and by his consenting to exercise such authority, he also virtually declares that he thinks himself superior. And, to establish this hypothesis of a compact, it is farther necessary that the whole assembly should concur in this opinion—a concurrence so extremely improbable that it seems to be barely possible. The supposition that a large concourse of people, in a rude and imperfect state of society, or even a majority of them, should thus rationally and unanimously concur to subject themselves to various restrictions, many of them irksome and unpleasant, and all of them contrary to all their former habits, is to suppose them possessed of more wisdom and virtue than multitudes in any instance in real life have every shown. Another difficulty respecting this notion may yet be mentioned. Without a power of life and death, it will, I presume, be readily admitted that there could be no government. Now, admitting it to be possible that men, from motives of public and private utility, may be induced to submit to many heavy penalties, and even to corporal punishment, inflicted by the sentence of the law, there is an insuperable objection to any man's giving to another a power over his life: this objection is that no man has such a power over his own life and cannot therefore transfer to another, or to others, be they few or many, on any conditions, a right which he does not himself possess. He only who gave life can give the authority to take it way; and as such authority is essential to government, this argument seems very decidedly to prove, not only that government did not originate in any compact, but also that is was originally from God. . . .

. . . The glory of God is much concerned that there should be good government in the world; it is, therefore, the uniform doctrine of the Scriptures that it is under the deputation and authority of God alone that *kings reign and princes decree justice.* Kings and princes (which are only other words for supreme magistrates) were doubtless created and appointed, not so much for their own sakes, as for the sake of the people committed to their charge; yet are they not, therefore, the creatures of the people. So far from deriving their authority from any supposed consent or suffrage of men, they receive their commission from Heaven; they receive it from God, the source and original of all power. However obsolete, therefore, either the sentiment or the language may now be deemed, it is with the most perfect propriety that the supreme magistrate, whether consisting of one or of many, and whether denominated an emperor, a king, an archon, a dictator, a consul, or a senate, is to be regarded and venerated as the vicegerent of God. . . .

Nor let this be deemed a degrading and servile principle: it is the very reverse; and it is this its superior dignity which proves its celestial origin. For, whilst other doctrines and other systems distract the world with disputes and debates which admit of no decision, and of *wars and fightings* which are almost as endless as they are useless, it is the glory of Christianity to teach her votaries patiently to bear imperfections, inconveniences, and evils in government, as in everything else that is human. This patient acquiescence under some remediless evils is not more our duty than it is our interest: for, the only very intolerable grievance in government is when men allow themselves to disturb and destroy the peace of the world by vain attempts to render that perfect which the laws of our nature have ordained to the imperfect. And there is more magnanimity, as well as more wisdom, in enduring some present and certain evils than can be manifested by any projects of redress that are uncertain; but which, if they fail, may bring down irretrievable ruin on thousands of others, as well as on ourselves, since to suffer nobly indicates more greatness of mind than can be shown even by acting valiantly. Wise men, therefore, in the words of a noted philosopher, will "rather choose to brook with patience some inconveniences under government" (because human affairs cannot possibly be without some) than self-opinionatedly disturb the quiet of the public. And, weighing the justice of those things you are about, not by the persuasion and advice of private men, but by the laws of the realm, you will no longer suffer amibitious men, through the streams of your blood, to wade to their own power but esteem it better to enjoy ourselves in the present state, though perhaps not the best, than, by waging war, endeavor to procure a reformation. . . .

All government, whether lodged in one or in many, is, in its nature, absolute and irresistible. It is not within the competency even of the supreme power to limit itself, because such limitation can emanate only from a superior. For any government to make itself irresistible, and to cease to be absolute, it must cease to be supreme, which is but saying, in other words, that it must dissolve itself or be destroyed. If, then, to resist government be to destroy it, every man who is a subject must necessarily owe to the government under which he lives an obedience either active or passive: active, where the duty enjoined may be performed without offending God; and passive (that is to say, patiently to submit to the penalties annexed to disobedience), where that which is commanded by man is forbidden by God. No government upon earth can rightfully compel any one of its subjects to an active compliance with anything that is, or that appears to his conscience to be, inconsistent with, or contradictory to, the known laws of God, because every man is under a prior and superior obligation to *obey God in all things*. When such cases of incompatible demands of duty occur, every well-informed person knows what he is to do; and every well-principled person will do what he ought, viz., he will submit to the ordinances of God rather than comply with the commandments of men. In thus acting, he cannot err, and this alone is "passive obedience," which I entreat you to observe is so far from being "unlimited obedience" (as its enemies wilfully persist to miscall it) that it is the direct contrary. Resolute not to disobey God, a man of good principles determines, in case of competition, as the lesser evil, to disobey man; but he knows that he sould also disobey God, were he not, at the same time, patiently to submit to any penalties incurred by his disobedience to man. . . .

A nonresisting spirit never yet made any man a bad subject. And if men of such mild and yielding tempers have shown less ardor than many others do, in the pursuit of that liberty which makes so conspicuous a figure in the effusions of orators and poets, it can be only for this reason: that they think it is precisely that kind of liberty which has so often set the world in an uproar, and that therefore it would be better for the world if it were never more heard of. If they are mistaken, their mistakes are at least harmless; and there is much justice, as well as great good sense, in Bishop Hall's remark that "some quiet errors are better than some unurly truths.". . .

Mr. Locke, like many inferior writers, when defending resistance, falls into inconsistencies and is at variance with himself. "Rebellion being," as he says, "an opposition not to persons, but to authority, which is founded only in the constitution and laws of the government, those, whoever they be, who by force break through, and by force justify their violation of them are truly and properly rebels." To this argument no one can object; but it should be attended to that, in political consideration, it is hardly possible to dissociate the ideas of authority in the abstract from persons vested with authority to resist a person legally vested with authority is, I conceive, to all intents and purposes, the same thing as to resist authority. Nothing but its success could have rescued the revolution from this foul imputation, had it not been for the abdication. Accordingly this great event has always hung like a millstone on the necks of those who must protest against rebellions; whilst yet their system of politics requires that they should approve of resistance, and the revolution. . . .

. . . "The Divine Author of our existence" has beyond all question given to "one part of the human race" to hold over another. Without some paramount and irresistible power, there can be no government. In our constitution this supremacy is vested in the king and the Parliament; and, subordinate to them, in our provincial legislatures. If you were now released from this constitutional power, you must differ from all others "of the human race" if you did not soon find yourselves under a necessity of submitting to a power no less absolute, though vested in other persons, and a government differently constituted. And much does it import you to consider whether those who are now so ready to promise to make *the grievous yoke of your fathers lighter* may not themselves verify Rehoboam's assertion and make you feel that *their little fingers are thicker than your father's loins.*

Be it (for the sake of argument) admitted that the government under which till now you have lived happily is, most unaccountably, all at once become *oppressive and severe;* did you, of yourselves, make the discovery? No. I affirm, without any apprehension of being contradicted, that you are acquainted with these oppressions only from the report of others. For what, then (admitting you have a right to resist in any case), are you now urged to resist and rise against those whom you have hitherto always regarded (and certainly not without reason) as your *nursing fathers and nursing mothers?* Often as you have already heard it repeated without expressing any disapprobation, I assure myself it will afford you no pleasure to be reminded that it is on account of an insignificant duty on tea, imposed by the British Parliament, and which, for aught we know, may or may not be constitutionally imposed, but which, we well know, two-thirds of the people of America can never be called on to pay. Is it the part of an *understanding people,* of loyal subjects, or of good Christians, instantly to resist and rebel for a cause so trivial? O my brethen, consult your own hearts and follow your own judgments! and learn not your "measures of obedience" from men who weakly or wickedly imagine there can be liberty unconnected with law—and whose aim it is to drive you on, step by step, to a resistance which will terminate, if it does not begin, in rebellion! On all such trying occasions, learn the line of conduct which it is your duty and interest to observe, from our constitution itself, which, in this particular, is a fair transcript or exemplification of the ordinance of God. Both the one and the other warn you against resistance; but you are not forbidden either to remonstrate or to petition. And can it be humilitating to any man, or any number of men, to ask when we have but to *ask and it shall be given?* Is prayer an abject duty, or do men ever appear either so great, or so amiable, as when they are modest and humble? However meanly this privilege of petitioning may be regarded by those who claim everything as a right, they are challenged to show an instance in which it has failed when it ought to have succeeded. If, however, our grievances, in any point of view, be of such moment as that other means of obtaining redress should be judged expedient, happily we enjoy those means. In a certain sense, some considerable portion of legislation is still in our own hands. We are supposed to have chosen "fit and able" persons to represent us in the great council of our country;

and they only can constitutionally interfere either to obtain the enacting of what is right or the repeal of what is wrong. If we, and our fellow-subjects, have been conscientiously faithful in the discharge of our duty, we can have no reason to doubt that our delegates will be equally faithful in the discharge of theirs. Our provincial assemblies, it is true, are but one part of our colonial legislature; they form, however, that part which is the most efficient. If the present general topic of complaint be in their estimation, well founded, and a real and great grievance, what reason have you to imagine that all the assemblies on the continent will not concur and be unanimous in so representing it? And if they should all concur so to represent it, it is hardly within the reach of supposition that all due attention will not be paid to their united remonstrances. So many and such large concessions have often been made, at the instance only of individual assemblies, that we are warranted in relying that nothing which is reasonable and proper will ever be withheld from us, provided only it be asked for with decency, and that we do not previously forfeit our title to attention by becoming refractory and rebellious.

Let it be supposed, however, that even the worst may happen, which can happen: that our remonstrances are disregarded, our petitions rejected, and our grievances unredressed: what, you will naturally ask—what, in such a case, would I advise you to do? . . . To your question, therefore, I hesitate not to answer that I wish and advise you to act the part of reasonable men and of Christians. You will be pleased to observe, however, that I am far from thinking that your virtue will ever be brought to so severe a test and trial. The question, I am aware, was an ensnaring one, suggested to you by those who are as little solicitous about your peace as they are for my safety; the answer which, in condescension to your wishes, I have given to it is direct and plain and not more applicable to you than it is to all the people of America. If you think the duty of three pence a pound upon tea laid on by the British Parliament a grievance, it is your duty to instruct your members to take all the constitutional means in their power to obtain redress; if those means fail of success, you cannot but be sorry and grieved, but you will better bear your disappointment by being able to reflect that it was not owing to any misconduct of your own. And, what is the whole history of human life, public or private, but a series of disappointments? It might be hoped that Christians would not think it grievous to be doomed to submit to disappointments and calamities, as their Master submitted, even if they were as innocent. His disciples and first followers shrunk from no trials nor dangers. Treading in the steps of him who, *whom he was reviled, blessed, and when he was persecuted, suffered it*, they willingly laid down their lives rather than resist some of the worst tyrants that ever disgraced the annals of history. Those persons are as little acquainted with general history, as they are with the particular doctrines of Christianity, who represent such submission as abject and servile. I affirm, with great authority, that "there can be no better way of asserting the people's lawful rights, than the disowning unlawful commands, by thus patiently suffering." When this doctrine was more generally embraced, our holy religion gained as much by submission as it is now in a fair way of losing for want of it. . . .

John Dickinson

Declaration On Taking Up Arms (1775)

By 1775 relations between the Mother Country and her American colonies had clearly reached a crisis. In Boston the arrival of ships bringing the now-taxed tea caused a sharp reaction. The famous "tea party" at which the Sons of Liberty, transparently disguised as Indians, dumped 342 chests of tea into the harbor took palce in December 1773. Although there were other acts of defiance that prevented the landing of tea throughout the colonies, when Parliament met the following March its anger was directed particularly toward Boston. The Coercive Acts—termed in America the Intolerable Acts—passed by Parliament closed the Port of Boston, revoked the Massachusetts Charter, provided that officials charged with capital offenses committed while performing their duties be sent to England for trial, and forced on all the colonists the quartering of troops. In Philadelphia the First Continental Congress gathered to denounce the Coercive Acts as illegal, to urge the citizens of Massachusetts to collect their own taxes and withhold them from the royal government, to advise the colonies to form and arm their own militia, and to call for economic sanctions against England. After preparing an address to King George and the British and American people, Congress adjourned with the determination to meet again in May 1775.

Before Congress reconvened, Virginians had been urged to prepare for war by Patrick Henry who, in his "Liberty or Death" speech, predicted that fighting would soon break out in New England. His prophecy proved accurate when the new military governor of Massachusetts, General Gage, sent a detachment to seize colonial military stores and arrest Samuel Adams and John Hancock. Encountering the local militia first at Lexington and then at Concord, the British dispersed the "Minutemen." On their return to Boston, however, the regulars were ambushed and harassed, and were saved from utter rout only by the arrival of reinforcements. Ninety-three colonials were dead and the British suffered over 250 casualties. The war had begun.

Massachusetts quickly took steps to raise an army, and Rhode Island, Connecticut, and New Hampshire almost immediately answered Massachusetts's call for assistance. The growing army was gathering at Cambridge when the Second Continental Congress met in Philadelphia in May. In June Congress accepted John Adams's proposal that the army become a Continental Army and approved George Washington as Commander-in-Chief. Deciding that a declaration should be prepared to be read to the troops—and to be published abroad—Congress appointed a committee to draft the document. The committee met with little success until John Dickinson of Pennsylvania was added and his draft subsequently was adopted.

John Dickinson was well suited to prepare a declaration that had to compromise the feelings of the radicals with those of the moderates, who were by no means ready to assert independence. Dickinson achieved fame in 1767 with the publication and widespread distribution throughout the colonies and in England of his *Letters from a Pennsylvania Farmer to the Inhabitants of the Colonies*. The *Farmer's Letters* argued against the right of Parliament to tax the colonies on constitutional grounds. Dickinson, however, was no radical. "The cause of liberty," he asserted, "is a cause of too much dignity to be sullied by turbulence and tumult," and he advised against "hot, rash, disorderly proceedings." A wealthy lawyer, educated in England and moving in the highest circles of colonial society, Dickinson strongly resisted attempts to break away from the Mother Country. His feelings in this regard led him to withhold his signature from the Declaration of Independence, although he did support the American cause in the war.

The "Declaration on Taking up Arms" not only reviews the causes of friction between Great Britain and her colonies, but specifically assures "friends and fellow subjects in any part of the Empire" that "we mean not to dissolve that union which has so long and so happily subsisted between us, and which we sincerely wished to see restored." It was not at all so clear that all the delegates wished to see the union restored or that they did not mean to dissolve the union, but Dickinson and the moderates were still in control and the Declaration is free of the vituperative attacks that characterize the speeches of such men as Samuel Adams and John Hancock.

If it was possible for men who exercise their reason to believe that the Divine Author of our existence intended a part of the human race to hold an absolute property in and an unbounded power over others, marked out by his infinite goodness and wisdom, as the objects of a legal domination never rightfully resistible, however severe and oppressive, the inhabitants of these colonies might at least require from the Parliament of Great Britain some evidence that this dreadful authority has been granted to that body. But a reverence for our great Creator, principles of humanity, and the dictates of common sense, must convince all those who reflect upon the subject that government was instituted to promote the welfare of mankind and ought to be administered for the attainment of that end. The legislature of Great Britain, however, stimulated by an inordinate passion for a power not only unjustifiable, but which they know to be peculiarly reprobated by the very constitution of that kingdom, and desperate of success in any mode of contest where regard should be had to truth, law, or right, have at length, deserting those, attempted to effect their cruel and impolitic purpose of enslaving these colonies by violence, and have thereby rendered it necessary for us to close with their last appeal from reason to arms. Yet, however blinded that assembly may be, by their intemperate rage for unlimited domination, so to slight justice and the opinion of mankind, we esteem ourselves bound by obligations of respect to the rest of the world to make known the justice of our cause.

Our forefathers, inhabitants of the island of Great Britain, left their native land to seek on these shores a residence for civil and religious freedom. At the expense of their blood; at the hazard of their fortunes; without the least charge to the country from which they removed; by unceasing labor and an unconquerable spirit, they effected settlements in the distant and inhospitable wilds of America, then filled with numerous and warlike nations of barbarians. Societies or governments, vested with perfect legislatures, were formed under charters from the crown, and an harmonious intercourse was established between the colonies and the kingdom from which they derived their origin.

The mutual benefits of this union became in a short time so extraordinary as to excite astonishment. It is universally confessed that the amazing increase of the wealth, strength, and navigation of the realm arose from this source; and the minister who so wisely and successfully directed the measures of Great Britain in the late war publicly declared that these colonies enabled her to triumph over her enemies. Toward the conclusion of that war it pleased our sovereign to make a change in his counsels. From that fatal moment the affairs of the British empire began to fall into confusion, and gradually sliding from the summit of glorious prosperity to which they had been advanced by the virtues and abilities of one man are at length distracted by the convulsions that now shake its deepest foundations. The new ministry, finding the brave foes of Britain, though frequently defeated, yet still contending, took up the unfortunate idea of granting them a hasty peace and of then subduing her faithful friends.

These devoted colonies were judged to be in such a state as to present victories without bloodshed and all the easy emoluments of statutable plunder. The uninterrupted tenor of their peaceable and respectful behavior from the beginning of colonization; their dutiful, zealous, and useful services during the war, though so recently and amply acknowledged in the most honorable manner by his Majesty, by the late King and by Parliament, could not save them from the meditated innovations. Parliament was influenced to adopt the pernicious project, and assuming a new power over them have in the course of eleven years given such decisive specimens of the spirit and consequences attending this power as to leave no doubt concerning the effects of acquiescence under it.

They have undertaken to give and grant our money without our consent, though we have ever exercised an exclusive right to dispose of our own property; statutes have been passed for extending the jurisdiction of courts of admiralty and vice-admiralty beyond their ancient limits; for depriving us of the accustomed and inestimable privilege of trial by jury in cases affecting both life and property; for suspending the legislature of one of the colonies; for interdicting all commerce to the capital of another, and for altering, fundamentally, the form of government established by charter and secured by acts of its own legislature, solemnly confirmed by the crown; for exempting the "murderers" of colonists from legal trial, and in effect from punishment; for erecting in a neighboring province, acquired by the joint arms of Great Britain and America, a despotism dangerous to our very existence; and for quartering soldiers upon the colonists in time of profound peace. It has also been resolved in Parliament that colonists charged with committing certain offences shall be transported to England to be tried.

But why should we enumerate our injuries in detail? By one statute it is declared that Parliament can "of right make laws to bind us in all cases whatsoever." What is to defend us against so enormous, so unlimited a power? Not a single man of those who assume it is chosen by us or is subject to our control or influence; but on the contrary they are all of them exempt from the operation of such laws, and an American revenue, if not diverted from the ostensible purposes for which it is raised, would actually lighten their own burden in proportion as they increase ours. We saw the misery to which such despotism would reduce us. We, for ten years, incessantly and ineffectually besieged the throne as supplicants; we reasoned, we remonstrated with Parliament in the most mild and decent language.

Administration, sensible that we should regard these oppressive measures as freemen ought to do, sent over fleets and armies to enforce them. The indignation of the Americans was roused, it is true, but it was the indignation of a virtuous, loyal, and affectionate people. A congress of delegates from the united colonies was assembled at Philadelphia on the 5th day of last September. We resolved again to offer an humble and dutiful petition to the King, and also addressed our fellow subjects of Great Britain. We have pursued every temperate, every respectful measure; we have even proceeded to break off our commercial intercourse with our fellow subjects, as the last peaceable admonition that our attachment to no nation upon earth should supplant our attachment to liberty. This, we flattered ourselves, was the ultimate step of the controversy, but subsequent events have shown how vain was this hope of finding moderation in our enemies.

Several threatening expressions against the colonies were inserted in his Majesty's speech; our petition, though we were told it was a decent one, and that his Majesty had been pleased to receive it graciously, and to promise laying it before his Parliament, was huddled into both Houses among a bundle of American papers and there neglected. The Lords and Commons in their address in the month of February said that "a rebellion at that time actually existed within the province of Massachusetts Bay, and that those concerned in it had been countenanced and encouraged by unlawful combinations and engagements entered into by his Majesty's subjects in several of the other colonies; and therefore they besought his Majesty that he would take the most effectual measures to enforce due obedience to the laws and authority of the supreme legislature." Soon after, the commercial intercourse of whole colonies with foreign countries and with each other was cut off by an act of Parliament; by another, several of them were entirely prohibited from the fisheries in the seas near their coasts, on which they always depended for their subsistence, and large reinforcements of ships and troops were immediately sent over to General Gage.

Fruitless were all the entreaties, arguments, and eloquence of an illustrious band of the most distinguished peers and commoners, who nobly and strenuously asserted the justice of our cause to stay or even to mitigate the heedless fury with which these accumulated and unexampled outrages were hurried on. Equally fruitless was the interference of the city of London, of Bristol, and many other respectable towns, in our favor. Parliament adopted an insidious manoeuvre, calculated to divide us, to establish a perpetual auction of taxations, where colony should bid against colony, all of them uninformed what ransom would redeem their lives; and thus to extort from us, at the point of the bayonet, the unknown sums that should be sufficient to gratify, if posible to gratify, ministerial rapacity, with the miserable indulgence left to us of raising in our own mode the prescribed tribute. What terms more rigid and humiliating could have been dictated by remorseless victors to conquered enemies? In our circumstances to accept them would be to deserve them.

Soon after the intelligence of these proceedings arrived on this continent, General Gage, who in the course of the last year had taken possession of the town of Boston, in the province of Massachusetts Bay, and still occupied it as a garrison, on the 19th day of April sent out from that place a large detachment of his army, who made an unprovoked assault on the inhabitants of the said province at the town of Lexington, as appears by the affidavits of a great number of persons, some of whom were officers and soliders of that detachment, murdered eight of the inhabitants and wounded many others. From thence the troops proceeded in warlike array to the town of Concord, where they set upon another party of the inhabitants of the same province, killing several and wounding more, until compelled to retreat by the country people suddenly assembled to repel this cruel aggression.

Hostilities thus commenced by the British troops have been since prosecuted by them without regard to faith or reputation. The inhabitants of Boston being confined within that town by the general, their governor, and having, in order to procure their dismission, entered into a treaty with him, it was stipulated that the said inhabitants, having deposited their arms with their own magistrates, should have liberty to depart, taking with them their other effects. They accordingly delivered up their arms, but in open violation of honor, in defiance of the obligation of treaties which even savage nations esteem sacred, the governor ordered the arms deposited as aforesaid, that they might be preserved for their owners, to be seized by a body of soliders, detained the greatest part of the inhabitants in the town, and compelled the few who were permitted to retire to leave their most valuable effects behind.

By this perfidy wives are separated from their husbands, children from their parents, the aged and the sick from their relations and friends who wish to attend and comfort them, and those who have been used to live in plenty and even elegance are reduced to deplorable distress.

The general, further emulating his ministerial masters, by a proclamation bearing date on the 12th day of June, after venting the grossest falsehoods and calumnies against the good people of these colonies, proceeds to "declare them all, either by name or description, to be rebels and traitors to supesede the course of common law, and instead thereof to publish and order the use and exercise of the law martial." His troops have butchered our countrymen, have wantonly burnt Charlestown, besides a considerable number of houses in other places; our ships and vessels are seized; the necessary supplies of provisions are intercepted, and he is exerting his utmost power to spread destruction and devastation around him.

We have received certain intelligence that General Carleton, the Governor of Canada, is instigating the people of that province and the Indians to fall upon us; and we have but too much reason to apprehend that schemes have been formed to excite domestic enemies against us. In brief, a part of these colonies now feel, and all of them are sure of feeling, as far as the vengeance of administration can inflict them, the complicated calamities of fire, sword, and famine. We are reduced to the alternative of choosing an unconditional submission to the tyranny of irritated ministers or resistance by force. The latter is our choice. We have counted the cost of this contest and find nothing so dreadful as voluntary slavery! Honor, justice, and humanity forbid us tamely to surrender that freedom which we received from our gallant ancestors, and which our innocent posterity have a right to receive from us. We cannot endure the infamy and guilt of resigning succeeding generations to that wretchedness which inevitably awaits them if we basely entail hereditary bondage upon them.

Our cause is just. Our union is perfect. Our internal resources are great, and, if necessary, foreign assistance is undoubtedly attainable. We gratefully acknowledge, as signal instances of Divine favor toward us, that his providence would not permit us to be called into his severe controversy until we were grown up to our present strength, had been previously exercised in warlike operations, and possessed the means of defending ourselves. With hearts fortified by these animating reflections we most solemnly, before God and the world, declare, that, exerting the utmost energy of those powers which our beneficient Creator has graciously bestowed upon us, the arms we have been compelled by our enemies to assume, we will, in definance of every hazard, with unabating firmness and perseverance, employ for the preservation of our liberties; being with one mind resolved to die freemen rather than to live slaves.

Lest this declaration should disquiet the minds of our friends and fellow subjects in any part of the Empire, we assure them that we mean not to dissolve that union which has so long and so happily subsisted between us, and which we sincerely wish to see restored. Necessity has not yet driven us into that desperate measure or induced us to excite any other nation to war against them. We have not raised armies with ambitious designs of separating from Great Britain and establishing independent states. We fight not for glory or for conquest. We exhibit to mankind the remarkable spectacle of a people attacked by unprovoked enemies, without any imputation or even suspicion of offense. They boast of their privileges and civilization, and yet proffer no milder conditions than servitude or death.

In our own native land, in defense of the freedom that is our birthright, and which we ever enjoyed till the late violation of it—for the protection of our property, acquired solely by the honest industry of our forefathers and ourselves, against violence actually offered, we have taken up arms. We shall lay them down when hostilities shall cease on the part of the aggressors and all danger of their being renewed shall be removed, and not before.

With an humble confidence in the mercies of the Supreme and impartial Judge and Ruler of the universe, we most devoutly implore his divine goodness to protect us happily through this great conflict, to dispose our adversaries to reconciliation on reasonable terms, and thereby to relieve the Empire from the calamities of civil war.

Samuel Adams

American Independence (1776)

By the time General Washington reached the Continental encampment at Cambridge at the beginning of July 1775, a battle between the colonists and the British had already been fought. Thwarting the efforts of the Americans to seize the high ground overlooking Boston, the British drove colonial forces from Breed's Hill and Bunker Hill at the cost of over 1,000 casualties. In Philadelphia moderates still held sway in the Congress, however, and John Dickinson's "Olive Branch Petition," begging the King to cease hostilities against the colonists and calling for reconciliation, was adopted on July 5. This was followed by the rejection of a plan of reconciliation offered by the British prime minister, Lord North, a plan that was recognized in the colonies as well as by North's critics in England as a ploy to destroy colonial unity. Congress also authorized General Philip Schuyler of New York to organize an expedition to march on Canada.

When George III was presented with the petition in August, he refused to receive it, instead issuing a royal proclamation that declared the American colonies to be in a state of rebellion. In November, upon hearing of the King's action, Congress reasserted its allegiance to the King but specifically disavowed American allegiance to Parliament. By the end of the year the rift between the colonies and Great Britain had grown: Americans were beginning to explore the possibility of enlisting French aid; Congress authorized the formation of a navy; Continental forces seized Montreal but were repulsed from Quebec; the Royal Governor of Virginia offered to free slaves who would desert their masters, fought and lost a pitched battle, and evacuated and burned Norfolk.

In January 1776 Thomas Paine's *Common Sense* appeared,

attacking monarchical government, stigmatizing the King as the "Royal Brute," and calling for American independence. In the months ahead—as the war spread to the South, as Howe evacuated Boston, as the Americans retreated from Canada, and as France cautiously indicated that support for the Americans would be forthcoming—the movement toward independence grew in strength. A Royal Proclamation closing colonial ports to all commerce was answered by a Congressional resolution opening American ports to all trade except with Britain. In April North Carolina, followed in May by Virginia, instructed its Congressional delegations to vote for independence, and in June Richard Henry Lee offered his famous resolution to Congress: that the colonies "are, and of right ought to be, free and independent States." There were still a few weeks of struggle while conservatives, such as John Dickinson, sought to prevent the adoption of a declaration of independence. Thomas Jefferson was delegated the task of preparing the draft declaration by a committee appointed for that purpose. Finally, on July 2, Congress formally voted for independence; Jefferson's Declaration was amended over the next two days and approved on July 4.

Among the delegates to Congress were those to whom the decision to declare independence was in no way painful and had, indeed, seemed long in coming. Samuel Adams had long been a thorn in the side of royal government in Massachusetts. He rejected as absurd the notion that "mankind submitted to government for the sake of being subordinate," arguing rather that "Mankind have entered into political society . . . for the sake of restoring equality." A shrewd organizer and propagandist, Adams took a leading part in agitation against Parliamentary attempts to control trade and raise revenue; he was a leader in forming the Non-Importation Association; he helped found the Sons of Liberty, promoted committees of correspondence, organized the agitation that produced the Boston Massacre and the commemorations that kept dissent alive, and instigated the Boston Tea Party. Anathema to authorities, Adams, along with John Hancock, was specifically excluded from a general amnesty offered by General Gage.

In the speech that follows, Adams dismissed both the political and religious arguments for the subordination of America to Britain. He condemned those who "wander into metaphysical labyrinths, or have recourse to original contracts, to determine the rights of men," and rejected the divine sanction offered for the actions of the "civil magistrate" who "has everywhere contaminated religion by making it an engine of policy." For the newly created nation, Adams laid down the precept that would animate a new, American creed: "The law is the will of the people." Adams pictured America as it would come to see itself, the haven for liberty and the seat of virtue, a nation that "shall neither be exposed to the necessary convulsions of elective monarchies, nor to the want of wisdom, fortitude, and virtue, to which hereditary succession is liable. In your hands it will be to perpetuate a prudent, active, and just legislature, and which will never expire until you yourselves lose the virtues which give it existence."

I would gladly have declined an honor to which I find myself unequal. I have not the calmness and impartiality which the infinite importance of this occasion demands. I will not deny the charge of my enemies, that resentment for the accumulated injuries of our country, and an ardor for her glory, rising to enthusiasm, may deprive me of that accuracy of judgment and expression which men of cooler passions may possess. Let me beseech you, then, to hear me with caution, to examine your prejudice, and to correct the mistakes into which I may be hurried by my zeal.

Truth loves an appeal to the common-sense of mankind. Your unperverted understandings can best determine on subjects of a practical nature. The positions and plans which are said to be above the comprehension of the multitude may be always suspected to be visionary and fruitless. He who made all men hath made the truths necessary to human happiness obvious to all.

Our forefathers threw off the yoke of Popery in religion; for you is reserved the honor of levelling the popery of politics. They opened the Bible to all, and maintained the capacity of every man to judge for himself in religion. Are we sufficient for the comprehension of the sublimest spiritual truths, and unequal to material and temporal ones?

Heaven hath trusted us with the management of things for eternity, and man denies us ability to judge of the present, or to know from our feelings the experience that will make us happy. "You can discern," they say, "objects distant and remote, but cannot perceive those within your grasp. Let us have the distribution of present goods, and cut out and manage as you please the interests of futurity." This day, I trust, the reign of political protestantism will commence. We have explored the temple of royalty, and found that the idol we have bowed down to has eyes which see not, ears that hear not our prayers, and a heart like the nether millstone. We have this day restored the Sovereign to whom alone men ought to be obedient. He reigns in heaven, and with a propitious eye beholds his subjects assuming that freedom of thought and dignity of self-direction which he bestowed on them. From the rising to the setting sun, may his kingdom come!

Having been a slave to the influence of opinion early acquired, and distinctions generally received, I am ever inclined not to despise but pity those who are yet in darkness. But to the eye of reason what can be more clear than that all men have an equal right to happiness? Nature made no other distinction than that of higher and lower degrees of power of mind and body. But what mysterious distribution of character has the craft of statesmen, more fatal than priestcraft, introduced?

According to their doctrine, the offspring of perhaps the lewd embraces of a successful invader shall, from generation to generation, arrogate the right of lavishing on their pleasures a proportion of the fruits of the earth, more than sufficient to supply the wants of thousands of their fellow-creatures; claim authority to manage them like beasts of burden, and, with superior industry, capacity, or virtue, nay, though disgraceful to humanity, by their ignorance, intemperance, and brutality, shall be deemed best calculated to frame laws and to consult for the welfare of society.

Were the talents and virtues which Heaven has bestowed on men given merely to make them more obedient drudges, to be sacrificed to the follies and ambition of a few? Or, were not the noble gifts so equally dispensed with a divine purpose and law, that they should as nearly as possible be equally exerted, and the blessings of Providence be equally enjoyed by all? Away, then, with those absurd systems which to gratify the pride of a few debase the greater part of our species below the order of men. What an affront to the King of the universe, to maintain that the happiness of a monster, sunk in debauchery and spreading desolation and murder among men, of a Caligula, a Nero, or a Charles, is more precious in his sight than that of millions of his suppliant creatures, who do justice, love mercy, and walk humbly with their God! No, in the judgment of Heaven there is no other superiority among men than a superiority in wisdom and virtue. And can we have a safer model in forming ours? The Deity, then, has not given any order or family of men authority over others; and if any men have given it, they only could give it for themselves. Our forefathers, 'tis said, consented to be subject to the laws of Great Britain. I will not, at present, dispute it, nor mark out the limits and conditions of their submission; but will it be denied that they contracted to pay obedience and to be under the control of Great Britain because it appeared to them most beneficial in their then present circumstances and situations? We, my countrymen, have the same right to consult and provide for our happiness which they had to promote theirs. If they had a view to posterity in their contracts, it must have been to advance the felicity of their descendants. If they erred in their expectations and prospects, we can never be condemned for a conduct which they would have recommended had they foreseen our present condition.

Ye darkeners of counsel, who would make the property, lives, and religion of millions depend on the evasive interpretations of musty parchments; who would send us to antiquated charters of uncertain and contradictory meaning, to prove that the present generation are not bound to be victims to cruel and unforgiving despotism, tell us whether our pious and generous ancestors bequeathed to us the miserable privilege of having the rewards of our honesty, industry, the fruits of those fields which they purchased and bled for, wrested from us at the will of men over whom we have no check. Did they contract for us that, with folded arms, we should expect that justice and mercy from brutal and inflamed invaders which have been denied to our supplications at the foot of the throne? Were we to hear our character as a people ridiculed with indifference? Did they promise for us that our meekness and patience should be insulted; our coasts harassed, our towns demolished and plundered, and our wives and offspring exposed to nakedness, hunger, and death, without our feeling the resentment of men, and exerting those powers of self-preservation which God has given us? No man had once a greater veneration for Englishmen than I entertained. They were dear to me as branches of the same parental trunk, and partakers of the same religion and laws; I still view with respect the remains of the Constitution as I would a lifeless body which had once been animated by a great and heroic soul. But when I am aroused by the din of arms; when I behold legions of foreign assassins, paid by Englishmen to imbrue their hands in our blood; when I tread over the uncoffined bodies of my countrymen, neighbors, and friends; when I see the locks of a venerable father torn by savage hands, and a feeble mother, clasping her infants to her bosom, and on her knees imploring their lives from her own slaves, whom Englishmen have allured to treachery and murder; when I behold my country, once the seat of industry, peace, and plenty, changed by Englishmen to a theatre of blood and misery, Heaven forgive me if I cannot root out those passions which it has implanted in my bosom, and detest submission to a people who have either ceased to be human, or have not virtue enough to feel their own wretchedness and servitude!

Men who content themselves with the semblance of truth, and a display of words, talk much of our obligations to Great Britain for protection. Had she a single eye to our advantage? A nation of shopkeepers are very seldom so disinterested. Let us not be so amused with words; the extension of her commerce was her object. When she defended our coasts, she fought for her customers, and convoyed our ships loaded with wealth, which we had acquired for her by our industry. She has treated us as beasts of burden, whom the lordly masters cherish that they may carry a greater load. Let us inquire also against whom she has protected us? Against her own enemies with whom we had no quarrel, or only on her account, and against whom we always readily exerted our wealth and strength when they were required. Were these colonies backward in giving assistance to Great Britain, when they were called upon in 1739 to aid the expedition against Carthagena? They at that time sent three thousand men to join the British army, although the war commenced without their consent. But the last war, 'tis said, was purely American. This is a vulgar error, which, like many others, has gained credit by being confidently repeated. The dispute between the courts of Great Britain and France related to the limits of Canada and Nova Scotia. The controverted territory was not claimed by any in the colonies, but by the crown of Great Britain. It was therefore their own quarrel. The infringement of a right which England had, by the treaty of Utrecht, of trading in the Indian country of Ohio, was another cause of the war. The French seized large quantities of British manufactures and took possession of a fort which a company of British merchants and factors had erected for the security of their commerce. The war was therefore waged in defence of lands claimed by the crown, and for the protection of British property. The French at that time had no quarrel with America, and, as appears by letters sent from their commander-in chief to some of the colonies, wished to remain in peace with us. The part, therefore, which we then took, and the miseries to which we exposed ourselves, ought to be charged to our affection to Britain. These colonies granted more than their proportion to the support of the war. They raised, clothed, and maintained nearly twenty-five thousand men, and so sensible were the people of England of our great exertions, that a message was annually sent to the House of Commons purporting, "that his Majesty, being highly satisfied with the zeal and vigor with which his faithful subjects in North America had exerted themselves in defence of his Majesty's just rights and possessions, recommends it to the House to take the same into consideration, and enable him to give them a proper compensation."

But what purpose can arguments of this kind answer? Did the protection we received annul our rights as men, and lay us under an obligation of being miserable?

Who among you, my countrymen, that is a father, would claim authority to make your child a slave because you had nourished him in infancy?

'Tis a strange species of generosity which requires a return infinitely more valuable than anything it could have bestowed; that demands as a reward for a defence of our property a surrender of those inestimable privileges, to the arbitrary will of vindictive tyrants, which alone give value to that very property.

Political right and public happiness are different words for the same idea. They who wander into metaphysical labyrinths, or have recourse to original contracts, to determine the rights of men, either impose on themselves or mean to delude others. Public utility is the only certain criterion. It is a test which brings disputes to a speedy decision, and makes its appeal to the feelings of mankind. The force of truth has obliged men to use arguments drawn from this principle who were combating it, in practice and speculation. The advocates for a despotic government and nonresistance to the magistrate employ reasons in favor of their systems drawn from a consideration of their tendency to promote public happiness.

The Author of Nature directs all his operations to the production of the greatest good, and has made human virtue to consist in a disposition and conduct which tends to the common felicity of his creatures. An abridgment of the natural freedom of men, by the institutions of political societies, is vindicable only on this foot. How absurd, then, is it to draw arguments from the nature of civil society for the annihilation of those very ends which society was intended to procure! Men associate for their mutual advantage. Hence, the good and happiness of the members, that is, the majority of the members, of any State, is the great standard by which everything relating to that State must finally be determined; and though it may be supposed that a body of people may be bound by a voluntary resignation (which they have been so infatuated as to make) of all their interests to a single person, or to a few, it can never be conceived that the resignation is obligatory to their posterity; because it is manifestly contrary to the good of the whole that it should be so.

These are the sentiments of the wisest and most virtuous champions of freedom. Attend to a portion on this subject from a book in our own defence, written, I had almost said, by the pen of inspiration. "I lay no stress," says he, "on charters; they derive their rights from a higher source. It is inconsistent with common-sense to imagine that any people would ever think of settling in a distant country on any such condition, or that the people from which they withdrew should forever be masters of their property, and have power to subject them to any modes of government they pleased. And had there been expressed stipulations to this purpose in all the charters of the colonies, they would, in my opinion, be no more bound by them, than if it had been stipulated with them that they should go naked, or expose themselves to the incursions of wolves and tigers."

Such are the opinions of every virtuous and enlightened patriot in Great Britain. Their petition to Heaven is, "That there may be one free country left upon earth, to which they may fly, when venality, luxury, and vice shall have completed the ruin of liberty there."

Courage, then, my countrymen, our contest is not only whether we ourselves shall be free, but whether there shall be left to mankind an asylum on earth for civil and religious liberty. Dismissing, therefore, the justice of our cause, as incontestable, the only question is, What is best for us to pursue in our present circumstances?

The doctrine of dependence on Great Britain is, I believe, generally exploded; but as I would attend to the honest weakness of the simplest of men, you will pardon me if I offer a few words on that subject.

We are now on this continent, to the astonishment of the world, three millions of souls united in one cause. We have large armies, well disciplined and appointed, with commanders inferior to none in military skill, and superior in activity and zeal. We are furnished with arsenals and stores beyond our most sanguine expectations, and foreign nations are waiting to crown our success by their alliances. There are instance of, I would say, an almost astonishing Providence in our favor; our success has staggered our enemies, and almost given faith to infidels; so we may truly say it is not our own arm which has saved us.

The hand of Heaven appears to have led us on to be, perhaps, humble instruments and means in the great Providential dispensation which is completing. We have fled from the political Sodom; let us not look back, lest we perish and become a monument of infamy and derision to the world. For can we ever expect more unanimity and better preparation for defence; more infatuation of counsel among our enemies, and more valor and zeal among ourselves? The same force and resistance which are sufficient to procure us our liberties will secure us a glorious independence and support us in the dignity of free, imperial States. We cannot suppose that our opposition has made a corrupt and dissipated nation more friendly to America, or created in them a greater respect for the rights of mankind. We can therefore expect a restoration and establishment of our privileges, and a compensation for the injuries we have received from their want of power, from their fears, and not from their virtues. The unanimity and valor which will effect an honorable peace can render a future contest for our liberties unnecessary. He who has strength to chain down the wolf is a madman if he let him loose without drawing his teeth and paring his nails.

From the day on which an accommodation takes place between England and America, on any other terms than as independent States, I shall date the ruin of this country. A politic minister will study to lull us into security, by granting us the full extent of our petitions. The warm sunshine of influence would melt down the virtue, which the violence of the storm rendered more firm and unyielding. In a state of tranquility, wealth, and luxury, our descendants would forget the arts of war and the noble activity and zeal which made their ancestors invincible. Every art of corruption would be employed to loosen the bond of union which renders our resistance formidable. When the spirit of liberty which now animates our hearts and gives success to our arms is extinct, our numbers will accelerate our ruin and render us easier victims to tyranny. Ye abandoned minions of an infatuated Ministry, if peradventure any should yet remain among us, remember that a Warren and Montgomery are numbered among the dead. Contemplate the mangled bodies of your countrymen, and then say, What should be the reward of such sacrifices? Bid us and our posterity bow the knee, supplicate the friendship, and plow, and sow, and reap, to glut the avarice of the men who have let loose on us the dogs of war to riot in our blood and hunt us from the face of the earth? If ye love wealth better than liberty, the tranquility of servitude than the animating contest of freedom—go from us in peace. We ask not your counsels or arms. Crouch down and lick the hands which feed you. May your chains sit lightly upon you, and may posterity forget that ye were our countrymen!

To unite the supremacy of Great Britain and the liberty of America is utterly impossible. So vast a continent, and of such a distance from the seat of empire, will every day grow morc unmanageable. The motion of so unwieldy a body cannot be directed with any despatch and uniformity without committing to the Parliament of Great Britain powers inconsistent with our freedom. The authority and force which would be absolutely necessary for the preservation of the peace and good order of this continent would put all our valuable rights within the reach of that nation.

As the administration of government requires firmer and more numerous supports in proportion to its extent, the burdens imposed on us would be excessive, and we should have the melancholy prospect of their increasing on our posterity. The scale of officers, from the rapacious and needy commissioner to the haughty governor, and from the governor, with his hungry train, to perhaps a licentious and prodigal viceroy, must be upheld by you and your children. The fleets and armies which will be employed to silence your murmurs and complaints must be supported by the fruits of your industry.

And yet with all this enlargement of the expense and powers of government, the administration of it at such a distance, and over so extensive a territory, must necessarily fail of putting the laws into vigorous execution, removing private oppressions, and forming plans for the advancement of agriculture and commerce, and preserving the vast empire in any tolerable peace and security. If our posterity retain any spark of patriotism, they can never tamely submit to such burdens. This country will be made the field of bloody contention till it gain that independence for which nature formed it. It is, therefore, injustice and cruelty to our offspring, and would stamp us with the character of baseness and cowardice, to leave the salvation of this country to be worked out by them with accumulated difficulty and danger.

Prejudice, I confess, may warp our judgments. Let us hear the decision of Englishmen on this subject, who cannot be suspected of partiality. "The Americans," they say, "are but little short of half our number. To this number they have grown from a small body of original settlers by a very rapid increase. The probability is that they will go on to increase, and that in fifty or sixty years they will be double our number, and form a mighty empire, consisting of a variety of States, all equal or superior to ourselves in all the arts and accomplishments which give dignity and happiness to human life. In that period will they be still bound to acknowledge that supremacy over them which we now claim? Can there by any person who will assert this, or whose mind does not revolt at the idea of a vast continent holding all that is valuable to it at the discretion of a handful of people on the other side of the Atlantic? But if at that period this would be unreasonable, what makes it otherwise now? Draw the line if you can. But there is still a greater difficulty."

Britain is now, I will suppose, the seat of liberty and virtue, and its legislature consists of a body of able and independent men, who govern with wisdom and justice. The time may come when all will be reversed; when its excellent constitution of government will be subverted; when, pressed by debts and taxes, it will be greedy to draw to itself an increase of revenue from every distant province, in order to ease its own burdens; when the influence of the crown, strengthened by luxury and a universal profligacy of manners, will have tainted every heart, broken down every fence of liberty, and rendered us a nation of tame and contented vassals; when a general election will be nothing but a general auction of boroughs, and when the Parliament, the grand council of the nation, and once the faithful guardian of the State, and a terror to evil ministers, will be degenerated into a body of sycophants, dependent and venal, always ready to confirm any measures, and little more than a public court for registering royal edicts. Such, it is possible, may, some time or other, be the state of Great Britain. What will, at that period, be the duty of the colonies? Will they be still bound to unconditional submission? Must they always continue an appendage to our government and follow it implicitly through every change that can happen to it? Wretched condition, indeed, of millions of freemen as good as ourselves! Will you say that we now govern equitably, and that there is no danger of such revolution? Would to God that this were true! But you will not always say the same. Who shall judge whether we govern equitably or not? Can you give the colonies any security that such a period will ever come? No. *The period, countrymen, is already come!* The calamities were at our door. The rod of oppression was raised over us. We were roused from our slumbers, and may we never sink into repose until we can convey a clear and undisputed inheritance to our posterity! This day we are called upon to give a glorious example of what the wisest and best of men were rejoiced to view, only in speculation. This day presents the world with the most august spectacle that its annals ever unfolded—millions of freemen, deliberately and voluntarily forming themselves into a society for their common defence and common happiness. Immortal spirits of Hampden, Locke, and Sidney, will it not add to your benevolent joys to behold your posterity rising to the dignity of men, and evincing to the world the reality and expediency of your systems, and in the actual enjoyment of that equal liberty, which you were happy, when on earth, in delineating and recommending to mankind?

Other nations have received their laws from conquerors; some are indebted for a constitution to the suffering of their ancestors through revolving centuries. The people of this country, alone, have formally and deliberately chosen a government for themselves, and with open and uninfluenced consent bound themselves into a social compact. Here no man proclaims his birth or wealth as a title of honorable distinction, or to sanctify ignorance and vice with the name of hereditary authority. He who has most zeal and ability to promote public felicity, let him be the servant of the public. This is the only line of distinction drawn by nature. Leave the bird of night to the obscurity for which nature intended him, and expect only from the eagle to brush the clouds with his wings and look boldly in the face of the sun.

Some who would persuade us that they have tender feelings for future generations, while they are insensible to the happiness of the present, are perpetually foreboding a train of dissensions under our popular system. Such men's reasoning amounts to this: Give up all that is valuable to Great Britain and then you will have no inducements to quarrel among yourselves; or, suffer yourselves to be chained down by your enemies that you may not be able to fight with your friends.

This is an insult on your virtue as well as your common-sense. Your unanimity this day and through the course of the war is a decisive refutation of such invidious predictions. Our enemies have already had evidence that our present Constitution contains in it the justice and ardor of freedom and the wisdom and vigor of the most absolute system.

When the law is the will of the people, it will be uniform and coherent; but fluctuation, contradiction, and inconsistency of councils must be expected under those governments where every revolution in the ministry of a court produces one in the State—such being the folly and pride of all ministers, that they ever pursue measures directly opposite to those of their predecessors.

We shall neither be exposed to the necessary convulsions of elective monarchies, nor to the want of wisdom, fortitude, and virtue, to which hereditary succession is liable. In your hands it will be to perpetuate prudent, active, and just legislature, and which will never expire until you yourselves lose the virtues which give it existence.

And, brethren and fellow-countrymen, if it was ever granted to mortals to trace the designs of Providence, and interpret its manifestations in favor of their cause, we may, with humility of soul, cry out, "Not unto us, not unto us, but to thy Name be the praise!" The confusion of the devices among our enemies, and the rage of the elements against them, have done almost as much toward our success as either our councils or our arms.

The time at which this attempt on our liberty was made, when we were ripened into maturity, had acquired a knowledge of war, and were free from the incursions of enemies in this country; the gradual advances of our oppressors enabling us to prepare for our defence; the unusual fertility of our lands and clemency of the seasons; the success which at first attended our feeble arms, producing unanimity among our friends and reducing our internal foes to acquiescence—these are all strong and palpable marks and assurances that Providence is yet gracious unto Zion, that it will turn away the captivity of Jacob.

Our glorious reformers when they broke through the fetters of superstition effected more than could be expected from an age so darkened. But they left much to be done by their posterity. They lopped off, indeed, some of the branches of Popery, but they left the root and stock when they left us under the domination of human systems and decisions, usurping the infallibility which can be attributed to Revelation alone. They dethroned one usurper only to raise up another; they refused allegiance to the Pope only to place the civil magistrate in the throne of Christ, vested with authority to enact laws and inflict penalties in his kingdom. And if we now cast our eyes over the nations of the earth, we shall find that, instead of possessing the pure religion of the Gospel, they may be divided either into infidels, who deny the truth; or politicians who make religion a stalking horse for their ambition; or professors, who walk in the trammels of orthodoxy, and are more attentive to traditions and ordinances of men than to the oracles of truth.

The civil magistrate has everywhere contaminated religion by making it an engine of policy; and freedom of thought and the right of private judgment, in matters of conscience, driven from every other corner of the earth, direct their course to this happy country as their last asylum. Let us cherish the noble guests, and shelter them under the wings of a universal toleration! Be this the seat of unbounded religious freedom. She will bring with her in her train, industry, wisdom, and commerce. She thrives most when left to shoot forth in her natural luxuriance, and asks for human policy only not to be checked in her growth by artificial encouragements.

Thus, by the beneficence of Providence, we shall behold our empire arising, founded on justice and the voluntary consent of the people, and giving full scope to the exercise of those faculties and rights which most ennoble our species. Besides the advantages of liberty and the most equal Constitution, Heaven has given us a country with every variety of climate and soil, pouring forth in abundance whatever is necessary for the support, comfort, and strength of a nation. Within our own borders we possess all the means of sustenance, defence, and commerce; at the same time, these advantages are so distributed among the different States of this continent, as if nature had in view to proclaim to us: Be united among yourselves and you will want nothing from the rest of the world.

The more northern States most amply supply us with every necessary, and many of the luxuries of life; with iron, timber, and masts for ships of commerce or of war; with flax for the manufacture of linen, and seed either for oil or exportation.

So abundant are our harvests, that almost every part raises more than double the quantity of grain requisite for the support of the inhabitants. From Georgia and the Carolinas we have, as well for our own wants as for the purpose of supplying the wants of other powers, indigo, rice, hemp, naval stores, and lumber.

Virginia and Maryland teem with wheat, Indian corn, and tobacco. Every nation whose harvest is precarious, or whose lands yield not those commodities which we cultivate, will gladly exchange their superfluities and manufactures for ours.

We have already received many and large cargoes of clothing, military stores, etc., from our commerce with foreign powers, and, in spite of the efforts of the boasted navy of England, we shall continue to profit by this connection.

The want of our naval stores has already increased the price of these articles to a great height, especially in Britain. Without our lumber, it will be impossible for those haughty islanders to convey the products of the West Indies to their own ports; for a while they may with difficulty effect it, but, without our assistance, their resources soon must fail. Indeed, the West India islands appear as the necessary appendages to this our empire. They must owe their support to it, and erelong, I doubt not, some of them will, from necessity, wish to enjoy the benefit of our protection.

These natural advantages will enable us to remain independent of the world, or make it the interest of European powers to court our alliance, and aid in protecting us against the invasion of others. What argument, therefore, do we want to show the equity of our conduct; or motive of interest to recommend it to our prudence? Nature points out the path, and our enemies have obliged us to pursue it.

If there is any man so base or so weak as to prefer a dependence on Great Britain to the dignity and happiness of living a member of a free and independent nation, let me tell him that necessity now demands what the generous principle of patriotism should have dictated.

We have no other alternative than independence, or the most ignominious and galling servitude. The legions of our enemies thicken on our plains; desolation and death mark their bloody career; while the mangled corpses of our countrymen seem to cry out to us as a voice from heaven:

"Will you permit our posterity to groan under the galling chains of our murderers?

Has our blood been expended in vain? Is the only benefit which our constancy till death has obtained for our country, that it should be sunk into a deeper and more ignominious vassalage? Recollect who are the men that demand your submission, to whose decrees you are invited to pay obedience. Men who, unmindful of their relation to you as brethren; of your long implicit submission to their laws; of the sacrifice which you and your forefathers made of your natural advantages for commerce to their avarice; formed a deliberate plan to wrest from you the small pittance of property which they had permitted you to acquire. Remember that the men who wish to rule over you are they who, in pursuit of this plan of despotism, annulled the sacred contracts which they had made with your ancestors; conveyed into your cities a mercenary soldiery to compel you to submission by insult and murder; who called your patience cowardice, your piety hypocrisy."

Countrymen, the men who now invite you to surrender your rights into their hands are the men who have let loose the merciless savages to riot in the blood of their brethren; who have dared to establish Popery triumphant in our land; who have taught treachery to your slaves, and courted them to assassinate your wives and children.

These are the men to whom we are exhorted to sacrifice the blessings which Providence holds out to us; the happiness, the dignity, of uncontrolled freedom and independence.

Let not your generous indignation be directed against any among us who may advise so absurd and maddening a measure. Their number is but few, and daily decreases; and the spirit which can render them patient of slavery will render them contemptible enemies.

Our Union is now complete; our Constitution composed, established, and approved. You are now the guardians of your own liberties. We may justly address you, as the *decemviri* did the Romans, and say, "Nothing that we propose can pass into a law without your consent. Be yourselves, O Americans, the authors of those laws on which your happiness depends."

You have now in the field armies sufficient to repel the whole force of your enemies and their base and mercenary auxiliaries. The hearts of your soldiers beat high with the spirit of freedom; they are animated with the justice of their cause, and while they grasp their swords can look up to Heaven for assistance. Your adversaries are composed of wretches who laugh at the rights of humanity, who turn religion into derision, and would, for higher wages, direct their swords against their leaders or their country. Go on, then, in your generous enterprise with gratitude to Heaven for past success, and confidence of it in the future. For my own part, I ask no greater blessing than to share with you the common danger and common glory. If I have a wish dearer to my soul than that my ashes may be mingled with those of a Warren and Montgomery, it is that these American States may never cease to be free and independent.

John Rutledge

Speech to the General Assembly of South Carolina (1782)

In February 1780 a British fleet carrying General Clinton and his army of 14,000 men arrived off the coast of Carolina. By May the city of Charleston, capital of South Carolina, fell; the British cavalry soon crushed a Virginia regiment at Waxhaw Creek. General Clinton returned to New York, leaving Lord Cornwallis to continue operations in the area.

There was little the Americans could do, other than harry the British lines of communication. An American force dispatched south to attack the British supply base at Camden was decisively beaten and it retreated to North Carolina. Cornwallis's attempt to mount an invasion of North Carolina was frustrated when a loyalist force covering the British general's flank was wiped out. Cornwallis retreated back into South Carolina and went into winter quarters. Congress, in October 1780, appointed Nathanael Greene to command the Continental Army in the south. By March 1781 Greene succeeded in restricting British control to the area around Charleston. Cornwallis became convinced that the key to controlling the Carolinas was the destruction of American power in Virginia, and in May 1781 he marched north in a campaign that was to end with the surrender of his entire army at Yorktown in October.

The war was not quite over when the South Carolina legislature met in January of 1782 in Jacksonburgh. The British were still in possession of the State capital from which the legislature, with Governor John Rutledge, had been forced to flee when the British took Charleston almost two years before. While victory seemed assured, it could not be taken for granted, and Americans could not know that within a few months Lord North's government would fall and Parliament would resolve not to continue the armed struggle.

Rutledge had been elected governor in 1779, after years of active opposition to British authority. Patrick Henry considered him "by far the greatest orator" in the First Continental Congress, which Rutledge had attended as a delegate from South Carolina. Previously he had sat in the Stamp Act Congress and had urged the South Carolina convention to support Massachusetts in 1774. His brother, Edward, was a signer of the Declaration of Independence.

In addressing the legislature in 1782, Rutledge was aware of the need to be prepared to resume the vigorous prosecution of the war if that proved necessary. He was also cognizant of the bitterness generated by the active participation of South Carolina loyalists who had fought alongside the King's troops. Along with forming local Tory militia companies, the British had not hesitated to use slaves and Indians in their attacks on the South Carolinians. The role of the loyalists and their association with the royal army in the vicious struggle engendered by what was, in large measure, a guerrilla war, created the hardest and most vindictive feelings. The governor's condemnation of the savagery of the enemy, along with his observation on the "extraordinary lenity" of the State in dealing with Tories, reflected the deeply held feelings of hostility in his audience. Those who had proclaimed their loyalty to the Crown were now branded as disloyal traitors on whom retribution was soon to be visited.

Honorable gentlemen of the Senate; Mr. Speaker and gentlemen of the House of Representatives,—Since the last meeting of a general assembly the good people of this State have not only felt the common calamities of war, but from the wanton and savage manner in which it has been prosecuted they have experienced such severities as are unpractised and will scarcely be credited by civilized nations.

The enemy unable to make any impression on the northern States, the number of whose inhabitants and the strength of whose country had baffled their repeated efforts, turned their views towards the southern, which a difference of circumstances afforded some expectation of conquering, or at least of greatly distressing. After a long resistance the reduction of Charleston was effected by the vast superiority of force with which it had been besieged. The loss of that garrison, as it consisted of the Continental troops of Virginia and the Carolinas, and a number of militia, facilitated the enemy's march into the country and their establishment of strong posts in the upper and interior parts of it, and the unfavorable issue of the action near Camden induced them vainly to imagine that no other army could be collected which they might not easily defeat.

The militia, commanded by the Brigadiers Sumter and Marion, whose enterprising spirit and unremitting perseverance under many difficulties are deserving of great applause, harassed and often defeated large parties; but the numbers of those militia were too few to contend effectually with the collected strength of the enemy.

Regardless, therefore, of the sacred ties of honor, destitute of the feelings of humanity, and determined to extinguish, if possible, every spark of freedom in this country; they, with the insolent pride of conquerors, gave unbounded scope to the exercises of their tyrannical disposition, infringed their public engagements, and violated the most solemn capitulations. Many of our worthiest citizens were, without cause, long and closely confined, some on board of prison ships, and others in the town and castle of St. Augustine, their properties disposed of at the will and caprice of the enemy, and their families sent to different and distant parts of the continent without the means of support. Many who had surrendered as prisoners of war were killed in cold blood; several suffered death in the most ignominious manner, and others were delivered up to savages and put to tortures under which they expired. Thus, the lives, liberties, and properties of the people were dependent solely on the pleasure of British officers, who deprived them of either or all on the most frivolous pretences. Indians, slaves, and a desperate banditti of the most profligate characters were caressed and employed by the enemy to execute their infamous purposes; devastation and ruin marked their progress and that of their adherents, nor were their violences restrained by the charms or influence of beauty and innocence; even the fair sex, whom it is the duty of all, and the pleasure and pride of the brave to protect, they and their tender offspring were victims to the inveterate malice of an unrelenting foe; neither the tears of mothers nor the cries of infants could excite in their breasts pity or compassion; not only the peaceful habitation of the widow, the aged, and the infirm, but the holy temples of the Most High were consumed, in flames kindled by their sacrilegious hands. They have tarnished the glory of the British arms, disgraced the profession of a soldier, and fixed indelible stigmas of rapine, cruelty, perfidy, and profaneness on the British name.

But I can now congratulate you, and I do most cordially on the pleasing change of affairs which, under the blessing of God, the wisdom, prudence, address, and bravery of the great and gallant General Greene, and the intrepidity of the officers and men under his command, have happily effected. A general who is justly entitled from his many signal services to honorable and singular marks of your approbation and gratitude, his successes have been more rapid and complete than the most sanguine could have expected; the enemy, compelled to surrender or evacuate every post which they held in the country, frequently defeated and driven from place to place, are obliged to seek refuge under the walls of Charleston and on islands in its vicinity. We have now the full and absolute possession of every other part of the State, and the legislative, executive, and judicial powers are in the free exercise of their respective authorities.

I also most heartily congratulate you on the glorious victory obtained by the combined forces of America and France over their common enemy; when the very general who was second in command at the reduction of Charleston, and to whose boasted prowess and highly extolled abilities the conquest of no less than three States had been arrogantly committed, was speedily compelled to accept of the same mortifying terms which had been imposed on that brave but unfortunate garrison; to surrender an army of many thousand regulars, and to abandon his wretched followers, whom he had artfully seduced from their allegiance by specious promises of protection which he could never have hoped to fulfil, to the justice or mercy of their country: on the naval superiority established by the illustrious ally of the

United States—a superiority in itself so decided, and in its consequences so extensive, as must inevitably soon oblige the enemy to yield to us the only post which they occupy in this State: and on the reiterated proofs of the sincerest friendship, and on the great support which America has received from that powerful monarch—a monarch whose magnanimity is universally acknowledged and admired, and on whose royal word we may confidently rely for every necessary assistance: on the perfect harmony which subsists between France and America: on the stability which her independence has acquired, and the certainty that it is too deeply rooted ever to be shaken; for, animated as they are by national honor, and united by one common interest, it must and will be maintained.

What may be the immediate effects on the British nation, of the events which I have mentioned, of their loss of territory in other parts of the world, and of their well-founded apprehensions from the powers of France, Spain, and Holland, it is impossible to foretell. If experience can teach wisdom to a haughty and infatuated people, and if they will now be governed by reason, they will have learnt they can have no solid ground of hope to conquer any State in the Union; for though their armies have obtained temporary advantages over our troops, yet the citizens of these States, firmly resolved as they are never to return to a domination which, near six years ago, they unanimously and justly renounced, cannot be subdued; and they must now be convinced that it is the height of folly and madness to persist in so ruinous a war.

If, however, we judge, as we ought, of their future by their past conduct, we may presume that they will not only endeavor to keep possession of our capital, but make another attempt, howsoever improbable the success of it may appear, to subjugate this country: it is therefore highly incumbent upon us to use our most strenuous efforts to frustrate so fatal a design; and I earnestly conjure you, by the sacred love which you bear to your country, by the constant remembrance of her bitter sufferings, and by the just detestation of British government which you and your posterity must forever possess, to exert your utmost faculties for that purpose by raising and equipping, with all possible expedition, a respectable permanent force, and by making ample provision for their comfortable subsistence.

I am sensible the expense will be great; but a measure so indispensable to the preservation of our freedom is above every pecuniary consideration.

The organization of our militia is likewise a subject of infinite importance: a clear and concise law, by which the burdens of service will be equally sustained and a competent number of men brought forth and kept in the field when their assistance may be required, is essential to our security, and therefore justly claims your immediate and serious attention: certain it is that some of our militia have, upon several occasions, exhibited symptoms of valor which would have reflected honor on veteran troops. The courage and conduct of the generals whom I have mentioned; the cool and determined bravery displayed by Brigadier Pickens, and, indeed, the behavior of many officers and men in every brigade, are unquestionable testimonies of the truth of this assertion. But such behavior cannot be expected from militia in general, without good order and strict discipline; nor can that order and discipline be established but by a salutary law steadily executed.

Another important matter for your deliberation is the conduct of such of our citizens as, voluntarily avowing their allegiance and even glorifying in their professions of loyalty and attachment to his Britannic Majesty, have offered their congratulations on the success of his arms, prayed to be embodied as loyal militia, accepted commissions in his service, or endeavored to subvert our constitution and establish his power in its stead; of those who have returned to this State, in defiance of law, by which such return was declared to be a capital offence, and have bettered the British interest, and of such whose behavior has been so reprehensible that justice and policy forbid their free re-admission to the rights and privileges of citizens.

The extraordinary lenity of this State has been remarkably conspicuous. Other States have thought it just and expedient to appropriate the property of British subjects to the public use; but we have forborne even to take the profits of the estates of our most implacable enemies. It is with you to determine whether the forfeiture and appropriation of their property should now take place: if such should be your determination, though many of our warmest friends have been reduced, for their inflexible attachment to the cause of their country, from opulence to inconceivable distress, and if the enemy's will and power had prevailed, would have been doomed to indigence and beggary, yet it will redound to the reputation of this State to provide a becoming support for the families of those whom you may deprive of their property.

The value of paper currency became of late so much depreciated that it was requisite, under the powers vested in the executive during the recess of the General Assembly, to suspend the laws by which it was made a tender. You will now consider whether it may not be proper to repeal those laws, and fix some equitable mode for the discharge of debts contracted whilst paper money was in circulation.

In the present scarcity of specie it would be difficult, if not impracticable, to levy a tax to any considerable amount, towards sinking the public debt, nor will the creditors of the State expect that such a tax should at this time be imposed; but it is just and reasonable that all unsettled demand should be liquidated, and satisfactory assurances of payment given to the public creditors.

The interest and honor, the safety and happiness of our country depend so much on the result of your deliberations, that I flatter myself you will proceed in the weighty business before you with firmness and temper, with vigor, unanimity, and despatch.

Foundations of Government

Benjamin Franklin

On the Constitution (1787)

Operating under the Articles of Confederation, the central government of the new United States was dependent upon the stronger state governments for financing and could take no significant actions without their unanimous approval. The weaknesses in this form of government, both in managing domestic matters and in conducting foreign affairs, were apparent. Many doubted that such a government could survive, although forces within the various states upholding the arrangement were strong. In 1786, when the country was in the grip of a severe economic depression, nine states agreed to a convention in Annapolis to discuss interstate commercial matters. The conference was poorly attended but, before adjourning, the delegates issued a call for a convention to consider all matters of government. Congress responded with a cautious endorsement of a convention to consider revision of the Articles.

Meeting in Philadelphia in May 1787, the convention included delegates from eleven states; New Hampshire's delegates didn't arrive until July and Rhode Island shunned the convention altogether. The convention quickly organized, electing George Washington as its president and agreeing to absolute secrecy in its proceedings. Throughout the summer, delegates debated issues that brought the various interests represented into conflict. The small states were fearful of the power of the large; the interests of the north and south differed; the extent to which the delegates even had the authority to move beyond mere amendment of the Articles was questioned. A plan concerning representation in the national legislature offered by Virginia was countered by a plan submitted by New Jersey. By the beginning of August a compromise was reached that established a legislature composed of two separate houses, one whose membership was determined by population and the other by equal representation of the states. The specific terms of the final constitution were laboriously debated over the next month. A committee on Style and Arrangement quickly prepared the final draft, which was considered clause by clause. When final approval came on September 17, it was clear that no one had achieved all that he wanted in this new constitution. The Constitution was clearly the result of painstaking compromise. It would soon be up to the various states to decide whether the compromise would be accepted, and many felt that the delegates, who had argued in secret, now must send forth their creation with as enthusiastic and unanimous support as possible.

The oldest delegate to the Constitutional Convention, the 81-year-old Benjamin Franklin, was well versed in the art of compromise and, like George Washington, was almost universally venerated and respected. Franklin's career had really been several careers. The printer and editor produced the famous *Poor Richard's Almanack*; the public-spirited cultural leader founded a debating society, a library, and an academy; the scientist-inventor devised the Franklin stove and unlocked the secrets of lightning and electricity; the politician was a member of the colonial Pennsylvania Assembly, postmaster general of the Colonies and, in later years, of the new United States, a drafter and signer of the Declaration of Independence, and, when the Convention met, president of the Executive Council of Pennsylvania; the diplomat served the colonies in London for years as a colonial agent before the Revolution and represented the fledgling United States in France at a time when French support was vital. At the Convention itself, Franklin played his part in bringing about the compromise that permitted the work to go forward.

With the deliberation completed, Franklin sought to launch the new Constitution successfully. Shrewdly observing that the new document could never be perfect while professing amazement at how near the work did come to perfection, Franklin appealed to solidarity in presenting and defending the fruit of their labors to the world. In his wisdom, he wished "that every member of the convention who may still have objections to it would with me on this occasion doubt a little of his own infallibility."

Mr. President:—I confess that I do not entirely approve of this Constitution at present; but, sir, I am not sure I shall never approve it; for, having lived long, I have experienced many instances of being obliged, by better information or fuller consideration, to change opinions even on important subjects, which I once thought right, but found to be otherwise. It is therefore that, the older I grow, the more apt I am to doubt my own judgment of others. Most men, indeed, as well as most sects in religion, think themselves in possession of all truth, and that wherever others differ from them, it is so far error. Steele, a Protestant, in a dedication, tells the Pope that the only difference between our two churches in their opinions of the certainty of their doctrine is, the Romish Church is *infallible,* and the Church of England is *never in the wrong*. But though many private persons think almost as highly of their own infallibility as that of their sect, few express it so naturally as a certain French lady, who, in a little dispute with her sister, said: "But I meet with nobody but myself that is *always* in the right." "*Je ne trouve que moi qui aie toujours raison.*"

In these sentiments, sir, I agree to this Constitution, with all its faults—if they are such;—because I think a general government necessary for us, and there is no *form* of government but what may be a blessing to the people, if well administered; and I believe further, that this is likely to be well administered for a course of years, and can only end in despotism, as other forms have done before it, when the people shall become so corrupted as to need despotic government, being incapable of any other. I doubt, too, whether any other convention we can obtain, may be able to make a better Constitution; for, when you assemble a number of men, to have the advantage of their joint wisdom, you inevitably assemble with those men, all their prejudices, their passions, their errors of opinion, their local interests, and their selfish views. From such an assembly can a *perfect* production be expected? It therefore astonishes me, sir, to find this system approaching so near to perfection as it does; and I think it will astonish our enemies, who are waiting with confidence to hear that our counsels are confounded like those of the builders of Babel, and that our States are on the point of separation, only to meet hereafter for the purpose of cutting one another's throats. Thus I consent, sir, to this Constitution, because I expect no better, and because I am not sure that it is not the best. The opinions I have had of its *errors* I sacrifice to the public good. I have never whispered a syllable of them abroad. Within these walls they were born, and here they shall die. If every one of us, in returning to our constituents, were to report the objections he has had to it, and endeavor to gain partisans in support of them, we might prevent its being generally received, and thereby lose all the salutary effects and great advantages resulting naturally in our favor among foreign nations, as well as among ourselves, from our real or apparent unanimity. Much of the strength and efficiency of any government in procuring and securing happiness to the people, depends on *opinion*, on the general opinion, of the goodness of that government, as well as of the wisdom and integrity of its governors. I hope, therefore, for our own sakes, as a part of the people, and for the sake of our posterity, that we shall act heartily and unanimously in recommending this Constitution, wherever our influence may extend, and turn our future thoughts and endeavors to the means of having it *well administered.*

On the whole, sir, I cannot help expressing a wish that every member of the convention who may still have objections to it would with me on this occasion doubt a little of his own infallibility, and, to make *manifest* our *unanimity*, put his name to this instrument.

Patrick Henry

Against the Federal Constitution (1788)

The constitution that emerged from the Philadelphia convention in 1787 was an intensely controversial document. The delegates had been charged only to modify the defects in the Articles of Confederation, not to draft a whole new charter for the government of the new nation. Not only had they exceeded their instructions, but they had put forward a document which limited the sovereignty of the individual states in order to strengthen the power of the central government. Although proponents of the new document described it as "federal," with powers divided between state and national governments, skeptics saw it as tending toward the consolidated government exemplified by the British monarchy.

There were many skeptics. When the Constitution was first submitted for ratification, its opponents, referred to as antifederalists, were in the majority in at least half the states. Supporters were often found in the cities, opponents in the rural areas and on the western frontier. Since the Constitution required approval from nine states before it could take effect, many uncommitted or hostile delegates to the state ratifying conventions had to be won over.

Each state held is own convention, and the first victories were easy. Delaware, Pennsylvania, New Jersey, Georgia, and Connecticut all ratified quickly. The first big test came in Massachusetts, where antifederalists held the edge but were outmaneuvered in the state convention, both by the superior advocacy of the federalists and by the promise that, once the Constitution had been duly ratified, amendments embodying a bill of rights would be proposed. In the end the Massachusetts convention ratified it by a 20-vote margin. Approval by Maryland and South Carolina followed in the spring of 1788.

The Virginia ratifying convention, which met in June 1788, was therefore critical. Virginia was potentially the ninth state, the one whose approval would put the Constitution in force. In any case, this state's ratification was crucial because of its large population, its geographic position in the center of the nation, its economy, and its influential leaders. Failure in Virginia would doom the new government, whereas success might set a precedent for the states to follow, particularly New York.

The antifederalists held the majority in Virginia but the state ratifying convention was almost evenly matched. Moreover, antifederalists labored under rhetorical disadvantages. They were debating whether or not the Constitution was the best answer to the problems of the Articles of Confederation, implicitly granting that there *were* problems. Also the convention voted to debate the document point by point, whereas opponents focused less on specific provisions than on the overall intent of the new charter.

Opponents of the Constitution were not without resources, however. The most significant antifederalist speaker was Patrick Henry. As a member of the House of Burgesses in 1765, he had authored resolutions denouncing the Stamp Act. He had served in the First and Second Continental Congresses, in the second revolutionary convention of Virginia, and as governor from 1776 to 1779 and again from 1784 to 1786. Chosen as a delegate to the Philadelphia convention, he had declined to serve because he feared that the delegates would exceed their instructions in just the way that they did. Now he directed his oratorical power against the Constitution, which he believed would impair the liberty of Virginians.

Henry spoke on June 5, 1788. His speech included the basic antifederalist arguments: too much power was invested in the central government, state sovereignty was not made explicit, the concentration of power could lead to tyranny, and there was no bill of rights. Henry's speech is particularly significant because he grounds many of his fears in vague phrases within the document and imagines the worst-case application which they might have. His fears may strike today's reader as farfetched, but only because we know how events came out. Henry's arguments are not fundamentally unlike those advanced during the 1980's against the calling of a new constitutional convention.

Mr. Chairman, I am much obliged to the very worthy gentleman for his encomium. I wish I was possessed with talents, or possessed of any thing that might enable me to elucidate this great subject. I am not free from suspicion: I am apt to entertain doubts. I rose yesterday to ask a question which arose in my own mind. When I asked that question, I thought the meaning of my interrogation was obvious. The fate of this question and of America may depend on this. Have they said, We, the states? Have they made a proposal of a compact between states? If they had, this would be a confederation. It is otherwise most clearly a consolidated government. The question turns, sir, on that poor little thing—the expression, We, the *people*, instead of the *states*, of America. I need not take much pains to show that the principles of this system are extremely pernicious, impolitic, and dangerous. Is this a monarchy, like England—a compact between prince and people, with checks on the former to secure the liberty of the latter? Is this a confederacy, like Holland—an association of a number of independent states, each of which retains its individual sovereignty? It is not a democracy, wherein the people retain all their rights securely. Had these principles been adhered to, we should not have been brought to this alarming transition, from a confederacy to a consolidated government. We have no detail of these great considerations, which, in my opinion, ought to have abounded before we should recur to a government of this kind. Here is a resolution as radical as that which separated us from Great Britain. It is radical in this transition; our rights and privileges are endangered, and the sovereignty of the states will be relinquished: and cannot we plainly see that this is actually the case? The rights of conscience, trial by jury, liberty of the press, all your immunities and franchises, all pretensions to human rights and privileges, are rendered insecure, if not lost, by this change, so loudly talked of by some, and inconsiderately by others. Is this tame relinquishment of rights worthy of freemen? Is it worthy of that manly fortitude that ought to characterize republicans? It is said eight states have adopted this plan. I declare that if twelve states and a half had adopted it, I would, with manly firmness, and in spite of an erring world, reject it. You are not to inquire how your trade may be increased, nor how you are to become a great and powerful people, but how your liberties can be secured; for liberty ought to be the direct end of your government.

Having premised these things, I shall, with the aid of my judgment and information, which, I confess, are not extensive, go into the discussion of this system more minutely. Is it necessary for your liberty that you should abandon those great rights by the adoption of this system? Is the relinquishment of the trial by jury and the liberty of the press necessary for your liberty? Will the abandonment of your most sacred rights tend to the security of your liberty? Liberty, the greatest of all earthly blessings—give us that precious jewel, and you may take every thing else! But I am fearful I have lived long enough to become an old-fashioned fellow. Perhaps an invincible attachment to the dearest rights of man may, in these refined, enlightened days, be deemed old-fashioned; if so, I am contented to be so. I say, the time has been when every pulse of my heart beat for American liberty, and which, I believe, had a counterpart in the breast of every true American; but suspicions have gone forth—suspicions of my integrity—publicly reported that my professions are not real. Twenty-three years ago was I supposed a traitor to my country? I was then said to be the bane of sedition, because I supported the rights of my country. I may be thought suspicious when I say our privileges and rights are in danger. But, sir, a number of the people of this country are weak enough to think these things are too true. I am happy to find that the gentleman on the other side declares they are groundless. But, sir, suspicion is a virtue as long as its object is the preservation of the public good, and as long as it stays within proper bounds: should it fall on me, I am contented: conscious rectitude is a powerful consolation. I trust there are many who think my professions for the public good to be real. Let your suspicion look to both sides. There are many on the other side, who possibly may have been persuaded to the necessity of these measures, which I conceive to be dangerous to your liberty. Guard with jealous attention the public liberty. Suspect every one who approaches that jewel. Unfortunately, nothing will preserve it but downright force. Whenever you give up that force, you are inevitably ruined. I am answered by gentlemen, that, though I might speak of terrors, yet the fact was, that we were surrounded by none of the dangers I apprehended. I conceive this new government to be one of those dangers: it has produced those horrors which distress many of our best citizens. We are come hither to preserve the poor commonwealth of Virginia, if it can be possibly done: something must be done to preserve your liberty and mine. The Confederation, this same despised government, merits, in my opinion, the highest encomium: it carried us through a long and dangerous war; it rendered us victorious in that bloody conflict with a powerful nation; it has secured us a territory greater than any European monarch possesses: and shall a government which has been thus strong and vigorous, be accused of imbecility, and abandoned for want of energy? Consider what you are about to do before you part with the government. Take longer time in reckoning things; revolutions like this have happened in almost every country in Europe; similar examples are to be found in ancient Greece and ancient Rome—instances of the people losing their liberty by their carelessness and the ambition of a few. We are cautioned by the honorable gentleman, who presides, against faction and turbulence. I acknowledge that licentiousness is dangerous, and that it ought to be provided against; I acknowledge, also, the new form of government may effectually prevent it: yet there is another thing it will as effectually do—it will oppress and ruin the people.

There are sufficient guards placed against sedition and licentiousness; for, when power is given to this government to suppress these, or for any other purpose, the language it assumes is clear, express, and unequivocal; but when this Constitution speaks of privileges, there is an ambiguity, sir, a fatal ambiguity—an ambiguity which is very astonishing. In the clause under consideration, there is the strangest language that I can conceive. I mean, when it says that there shall not be more representatives than one for every thirty thousand. Now, sir, how easy is it to evade this privilege! "The number shall not exceed one for every thirty thousand." This may be satisfied by one representative from each state. Let our numbers be ever so great, this immense continent may, by this artful expression, be reduced to have but thirteen representatives. I confess this construction is not natural; but the ambiguity of the expression lays a good ground for a quarrel. Why was it not clearly and unequivocally expressed, that they should be entitled to have one for every thirty thousand? This would have obviated all disputes; and was this difficult to be done? What is the inference? When population increases, and a state shall send representatives in this proportion, Congress *may* remand them, because the right of having one for every thirty thousand is not clearly expressed. This possibility of reducing the number to one for each state approximates to probability by that other expression—"but each state shall at least have one representative." Now, is it not clear that, from the first expression, the number might be reduced so much that some states should have no representatives at all, were it not for the insertion of this last expression? And as this is the only restriction upon them, we may fairly conclude that they *may* restrain the number to one from each state. Perhaps the same horrors may hang over my mind again. I shall be told I am continually afraid: but, sir, I have strong cause of apprehension. In some parts of the plan before you, the great rights of freemen are endangered; in other parts, absolutely taken away. How does your trial by jury stand? In civil cases gone—not sufficiently secured in criminal—this best privilege is gone. But we are told that we need not fear; because those in power, being our representatives, will not abuse the power we put in their hands. I am not well versed in history, but I will submit to your recollection, whether liberty has been destroyed most often by the licentiousness of the people, or by the tyranny of rulers. I imagine, sir, you will find the balance on the side of tyranny. Happy will you be if you miss the fate of those nations, who, omitting to resist their oppressors, or negligently suffering their liberty to be wrested from them, have groaned under intolerable despotism! Most of the human race are now in this deplorable condition; and those nations who have gone in search of grandeur, power, and splendor, have also fallen a sacrifice, and been the victims of their own folly. While they acquired those visionary blessings, they lost their freedom. My great objection to this government is, that it does not leave us the means of defending our rights, or of waging war against tyrants. It is urged by some gentlemen, that this new plan will brings us an acquisition of strength—an army, and the militia of the states. This is an idea extremely ridiculous: gentlemen cannot be earnest. This acquisition will trample on our fallen liberty. Let my beloved Americans guard against that fatal lethargy that has pervaded the universe. Have we the means of resisting disciplined armies, when our only defence, the militia, is put into the hands of Congress? The honorable gentleman said that great danger would ensue if the Convention rose without adopting this system. I ask, Where is that danger? I see none. Other gentlemen have told us, within these walls, that the union is gone, or that the union will be gone. Is not this trifling with the judgment of their fellow-citizens? Till they tell us the grounds of their fears, I will consider them as imaginary. I rose to make inquiry where those dangers were; they could make no answer: I believe I never shall have that answer. Is there a disposition in the people of this country to revolt against the dominion of laws? Has there been a single tumult in Virginia? Have not the people of Virginia, when laboring under the severest pressure of accumulated distresses, manifested the most cordial acquiescence in the execution of the laws? What could be more awful than their unanimous acquiescence under general distresses? Is there any revolution in Virginia? Whither is the spirit of America gone? Whither is the genius of America fled? It was but yesterday, when our enemies marched in triumph through our country. Yet the people of this country could not be appalled by their pompous armaments: they stopped their career, and victoriously captured them. Where is the peril, now, compared to that? Some minds are agitated by foreign alarms. Happily for us, there is no real danger from Europe; that country is engaged in more arduous business: from that quarter there is no cause of fear: you may sleep in safety forever for them.

Where is the danger? If, sir, there was any, I would recur to the Americans spirit to defend us; that spirit which has enabled us to surmount the greatest difficulties: to that illustrious spirit I address my most fervent prayer to prevent our adopting a system destructive to liberty. Let no gentlemen be told that it is not safe to reject this government. Wherefore is it not safe? We are told there are dangers, but those dangers are ideal; they cannot be demonstrated. To encourage us to adopt it, they tell us that there is a plain, easy way of getting amendments. When I come to contemplate this part, I suppose that I am mad, or that my countrymen are so. The way to amendment is, in my conception, shut. Let us consider this plain, easy way. "The Congress, whenever two thirds of both houses shall deem it necessary, shall propose amendments to this Constitution, or on the application of the legislatures of two thirds of the several states, shall call a Convention for proposing amendments, which, in either case, shall be valid to all intents and purposes, as part of this Constitution, when ratified by the legislatures of three fourths of the several states, or by the Conventions in three fourths thereof, as the one or the other mode of ratification may be proposed by the Congress. Provided, that no amendment which may be made prior to the year 1808, shall in any manner affect the 1st and 4th clauses in the 9th section of the 1st article; and that no state, without its consent, shall be deprived of its equal suffrage in the Senate."

Hence it appears that three fourths of the states must ultimately agree to any amendments that may be necessary. Let us consider the consequence of this. However uncharitable it may appear, yet I must tell my opinion—that the most unworthy character may get into power, and prevent the introduction of amendments. Let us suppose—for the case is supposable, possible, and probable—that you happen to deal those powers to unworthy hands; will they relinquish powers already in their possession, or agree to amendments? Two thirds of the Congress, or of the state legislatures, are necessary even to propose amendments. If one third of these be unworthy men, they may prevent the application for amendments; but what is destructive and mischievous, is, that three fourths of the state legislatures, or of the state conventions, must concur in the amendments when proposed! In such numerous bodies, there must necessarily be some designing, bad men. To suppose that so large a number as three fourths of the states will concur, is to suppose that they will possess genius, intelligence, and integrity, approaching to miraculous. It would indeed be miraculous that they should concur in the same amendments, or even in such as would bear some likeness to one another; for four of the smallest states, that do not collectively contain one tenth part of the population of the United States, may obstruct the most salutary and necessary amendments. Nay, in these four states, six tenths of the people may reject these amendments; and suppose that amendments shall be opposed to amendments, which is highly probable,—is it possible that three fourths can ever agree to the same amendments? A bare majority in these four small states may hinder the adoption of amendments; so that we may fairly and justly conclude that one twentieth part of the American people may prevent the removal of the most grievous inconveniences and oppression, by refusing to accede to amendments. A trifling minority may reject the most salutary amendments. Is this an easy mode of securing the public liberty? It is, sir, a most fearful situation, when the most contemptible minority can prevent the alteration of the most oppressive government; for it may, in many respects, prove to be such. Is this the spirit of republicanism?

What, sir, is the genius of democracy? Let me read that clause of the bill of rights of Virginia which relates to this: 3d clause:—that government is, or ought to be, instituted for the common benefit, protection, and security of the people, nation, or community. Of all the various modes and forms of government, that is best, which is capable of producing the greatest degree of happiness and safety, and is most effectually secured against the danger of mal-administration; and that whenever any government shall be found inadequate, or contrary to those purposes, a majority of the community hath an indubitable, unalienable, and indefeasible right to reform, alter, or abolish it, in such manner as shall be judged most conducive to the public weal.

This, sir, is the language of democracy—that a majority of the community have a right to alter government when found to be oppressive. But how different is the genius of your new Constitution form this! How different from the sentiments of freemen, that a contemptible minority can prevent the good of the majority! If, then, gentlemen, standing on this ground, are come to that point, that they are willing to bind themselves and their posterity to be oppressed, I am amazed and inexpressibly astonished. If this be the opinion of the majority, I must submit; but to me, sir, it appears perilous and destructive. I cannot help thinking so. Perhaps it may be the result of my age. These may be feelings natural to a man of my years, when the American spirit has left him, and his mental powers, like the members of the body, are decayed. If, sir, amendments are left to the twentieth, or tenth part of the people of America, your liberty is gone forever. We have heard that there is a great deal of bribery practised in the House of Commons, in England, and that many of the members raise themselves to preferments by selling the rights of the whole of the people. But, sir, the tenth part of that body cannot continue oppressions on the rest of the people. English liberty is, in this case, on a firmer foundation than American liberty. It will be easily contrived to procure the opposition of one tenth of the people to any alteration, however judicious. The honorable gentleman who presides told us that, to prevent abuses in our government, we will assemble in Convention, recall our delegated powers, and punish our servants for abusing the trust reposed in them. O sir, we should have fine times, indeed, if, to punish tyrants, it were only sufficient to assemble the people! Your arms, wherewith you could defend yourselves are gone; and you have no longer an aristocratical, no longer a democratical spirit. Did you ever read of any revolution in a nation, brought about by the punishment of those in power, inflicted by those who had no power at all? You read of a riot act in a country which is called one of the freest in the world, where a few neighbors cannot assemble without the risk of being shot by a hired soldiery, the engines of despotism. We may see such an act in America.

A standing army we shall have, also, to execute the execrable commands of tyranny; and how are you to punish them? Will you order them to be punished? Who shall obey these orders? Will your macebearer be a match for a disciplined regiment? In what situation are we to be? The clause before you gives a power of direct taxation, unbounded and unlimited, exclusive power of legislation, in all cases whatsoever, for ten miles square, and over all places purchased for the erection of forts, magazines, arsenals, dockyards, &c. What resistance could be made? The attempt would be madness. You will find all the strength of this country in the hands of your enemies; their garrisons will naturally be the strongest places in the country. Your militia is given up to Congress, also, in another part of this plan: they will therefore act as they think proper: all power will be in their own possession. You cannot force them to receive their punishment: of what service would militia be to you, when, most probably, you will not have a single musket in the state? for, as arms are to be provided by Congress, they may or may not furnish them.

Let me here call your attention to that part which gives the Congress power "to provide for organizing, arming, and disciplining the militia, and for governing such part of them as may be employed in the service of the United States—reserving to the states, respectively, the appointment of the officers, and the authority of training the militia according to the discipline prescribed by Congress." By this, sir, you see that their control over our last and best defence is unlimited. If they neglect or refuse to discipline or arm our militia, they will be useless: the states can do neither—this power being exclusively given to Congress. The power of appointing officers over men not disciplined or armed is ridiculous; so that this pretended little remains of power left to the states may, at the pleasure of Congress, be rendered nugatory. Our situation will be deplorable indeed: nor can we ever expect to get this government amended, since I have already shown that a very small minority may prevent it, and that small minority interested in the continuance of the oppression. Will the oppressor let go the oppressed? Was there even an instance? Can the annals of mankind exhibit one single example where rulers overcharged with power willingly let go the oppressed, though solicited and requested most earnestly? The application for amendments will therefore be fruitless. Sometimes, the oppressed have got loose by one of those bloody struggles that desolate a country; but a willing relinquishment of power is one of those things which human nature never was, nor ever will be, capable of.

The honorable gentleman's observations, respecting the people's right of being the agents in the formation of this government, are not accurate, in my humble conception. The distinction between a national government and confederacy is not sufficiently discerned. Had the delegates, who were sent to Philadelphia, a power to propose a consolidated government instead of a confederacy? Were they not deputed by states, and not by the people? The assent of the people, in their collective capacity, is not necessary to the formation of a federal government. The people have no right to enter into leagues, alliances, or confederations; they are not the proper agents for this purpose. States and foreign powers are the only proper agents for this kind of government. Show me an instance where the people have exercised this business. Has it not always gone through the legislatures? I refer you to the treaties with France, Holland, and other nations. How were they made? Were they not made by the states? Are the people, therefore, in their aggregate capacity, the proper persons to form a confederacy? This, therefore, ought to depend on the consent of the legislatures, the people having never sent delegates to make any proposition for changing the government. Yet I must say, at the same time, that it was made on grounds the most pure; and perhaps I might have been brought to consent to it so far as to the change of government. But there is one thing in it which I never would acquiesce in. I mean, the changing it into a consolidated government, which is so abhorrent in my mind. [*The honorable gentleman then went on to the figure we make with foreign nations; the contemptible one we make in France and Holland; which, according to the substance of the notes, he attributes to the present feeble government.*] An opinion has gone forth, we find, that we are contemptible people: the time has been when we were thought otherwise. Under the same despised government, we commanded the respect of all Europe: wherefore are we now reckoned otherwise? The American spirit has fled from hence: it has gone to regions where it has never been expected; it has gone to the people of France, in search of a splendid government—a strong, energetic government. Shall we imitate the example of those nations who have gone from a simple to a splendid government? Are those nations more worthy of our imitation? What can make an adequate satisfaction to them for the loss they have suffered in attaining such a government—for the loss of their liberty? If we admit this consolidated government, it will be because we like a great, splendid one. Some way or other we must be a great and mighty empire; we must have an army, and a navy, and a number of things. When the American spirit was in its youth, the language of America was different: liberty, sir, was then the primary object. We are descended from a people whose government was founded on liberty: our glorious forefathers of Great Britain made liberty the foundation of every thing. That country is become a great, mighty, and splendid nation; not because their government is strong and energetic, but, sir, because liberty is its direct end and foundation. We drew the spirit of liberty from our British ancestors: by that spirit we have triumphed over every difficulty. But now, sir, the American spirit, assisted by the ropes and chains of consolidation, is about to convert this country into a powerful and mighty empire. If you make the citizens of this country agree to become the subjects of one great consolidated empire of America, your government will not have sufficient energy to keep them together. Such a government is incompatible with the genius of republicanism. There will be no checks, no real balances, in this government. What can avail your specious, imaginary balance, your rope-dancing, chain-rattling, ridiculous ideal checks and contrivances? But, sir, we are not feared by foreigners; we do not make nations tremble. Would this constitute happiness, or secure liberty? I trust, sir, our political hemisphere will ever direct their operations to the security of those objects.

Consider our situation, sir: go to the poor man, and ask him what he does. He will inform you that he enjoys the fruits of his labor, under his own fig-tree, with his wife and children around him, in peace and security. Go to every other member of society,—you will find the same tranquil ease and content; you will find no alarms or disturbances. Why, then, tell us of danger, to terrify us into an adoption of this new form of government? And yet who knows the dangers that this new system may produce? They are out of the sight of the common people: they cannot foresee latent consequences. I dread the operation of it on the middling and lower classes of people: it is for them I fear the adoption of this system. I fear I tire the patience of the committee; but I beg to be indulged with a few more observations. When I thus profess myself an advocate for the liberty of the people, I shall be told I am a designing man, that I am to be a great man, that I am to be a demagogue; and many similar illiberal insinuations will be thrown out: but, sir, conscious rectitude outweighs those things with me. I see great jeopardy in this new government. I see none from our present one. I hope some gentleman or other will bring forth, in full array, those dangers, if there by any, that we may see and touch them. I have said that I thought this is a consolidated government: I will now prove it. Will the greats rights of the people be secured by this government? Suppose it should prove oppressive, how can it be altered? Our bill of rights declares, "that a majority of the community hath an indubitable, unalienable, and indefeasible right to reform, alter, or abolish it, in such manner as shall be judged most conducive to the public weal."

I have just proved that one tenth, or less, of the people of America—a most despicable minority—may prevent this reform or alteration. Suppose the people of Virginia should wish to alter their government; can a majority of them do it? No; because they are connected with other men, or, in other words, consolidated with other states. When the people of Virginia, at a future day, shall wish to alter their government, though they should be unanimous in this desire, yet they may be prevented therefrom by a despicable minority at the extremity of the United States. The founders of your Constitution made your government changeable: but the power of changing it is gone from you. Whither is it gone? It is placed in the same hands that hold the rights of twelve other states; and those who hold those rights have right and power to keep them. It is not the particular government of Virginia: one of the leading features of that government is, that a majority can alter it, when necessary for the public good. This government is not a Virginian, but an American government. Is it not, therefore, a consolidated government? The sixth clause of your bill of rights tells you, "that elections of members to serve as representatives of the people in the Assembly ought to be free, and that all men having sufficient evidence of permanent common interest with, and attachment to, the community, have the right of suffrage, and cannot be *taxed*, or deprived of their property for public uses, without their own consent, or that of their representatives so elected, nor bound by any law to which they have not in like manner assented for the public good." But what does this Constitution say? The clause under consideration gives an unlimited and unbounded power of taxation. Suppose every delegate from Virginia opposes a law laying a tax; what will it avail? They are opposed by a majority; eleven members can destroy their efforts; those feeble ten cannot prevent the passing the most oppressive tax law; so that, in direct opposition to the spirit and express language of your declaration of rights, you are taxed, not by your own consent, but by people who have no connection with you.

The next clause of the bill of rights tells you, "that all power of suspending law, or the execution of laws, by any authority, without the consent of the representatives of the people, is injurious to their rights, and ought not to be exercised." This tells us that there can be no suspension of government or laws without our own consent; yet this Constitution can counteract and suspend any of our laws that contravene its oppressive operation; for they have the power of direct taxation, which suspends our bill of rights; and it is expressly provided that they can make all laws necessary for carrying their powers into execution; and it is declared paramount to the laws and constitutions of the states. Consider how the only remaining defence we have left is destroyed in this manner. Besides the expenses of maintaining the Senate and other house in as much splendor as they please, there is to be a great and mighty President, with very extensive powers—the powers of a king. He is to be supported in extravagant magnificence; so that the whole of our property may be taken by this American government, by laying what taxes they please, giving themselves what salaries they please, and suspending our laws at their pleasure. I might be thought too inquisitive, but I believe I should take up very little of your time in enumerating the little power that is left to the government of Virginia; for this power is reduced to little or nothing: their garrisons, magazines, arsenals, and forts, which will be situated in the strongest places within the states; their ten miles square, with all the fine ornaments of human life, added to their powers, and taken from the states, will reduce the power of the latter to nothing.

The voice of tradition, I trust, will inform posterity of our struggles for freedom. If our descendants be worthy the name of Americans, they will preserve, and hand down to their latest posterity, the transactions of the present times; and, though I confess my exclamations are not worthy the hearing, they will see that I have done my utmost to preserve their liberty; for I never will give up the power of direct taxation but for the scourge. I am willing to give it conditionally; that is, after non-compliance with requisitions. I will do more, sir, and what I hope will convince the most skeptical man that I am a lover of the American Union—that, in case Virginia shall not make punctual payment, the control of our custom-houses, and the whole regulation of trade, shall be given to Congress, and that Virginia shall depend on Congress even for passports, till Virginia shall have paid the last farthing, and furnished the last soldier. Nay, sir, there is another alternative to which I would consent;—even that they should strike us out of the Union, and take away from us all federal privileges, till we comply with federal requisitions: but let it depend upon our own pleasure to pay our money in the most easy manner for our people. Were all the states, more terrible than the mother country, to join against us, I hope Virginia could defend herself; but, sir, the dissolution of the Union is most abhorrent to my mind. The first thing I have at heart is American liberty: the second thing is American union; and I hope the people of Virginia will endeavor to preserve that union. The increasing population of the Southern States is far greater than that of New England; consequently, in a short time, they will be far more numerous than the people of that country. Consider this, and you find this state more particularly interested to support American liberty, and not bind our posterity by an improvident relinquishment of our rights. I would give the best security for a punctual compliance with requisitions; but I beseech gentlemen, at all hazards, not to give up this unlimited power of taxation. The honorable gentleman has told us that these powers, given to Congress, are accompanied by a judiciary which will correct all. On examination, you will find this very judiciary oppressively constructed; your jury trial destroyed, and the judges dependent on Congress.

In this scheme of energetic government, the people will find two sets of tax-gatherers—the state and the federal sheriffs. This, it seems to me, will produce such dreadful oppression as the people cannot possibly bear. The federal sheriff may commit what oppression, make what distresses, he pleases, and ruin you with impunity; for how are you to tie his hands? Have you any sufficiently decided means of preventing him from sucking your blood by speculations, commissions, and fees? Thus thousands of your people will be most shamefully robbed: our state sheriffs, those unfeeling blood-suckers, have, under the watchful eye of our legislature, committed the most horrid and barbarous ravages on our people. It has required the most constant vigilance of the legislature to keep them from totally ruining the people; a repeated succession of laws has been made to suppress their iniquitous speculations and cruel extortions; and as often has their nefarious ingenuity devised methods of evading the force of those laws: in the struggle they have generally triumphed over the legislature.

It is a fact that lands have been sold for five shillings, which were worth one hundred pounds: if sheriffs, thus immediately under the eye of our state legislature and judiciary, have dared to commit these outrages, what would they not have done if their masters had been at Philadelphia or New York? If they perpetrate the most unwarrantable outrage on your person or property, you cannot get redress on this side of Philadelphia or New York; and how can you get it there? If your domestic avocations could permit you to go thither, there you must appeal to judges sworn to support this Constitution, in opposition to that of any state, and who may also be inclined to favor their own officers. When these harpies are aided by excisemen, who may search, at any time, your houses, and most secret recesses, will the people bear it? If you think so, you differ from me. Where I thought there was a possibility of such mischiefs, I would grant power with a niggardly hand; and here there is a strong probability that these oppressions shall actually happen. I may be told that it is safe to err on that side, because such regulations may be made by Congress as shall restrain these officers, and because laws are made by our representatives, and judged by righteous judges: but sir, as these regulations may be made, so they may not; and many reasons there are to induce a belief that they will not. I shall therefore be an infidel on that point till the day of my death.

This Constitution is said to have beautiful features; but when I come to examine these features, sir, they appear to me horribly frightful. Among other deformities, it has an awful squinting; it squints toward monarchy; and does not this raise indignation in the breast of every true American?

Your President may easily become king. Your Senate is so imperfectly constructed that your dearest rights may be sacrificed by what may be a small minority; and a very small minority may continue forever unchangeably this government, although horridly defective. Where are your checks in this government? Your strongholds will be in the hands of your enemies. It is on a supposition that your American governors shall be honest, that all the good qualities of this government are founded; but its defective and imperfect construction puts it in their power to perpetrate the worst of mischiefs, should they be bad men; and, sir, would not all the world, from the eastern to the western hemisphere, blame our distracted folly in resting our rights upon the contingency of our rulers being good or bad? Show me that age and country where the rights and liberties of the people were placed on the sole chance of their rulers being good men, without a consequent loss of liberty! I say that the loss of that dearest privilege has ever followed, with absolute certainty, every such mad attempt.

If your American chief be a man of ambition and abilities, how easy is it for him to render himself absolute! The army is in his hands, and if he be a man of address, it will be attached to him, and it will be the subject of long mediation with him to seize the first auspicious moment to accomplish his design; and, sir, will the

American spirit solely relieve you when this happens? I would rather infinitely—and I am sure most of this Convention are of the same opinion—have a king, lords, and commons, than a government so replete with such insupportable evils. If we make a king, we may prescribe the rules by which he shall rule his people, and interpose such checks as shall prevent him from infringing them; but the President, in the field, at the head of his army, can prescribe the terms on which he shall reign master, so far that it will puzzle any American ever to get his neck from under the galling yoke. I cannot with patience think of this idea. If ever he violates the laws, one of two things will happen: he will come at the head of his army, to carry every thing before him; or he will give bail, or do what Mr. Chief Justice will order him. If he be guilty, will not the recollection of his crimes teach him to make one bold push for the American throne? Will not the immense difference between being master of every thing, and being ignominiously tried and punished, powerfully excite him to make this bold push? But, sir, where is the existing force to punish him? Can he not, at the head of his army, beat down every opposition? Away with your President! we shall have a king: the army will salute him monarch: your militia will leave you, and assist in making him king, and fight against you: and what have you to oppose this force? What will then become of you and your rights? Will not absolute despotism ensue? [*Here Mr. Henry strongly and pathetically expatiated on the probability of the President's enslaving America, and the horrid consequences that must result.*]

What can be more defective than the clause concerning the elections? The control given to Congress over the time, place, and manner of holding elections, will totally destroy the end of suffrage. The elections may be held at one place, and the most inconvenient in the state; or they may be at remote distances from those who have a right of suffrage: hence nine out of ten must either not vote at all, or vote for strangers; for the most influential characters will be applied to, to know who are the most proper to be chosen. I repeat, the control of Congress over the *manner*, &c., of electing, well warrants this idea. The natural consequence will be, that this democratic branch will possess none of the public confidence; the people will be prejudiced against representatives chosen in such an injudicious manner. The proceedings in the northern conclave will be hidden from the yeomanry of this country. We are told that the yeas and nays shall be taken, and entered on the journals. This, sir, will avail nothing: it may be locked up in their chests, and concealed forever from the people; for they are not to publish what parts they think require secrecy: they *may* think, and *will think*, the whole requires it. Another beautiful feature of this Constitution is, the publication from time to time of the receipts and expenditures of the public money.

This expression, *from time to time*, is very indefinite and indeterminate: it may extend to a century. Grant that any of them are wicked; they may squander the public money so as to ruin you, and yet this expression will give you no redress. I say they may ruin you; for where, sir, is the responsibility? The yeas and nays will show you nothing, unless they be fools as well as knaves; for, after having wickedly trampled on the rights of the people, they would act like fools indeed, were they to publish and divulge their iniquity, when they have it equally in their power to suppress and conceal it. Where is the responsibility—that leading principle in the British government? In that government, a punishment certain and inevitable is provided; but in this, there is no real, actual punishment for the grossest mal-administration. They may go without punishment, though they commit the most outrageous violation on our immunities. That paper may tell me they will be punished. I ask, By what law? They must make the law, for there is no existing law to do it. What! will they make a law to punish themselves?

This, sir, is my great objection to the Constitution, that there is no true responsibility—and that the preservation of our liberty depends on the single chance of men being virtuous enough to make laws to punish themselves.

In the country from which we are descended, they have real and not imaginary responsibility; for the mal-administration has cost their heads to some of the most saucy geniuses that ever were. The Senate, by making treaties, may destroy your liberty and laws for want of responsibility. Two thirds of those that shall happen to be present, can, with the President, make treaties that shall be the supreme law of the land; they may make the most ruinous treaties; and yet there is no punishment for them. Whoever shows me a punishment provided for them will oblige me. So, sir, notwithstanding there are eight pillars, they want another. Where will they make another? I trust, sir, the exclusion of the evils wherewith this system is replete in its present form, will be made a condition precedent to its adoption by this or any other state. The transition, from a general unqualified admission to offices, to a consolidation of government, seems easy; for, though the American states are dissimilar in their structure, this will assimilate them. This, sir, is itself a strong consolidating feature, and is not one of the least dangerous in that system. Nine states are sufficient to establish this government over those nine. Imagine that nine have come into it. Virginia has certain scruples. Suppose she will, consequently, refuse to join with those states; may not she still continue in friendship and union with them? If she sends her annual requisitions in dollars, do you think their stomachs will be so squeamish as to refuse her dollars? Will they not accept her regiments? They would intimidate you into an inconsiderate adoption, and frighten you with ideal evils, and that the Union shall be dissolved. 'Tis a bugbear, sir: the fact is, sir, that the eight adopting states can hardly stand on their own legs. Public fame tells us that the adopting states have already heart-burnings and animosity, and repent their precipitate hurry: this, sir, may occasion exceeding great mischief. When I reflect on these and many other circumstances, I must think those states will be found to be in confederacy with us. If we pay our quota of money annually, and furnish our ratable number of men, when necessary, I can see no danger from a rejection.

The history of Switzerland clearly proves that we might be in amicable alliance with those states without adopting this Constitution. Switzerland is a confederacy, consisting of dissimilar governments. This is an example which proves that governments of dissimilar structures may be confederated. That confederate republic has stood upwards of four hundred years; and, although several of the individual republics are democratic, and the rest aristocratic, no evil has resulted from this dissimilarity; for they have braved all the power of France and Germany during that long period. The Swiss spirit, sir, has kept them together; they have encountered and overcome immense difficulties with patience and fortitude. In the vicinity of powerful and ambitious monarchs, they have retained their independence, republican simplicity, and valor. [*Here he makes a comparison of the people of that country and those of France, and makes a quotation from Addison illustrating the subject.*] Look at the peasants of that country and of France; and mark the difference. You will find the condition of the former far more desirable and comfortable. No matter whether the people be great, splendid, and powerful, if they enjoy freedom. The Turkish Grand Signior, alongside of our President, would put us to disgrace; but we should be as abundantly consoled for this disgrace, when our citizens have been put in contrast with the Turkish slave. The most valuable end of government is the liberty of the inhabitants. No possible advantages can compensate for the loss of this privilege. Show me the reason why the American Union is to be dissolved. Who are those eight adopting states? Are they averse to give us a little time to consider, before we conclude? Would such a disposition render a junction with them eligible; or is it the genius of that kind of government to precipitate people hastily into measures of the utmost importance, and grant no indulgence? If it be, sir, is it for us to accede to such a government? We have a right to have time to consider: we shall therefore insist upon it. Unless the government be amended, we can never accept it. The adopting states will doubtless accept our money and our regiments; and what is to be the consequence, if we are disunited? I believe it is yet doubtful, whether it is not proper to stand by a while, and see the effect of its adoption in other states. In forming a government, the utmost care should be taken to prevent its becoming oppressive; and this government is of such an intricate and complicated nature, that no man on this earth can know its real operation. The other states have no reason to think, from the antecedent conduct of Virginia, that she has any intention of seceding from the Union, or of being less active to support the general welfare. Would they not, therefore, acquiesce in our taking time to deliberate—deliberate whether the measure be not perilous, not only for us, but the adopting states?

Permit me, sir, to say, that a great majority of the people, even in the adopting states, are averse to this government. I believe I would be right to say, that they have been egregiously misled. Pennsylvania has, *perhaps*, been tricked into it. If the other states who have adopted it have not been tricked, still they were too much hurried into its adoption. There were very respectable minorities in several of them; and if reports be true, a clear majority of the people are averse to it. If we also accede, and it should prove grievous, the peace and prosperity of our country, which we all love, will be destroyed. This government has not the affection of the people at present. Should it be oppressive, their affections will be totally estranged from it; and, sir, you know that a government, without their affections, can neither be durable nor happy. I speak as one poor individual; but when I speak, I speak the language of thousands. But, sir, I mean not to breathe the spirit, nor utter the language, of secession.

I have trespassed so long on your patience, I am really concerned that I have something yet to say. The honorable member has said, we shall be properly represented. Remember, sir, that the number of our representatives is but ten, whereof six is a majority. Will those men be possessed of sufficient information? A particular knowledge of particular districts will not suffice. They must be well acquainted with agriculture, commerce, and a great variety of other matters throughout the continent; they must know not only the actual state of nations in Europe and America, the situations of their farmers, cottagers, and mechanics, but also the relative situations and intercourse of those nations. Virginia is as large as England. Our proportion of representatives is but ten men. In England they have five hundred and fifty-eight. The House of Commons, in England, numerous as they are, we are told, are bribed, and have bartered away the rights of their constituents: what, then, shall become of us? Will these few protect our rights? Will they be incorruptible? You say they will be better men than the English commoners. I say they will be infinitely worse men, because they are to be chosen blindfolded: their election (the term, as applied to their appointment, is inaccurate) will be an involuntary nomination, and not a choice.

I have, I fear, fatigued the committee; yet I have not said the one hundred thousandth part of what I have on my mind, and wish to impart. On this occasion, I conceived myself bound to attend strictly to the interest of the state, and I thought her dearest rights at stake. Having lived so long—been so much honored—my efforts, though small, are due to my country. I have found my mind hurried on, from subject to subject, on this very great occasion. We have been all out of order, from the gentleman who opened to-day to myself. I did not come prepared to speak, on so multifarious a subject, in so general a manner. I trust you will indulge me another time. Before you abandon the present system, I hope you will consider not only its defects, most maturely, but likewise those of that which you are to substitute for it. May you be fully apprized of the dangers of the latter, not by fatal experience, but by some abler advocate than I!

James Madison

For the Federal Constitution (1788)

Although the Virginia ratifying convention had begun with a majority opposing the Constitution, the attack led by Patrick Henry and others was ultimately repulsed. To those who wished to make Virginia's support contingent on adoption of a bill of rights, supporters answered that the hour was too late for that strategy since eight states already had ratified. Instead, the preferred stance was that of the Massachusetts convention: unconditional acceptance of the document, coupled with recommended amendments to the new government.

One of Henry's most important antagonists was James Madison. Madison had helped to draft the Virginia state convention of 1776, had served in the Continental Congress and the Virginia legislature, and had been instrumental in the call for the Constitutional Convention in Philadelphia, where he kept a journal of the assembly's proceedings. The Virginia Plan for the national legislature, which became the basis for Article I of the Constitution, was written largely by Madison. During 1788 Madison collaborated with Alexander Hamilton and John Jay in writing *The Federalist Papers*, a series of essays supporting the Constitution which were published in New York newspapers in an attempt to promote the cause of ratification in that state. Madison conducted an active correspondence with other Virginia federalists, and he realized that a favorable outcome in Virginia could sway the delegates in New York.

The speech that follows was delivered on June 6, 1788, in response to Patrick Henry. Madison emphasized the seriousness of current economic conditions and explained that the Constitution, unlike the Articles of Confederation, gave the central government the ability to raise revenue in order to retire the war debt. He argued that representation would be fairer under the new document because it was based on population. And he answered the criticism that the federal government would be tyrannical by observing that the multiplication of factions and interests would greatly reduce the likelihood that a tyrannical majority might form.

Neither side in the convention was sure that it had a majority, so both tended to prolong debate. Not until nineteen days after Madison's speech did the delegates finally vote. New Hampshire meanwhile had been the ninth state to ratify the Constitution, thereby putting it into effect and denying Virginia that pivotal role. This fact, however, was not well-known among the Virginia delegates until after their own vote. Nor was it known that New York Governor George Clinton, an antifederalist, had urged calling a second national convention to discuss the Articles of Confederation. In any case, Virginia's support for the new document remained crucial. By the narrow margin of 89–79, Virginia became the tenth state to ratify. Several delegates, especially from the rural western regions, in the end voted against the wishes of their constituents.

I shall not attempt to make impressions by any ardent professions of zeal for the public welfare. We know the principles of every man will, and ought to be, judged, not by his professions and declarations, but by his conduct; by that criterion I mean, in common with every other member, to be judged; and should it prove unfavorable to my reputation, yet it is a criterion from which I will by no means depart. Comparisons have been made between the friends of this Constitution and those who oppose it: although I disapprove of such comparisons, I trust that, in point of truth, honor, candor, and rectitude of motives, the friends of this system, here and in other states, are not inferior to its opponents. But professions of attachment to the public good, and comparisons of parties, ought not to govern or influence us now. We ought, sir, to examine the Constitution on its own merits solely: we are to inquire whether it will promote the public happiness: its aptitude to produce this desirable object ought to be the exclusive subject of our present researches. In this pursuit, we ought not to address our arguments to the feelings and passions, but to those understandings and judgments which were selected by the people of this country, to decide this great question by a calm and rational investigation. I hope that gentlemen, in displaying their abilities on this occasion, instead of giving opinions and making assertions, will condescend to prove and demonstrate, by a fair and regular discussion. It gives me pain to hear gentlemen continually distorting the natural construction of language; for it is sufficient if any human production can stand a fair discussion. Before I proceed to make some additions to the reasons which have been adduced by my honorable friend over the way, I must take the liberty to make some observations on what was said by another gentleman [Mr. Henry]. He told us that this Constitution ought to be rejected because it endangered the public liberty, in his opinion, in many instances. Give me leave to make one answer to that observation: Let the dangers which this system is supposed to be replete with be clearly pointed out: if any dangerous and unnecessary powers be given to the general legislature, let them be plainly demonstrated, and let us not rest satisfied with general assertions of danger, without examination. If powers be necessary, apparent danger is not a sufficient reason against conceding them. He has suggested that licentiousness has seldom produced the loss of liberty; but that the tyranny of rulers has almost always effected it. Since the general civilization of mankind, I believe there are more instances of the abridgement of the freedom of the people by gradual and silent encroachments of those in power, than by violent and sudden usurpations; but, on a candid examination of history, we shall find that turbulence, violence, and abuse of power, by the majority trampling on the rights of the minority, have produced factions and commotions, which, in republics, have, more frequently than any other cause, produced despotism. If we go over the whole history of ancient and modern republics, we shall find their destruction to have generally resulted from those causes. If we consider the peculiar situation of the United States, and what are the sources of the diversity of sentiment which pervades its inhabitants, we shall find great danger to fear that the same causes may terminate here in the same fatal effects which they produced in those republics. This danger ought to be wisely guarded against. Perhaps, in the progress of this discussion, it will appear that the only possible remedy for those evils, and means of preserving and protecting the principles of republicanism, will be found in that very system which is now exclaimed against as the parent of oppression.

I must confess I have not been able to find his usual consistency in the gentleman's argument on this occasion. He informs us that the people of the country are at perfect repose,—that is, every man enjoys the fruits of his labor peaceably and securely, and that every thing is in perfect tranquillity and safety. I wish sincerely, sir, this were true. If this be their happy situation, why has every state acknowledged the contrary? Why were deputies from all the states sent to the general Convention? Why have complaints of national and individual distresses been echoed and reechoed throughout the continent? Why has our general government been so shamefully disgraced, and our Constitution violated? Wherefore have laws been made to authorize a change, and wherefore are we now assembled here? A federal government is formed for the protection of its individual members. Ours has attacked itself with impunity. Its authority has been disobeyed and despised. I think I perceive a glaring inconsistency in another of his arguments. He complains of this Constitution, because it requires the consent of at least three fourths of the states to introduce amendments which shall be necessary for the happiness of the people. The assent of so many he urges as too great an obstacle to the admission of salutary amendments, which, he strongly insists, ought to be at the will of a bare majority. We hear this argument, at the very moment we are called upon to assign reasons for proposing a constitution which puts it in the power of nine states to abolish the present inadequate, unsafe, and pernicious Confederation! In the first case, he asserts that a majority ought to have the power of altering the government, when found to be inadequate to the security of public happiness. In the last case, he affirms that even three fourths of the community have not a right to alter a government which experience has proved to be subversive of national felicity! nay, that the most necessary and urgent alterations cannot be made without the absolute unanimity of all the states! Does not the thirteenth article of the Confederation expressly require that no alteration shall be made without the unanimous consent of all the states? Could any thing in theory be more perniciously improvident and injudicious than this submission of the will of the majority to the most trifling minority? Have not experience and practice actually manifested this theoretical inconvenience to be extremely impolitic? Let me mention one fact, which I conceive must carry conviction to the mind of any one: the smallest state in the Union has obstructed every attempt to reform the government; that little member has repeatedly disobeyed and counteracted the general authority; nay, has even supplied the enemies of its country with provisions. Twelve states had agreed to certain improvements which were proposed, being thought absolutely necessary to preserve the existence of the general government; but as these improvements, though really indispensable, could not, by the Confederation, be introduced into it without the consent of every state, the refractory dissent of that little state prevented their adoption. The inconveniences resulting from this requisition, of unanimous concurrence in alterations in the Confederation, must be known to every member in this Convention; it is therefore needless to remind them of them. Is it not self-evident that a trifling minority ought not to bind the majority? Would not foreign influence be exerted with facility over a small minority? Would the honorable gentleman agree to continue the most radical defects in the old system, because the petty sate of Rhode Island would not agree to remove them?

He next objects to the exclusive legislation over the district where the seat of government may be fixed. Would he submit that the representatives of this state should carry on their deliberations under the control of any other member of the Union? If any state had the power of legislation over the place where Congress should fix the general government, this would impair the dignity, and hazard the safety, of Congress. If the safety of the Union were under the control of any particular state, would not foreign corruption probably prevail, in such a state, to induce it to exert its controlling influence over the members of the general government? Gentlemen cannot have forgotten the disgraceful insult which Congress received some years ago. When we also reflect that the previous cession of particular states is necessary before Congress can legislate exclusively any where, we must, instead of being alarmed at this part, heartily approve of it.

But the honorable member sees great danger in the provision concerning the militia. This I conceive to be an additional security to our liberty, without diminishing the power of the states in any considerable degree. It appears to me so highly expedient that I should imagine it would have found advocates even in the warmest friends of the present system. The authority of training the militia, and appointing the officers, is reserved to the states. Congress ought to have the power to establish a uniform discipline throughout the states, and to provide for the execution of the laws, suppress insurrections, and repel invasions: these are the only cases wherein they can interfere with the militia; and the obvious necessity of their having power over them in these cases must convince any reflecting mind. Without uniformity of discipline, military bodies would be incapable of action: without a general controlling power to call forth the strength of the Union to repel invasions, the country might be overrun and conquered by foreign enemies: without such a power to suppress insurrections, our liberties might be destroyed by domestic faction, and domestic tyranny be established.

The honorable member then told us that there was no instance of power once transferred being voluntarily renounced. Not to produce European examples, which may probably be done before the rising of this Convention, have we not seen already, in seven states (and probably in an eighth state) legislatures surrendering some of the most important powers they possessed? But, sir, by this government, powers are not given to any particular set of men; they are in the hands of the people; delegated to their representatives chosen for short terms: to representatives responsible to the people, and whose situation is perfectly similar to their own. As long as this is the case we have no danger to apprehend. When the gentleman called our recollection to the usual effects of the concession of powers, and imputed the loss of liberty generally to open tyranny, I wish he had gone on farther. Upon his review of history, he would have found that the loss of liberty very often resulted from factions and divisions; from local considerations, which eternally lead to quarrels; he would have found internal dissensions to have more frequently demolished civil liberty, than a tenacious disposition in rulers to retain any stipulated powers. [*Here Mr. Madison enumerated the various means whereby nations had lost their liberties.*]

The power of raising and supporting armies is exclaimed against as dangerous and unnecessary. I wish there were no necessity of vesting this power in the general government. But suppose a foreign nation to declare war against the United States; must not the general legislature have the power of defending the United States? Ought it to be known to foreign nations that the general government of the United States of America has no power to raise and support an army, even in the utmost danger, when attacked by external enemies? Would not their knowledge of such a circumstance stimulate them to fall upon us? If, sir, Congress be not invested with this power, any powerful nation, prompted by ambition or avarice, will be invited, by our weakness, to attack us; and such an attack, by disciplined veterans, would certainly be attended with success, when only opposed by irregular, undisciplined militia. Whoever considers the peculiar situation of this country, the multiplicity of its excellent inlets and harbors, and the uncommon facility of attacking it,—however much he may regret the necessity of such a power, cannot hesitate a moment in granting it. One fact may elucidate this argument. In the course of the late war, when the weak parts of the Union were exposed, and many states were in the most deplorable situation by the enemy's ravages, the assistance of foreign nations was thought so urgently necessary for our protection, that the relinquishment of territorial advantages was not deemed too great a sacrifice for the acquisition of one ally. This expedient was admitted with great reluctance, even by those states who expected advantages from it. The crisis, however, at length arrived, when it was judged necessary for the salvation of this country to make certain cessions to Spain; whether wisely or otherwise is not for me to say; but the fact was, that instructions were sent to our representative at the court of Spain, to empower him to enter into negotiations for that purpose. How it terminated is well known. This fact shows the extremities to which nations will go in cases of imminent danger, and demonstrates the necessity of making ourselves more respectable. The necessity of making dangerous cessions, and of applying to foreign aid, ought to be excluded.

The honorable member then told us that there are heart-burnings in the adopting states, and that Virginia may, if she does not come into the measure, continue in amicable confederacy with the adopting sates. I wish as seldom as possible to contradict the assertions of gentlemen; but I can venture to affirm, without danger of being in error, that there is the most satisfactory evidence that the satisfaction of those states is increasing every day, and that, in that state where it was adopted only by a majority of nineteen, there is not one fifth of the people dissatisfied. There are some reasons which induce us to conclude that the grounds of proselytism extend every where; its principles begin to be better understood; and the inflammatory violence wherewith it was opposed by designing, illiberal, and unthinking minds, begins to subside. I will not enumerate the causes from which, in my conception, the heart-burnings of a majority of its opposers have originated. Suffice it to say, that in all they were founded on a misconception of its nature and tendency. Had it been candidly examined and fairly discussed, I believe, sir, that but a very inconsiderable minority of the people of the United States would have opposed it. With respect to the Swiss, whom the honorable gentleman has proposed for our example, as far as historical authority may be relied on, we shall find their government quite unworthy of our imitation. I am sure, if the honorable gentleman had adverted to their history and government, he never would have quoted their example here; he would have found that, instead of respecting the rights of mankind, their government (at least of several of their cantons) is one of the vilest aristocracies that ever was instituted: the peasants of some of their cantons are more oppressed and degraded than the subjects of any monarch in Europe; nay, almost as much so as those of any Eastern despot. It is a novelty in politics, that from the worst of systems the happiest consequences should ensure. Their artistocratical rigor, and the peculiarity of their situation, have so long supported their union: without the closest alliance and amity, dismemberment might follow; their powerful and ambitious neighbors would immediately avail themselves of their least jarrings. As we are not circumstanced like them, no conclusive precedent can be drawn from their situation. I trust the gentleman does not carry his idea so far as to recommend a separation from the adopting states. This government may secure our happiness; this is at least as probable as it shall be oppressive. If eight states have, from a persuasion of its policy and utility, adopted it, shall Virginia shrink from it, without a full conviction of danger and inutility? I hope she will never shrink from any duty: I trust she will not determine without the most serious reflection and deliberation.

I confess to you, sir, were uniformity of religion to be introduced by this system, it would, in my opinion, be ineligible; but I have no reason to conclude that uniformity of government will produce that of religion. This subject is, for the honor of America, perfectly free and unshackled. The government has no jurisdiction over it: the least reflection will convince us there is no danger to be feared on this ground.

But we are flattered with the probability of obtaining previous amendments. This calls for the most serious attention of this house. If amendments are to be proposed by one state, other states have the same right, and will also propose alterations. These cannot but be dissimilar, and opposite in their nature. I beg leave to remark, that the governments of the different states are in many respects dissimilar in their structure; their legislative bodies are not similar; their executive are more different. In several of the states, the first magistrate is elected by the people at large; in others, by joint ballot of the members of both branches of the legislature; and in others, in other different manners. This dissimilarity has occasioned a diversity of opinion on the theory of government, which will, without many reciprocal concessions, render a concurrence impossible. Although the appointment of an executive magistrate has not been thought destructive to the principles of democracy in many of the states, yet, in the course of the debate, we find objections made to the federal executive: it is urged that the President will degenerate into a tyrant. I intended, in compliance with the call of the honorable member, to explain the reasons of proposing this Constitution, and develop its principles; but I shall postpone my remarks till we hear the supplement which, he has informed us, he intends to add to what he has already said.

Give me leave to say something of the nature of the government, and to show that it is safe and just to vest it with the power of taxation. There are a number of opinions; but the principal question is, whether it be a federal or consolidated government. In order to judge properly of the question before us, we must consider it minutely in its principal parts. I conceive myself that it is of a mixed nature; it is in a manner unprecedented; we cannot find one express example in the experience of the world. It stands by itself. In some respects it is a government of a federal nature; in others, it is of a consolidated nature. Even if we attend to the manner in which the Constitution is investigated, ratified, and made the act of the people of America, I can say, notwithstanding what the honorable gentleman has alleged, that this government is not completely consolidated, nor is it entirely federal. Who are parties to it? The people—but not the people as composing one great body; but the people as composing thirteen sovereignties. Were it, as the gentleman asserts, a consolidated government, the assent of a majority of the people would be sufficient for its establishment; and, as a majority have adopted it already, the remaining states would be bound by the act of the majority, even it they unanimously reprobated it. Were it such a government as is suggested, it would be now binding on the people of this state, without having had the privilege of deliberating upon it. But, sir, no state is bound by it, as it is, without its own consent. Should all the states adopt it, it will then be a government established by the thirteen states of America, not through the intervention of the legislatures, but by the people at large. In this particular respect, the distinction between the existing and proposed government is very material. The existing system has been derived from the dependent derivative authority of the legislatures of the states; whereas this is derived from the superior power of the people. If we look at the manner in which alterations are to be made in it, the same idea is, in some degree, attended to. By the new system, a majority of the states cannot introduce amendments; nor are all the states required for that purpose; three fourths of them must concur in alterations; in this there is a departure from the federal idea. The members to the national House of Representatives are to be chosen by the people at large, in proportion to the numbers in the respective districts. When we come to the Senate, its members are elected by the states in their equal and political capacity. But had the government been completely consolidated, the Senate would have been chosen by the people in their individual capacity, in the same manner as the members of the other house. Thus it is of a complicated nature; and this complication, I trust, will be found to exclude the evils of absolute consolidation, as well as of a mere confederacy. If Virginia was separated from all the states, her power and authority would extend to all cases: in like manner, were all powers vested in the general government, it would be a consolidated government; but the powers of the federal government are enumerated; it can only operate in certain cases; it has legislative powers on defined and limited objects, beyond which it cannot extend its jurisdiction.

But the honorable member has satirized, with peculiar acrimony, the powers given to the general government by this Constitution. I conceive that the first question on this subject is, whether these powers be necessary; if they be, we are reduced to the dilemma of either submitting to the inconvenience or losing the Union. Let us consider the most important of these reprobated powers; that of direct taxation is most generally objected to. With respect to the exigencies of government, there is no question but the most easy mode of providing for them will be adopted. When, therefore, direct taxes are not necessary, they will not be recurred to. It can be of little advantage to those in power to raise money in a manner oppressive to the people. To consult the conveniences of the people will cost them nothing, and in many respects will be advantageous to them. Direct taxes will only be recurred to for great purposes. What has brought on other nations those immense debts, under the pressure of which many of them labor? Not the expenses of their governments, but war. If this country should be engaged in war,—and I conceive we ought to provide for the possibility of such a case,—how would it be carried on? By the usual means provided from year to year? As our imports will be necessary for the expenses of government and other common exigencies, how are we to carry on the means of defence? How is it possible a war could be supported without money or credit? And would it be possible for a government to have credit without having the power of raising money? No; it would be impossible for any government, in such a case, to defend itself. Then, I say, sir, that it is necessary to establish funds for extraordinary exigencies, and to give this power to the general government; for the utter inutility of previous requisitions on the states is too well known. Would it be possible for those countries, whose finances and revenues are carried to the highest perfection, to carry on the operations of government on great emergencies, such as the maintenance of a war, without an uncontrolled power of raising money? Has it not been necessary for Great Britain, notwithstanding the facility of the collection of her taxes, to have recourse very often to this and other extraordinary methods of procuring money? Would not her public credit have been ruined, if it was known that her power to raise money was limited? Has not France been obliged, on great occasions, to use unusual means to raise funds? It has been the case in many countries, and no government can exist unless its powers extend to make provisions for every contingency. If we were actually attacked by a powerful nation, and our general government had not the power of raising money, but depended solely on requisitions, our condition would be truly deplorable: if the revenue of this commonwealth were to depend on twenty distinct authorities, it would be impossible for it to carry on its operations. This must be obvious to every member here; I think, therefore, that it is necessary, for the preservation of the Union, that this power shall be given to the general government.

But it is urged that its consolidated nature, joined to the power of direct taxation, will give it a tendency to destroy all subordinate authority; that its increasing influence will speedily enable it to absorb the state governments. I cannot think this will be the case. If the general government were wholly independent of the governments of the particular states, then, indeed, usurpation might be expected to the fullest extent. But, sir, on whom does this general government depend? It derives its authority from these governments, and from the same sources from which their authority is derived. The members of the federal government are taken from the same men from whom those of the state legislatures are taken. If we consider the mode in which the federal representatives will be chosen, we shall be convinced that the general will never destroy the individual governments; and this conviction must be strengthened by an attention to the construction of the Senate. The representatives will be chosen probably under the influence of the members of the state legislatures; but there is not the least probability that the election of the latter will be influenced by the former. One hundred and sixty members represent this commonwealth in one branch of the legislature, are drawn from the people at large, and must ever possess more influence than the few men who will be elected to the general legislature.

The reasons offered on this subject, by a gentleman on the same side, [*Mr. Nicholas*] were unanswerable, and have been so full that I shall add but little more on the subject. Those who wish to become federal representatives must depend on their credit with that class of men who will be the most popular in their counties, who generally represent the people in the state governments; they can, therefore, never succeed in any measure contrary to the wishes of those on whom they depend. It is almost certain, therefore, that the deliberations of the members of the federal House of Representatives will be directed to the interest of the people of America. As to the other branch, the senators will be appointed by the legislatures; and, though elected for six years, I do not conceive they will so soon forget the source from whence they derive their political existence. This election of one branch of the federal by the state legislatures, secures an absolute dependence of the former on the latter. The biennial exclusion of one third will lessen the facility of a combination, and may put a stop to intrigues. I appeal to our past experience, whether they will attend to the interests of their constituent states. Have not those gentlemen, who have been honored with seats in Congress, *often signalized themselves by their attachment to their seats?* I wish this government may answer the expectation of its friends, and foil the apprehension of its enemies. I hope the patriotism of the people will continue, and be a sufficient guard to their liberties. I believe its tendency will be, that the state governments will counteract the general interest, and ultimately prevail. The number of the representatives is yet sufficient for our safety, and will gradually increase; and, if we consider their different sources of information, the number will not appear too small.

Thomas Jefferson

First Inaugural Address (1801)

In the early morning hours of March 4, 1801, the second President of the United States, John Adams, left the new federal capital of Washington rather than witness the inauguration of the man who had defeated him in his bid for reelection. The election of 1800 was a bitter one, fought by the two parties that emerged out of the clash of political principles and personal ambitions and inclinations in the early years of the Republic. In spite of Washington's distaste for "faction," political harmony between members of his administration, such as Jefferson on one hand and Alexander Hamilton on the other, could not easily be maintained.

Jefferson's view, and that of the Democratic-Republican party that he led, was fundamentally democratic and agrarian with a distrust of strong central government and a profound conviction that the people could safely govern themselves. Hamiltonian principles, which animated the Federalist Party, held that a strong national government should be actively supportive of commercial and industrial interests, and were suspicious of popular government.

The events of the French Revolution served as a catalyst in the formation of American political parties. Republicans welcomed the destruction of the old monarchy and the promise that the new Republic held for extending the rights of man. Federalists were horrified by the excesses of the French Revolution and the clear threat it posed for public order and the rights of property. When France went to war with Great Britain, President Washington issued a Neutrality Proclamation and sought to maintain peace with both nations. However, the sympathies of the Republicans were clearly with France, while the Federalists favored Britain.

During John Adams's term as President, relations with France deteriorated and a virtual, if undeclared, naval war with France raged. Nevertheless, the President resisted pressures from Federalist hawks and maintained an uneasy peace. The threat of war, however, raised Federalist suspicions of aliens; the Federalists seized the opportunity to pass the Alien and Sedition Acts in 1798. Most obnoxious to Republicans was the provision that imposed fines and imprisonment on any who were guilty of "false, scandalous, or malicious writing" directed against the government, Congress, or President. Since all 25 of those prosecuted were Republican editors and printers, Republican fears that the act was an attempt to suppress dissent seemed justified. Jefferson himself drafted a set of Resolutions passed by the Kentucky legislature arguing that the Alien and Sedition Acts were unconstitutional. These Resolutions, and those in a similar vein that followed from Virginia, implied that the states had the right to nullify unconstitutional acts, but no direct action was taken by either state to obstruct their execution.

Debate during the Presidential election of 1800 centered on the Alien and Sedition Acts and American relations with France and Britain. The fact that problems with France had sharply reduced trade with that country and that preparations for a possible war brought about an increase in taxes were related issues in the contest. The election became heated as Republicans proclaimed that "the friends of peace will vote for Jefferson—the friends of war will vote for Adams." For their part, the Federalists recoiled at the thought of a "Jacobin President" and asserted that Jefferson's election would "destroy religion, introduce immorality, and loosen all the bonds of society." The election ended with a tie in electoral votes between Jefferson and the man who Republicans assumed would be elected vice-president, Aaron Burr, throwing the election into the House of Representatives and drawing out the final result until February 17, 1800.

Plainly dressed on that March day when he took the oath of office—he wore no ceremonial sword, for example, as Washington and Adams had done for their inaugurations—Thomas Jefferson symbolized the simple virtues of republican democracy. Like many of the founding fathers, Jefferson was a lawyer who had been active as a colonial politician and propagandist before the revolution. The author of the Declaration of Independence, Jefferson returned to Virginia to serve as a member of the legislature, where he helped to frame measures that he believed would make the new state government "truly republican." He succeeded Patrick Henry as governor, served briefly in the old Congress at the conclusion of the war, and went to France in 1785 to replace Franklin as Minister to France. He generally approved of the new Constitution that was written in his absence and returned to America to become Secretary of State in Washington's cabinet, from which he finally resigned when he came in conflict with

Hamilton's economic policy and the latter's efforts to increase centralization of government. Leading the growing Republican-Democratic opposition, he was defeated by Adams for the Presidency in 1796 and became vice-president. His opposition to the Alien and Sedition Acts was well-known, as were his generally sympathetic views toward France.

Jefferson's inaugural address was his attempt to heal some of the wounds that the election has opened and to set forth the basic principles upon which democratic government should be built. Calling on his fellow citizens to "unite with one heart and one mind," President Jefferson outlined the "creed of our political faith," a creed that embodied the ideal, if not always the practice, of American democracy in the years to come.

Friends and fellow-citizens, called upon to undertake the duties of the first executive office of our country, I avail myself of the presence of that portion of my fellow-citizens which is here assembled to express my grateful thanks for the favor with which they have been pleased to look toward me, to declare a sincere consciousness that the task is above my talents, and that I approach it with those anxious and awful presentiments which the greatness of the charge and the weakness of my powers so justly inspire. A rising nation, spread over a wide and fruitful land, traversing all the seas with the rich productions of their industry, engaged in commerce with nations who feel power and forget right, advancing rapidly to destinies beyond the reach of mortal eye—when I contemplate these transcendent objects, and see the honor, the happiness, and the hopes of this beloved country committed to the issue, and the auspices of this day, I shrink from the contemplation, and humble myself before the magnitude of the undertaking. Utterly, indeed, should I despair did not the presence of many whom I here see remind me that in the other high authorities provided by our Constitution I shall find resources of wisdom, of virtue, and of zeal on which to rely under all difficulties. To you, then, gentlemen, who are charged with the sovereign functions of legislation, and to those associated with you, I look with encouragement for that guidance and support which may enable us to steer with safety the vessel in which we are all embarked amidst the conflicting elements of a troubled world.

During the contest of opinion through which we have passed the animation of discussions and of exertions has sometimes worn an aspect which might impose on strangers unused to think freely and to speak and to write what they think; but this being now decided by the voice of the nation, announced according to the rules of the Constitution, all will, of course, arrange themselves under the will of the law, and unite in common efforts for the common good. All, too, will bear in mind this sacred principle, that though the will of the majority is in all cases to prevail, that will to be rightful must be reasonable; that the minority possesses their equal rights, which equal law must protect, and to violate would be oppression. Let us, then, fellow-citizens, unite with one heart and one mind. Let us restore to social intercourse that harmony and affection without which liberty and even life itself are but dreary things. And let us reflect that, having banished from our land that religious intolerance under which mankind so long bled and suffered, we have yet gained little if we countenance a political intolerance as despotic, as wicked, and capable of as bitter and bloody persecutions. During the throes and convulsions of the ancient world, during the agonizing spasms of infuriated man, seeking through blood and slaughter his long-lost liberty, it was not wonderful that the agitation of the billows should reach even this distant and peaceful shore; that this should be more felt and feared by some and less by others, and should divide opinions as to measures of safety. But every difference of opinion is not a difference of principle. We have called by different names brethren of the same principle. We are all Republicans, we are all Federalists. If there be any among us who would wish to dissolve this Union or to change its republican form, let them stand undisturbed as monuments of the safety with which error of opinion may be tolerated where reason is left free to combat it. I know, indeed, that some honest men fear that a republican government can not be strong, that this Government is not strong enough; but would the honest patriot, in the full tide of successful experiment, abandon a government which has so far kept us free and firm on the theoretic and visionary fear that this Government, the world's best hope, may by possibility want energy to preserve itself? I trust not. I believe this, on the contrary, the strongest Government on earth. I believe it the only one where every man, at the call of the law, would fly to the standard of the law, and would meet invasions of the public order as his own personal concern. Sometimes it is said that man can not be trusted with the government of himself. Can he, then, be trusted with the government of others? Or have we found angels in the forms of kings to govern him? Let history answer this question.

Let us, then, with courage and confidence pursue our own federal and Republican principles, our attachment to union and representative government. Kindly separated by nature and a wide ocean from the exterminating havoc of one quarter of the globe; too high-minded to endure the degradations of the others; possessing a chosen country, with room enough for our descendants to the thousandth and thousandth generation; entertaining a due sense of our equal right to the use of our own faculties, to the acquisitions of our own industry, to honor and confidence from our fellow-citizens, resulting not from birth, but from our actions and their sense of them; enlightened by a benign religion, professed, indeed, and practiced in various forms, yet all of them inculcating honesty, truth, temperance, gratitude, and the love of man; acknowledging and adoring an overruling Providence, which by all its dispensations proves that it delights in the happiness of man here and his greater happiness hereafter—with all these blessings, what more is necessary to make us a happy and prosperous people? Still one thing more, fellow-citizens—a wise and frugal Government, which shall restrain men from injuring one another, shall leave them otherwise free to regulate their own pursuits of industry and improvement, and shall not take from the mouth of labor the bread it has earned. This is the sum of good government, and this is necessary to close the circle of our felicities.

About to enter, fellow-citizens, on the exercise of duties which comprehend everything dear and valuable to you, it is proper you should understand what I deem essential principles of our Government, and consequently those which ought to shape its Administration, I will compress them within the narrowest compass they will bear, stating the general principle, but not all its limitations. Equal and exact justice to all men, of whatever state or persuasion, religious or political, peace, commerce, and honest friendship with all nations, entangling alliances with none; the support of the State governments in all their rights, as the most competent administrations for our domestic concerns and the surest bulwarks against antirepublican tendencies; the preservation of the General Government in its whole constitutional vigor, as the sheet anchor of our peace at home and safety abroad; a jealous care of the right of election by the people—a mild and safe corrective of abuses which are lopped by the sword of revolution where peaceable remedies are unprovided; absolute acquiescence in the decisions of the majority, the vital principle of republics, from which is no appeal but to force, the vital principle and immediate parent of despotism; a well-disciplined militia, our best reliance in peace and for the first moments of war, till regulars may relieve them; the supremacy of the civil over the military authority; economy in the public expense, that labor may be lightly burthened; the honest payment of our debts and sacred preservation of the public faith; encouragement of agriculture and of commerce as its handmaid; the diffusion of information and arraignment of all abuses at the bar of the public reason; freedom of religion; freedom of the press, and freedom of person under the protection of the habeas corpus, and trial by juries impartially selected. These principles form the bright constellation which has gone before us and guided our steps through an age of revolution and reformation. The wisdom of our sages and blood of our heroes have been devoted to their attainment. They should be the creed of our political faith, the text of civic instruction, the touchstone by which to try the services of those we trust; and should we wander from them in moments of error or of alarm, let us hasten to retrace our steps and to regain the road which alone leads to peace, liberty, and safety.

I repair, then, fellow-citizens, to the post you have assigned me. With experience enough in subordinate offices to have seen the difficulties of this the greatest of all, I have learnt to expect that it will rarely fall to the lot of imperfect man to retire from this station with the reputation and the favor which bring him into it. Without pretentions to that high confidence you reposed in our first and greatest revolutionary character, whose preeminent services had entitled him to the first place in his country's love and destined for him the fairest page in the volume of faithful history, I ask so much confidence only as may give firmness and effect to the legal administration of your affairs. I shall often go wrong through defect of judgment. When right, I shall often be thought wrong by those whose positions will not command a view of the whole ground. I ask your indulgence for my own errors, which will never be intentional, and your support against the errors of others, who may condemn what they would not if seen in all its parts. The approbation implied by your suffrage is a great consolation to me for the past, and my future solicitude will be to retain the good opinion of those who have bestowed it in advance, to conciliate that of others by doing them all the good in my power, and to be instrumental to the happiness and freedom of all.

Relying, then, on the patronage of your good will, I advance with obedience to the work, ready to retire from it whenever you become sensible how much better choice it is in your power to make. And may that Infinite Power which rules the destinies of the universe lead our councils to what is best, and give them a favorable issue for your peace and prosperity.

The Young Republic

Sagoyewatha (Red Jacket)

On the White Man's and Red Man's Religion (1805)

From the time of the earliest settlement in North America the new colonists came into conflict with the indigenous culture of the American Indians. This culture was rich and varied and much more complex than would be suggested by the stereotyping myths of white men, which tended to lump all Indians together. Over a period of twelve millennia, as the anthropologist Brian M. Fagan points out, the Indians, "with the simplest of bone and stone technologies," were "capable of colonizing, populating and adapting successfully to a vast continent without all the elaborate artifices of modern industrial civilization." In only a few centuries, however, European hunger for land—not land over which to roam and hunt, but land to clear and farm—supported by European technology, pushed back, overwhelmed, and virtually obliterated the Native American culture.

To the settlers and then the citizens of the new Republic, Indians were savages, sometimes romanticized as "noble" ones, but almost universally viewed as inferior beings to be subjugated or "civilized" by the white man. That is not to say that there were not those among the new Americans who were animated by sincere and humane values. The Quakers, for example, labored to save the frontier Indians from the evils that the white man's introduction of liquor had visited upon the natives. The missionaries believed that conversion and civilization went hand in hand and could only benefit the converts. However, whether they were well intentioned or just greedy, the settlers' actions, rationalized by a pervasive if unperceived cultural arrogance, led inexorably to the demise of Indian society.

Among the many Indian leaders who resisted the territorial and cultural incursions of the white man was a Seneca chief known as Red Jacket, a name derived from an army tunic he wore which was given to him by his British allies during the years of the American Revolution. Sagoyewatha finally made peace with the new Republic, however, and even visited George Washington in 1792; when war with the British broke out in 1812 he took the American side. Nevertheless, he strenuously and consistently resisted attempts to introduce white customs and religion among his people.

In the summer of 1805 a council of chiefs of the Six Nations of the Iroquois—the Mohawk, Oneida, Onondaga, Cayuga, Seneca, and Tuscarora—met and were addressed by a missionary named Cram, who planned to work among them. In his effort to discourage Cram, Sagoyewatha chronicled, from the Indian point of view, the unhappy history of relations between the two races and argued against the substitution of the white man's religion for the Indian's. His plea was for religious toleration, the right to be left alone, and it contained the shrewd challenge to the missionary to convert by example. The text of the speech, of course, is a white man's translation and therefore can only be an approximation of what was said.

Friend and Brother:—It was the will of the Great Spirit that we should meet together this day. He orders all things and has given us a fine day for our council. He has taken His garment from before the sun and caused it to shine with brightness upon us. Our eyes are opened that we see clearly; our ears are unstopped that we have been able to hear distinctly the words you have spoken. For all these favors we thank the Great Spirit, and Him only.

Brother, this council fire was kindled by you. It was at your request that we came together at this time. We have listened with attention to what you have said. You requested us to speak our minds freely. This gives us great joy; for we now consider that we stand upright before you and can speak what we think. All have heard your voice and all speak to you now as one man. Our minds are agreed.

Brother, you say you want an answer to your talk before you leave this place. It is right you should have one, as you are a great distance from home and we do not wish to detain you. But first we will look back a little and tell you what our fathers have told us and what we have heard from the white people.

Brother, listen to what we say. There was a time when our forefathers owned this great island. Their seats extended from the rising to the setting sun. The Great Spirit had made it for the use of Indians. He had created the buffalo, the deer, and other animals for food. He had made the bear and the beaver. Their skins served us for clothing. He had scattered them over the country and taught us how to produce corn for bread. All this He had done for His red children because He loved them. If we had some disputes about our hunting-ground they were generally settled without the shedding of much blood.

But an evil day came upon us. Your forefathers crossed the great water and landed on this island. Their numbers were small. They found friends and not enemies. They told us they had fled from their own country for fear of wicked men and had come here to enjoy their religion. They asked us for a small seat. We took pity on them, granted their request, and they sat down among us. We gave them corn and meat; they gave us poison in return.

The white people, brother, had now found our country. Tidings were carried back and more came among us. Yet we did not fear them. We took them to be friends. They called us brothers. We believed them and gave them a larger seat. At length their numbers had greatly increased. They wanted more land; they wanted our country. Our eyes were opened and our minds became uneasy. Wars took place. Indians were hired to fight against Indians, and many of our people were destroyed. They also brought strong liquor among us. It was strong and powerful, and has slain thousands.

Brother, our seats were once large and yours were small. You have now become a great people, and we have scarcely a place left to spread our blankets. You have got our country, but are not satisfied; you want to force your religion upon us.

Brother, continue to listen. You say that you are sent to instruct us how to worship the Great Spirit agreeably to His mind; and, if we do not take hold of the religion which you white people teach we shall be unhappy hereafter. You say that you are right and we are lost. How do you know this to be true? We understand that your religion is written in a Book. If it was intended for us, as well as you, why has not the Great Spirit given to us, and not only to us, but why did He not give to our forefathers the knowledge of that Book, with the means of understanding it rightly. We only know what you tell us about it. How shall we know when to believe, being so often deceived by the white people?

Brother, you say there is but one way to worship and serve the Great Spirit. If there is but one religion, why do you white people differ so much about it? Why not all agreed, as you can all read the Book?

Brother, we do not understand these things. We are told that your religion was given to your forefathers and has been handed down from father to son. We also have a religion which was given to our forefathers and has been handed down to us, their children. We worship in that way. It teaches us to be thankful for all the favors we receive, to love each other, and to be united. We never quarrel about religion.

Brother, the Great Spirit has made us all, but He has made a great difference between His white and His red children. He has given us different complexions and different customs. To you He has given the arts. To these He has not opened our eyes. We know these things to be true. Since He has made so great a difference between us in other things, why may we not conclude that He has given us a different religion according to our understanding? The Great Spirit does right. He knows what is best for His children; we are satisfied.

Brother, we do not wish to destroy your religion or take it from you. We only want to enjoy our own.

Brother, you say you have not come to get our land or our money, but to enlighten our minds. I will now tell you that I have been at your meetings and saw you collect money from the meeting. I can not tell what this money was intended for, but suppose that it was for your minister; and, if we should conform to your way of thinking, perhaps you may want some from us.

Brother, we are told that you have been preaching to the white people in this place. These people are our neighbors. We are acquainted with them. We will wait a little while and see what effect your preaching has upon them. If we find it does them good, make them honest, and less disposed to cheat Indians, we will then consider again of what you have said.

Brother, you have now heard our answer to your talk, and this is all we have to say at present. As we are going to part, we will come and take you by the hand, and hope the Great Spirit will protect you on your journey and return you safe to your friends.

Daniel Webster

Bunker Hill Monument Oration (1825)

In the early years of the nineteenth century America grew more confident as the republican experiment not only appeared to be working but gave every sign of enduring. The Revolution secured independence; the Constitution stabilized the process of government; a second war with Great Britain had been fought successfully. Although the seeds of sectional strife and discord were germinating, a spirit of nationalism infused American life. The West was rapidly opening up. The "American System" encouraged the growth of American industry and stimulated internal improvements. Americans were proud of themselves and what they had accomplished—overly proud, thought some Europeans, such as the British observer who found an excess of "national vanity."

This patriotic impulse was indulged by Americans who were pleased to remind themselves of their great achievement. Ceremonial speaking, such as July Fourth orations, was at a peak of popularity as new voices extolled those who had gone before. John Quincy Adams in his 1825 inaugural address paid typical reverence to America's "precious inheritance" and felt "gratification and encouragement" in observing "that the great result of this experiment upon the theory of human rights has at the close of the generation by which it was formed been crowned with success equal to the most sanguine expectations of its founders." A new generation had succeeded the Revolutionary one and was generous in praise of their inheritance.

The theme of almost miraculous success—the wonder at what was done, what had been accomplished, and what lay ahead—was nowhere better expressed than in a speech given at a ceremony celebrating the laying of the cornerstone of a new monument commemorating the Battle of Bunker Hill. The speaker on that day in June 1825 was one of the greatest orators in American history, Daniel Webster, who excelled in all branches of speaking—legal, ceremonial, and political.

The "God-like Daniel," as he came to be known to his admirers, established himself as a great legal speaker, appearing before the Supreme Court to argue on behalf of his alma mater in the celebrated *Dartmouth College Case*. In 1820 his ceremonial speech at Plymouth placed him at the forefront of American orators of his day. In 1825, the date of his Bunker Hill oration, Webster's most famous political orations—his reply to Senator Hayne of South Carolina and his speech on behalf of the Compromise of 1850—were still in the future.

Daniel Webster had been a member of Congress for two years when he was invited to speak at the Bunker Hill commemoration before an audience that included not only Revolutionary War veterans, some of whom had actually been at the famous battle, but also the Marquis de Lafayette himself. Webster took this opportunity to pay tribute to the "value and importance of the achievements of our ancestors" and to extol "the character of our people," a character "admirably . . . calculated for setting the great example of popular governments." The theme that dominated much of early American rhetoric and captivated the American imagination down to the present time emerged from Webster's oration: with this new country, exemplifying by its very existence "that with wisdom and knowledge men may govern themselves," rested "the last hopes of mankind" for "popular liberty."

This uncounted multitude before me and around me proves the feeling which the occasion has excited. These thousands of human faces, glowing with sympathy and joy, and from the impulses of a common gratitude turned reverently to heaven in this spacious temple of the firmament, proclaim that the day, the place, and the purpose of our assembling have made a deep impression on our hearts.

If, indeed, there by any thing in local association fit to affect the mind of man, we need not strive to repress the emotions which agitate us here. We are among the sepulchres of our fathers. We are on ground, distinguished by their valor, their constancy, and the shedding of their blood. We are here, not to fix an uncertain date in our annals, nor to draw into notice an obscure and unknown spot. If our humble purpose had never been conceived, if we ourselves had never been born, the 17th of June, 1775, would have been a day on which all subsequent history would have poured its light, and the eminence where we stand a point of attraction to the eyes of successive generations. But we are Americans. We live in what may be called the early age of this great continent; and we know that our posterity, through all time, are here to enjoy and suffer the allotments of humanity. We see before us a probable train of great events; we know that our own fortunes have been happily cast; and it is natural, therefore, that we should be moved by the contemplation of occurrences which have guided our destiny before many of us were born, and settled the condition in which we should pass that portion of our existence which God allows to men on earth.

We do not read even of the discovery of this continent, without feeling something of a personal interest in the event; without being reminded how much it has affected our own fortunes and our own existence. It would be still more unnatural for us, therefore, than for others, to contemplate with unaffected minds that interesting, I may say that most touching and pathetic scene, when the great discoverer of America stood on the deck of his shattered bark, the shades of night falling on the sea, yet no man sleeping; tossed on the billows of an unknown ocean, yet the stronger billows of alternate hope and despair tossing his own troubled thoughts; extending forward his harassed frame, straining westward his anxious and eager eyes, till Heaven at last granted him a moment of rapture and ecstasy, in blessing his vision with the sight of the unknown world.

Nearer to our times, more closely connected with our fates, and therefore still more interesting to our feelings and affections, is the settlement of our country by colonists from England. We cherish every memorial of these worthy ancestors; we celebrate their patience and fortitude; we admire their daring enterprise; we teach our children to venerate their piety; and we are justly proud of being descended from men who have set the world an example of founding civil institutions on the great and united principles of human freedom and human knowledge. To us, their children, the story of their labors and sufferings can never be without its interest. We shall not stand unmoved on the shore of Plymouth, while the sea continues to wash it; nor will our brethren in another early and ancient Colony forget the place of its first establishment, till their river shall cease to flow by it. No vigor of youth, no maturity of manhood, will lead the nation to forget the spots where its infancy was cradled and defended

But the great event in the history of the continent, which we are now met here to commemorate, that prodigy of modern times, at once the wonder and the blessing of the world, is the American Revolution. In a day of extraordinary prosperity and happiness, of high national honor, distinction, and power, we are brought together, in this place, by our love of country, by our admiration of exalted character, by our gratitude for signal services and patriotic devotion.

The Society whose organ I am was formed for the purpose of rearing some honorable and durable monument to the memory of the early friends of American Independence. They have thought, that for this object no time could be more propitious than the present prosperous and peaceful period; that no place could claim preference over this memorable spot; and that no day could be more auspicious to the undertaking, than the anniversary of the battle which was here fought. The foundation of that monument we have now laid. With solemnities suited to the occasion, with prayers to Almighty God for his blessing and in the midst of this cloud of witnesses, we have begun the work. We trust it will be prosecuted, and that, springing from a broad foundation, rising high in massive solidity and unadorned grandeur, it may remain as long as Heaven permits the works of man to last, a fit emblem, both of the events in memory of which it is raised, and of the gratitude of those who have reared it.

We know, indeed, that the record of illustrious actions is most safely deposited in the universal remembrance of mankind. We know, that if we could cause this structure to ascend, not only till it reached the skies, but till it pierced them, its broad surfaces could still contain but part of that which, in an age of knowledge, hath already been spread over the earth, and which history charges itself with making known to all future times. We know that no inscription on entablatures less broad than the earth itself can carry information of the events we commemorate where it has not already gone; and that no structure, which shall not outlive the duration of letters and knowledge among men, can prolong the memorial. But our object is, by this edifice, to show our own deep sense of the value and importance of the achievements of our ancestors; and, by presenting this work of gratitude to the eye, to keep alive similar sentiments, and to foster a constant regard for the principles of the Revolution. Human beings are composed, not of reason only, but of imagination also, and sentiment; and that is neither wasted nor misapplied which is appropriated to the purpose of giving right direction to sentiments, and opening proper springs of feeling in the heart. Let it not be supposed that our object is to perpetuate national hostility, or even to cherish a mere military spirit. It is higher, purer, nobler. We consecrate our work to the spirit of national independence, and we wish that the light of peace may rest upon it for ever. We rear a memorial of our conviction of that unmeasured benefit which has been conferred on our own land, and of the happy influences which have been produced, by the same events, on the general interests of mankind. We come, as Americans, to mark a spot which must for ever be dear to us and our posterity. We wish that whosoever, in all coming time, shall turn his eye hither, may behold that the place is not undistinguished where the first great battle of the Revolution was fought. We wish that this structure may proclaim the magnitude and importance of that event to every class and every age. We wish that infancy may learn the purpose of its erection from maternal lips, and that weary and withered age may behold it, and be solaced by the recollections which it suggests. We wish that labor may look up here, and be proud, in the midst of its toil. We wish that, in those days of disaster, which, as they come upon all nations, must be expected to come upon us also, desponding patriotism may turn its eyes hitherward, and be assured that the foundations of our national power are still strong. We wish that this column, rising towards heaven among the pointed spires of so many temples dedicated to God, may contribute also to produce, in all minds, a pious feeling of dependence and gratitude. We wish, finally, that the last object to the sight of him who leaves his native shore, and the first to gladden his who revisits it, may be something which shall remind him of the liberty and the glory of his country. Let it rise! let it rise, till it meet the sun in his coming; let the earliest light of the morning gild it, and parting day linger and play on its summit.

We live in a most extraordinary age. Events so various and so important that they might crowd and distinguish centuries, are, in our times, compressed within the compass of a single life. When has it happened that history has had so much to record, in the same term of years, as since the 17th of June, 1775? Our own Revolution, which, under other circumstances, might itself have been expected to occasion a war of half a century, has been achieved; twenty-four sovereign and independent States erected; and a general government established over them, so safe, so wise, so free, so practical, that we might well wonder its establishment should have been accomplished so soon, were it not for the greater wonder that it should have been established at all. Two or three millions of people have been augmented to twelve, the great forests of the West prostrated beneath the arm of successful industry, and the dwellers on the banks of the Ohio and the Mississippi become fellow-citizens and neighbors of those who cultivate the hills of New England. We have commerce, that leaves no sea unexplored; navies, which take no law from superior force; revenues, adequate to all the exigencies of government, almost without taxation; and peace with all nations, founded on equal rights and mutual respect.

Europe, within the same period, has been agitated by a mighty revolution, which, while it has been felt in the individual condition and happiness of almost every man, has shaken to the centre her political fabric, and dashed against one another thrones which had stood tranquil for ages. On this, our continent, our own example has been followed, and colonies have sprung up to be nations. Unaccustomed sounds of liberty and free government have reached us from beyond the track of the sun; and at this moment the dominion of European power in this continent, from the place where we stand to the south pole, is annihilated for ever.

In the mean time, both in Europe and America, such has been the general progress of knowledge, such the improvement in legislation, in commerce, in the arts, in letters, and, above all, in liberal ideas and the general spirit of the age, that the whole world seems changed.

Yet, notwithstanding that this is but a faint abstract of the things which have happened since the day of the battle of Bunker Hill, we are but fifty years removed from it; and we now stand here to enjoy all the blessings of our own condition, and to look abroad on the brightened prospects of the world, while we still have among us some of those who were active agents in the scenes of 1775, and who are now here, from every quarter of New England, to visit once more, and under circumstances so affecting, I had almost said so overwhelming, this renowned theatre of their courage and patriotism.

Venerable men! you have come down to us from a former generation. Heaven has bounteously lengthened out your lives, that you might behold this joyous day. You are now where you stood fifty years ago, this very hour, with your brothers and your neighbors, shoulder to shoulder, in the strife for your country. Behold, how altered! The same heavens are indeed over your heads; the same ocean rolls at your feet; but all else how changed! You hear now no roar of hostile cannon, you see no mixed volumes of smoke and flame rising from burning Charlestown. The ground strowed with the dead and the dying; the impetuous charge; the steady and successful repulse; the loud call to repeated assault; the summoning of all that is manly to repeated resistance; a thousand bosoms freely and fearlessly bared in an instant to whatever of terror there may be in war and death;—all these you have witnessed, but you witness them no more. All is peace. The heights of yonder metropolis, its towers and roofs, which you then saw filled with wives and children and countrymen in distress and terror, and looking with unutterable emotions for the issue of the combat, have presented you to-day with the sight of its whole happy population, come out to welcome and greet you with a universal jubilee. Yonder proud ships, by a felicity of position appropriately lying at the foot of this mount, and seeming fondly to cling around it, are not means of annoyance to you, but your country's own means of distinction and defence. All is peace; and God has granted you this sight of your country's happiness, ere you slumber in the grave. He has allowed you to behold and to partake the reward of your patriotic toils; and He has allowed us, your sons and countrymen, to meet you here, and in the name of the present generation, in the name of your country, in the name of liberty, to thank you!

But, alas! you are not all here! Time and the sword have thinned your ranks. Prescott, Putnam, Stark, Brooks, Read, Pomeroy, Bridge! our eyes seek for you in vain amid this broken band. You are gathered to your fathers, and live only to your country in her grateful remembrance and your own bright example. But let us not too much grieve, that you have met the common fate of men. You lived at least long enough to know that your work had been nobly and successfully accomplished. You lived to see your country's independence established, and to sheathe your swords from war. On the light of Liberty you saw arise the light of Peace, like

> another morn,
> Risen on mid-noon;

and the sky on which you closed your eyes was cloudless.

But ah! Him! the first great martyr in this great cause! Him! the premature victim of his own self-devoting heart! Him! the head of our civil councils, and the destined leader of our military bands, whom nothing brought hither but the unquenchable fire of his own spirit! Him! cut off by Providence in the hour of overwhelming anxiety and thick gloom; falling ere he saw the star of his country rise; pouring out his generous blood like water, before he knew whether it would fertilize a land of freedom or of bondage!—how shall I struggle with the emotions that stifle the utterance of thy name! Our poor work may perish; but thine shall endure! This monument may moulder away; the solid ground it rests upon may sink down to a level with the sea; but thy memory shall not fail! Wheresoever among men a heart shall be found that beats to the transports of patriotism and liberty, its aspirations shall be to claim kindred with thy spirit!

But the scene amidst which we stand does not permit us to confine our thoughts or our sympathies to those fearless spirits who hazarded or lost their lives on this consecrated spot. We have the happiness to rejoice here in the presence of a most worthy representation of the survivors of the whole Revolutionary army.

Veterans! you are the remnant of many a well-fought field. You bring with you marks of honor from Trenton and Monmouth, from Yorktown, Camden, Bennington, and Saratoga. Veterans of half a century! when in your youthful days you put everything at hazard in your country's cause, good as that cause was, and sanguine as youth is, still your fondest hopes did not stretch onward to an hour like this! At a period to which you could not reasonably have expected to arrive, at a moment of national prosperity such as you could never have foreseen, you are now met here to enjoy the fellowship of old soldiers, and to receive the overflowings of a universal gratitude.

But your agitated countenances and your heaving breasts inform me that even this is not an unmixed joy. I perceive that a tumult of contending feelings rushes upon you. The images of the dead, as well as the persons of the living, present themselves before you. The scene overwhelms you, and I turn from it. May the Father of all mercies smile upon your declining years, and bless them! And when you shall here have exchanged your embraces, when you shall once more have pressed the hands which have been so often extended to give succor in adversity, or grasped in the exultation of victory, then look abroad upon this lovely land which your young valor defended, and mark the happiness with which it is filled; yea, look abroad upon the whole earth, and see what a name you have contributed to give to your country, and what a praise you have added to freedom, and then rejoice in the sympathy and gratitude which beam upon your last days from the improved condition of mankind!

This occasion does not require of me any particular account of the battle of the 17th of June, 1775, nor any detailed narrative of the events which immediately preceded it. These are familiarly known to all. In the progress of the great and interesting controversy, Massachusetts and the town of Boston had become early and marked objects of the displeasure of the British Parliament. This had been manifested in the act for altering the government of the Province, and in that for shutting up the port of Boston. Nothing sheds more honor on our early history, and nothing better shows how little the feelings and sentiments of the Colonies were known or regarded in England, than the impression which these measures everywhere produced in America. It had been anticipated, that while the Colonies in general would be terrified by the severity of the punishment inflicted on Massachusetts, the other seaports would be governed by a mere spirit of gain; and that, as Boston was now cut off from all commerce, the unexpected advantage which this blow on her was calculated to confer on other towns would be greedily enjoyed. How miserably such reasoners deceived themselves! How little they knew of the depth, and the strength, and the intenseness of that feeling of resistance to illegal acts of power, which possessed the whole American people! Everywhere the unworthy boon was rejected with scorn. The fortunate occasion was seized, everywhere, to show to the whole world that the Colonies were swayed by no local interest, no partial interest, no selfish interest. The temptation to profit by the punishment of Boston was strongest to our neighbors of Salem. Yet Salem was precisely the place where this miserable proffer was spurned, in a tone of the most lofty self-respect and the most indignant patriotism. "We are deeply affected," said its inhabitants, "with the sense of our public calamities; but the miseries that are now rapidly hastening on our brethren in the capital of the Province greatly excite our commiseration. By shutting up the port of Boston, some imagine that the course of trade might be turned hither and to our benefit; but we must be dead to every idea of justice, lost to all feelings of humanity, could we indulge a thought to seize on wealth and raise our fortunes on the ruin of our suffering neighbors." These noble sentiments were not confined to our immediate vicinity. In that day of general affection and brotherhood, the blow given to Boston smote on every patriotic heart from one end of the country to the other. Virginia and the Carolinas, as well as Connecticut and New Hampshire, felt and proclaimed the cause to be their own. The Continental Congress, then holding its first session in Philadelphia, expressed its sympathy for the suffering inhabitants of Boston, and addresses were received from all quarters, assuring them that the cause was a common one, and should be met by common efforts and common sacrifices. The Congress of Massachusetts responded to these assurances;

and in an address to the Congress at Philadelphia, bearing the official signature, perhaps among the last, of the immortal Warren, notwithstanding the severity of its suffering and magnitude of the dangers which threatened it, it was declared, that this Colony "is ready, at all times, to spend and to be spent in the cause of America."

But the hour drew nigh which was to put professions to the proof and to determine whether the authors of these mutual pledges were ready to seal them in blood. The tidings of Lexington and Concord had no sooner spread, than it was universally felt that the time was at last come for action. A spirit pervaded all ranks, not transient, not boisterous, but deep, solemn, determined,

> totamque infusa per artus
> Mens agitat molem, et magno se
> corpore miscet.

War, on their own soil and at their own doors, was, indeed, a strange work to the yeomanry of New England; but their consciences were convinced of its necessity, their country called them to it, and they did not withhold themselves from the perilous trial. The ordinary occupations of life were abandoned; the plough was staid in the unfinished furrow; wives gave up their husbands, and mothers gave up their sons, to the battles of a civil war. Death might come, in honor, on the field; it might come, in disgrace, on the scaffold. For either and for both they were prepared. The sentiment of Quincy was full in their hearts. "Blandishments," said that distinguished son of genius and patriotism, "will not fascinate us, nor will threats of a halter intimidate; for, under God, we are determined that, wheresoever, whensoever, or howsoever we shall be called to make our exit, we will die free men."

The 17th of June saw the four New England Colonies standing here, side by side, to triumph or to fall together; and there was with them from that moment to the end of the war, what I hope will remain with them for ever, one cause, one country, one heart.

The battle of Bunker Hill was attended with the most important effects beyond its immediate results as a military engagement. It created at once a state of open, public war. There could now be no longer a question of proceeding against individuals, as guilty of treason or rebellion. That fearful crisis was past. The appeal lay to the sword, and the only question was, whether the spirit and the resources of the people would hold out, till the object should be accomplished. Nor were its general consequences confined to our own country. The previous proceedings of the Colonies, their appeals, resolutions, and addresses, had made their cause known to Europe. Without boasting, we may say, that in no age or country has the public cause been maintained with more force of argument, more power of illustration, or more of that persuasion which excited feeling and elevated principle can alone bestow, than the Revolutionary state papers exhibit. These papers will for ever deserve to be studied, not only for the spirit which they breathe, but for the ability with which they were written.

To this able vindication of their cause, the Colonies had now added a practical and severe proof of their own true devotion to it, and given evidence also of power which they could bring to its support. All now saw, that if America fell, she would not fall without a struggle. Men felt sympathy and regard, as well as surprise, when they beheld these infant states, remote, unknown, unaided, encounter the power of England, and, in the first considerable battle, leave more of their enemies dead on the field, in proportion to the number of combatants, than had been recently known to fall in the wars of Europe.

Information of these events, circulating throughout the world, at length reached the ears of one who now hears me. He has not forgotten the emotion which the fame of Bunker Hill, and the name of Warren, excited in his youthful breast.

Sir, we are assembled to commemorate the establishment of great public principles of liberty, and to do honor to the distinguished dead. The occasion is too severe for eulogy of the living. But, Sir, your interesting relation to this country, the peculiar circumstances which surround you and surround us, call on me to express the happiness which we derive from your presence and aid in this solemn commemoration.

Fortunate, fortunate man! with what measure of devotion will you not thank God for the circumstances of your extraordinary life! You are connected with both hemispheres and with two generations. Heaven saw fit to ordain, that the electric spark of liberty should be conducted, through you, from the New World to the Old; and we, who are now here to perform this duty of patriotism, have all of us long ago received it in charge from our father to cherish your name and your virtues. You will account it an instance of your good fortune, Sir, that you crossed the seas to visit us at a time which enables you to be present at this solemnity. You now behold the field, the renown of which reached you in the heart of France, and caused a thrill in your ardent bosom. You see the lines of the little redoubt thrown up by the incredible diligence of Prescott; defended, to the last extremity, by his lion-hearted valor; and within which the corner-stone of our monument has now taken its position. You see where Warren fell, and where Parker, Gardner, McCleary, Moore, and other early patriots, fell with him. Those who survived that day, and whose lives have been prolonged to the present hour, are now around you. Some of them you have known in the trying scenes of war. Behold! they now stretch forth their feeble arms to embrace you. Behold! they raise their trembling voices to invoke the blessing of God on you and yours for ever.

Sir, you have assisted us in laying the foundation of this structure. You have heard us rehearse, with our feeble commendation, the names of departed patriots. Monuments and eulogy belong to the dead. We give them this day to Warren and his associates. On other occasions they have been given to your more immediate companions in arms, to Washington, to Greene, to Gates, to Sullivan, and to Lincoln. We have become reluctant to grant these, our highest and last honors, further. We would gladly hold them yet back from the little remnant of that immortal band. *Serus in cælum redeas.* Illustrious as are your merits, yet far, O, very far distant be the day, when any inscription shall bear your name, or any tongue pronounce its eulogy!

The leading reflection to which this occasion seems to invite us, respects the great changes which have happened in the fifty years since the battle of Bunker Hill was fought. And it peculiarly marks the character of the present age, that, in looking at these changes, and in estimating their effect on our condition, we are obliged to consider, not what has been done in our own country only, but in others also. In these interesting times, while nations are making separate and individual advances in improvement, they make, too, a common progress; like vessels on a common tide, propelled by the gales at different rates, according to their several structure and management, but all moved forward by one mighty current, strong enough to bear onward whatever does not sink beneath it.

A chief distinction of the present day is a community of opinions and knowledge amongst men in different nations, existing in a degree heretofore unknown. Knowledge has, in our time, triumphed, and is triumphing, over distance, over difference of languages, over diversity of habits, over prejudice, and over bigotry. The civilized and Christian world is fast learning the great lesson, that difference of nation does not imply necessary hostility, and that all contact need not be war. The whole world is becoming a common field for intellect to act in. Energy of mind, genius, power, wheresoever it exists, may speak out in any tongue, and the *world* will hear it. A great chord of sentiment and feeling runs through two continents, and vibrates over both. Every breeze wafts intelligence from country to country; every wave rolls it; all give it forth, and all in turn receive it. There is a vast commerce of ideas; there are marts and exchanges for intellectual discoveries, and a wonderful fellowship of those individual intelligences which make up the mind and opinion of the age. Mind is the great lever of all things; human thought is the process by which human ends are ultimately answered; and the diffusion of knowledge, so astonishing in the last half-century, has rendered innumerable minds, variously gifted by nature, competent to be competitors or fellow-workers on the theatre of intellectual operation.

From these causes important improvements have taken place in the personal condition of individuals. Generally speaking, mankind are not only better fed and better clothed, but they are able to enjoy more leisure; they possess more refinement and more self-respect. A superior tone of education, manners, and habits prevails. This remark, most true in its application to our own country, is also partly true when applied elsewhere. It is proved by the vastly augmented consumption of those articles of manufacture and of commerce which contribute to the comforts and the decencies of life; an augmentation which has far outrun the progress of population. And while the unexampled and almost incredible use of machinery would seem to supply the place of labor, labor still finds its occupation and its reward; so wisely has Providence adjusted men's wants and desires to their condition and their capacity.

Any adequate survey, however, of the progress made during the last half-century in the polite and the mechanic arts, in machinery and manufactures, in commerce and agriculture, in letters and in science, would require volumes. I must abstain wholly from these subjects, and turn for a moment to the contemplation of what has been done on the great question of politics and government. This is the master topic of the age; and during the whole fifty years it has intensely occupied the thoughts of men. The nature of civil government, its ends and uses, have been canvassed and investigated; ancient opinions attacked and defended; new ideas recommended and resisted, by whatever power the mind of man could bring to the controversy. From the closet and the public halls the debate has been transferred to the field; and the world has been shaken by wars of unexampled magnitude, and the greatest variety of fortune. A day of peace has at length succeeded; and now that the strife has subsided, and the smoke cleared away, we may begin to see what has actually been done, permanently changing the state and condition of human society. And, without dwelling on particular circumstances, it is most apparent, that, from the before-mentioned causes of augmented knowledge and improved individual condition, a real, substantial, and important change has taken place, and is taking place, highly favorable, on the whole, to human liberty and human happiness.

The great wheel of political revolution began to move in America. Here its rotation was guarded, regular, and safe. Transferred to the other continent, from unfortunate but natural causes, it received an irregular and violent impulse; it whirled along with a fearful celerity; till at length, like the chariot-wheels in the races of antiquity, it took fire from the rapidity of its own motion, and blazed onward, spreading conflagration and terror around.

We learn from the result of this experiment, how fortunate was our own condition, and how admirably the character of our people was calculated for setting the great example of popular governments. The possession of power did not turn the heads of the American people, for they had long been in the habit of exercising a great degree of self-control. Although the paramount authority of the parent state existed over them, yet a large field of legislation had always been open to our Colonial assemblies. They were accustomed to representative bodies and the forms of free government; they understood the doctrine of the division of power among different branches, and the necessity of checks on each. The character of our countrymen, moreover, was sober, moral, and religious; and there was little in the change to shock their feelings of justice and humanity, or even to disturb an honest prejudice. We had no domestic throne to overturn, no privileged orders to cast down, no violent changes of property to encounter. In the American Revolution, no man sought or wished for more than to defend and enjoy his own. None hoped for plunder or for spoil. Rapacity was unknown to it; the axe was not among the instruments of its accomplishment; and we all know that it could not have lived a single day under any well-founded imputation of possessing a tendency adverse to the Christian religion.

It need not surprise us, that, under circumstances less auspicious, political revolutions elsewhere, even when well intended, have terminated differently. It is, indeed, a great achievement, it is the master-work of the world, to establish governments entirely popular on lasting foundations; nor is it easy, indeed, to introduce the popular principle at all into governments to which it has been altogether a stranger. It cannot be doubted, however, that Europe has come out of the contest, in which she has been so long engaged, with greatly superior knowledge, and, in many respects, in a highly improved condition. Whatever benefit has been acquired is likely to be retained, for it consists mainly in the acquisition of more enlightened ideas. And although kingdoms and provinces may be wrested from the hands that hold them, in the same manner they were obtained; although ordinary and vulgar power may, in human affairs, be lost as it has been won; yet it is the glorious prerogative of the empire of knowledge, that what it gains it never loses. On the contrary, it increases by the multiple of its own power; all its ends become means; all its attainments, helps to new conquests. Its whole abundant harvest is but so much seed wheat, and nothing has limited, and nothing can limit, the amount of ultimate product.

Under the influence of this rapidly increasing knowledge, the people have begun, in all forms of government, to think, and to reason, on affairs of state. Regarding government as an institution for the public good, they demand a knowledge of its operations, and a participation in its exercise. A call for the representative system, wherever it is not enjoyed, and where there is already intelligence enough to estimate its value, is perseveringly made. Where men may speak out, they demand it; where the bayonet is at their throats, they pray for it.

When Louis the Fourteenth said, "I am the state," he expressed the essence of the doctrine of unlimited power. By the rules of that system, the people are disconnected from the state; they are its subjects; it is their lord. These ideas, founded in the love of power, and long supported by the excess and the abuse of it, are yielding, in our age, to other opinions; and the civilized world seems at last to be proceeding to the conviction of that fundamental and manifest truth, that the powers of government are but a trust, and that they cannot be lawfully exercised but for the good of the community. As knowledge is more and more extended, this conviction becomes more and more general. Knowledge, in truth, is the great sun in the firmament. Life and power are scattered with all its beams. The prayer of the Grecian champion, when enveloped in unnatural clouds and darkness, is the appropriate political supplication for the people of every country not yet blessed with free institutions:—

> Dispel this cloud, the light of heaven restore,
> Give me to SEE,—and Ajax asks no more.

We may hope that the growing influence of enlightened sentiment will promote the permanent peace of the world. Wars to maintain family alliances, to uphold or to cast down dynasties, and to regulate successions to thrones, which have occupied so much room in the history of modern times, if not less likely to happen at all, will be less likely to become general and involve many nations, as the great principle shall be more and more established, that the interest of the world is peace, and its first great statute, that every nation possesses the power of establishing a government for itself. But public opinion has attained also an influence over governments which do not admit the popular principle into their organization. A necessary respect for the judgment of the world operates, in some measure, as a control over the most unlimited forms of authority. It is owing, perhaps, to this truth, that the interesting struggle of the Greeks has been suffered to go on so long, without a direct interference, either to wrest that country from it present masters, or to execute the system of pacification by force, and, with united strength, lay the neck of Christian and civilized Greek at the foot of the barbarian Turk. Let us thank God that we live in an age when something has influence besides the bayonet, and when the sternest authority does not venture to encounter the scorching power of public reproach. Any attempt of the kind I have mentioned should be met by one universal burst of indignation; the air of the civilized world ought to be made too warm to be comfortably breathed by any one who would hazard it.

It is, indeed, a touching reflection, that, while, in the fulness of our country's happiness, we rear this monument to her honor, we look for instruction in our undertaking to a country which is now in fearful contest, not for works of art or memorials of glory, but for her own existence. Let her be assured, that she is not forgotten in the world; that her efforts are applauded, and that constant prayers ascend for her success. And let us cherish a confident hope for her final triumph. If the true spark of religious and civil liberty be kindled, it will burn. Human agency cannot extinguish it. Like the earth's central fire, it may be smothered for a time; the ocean may overwhelm it; mountains may press it down; but its inherent and unconquerable force will heave both the ocean and the land, and at some time or other, in some place or other, the volcano will break out and flame up to heaven.

Among the great events of the half-century, we must reckon, certainly, the revolution of South America; and we are not likely to overrate the importance of that revolution, either to the people of the country itself or to the rest of the world. The late Spanish colonies, now independent states, under circumstances less favorable, doubtless, than attended our own revolution, have yet successfully commenced their national existence. They have accomplished the great object of establishing their independence; they are known and acknowledged in the world; and although in regard to their systems of government, their sentiments on religious toleration, and their provisions for public instruction, they may have yet much to learn, it must be admitted that they have risen to the condition of settled and established states more rapidly than could have been reasonably anticipated. They already furnish an exhilarating example of the difference between free governments and despotic misrule. Their commerce, at this moment, creates a new activity in all the great marts of the world. They show themselves able, by an exchange of commodities, to bear a useful part in the intercourse of nations.

A new spirit of enterprise and industry begins to prevail; all the great interests of society receive a salutary impulse; and the progress of information not only testifies to an improved condition, but itself constitutes the highest and most essential improvement.

When the battle of Bunker Hill was fought, the existence of South America was scarcely felt in the civilized world. The thirteen little Colonies of North America habitually called themselves the "Continent." Borne down by colonial subjugation, monopoly, and bigotry, these vast regions of the South were hardly visible above the horizon. But in our day there has been, as it were, a new creation. The southern hemisphere emerges from the sea. Its lofty mountains begin to life themselves into the light of heaven; its broad and fertile plains stretch out, in beauty, to the eye of civilized man, and at the mighty bidding of the voice of political liberty the waters of darkness retire.

And, now, let us indulge an honest exultation in the conviction of the benefit which the example of our country has produced, and is likely to produce, on human freedom and human happiness. Let us endeavor to comprehend in all its magnitude, and to feel in all its importance, the part assigned to us in the great drama of human affairs. We are placed at the head of the system of representative and popular governments. Thus far our example shows that such governments are compatible, not only with respectability and power, but with repose, with peace, with security of personal rights, with good laws, and a just administration.

We are not propagandists. Wherever other systems are preferred, either as being thought better in themselves, or as better suited to existing conditions, we leave the preference to be enjoyed. Our history hitherto proves, however, that the popular form is practicable, and that with wisdom and knowledge men may govern themselves; and the duty incumbent on us is, to preserve the consistency of this cheering example, and take care that nothing may weaken its authority with the world. If, in our case, the representative system ultimately fail, popular governments must be pronounced impossible. No combination of circumstances more favorable to the experiment can ever be expected to occur. The last hopes of mankind, therefore, rest with us; and if it should be proclaimed, that our example had become an argument against the experiment, the knell of popular liberty would be sounded throughout the earth.

These are excitements to duty; but they are not suggestions of doubt. Our history and our condition, all that is gone before us, and all that surrounds us, authorize the belief, that popular governments, though subject to occasional variations, in form perhaps not always for the better, may yet, in their general character, be as durable and permanent as other systems. We know, indeed, that in our country any other is impossible. The *principle* of free governments adheres to the American soil. It is bedded in it, immovable as its mountains.

And let the sacred obligations which have devolved on this generation, and on us, sink deep into our hearts. Those who established our liberty and our government are daily dropping from among us. The great trust now descends to new hands. Let us apply ourselves to that which is presented to us, as our appropriate object. We can win no laurels in a war for independence. Earlier and worthier hands have gathered them all. Nor are there places for us by the side of Solon, and Alfred, and other founders of states. Our fathers have filled them. But there remains to us a great duty of defence and preservation, and there is opened to us, also, a noble pursuit, to which the spirit of the times strongly invites us. Our proper business is improvement. Let our age be the age of improvement. In a day of peace, let us advance the arts of peace and the works of peace. Let us develop the resources of our land, call forth its powers, build up its institutions, promote all its great interests, and see whether we also, in our day and generation, may not perform something worthy to be remembered. Let us cultivate a true spirit of union and harmony. In pursuing the great objects which our condition points out to us, let us act under a settled conviction, and an habitual feeling, that these twenty-four States are one country. Let our conceptions be enlarged to the circle of our duties. Let us extend our ideas over the whole of the vast field in which we are called to act. Let our object be our country, our whole country, and nothing but our country. And, by the blessing of God, may that country itself become a vast and splendid monument, not of oppression and terror, but of Wisdom, of Peace, and of Liberty, upon which the world may gaze with admiration for ever!

John C. Calhoun

On the Force Bill: Nationalism and States' Rights (1833)

When Congress passed a tariff act in 1828 that embodied the principles of protectionism, it was quickly dubbed the "Tariff of Abominations" by disgruntled Southerners, who saw it as unjust and oppressive. They were convinced that a tariff that protected northern industries from foreign competition worked against the South. The tariff would reduce, Southerners believed, the purchasing power of foreign cotton customers—particularly England—while, at the same time, raise prices on manufactured goods for Southern consumers. The South Carolina legislature passed a series of resolutions declaring the tariff unconstitutional, and John C. Calhoun authored the *South Carolina Exposition and Protest*. In this document Calhoun set forth the theory of state sovereignty and argued the right of a state to nullify unconstitutional laws, a theory largely derived from the debates over the ratification of the Federal Constitution.

John Calhoun began his political career as a member of the South Carolina legislature and then served in the U.S. House of Representatives from 1811 to 1817; there, as chairman of the Foreign Relations Committee, he took the lead among the "War Hawks" who favored war with Great Britain. From the House, Calhoun moved to the Cabinet of President James Monroe as Secretary of War. In 1825 he was elected vice-president of the United States under President John Quincy Adams and was serving in that office when he wrote the *Exposition*. Although Calhoun supported Andrew Jackson and was elected as his vice-president, he broke with Jackson in 1830 and became the leading spokesman for states' rights and nullification.

President Jackson affirmed the constitutionality of the 1828 Tariff in his annual message in 1830, but later he recommended tariff revision that was embodied in a new tariff bill passed in 1832. This new bill, although less objectionable than the 1828 measure, still met with concerted opposition in South Carolina. A special state convention passed the Ordinance of Nullification, voiding both tariff acts and claiming that the use of force to implement them would be a cause for secession from the Union. The state legislature promptly passed laws to ensure the enforcement of the Nullification Ordinance and authorized raising a military force.

President Jackson responded with firmness. He gave command of the army in South Carolina to General Winfield Scott and issued a Proclamation to the People of South Carolina in which he denounced nullification as absurd and declared that "disunion by armed force is treason." He followed the proclamation with a request to Congress to enforce the revenue laws by military action. At the same time, however, he sent a message to Congress urging downward revision of the tariff. At the height of the controversy, in December 1832, Calhoun resigned as vice-president in order to take the Senate seat vacated by the new governor of South Carolina, Robert Hayne. In the Senate, Calhoun led the fight against what come to be known as the "Force Bill."

Calhoun used the debate to lay out his conception of the rights of states against the federal or "general" government. He saw the conflict as between "the southern and other sections" of the country. The South, he reasoned, would be a permanent minority and must therefore stand against the power of the general government which would be in the hands of the majority. Arguing from the example of Roman history, he virtually demanded the right of veto by the South over the passage and execution of laws. If the South was able to "restrain . . . [the central government] within its constitutional limits," the "weaker section" would be able to maintain "all that can be dear to freeman." Failure to do so would render the South "wretched." In short, Calhoun saw the struggle as between "power and liberty."

The bill was passed; however, along with it, a compromise tariff that mollified the South was also passed. South Carolina then rescinded the Nullification Ordinance. By rescinding the Ordinance, the need for legislation to enforce the collection of revenue no longer exited, rendering the Force Bill a dead letter. Nevertheless, in a face-saving gesture, the South Carolina legislature declared the now irrelevant Force Bill null and void. Thus, both sides were able to declare themselves victorious in this exchange. The issue, however, was far from settled, and the question of the powers of the central government vis-a-vis the states was one that was to continue to intrude itself into the stream of American rhetoric.

At the last session of Congress, it was avowed on all sides that the public debt, as to all practical purposes, was in fact paid, the small surplus remaining being nearly covered by the money in the Treasury and the bonds for duties which had already accrued; but with the arrival of this event our last hope was doomed to be disappointed. After a long session of many months, and the most earnest effort on the part of South Carolina and the other Southern States to obtain relief, all that could be effected was a small reduction in the amount of the duties, but a reduction of such a character that, while it diminished the amount of burden, it distributed that burden more unequally than even the obnoxious Act of 1828; reversing the principle adopted by the Bill of 1816, of laying higher duties on the unprotected than the protected articles, by repealing almost entirely the duties laid upon the former, and imposing the burden almost entirely on the latter. It was thus that, instead of relief—instead of an equal distribution of burdens and benefits of the government, on the payment of the debt, as had been fondly anticipated—the duties were so arranged as to be, in fact, bounties on one side and taxation on the other; thus placing the two great sections of the country in direct conflict in reference to its fiscal action, and thereby letting in that flood of political corruption which threatens to sweep away our Constitution and our liberty.

This unequal and unjust arrangement was pronounced, both by the administration, through its proper organ, the Secretary of the Treasury, and by the opposition, to be a *permanent* adjustment; and it was thus that all hope of relief through the action of the general government terminated; and the crisis so long apprehended at length arrived, at which the State was compelled to choose between absolute acquiescence in a ruinous system of oppression, or a resort to her reserved powers—powers of which she alone was the rightful judge, and which only, in this momentous juncture, could save her. She determined on the latter.

The consent of two-thirds of her Legislature was necessary for the call of a convention, which was considered the only legitimate organ through which the people, in their sovereignty, could speak. After an arduous struggle the States-right party succeeded; more than two-thirds of both branches of the Legislature favorable to a convention were elected; a convention was called—the ordinance adopted. The convention was succeeded by a meeting of the Legislature, when the laws to carry the ordinance into execution were enacted—all of which have been communicated by the President, have been referred to the Committee on the Judiciary, and this bill is the result of their labor.

Having now corrected some of the prominent misrepresentations as to the nature of this controversy, and given a rapid sketch of the movement of the State in reference to it, I will next proceed to notice some objections connected with the ordinance and the proceedings under it.

The first and most prominent of these is directed against what is called the test oath, which an effort has been made to render odious. So far from deserving the denunciation that has been levelled against it, I view this provision of the ordinance as but the natural result of the doctrines entertained by the State, and the position which she occupies. The people of Carolina believe that the Union is a union of States, and not of individuals; that it was formed by the States, and that the citizens of the several States were bound to it through the acts of their several States; that each State ratified the Constitution for itself, and that it was only by such ratification of a State that any obligation was imposed upon its citizens. Thus believing, it is the opinion of the people of Carolina that it belongs to the State which has imposed the obligation to declare, in the last resort, the extent of this obligation, as far as her citizens are concerned; and this upon the plain principles which exist in all analogous cases of compact between sovereign bodies. On this principle the people of the State, acting in their sovereign capacity in convention, precisely as they did in the adoption of their own and the Federal Constitution, have declared, by the ordinance, that the acts of Congress which imposed duties under the authority to lay imposts, were acts not for revenue, as intended by the Constitution, but for protection, and therefore null and void. The ordinance thus enacted by the people of the State themselves, acting as a sovereign community, is as obligatory on the citizens of the State as any portion of the Constitution. In prescribing, then, the oath to obey the ordinance, no more was done than to prescribe an oath to obey the Constitution. It is, in fact, but a particular oath of allegiance, and in every respect similar to that which is prescribed, under the Constitution of the United States, to be administered to all the officers of the State and Federal governments; and is no more deserving the harsh and bitter epithets which have been heaped upon it than that or any similar oath. It ought to be borne in mind that, according to the opinion which prevails in Carolina, the right of resistance to the unconstitutional acts of Congress belongs to the State, and not to her individual citizens; and that, though the latter may, in a mere question of *meum* and *tuum*, resist through the courts an unconstitutional encroachment upon their rights, yet the final stand against usurpation rests not with them, but with the State of which they are members; and such act of resistance by a State binds the conscience and allegiance of the citizen. But there appears to be a general misapprehension as to the extent to which the State has acted under this part of the ordinance. Instead of sweeping every officer by a general proscription of the minority, as has been represented in debate, as far as my knowledge extends, not a single individual has been removed. The State has, in fact, acted with the greatest tenderness, all circumstances considered, toward citizens who differed from the majority; and, in that spirit, has directed the oath to be administered only in the case of some official act directed to be performed in which obedience to the ordinance is involved. . . .

It is next objected that the enforcing acts have legislated the United States out of South Carolina. I have already replied to this objection on another occasion, and will now but repeat what I then said: that they have been legislated out only to the extent that they had no right to enter. The Constitution has admitted the jurisdiction of the United States within the limits of the several States only so far as the delegated powers authorize; beyond that they are intruders, and may rightfully be expelled; and that they have been efficiently expelled by the legislation of the State through her civil process, as has been acknowledged on all sides in the debate, is only a confirmation of the truth of the doctrine for which the majority in Carolina have contended.

The very point at issue between the two parties there is, whether nullification is a peaceful and an efficient remedy against an unconstitutional act of the general government, and may be asserted, as such, through the State tribunals. Both parties agree that the acts against which it is directed are unconstitutional and oppressive. The controversy is only as to the means by which our citizens may be protected against the acknowledged encroachments on their rights. This being the point at issue between the parties, and the very object of the majority being an efficient protection of the citizens through the State tribunals, the measures adopted to enforce the ordinance, of course, received the most decisive character. We were not children, to act by halves. Yet for acting thus efficiently the State is denounced, and this bill reported, to overrule, by military force, the civil tribunal and civil process of the State! Sir, I consider this bill, and the arguments which have been urged on this floor in its support, as the most triumphant acknowledgement that nullification is peaceful and efficient, and so deeply intrenched in the principles of our system, that it cannot be assailed but by prostrating the Constitution, and substituting the supremacy of military force in lieu of the supremacy of the laws. In fact, the advocates of this bill refute their own argument. They tell us that the ordinance in unconstitutional; that it infracts the Constitution of South Carolina, although, to me, the objection appears absurd, as it was adopted by the very authority which adopted the Constitution itself. They also tell us that the Supreme Court is the appointed arbiter of all controversies between a State and the general government. Why, then, do they not leave this controversy to that tribunal? Why do they not confide to them the abrogation of the ordinance, and the laws made in pursuance of it, and the assertion of that supremacy which they claim for the laws of Congress? The State stands pledged to resist no process of the court. Why, then, confer on the President the extensive and unlimited powers provided in this bill? Why authorize him to use military force to arrest the civil process of the State? But one answer can be given: That, in a contest between the State and the general government, if the resistance be limited on both sides to the civil process, the State, by its inherent sovereignty, standing upon its reserved powers, will prove too powerful in such a controversy, and must triumph over the Federal government, sustained by its delegated and limited authority; and in this answer we have an acknowledgement of the truth of those great principles for which the State has so firmly and nobly contended. . . .

Notwithstanding all that has been said, I may say that neither the Senator from Delaware [Mr. Clayton], nor any other who has spoken on the same side, has directly and fairly met the great question at issue: Is this a Federal Union? a union of States, as distinct from that of individuals? Is the sovereignty in the several States, or in the American people in the aggregate? The very language which we are compelled to use when speaking of our political institutions affords proof conclusive as to its real character. The terms union, federal, united, all imply a combination of sovereignties, a confederation of States. They never apply to an association of individuals. Who ever heard of the United State of New York, of Massachusetts, or of Virginia? Who ever heard the term federal or union applied to the aggregation of individuals into one community? Nor is the other point less clear—that the sovereignty is in the several States, and that our system is a union of twenty-four sovereign powers, under a constitutional compact, and not of a divided sovereignty between the States severally and the United States? In spite of all that has been said, I maintain that sovereignty is in its nature indivisible. It is the supreme power in a State, and we might just as well speak of half a square, or half of a triangle, as of half a sovereignty. It is a gross error to confound the *exercise* of sovereign powers with *sovereignty* itself, or the *delegation* of such powers with the *surrender* of them. A sovereign may delegate his powers to be exercised by as many agents as he may think proper, under such conditions and with such limitations as he may impose; but to surrender any portion of his sovereignty to another is to annihilate the whole. The Senator from Delaware [Mr. Clayton] calls this metaphysical reasoning, which he says he cannot comprehend. If by metaphysics he means that scholastic refinement which makes distinctions without difference, no one can hold it in more utter contempt than I do; but if, on the contrary, he means the power of analysis and combination—that power which reduces the most complex idea into its elements, which traces causes to their first principle, and, by the power of generalization and combination, unites the whole in one harmonious system—then, so far from deserving contempt, it is the highest attribute of the human mind. It is the power which raises man above the brute—which distinguishes his faculties from mere sagacity, which he holds in common with inferior animals. It is this power which has raised the astronomer from being a mere gazer at the stars to the high intellectual eminence of a Newton or a Laplace, and astronomy itself from a mere observation of isolated facts into that noble science which displays to our admiration the system of the universe. And shall this high power of the mind, which has effected such wonders when directed to the laws which control the material world, be forever prohibited, under a senseless cry of metaphysics, from being applied to the high purposes of political science and legislation? I hold them to be subject to laws as fixed as matter itself, and to be as fit a subject for the application of the highest intellectual power. Denunciation may, indeed, fall upon the philosophical inquirer into these first principles, as it did upon Galileo and Bacon, when they first unfolded the great discoveries which have immortalized their names; but the time will come when truth will prevail in spite of prejudice and denunciation, and when politics and legislation will be considered as much a science as astronomy and chemistry.

In connection with this part of the subject, I understood the Senator from Virginia [Mr. Rives] to say that sovereignty was divided, and that a portion remained with the States severally, and that the residue was vested in the Union. By Union, I suppose, the Senator meant the United States. If such be his meaning—if he intended to affirm that the sovereignty was in the twenty-four States, in whatever light he may view them, our opinions will not disagree; but according to my conception, the whole sovereignty is in the several States, while the exercise of sovereign power is divided—a part being exercised under compact, through this general government, and the residue through the separate State governments. But if the Senator from Virginia [Mr. Rives] means to assert that the twenty-four States form but one community, with a single sovereign power as to the objects of the Union, it will be but the revival of the old question, of whether the Union is a union between States, as distinct communities, or a mere aggregate of the American people, as a mass of individuals; and in this light his opinions would lead directly to consolidation. . . .

Disguise it as you may, the controversy is one between power and liberty; and I tell the gentlemen who are opposed to me, that, as strong as may be the love of power on their side, the love of liberty is still stronger on ours. History furnishes many instances of similar struggles, where the love of liberty has prevailed against power under every disadvantage, and among them few more striking than that of our own Revolution; where, as strong as was the parent country, and feeble as were the Colonies, yet, under the impulse of liberty, and the blessing of God, they gloriously triumphed in the contest. There are, indeed, many striking analogies between that and the present controversy. They both originated substantially in the same cause—with this difference—in the present case, the power of taxation is converted into that of regulating industry; in the other the power of regulating industry, by the regulation of commerce, was attempted to be converted into the power of taxation. Were I to trace the analogy further, we should find that the perversion of the taxing power, in the one case, has given precisely the same control to the northern section over the industry of the southern section of the Union, which the power to regulate commerce gave to Great Britain over the industry of the Colonies in the other; and that the very articles in which the Colonies were permitted to have a free trade, and those in which the mother-country had a monopoly, are almost identically the same as those in which the Southern States are permitted to have a free trade by the Act of 1832, and in which the Northern States have, by the same act, secured a monopoly. The only difference is in the means. In the former, the Colonies were permitted to have a free trade with all countries south of Cape Finisterre, a cape in the northern part of Spain; while north of that, the trade of the Colonies was prohibited, except through the mother-country, by means of her commercial regulations. If we compare the products of the country north and south of Cape Finisterre, we shall find them almost identical with the list of the protected and unprotected articles contained in the list of last year. Nor does the analogy terminate here. The very arguments resorted to at the commencement of the American Revolution, and the measures adopted, and the motives assigned to bring on that contest (to enforce the law), are almost identically the same.

But to return from this digression to the consideration of the bill. Whatever difference of opinion may exist upon other points, there is one on which I should suppose there can be none; that this bill rests upon principles which, if carried out, will ride over State sovereignties, and that it will be idle for any advocates hereafter to talk of State rights. The Senator from Virginia [Mr. Rives] says that he is the advocate of State rights; but he must permit me to tell him that, although he may differ in premises from the other gentlemen with whom he acts on this occasion, yet, in supporting this bill, he obliterates every vestige of distinction between him and them, saving only that, professing the principles of '98, his example will be more pernicious than that of the most open and bitter opponent of the rights of the States. I will also add, what I am compelled to say, that I must consider him (Mr. Rives) as less consistent than our old opponents, whose conclusions were fairly drawn from their premises, while his premises ought to have led him to opposite conclusions. The gentleman has told us that the new-fangled doctrines, as he chooses to call them, have brought State rights into disrepute. I must tell him, in reply, that what he calls new-fangled are but the doctrines of '98; and that it is he [Mr. Rives], and others with him, who, professing these doctrines, have degraded them by explaining away their meaning and efficacy. He [Mr. R.] has disclaimed, in behalf of Virginia, the authorship of nullification. I will not dispute that point. If Virginia chooses to throw away one of her brightest ornaments, she must not hereafter complain that it has become the property of another. But while I have, as a representative of Carolina, no right to complain of the disavowal of the Senator from Virginia, I must believe that he [Mr. R.] has done his native State great injustice by declaring on this floor, that when she gravely resolved, in '98, that "in cases of deliberate and dangerous infractions of the Constitution, the States, as parties to the compact, have the right, and are in duty bound, to interpose to arrest the progress of the evil, and to maintain within their respective limits the authorities, rights, and liberties appertaining to them," she meant no more than to proclaim the right to protest and to remonstrate. To suppose that, in putting forth so solemn a declaration, which she afterward sustained by so able and elaborate an argument, she meant no more than to assert what no one had ever denied, would be to suppose that the State had been guilty of the most egregious trifling that ever was exhibited on so solemn an occasion.

Wendell Phillips

The Murder of Lovejoy (1837)

Those who argued that slavery was an evil that stained the American character and should be abolished were not numerous, and certainly were not popular in the early years of the nineteenth century. An ingrained racism led whites—North and South—to regard blacks as inferior, and many feared that agitation over the slavery issue would intensify sectional conflict and destroy the union. Most Americans, therefore, looked with suspicion and hostility on the abolitionists. For their part, however, the abolitionists were willing to suffer beatings and abuse, to face the threat of mob violence, to endure the wrath not only of Southerners but of their Northern neighbors, as well, in order to argue in the strongest terms against the dreadful proposition that human beings could legally and morally be held as property.

Men and women willing to endure social ostracism and physical attack were hard to silence, but their opponents were convinced that to do so was essential to the preservation of American government and society. Abolitionists were particularly aggrieved by the spectacle of slaves being bought and sold in the nation's capital, and petitions rained on Congress calling for the abolition of slavery and the slave trade in the District of Columbia. The Senate adopted the practice of receiving the petitions and quickly voting to deny them, but the House, in 1836, adopted a "gag rule" that automatically tabled, without discussion, any petition that related in any way to slavery. This was done over the strenuous objections of former President John Quincy Adams, now a Representative from Massachusetts, who considered such action "a violation of the Constitution."

When Congress reconvened in December 1837, the abolitionist agitation in the North had been intensified by an event in Alton, Illinois, producing more petitions and the reinstatement of an even harsher gag rule. In Alton, an abolitionist editor, Elijah P. Lovejoy, was murdered by a mob augmented by men who crossed the river from Missouri to destroy Lovejoy's press—as similar Missouri mobs had before done, forcing Lovejoy to leave St. Louis. Lovejoy was shot as he and a band of supporters attempted to defend his printing press. When the news of this assault reached Boston, a group of prominent citizens, led by Dr. William Ellery Channing, called a meeting in Faneuil Hall to offer resolutions denouncing the attack on Lovejoy. Although a center of abolitionist activity, Boston was not without bitter enemies of the antislavery movement. It was only two years before, for example, that William Lloyd Garrison was himself mobbed in the streets of Boston.

That particular scene had been witnessed by a young lawyer who deplored the fact that some of the best people of Boston were among the crowd that manhandled Garrison. Wendell Phillips was a descendant of an old Boston family, a family that had produced generations of ministers and lawyers. Phillips was a graduate of Harvard Law School and was on his way to becoming a prominent attorney himself when the Garrison incident, coupled with Phillip's marriage to Anne Terry Greene, a passionate abolitionist, converted him to the antislavery cause.

Phillips gave his first abolitionist speech in June 1837 at a meeting of the Lynn, Massachusetts, abolitionist society and was among the crowd that packed Faneuil Hall in December. Phillips did not intend to speak, but the attack on the petition by the attorney general of Massachusetts, James Austin, moved Phillips to action. Austin had compared slaves to wild beasts and identified the mob at Alton with the Boston patriots who dumped the British tea in the harbor. Further, Austin labeled Lovejoy "presumptuous and imprudent" and asserted that the abolitionist editor had "died as the fool dieth." The attorney general also dismissed Dr. Channing, who, as a clergyman, was considered by Austin to be "out of place" in such proceedings.

The hall was liberally sprinkled with Austin supporters; they raised such a tumult that Phillips had a hard time replying. But reply he did, recognizing that both slavery and freedom of the press were at issue. "When Liberty is in danger," Phillips asserted, "Faneuil Hall has the right, it is her duty, to strike the key-note for these United States." Phillips's indignant rebuttal helped to secure the passage of the resolutions condemning the "outrage" and launched Phillips himself on a career as one of the foremost antislavery agitators.

Mr. Chairman:—We have met for the freest discussion of these resolutions, and the events which gave rise to them. [*Cries of "Question," "Hear him," "Go on," "No gagging," etc.*] I hope I shall be permitted to express my surprise at the sentiments of the last speaker,—surprise not only at such sentiments from such a man, but at the applause they have received within these walls. A comparison has been drawn between the events of the Revolution and the tragedy at Alton. We have heard it asserted here, in Faneuil Hall, that Great Britain had a right to tax the Colonies, and we have heard the mob at Alton, the drunken murderers of Lovejoy, compared to those patriot fathers who threw the tea overboard! [*Great applause.*] Fellow-citizens, is this Faneuil Hall doctrine? [*"No, no."*] The mob at Alton were met to wrest from a citizen his just rights,—met to resist the laws. We have been told that our fathers did the same; and the glorious mantle of Revolutionary precedent has been thrown over the mobs of our day. To make out their title to such defence, the gentleman says that the British Parliament had a *right* to tax these Colonies. It is manifest that, without this, his parallel falls to the ground; for Lovejoy had stationed himself within constitutional bulwarks. He was not only defending the freedom of the press, but he was under his own roof, in arms with the sanction of the civil authority. The men who assailed him went against and over the laws. The *mob*, as the gentleman terms it,—mob, forsooth! certainly we sons of the tea-spillers are a marvellously patient generation!—the "orderly mob" which assembled in the Old South to destroy the tea were met to resist, not the laws, but illegal exactions. Shame on the American who calls the tea-tax and stamp-act *laws!* Our fathers resisted, not the King's prerogative, but the King's usurpation. To find any other account, you must read our Revolutionary history upside down. Our State archives are loaded with arguments of John Adams to prove the taxes laid by the British Parliament unconstitutional,—beyond its power. It was not till this was made out that the men of New England rushed to arms. The arguments of the Council Chamber and the House of Representatives preceded and sanctioned the contest. To draw the conduct of our ancestors into a precedent for mobs, for a right to resist laws we ourselves have enacted, is an insult to their memory. The difference between the excitements of those days and our own, which the gentleman in kindness to the latter has overlooked, is simply this: the men of that day went for the right, as secured by the laws. They were the people rising to sustain the laws and constitution of the Province. The rioters of our day go for their own wills, right or wrong. Sir, when I heard the gentleman lay down principles which place the murderers of Alton side by side with Otis and Hancock, with Quincy and Adams, I thought those pictured lips [*pointing to the portraits in the Hall*] would have broken into voice to rebuke the recreant American,—the slanderer of the dead. [*Great applause and counter applause.*] The gentleman said that he should sink into insignificance if he dared to gainsay the principles of these resolutions. Sir, for the sentiments he has uttered, on soil consecrated by the prayers of Puritans and the blood of patriots, the earth should have yawned and swallowed him up.

[*Applause and hisses, with cries of "Take that back."*]

Fellow-citizens, I cannot take back my words. Surely the Attorney-General, so long and well known here, needs not the aid of your hisses against one so young as I am,—my voice never before heard within these walls!

Another ground has been taken to excuse the mob, and throw doubt and discredit on the conduct of Lovejoy and his associates. Allusion has been made to what lawyers understand very well,—the "conflict of laws." We are told that nothing but the Mississippi River rolls between St. Louis and Alton; and the conflict of laws somehow or other gives the citizens of the former a right to find fault with the defender of the press for publishing his opinions so near their limits. Will the gentleman venture that argument before lawyers? How the laws of the two States could be said to come into conflict in such circumstances I question whether any lawyer in this audience can explain or understand. No matter whether the line that divides one sovereign State from another be an imaginary one or ocean-wide, the moment you cross it the State you leave is blotted out of existence, so far as you are concerned. The Czar might as well claim to control the deliberations in Faneuil Hall, as the laws of Missouri demand reverence, or the shadow of obedience from an inhabitant of Illinois.

I must find some fault with the statement which has been made of the events at Alton. It has been asked why Lovejoy and his friends did not appeal to the executive,—trust their defence to the police of the city. It has been hinted that, from hasty and ill-judged excitement, the men within the building provoked a quarrel, and that he fell in the course it, one mob resisting another. Recollect, Sir, that they did act with the approbation and sanction of the Mayor. In strict truth, there was no executive to appeal to for protection. The Mayor acknowledged that he could not protect them. They asked him if it was lawful for them to defend themselves. He told them it was, and sanctioned their assembling in arms to do so. They were not, then, a mob; they were not merely citizens definding their own property; they were in some sense the *posse comitatus*, adopted for the occasion into the police of the city, acting under the order of a magistrate. It was civil authority resisting lawless violence. Where, then, was the imprudence? Is the doctrine to be sustained here, that it is *imprudent* for men to aid magistrates in executing the laws?

Men are continually asking each other, Had Lovejoy a right to resist? Sir, I protest against the question, instead of answering it. Lovejoy did not resist, in the sense they mean. He did not throw himself back on the natural right of self-defence. He did not cry anarchy, and let slip the dogs of civil war, careless of the horrors which would follow.

Sir, as I understand this affair, it was not an individual protecting his property; it was not one body of armed men resisting another, and making the streets of a peaceful city run blood with their contentions. It did not bring back the scenes in some old Italian cities, where family met family, and faction met faction, and mutually trampled the laws under foot. No; the men in that house were regularly *enrolled*, under the sanction of the Mayor. There being no militia in Alton, about seventy men were enrolled with the approbation of the Mayor. These relieved each other every other night. About thirty men were in arms on the night of the sixth, when the press was landed. The next evening, it was not thought necessary to summon more than half that number; among these was Lovejoy. It was, therefore, you perceive, Sir, the police of the city resisting rioters,—civil government breasting itself to the shock of lawless men.

Here is no question about the right of self-defence. It is in fact simply this: Has the civil magistrate a right to put down a riot?

Some persons seem to imagine that anarchy existed at Alton from the commencement of these disputes. Not at all. "No one of us," says an eyewitness and a comrade of Lovejoy, "has taken up arms during these disturbances but at the command of the Mayor." Anarchy did not settle down on that devoted city till Lovejoy breathed his last. Till then the law, represented in his person, sustained itself against its foes. When he fell, civil authority was trampled under foot. He had "planted himself on his constitutional rights,"—appealed to the laws,—claimed the protection of the civil authority,—taken refuge under "the broad shield of the Constitution. When through that he was pierced and fell, he fell but one sufferer in a common catastrophe." He took refuge under the banner of liberty,—amid its folds; and when he fell, its glorious stars and stripes, the emblem of free institutions, around which cluster so many heart-stirring memories, were blotted out in the martyr's blood.

It has been stated, perhaps inadvertently, that Lovejoy or his comrades fired first. This is denied by those who have the best means of knowing. Guns were first fired by the mob. After being twice fired on, those within the building consulted together and deliberately returned the fire. But suppose they did fire first. They had a right so to do; not only the right which every citizen has to defend himself, but the further right which every civil officer has to resist violence. Even if Lovejoy fired the first gun, it would not lessen his claim to our sympathy, or destroy his title to be considered a martyr in defence of a free press. The question now is, Did he act within the Constitution and the laws? The men who fell in State Street on the 5th of March 1770, did more than Lovejoy is charged with. They were the *first* assailants. Upon some slight quarrel they pelted the troops with every missle within reach. Did this bate one jot of the eulogy with which Hancock and Warren hallowed their memory, hailing them as the first martyrs in the cause of American liberty?

If, Sir, I had adopted what are called Peace principles, I might lament the circumstances of this case. But all you who believe, as I do, in the right and duty of magistrates to execute the laws, join with me and brand as base hypocrisy the conduct of those who assemble year after year on the 4th of July, to fight over the battles of the Revolution and yet "damn with faint praise," or load with obloquy, the memory of this man, who shed his blood in defence of life, liberty, property, and the freedom of the press!

Throughout that terrible night I find nothing to regret but this, that within the limits of our country, civil authority should have been so prostrated as to oblige a citizen to arm in his own defence, and to arm in vain. The gentleman says Lovejoy was presumptuous and imprudent,—he "died as a fool dieth." And a reverend clergyman of the city tells us that no citizen has a right to publish opinions disagreeable to the community! If any mob follows such publication, on *him* rests its guilt! He must wait, forsooth, till the people come up to it and agree with him! This libel on liberty goes on to say that the want of right to speak as we think is an evil inseparable from republican institutions! If this be, what are they worth? Welcome the despotism of the Sultan, where one knows what he may publish and what he may not, rather than the tyranny of this many-headed monster, the mob, where we know not what we may do or say, till some fellow-citizen has tried it, and paid for the lesson with his life. This clerical absurdity chooses as a check for the abuses of the press, not the *law*, but the dread of a mob. By so doing, it deprives not only the individual and the minority of their rights, but the majority also, since the expression of *their* opinion may sometimes provoke disturbance from the minority. A few men may make a mob as well as many. The majority, then, have no right, as Christian men, to utter their sentiments, if by any possibility it may lead to a mob! Shades of Hugh Peters and John Cotton, save us from such pulpits!

Imprudent to defend the liberty of the press! Why? Because the defence was unsuccessful? Does success gild crime into patriotism, and the want of it change heroic self-devotion to imprudence? Was Hampden imprudent when he drew the sword and threw away the scabbard? Yet he, judged by that single hour, was unsuccessful. After a short exile, the race he hated sat again upon the throne.

Imagine yourself present when the first news of Bunker Hill battle reached a New England town. The tale would have run thus: "The patriots are routed,—the redcoats victorious,—Warren lies dead upon the field." With what scorn would that *Tory* have been received, who should have charged Warren with *imprudence!* who should have said that, bred a physician, he was "out of place" in that battle, and "died as the *fool dieth*"! [Great applause.] How would the intimation have been received, that Warren and his associates should have waited a better time? But if success be indeed the only criterion of prudence, *Respice finem*,—wait till the end.

Presumptuous to assert the freedom of the press on American ground! Is the assertion of such freedom before the age? So much before the age as to leave one no right to make it because it displeases the community? Who invents this libel on his country? It is this very thing which entitles Lovejoy to greater praise. The disputed right which provoked the Revolution—taxation without representation—is far beneath that for which he died. [Here there was a strong and general expression of disapprobation.] One word, gentlemen. As much as *thought* is better than money, so much is the cause in which Lovejoy died nobler than a mere question of taxes. James Otis thundered in this Hall when the King did but touch his *pocket*. Imagine, if you can, his indignant eloquence, had England offered to put a gag upon his lips. [Great applause.]

The question that stirred the Revolution touched our civil interests. *This* concerns us not only as citizens, but as immortal beings. Wrapped up in its fate, saved or lost with it, are not only the voice of the statesman, but the instructions of the pulpit, and the progress of our faith.

The clergy "marvellously out of place" where free speech is battled for,—liberty of speech on national sins? Does the gentleman remember that freedom to preach was first gained, dragging in its train freedom to print? I thank the clergy here present, as I reverence their predecessors, who did not so far forget their country in their immediate profession as to deem it duty to separate themselves from the struggle of '76,—the Mayhews and Coopers, who remembered they were citizens before they were clergymen.

Mr. Chairman, from the bottom of my heart I thank that brave little band at Alton for resisting. We must remember that Lovejoy had fled from city to city,—suffered the destruction of three presses patiently. At length he took counsel with friends, men of character, of tried integrity, of wide views, of Christian principle. They thought the crisis had come: it was full time to assert the laws. They saw around them, not a community like our own, of fixed habits, of character moulded and settled, but one "in the gristle, not yet hardened into the bone of manhood." The people there, children of our older States, seem to have forgotten the blood-tried principles of their fathers the moment they lost sight of our New England hills. Something was to be done to show them the priceless value of the freedom of the press, to bring back and set right their wandering and confused ideas. He and his advisers looked out on a community, staggering like a drunken man, indifferent to their rights and confused in their feelings. Deaf to argument, haply they might be stunned into sobriety. They saw that of which we cannot judge, the *necessity* of resistance. Insulted law called for it. Public opinion, fast hastening on the downward course, must be arrested.

Does not the event show they judged rightly? Absorbed in a thousand trifles, how has the nation all at once come to a stand? Men begin, as in 1776 and 1640, to discuss principles, to weigh characters, to find out where they are. Haply we may awake before we are borne over the precipice.

I am glad, Sir, to see this crowded house. It is good for us to be here. When Liberty is in danger, Faneuil Hall has the right, it is her duty, to strike the key-note for these United States. I am glad, for one reason, that remarks such as those to which I have alluded have been uttered here. The passage of these resolutions, in spite of this opposition, led by the Attorney-General of the Commonwealth, will show more clearly, more decisively, the deep indignation with which Boston regards this outrage.

Ralph Waldo Emerson

The American Scholar (1837)

For over a century and a half, from the first settlements until the very eve of the Revolution, colonists tended to think of themselves as Englishmen, often arguing for the same rights that Englishmen had back in the Mother Country. During this time, however, a gradual process of transformation was at work, turning the British in America into Americans. Political separation, of course, did not complete the task, and Americans continued to struggle with their own definition of themselves.

One of the boldest and most eloquent statements of what it meant to be an American came from a lecturer and author, a former minister, a man who was to become the preeminent philosophical and literary voice of the nineteenth century, Ralph Waldo Emerson.

Emerson was born in Boston in 1803 and attended Harvard, where his dislike of mathematics and Greek and his aversion to rote memorization led him to place thirtieth out of a class of 59. Perhaps his most significant education came from his own reading of the great literary and philosophical works of the past. He was, for a brief time, a teacher, attended Harvard Divinity School, and then, as a Unitarian minister, accepted the pastorate of the Second Church of Boston. After three years, in 1831, he resigned. The immediate cause was a theological issue—his unwillingness to administer the Last Supper as a sacrament—but he had felt uncomfortable with the restrictions imposed by his position for some time; he preferred the freedom to work, think, and lecture without intellectual restraint. He toured Europe, where he met and formed friendships with some of the leading literary figures of the time. After his return to Boston he devoted more of his time to study and to lecturing. In 1835 he moved to Concord, and it was in Concord that he was surrounded by creative, imaginative, philosophic intellects; he numbered among his friends Thoreau, Nathaniel Hawthorne, Bronson Alcott, and Margaret Fuller.

In 1836 Emerson published a small book of essays under the title *Nature*, which laid the groundwork for the school of thought with which Emerson and the Concord group was associated, Transcendentalism. Emerson's real introduction to public notice came a year later, however, when he was invited to deliver the annual Phi Beta Kappa address at Harvard. Frankly, not much was expected of Emerson. He was not the first choice of the organizers of the event, and some of the more distinguished members of the Harvard community didn't come to the lecture. No one seemed prepared for what was later to be called by Justice Oliver Wendell Holmes "the declaration of American intellectual independence," a call for Americans to use their own experience to create and evaluate their own literature. In "The American Scholar" Emerson advised the students of his time to seek "to know all . . . to dare all." Urging those who would seek to know and influence their own world to reject the "courtly Muses of Europe," Emerson declared: "We will walk on our own feet; we will work with our own hands; we will speak our own minds."

Mr. President and gentlemen,—I greet you on the recommencement of our literary year. Our anniversary is one of hope, and perhaps not enough of labor. We do not meet for games of strength or skill, for the recitation of histories, tragedies, and odes, like the ancient Greeks; for parliaments of love and poesy, like the Troubadours; nor for the advancement of science, like our contemporaries in the British and European capitals. Thus far our holiday has been simply a friendly sign of the survival of the love of letters amongst a people too busy to give to letters any more. As such it is precious as the sign of an indestructible instinct. Perhaps the time has already come when it ought to be and will be something else; when the sluggard intellect of this continent will look from under its iron lids and fill the postponed expectation of the world with something better than the exertions of mechanical skill. Our day of dependence, our long apprenticeship to the learning of other lands, draws to a close. The millions that around us are rushing into life cannot always be fed on the sere remains of foreign harvests. Events, actions arise, that must be sung, that will sing themselves. Who can doubt that poetry will revive and lead in a new age, as the star in the constellation Harp, which now flames in our zenith, astronomers announce, shall one day be the pole-star for a thousand years?

In this hope I accept the topic which not only usage, but the nature of our association, seem to prescribe to this day—the American Scholar. Year by year we come up hither to read one more chapter of his biography. Let us inquire what light new days and events have thrown on his character and his hopes.

It is one of those fables which, out of an unknown antiquity, convey an unlooked-for-wisdom, that the gods in the beginning divided Man into men, that he might be more helpful to himself; just as the hand was divided into fingers, the better to answer its end.

The old fable covers a doctrine ever new and sublime; that there is One Man—present to all particular men only partially, or through one faculty; and that you must take the whole society to find the whole man. Man is not a farmer, or professor, or an engineer, but he is all. Man is priest, and scholar, and statesman, and producer, and soldier. In the divided or social state these functions are parcelled out to individuals, each of whom aims to do his stint of the joint work, whilst each other performs his. The fable implies, that the individual to possess himself must sometimes return from his own labor to embrace all the other laborers. But unfortunately, this original unit, this fountain of power, has been so distributed to multitudes, has been so minutely subdivided and peddled out, that it is spilled into drops, and cannot be gathered. The state of society is one in which the members have suffered amputation from the trunk, and strut about, so many walking monsters—a good finger, a neck, a stomach, an elbow, but never a man.

Man is thus metamorphosed into a thing, into many things. The planter, who is Man sent out into the field to gather food, is seldom cheered by any idea of the true dignity of his ministry. He sees his bushel and his cart, and nothing beyond, and sinks into the farmer, instead of Man on the farm. The tradesman scarcely ever gives an ideal worth to his work, but is ridden by the routine of his craft and the soul is subject to dollars. The priest becomes a form; the attorney, a statute book; the mechanic, a machine; the sailor, a rope of a ship.

In this distribution of functions the scholar is the delegated intellect. In the right state he is Man Thinking. In the degenerate state, when the victim of society, he tends to become a mere thinker, or, still worse, the parrot of other men's thinking.

In this view of him, as Man Thinking, the theory of his office is contained. Him nature solicits with all her placid, all her monitory pictures; him the past instructs; him the future invites. Is not, indeed, every man a student, and do not all things exist for the student's behoof? And finally is not the true scholar the only true master? But the old oracle said, "All things have two handles: beware of the wrong one." In life too often the scholar errs with mankind and forfeits his privilege. Let us see him in his school and consider him in reference to the main influences he receives.

I. The first in time and the first in importance of the influences upon the mind is that of nature. Every day, the sun; and after sunset, night and her stars. Ever the winds blow; ever the grass grows. Every day men and women conversing, beholding and beholden. The scholar is he of all men whom this spectacle most engages. He must settle its value in his mind. What is nature to him? There is never a beginning, there is never an end to the inexplicable continuity of this web of God, but always circular power returning into itself. Therein it resembles his own spirit, whose beginning, whose ending, he never can find—so entire, so boundless. Far, too, as her splendors shine, system on system shooting like rays, upward, downward, without centre, without circumference—in the mass and in the particle nature hastens to render account of herself to the mind. Classification begins. To the young mind everything is individual, stands by itself. By and by it finds how to join two things and see in them one nature, then three, then three thousand; and so, tyrannized over by its own unifying instinct, it goes on tying things together, diminishing anomalies, discovering roots running under ground, whereby contrary and remote things cohere and flower out from one stem. It presently learns that since the dawn of history there has been a constant accumulation and classifying of facts. But what is classification but the perceiving that these objects are not chaotic and are not foreign, but have a law which is also a law of the human mind? The astronomer discovers that geometry, a pure abstraction of the human mind, is the measure of planetary motion. The chemist finds proportions and intelligible method throughout matter; and science is nothing but the finding of analogy, identity, in the most remote parts. The ambitious soul sits down before each refractory fact; one after another, reduces all strange constitutions, all new powers, to their class and their law, and goes on forever to animate the last fibre of organization, the outskirts of nature, by insight.

Thus to him, to this school-boy under the bending dome of day, is suggested that he and it proceed from one root; one is leaf and one is flower; relation, sympathy, stirring in every vein. And what is that Root? Is not that the soul of his soul?—a thought too bold,—a dream too wild. Yet when this spiritual light shall have revealed the law of more earthly natures,—when he has learned to worship the soul, and to see that the natural philosophy that now is, is only the first gropings of its gigantic hand, he shall look forward to an ever expanding knowledge as to a becoming creator. He shall see that nature is the opposite of the soul, answering to it part for part. One is seal and one is print. Its beauty is the beauty of his own mind. Its laws are the laws of his own mind. Nature then becomes to him the measure of his attainments. So much of nature as he is ignorant of, so much of his own mind does he not yet possess. And in fine the ancient precept, "Know thyself," and the modern precept, "Study nature," become at last one maxim.

II. The next great influence into the spirit of the scholar is the mind of the Past,—in whatever form, whether of literature, of art, of institutions, that mind is inscribed. Books are the best type of the influence of the past, and perhaps we shall get at the truth,—learn the amount of this influence more conveniently,—by considering their value alone.

The theory of books is noble. The scholar of the first age received into him the world around; brooded thereon; gave it the new arrangement of his own mind and uttered it again. It came into him, life; it went out from him, truth. It came to him, short-lived actions; it went out from him, immortal thoughts. It came to him, business; it went from him, poetry. It was dead fact; now, it is quick thought. It can stand and it can go. It now endures, it now flies, it now inspires. Precisely in proportion to the depth of mind from which it issued, so high does it soar, so long does it sing.

Or, I might say, it depends on how far the process had gone, of transmuting life into truth. In proportion to the completeness of the distillation, so will the purity and imperishableness of the product be. But none is quite perfect. As no air-pump can by any means make a perfect vacuum, so neither can any artist entirely exclude the conventional, the local, the perishable from his book, or write a book of pure thought, that shall be as efficient, in all respects, to a remote posterity, as to contemporaries, or rather to the second age. Each age, it is found, must write its own books; or rather, each generation for the next succeeding. The books of an older period will not fit this.

Yet hence arises a grave mischief. The sacredness which attaches to the act of creation,—the act of thought,—is transferred to the record. The poet chanting, was felt to be a divine man: henceforth the chant is divine also. The writer was a just and wise spirit: henceforward it is settled, the book is perfect; as love of the hero corrupts into worship of his statue. Instantly the book becomes noxious: the guide is a tyrant. The sluggish and perverted mind of the multitude, slow to open to the incursions of Reason, having once so opened, having once received this book, stands upon it and makes an outcry if it is disparaged. Colleges are built on it. Books are written on it by thinkers, not by Man Thinking; by men of talent, that is, who start wrong, who set out from accepted dogmas, not from their own sight of principles. Meek young men grow up in libraries, believing it their duty to accept the views which Cicero, which Locke, which Bacon have given, forgetful that Cicero, Locke, and Bacon were only young men in libraries when they wrote these books.

Hence, instead of Man Thinking, we have the bookworm. Hence, the book-learned class who value books, as such; not as related to nature and the human constitution, but as making a sort of Third Estate with the world and the soul. Hence, the restorers of readings, the emendators, the bibliomaniacs of all degrees.

Books are the best of things, well used; abused, among the worst. What is the right use! What is the one end, which all means go to effect? They are for nothing but to inspire. I had better never see a book than to be warped by its attraction clean out of my own orbit and made a satellite instead of a system. The one thing in the world of value is the active soul. This every man is entitled to; this every man contains within him, although, in almost all men, obstructed, and as yet unborn. The soul active sees absolute truth; and utters truth, or creates. In this action, it is genius; not the privilege of here and there a favorite, but the sound estate of every man. In its essence, it is progressive. The book, the college, the school of art, the institution of any kind, stop with some past utterance of genius. This is good, say they,—let us hold by this. They pin me down. They look backward and not forward. But genius looks forward: the eyes of man are set in his forehead, not in his hindhead; man hopes, genius creates. Whatever talents may be, if the man create not, the pure efflux of the Deity is not his; cinders and smoke there maybe, but not yet flame. There are creative manners, there are creative actions, and creative words; manners, actions, words, that is, indicative of no custom or authority, but springing spontaneous from the mind's own sense of good and fair.

On the other part, instead of being its own seer, let it receive from another mind its truth, though it were in torrents of light, without periods of solitude, inquest, and self-recovery, and a fatal disservice is done. Genius is always sufficiently the enemy of genius by over-influence. The literature of every nation bear me witness. The English dramatic poets have Shakspearized now for two hundred years.

Undoubtedly there is a right way of reading, so it be sternly subordinated. Man Thinking must not be subdued by his instruments. Books are for the scholar's idle times. When he can read God directly, the hour is too precious to be wasted in other men's transcripts of their readings. But when the intervals of darkness come, as come they must,—when the sun is hid, and the stars withdraw their shining,—we repair to the lamps which were kindled by their ray, to guide our steps to the East again, where the dawn is. We hear, that we may speak. The Arabian proverb says, "A fig-tree, looking on a fig-tree, becomes fruitful."

It is remarkable, the character of the pleasure we derive from the best books. They impress us with the conviction, that one nature wrote and the same reads. We read the verses of one of the great English poets, of Chaucer, of Marvell, of Dryden, with the most modern joy,—with a pleasure, I mean, which is in great part caused by the abstraction of all time from their verses. There is some awe mixed with the joy of our surprise, when this poet, who lived in some past world, two or three hundred years ago, says that which lies close to my own soul, that which I also had wellnigh thought and said. But for the evidence thence afforded to the philosophical doctrine of the identity of all minds, we should suppose some pre-established harmony, some foresight of souls that were to be, and some preparation of stores for their future wants, like the fact observed in insects, who lay up food before death for the young grub they shall never see.

I would not be hurried by any love of system, by any exaggeration of instincts, to underrate the Book. We all know that, as the human body can be nourished on any food, though it were boiled grass and the broth of shoes, so the human mind can be fed by any knowledge. And great and heroic men have existed who had almost no other information than by the printed page. I only would say, that it needs a strong head to bear that diet. One must be an inventor to read well. As the proverb says, "He that would bring home the wealth of the Indies, must carry out the wealth of the Indies." There is, then, creative reading as well as creative writing. When the mind is braced by labor and invention, the page of whatever book we read becomes luminous with manifold allusion. Every sentence is doubly significant, and the sense of our author is as broad as the world. We then see, what is always true, that, as the seer's hour of vision is short and rare among heavy days and months, so is its record, perchance, the least part of his volume. The discerning will read, in his Plato or Shakespeare, only that least part,—only the authentic utterances of the oracle; all the rest he rejects, were it never so many times Plato's and Shakespeare's.

Of course there is a portion of reading quite indispensable to a wise man. History and exact science he must learn by laborious reading. Colleges, in like manner, have their indispensable office,—to teach elements. But they can only highly serve us when they aim not to drill, but to create; when they gather from far every ray of various genius to their hospitable halls, and, by the concentrated fires, set the hearts of their youth on flame. Thought and knowledge are natures in which apparatus and pretension avail nothing. Gowns and pecuniary foundations, though of towns of gold, can never countervail the least sentence or syllable of wit. Forget this, and our American colleges will recede in their public importance, whilst they grow richer every year.

III. There goes in the world a notion that the scholar should be a recluse, a valetudinarian,—as unfit for any handiwork or public labor as a penknife for an axe. The so-called "practical men" sneer at speculative men as if, because they speculate or see, they could do nothing. I have heard it said that the clergy,—who are always, more universally than any other class, the scholars of their day,—are addressed as women; that the rough, spontaneous conversation of men they do not hear, but only a mincing and diluted speech. They are often virtually disfrancised; and, indeed, there are advocates for their celibacy. As far as this is true of the studious classes, it is not just and wise. Action is with the scholar subordinate, but it is essential. Without it, he is not yet man. Without it, thought can never ripen into truth. Whilst the world hangs before the eye as a cloud of beauty, we cannot even see its beauty. Inaction is cowardice, but there can be no scholar without the heroic mind. The preamble of thought, the transition through which it passes from the unconscious to the conscious, is action. Only so much do I know as I have lived. Instantly, we know whose words are loaded with life, and whose not.

The world,—this shadow of the soul, or *other me*, lies wide around. Its attractions are the keys which unlock my thoughts and make me acquainted with myself. I run eagerly into this resounding tumult. I grasp the hands of those next me, and take my place in the ring to suffer and to work, taught by an instinct, that so shall the dumb abyss be vocal with speech. I pierce its order; I dissipate its fear; I dispose of it within the circuit of my expanding life. So much only of life as I know by experience, so much of the wilderness have I vanquished and planted, or so far have I extended my being, my dominion. I do not see how any man can afford, for the sake of his nerves and his nap, to spare any action in which he can partake. It is pearls and rubies to his discourse. Drudgery, calamity, exasperation, want, are instructors in eloquence and wisdom. The true scholar grudges every opportunity of action past by as a loss of power.

It is the raw material out of which the intellect moulds her splendid products. A strange process too, this, by which experience is converted into thought, as a mulberry leaf is converted into satin. The manufacture goes forward at all hours.

The actions and events of our childhood and youth are now matters of calmest observation. They lie like fair pictures in the air. Not so with our recent actions,—with the business which we now have in hand. On this we are quite unable to speculate. Our affections as yet circulate through it. We no more feel or know it than we feel the feet or the hand or the brain of our body. The new deed is yet a part of life,—remains for a time immersed in our unconscious life. In some contemplative hour, it detaches itself from the life like a ripe fruit, to become a thought of the mind. Instantly, it is raised, transfigured; the corruptible has put on incorruption. Henceforth it is an object of beauty, however base its origin and neighborhood. Observe, too, the impossibility of antedating this act. In its grub state it cannot fly, it cannot shine, it is a dull grub. But suddenly, without observation, the selfsame thing unfurls beautiful wings and is an angel of wisdom. So is there no fact, no event in our private history, which shall not, sooner or later, lose its adhesive, inert form, and astonish us by soaring from our body into the empyrean. Cradle and infancy, school and playground, the fear of boys, and dogs, and ferules, the love of little maids and berries, and many another fact that once filled the whole sky, are gone already; friend and relative, profession and party, town and country, nation and world, must also soar and sing.

Of course he who has put forth his total strength in fit actions has the richest return of wisdom. I will not shut myself out of this globe of action and transplant an oak into a flower-pot, there to hunger and pine; nor trust the revenue of some single faculty, and exhaust one vein of thought, much like those Savoyards, who, getting their livelihood by carving shepherds, shepherdesses, and smoking Dutchmen, for all Europe, went out one day to the mountain to find stock and discovered that they had whittled up the last of their pine-trees. Authors we have in numbers who have written out their vein, and who, moved by a commendable prudence, sail for Greece or Palestine, follow the trapper into the prairie, or ramble around Algiers, to replenish their merchantable stock.

If it were only for a vocabulary, the scholar would be covetous of action. Life is our dictionary. Years are well spent in country labors; in town, in the insight into trades and manufactures; in frank intercourse with many men and women; in science; in art; to the one end of mastering in all their facts a language by which to illustrate and embody our perceptions. I learn immediately from any speaker how much he has already lived, through the poverty or the splendor of his speech. Life lies behind us as the quarry from whence we get titles and cope-stones for the masonry of to-day. This is the way to learn grammar. Colleges and books only copy the language which the field and the work-yard made.

But the final value of action, like that of books, and better than books, is, that it is a resource. That great principle of Undulation in nature that shows itself in the inspiring and expiring of the breath; in desire and satiety; in the ebb and flow of the sea; in day and night; in heat and cold; and as yet more deeply ingrained in every atom and every fluid, is known to us under the name of Polarity,—these "fits of easy transmission and reflection," as Newton called them, are the law of nature because they are the law of spirit.

The mind now thinks; now acts; and each fit reproduces the other. When the artist has exhausted his materials, when the fancy no longer paints, when thoughts are no longer apprehended, and books are a weariness,—he has always the resource to live. Character is higher than intellect. Thinking is the function. Living is the functionary. The stream retreats to its source. A great soul will be strong to live, as well as strong to think. Does he lack organ or medium to impart his truths? He can still fall back on this elemental force of living them. This is a total act. Thinking is a partial act. Let the grandeur of justice shine in his affairs. Let the beauty of affection cheer his lowly roof. Those "far from fame," who dwell and act with him, will feel the force of his constitution in the doings and passages of the day better than it can be measured by any public and designed display. Time shall teach him that the scholar loses no hour which the man lives. Herein he unfolds the sacred germ of his instinct, screened from influence. What is lost in seemliness is gained in strength. Not out of those on whom systems of education have exhausted their culture comes the helpful giant to destroy the old or to build the new, but out of unhandselled savage nature, out of terrible Druids and berserkirs, come at last Alfred and Shakespeare.

I hear, therefore, with joy whatever is beginning to be said of the dignity and necessity of labor to every citizen. There is virtue yet in the hoe and the spade, for learned as well as for unlearned hands. And labor is everywhere welcome; always we are invited to work; only be this limitation observed, that a man shall not for the sake of wider activity sacrifice any opinion to the popular judgments and modes of action.

I have now spoken of the education of the scholar by nature, by books, and by action. It remains to say somewhat of his duties.

They are such as become Man

Thinking. They may all be comprised in self-trust. The office of the scholar is to cheer, to raise, and to guide men by showing them facts amidst appearances. He plies the slow, unhonored, and unpaid task of observation. Flamsteed and Herschel, in their glazed observatories, may catalogue the stars with the praise of all men, and, the results being splendid and useful, honor is sure. But he, in his private observatory, cataloguing obscure and nebulous stars of the human mind, which as yet no man has thought of as such,—watching days and months, sometimes, for a few facts; correcting still his old records;—must relinquish display and immediate fame. In the long period of his preparation he must betray often an ignorance and shiftlessness in popular arts, incurring the disdain of the able who shoulder him aside. Long he must stammer in his speech; often forego the living for the dead. Worse yet, he must accept,—how often! poverty and solitude. For the ease and pleasure of treading the old road, accepting the fashions, the education, the religion of society, he takes the cross of making his own, and, of course, the self-accusation, the faint heart, the frequent uncertainty and loss of time, which are the nettles and tangling vines in the way of the self-relying and self-directed; and the state of virtual hostility in which he seems to stand to society, and especially to educated society. For all this loss and scorn, what offset? He is to find consolation in exercising the highest functions of human nature. He is one who raises himself from private considerations, and breathes and lives on public and illustrious thoughts. He is the world's eye. He is the world's heart. He is to resist the vulgar prosperity that retrogrades ever to barbarism, by preserving and communicating heroic sentiments, noble biographies, melodious verse, and the conclusions of history. Whatsoever oracles the human heart, in all emergencies, in all solemn hours, has uttered as its commentary on the world of actions,—these he shall receive and impart. And whatsoever new verdict Reason from her inviolable seat pronounces on the passing men and events of to-day,—this he shall hear and promulgate.

These being his functions, it becomes him to feel all confidence in himself, and to defer never to the popular cry. He and he only knows the world. The world of any moment is the merest appearance. Some great decorum, some fetish of a government, some ephemeral trade, or war, or man, is cried up by half mankind and cried down by the other half, as if all depended on this particular up and down. The odds are that the whole question is not worth the poorest thought which the scholar has lost in listening to the controversy. Let him not quit his belief that a popgun is a popgun, though the ancient and honorable of the earth affirm it to be the crack of doom. In silence, in steadiness, in severe abstraction, let him hold by himself; add observation to observation, patient of neglect, patient of reproach; and bide his own time,—happy enough, if he can satisfy himself alone, that this day he has seen something truly. Success treads on every right step. For the instinct is sure that prompts him to tell his brother what he thinks. He then learns that in going down into the streets of his own mind, he has descended into the secrets of all minds. He learns that he who has mastered any law in his private thoughts is master to that extent of all men whose language he speaks and of all into whose language his own can be translated. The poet, in utter solitude remembering his spontaneous thoughts and recording them, is found to have recorded that which men in crowded cities find true for them also. The orator distrusts at first the fitness of his frank confessions,—his want of knowledge of the persons he addresses,—until he finds that he is the complement of his hearers; that they drink his words because he fulfils for them their own nature; the deeper he dives into his privatest, secretest presentiment, to his wonder he finds this is the most acceptable, most public, and universally true. The people delight in it; the better part of every man feels, This is my music; this is myself.

In self-trust all the virtues are comprehended. Free should the scholar be,—free and brave. Free even to the definition of freedom, "without any hindrance that does not arise out of his own constitution." Brave; for fear is a thing which a scholar by his very function puts behind him. Fear always springs from ignorance. It is a shame to him if his tranquillity, amid dangerous times, arise from the presumption that, like children and women, his is a protected class; or if he seek a temporary peace by the diversion of his thoughts from politics or vexed questions, hiding his head like an ostrich in the flowering bushes, peeping into microscopes, and turning rhymes, as a boy whistles to keep his courage up. So is the danger a danger still; so is the fear worse. Manlike let him turn and face it. Let him look into its eye and search its nature, inspect its origin,—see the whelping of this lion, which lies no great way back; he will then find in himself a perfect comprehension of its nature and extent; he will have made his hands meet on the other side, and can henceforth defy it and pass on superior. The world is his who can see through its pretension. What deafness, what stone-blind custom, what overgrown error you behold is there only by sufferance,—by your sufferance. See it to be a lie, and you have already dealt it its mortal blow.

Yes, we are the cowed,—we the trustless. It is a mischievous notion that we are come late into nature; that the world was finished a long time ago. As the world was plastic and fluid in the hands of God, so it is ever to so much of his attributes as we bring to it. To ignorance and sin, it is flint. They adapt themselves to it as they may; but in proportion as man has anything in him divine, the firmament flows before him and takes his signet and form. Not he is great who can alter matter, but he who can alter my state of mind. They are the kings of the world who give the color of their present thought to all nature and all art, and persuade men by the cheerful serenity of their carrying the matter, that this thing which they do is the apple which the ages have desired to pluck, now at last ripe, and inviting nations to the harvest. The great man makes the great thing. Wherever Macdonald sits, there is the head of the table. Linnæus makes botany the most alluring of studies, and wins it from the farmer and the herb-woman; Davy, chemistry; and Cuvier, fossils. The day is always his who works in it with serenity and great aims. The unstable estimates of men crowd to him whose mind is filled with a truth, as the heaped waves of the Atlantic follow the moon.

For this self-trust, the reason is deeper than can be fathomed,—darker than can be enlightened. I might not carry with me the feeling of my audience in stating my own belief. But I have already shown the ground of my hope, in adverting to the doctrine that man is one. I believe man has been wronged; he has wronged himself. He has almost lost the light that can lead him back to his prerogatives. Men are become of no account. Men in history, men in the world of to-day are bugs, are spawn, and are called "the mass" and "the herd." In a century, in a millennium, one or two men; that is to say,—one or two approximations to the right state of every man. All the rest behold in the hero or the poet their own green and crude being,—ripened; yes, and are content to be less, so *that* may attain to its full stature. What a testimony,—full of grandeur, full of pity, is borne to the demands of his own nature, by the poor clansman, the poor partisan, who rejoices in the glory of his chief. The poor and the low find some amends to their immense moral capacity, for their acquiescence in a political and social inferiority. They are content to be brushed like flies from the path of a great person, so that justice shall be done by him to that common nature which is the dearest desire of all to see enlarged and glorified. They sun themselves in the great man's light, and feel it to be their own element. They cast the dignity of man from their downtrod selves upon the shoulders of a hero, and will perish to add one drop of blood to make that great heart beat, those giant sinews combat and conquer. He lives for us, and we live in him.

Men such as they are, very naturally seek money or power; and power because it is as good as money,—the "spoils," so called, "of office." And why not? for they aspire to the highest, and this, in their sleep-walking, they dream is highest. Wake them, and they shall quit the false good and leap to the true, and leave governments to clerks and desks. This revolution is to be wrought by the gradual domestication of the idea of Culture. The main enterprise of the world for splendor, for extent, is the upbuilding of a man. Here are the materials strown along the ground. The private life of one man shall be a more illustrious monarchy,—more formidable to its enemy, more sweet and serene in its influence to its friend, than any kingdom in history. For a man, rightly viewed, comprehendeth the particular natures of all men. Each philosopher, each bard, each actor, has only done for me, as by a delegate, what one day I can do for myself. The books which once we valued more than the apple of the eye we have quite exhausted. What is that but saying that we have come up with the point of view which the universal mind took through the eyes of one scribe; we have been that man, and have passed on. First, one; then, another; we drain all cisterns, and, waxing greater by all these supplies, we crave a better and more abundant food. The man has never lived that can feed us ever. The human mind cannot be enshrined in a person, who shall set a barrier on any one side to this unbounded, unboundable empire. It is one central fire, which, flaming now out of the lips of Etna, lightens the capes of Sicily; and, now out of the throat of Vesuvius, illuminates the towers and vineyards of Naples. It is one light which beams out of a thousand stars. It is one soul which animates all men.

But I have dwelt perhaps tediously upon this abstraction of the Scholar. I ought not to delay longer to add what I have to say, of nearer reference to the time and to this country.

Historically, there is thought to be a difference in the ideas which predominate over successive epochs, and there are data for marking the genius of the Classic, of the Romantic, and now of the Reflective or Philosophical age. With the views I have intimated of the oneness or the identity of the mind through all individuals, I do not much dwell on these differences. In fact, I believe each individual passes through all three. The boy is a Greek; the youth, romantic; the adult, reflective. I deny not, however, that a revolution in the leading idea may be distinctly enough traced.

Our age is bewailed as the age of Introversion. Must that needs be evil? We, it seems, are critical; we are embarrassed with second thoughts; we cannot enjoy anything for hankering to know whereof the pleasure consists; we are lined with eyes; we see with our feet; the time is infected with Hamlet's unhappiness—

> Sicklied o'er with the pale cast of thought.

Is it so bad then? Sight is the last thing to be pitied. Would we be blind? Do we fear lest we should outsee nature and God, and drink truth dry? I look upon the discontent of the literary class as a mere announcement of the fact that they find themselves not in the state of mind of their fathers, and regret the coming state as untried, as a boy dreads the water before he has learned that he can swim. If there is any period one would desire to be born in, is it not the age of Revolution; when the old and the new stand side by side, and admit of being compared; when the energies of all men are searched by fear and by hope; when the historic glories of the old can be compensated by the rich possibilities of the new era? This time, like all times, is a very good one, if we but know what to do with it.

I read with joy some of the auspicious signs of the coming days, as they glimmer already through poetry and art, through philosophy and science, through church and state.

One of these signs is the fact that the same movement which effected the elevation of what was called the lowest class in the state assumed in literature a very marked and as benign an aspect. Instead of the sublime and beautiful, the near, the low, the common, was explored and poetized. That which had been negligently trodden under foot by those who were harnessing and provisioning themselves for long journeys into far countries is suddenly found to be richer than all foreign parts. The literature of the poor, the feelings of the child, the philosophy of the street, the meaning of household life, are the topics of the time. It is a great stride. It is a sign, is it not? of new vigor when the extremities are made active, when currents of warm life run into the hands and the feet. I ask not for the great, the remote, the romantic, what is doing in Italy or Arabia, what is Greek art or Provencal minstrelsy; I embrace the common; I explore and sit at the feet of the familiar, the low. Give me insight into to-day, and you may have the antique and future worlds. What would we really know the meaning of? The meal in the firkin, the milk in the pan, the ballad in the street, the news of the boat, the glance of the eye, the form and the gait of the body; show me the ultimate reason of these matters; show me the sublime presence of the highest spiritual cause lurking, as always it does lurk, in these suburbs and extremities of nature; let me see every trifle bristling with the polarity that ranges it instantly on an eternal law; and the shop, the plough, and the ledger, referred to the like cause by which light undulates and poets sing—and the world lies no longer a dull miscellany and lumber-room, but has form and order; there is no trifle; there is no puzzle; but one design unites and animates the farthest pinnacle and the lowest trench.

This idea has inspired the genius of Goldsmith, Burns, Cowper, and, in a newer time, of Goethe, Wordsworth, and Carlyle. This idea they have differently followed and with various success. In contrast with their writing, the style of Pope, of Johnson, of Gibbon, looks cold and pedantic. This writing is blood-warm. Man is surprised to find that things near are not less beautiful and wondrous than things remote. The near explains the far. The drop is a small ocean. A man is related to all nature. This perception of the worth of the vulgar is fruitful in discoveries. Goethe, in this very thing the most modern of the moderns, has shown us, as none ever did, the genius of the ancients.

There is one man of genius who has done much for this philosophy of life, whose literary value has never yet been rightly estimated; I mean Emanuel Swedenborg. The most imaginative of men, yet writing with the precision of a mathematician, he endeavored to engraft a purely philosophical Ethics on the popular Christianity of his time. Such an attempt, of course, must have difficulty which no genius could surmount. But he saw and showed the connection between nature and the affections of the soul. He pierced the emblematic or spiritual character of the visible, audible, tangible world. Especially did his shade-loving muse hover over and interpret the lower parts of nature; he showed the mysterious bond that allies moral evil to the foul material forms, and has given in epical parables a theory of insanity, of beasts, of unclean and fearful things.

Another sign of our times, also marked by an analogous political movement, is the new importance given to the single person. Everything that tends to insulate the individual—to surround him with barriers of natural respect, so that each man shall feel the world is his, and man shall treat with man as a sovereign State with a sovereign State—tends to true union as well as greatness. "I learned," said the melancholy Pestalozzi, "that no man in God's wide earth is either willing or able to help any other man." Help must come from the bosom alone. The scholar is that man who must take up into himself all the ability of the time, all the contributions of the past, all the hopes of the future. He must be an university of knowledges. If there be one lesson more than another which should pierce his ear, it is, The world is nothing, the man is all; in yourself is the law of all nature, and you know not yet how a globule of sap ascends; in yourself slumbers the whole of Reason; it is for you to know all, it is for you to dare all. Mr. President and gentlemen, this confidence in the unsearched might of man belongs, by all motives, by all prophecy, by all preparation, to the American Scholar. We have listened too long to the courtly muses of Europe. The spirit of the American freeman is already suspected to be timid, imitative, tame. Public and private avarice make the air we breathe thick and fat. The scholar is decent, indolent, complaisant. See already the tragic consequence. The mind of this country, taught to aim at low objects, eats upon itself. There is no work for any but the decorous and the complaisant. Young men of the fairest promise, who begin life upon our shores, inflated by the mountain winds, shined upon by all the stars of God, find the earth below not in unison with these, but are hindered from action by the disgust which the principles on which business is managed inspire, and turn drudges, or die of disgust—some of them suicides. What is the remedy? They did not yet see, and thousands of young men as hopeful now crowding to the barriers for the career, do not yet see that if the single man plant himself indomitably on his instincts, and there abide, the huge world will come round to him. Patience—patience; with the shades of all the good and great for company; and for solace, the perspective of your own infinite life; and for work, the study and the communication of principles, the making those instincts prevalent, the conversion of the world. Is it not the chief disgrace in the world not to be an unit; not to be reckoned one character; not to yield that peculiar fruit which each man was created to bear, but to be reckoned in the gross, in the hundred, or the thousand, of the party, the section, to which we belong; and our opinion predicted geographically, as the north, or the south! Not so, brothers and friends; please God ours shall not be so! We will walk on our own feet; we will work with our own hands; we will speak our own minds. The study of letters shall be no longer a name for pity, for doubt, and for sensual indulgence. The dread of man and the love of man shall be a wall of defence and a wreath of joy around all. A nation of men will for the first time exist, because each believes himself inspired by the Divine Soul, which also inspires all men.

Frederick Douglass

American Slavery (1850)

The institution of slavery gradually took root in colonial America, with the importation of slaves growing throughout the eighteenth century. Following the invention of the cotton gin in 1793, the output of cotton was dramatically increased and, as the cotton kingdom expanded, slaveholding became concentrated in the great plantations that formed an economic mainstay of the South. Along with the growth of slavery, however, went increasing concern for the moral and political issues that it raised. Slavery had long troubled the American mind. The first American antislavery society was formed in 1775 by Quakers, who had voiced their opposition to slavery as unchristian as early as 1688. Thomas Jefferson's catalogue of Royal offences included an attack on the King for disallowing laws to prohibit the slave trade, but, upon the insistence of Southern delegates, this passage was deleted from the final draft of the Declaration of Independence.

It was in the first half of the nineteenth century, however, that the argument over slavery grew bitter and intense. On January 1, 1831, William Lloyd Garrison published the first issue of *The Liberator* and established himself as the leading voice of radical abolitionism with his declaration, "I will not retreat a single inch—and I will be heard." In the same year a bloody slave insurrection led by Nat Turner in Virginia terrified the South. When a Virginia convention met later that year to consider the slave question, every proposal for emancipation was defeated, and soon restrictive slave codes were passed in states throughout the South.

Abolitionists took the rhetorical offensive. Garrison's New England Anti-Slavery Society, and the American and Foreign Antislavery Society launched by Theodore Weld, sponsored meetings and conventions and sent speakers to spread the abolitionist message throughout the country. Defenders of slavery produced their own tracts purporting to show that slavery was benign, even beneficial to blacks, who were portrayed as inferior to whites. Throughout the South, severe measures were taken to see that no abolitionist literature or lecturers were allowed within its borders.

In 1841, in Nantucket, a convention of the Massachusetts Anti-Slavery Society was addressed by a black speaker named Frederick Douglass, who so impressed the gathering that he was engaged as an antislavery lecturer. Over the course of the next twenty years Douglass, a former slave who had escaped from his Baltimore master in 1838, became living refutation of the argument for black inferiority. He published his autobiography, edited an abolitionist newspaper, *The North Star,* and carried out a successful lecture tour of England. But it was his speaking throughout the North, often under the most threatening conditions, to hostile, ugly crowds that established him as one of the most significant voices raised against the evils of slavery.

His speech in Rochester, New York, in 1850 was delivered to a generally sympathetic audience, the first lecture in a series on slavery. It was given against the backdrop of the momentous debate in Congress that had produced, that year, the Great Compromise. Among other things, the Compromise of 1850 strengthened the Fugitive Slave Law, anathema to Northern abolitionists. The political settlement of 1850 did not resolve the deeper moral issues; this situation led Douglass to conclude that "While this nation is guilty of the enslavement of three millions of innocent men and women, it is . . . idle to think of having a sound and lasting peace."

I come before you this evening to deliver the first lecture of a course which I purpose to give in this city, during the present winter, on the subject of American Slavery.

I make this announcement with no feelings of self-sufficiency. If I do not mistake my own emotions, they are such as result from a profound sense of my incompetency to do justice to the task which I have just announced, and now entered upon.

If any, then, demand of me why I speak, I plead as my apology, the fact that abler and more eloquent men have failed to speak, or what, perhaps, is more true, and therefore more strong, such men have spoken only on the wrong side of the question, and have thus thrown their influence against the cause of liberty, humanity and benevolence.

There are times in the experience of almost every community, when even the humblest member thereof may properly presume to teach—when the wise and great ones, the appointed leaders of the prople, exert their powers of mind to complicate, mystify, entangle and obscure the simple truth—when they exert the noblest gifts which heaven has vouchsafed to man to mislead the popular mind, and to corrupt the public heart,—*then* the humblest may stand forth and be excused for opposing even his weakness to the torrent of evil.

That such a state of things exists in this

community, I have abundant evidence. I learn it from the Rochester press, from the Rochester pulpit, and in my intercourse with the people of Rochester. Not a day passes over me that I do not meet with apparently good men, who utter sentiments in respect to this subject which would do discredit to savages. They speak of the enslavement of their fellow-men with an indifference and coldness which might be looked for only in men hardened by the most atrocious and villainous crimes.

The fact is, we are in the midst of a great struggle. The public mind is widely and deeply agitated; and bubbling up from its perturbed waters, are many and great impurities, whose poisonous miasma demands a constant antidote.

Whether the contemplated lectures will in any degree contribute towards answering this demand, time will determine.

Of one thing, however, I can assure my hearers—that I come up to this work at the call of duty, and with an honest desire to promote the happiness and well-being of every member of this community, as well as to advance the emancipation of every slave.

The audience will pardon me if I say one word more by way of introduction. It is my purpose to give this subject a calm, candid and faithful discussion. I shall not aim to shock nor to startle my hearers; but to convince their judgment and to secure their sympathies for the enslaved. I shall aim to be as stringent as truth, and as severe as justice; and if at any time I shall fail of this, and do injustice in any respect, I shall be most happy to be set right by any gentleman who shall hear me, subject, of course to order and decorum. I shall deal, during these lectures, alike with individuals and institutions—men shall no more escape me than things. I shall have occasion, at times, to be even personal, and to rebuke sin in high places. I shall not hesitate to arraign either priests or politicians, church or state, and to measure all by the standard of justice, and in the light of truth. I shall not forget to deal with the unrighteous spirit of *caste* which prevails in this community; and I shall give particular attention to the recently enacted fugitive slave bill. I shall keep my eye upon the Congress which is to commence to-morrow, and fully inform myself as to its proceedings. In a word, the whole subject of slavery, in all its bearings, shall have a full and impartial discussion.

A very slight acquaintance with the history of American slavery is sufficient to show that it is an evil of which it will be difficult to rid this country. It is not the creature of a moment, which to-day is, and to-morrow is not; it is not a pigmy, which a slight blow may demolish; it is no youthful upstart, whose impertinent pratings may be silenced by a dignified contempt. No: it is an evil of gigantic proportions, and of long standing.

Its origin in this country dates back to the landing of the pilgrims on Plymouth rock.—It was here more than two centuries ago. The first spot poisoned by its leprous presence, was a small plantation in Virginia. The slaves, at that time, numbered only twenty. They have now increased to the frightful number of three millions; and from that narrow plantation, they are now spread over by far the largest half of the American Union. Indeed, slavery forms an important part of the entire history of the American people. Its presence may be seen in all American affairs. It has become interwoven with all American institutions, and has anchored itself in the very soil of the American Constitution. It has thrown its paralysing arm over freedom of speech, and the liberty of the press; and has created for itself morals and manners favorable to its own continuance. It has seduced the church, corrupted the pulpit, and brought the powers of both into degrading bondage; and now, in the pride of its power, it even threatens to bring down that grand political edifice, the American Union, unless every member of this republic shall so far disregard his conscience and his God as to yield to its infernal behests.

That must be a powerful influence which can truly be said to govern a nation; and that slavery governs the American people, is indisputably true. If there were any doubt on this point, a few plain questions (it seems to me) could not fail to remove it. *What* power has given this nation its Presidents for more than fifty years? *Slavery*. What power is that to which the present aspirants to presidential honors are bowing? *Slavery*. We may call it "Union," "Constitution," "Harmony," or "American institutions," that to which such men as Cass, Dickinson, Webster, Clay and other distinguished men of this country, are devoting their energies, is nothing more nor less than American slavery. It is for this that they are writing letters, making speeches, and promoting the holding of great mass meetings, professedly in favor of "*the Union*." These men know the service most pleasing to their master, and that which is most likely to be richly rewarded. Men may "serve God for nought," as did Job; but he who serves the devil has an eye to his reward. "Patriotism," "obedience to the law," "prosperity to the country," have come to mean, in the mouths of these distinguished statesmen, a mean and servile acquiescence in the most flagitious and profligate legislation in favor of slavery. I might enlarge here on this picture of slave power, and tell of its influence upon the press in the free States, and upon the condition and rights of the free colored people of the North; but I forbear for the present.—Enough has been said, I trust, to convince all that the abolition of this evil will require time, energy, zeal, perserverance and patience; that it will require fidelity, a martyr-like spirit of self-sacrifice, and a firm reliance on Him who has declared Himself to be "*the God of the oppressed*." Having said thus much upon the power and prevalence of slavery, allow me to speak of the nature of slavery itself; and here I can speak, in part, from experience—I can speak with the authority of positive knowledge. . . .

First of all, I will state, as well as I can, the legal and social relation of master and slave. A master is one (to speak in the vocabulary of the Southern States) who claims and exercises a right of property in the person of a fellow man. This he does with the force of the law and the sanction of Southern religion. The law gives the master absolute power over the slave. He may work him, flog him, hire him out, sell him, and, in certain contingencies, *kill* him, with perfect impunity. The slave is a human being, divested of all rights—reduced to the level of a brute—a mere "chattel" in the eye of the law—placed beyond the circle of human brotherhood—cut off from his kind—his name, which the "recording angel" may have enrolled in heaven, among the blest, is impiously inserted in a *master's ledger*, with horses, sheep and swine. In law, the slave has no wife, no children, no country, and no home. He can own nothing, possess nothing, acquire nothing, but what must belong to another. To eat the fruit of his own toil, to clothe his person with the work of his own hands, is considered stealing. He toils that another may reap the fruit; he is industrious that another may live in idleness; he eats unbolted meal, that another may eat the bread of fine flour; he labors in chains at home, under a burning sun and a biting lash, that another may ride in ease and splendor abroad; he lives in ignorance, that another may be educated; he is abused, that another may be exalted; he rests his toil-worn limbs on the cold, damp ground, that another may repose on the softest pillow; he is clad in coarse and tattered raiment, that another may be arrayed in purple and fine linen; he is sheltered only by the wretched hovel, that a master may dwell in a magnificent mansion; and to this condition he is bound down as by an arm of iron.

From this monstrous relation, there springs an unceasing stream of most revolting cruelties. The very accompaniments of the slave system, stamp it as the offspring of hell itself. To ensure good behavior, the slaveholder relies on *the whip*; to induce proper humility, he relies on *the whip*; to rebuke what he is pleased to term insolence, he relies on *the whip*; to supply the place of wages, as an incentive to toil, he relies on *the whip*; to bind down the spirit of the slave, to imbrute and to destroy his manhood, he relies on *the whip*, the chain, the gag, the thumb-screw, the pillory, the bowie-knife, the pistol, and the bloodhound. These are the necessary and unvarying accompaniments of the system. . . .

Nor is slavery more adverse to the conscience than it is to the mind.

This is shown by the fact that in every State of the American Union, where slavery exists, except the State of Kentucky, there are laws, *absolutely* prohibitory of education among the slaves. The crime of teaching a slave to read is punishable with severe fines and imprisonment, and, in some instances, with *death itself*.

Nor are the laws respecting this matter, a dead letter. Cases may occur in which they are disregarded, and a few instances may be found where slaves may have learned to read; but such are isolated cases, and only prove the rule. The great mass of slaveholders look upon education among the slaves as utterly subversive of the slave system. I *well* remember when my mistress first announced to my master that she had discovered that I could read. His face colored at once, with surprise and chagrin. He said that "I was ruined, that my value as a slave was destroyed; that a slave should know nothing but to obey his master; that to give a Negro an inch would lead him to take an ell; that having learned how to read, I would soon want to know how to write; and that, bye and bye, I would be running away." I think my audience will bear witness to the correctness of this philosophy, and to the literal fulfilment of this prophecy.

It is perfectly well understood at the South that to educate a slave is to make him discontented with slavery, and to invest him with a power which shall open to him the treasures of freedom; and since the object of the slaveholder is to maintain complete authority over his slave, his constant vigilance is exercised to prevent everything which militates against, or endangers the stability of his authority. Education being among the menacing influences, and, perhaps, the most dangerous, is therefore, the most cautiously guarded against.

It is true that we do not often hear of the enforcement of the law, punishing as crime the teaching of slaves to read, but this is not because of a want of disposition to enforce it. The true reason, or explanation of the matter is this, there is the greatest unanimity of opinion among the white population of the South, in favor of the policy of keeping the slave in ignorance. There is, perhaps, another reason why the law against education is so seldom violated. The slave is *too* poor to be able to offer a temptation sufficiently strong to induce a white man to violate it; and it is not to be supposed that in a community where the moral and religious sentiment is in favor of slavery, many martyrs will be found sacrificing their liberty and lives by violating those prohibitory enactments.

As a general rule, then, darkness reigns over the abodes of the enslaved, and "how great is that darkness!"

We are sometimes told of the contentment of the slaves, and are entertained with vivid pictures of their happiness. We are told that they often dance and sing; that their masters frequently give them wherewith to make merry; in fine, that they have little of which to complain. I admit that the slave *does* sometimes sing, dance, and appear to be merry. But what does this prove? It only proves to my mind, that though slavery is armed with a thousand stings, it is not able entirely to kill the elastic spirit of the bondman. That spirit will rise and walk abroad, despite of whips and chains, and extract from the cup of nature, occasional drops of joy and gladness. No thanks to the slaveholder, nor to slavery, that the vivacious captive may sometimes dance in his chains, his very mirth in such circumstances, stands before God, as an accusing angel against his enslaver.

But *who* tell us of the extraordinary contentment and happiness of the slave? What traveller has explored the balmy regions of our Southern country and brought back "these glad tidings of joy"? Bring him on the platform, and bid him answer a few plain questions, we shall then be able to determine the weight and importance that attach to his testimony. Is he a minister? Yes. Were you ever in a slave State, sir? Yes. May I inquire the object of your mission South? To preach the gospel, sir. Of what denomination are you? A Presbyterian, sir. To whom were you introduced? To the Rev. Dr. Plummer. Is he a slaveholder, sir? Yes, sir. Has slaves about his house? Yes, sir. Were you than the guest of Dr. Plummer? Yes, sir. Waited on by slaves while there? Yes, sir. Did you preach for Dr. Plummer? Yes, sir. Did you spend your nights at the great house, or at the quarter among the slaves? At the great house. You had, then, no social intercourse with the slaves? No, sir. You fraternized, then, wholly with the *white* portion of the population while there? Yes, sir. This is sufficient, sir; you can leave the platform.

Nothing is more natural than that those who go into slave States, and enjoy the hospitality of slaveholders, should bring back favorable reports of the condition of the slave. If that ultra republican, the Hon. Lewis Cass could not return from the Court of France, without paying a compliment to royalty simply because King Louis Phillippe patted him on the shoulder, called him "friend," and invited him to dinner, it is not to be expected that those hungry shadows of men in the shape of ministers, that go South, can escape a contamination even more beguiling and insidious. Alas! for the weakness of poor human nature! "Pleased with a rattle, tickled with a straw!"

Why is it that all the reports of contentment and happiness among the slaves at the South come to us upon the authority of slaveholders, or (what is equally significant), of slaveholders' friends? *Why* is it that we do not hear from the slaves direct? The answer to this question furnishes the darkest features in the American slave system.

Is is often said, by the opponents of the anti-slavery cause, that the condition of the people of Ireland is more deplorable than that of the American slaves. *Far* be it from me to underrate the sufferings of the Irish people. They have been long oppressed; and the same heart that prompts me to plead the cause of the American bondman, makes it impossible for me *not* to sympathize with the oppressed of all lands. Yet I must say that there is no analogy between the two cases. The Irishman is poor, but he is *not* a slave. He *may* be in rags, but he is *not* a slave. He is still the master of his own body, and can say with the poet, "The hand of Douglass is his own." "The world is all before him, where to choose," and poor as may be my opinion of the British Parliament, I cannot believe that it will ever sink to such a depth of infamy as to pass a law for the recapture of Fugitive Irishmen! The shame and scandal of kidnapping will long remain wholly monopolized by the American Congress! The Irishman has not only the liberty to emigrate from his country, but he has liberty at home. He can write, and speak, and co-operate for the attainment of his rights and the redress of his wrongs.

The multitude can assembly upon all the green hills, and fertile plains of the Emerald Isle—they can pour out their grievances, and proclaim their wants without molestation; and the press, that "swift-winged messenger," can bear the tidings of their doings to the extreme bounds of the civilized world. They have their "Conciliation Hall" on the banks of the Liffey, their reform Clubs, and the newspapers; they pass resolutions, send forth addresses, and enjoy the right of petition. But how is it with the American slave? *Where* may he assemble? *Where* is his Conciliation Hall? Where are his newspapers? Where is his right of petition? Where is his freedom of speech? his liberty of the press? and his right of locomotion? He is said to be happy; happy men can speak. But ask the slave—*what* is his condition?—*what* his state of mind?—*what* he thinks of his enslavement? and you had as well address your inquiries to the *silent dead*. There comes no *voice* from the enslaved, we are left to gather his feelings by imagining what ours would be, were our souls in his soul's stead.

If there were no other fact descriptive of slavery, than that the slave is dumb, this alone would be sufficient to mark the slave system as a grand aggregation of human horrors.

Most who are present will have observed that leading men, in this country, have been putting forth their skill to secure quiet to the nation. A system of measures to promote this object was adopted a few months ago in Congress.

The result of those measures is known. Instead of quiet, they have produced alarm; instead of peace, they have brought us war, and so must ever be.

While this nation is guilty of the enslavement of three millions of innocent men and women, it is as idle to think of having a sound and lasting peace, as it is to think there is no God, to take cognizance of the affairs of men. There can be no peace to the wicked while slavery continues in the land, it will be condemned, and while it is condemned there will be agitation; Nature must cease to be nature; Men must become monsters; Humanity must be transformed; Christianity must be exterminated; all ideas of justice, and the laws of eternal goodness must be utterly blotted out from the human soul, ere a system so foul and infernal can escape condemnation, or this guilty Republic can have a sound and enduring Peace.

Henry Clay

On the Compromise Measures (1850)

Victory in the Mexican War brought the United States a vast addition of territory in the southwest, stretching westward from Texas all the way to the Pacific Ocean. Even while the war was still underway, the prospect of territorial gains was widely recognized, and debate began on the question of how to establish civil government in lands to be acquired from Mexico. Almost immediately this debate became entangled with the growing moral abhorrence, in the North, of slavery. Previously the Missouri Compromise line (latitute 36°30′) had been regarded as the dividing line between slave states and free ones. Most of the land obtained after the Mexican War lay south of that line. In August 1846, however, Pennsylvania Congressman David Wilmot introduced a measure which came to be known as the Wilmot Proviso, stipulating that slavery be excluded from any territory that might be acquired from Mexico.

The Wilmot Proviso controversy effectively blocked any Congressional attempt to provide for territorial organization and government. The House, in which antislavery forces had the edge, repeatedly attached the Proviso to other legislation; the Senate, with an equal number of free and slave state members, repeatedly rejected it, and the two bodies were unable to compromise. This stalemate might not have been a serious problem so long as the territory remained largely unpopulated, but the discovery of gold in California in 1848 sparked such a wave of settlement that within a year California had population sufficient to apply for immediate admission to the Union as a state. In the face of immigration, disputed land claims, and frontier lawlessness, the absence of civil government became a serious concern and the Wilmot Proviso controversy became a major stumbling block to Congressional action.

In the midst of this crisis, Kentucky had called Henry Clay, the "Great Compromiser," out of retirement and had returned him to the Senate. In January 1850 Clay proposed to the Senate a series of steps which he hoped would resolve several problems at once and break the Congressional logjam. First, California was to be admitted to the Union as a free state, as she had requested. Since this move would cause free states to outnumber slave, it threatened Southern dominance of the Senate. Second, the rest of the land obtained from Mexico would be organized into two territories, Utah and New Mexico, in each of which the decision for or against slavery would be made by the people actually living there. Although this step might open new lands to slavery, for the time being it was a decision not to decide. Third, in settlement of the disputed Texas boundary, the area claimed by Texas would be reduced, but in return the national government would assume the debt which the Republic of Texas had incurred prior to admission to the Union. Fourth, a stronger fugitive slave law reaffirmed the right of masters to capture runaway slaves. Finally, the slave trade (though not slavery itself) was to be abolished in the District of Columbia.

The 73-year-old Clay was well suited to to the task of compromiser. Even though he was a slaveholder from a slave state, Clay had never been identified with the most radical Southern element and was generally viewed as a spokesman for the West. He had publicly asserted that he would not personally support the introduction of slavery into a territory where it did not exist, while at the same time maintaining that the people of the territories had the right to do so if they wished.

Twice before, Clay was instrumental in effecting compromise: in 1821 he smoothed the way for the admission of Missouri by inducing the state legislature to rescind, in effect, a provision of its constitution which prohibited free blacks from entering the state; in 1833 it was Clay who crafted the compromise tariff that blunted the confrontation between President Jackson and the Southern nullifiers. After a long career in public life, a career that included membership in both houses of Congress, service as Secretary of State, and several unsuccessful attempts to become President, Clay retired to his home in Kentucky in 1848.

His return to the Senate at the end of 1849 was prompted by his desire to settle the slavery issue and lay to rest the disquieting threats of disunion. The speech introducing the resolutions was given over two days, February 5–6, and the debate continued in the succeeding months, with final passage in September of the acts resulting from the resolutions. Clay's was a plea for concessions on both sides and a warning that secession was not a remedy for the abuses to which Southerners believed they were subjected. Opposition to the measures came from both sides. Calhoun, who was dying and too ill to deliver his own speech, demanded a halt to all agitation on the slavery issue and favored a constitutional amendment that would ensure Southern political equality, a position echoed by the senator from Mississippi, Jefferson Davis. Northern Senators such as Seward of New York and Chase of Ohio upheld the right of Congress to limit slavery. But Clay had support as well, most notably from Daniel Webster of Massachusetts.

The passage of the compromise measures dampened the fires of secession but did not, of course, finally resolve the issues of slavery and union. Many hoped that the compromise would bring the fierce sectional antagonisms to an end and with them the threat to economic growth and stability. The abolitionists, however, continued their moral assault on slavery, and Daniel Webster experienced the deep hostility felt by many in the North against the new Fugitive Slave law. The question of the extension of slavery into the territories was raised again only four years later in the debate over the Kansas-Nebraska Act, passage of which contributed to the founding of the new Republican Party. Clay's efforts may have warded off the impending crisis, but the controversy was too far-reaching and the "tyranny of passion" Clay deplored too deep to yield ultimately to the arguments of conciliation.

Mr. President: Never on any former occasion have I risen under feelings of such painful solicitude. I have seen many periods of great anxiety, of peril, and of danger in this country, and I have never before risen to address any assemblage so oppressed, so appalled, and so anxious; and, sir, I hope it will not be out of place to do here, what again and again I have done in my private chamber, to implore of Him who holds the destinies of nations and individuals in His hands, to bestow upon our country His blessings, to calm the violence and rage of party, to still passion, to allow reason once more to resume its empire. . . . I know, sir, the jealousies, the fears, the apprehensions which are engendered by the existence of that party spirit to which I have referred; but if there be in my hearing now, in or out of this Capitol, any one who hopes, in his race for honors and elevation, for higher honors and higher elevation than that which he now occupies, I beg him to believe that I, at least, will never jostle him in the pursuit of those honors or that elevation. I beg him to be perfectly persuaded that, if my wishes prevail, my name shall never be used in competition with his. I beg to assure him that when my service is terminated in this body, my mission, so far as respects the public affairs of this world and upon this earth is closed, and closed, if my wishes prevail, forever. . . .

From the beginning of the session to the present time my thoughts have been anxiously directed to the object of finding some plan, of proposing some mode of accomodation which would once more restore the blessings of concord, harmony, and peace to this great country. I am not vain enough to suppose that I have been successful in the accomplishment of this object, but I have presented a scheme; and allow me to say to honorable Senators that, if they find in that plan anything that is defective, if they find in it anything that is worthy of acceptance, but is susceptible of improvement by amendment, it seems to me that the true and patriotic course is not to denounce it, but to improve it—not to reject without examination any project of accomodation having for its object the restoration of harmony in this country, but to look at it to see if it be susceptible of elaboration or improvement, so as to accomplish the object which I indulge the hope is common to all and every one of us, to restore peace and quiet, and harmony and happiness to this country.

Sir, when I came to consider this subject, there were two or three general purposes which it seemed to me to be most desirable, if possible, to accomplish. The one was, to settle all the controverted questions arising out of the subject of slavery. It seemed to me to be doing very little if we settled one question and left other distracting questions unadjusted; it seemed to me to be doing but little if we stopped one leak only in the ship of State, and left other leaks capable of producing danger, if not destruction, to the vessel. I therefore turned my attention to every subject connected with the institution of slavery, and out of which controverted questions had sprung, to see if it were possible or practicable to accomodate and adjust the whole of them. Another principal object which attracted my attention was, to endeavor to form such a scheme of accommodation that neither of the two classes of States into which our country is so unhappily divided should make any sacrifice to any great principle. I believe, sir, the series of resolutions which I have had the honor to present to the Senate accomplishes that object.

Sir, another purpose which I have had in view was this: I was aware of the difference of opinion prevailing between these two classes of States. I was aware that, while one portion of the Union was pushing matters, as it seemed to me, to the greatest extremity, another portion of the Union was pushing them to an opposite, perhaps not less dangerous extremity. It appeared to me, then, that if any arrangement, any satisfactory adjustment could be made of the controverted questions between the two classes of States, that adjustment, that arrangement, could only be successful and effectual by extracting from both parties some concession—not of principle, not of principle at all, but of feeling, of opinion, in relation to matters in controversy between them. Sir, I believe the resolutions which I have prepared fulfill that object. I believe, sir, that you will find, upon that careful, rational, and attentive examination of them which I think they deserve, that neither party in some of them make any concession at all; in others the concessions of forbearance are mutual; and in the third place, in reference to the slaveholding States, there are resolutions making concessions to them by the opposite class of States, without any compensation whatever being rendered by them to the non-slaveholding States. I think every one of these characteristics which I have assigned, and the measures which I proposed, is susceptible of clear and satisfactory demonstration by an attentive perusal and critical examination of the resolutions themselves. Let us take up the first resolution.

The first resolution, Mr. President, as you are aware, relates to California, and it declares that California, with suitable limits, ought to be admitted as a member of this Union, without the imposition of any restriction either to interdict or to introduce slavery within her limits. Well, now, is there any concession in this resolution by either party to the other? I know that gentlemen who come from slaveholding States say the North gets all that it desires; but by whom does it get it? Does it get it by any action of Congress? If slavery be interdicted within the limits of California, has it been done by Congress—by this government? No, sir. That interdiction is imposed by California herself. And has it not been the doctrine of all parties that when a State is about to be admitted into the Union, that State has a right to decide for itself whether it will or will not have slavery within its limits?

Mr. President, the next resolution in the series which I have offered I beg gentlemen candidly now to look at. I was aware, perfectly aware, of the perseverance with which the Wilmot proviso was insisted upon. I knew that every one of the free States in this Union, without exception, had by its legislative body passed resolutions instructing their Senators and requesting their Representatives to get that restriction incorporated in any Territorial government which might be established under the auspices of Congress. I knew how much, and I regretted how much, the free States had put their hearts upon the adoption of this measure. In the second resolution I call upon them to waive persisting in it. I ask them, for the sake of peace and in the spirit of mutual forbearance to other members of the Union, to give it up—to no longer insist upon it—to see, as they must see, if their eyes are open, the dangers which lie ahead, if they persevere in insisting upon it.

When I called upon them in this resolution to do this, was I not bound to offer, for a surrender of that favorite principle or measure of theirs, some compensation, not as an equivalent by any means, but some compensation in the spirit of mutual forbearance, which, animating one side, ought at the same time to actuate the other side? Well, sir, what is it that is offered them? It is a declaration of what I characterized, and must still characterize, with great deference to all those who entertain opposite opinions, as two truths, I will not say incontestable, but to me clear, and I think they ought to be regarded as indisputable truths. What are they? The first is, that by law slavery no longer exists in any part of the acquisitions made by us from the Republic of Mexico; and the other is, that in our opinion, according to the probabilities of the case, slavery never will be introduced into any portion of the territories so acquired from Mexico. . . .

Allow me to say that, in my humble judgment, the institution of slavery presents two questions totally distinct and resting on entirely different grounds—slavery within the States, and slavery without the States. Congress, the general government, has no power, under the Constitution of the United States, to touch slavery within the States, except in three specified particulars in that instrument: to adjust the subject of representation; to impose taxes when a system of direct taxation is made; and to perform the duty of surrendering, or causing to be delivered up, fugitive slaves that may escape from service which they owe in slave States, and take refuge in free States. And, sir, I am ready to say that if Congress were to attack, within the States, the institution of slavery, for the purpose of the overthrow or extinction of slavery, then, Mr. President, my voice would be for war; then would be made a case which would justify in the sight of God, and in the presence of the nations of the earth, resistance on the part of the slave States to such an unconstitutional and usurped attempt as would be made on the supposition which I have stated.

Then we should be acting in defense of our rights, our domicils, our safety, our lives; and then, I think, would be furnished a case in which the slaveholding States would be justified, by all considerations which pertain to the happiness and security of man, to employ every instrument which God or nature had placed in their hands to resist such an attempt on the part of the free States. And then, if unfortunately civil war should break out, and we should present to the nations of the earth the spectacle of one portion of this Union endeavoring to subvert an institution in violation of the Constitution and the most sacred obligations which can bind men; we should present the spectacle in which we should have the sympathies, the good wishes, and the desire for our success of all men who love justice and truth. Far different, I fear, would be our case if unhappily we should be plunged into civil war—if the two parts of this country should be placed in a position hostile toward each other—in order to carry slavery into the new territories acquired from Mexico. . . .

The government has no right to touch the institution within the States; but whether she has, and to what extent she has the right or not to touch it outside of the States, is a question which is debatable, and upon which men may honestly and fairly differ, but which, decided however it may be decided, furnishes, in my judgment, no just occasion for breaking up this happy and glorious Union of ours. . . .

Mr. President, I shall not take up time, of which already so much has been consumed, to show that, according to the sense of the Constitution of the United States, or rather according to the sense in which the clause has been interpreted for the last fifty years, the clause which confers on Congress the power to regulate the Territories and other property of the United States conveys the authority. . . .

I said there is another source of power equally satisfactory, equally conclusive in my mind, as that which relates to the Territories; and that is the treaty-making power—the acquiring power. Now I put it to gentlemen, is there not at this moment a power somewhere existing either to admit or exclude slavery from a ceded territory? It is not an annihilated power. This is impossible. It is a subsisting, actual, existing power; and where does it exist? It existed, I presume no one will controvert, in Mexico prior to the cession of these territories. Mexico could have abolished slavery or introduced slavery either in California or New Mexico. That must be conceded. Who will controvert this position? Well, Mexico has parted from the territory and from sovereignty over the territory; and to whom did she transfer it? She transferred the territory and the sovereignty of the territory to the government of the United States.

The government of the United States acquires in sovereignty and in territory over California and New Mexico, all, either in sovereignty or territory, that Mexico held in California or New Mexico, by the cession of those territories. Sir, dispute that who can. The power exists or it does not; no one will contend for its annihilation. It existed in Mexico. No one, I think, can deny that. Mexico alienates the sovereignty over the territory, and her alienee is the government of the United States. The government of the United States, then, possesses all power which Mexico possessed over the ceded territories, and the government of the United States can do in reference to them—within, I admit, certain limits of the Constitution—whatever Mexico could have done. There are prohibitions upon the power of Congress within the Constitution, which prohibitions, I admit, must apply to Congress whenever she legislates, whether for the old States or for new territories; but, within those prohibitions, the powers of the United States over the ceded territories are coextensive and equal to the power of Mexico in the ceded territories, prior to the cession.

I pass on from the second resolution to the third and fourth, which relate to Texas: and allow me to say, Mr. President, that I approach the subject with a full knowledge of all its difficulties; and of all the questions connected with or growing out of this institution of slavery which Congress is called upon to pass upon and decide, there are none so difficult and troublesome as those which relate to Texas, because, sir, Texas has a question of boundary to settle, and the question of slavery, or the feelings connected with it, run into the question of boundary. The North, perhaps, will be anxious to contract Texas within the narrowest possible limits, in order to exclude all beyond her to make it a free Territory; the South, on the contrary, may be anxious to extend those sources of Rio Grande, for the purpose of creating an additional theater for slavery; and thus, to the question of the limits of Texas, and the settlement of her boundary, the slavery question, with all its troubles and difficulties, is added, meeting us at every step we take.

There is, sir, a third question, also, adding to the difficulty. By the resolution of annexation, slavery was interdicted in all north of 36 degrees 30 minutes; but of New Mexico, that portion of it which lies north of 36 degrees 30 minutes embraces, I think, about one-third of the whole of New Mexico east of the Rio Grande; so that you have free and slave territory mixed, boundary and slavery mixed together, and all these difficulties are to be encountered.

Sir, the other day my honorable friend who represents so well the State of Texas said that we had no more right to touch the limits of Texas than we had to touch the limits of Kentucky. I think that was the illustration he gave us—that a State is one and indivisible, and that the general government has no right to sever it. I agree with him, sir, in that; where the limits are ascertained and certain, where they are undisputed and indisputable. The general government has no right, nor has any other earthly power the right, to interfere with the limits of a State whose boundaries are thus fixed, thus ascertained, known, and recognized. The whole power, at least, to interfere with it is voluntary. The extreme case may be put—one which I trust in God may never happen in this nation—of a conquered nation, and of a constitution adapting itself to a state of subjugation or conquest to which it has been reduced; and giving up whole States, as well as parts of States, in order to save from the conquering arms of the invader what remains. I say such a power in case of extremity may exist. But I admit that, short of such extremity, voluntarily, the general government has no right to separate a State—to take a portion of its territory from it, or to regard it otherwise than as integral, one and indivisible, and not to be affected by any legislation of ours. But, then, I assume what does not exist in the case of Texas, and these boundaries must be known, ascertained, and indisputable. With regard to Texas, all was open, all was unfixed; all is unfixed at this moment, with respect to her limits west and north of the Nueces. . . . In the resolution, what is proposed? To confine her to the Nueces? No, sir. To extend her boundary to the mouth of the Rio Grande, and thence up that river to the southern limit of New Mexico; and thence along that limit to the boundary between the United States and Spain, as marked under the treaty of 1819.

Why, sir, here is a vast country. I

believe—although I have made no estimate about it—that it is not inferior in extent of land, of acres, of square miles, to what Texas east of the river Nueces, extending to the Sabine, had before. And who is there can say with truth and justice that there is no reciprocity, nor mutuality, no concession in this resolution, made to Texas, even in reference to the question of boundary alone? You give her a vast country, equal, I repeat, in extent nearly to what she indisputably possessed before; a country sufficiently large, with her consent, hereafter to carve out of it some two or three additional States when the condition of the population may render it expedient to make new States. Sir, is there not in this resolution concession, liberality, justice? But this is not all that we propose to do. The second resolution proposes to pay off a certain amount of the debt of Texas. A blank is left in the resolution, because I have not heretofore been able to ascertain the amount.

I pass to the consideration of the next resolution in the series which I have had the honor to submit, and which relates, if I am not mistaken, to this District.

"Resolved, That it is inexpedient to abolish slavery in the District of Columbia, while that institution continues to exist in the State of Maryland, without the consent of that State, without the consent of the people of the District, and without just compensation to the owners of slaves within the District."

Mr. President, an objection at the moment was made to this resolution, by some honorable Senator on the other side of the body, that it did not contain an assertion of the unconstitutionality of the exercise of the power of abolition. I said then, as I have uniformly maintained in this body, as I contended for in 1838, and ever have done, that the power to abolish slavery within the District of Columbia has been vested in Congress by language too clear and explicit to admit, in my judgment, of any rational doubt whatever. What, sir, is the language of the Constitution? "To exercise exclusive legislation, in all cases whatever, over such District (not exceeding ten miles square) as may, by cession of particular States and the acceptance of Congress, become the seat of the government of the United States." Now, sir, Congress, by this grant of power, is invested with all legislation whatsoever over the District.

Can we conceive of human language more broad and comprehensive than that which invests a legislative body with exclusive power, in all cases whatsoever, of legislature over a given district of territory or country? Let me ask, sir, is there any power to abolish slavery in this District? Let me suppose, in addition to what I suggested the other day, that slavery had been abolished in Maryland and Virginia—let me add to it the supposition that it was abolished in all the States in the Union; is there any power then to abolish slavery within the District of Columbia, or is slavery planted here to all eternity, without the possibility of the exercise of any legislative power for its abolition? It can not be invested in Maryland, because the power with which Congress is invested is exclusive. Maryland, therefore, is excluded, and so all the other States of the Union are excluded. It is here, or it is nowhere.

This was the view which I took in 1838, and I think there is nothing in the resolution which I offered on that occasion incompatible with the view which I now present, and which the resolution contains. While I admitted the power to exist in Congress, and exclusively in Congress, to legislate in all cases whatsoever, and consequently in the abolition of slavery in this District, if it is deemed proper to do so, I admitted on that occasion, as I contend now, that it is a power which Congress can not, in conscience and good faith, exercise while the institution of slavery continues within the State of Maryland. . . .

This resolution requires . . . that slavery shall not be abolished within the District of Columbia, although Maryland consents, although the people of the District of Columbia themselves consent, without the third condition of making compensation to the owners of the slaves within the District. Sir, it is immaterial to me upon what basis this obligation to compensate for the slaves who may be liberated by the authority of Congress is placed. There is a clause in the Constitution of the United States, of the amendments to the Constitution, which declares that no private property shall be taken for public use, without just compensation being made to the owner of the property. . . .

I know it has been argued that the clause of the Constitution which requires compensation for property taken by the public, for its use, would not apply to the case of the abolition of slavery in the District of Columbia, because the property is not taken for the use of the public. Literally, perhaps, it would not be taken for the use of the public; but it would be taken in consideration of a policy and purpose adopted by the public, as one which it was deemed expedient to carry into full effect and operation; and, by a liberal interpretation of the clause, it ought to be so far regarded as taken for the use of the public, at the instance of the public, as to demand compensation to the extent of the value of the property. . . .

The second clause of this resolution [the sixth], provides "that it is expedient to prohibit within the District the trade in slaves brought into it from States or places beyond the limits of the District, either to be sold therein as merchandise, or to be transported to other markets."

Well, Mr. President, if the concession be made that Congress has the power of legislation, and exclusive legislation, in all cases whatsoever, how can it be doubted that Congress has authority to prohibit what is called the slave-trade in the District of Columbia? Sir, my interpretation of the Constitution is this: that with regard to all parts of it which operate upon the States, Congress can exercise no power which is not granted, or which is not a necessary implication from a granted power. That is the rule for the action of Congress in relation to its legislation upon the States, but in relation to its legislation upon this District, the reverse. I take it to be the rule that Congress has all power over the District which is not prohibited by some part of the Constitution of the United States; in other words, that Congress has a power within the District equivalent to, and co-extensive with, the power which any State itself possesses within its own limits. Well, sir, does any one doubt the power and the right of any slaveholding State in this Union to forbid the introduction, as merchandise, of slaves within their limits? Why, sir, almost every slaveholding State in the Union has exercised its power to prohibit the introduction of slaves as merchandise. . . .

Sir, the power exists; the duty, in my opinion, exists; and there has been no time—as I may, in language coincident with that used by the honorable Senator from Alabama—there has been no time in my public life when I was not willing to concur in the abolition of the slave-trade in this District. . . . Why are the feelings of citizens here outraged by the scenes exhibited, and the corteges which pass along our avenues, of manacled human beings, not collected at all in our own neighborhood, but brought from distant parts of neighboring States? Why should they be outraged? And who is there, that has a heart, that does not contemplate a spectacle of that kind with horror and indignation? Why should they be outraged by a scene so inexcusable and detestable as this?

Sir, it is no concession, I repeat, from one class of States or from the other. It is an object in which both of them, it seems to me, should heartily unite, and which the one side as much as the other should rejoice in adopting, inasmuch as it lessens one of the causes of inquietude and dissatisfaction which are connected with this District.

The next resolution is:

> That more effectual provision ought to be made by law, according to the requirement of the Constitution, for the restitution and delivery of persons bound to service or labor in any State, who may escape into any other State or Territory in the Union.

Now, Mr. President, upon that subject I go with him who goes furthest in the interpretation of that clause in the Constitution. In my humble opinion, sir, it is a requirement by the Constitution of the United States which is not limited in its operation to the Congress of the United States, but extends to every State in the Union and to the officers of every State in the Union; and I go one step further: it extends to every man in the Union, and devolves upon them all an obligation to assist in the recovery of a fugitive from labor who takes refuge in or escapes into one of the free states. And, sir, I think I can maintain all this by a fair interpretation of the Constitution. It provides:

> That no person held to service or labor in one State under the laws thereof, escaping into another, shall, in consequence of any law or regulation therein, be discharged from service or labor, but shall be delivered up on claim of the party to whom such service or labor may be due.

It will be observed, Mr. President, that this clause in the Constitution is not among the enumerated powers granted to Congress, for, if that had been the case, it might have been urged that Congress alone could legislate to carry it into effect; but it is one of the general powers or one of the general rights secured by this constitutional instrument, and it addresses itself to all who are bound by the Constitution of the United States. Now, sir, the officers of the general government are bound to take an oath to support the Constitution of the United States. All State officers are required by the Constitution to take an oath to support the Constitution of the United States; and all men who love their country and are obedient to its laws, are bound to assist in the execution of those laws, whether they are fundamental or derivative. I do not say that a private individual is bound to make the tour of his State in order to assist an owner of a slave to recover his property; but I do say, if he is present when the owner of a slave is about to assert his rights and endeavor to obtain possession of his property, every man present, whether he be an officer of the general government or the State government, or a private individual, is bound to assist, if men are bound at all to assist in the execution of the laws of their country.

Now what is this provision? It is that such fugitive shall be delivered upon claim of the party to whom such service or labor may be due. As has been already remarked in the course of the debate upon the bill upon this subject which is now pending, the language used in regard to fugitives from criminal offenses and fugitives from labor is precisely the same. The fugitive from justice is to be delivered up, and to be removed to the State having jurisdiction; the fugitive from labor is to be delivered up on claim of the party to whom such service is due. Well, has it ever been contended on the part of any State that she is not bound to surrender a fugitive from justice, upon demand from the State from which he fled? I believe not. There have been some exceptions to the performance of this duty, but they have not denied the general right; and if they have refused in any instance to give up the person demanded, it has been upon some technical or legal ground, not at all questioning the general right to have the fugitive surrendered, or the obligation to deliver him up as intended by the Constitution.

I think, then, Mr. President, that with regard to the true interpretation of this provision of the Constitution there can be no doubt. It imposes an obligation upon all the States, free or slaveholding; it imposes an obligation upon all officers of the government, State or Federal; and, I will add, upon all the people of the United States, under particular circumstances, to assist in the surrender and recovery of a fugitive slave from his master. . . .

Mr. President, I do think that that whole class of legislation, beginning in the Northern States and extending to some of the Western States, by which obstructions and impediments have been thrown in the way of the recovery of fugitive slaves, is unconstitutional and has originated in a spirit which I trust will correct itself when those States come calmly to consider the nature and extent of their federal obligations. Of all the States in this Union, unless it be Virginia, the State of which I am a resident suffers most by the escape of their slaves to adjoining States.

I have very little doubt, indeed, that the extent of loss to the State of Kentucky, in consequence of the escape of her slaves is greater, at least, in proportion to the total number of slaves which are held within that commonwealth, even than in Virginia. I know full well, and so does the honorable Senator from Ohio know, that it is at the utmost hazard, and insecurity of life itself, that a Kentuckian can cross the river and go into the interior to take back his fugitive slave to the place from whence he fled. Recently an example occurred even in the city of Cincinnati, in respect to one of our most respectable citizens. Not having visited Ohio at all, but Covington, on the opposite side of the river, a little slave of his escaped over to Cincinnati. He pursued it; he found it in the house in which it was concealed; he took it out, and it was rescued by the violence and force of a negro mob from his possession—the police of the city standing by, and either unwilling or unable to afford the assistance which was requisite to enable him to recover his property.

Upon this subject I do think that we have just a serious cause of complaint against the free States. I think they fail in fulfilling a great obligation, and the failure is precisely upon one of those subjects which in its nature is the most irritating and inflaming to those who live in the slave States.

Now, sir, I think it is a mark of no good neighborhood, of no kindness, of no courtesy, that a man living in a slave State can not now, with any sort of safety, travel in the free States with his servants, although he has no purpose whatever of stopping there longer than a short time. And on this whole subject, sir, how has the legislation of the free States altered for the worse within the course of the last twenty or thirty years? Why, sir, most of those States, until within a period of the last twenty or thirty years, had laws for the benefit of sojourners, as they were called, passing through or abiding for the moment in the free States, with their servants. . . . Well, now, sir, all these laws in behalf of these sojourners through the free States are swept away, except I believe in the State of Rhode Island.

MR. DAYTON: And New Jersey.

MR. CLAY: Ay, and in New Jersey. . . .

Then, Mr. President, I think that the existing laws upon the subject, for the recovery of fugitive slaves, and the restoration and delivering of them up to their owners, being found inadequate and ineffective, it is incumbent on Congress—and I hope hereafter, in a better state of feeling, when more harmony and good will prevail among the members of this confederacy, it will be regarded by the free States themselves as a part of their duty also—to assist in allaying this irritating and disturbing subject to the peace of our Union; but, at all events, whether they do it or not, it is our duty to do it. It is our duty to make the law more effective, and I shall go with the Senator from the South who goes furthest in making penal laws and imposing the heaviest sanctions for the recovery of fugitive slaves, and the restoration of them to their owners.

Mr. President, upon this part of the subject, however, allow me to make an observation or two. I do not think the States, as States, ought to be responsible for all the misconduct of particular individuals within those States. I think that the States are only to be held responsible when they act in their sovereign capacity. If there are a few persons, indiscreet, mad if you choose—fanatics if you choose so to call them—who are for dissolving this Union, as we know there are some at the North, and for dissolving it in consequence of the connection which exists between the free and slaveholding States, I do not think that any State in which such madmen as they are to be found, ought to be held responsible for the doctrines they propagate, unless the State itself adopts those doctrines.

Mr. President, I have a great deal yet to say, and I shall, therefore, pass from the consideration of this seventh resolution, with the observation, which I believe I have partly made before, that the most stringent provision upon this subject which can be devised will meet with my hearty concurrence and co-operation, in the passage of the bill which is under the consideration of the Senate. The last resolution declares:

> That Congress has no power to prohibit or obstruct the trade in slaves between the slaveholding States; but that the admission or exclusion of slaves brought from one into another of them, depends exclusively upon their own particular laws.

This is a concession, not, I admit, of any real constitutional provision, but a concession from the North to the South of what is understood, I believe, by a great number at the North, to be a constitutional provision. If the resolution should be adopted, take away the decision of the Supreme Court of the United States on this subject, and there is a great deal, I know, that might be said on both sides, as to the right of Congress to regulate the trade between the States, and, consequently, the trade in slaves between the States; but I think the decision of the Supreme Court has been founded upon correct principles, and I trust it will forever put an end to the question whether Congress has or has not the power to regulate the intercourse and trade in slaves between the different States.

Such, Mr. President, is the series of resolutions which, in an earnest and anxious desire to present the olive branch to both parts of this distracted, and at the present moment, unhappy country, I have thought it my duty to offer. Of all men upon the earth I am the least attached to any productions of my own mind. No man upon earth is more ready than I am to surrender anything which I have proposed, and to accept in lieu of it anything that is better; but I put it to the candor of honorable Senators on the other side and upon all sides of the House, whether their duty will be performed by simply limiting themselves to objections to any one or to all of the series of resolutions that I have offered. If my plan of peace, and accomodation, and harmony, is not right, present us your plan. Let us see the counter project. Let us see how all the questions that have arisen out of this unhappy subject of slavery can be better settled, more fairly and justly settled to all quarters of the Union, than on the plan proposed in the resolutions which I have offered. Present me such a scheme, and I will hail it with pleasure, and will accept it without the slightest feeling of regret that my own was abandoned.

Now, sir, when I came to consider the subject and to compare the provisions of the line of 36 degrees 30 minutes—the Missouri Compromise line—with the plan which I propose for the accommodation of this question, what said I to myself? Why sir, if I offer the line of 36 degrees 30 minutes, interdicting slavery north of it, and leaving the question open south of that line, I offer that which is illusory to the South; I offer that which will deceive them, if they suppose that slavery will be introduced south of that line. It is better for them, I said to myself—it is better for the whole South, that there should be non-action on both sides, than that there should be action interdicting slavery on one side, without action for admission of slavery on the other side of the line. Is it not so? What, then, is gained by the South, if the Missouri line is extended to the Pacific, with an interdiction of slavery north of it? Why, sir, one of the very arguments which have been most often and most seriously urged by the South has been this, that we do not want you to legislate upon the subject at all; you ought not to touch it; you have no power over it. I do not concur, as is well known from what I have said upon this occasion, in this view of the subject. But that is the Southern argument. We do not want you to legislate at all on the subject of slavery. But if you adopt the Missouri line and extend it to the Pacific, and interdict slavery north of that line, you do legislate upon the subject of slavery, and you legislate without a corresponding equivalent of legislation on the subject south of the line. For, if there be legislation interdicting slavery north of the line, the principle of equality would require that there should be legislation admitting slavery south of the line.

Sir, I have said that I never could vote for it, and I repeat that I never can, and never will vote for it; and no earthly power shall ever make me vote to plant slavery where slavery does not exist. Still, if there be a majority—and there ought to be such a majority—for interdicting slavery north of the line, there ought to be an equal majority—if equality and justice be done to the South—to admit slavery south of the line. And if there be a majority ready to accomplish both of these purposes, though I can not concur in the action, yet I would be one of the last to create any disturbance, I would be one of the first to acquiesce in such legislation, though it is contrary to my own judgment and my own conscience. I think, then, it would be better to keep the whole of these territories untouched by any legislation by Congress on the subject of slavery, leaving it open, undecided, without any action of Congress in relation to it; that it would be best for the South, and best for all the views which the South has, from time to time, disclosed to us as correspondent with her wishes. . . .

And, sir, I must take occasion here to say that in my opinion there is no right on the part of any one or more of the States to secede from the Union. War and dissolution of the Union are identical and inevitable, in my opinion. There can be a dissolution of the Union only by consent or by war. Consent no one can anticipate, from any existing state of things, is likely to be given; and war is the only alternative by which a dissolution could be accomplished. If consent were given—if it were possible that we were to be separated by one great line—in less than sixty days after such consent was given war would break out between the slaveholding and non-slaveholding portions of this Union—between two independent parts into which it would be erected in virtue of the act of separation. In less than sixty days, I believe, our slaves from Kentucky, flocking over in numbers to the other side of the river, would be pursued by their owners. Our hot and ardent spirits would be restrained by no sense of the right which appertains to the independence of the other side of the river, should that be the line of separation. They would pursue their slaves into the adjacent free States; they would be repelled; and the consequence would be that, in less than sixty days, war would be blazing in every part of this now happy and peaceful land.

And, sir, how are you going to separate the States of this confederacy? In my humble opinion, Mr. President, we should begin with at least three separate confederacies. There would be a confederacy of the North, a confederacy of the Southern Atlantic slaveholding States, and a confederacy of the valley of the Mississippi. My life upon it, that the vast population which has already concentrated and will concentrate on the head-waters and the tributaries of the Mississippi will never give their consent that the mouth of that river shall be held subject to the power of any foreign State or community whatever. Such, I believe, would be the consequences of a dissolution of the Union, immediately ensuing; but other confederacies would spring up from time to time, as dissatisfaction and discontent were disseminated throughout the country—the confederacy of the lakes, perhaps the confederacy of New England, or of the middle States. Ah, sir, the veil which covers these sad and disastrous events that lie beyond it, is too thick to be penetrated or lifted by any mortal eye or hand. . . .

Mr. President, I have said, what I solemnly believe, that dissolution of the Union and war are identical and inevitable; and they are convertible terms; and such a war as it would be, following a dissolution of the *Union!* Sir, we may search the pages of history, and none so ferocious, so bloody, so implacable, so exterminating—not even the wars of Greece, including those of the Commoners of England and the revolutions of France—none, none of them all would rage with such violence, or be characterized with such bloodshed and enormities as would the war which must succeed, if that ever happens, the dissolution of the Union. And what would be its termination? Standing armies, and navies, to an extent stretching the revenues of each portion of the dissevered members, would take place. An exterminating war would follow—not sir, a war of two or three years' duration, but a war of interminable duration—and exterminating wars would ensue, until, after the struggles and exhaustion of both parties, some Philip or Alexander, some Cæsar or Napoleon, would arise and cut the Gordian knot, and solve the problem of the capacity of man for self-government, and crush the liberties of both the severed portions of this common empire. Can you doubt it?

Look at all history—consult her pages, ancient or modern—look at human nature; look at the contest in which you would be engaged in the supposition of war following upon the dissolution of the Union, such as I have suggested; and I ask you if it is possible for you to doubt that the final disposition of the whole would be some despot treading down the liberties of the people—the final result would be the extinction of this last and glorious light which is leading all mankind, who are gazing upon it, in the hope and anxious expectation that the liberty which prevails here will sooner or later be diffused throughout the whole of the civilized world. Sir, can you lightly contemplate these consequences? Can you yield yourself to the tyranny of passion, amid dangers which I have depicted, in colors far too tame, of what the result would be if that direful event to which I have referred should ever occur? Sir, I implore gentlemen, I adjure them, whether from the South or the North, by all that they hold dear in this world—by all their love of liberty—by all their veneration for their ancestors—by all their regard for posterity—by all their gratitude to Him who has bestowed on them such unnumbered and countless blessings—by all the duties which they owe to mankind—and by all the duties which they owe to themselves, to pause, solemnly to pause at the edge of the precipice, before the fearful and dangerous leap be taken into the yawning abyss below, from which none who ever take it shall return in safety.

Finally, Mr. President, and in conclusion, I implore, as the best blessing which Heaven can bestow upon me upon earth, that if the direful event of the dissolution of this Union is to happen, I shall not survive to behold the sad and heart-rending spectacle.

Daniel Webster

On the Compromise Measures: The Seventh of March Speech (1850)

The Clay compromise proposals became the focus of Congressional debate for several months in 1850. On March 4 the dying John C. Calhoun indicated his opposition. In a speech he was too ill to read, Calhoun dismissed the measure as a siren song which threatened Southern dominance and autonomy. The chances for success then depended largely on finding prominent support in the North, and attention focused on Daniel Webster, who had announced he would speak on March 7. Webster was an antislavery man avowedly opposed to permitting any more slave territory in the Union. No one knew what he would say, and a great sense of anticipation and excitement filled the Senate chamber when he rose to speak.

To the surprise of some of his most influential constituents, Webster supported the compromise. He saw the Union in jeopardy and argued that preserving the Union transcended any sectional considerations. For this reason, he said, he was speaking "not as a Massachusetts man, but as an American." Besides, he maintained, the compromise gave each section what it wanted most, and it required each to make only incidental concessions. In particular, he reassured his home-state supporters that even though Utah and New Mexico technically were open to slavery, still the soil and climate effectively precluded the peculiar institution from the region. As for the fugitive slave law, he pointed out that the right to reclaim fugitives was clearly set out in the Constitution and that the only way to preserve the Union was to defer to the Constitution.

Webster's speech received mixed reactions. He was denounced by the intellectual and literary elite of Massachusetts, many of whom decried his sacrifice of principle and assumed that his true motive was wooing Southern support for a Presidential bid in 1852. But he was strongly supported by the moderates and especially by the commercial interests who saw the end of the stalemated controversy as a boon to the nation's economic health. Webster himself despaired of the prospects for the compromise and left Washington in midsummer. While he was gone, the package proposal was divided into separate bills which were passed by different majorities, largely through the leadership of Stephen A. Douglas.

Webster did seek the Presidency in 1852 but the Whig convention, deadlocked between him and incumbent President Millard Fillmore, turned to the popular Mexican War hero, General Winfield Scott. Webster returned to his home in Massachusetts and died before Election Day.

I wish to speak to-day, not as a Massachusetts man, nor as a Northern man, but as an American, and a member of the Senate of the United States. It is fortunate that there is a Senate of the United States; a body not yet moved from its propriety, not lost to a just sense of its own dignity and its own high responsibilities, and a body to which the country looks, with confidence, for wise, moderate, patriotic, and healing counsels. It is not to be denied that we live in the midst of strong agitations, and are surrounded by very considerable dangers to our institutions and government. The imprisoned winds are let loose. The East, the North, and the stormy South combine to throw the whole sea into commotion, to toss its billows to the skies, and disclose its profoundest depths. I do not affect to regard myself, Mr. President, as holding, or as fit to hold, the helm in this combat with the political elements; but I have a duty to perform, and I mean to perform it with fidelity, not without a sense of existing dangers, but not without hope. I have a part to act, not for my own security or safety, for I am looking out for no fragment upon which to float away from the wreck, if wreck there must be, but for the good of the whole, and the preservation of all, and there is that which will keep me to my duty during this struggle, whether the sun and the stars shall appear, or shall not appear, for many days. I speak to-day for the preservation of the Union. "Hear me for my cause." I speak to-day, out of a solicitous and anxious heart, for the restoration to the country of that quiet and that harmony which make the blessings of this Union so rich, and so dear to us all. These are the topics that I propose to myself to discuss; these are the motives, and the sole motives, that influence me in the wish to communicate my opinions to the Senate and the country; and if I can do anything, however little, for the promotion of these ends, I shall have accomplished all that I expect.

Mr. President, it may not be amiss to recur very briefly to the events which, equally sudden and extraordinary, have brought the country into its present political condition. In May, 1846, the United States declared war against Mexico. Our armies, then on the frontiers, entered the provinces of that republic, met and defeated all her troops, penetrated her mountain passes, and occupied her capital. The marine force of the United States took possession of her forts and her towns, on the Atlantic and on the Pacific. In less than two years a treaty was negotiated, by which

Mexico ceded to the United States a vast territory, extending seven or eight hundred miles along the shores of the Pacific, and reaching back over the mountains, and across the desert, until it joins the frontier of the State of Texas. It so happened, in the distracted and feeble condition of the Mexican Government, that, before the declaration of war by the United States against Mexico had become known in California, the people of California, under the lead of American officers, overthrew the existing Mexican provincial government, and raised an independent flag. When the news arrived at San Francisco that war had been declared by the United States against Mexico, this independent flag was pulled down, and the Stars and Stripes of this Union hoisted in its stead. So, sir, before the war was over, the forces of the United States, military and naval, had possession of San Francisco and Upper California, and a great rush of emigrants from various parts of the world took place into California in 1846 and 1847. But now behold another wonder.

In January of 1848, a party of Mormons made a discovery of an extraordinary rich mine of gold, or rather of a great quantity of gold, hardly proper to be called a mine, for it was spread near the surface, on the lower part of the south or American branch of the Sacramento. They attempted to conceal their discovery for some time; but soon another discovery of gold, perhaps of greater importance was made, on another part of the American branch of the Sacramento, and near Sutters Fort, as it is called. The fame of these discoveries spread far and wide. They inflamed more and more the spirit of emigration toward California, which had already been excited; and adventurers crowded into the country by hundreds, and flocked toward the bay of San Francisco. This, as I have said, took place in the winter and spring of 1848. The digging commenced in the spring of that year, and from that time to this the work of searching for gold has been prosecuted with a success not heretofore known in the history of this globe. You recollect, sir, how incredulous at first the American public was at the accounts which reached us of these discoveries; but we all know, now, that these accounts received, and continue to receive, daily confirmation, and down to the present moment I suppose the assurance is as strong, after the experience of these several months, of the existence of deposits of gold apparently inexhaustible in the regions near San Francisco, in California, as it was at any period of the earlier dates of the accounts.

It so happened, sir, that although, after the return of peace, it became a very important subject for legislative consideration and legislative decision to provide a proper Territorial government for California, yet differences of opinion between the two Houses of Congress prevented the establishment of any such Territorial government at the last session. Under this state of things, the inhabitants of California, already amounting to a considerable number, thought it to be their duty, in the summer of last year, to establish a local government. Under the proclamation of General Riley, the people chose delegates to a convention and that convention met at Monterey. It formed a Constitution for the State of California, which, being referred to the people, was adopted by them in their primary assemblages. Desirous of immediate connection with the United States, its Senators were appointed and Representatives chosen, who have come hither, bringing with them the authentic Constitution of the State of California; and they now present themselves, asking, in behalf of their constituents, that it may be admitted into this Union as one of the United States. This Constitution, sir, contains an express prohibition of slavery, or involuntary servitude, in the State of California. It is said, and I suppose truly, that, of the members who composed that convention, some sixteen were natives of, and had been residents in, the slaveholding States, about twenty-two were from the non-slaveholding States, and the remaining ten members were either native Californians or old settlers in that country. This prohibition of slavery, it is said, was inserted with entire unanimity.

It is this circumstance, sir, the prohibition of slavery, which has contributed to raise, I do not say it has wholly raised, the dispute as to the propriety of the admission of California into the Union under this Constitution. It is not to be denied, Mr. President, nobody thinks of denying, that, whatever reasons were assigned at the commencement of the late war with Mexico, it was prosecuted for the purpose of the acquisition of territory, and under the alleged argument that the cession of territory was the only form in which proper compensation could be obtained by the United States, from Mexico, for the various claims and demands which the people of this country had against that government. At any rate, it will be found that President Polk's message, at the commencement of the session of December, 1847, avowed that the war was to be prosecuted until some acquisition of territory should be made. As the acquisition was to be south of the line of the United States, in warm climates and countries, it was naturally, I suppose, expected by the South, that whatever acquisitions were made in that region would be added to the slaveholding portion of the United States. Very little of accurate information was possessed of the real physical character, either of California or New Mexico, and events have not turned out as was expected. Both California and New Mexico are likely to come in as free States; and therefore some degree of disappointment and surprise has resulted. In other words, it is obvious that the question which has so long harassed the country, and at some times very seriously alarmed the minds of wise and good men, has come upon us for a fresh discussion—the question of slavery in these United States.

Now, sir, I propose, perhaps at the expense of some detail and consequent detention of the Senate, to review historically this question, which, partly in consequence of its own importance, and partly, perhaps mostly, in consequence of the manner in which it has been discussed in different portions of the country, has been a source of so much alienation and unkind feeling between them.

We all know, sir, that slavery has existed in the world from time immemorial. There was slavery, in the earliest periods of history, among the Oriental nations. There was slavery among the Jews; the theocratic government of that people issued no injunction against it. There was slavery among the Greeks; and the ingenious philosophy of the Greeks found, or sought to find, a justification for it exactly upon the grounds which have been assumed for such a justification in this country; that is, a natural and original difference among the races of mankind, and the inferiority of the black or colored race to the white. The Greeks justified their system of slavery upon that idea precisely. They held the African and some of the Asiatic tribes to be inferior to the white race; but they did not show, I think, by any close process of logic, that, if this were true, the more intelligent and the stronger had therefore a right to subjugate the weaker.

The more manly philosophy and jurisprudence of the Romans placed the justification of slavery on entirely different grounds. The Roman jurists, from the first and down to the fall of the empire, admitted that slavery was against the natural law, by which, as they maintained, all men, of whatsoever clime, color, or capacity, were equal; but they justified slavery, first, upon the ground and authority of the law of nations, arguing, and arguing truly, that at that day the conventional law of nations admitted that captives in war, whose lives, according to the notions of the times, were at the absolute disposal of the captors, might, in exchange for exemption from death, be made slaves for life, and that such servitude might descend to their posterity. The jurists of Rome also maintained, that, by the civil law, there might be servitude or slavery, personal and hereditary; first, by the voluntary act of the individual, who might sell himself into slavery; secondly, by his being reduced into a state of slavery by his creditors, in satisfaction of his debts; and, thirdly, by being placed in a state of servitude or slavery for crime. At the introduction of Christianity, the Roman world was full of slaves, and I suppose there is to be found no injunction against that relation between man and man in the teachings of the Gospel of Jesus Christ or of any of his Apostles. The object of the instruction imparted to mankind by the Founder of Christianity was to touch the heart, purify the soul, and improve the lives of individual men. That object went directly to the first fountain of all the political and social relations of the human race, as well as of all true religious feeling, the individual heart and mind of man.

Now, sir, upon the general nature and influence of slavery there exists a wide difference of opinion between the northern portion of this country and the southern. It is said on the one side, that, although not the subject of any injunction or direct prohibition in the New Testament, slavery is a wrong; that it is founded merely in the right of the strongest; and that it is an oppression, like unjust wars, like all those conflicts by which a powerful nation subjects a weaker to its will; and that, in its nature, whatever may be said of it in the modifications which have taken place, it is not according to the meek spirit of the Gospel. It is not "kindly affectioned"; it does not "seek another's, and not its own"; it does not "let the oppressed go free." These are sentiments that are cherished, and of late with greatly augmented force, among the people of the Northern States. They have taken hold of the religious sentiment of that part of the country, as they have, more or less, taken hold of the religious feelings of a considerable portion of mankind. The South, upon the other side, having been accustomed to this relation between the two races all their lives, from their birth, having been taught, in general, to treat the subjects of this bondage with care and kindness, and I believe, in general, feeling great kindness for them, have not taken the view of the subject which I have mentioned. There are thousands of religious men, with consciences as tender as any of their brethren at the North, who do not see the unlawfulness of slavery; and there are more thousands, perhaps, that, whatsoever they may think of it in its origin, and as a matter depending upon natural right, yet take things as they are, and finding slavery to be an established relation of the society in which they live, can see no way in which, let their opinions on the abstract question be what they may, it is in the power of the present generation to relieve themselves from this relation. And candor obliges me to say, that I believe they are just as conscientious, many of them, and the religious people, all of them, as they are at the North who hold different opinions.

The honorable Senator from South Carolina the other day alluded to the separation of that great religious community, the Methodist Episcopal Church. That separation was brought about by differences of opinion upon this particular subject of slavery. I felt great concern, as that dispute went on, about the result. I was in hopes that the difference of opinion might be adjusted, because I looked upon that religious denomination as one of the great props of religion and morals throughout the whole country, from Maine to Georgia, and westward to our utmost western boundary. The result was against my wishes and against my hopes. I have read all their proceedings and all their arguments; but I have never yet been able to come to the conclusion that there was any real ground for that separation; in other words, that any good could be produced by that separation. I must say I think there was some want of candor and charity. Sir, when a question of this kind seizes on the religious sentiments of mankind, and comes to be discussed in religious assemblies of the clergy and laity, there is always to be expected, or always to be feared, a great degree of excitement. It is in the nature of man, manifested by his whole history, that religious disputes are apt to become warm in proportion to the strength of the convictions which men entertain of the magnitude of the questions at issue. In all such disputes, there will sometimes be found men with whom everything is absolute; absolutely wrong or absolutely right. They see the right clearly; they think others ought so to see it, and they are disposed to establish a broad line of distinction between what is right and what is wrong. They are not seldom willing to establish that line upon their own convictions of truth and justice; and are ready to mark and guard it by placing along it a series of dogmas, as lines of boundary on the earth's surface are marked by posts and stones. There are men who, with clear perceptions, as they think, of their own duty, do not see how too eager a pursuit of one duty may involve them in the violation of others, or how too warm an embracement of one truth may lead to a disregard of other truths equally important. As I heard it stated strongly, not many days ago, these persons are disposed to mount upon some particular duty, as upon a war-horse, and to drive furiously on and upon and over all the other duties that may stand in the way. There are men who, in reference to disputes of that sort, are of opinion that human duties may be ascertained with the exactness of mathematics. They deal with morals as with mathematics; and they think what is right may be distinguished from what is wrong with the precision of an algebraic equation. They have, therefore, none too much charity toward others who differ with them. They are apt, too, to think that nothing is good but what is perfect, and that there are no compromises or modifications to be made in consideration of difference of opinion or in deference to other men's judgment. If their perspicacious vision enables them to detect a spot on the face of the sun, they think that a good reason why the sun should be struck down from heaven. They prefer the chance of running into utter darkness to living in heavenly light, if that heavenly light be not absolutely without any imperfection. There are impatient men; too impatient always to give heed to the admonition of St. Paul, that we are not to "do evil that good may come"; too impatient to wait for the slow progress of moral causes in the improvement of mankind. They do not remember that the doctrines and miracles of Jesus Christ have, in eighteen hundred years, converted only a small portion of the human race; and among the nations that are converted to Christianity, they forget how many vices and crimes, public and private, still prevail, and that many of them, public crimes especially, which are so clearly offences against the Christian religion, pass without exciting particular indignation. Thus wars are waged, and unjust wars. I do not deny that there may be just wars. There certainly are; but it was the remark of an eminent person, not many years ago, on the other side of the Atlantic, that it is one of the greatest reproaches to human nature that wars are sometimes just. The defence of nations sometimes causes a just war against the injustice of other nations. In this state of sentiment upon the general nature of slavery lies the cause of a great part of those unhappy divisions, exasperations, and reproaches which find vent and support in different parts of the Union.

But we must view things as they are. Slavery does exist in the United States. It did exist in the States before the adoption of this Constitution, and at that time. Let us, therefore, consider for a moment what was the state of sentiment, North and South, in regard to slavery, at the time this Constitution was adopted. A remarkable change has taken place since; but what did the wise and great men of all parts of the country think of slavery then? In what estimation did they hold it at the time when this Constitution was adopted? It will be found, sir, if we will carry ourselves by historical research back to that day, and ascertain men's opinions by authentic records still existing among us, that there was then no diversity of opinion between the North and the South upon the subject of slavery. It will be found that both parts of the country held it equally an evil—a moral and political evil. It will not be found that, either at the North or at the South, there was much, though there was some, invective against slavery as inhuman and cruel. The great ground of objection to it was political; that it weakened the social fabric; that, taking the place of free labor, society became less strong and labor less productive; and therefore we find from all the eminent men of the time the clearest expression of their opinion that slavery is an evil. They ascribed its existence here, not without truth, and not without some acerbity of temper and force of language, to the injurious policy of the mother country, who, to favor the navigator, had entailed these evils upon the Colonies. I need hardly refer, sir, particularly to the publications of the day. They are matters of history on the record. The eminent men, the most eminent men, and nearly all the conspicuous politicians of the South held the same sentiments—that slavery was an evil, a blight, a scourge, and a curse. There are no terms of reprobation of slavery so vehement in the North at that day as in the South. The North was not so much excited against it as the South; and the reason is, I suppose, that there was much less of it at the North, and the people did not see, or think they saw, the evils so prominently as they were seen, or thought to be seen, at the South.

Then, sir, when this Constitution was framed, this was the light in which the Federal Convention viewed it. That body reflected the judgment and sentiments of the great men of the South. A member of the other House, whom I have not the honor to know, has, in a recent speech, collected extracts from these public documents. They prove the truth of what I am saying, and the question then was, how to deal with it, and how to deal with it as an evil. They came to this general result. They thought that slavery could not be continued in the country if the importation of slaves was made to cease, and therefore they provided that, after a certain period, the importation might be prevented by the act of the new government. The period of twenty years was proposed by some gentleman from the North, I think, and many members of the Convention from the South opposed it as being too long. Mr. Madison especially was somewhat warm against it. He said it would bring too much of this mischief into the country to allow the importation of slaves for such a period. Because we must take along with us, in the whole of this discussion, when we are considering the sentiments and opinions in which the constitutional provision originated, that the conviction of all men was, that, if the importation of slaves ceased, the white race would multiply faster than the black race, and that slavery would therefore gradually wear out and expire. It may not be improper here to allude to that, I had almost said, celebrated opinion of Mr. Madison. You observe, sir, that the term slave, or slavery, is not used in the Constitution. The Constitution does not require that "fugitive slaves" shall be delivered up. It requires that persons held to service in one State, and escaping into another, shall be delivered up. Mr. Madison opposed the introduction of the term slave, or slavery, into the Constitution; for he said that he did not wish to see it recognized by the Constitution of the United States of America that there could be property in men.

Now, sir, all this took place in the Convention in 1787; but connected with this, concurrent and contemporaneous, is another important transaction, not sufficiently attended to. The Convention for framing this Constitution assembled in Philadalphia in May, and sat until September, 1787. During all that time the Congress of the United States was in session at New York. It was a matter of design, as we know, that the Convention should not assemble in the same city where Congress was holding its sessions. Almost all the public men of the country, therefore, of distinction and eminence, were in one or the other of these two assemblies; and I think it happened, in some instances, that the same gentlemen were members of both bodies. If I mistake not, such was the case with Mr. Rufus King, then a member of Congress from Massachusetts. Now, at the very time when the Convention in Philadelphia was framing this Constitution, the Congress in New York was framing the Ordinance of 1787, for the organization and government of the territory northwest of the Ohio. They passed that Ordinance on the 13th of July, 1787, at New York, the very month, perhaps the very day, on which these questions about the importation of slaves and the character of slavery were debated in the Convention of Philadelphia. So far as we can now learn, there was a perfect concurrence of opinion between these two bodies; and it resulted in this Ordinance of 1787, excluding slavery from all the territory over which the Congress of the United States had jurisdiction, and that was all the territory northwest of the Ohio. Three years before, Virginia and other States had made a cession of that great territory to the United States; and a most munificent act it was. I never reflect upon it without a disposition to do honor and justice, and justice would be the highest honor, to Virginia, for the cession of her northwestern territory. I will say, sir, it is one of her fairest claims to the respect and gratitude of the country, and that, perhaps, it is only second to that other claim which belongs to her—that from her counsels, and from the intelligence and patriotism of her leading statesmen, proceeded the first idea put into practice of the formation of a general Constitution of the United States. The Ordinance of 1787 applied to the whole territory over which the Congress of the United States had jurisdiction. It was adopted two years before the Constitution of the United States went into operation; because the Ordinance took effect immediately on its passage, while the Constitution of the United States, having been framed, was to be sent to the States to be adopted by their conventions; and then a government was to be organized under it. This Ordinance, then, was in operation and force when the Constitution was adopted, and the government put in motion, in April, 1789.

Mr. President, three things are quite clear as historical truths. One is, that there was an expectation that, on the ceasing of the importation of slaves from Africa, slavery would begin to run out here. That was hoped and expected. Another is, that, as far as there was any power in Congress to prevent the spread of slavery in the United States, that power was executed in the most absolute manner, and to the fullest extent. An honorable member [Mr. Calhoun], whose health does not allow him to be here to-day—

A Senator: He is here.

I am very happy to hear that he is; may he long be here, and in the enjoyment of health to serve his country! The honorable member said, the other day, that he considered this Ordinance as the first in a series of measures calculated to enfeeble the South, and deprive them of their just participation in the benefits and privileges of this government. He says, very properly, that it was enacted under the old Confederation, and before this Constitution went into effect; but my present purpose is only to say, Mr. President, that it was established with the entire the unanimous concurrence of the whole South. Why, there it stands! The vote of every State in the Union was unanimous in favor of the Ordinance, with the exception of a single individual vote, and that individual vote was given by a Northern man. This Ordinance prohibiting slavery forever northwest of the Ohio has the hand and seal of every Southern member in Congress. It was therefore no aggression of the North on the South. The other and third clear historical truth is, that the Convention meant to leave slavery in the States as they found it, entirely under the authority and control of the States themselves.

This was the state of things, sir, and this the state of opinion, under which those very important matters were arranged, and those three important things done; that is, the establishment of the Constitution of the United States with a recognition of slavery as it existed in the States; the establishment of the ordinance for the government of the Northwestern Territory, prohibiting, to the full extent of all territory owned by the United States, the introduction of slavery into that territory, while leaving to the States all power over slavery in their own limits; and creating a power, in the new government, to put an end to the importation of slaves, after a limited period. There was entire coincidence and concurrence of sentiment between the North and South, upon all these questions, at the period of the adoption of the Constitution. But opinions, sir, have changed, greatly changed; changed North and changed South. Slavery is not regarded in the South now as it was then. I see an honorable member of this body paying me the honor of listening to my remarks; he brings to my mind, sir, freshly and vividly, what I have learned of his great ancestor, so much distinguished in his day and generation, so worthy to be succeeded by so worthy a grandson, and of the sentiments he expressed in the Convention in Philadelphia.

Here we may pause. There was, if not an entire unanimity, a general concurrence of sentiment running through the whole community, and especially entertained by the eminent men of all parts of the country. But soon a change began, at the North and the South, and a difference of opinion showed itself; the North growing much more warm and strong against slavery, and the South growing much more warm and strong in its support. Sir, there is no generation of mankind whose opinions are not subject to be influenced by what appear to them to be their present emergent and exigent interests. I impute to the South no particularly selfish view in the change which has come over her. I impute to her certainly no dishonest view. All that has happened has been natural. It has followed those causes which always influence the human mind and operate upon it. What, then, have been the causes which have created so new a feeling in favor of slavery in the South, which have changed the whole nomenclature of the South on that subject, so that, from being thought and described in the terms I have mentioned and will not repeat, it has now become an institution, a cherished institution, in that quarter; no evil, no scourge, but a great religious, social, and moral blessing, as I think I have heard it latterly spoken of? I suppose this, sir, is owing to the rapid growth and sudden extension of the cotton plantations of the South. So far as any motive consistent with honor, justice, and general judgment could act, it was the cotton interest that gave a new desire to promote slavery, to spread it, and to use its labor. I again say that this change was produced by causes which must always produce like effects. The whole interest of the South became connected, more or less, with the extension of slavery. If we look back to the history of the commerce of this country in the early years of this government, what were our exports? Cotton was hardly, or but to a very limited extent, known. In 1791 the first parcel of cotton of the growth of the United States was exported, and amounted only to 19,200 pounds. It has gone on increasing rapidly, until the whole crop may now, perhaps, in a season of great product and high prices, amount to a hundred millions of dollars. In the years I have mentioned, there was more of wax, more of indigo, more of rice, more of almost every article of export from the South, than of cotton. When Mr. Jay negotiated the treaty of 1794 with England, it is evident from the twelfth article of the treaty, which was suspended by the Senate, that he did not know that cotton was exported at all from the United States.

Well, sir, we know what followed. The age of cotton became the golden age of our Southern brethren. It gratified their desire for improvement and accumulation, at that same time that it excited it. The desire grew by what it fed upon, and there soon came to be an eagerness for other territory, a new area or new areas for the cultivation of the cotton crop; and measures leading to this result were brought about rapidly, one after another, under the lead of Southern men at the head of the government, they having a majority in both branches of Congress to accomplish their ends. The honorable member from South Carolina observed that there has been a majority all along in favor of the North. If that be true, sir, the North has acted either very liberally and kindly, or very weakly; for they never exercised that majority efficiently five times in the history of the government, when a division or trial of strength arose. Never.

Whether they were outgeneralled, or whether it was owing to other causes, I shall not stop to consider; but no man acquainted with the history of the Union can deny that the general lead in the politics of the country, for three-fourths of the period that has elapsed since the adoption of the Constitution, has been a Southern lead.

In 1802, in pursuit of the idea of opening a new cotton region, the United States obtained a cession from Georgia of the whole of her western territory, now embracing the rich and growing States of Alabama and Mississippi. In 1803 Louisiana was purchased from France, out of which the States of Louisiana, Arkansas, and Missouri have been framed, as slaveholding States. In 1819 the cession of Florida was made, bringing in another region adapted to cultivation by slaves. Sir, the honorable member from South Carolina thought he saw in certain operations of the government, such as the manner of collecting the revenue, and the tendency of measures calculated to promote emigration into the country, what accounts for the more rapid growth of the North than the South. He ascribes that more rapid growth, not to the operation of time, but to the system of government and administration established under this Constitution. That is matter of opinion. To a certain extent it may be true; but it does seem to me that, if any operation of the government can be shown in any degree to have promoted the population, and growth, and wealth of the North, it is much more sure that there are sundry important and distinct operations of the government, about which no man can doubt, tending to promote, and which absolutely have promoted, the increase of the slave interest and the slave territory of the South. It was not time that brought in Louisiana; it was the act of men. It was not time that brought in Florida; it was the act of men. And lastly, sir, to complete those acts of legislation which have contributed so much to enlarge the area of the institution slavery, Texas, great and vast and illimitable Texas, was added to the Union as a slave State in 1845; and that, sir, pretty much closed the whole chapter, and settled the whole account.

That closed the whole chapter and settled the whole account, because the annexation of Texas, upon the conditions and under the guarantees upon which she was admitted, did not leave within the control of this government an acre of land, capable of being cultivated by slave labor, between this Capitol and the Rio Grande or the Nueces, or whatever is the proper boundary of Texas; not an acre. From that moment, the whole country, from this place to the western boundary of Texas, was fixed, pledged, fastened, decided, to be slave territory forever, by the solemn guarantees of law. And I now say, sir, as the proposition upon which I stand this day, and upon the truth and firmness of which I intend to act until it is overthrown, that there is not at this moment within the United States, or any Territory of the United States, a single foot of land, the character of which, in regard to its being free territory or slave territory, is not fixed by some law, and some irrepealable law, beyond the power of the action of the government. Is it not so with respect to Texas? It is most manifestly so. The honorable member from South Carolina, at the time of the admission of Texas, held an important post in the executive department of the government; he was Secretary of State. Another eminent person of great activity and adroitness in affairs, I mean the late Secretary of the Treasury, was a conspicuous member of this body, and took the lead in the business of annexation, in co-operation with the Secretary of State; and I must say that they did their business faithfully and thoroughly; there was no botch left in it. They rounded it off, and made as close joiner-work as ever was exhibited. Resolutions of annexation were brought into Congress, fitly joined together, compact, efficient, conclusive upon the great object which they had in view, and those resolutions passed.

Allow me to read a part of these resolutions. It is the third clause of the second section of the resolution of the 1st of March, 1845, for the admission of Texas, which applies to this part of the case. That clause is as follows:

> New States, of convenient size, not exceeding four in number, in addition to said State of Texas, and having sufficient population, may hereafter, by the consent of said State, be formed out of the territory thereof, which shall be entitled to admission under the provisions of the Federal Constitution. And such States as may be formed out of that portion of said territory lying south of thirty-six degrees thirty minutes north latitude, commonly known as the Missouri Compromise line, shall be admitted into the Union with or without slavery, as the people of each State asking admission may desire; and in such State or States as shall be formed out of said territory north of said Missouri Compromise line, slavery or involuntary servitide (except for crime) shall be prohibited.

Now what is here stipulated, enacted, and secured? It is, that all Texas south of 36°30′, which is nearly the whole of it, shall be admitted into the Union as a slave State. It was a slave State, and therefore came in as a slave State; and the guarantee is, that new States shall be made out of it, to the number of four, in addition to the State then in existence and admitted at that time by these resolutions, and that such States as are formed out of that portion of Texas lying south of 36°30′ may come in as slave States. I know no form of legislation which can strengthen this. I know no mode of recognition that can add a tittle of weight to it. I listened respectfully to the resolutions of my honorable friend from Tennessee. He proposed to recognize that stipulation with Texas. But any additional recognition would weaken the force of it; because it stands here on the ground of a contract, a thing done for consideration. It is a law founded on a contract with Texas, and designed to carry that contract into effect. A recognition now, founded not on any consideration, or any contract, would not be so strong as it now stands on the face of the resolution. I know no way, I candidly confess, in which this government, acting in good faith, as I trust it always will, can relieve itself from that stipulation and pledge, by any honest course of legislation whatever. And therefore I say again, that, so far as Texas is concerned, in the whole of that State south of 36°30′, which I suppose, embraces all the territory capable of slave cultivation, there is no land, not an acre, the character of which is not established by law; a law which cannot be repealed without the violation of a contract, and plain disregard of the public faith.

I hope, sir, it is now apparent that my proposition, so far as it respects Texas, has been maintained, and that the provision in this article is clear and absolute; and it has been well suggested by my friend from Rhode Island, that that part of Texas which lies north of 36°30′ of north latitude, and which may be formed into free States, is dependent, in like manner, upon the consent of Texas, herself a slave State.

Now, sir, how came this? How came it to pass that within these walls, where it is said by the honorable member from South Carolina that the free States have always had a majority, this resolution of annexation, such as I have described it, obtained a majority in both Houses of Congress? Sir, it obtained that majority by the great number of Northern votes added to the entire Southern vote, or at least nearly the whole of the Southern vote. The aggregate was made up of Northern and Southern votes. In the House of Representatives there were about eighty Southern votes and about fifty Northern votes for the admission of Texas. In the Senate the vote for the admission of Texas was twenty-seven, and twenty-five against it; and of those twenty-seven votes, constituting the majority, no less than thirteen came from the free States, and four of them were from New England. The whole of these thirteen Senators, constituting within a fraction, you see, one-half of all the votes in this body for the admission of this immeasurable extent of slave territory, were sent here by free States.

Sir, there is not so remarkable a chapter in our history of political events, political parties, and political men as is afforded by this admission of a new slaveholding Territory, so vast that a bird cannot fly over it in a week. New England, as I have said, with some of her own votes, supported this measure. Three-fourths of the votes of liberty-loving Connecticut were given for it in the other House, and one-half here. There was one vote for it from Maine, but I am happy to say, not the vote of the honorable member who addressed the Senate the day before yesterday, and who was then a Representative from Maine in the House of Representatives; but there was one vote from Maine, aye, and there was one vote for it from Massachusetts, given by a gentleman then representing, and now living in, the district in which the prevalence of Free Soil sentiment for a couple of years or so has defeated the choice of any member to represent it in Congress. Sir, that body of Northern and Eastern men who gave those votes at that time are now seen taking upon themselves, in the nomenclature of politics, the appellation of the Northern Democracy. They undertook to wield the destinies of this empire, if I may give that name to a republic, and their policy was, and they persisted in it, to bring into this country and under this government all the territory they could. They did it, in the case of Texas, under pledges, absolute pledges, to the slave interest, and they afterward lent their aid in bringing in these new conquests, to take their chance for slavery or freedom. My honorable friend from Georgia, in March, 1847, moved the Senate to declare that the war ought not to be prosecuted for the conquest of territory, or for the dismemberment of Mexico. The whole of the Northern Democracy voted against it. He did not get a vote from them. It suited the patriotic and elevated sentiments of the Northern Democracy to bring in a world from among the mountains and valleys of California and New Mexico, or any other part of Mexico, and then quarrel about it; to bring it in, and then endeavor to put upon it the saving grace of the Wilmot Proviso. There were two eminent and highly respectable gentlemen from the North and East, then leading gentlemen in the Senate (I refer, and I do so with entire respect, for I entertain for both of those gentlemen, in general, high regard, to Mr. Dix of New York and Mr. Niles of Connecticut), who both voted for the admission of Texas. They would not have that vote any other way than as it stood; and they would have it as it did stand. I speak of the vote upon the annexation of Texas. Those two gentlemen would have the resolution of annexation just as it is, without amendment; and they voted for it just as it is, and their eyes were all open to its true character. The honorable member from South Carolina who addressed us the other day was then Secretary of State. His correspondence with Mr. Murphy, the Chargé d'Affaires of the United States in Texas, had been published. That correspondence was all before those gentlemen, and the Secretary had the boldness and candor to avow in that correspondence, that the great object sought by the annexation of Texas was to strengthen the slave interest of the South. Why, sir, he said so in so many words—

MR. CALHOUN: Will the honorable Senator permit me to interrupt him for a moment?

Certainly.

MR. CALHOUN: I am very reluctant to interrupt the honorable gentleman; but, upon a point of so much importance, I deem it right to put myself *rectus in curia*. I did not put it upon the ground assumed by the Senator. I put it upon this ground; that Great Britain had announced to this country, in so many words, that her object was to abolish slavery in Texas, and, through Texas, to accomplish the abolition of slavery in the United States and the world. The ground I put it on was, that it would make an exposed frontier, and, if Great Britain succeeded in her object, it would be impossible that that frontier could be secured against the aggressions of the Abolitionists; and that this government was bound, under the guarantees of the Constitution, to protect us against such a state of things.

That comes, I suppose, sir, to exactly the same thing. It was, that Texas must be obtained for the security of the slave interest of the South.

MR. CALHOUN: Another view is very distinctly given.

That was the object set forth in the correspondence of a worthy gentleman not now living, who preceded the honorable member from South Carolina in the Department of State. There repose on the files of the Department, as I have occasion to know, strong letters from Mr. Upshur to the United States Minister in England, and I believe there are some to the same Minister from the honorable Senator himself, asserting to this effect the sentiments of this government; namely, that Great Britain was expected not to interfere to take Texas out of the hands of its then existing government and make it a free country. But my argument, my suggestion, is this: that those gentlemen who composed the Northern Democracy when Texas was brought into the Union saw clearly that it was brought in as a slave country, and brought in for the purpose of being maintained as slave territory, to the Greek Kalends. I rather thank the honorable gentleman who was then Secretary of State might, in some of his correspondence with Mr. Murphy, have suggested that it was not expedient to say too much about this object, lest it should create some alarm. At any rate, Mr. Murphy wrote to him that England was anxious to get rid of the Constitution of Texas, because it was a constitution establishing slavery; and what the United States had to do was to aid the people of Texas in upholding their Constitution; but that nothing should be said which should offend the fanatical men of the North. But, sir, the honorable member did avow this object himself, openly, boldly, and manfully; he did not disguise his conduct or his motives.

MR. CALHOUN: Never, never.

What he means he is very apt to say.

MR. CALHOUN: Always, always.

And I honor him for it.

This admission of Texas was in 1845. Then in 1847, *flagrante bello* between the United States and Mexico, the proposition I have mentioned was brought forward by my friend from Georgia, and the Northern Democracy voted steadily against it. Their remedy was to apply to the acquisitions, after they should come in, the Wilmot Proviso. What follows? These two gentlemen, worthy and honorable and influential men (and if they had not been they could not have carried the measure), these two gentlemen, members of this body, brought in Texas, and by their votes they also prevented the passage of the resolution of the honorable member from Georgia, and then they went home and took the lead in the Free Soil party. And there they stand, sir! They leave us here, bound in honor and conscience by the resolutions of annexation; they leave us here, to take the odium of fulfilling the obligations in favor of slavery which they voted us into, or else the greater odium of violating those obligations, while they are at home making capital and rousing speeches for free soil and no slavery. And therefore I say, sir, that there is not a chapter in our history, respecting public measures and public men, more full of what would create surprise, more full of what does create in my mind extreme mortification, than that of the conduct of the Northern Democracy on this subject.

Mr. President, sometimes, when a man is found in a new relation to things around him and to other men, he says the world has changed, and that he has not changed. I believe, sir, that our self-respect leads us often to make this declaration in regard to ourselves when it is not exactly true. An individual is more apt to change, perhaps, than all the world around him. But under the present circumstances, and under the responsibility which I know I incur by what I am stating here, I feel at liberty to recur to the various expressions and statements, made at various times, of my own opinions and resolutions respecting the admission of Texas, and all that has followed. Sir, as early as 1836, or in the early part of 1837, there was conversation and correspondence between myself and some private friends on this project of annexing Texas to the United States; and an honorable gentleman with whom I have had a long acquaintance, a friend of mine, now perhaps in this Chamber, I mean General Hamilton, of South Carolina, was privy to that correspondence. I had voted for the recognition of Texan independence, because I believed it to be an existing fact, surprising and astonishing as it was, and I wished well to the new republic; but I manifested from the first utter opposition to bringing her, with her slave territory, into the Union. I happened, in 1837, to make a public address to political friends in New York, and I then stated my sentiments upon the subject. It was the first time that I had occasion to advert to it; and I will ask a friend near me to have the kindness to read an extract from the speech made by me on that occasion. It was delivered in Niblo's Saloon, in 1837.

Mr. Greene then read the following extract from the speech of Mr. Webster to which he referred:

> Gentlemen, we all see that, by whomsoever possessed, Texas is likely to be a slaveholding country; and I frankly avow my entire unwillingness to do anything that shall extend the slavery of the African race on this Continent, or add other slaveholding States to the Union. When I say that I regard slavery in itself as a great moral, social, and political evil, I only use language which has been adopted by distinguished men, themselves citizens of slaveholding States. I shall do nothing, therefore, to favor or encourage its further extension. We have slavery already among us. The Constitution found it in the Union; it recognized it, and gave it solemn guarantees. To the full extent of these guarantees we are all bound, in honor, in justice, and by the Constitution. All the stipulations contained in the Constitution in favor of the slaveholding States which are already in the Union ought to be fulfilled, and, so

> far as depends on me, shall be fulfilled, in the fulness of their spirit, and to the exactness of their letter. Slavery, as it exists in the States, is beyond the reach of Congress. It is a concern of the States themselves; they have never submitted it to Congress, and Congress has no rightful power over it. I shall concur, therefore, in no act, no measure, no menace, no indication of purpose, which shall interfere or threaten to interfere with the exclusive authority of the several States over the subject of slavery as it exists within their respective limits. All this appears to me to be matter of plain and imperative duty.
>
> But when we come to speak of admitting new States, the subject assumes an entirely different aspect. Our rights and our duties are then both different. . . .
>
> I see, therefore, no political necessity for the annexation of Texas to the Union; no advantages to be derived from it; and objections to it of a strong, and, in my judgment, decisive character.

I have nothing, sir, to add to, or to take from, those sentiments. That speech, the Senate will perceive, was made in 1837. The purpose of immediately annexing Texas at that time was abandoned or postponed; and it was not revived with any vigor for some years. In the meantime it happened that I had become a member of the executive administration, and was for a short period in the Department of State. The annexation of Texas was a subject of conversation, not confidential, with the President and heads of departments, as well as with other public men. No serious attempt was then made, however, to bring it about. I left the Department of State in May, 1843, and shortly after I learned, though by means which were no way connected with official information, that a design had been taken up of bringing Texas, with her slave territory and population, into this Union. I was in Washington at the time, and persons are now here who will remember that we had an arranged meeting for conversation upon it. I went home to Massachusetts and proclaimed the existence of that purpose, but I could get no audience and but little attention. Some did not believe it, and some were too much engaged in their own pursuits to give it any heed. They had gone to their farms or to their merchandise, and it was impossible to arouse any feeling in New England, or in Massachusetts, that should combine the two great political parties against this annexation; and, indeed, there was no hope of bringing the Northern Democracy into that view, for their leaning was all the other way. But, sir, even with Whigs, and leading Whigs, I am ashamed to say, there was a great indifference toward the admission of Texas, with slave territory, into this Union.

The project went on. I was then out of Congress. The annexation resolutions passed on the 1st of March, 1845; the Legislature of Texas complied with the conditions and accepted the guarantees; for the language of the resolution is, that Texas is to come in "upon the conditions and under the guarantees herein prescribed." I was returned to the Senate in March, 1845, and was here in December following, when the acceptance by Texas of the conditions proposed by Congress was communicated to us by the President, and an act for the consummation of the union was laid before the two Houses. The connection was then not completed. A final law, doing the deed of annexation ultimately, had not been passed; and when it was put upon its final passage here, I expressed my opposition to it, and recorded my vote in the negative; and there that vote stands, with the observations that I made upon that occasion. Nor is this the only occasion on which I have expressed myself to the same effect. It has happened that, between 1837 and this time, on various occasions, I have expressed my entire opposition to the admission of slave States, or the acquisition of new slave territories, to be added to the United States. I know, sir, no change in my own sentiments, or my own purposes, in that respect. I will now ask my friend from Rhode Island to read another extract from a speech of mine made at a Whig convention in Springfield, Massachusetts, in the month of September, 1847.

Mr. Greene here read the following extract:

> We hear much just now of a panacea for the dangers and evils of slavery and slave annexation, which they call the "Wilmot Proviso." That certainly is a just sentiment, but it is not a sentiment to found any new party upon. It is not a sentiment on which Massachusetts Whigs differ. There is not a man in this hall who holds to it more firmly than I do, nor one who adheres to it more than another.
>
> I feel some little interest in this matter, sir. Did I not commit myself in 1837 to the whole doctrine, fully, entirely? And I must be permitted to say that I cannot quite consent that more recent discoverers should claim the merit and take out a patent.
>
> I deny the priority of their invention. Allow me to say, sir, it is not their thunder. . . .
>
> We are to use the first and the last and every occasion which offers to oppose the extension of slave power.
>
> But I speak of it here, as in Congress, as a political question, a question for statesmen to act upon. We must so regard it. I certainly do not mean to say that it is less important in a moral point of view, that it is not more important in many other points of view; but as a legislator, or in any official capacity, I must look at it, consider it, and decide it as a matter of political action.

On other occasions, in debates here, I have expressed my determination to vote for no acquisition, cession, or annexation, north or south, east or west. My opinion has been, that we have territory enough, and that we should follow the Spartan maxim, "Improve, adorn, what you have," seek no further. I think that it was in some observations that I made on the three-million loan bill that I avowed this sentiment. In short, sir, it has been avowed quite as often, in as many places, and before as many assemblies, as any humble opinions of mine ought to be avowed.

But now that, under certain conditions, Texas is in the Union, with all her territory, as a slave State, with a solemn pledge, also, that, if she shall be divided into many States, those States may come in as slave States south of 36°30′, how are we to deal with this subject? I know no way of honest legislation, when the proper time comes for the enactment, but to carry into effect all that we have stipulated to do. I do not entirely agree with my honorable friend from Tennessee, that, as soon as the time comes when she is entitled to another Representative, we should create a new State. On former occasions, in creating new States out of Territories, we have generally gone upon the idea that, when the population of the Territory amounts to about sixty thousand, we would consent to its admission as a State. But it is quite a different thing when a State is divided, and two or more States made out of it. It does not follow in such a case that the same rule of apportionment should be applied. That, however, is a matter for the consideration of Congress, when the proper time arrives. I may not then be here; I may have no vote to give on the occasion; but I wish it to be distinctly understood, that, according to my view of the matter, this government is solemnly pledged, by law and contract, to create new States out of Texas, with her consent, when her population shall justify and call for such a proceeding, and, so far as such States are formed out of Texan territory lying south of 36°30′, to let them come in as slave States. That is the meaning of the contract which our friends, the Northern Democracy, have left us to fulfil; and I, for one, mean to fulfil it, because I will not violate the faith of the government. What I mean to say is, that the time for the admission of new States formed out of Texas, the number of such States, their boundaries, the requisite amount of population, and all other things connected with the admission, are in the free discretion of Congress, except this, to wit, that, when new States formed out of Texas are to be admitted, they have a right, by legal stipulation and contract, to come in as slave States.

Now, as to California and New Mexico, I hold slavery to be excluded from those Territories by a law even superior to that which admits and sanctions it in Texas. I mean the law of nature, of physical geography, the law of the formation of the earth. That law settles forever, with a strength beyond all terms of human enactment, that slavery cannot exist in California or New Mexico. Understand me, sir; I mean slavery as we regard it; the slavery of the colored race as it exists in the Southern States. I shall not discuss the point, but leave it to the learned gentlemen who have undertaken to discuss it; but I suppose there is no slavery of that description in California now. I understand that *peonism*, a sort of penal servitude, exists there, or rather a sort of voluntary sale of a man and his offspring for debt, an arrangement of a peculiar nature known to the law of Mexico. But what I mean to say is, that it is as impossible that African slavery, as we see it among us, should find its way, or be introduced, into California and New Mexico, as any other natural impossibility. California and New Mexico are Asiatic in their formation and scenery. They are composed of vast ridges of mountains, of great height, with broken ridges and deep valleys. The sides of these mountains are entirely barren; their tops capped by perennial snow. There may be in California, now made free by its Constitution, and no doubt there are, some tracts of valuable land. But it is not so in New Mexico. Pray, what is the evidence which every gentleman must have obtained on this subject, from information sought by himself or communicated by others? I have inquired and read all I could find, in order to acquire information on this important subject. What is there in New Mexico that could, by any possibility, induce anybody to go there with slaves? There are some narrow strips of tillable land on the borders of the rivers; but the rivers themselves dry up before midsummer is gone. All that the people can do in that region is to raise some little articles, some little wheat for their *tortillas*, and that by irrigation. And who expects to see a hundred black men cultivating tobacco, corn, cotton, rice, or anything else, on lands in New Mexico, made fertile only by irrigation?

I look upon it, therefore, as a fixed fact, to use the current expression of the day, that both California and New Mexico are destined to be free, so far as they are settled at all, which I believe, in regard to New Mexico, will be but partially for a great length of time; free by the arrangement of things ordained by the Power above us. I have therefore to say, in this respect also, that this country is fixed for freedom, to as many persons as shall ever live in it, by a less repealable law than that which attaches to the right of holding slaves in Texas; and I will say further, that, if a resolution or a bill were now before us, to provide a Territorial government for New Mexico, I would not vote to put any prohibition into it whatever. Such a prohibition would be idle, as it respects any effect it would have upon the Territory; and I would not take pains uselessly to re-affirm an ordinance of nature, nor to re-enact the will of God. I would put in no Wilmot Proviso for the mere purpose of a taunt or a reproach. I would put into it no evidence of the votes of superior power, exercised for no purpose but to wound the pride, whether a just and rational pride, or an irrational pride, of the citizens of the Southern States. I have no such object, no such purpose. They would think it a taunt, an indignity; they would think it to be an act taking away from them what they regard as a proper equality of privilege. Whether they expect to realize any benefit from it or not, they would think it at least a plain theoretic wrong; that something more or less derogatory to their character and their rights had taken place. I propose to inflict no such wound upon anybody, unless something essentially important to the country, and efficient to the preservation of liberty and freedom, is to be effected. I repeat, therefore, sir, and, as I do not propose to address the Senate often on this subject, I repeat it because I wish it to be distinctly understood, that, for the reasons stated, if a proposition were now here to establish a government for New Mexico, and it was moved to insert a provision for a prohibition of slavery, I would not vote for it.

Sir, if we were now making a government for New Mexico, and anybody should propose a Wilmot Proviso, I should treat it exactly as Mr. Polk treated that provision for excluding slavery from Oregon. Mr. Polk was known to be in opinion decidedly averse to the Wilmot Proviso; but he felt the necessity of establishing a government for the Territory of Oregon. The proviso was in the bill, but he knew it would be entirely nugatory; and, since it must be entirely nugatory, since it took away no right, no describable, no tangible, no appreciable right of the South, he said he would sign the bill for the sake of enacting a law to form a government in that Territory, and let that entirely useless, and, in that connection, entirely senseless, proviso remain. Sir, we hear occasionally of the annexation of Canada; and if there be any man, any of the Northern Democracy, or any one of the Free Soil party, who supposes it necessary to insert a Wilmot Proviso in a territorial government for New Mexico, that man would of course be of opinion that it is necessary to protect the everlasting snows of Canada from the foot of slavery by the same overspreading wing of an act of Congress. Sir, wherever there is a substantive good to be done, wherever there is a foot of land to be prevented from becoming slave territory, I am ready to assert the principle of the exclusion of slavery. I am pledged to it from the year 1837; I have been pledged to it again and again; and I will perform those pledges; but I will not do a thing unnecessarily that wounds the feelings of others, or that does discredit to my own understanding.

Now, Mr. President, I have established, so far as I proposed to do so, the proposition with which I set out, and upon which I intend to stand or fall; and that is, that the whole territory within the former United States, or in the newly acquired Mexican provinces, has a fixed and settled character, now fixed and settled by law which cannot be repealed—in the case of Texas without a violation of public faith, and by no human power in regard to California or New Mexico; that, therefore, under one or other of these laws, every foot of land in the States or in the Territories has already received a fixed and decided character.

Mr. President, in the excited times in which we live, there is found to exist a state of crimination and recrimination between the North and South. There are lists of grievances produced by each, and those grievances, real or supposed, alienate the minds of one portion of the country from the other, exasperate the feelings, and subdue the sense of fraternal affection, patriotic love, and mutual regard. I shall bestow a little attention, sir, upon these various grievances existing on the one side and on the other. I begin with complaints of the South. I will not answer, further than I have, the general statements of the honorable Senator from South Carolina, that the North has prospered at the expense of the South in consequence of the manner of administering this government, in the collecting of its revenues, and so forth. These are disputed topics, and I have no inclination to enter into them. But I will allude to other complaints of the South, and especially to one which has in my opinion just foundation; and that is, that there has been found at the North, among individuals and among legislators, a disinclination to perform fully their constitutional duties in regard to the return of persons bound to service who have escaped into the free States. In that respect, the South, in my judgment, is right, and the North is wrong. Every member of every Northern Legislature is bound by oath, like every other officer in the country, to support the Constitution of the United States; and the article of the Constitution which says to these States that they shall deliver up fugitives from service is as binding in honor and conscience as any other article. No man fulfils his duty in any Legislature who sets himself to find excuses, evasions, escapes from this Constitutional obligation. I have always thought that the Constitution addressed itself to the Legislatures of the States or to the States themselves. It says that those persons escaping to other States "shall be delivered up," and I confess I have always been of the opinion that it was an injunction upon the States themselves. When it is said that a person escaping into another State, and coming therefore within the jurisdiction of that State, shall be delivered up, it seems to me the import of the clause is, that the State itself, in obedience to the Constitution, shall cause him to be delivered up. That is my judgment. I have always entertained that opinion, and I entertain it now. But when the subject, some years ago, was before the Supreme Court of the United States the majority of the judges held that the power to cause fugitives from service to be delivered up was a power to be exercised under the authority of this government. I do not know, on the whole, that it may not have been a fortunate decision. My habit is to respect the result of judicial deliberations and the solemnity of judicial decisions. As it now stands, the business of seeing that these fugitives are delivered up resides in the power of Congress and the national judicature, and my friend at the head of the Judiciary Committee has a bill on the subject now before the Senate, which, with some amendments to it, I propose to support, with all its provisions, to the fullest extent. And I desire to call the attention of all sober-minded men at the North, of all conscientious men, of all men who are not carried away by some fanatical idea or some false impression, to their Constitutional obligations. I put it to all the sober and sound minds at the North as a question of morals and a question of conscience. What right have they, in their legislative capacity or any other capacity, to endeavor to get round this Constitution, or to embarrass the free exercise of the rights secured by the Constitution to the persons whose slaves escape from them? None at all; none at all. Neither in the forum of conscience, nor before the face of the Constitution, are they, in my opinion, justified in such an attempt. Of course it is a matter for their consideration. They probably, in the excitement of the times, have not stopped to consider of this. They have followed what seemed to be the current of thought and of motives, as the occasion arose, and they have neglected to investigate fully the real question, and to consider their Constitutional obligations; which, I am sure, if they did consider, they would fulfil with alacrity. I repeat, therefore, sir, that here is a well-founded ground of complaint against the North, which ought to be removed, which it is now in the power of the different departments of this government to remove; which calls for the enactment of proper laws authorizing the judicature of this government, in the several States, to do all that is necessary for the recapture of fugitive slaves and for their restoration to those who claim them. Wherever I go, and whenever I speak on the subject, and when I speak here I desire to speak to the whole North, I say that the South has been injured in this respect, and has a right to complain; and the North has been too careless of what I think the Constitution peremptorily and emphatically enjoins upon her as a duty.

Complaint has been made against certain resolutions that emanate from Legislatures at the North, and are sent here to us, not only on the subject of slavery in this District, but sometimes recommending Congress to consider the means of abolishing slavery in the States. I should be sorry to be called upon to present any resolutions here which could not be referable to any committee or any power in Congress; and therefore I should be unwilling to receive from the Legislature of Massachusetts any instructions to present resolutions expressive of any opinion whatever on the subject of slavery, as it exists at the present moment in the States, for two reasons: first, because I do not consider that the Legislature of Massachusetts has anything to do with it; and next, because I do not consider that I, as her representative here, have anything to do with it. It has become, in my opinion, quite too common; and if the Legislatures of the States do not like that opinion, they have a great deal more power to put it down than I have to uphold it; it has become, in my opinion, quite too common a practice for the State Legislatures to present resolutions here on all subjects and to instruct us on all subjects. There is no public man that requires instruction more than I do, or who requires information more than I do, or desires it more heartily; but I do not like to have it in too imperative a shape. I took notice, with pleasure, of some remarkes made upon this subject, the other day, in the Senate of Massachusetts, by a young man of talent and character, of whom the best hopes may be entertained. I mean Mr. Hillard. He told the Senate of Massachusetts that he would vote for no instructions whatever to be forwarded to members of Congress, nor for any resolutions to be offered expressive of the sense of Massachusetts as to what her members of Congress ought to do. He said that he saw no propriety in one set of public servants giving instructions and reading lectures to another set of public servants. To his own master each of them must stand or fall, and that master is his constituents. I wish these sentiments could become more common. I have never entered into the question, and never shall, as to the binding force of instructions. I will, however, simply say this: if there by any matter pending in this body, while I am a member of it, in which Massachusetts has an interest of her own not adverse to the general interests of the country, I shall pursue her instructions with gladness of heart and with all the efficiency which I can bring to the occasion. But if the question be one which affects her interest, and, at the same time equally affects the interests of all the other States, I shall no more regard her particular wishes or instructions than I should regard the wishes of a man who might appoint me an arbitrator or referee to decide some question of important private right between him and his neighbor, and then instruct me to decide in his favor. If ever there was a government upon earth it is this government, if ever there was a body upon earth it is this body, which should consider itself as composed by agreement of all, each member appointed by some, but organized by the general consent of all sitting here, under the solemn obligations of oath and conscience, to do that which they think to be best for the good of the whole.

Then, sir, there are the Abolition societies, of which I am unwilling to speak, but in regard to which I have very clear notions and opinions. I do not think them useful. I think their operations for the last twenty years have produced nothing good or valuable. At the same time, I believe thousands of their members to be honest and good men, perfectly well-meaning men. They have excited feelings; they think they must do something for the cause of liberty; and, in their sphere of action, they do not see what else they can do than to contribute to an Abolition press, or an Abolition society, or to pay an Abolition lecturer. I do not mean to impute gross motives even to the leaders of these societies; but I am not blind to the consequences of their proceedings. I cannot but see what mischiefs their interference with the South has produced. And is it not plain to every man? Let any gentleman who entertains doubts on this point recur to the debates in the Virginia House of Delegates in 1832, and he will see with what freedom a proposition made by Mr. Jefferson Randolph for the gradual abolition of slavery was discussed in that body. Every one spoke of slavery as he thought; very ignominious and disparaging names and epithets were applied to it. The debates in the House of Delegates on that occasion, I believe, were all published. They were read by every colored man who could read; and to those who could not read, those debates were read by others. At that time Virginia was not unwilling or afraid to discuss this question, and to let that part of her population know as much of the discussion as they could learn. That was in 1832. As has been said by the honorable member from South Carolina, these Abolition societies commenced their course of action in 1835. It is said, I do not know how true it may be, that they sent incendiary publications into the slave States; at any rate, they attempted to arouse, and did arouse, a very strong feeling; in other words, they created great agitation in the North against Southern slavery. Well, what was the result? The bonds of the slaves were bound more firmly than before, their rivets were more strongly fastened. Public opinion, which in Virginia had begun to be exhibited against slavery, and was opening out for the discussion of the question, drew back and shut itself up in its castle. I wish to know whether anybody in Virginia can now talk openly as Mr. Randolph, Governor McDowell, and others talked in 1832, and sent their remarks to the press? We all know the fact, and we all know the cause; and everything that these agitating people have done has been, not to enlarge, but to restrain, not to set free, but to bind faster, the slave population of the South.

Again, sir, the violence of the Northern press is complained of. The press violent! Why, sir, the press is violent everywhere. There are outrageous reproaches in the North against the South, and there are reproaches as vehement in the South against the North. Sir, the extremists of both parts of this country are violent; they mistake loud and violent talk for eloquence and for reason. They think that he who talks loudest reasons best. And this we must expect, when the press is free, as it is here, and I trust always will be; for, with all its licentiousness and all its evil, the entire and absolute freedom of the press is essential to the preservation of government on the basis of a free constitution. Wherever it exists there will be foolish and violent paragraphs in the newspapers, as there are, I am sorry to say, foolish and violent speeches in both Houses of Congress. In truth, sir, I must say that, in my opinion, the vernacular tongue of the country has become greatly vitiated, depraved, and corrupted by the style of our Congressional debates. And if it were possible for those debates to vitiate the principles of the people as much as they have depraved their tastes, I should cry out, "God save the Republic!"

Well, in all this I see no solid grievance, no grievance presented by the South, within the redress of the government, but the single one to which I have referred; and that is, the want of a proper regard to the injunction of the Constitution for the delivery of fugitive slaves.

There are also complaints of the North against the South. I need not go over them particularly. The first and gravest is, that the North adopted the Constitution, recognizing the existence of slavery in the States, and recognizing the right, to a certain extent, of the representation of slaves in Congress, under a state of sentiment and expectation which does not now exist; and that, by events, by circumstances, by the eagerness of the South to acquire territory and extend her slave population, the North finds itself, in regard to the relative influence of the South and the North, of the free States and the slave States, where it never did expect to find itself when they agreed to the compact of the Constitution. They complain, therefore, that, instead of slavery being regarded as an evil, as it was then, an evil which all hoped would be extinguished gradually, it is now regarded by the South as an institution to be cherished, and preserved, and extended; an institution which the South has already extended to the utmost of her power by the acquisition of new territory.

Well, then, passing from that, everybody in the North reads; and everybody reads whatsoever the newspapers contain; and the newspapers, some of them, especially those presses to which I have alluded, are careful to spread about among the people every reproachful sentiment uttered by any Southern man bearing at all against the North; everything that is calculated to exasperate and to alienate; and there are many such things, as everybody will admit, from the South, or some portion of it, which are disseminated among the reading people; and they do exasperate, and alienate, and produce a most mischievous effect upon the public mind at the North. Sir, I would not notice things of this sort appearing in obscure quarters; but one thing has occurred in this debate which struck me very forcibly. An honorable member from Louisiana addressed us the other day on this subject. I suppose there is not a more amiable and worthy gentleman in this chamber, nor a gentleman who would be more slow to give offence to anybody, and he did not mean in his remarks to give offence. But what did he say? Why, sir, he took pains to run a contrast between the slaves of the South and the laboring people of the North, giving the preference, in all points of condition, and comfort, and happiness, to the slaves of the South. The honorable member, doubtless, did not suppose that he gave any offense, or did any injustice. He was merely expressing his opinion. But does he know how remarks of that sort will be received by the laboring people of the North? Why, who are the laboring people of the North? They are the whole North. They are the people who till their own farms with their own hands; freeholders, educated men, independent men. Let me say, sir, that five-sixths of the whole property of the North is in the hands of the laborers of the North; they cultivate their farms, they educate their children, they provide the means of independence. If they are not freeholders, they earn wages; these wages accumulate, are turned into capital, into new freeholds, and small capitalists are created. Such is the case, and such the course of things, among the industrious and frugal. And what can these people think when so respectable and worthy a gentleman as the member from Louisiana undertakes to prove that the absolute ignorance and the abject slavery of the South are more in conformity with the high purposes and destiny of immortal, rational human beings, than the educated, the independent free labor of the North?

There is a more tangible and irritating cause of grievance at the North. Free blacks are constantly employed in the vessels of the North, generally as cooks or stewards. When the vessel arrives at a Southern port, these free colored men are taken on shore, by the police or municipal authority, imprisoned, and kept in prison till the vessel is again ready to sail. This is not only irritating, but exceedingly unjustifiable and oppressive. Mr. Hoar's mission, some time ago, to South Carolina, was a well-intended effort to remove this cause of complaint. The North thinks such imprisonments illegal and unconstitutional; and as the cases occur constantly and frequently, they regard it as a great grievance.

Now, sir, so far as any of these grievances have their foundation in matters of law, they can be redressed, and ought to be redressed; and so far as they have their foundation in matters of opinion, in sentiment, in mutual crimination and recrimination, all that we can do is to endeavor to allay the agitation, and cultivate a better feeling and more fraternal sentiments between the South and the North.

Mr. President, I should much prefer to have heard from every member on this floor declarations of opinion that this Union could never be dissolved, than the declaration of opinion by anybody, that, in any case, under the pressure of any circumstances, such a dissolution was possible. I hear with distress and anguish the word "secession," especially when it falls from the lips of those who are patriotic, and known to the country, and known all over the world, for their political services. Secession! Peaceable secession! Sir, your eyes and mine are never destined to see that miracle. The dismemberment of this vast country without convulsion! The breaking up of the fountains of the great deep without ruffling the surface! Who is so foolish, I beg everybody's pardon, as to expect to see any such thing? Sir, he who sees these States, now revolving in harmony around a common centre, and expects to see them quit their places and fly off without convulsion, may look the next hour to see the heavenly bodies rush from their spheres, and jostle against each other in the realms of space, without causing the wreck of the universe. There can be no such thing as a peaceable secession. Peaceable secession is an utter impossibility. Is the great Constitution under which we live, covering this whole country—is it to be thawed and melted away by secession, as the snows on the mountain melt under the influence of a vernal sun, disappear almost unobserved, and run off? No, sir! No, sir! I will not state what might produce the disruption of the Union; but, sir, I see as plainly as I see the sun in heaven what that disruption itself must produce; I see that it must produce war, and such a war as I will not describe, in its twofold character.

Peaceable seccession! Peaceable secession! The concurrent agreement of all the members of this great Republic to separate! A voluntary separation, with alimony on one side and on the other. Why, what would be the result? Where is the line to be drawn? What States are to secede? What is to remain American? What am I to be? An American no longer? Am I to become a sectional man, a local man, a separatist, with no country in common with the gentlemen who sit around me here, or who fill the other House of Congress? Heaven forbid! Where is the flag of the Republic to remain? Where is the eagle still to tower? or is he to cower, and shrink, and fall to the ground? Why, sir, our ancestors, our fathers and our grandfathers, those of them that are yet living among us with prolonged lives, would rebuke and reproach us; and our children and our granchildren would cry out shame upon us, if we of this generation should dishonor these ensigns of the power of the government and the harmony of that Union which is every day felt among us with so much joy and gratitude. What is to become of the army? What is to become of the navy? What is to become of the public lands? How is each of the thirty States to defend itself? I know, although the idea has not been stated distinctly, there is to be, or it is supposed possible that there will be, a Southern Confederacy. I do not mean, when I allude to this statement, that any one seriously contemplates such a state of things. I do not mean to say that it is true, but I have heard it suggested elsewhere, that the idea has been entertained, that, after the dissolution of this Union, a Southern Confederacy might be formed. I am sorry, sir, that it has ever been though of, talked of, or dreamed of, in the wildest flights of human imagination. But the idea, so far as it exists, must be of a separation, assigning the slave States to one side and the free States to the other. Sir, I may express myself too strongly, perhaps, but there are impossibilities in the natural as well as in the physical world, and I hold the idea of a separation of these States, those that are free to form one government, and those that are slaveholding to form another, as such an impossibility. We could not separate the States by any such line, if we were to draw it. We could not sit down here to-day and draw a line of separation that would satisfy any five men in the country. There are natural causes that would keep and tie us together, and there are social and domestic relations which we could not break if we would, and which we should not if we could.

Sir, nobody can look over the face of this country at the present moment, nobody can see where its population is the most dense and growing, without being ready to admit, and compelled to admit, that erelong the strength of America will be in the Valley of the Mississippi. Well, now, sir, I beg to inquire what the wildest enthusiast has to say on the possibility of cutting that river in two, and leaving free States at its source and on its branches, and slave States down near its mouth, each forming a separate government? Pray, sir, let me say to the people of this country, that these things are worthy of their pondering and of their consideration. Here, sir, are five millions of freemen in the free States north of the river Ohio. Can anybody suppose that this population can be severed, by a line that divides them from the territory of a foreign and an alien government, down somewhere, the Lord knows where, upon the lower banks of the Mississippi? What would become of Missouri? Will she join the arrondissement of the slave States? Shall the man from the Yellowstone and the Platte be connected, in the new republic, with the man who lives on the southern extremity of the Cape of Florida? Sir, I am ashamed to pursue this line of remark. I dislike it, I have an utter disgust for it. I would rather hear of natural blasts and mildews, war, pestilence, and famine, than to hear gentlemen talk of secession. To break up this great government! to dismember this glorious country! to astonish Europe with an act of folly such as Europe for two centuries has never beheld in any government or any people! No, sir! no, sir! There will be no secession! Gentlemen are not serious when they talk of secession.

Sir, I hear there is to be a convention held at Nashville. I am bound to believe that, if worthy gentlemen meet at Nashville in convention, their object will be to adopt conciliatory counsels; to advise the South to forbearance and moderation; and to advise the North to forbearance and moderation; and to inculcate principles of brotherly love and affection, and attachment to the Constitution of the country as it now is. I believe, if the convention meet at all, it will be for this purpose; for certainly, if they meet for any purpose hostile to the Union, they have been singularly inappropriate in their selection of a place. I remember, sir, that, when the treaty of Amiens was concluded between France and England, a sturdy Englishman and a distinguished orator, who regarded the conditions of the peace as ignominious to England, said in the House of Commons, that, if King William could know the terms of that treaty, he would turn in his coffin! Let me commend this saying of Mr. Windham, in all its emphasis and in all its force, to any persons who shall meet at Nashville for the purpose of concerting measures for the overthrow of this Union over the bones of Andrew Jackson!

Sir, I wish now to make two remarks, and hasten to a conclusion. I wish to say, in regard to Texas, that if it should be hereafter, at any time, the pleasure of the government of Texas to cede to the United States a portion, larger or smaller, of her territory which lies adjacent to New Mexico, and north of 36°30′ of north latitude, to be formed into free States, for a fair equivalent in money or in the payment of her debt, I think it an object well worthy the consideration of Congress, and I shall be happy to concur in it myself, if I should have a connection with the government at that time.

I have one other remark to make. In my observations upon slavery as it has existed in this country, and as it now exists, I have expressed no opinion of the mode of its extinguishment or melioration. I will say, however, though I have nothing to propose, because I do not deem myself so competent as other gentlemen to take any lead on this subject, that if any gentlemen from the South shall propose a scheme, to be carried on by this government upon a large scale, for the transportation of free colored people to any colony or any place in the world, I should be quite disposed to incur almost any degree of expense to accomplish that object. Nay, sir, following an example set more than twenty years ago by a great man, then a Senator from New

York, I would return to Virginia, and through her to the whole South, the money received from the lands and territories ceded by her to this government, for any such purpose as to remove, in whole or in part, or in any way to diminish to deal beneficially with, the free colored population of the Southern States. I have said that I honor Virginia for her cession of this territory. There have been received into the treasury of the United States eighty millions of dollars, the proceeds of the sales of the public lands ceded by her. If the residue should be sold at the same rate, the whole aggregate will exceed two hundred millions of dollars. If Virginia and the South see fit to adopt any proposition to relieve themselves from the free people of color among them, or such as may be made free, they have my full consent that the government shall pay them any sum of money out of the proceeds of that cession which may be adequate to the purpose.

And now, Mr. President, I draw these observations to a close. I have spoken freely, and I meant to do so. I have sought to make no display. I have sought to enliven the occasion by no animated discussion, nor have I attempted any train of elaborate argument. I have wished only to speak my sentiments, fully and at length, being desirous, once and for all, to let the Senate know, and to let the country know, the opinions and sentiments which I entertain on all these subjects. These opinions are not likely to be suddenly changed. If there be any future service that I can render to the country, consistently with these sentiments and opinions, I shall cheerfully render it. If there be not, I shall still be glad to have had an opportunity to disburden myself from the bottom of my heart, and to make known every political sentiment that therein exists.

And now, Mr. President, instead of speaking of the possibility or utility of secession, instead of dwelling in those caverns of darkness, instead of groping with those ideas so full of all that is horrid and horrible, let us come out into the light of day; let us enjoy the fresh air of Liberty and Union; let us cherish those hopes which belong to us; let us devote ourselves to those great objects that are fit for our consideration and our action; let us raise our conceptions to the magnitude and the importance of the duties that devolve upon us; let our comprehension be as broad as the country for which we act, our aspirations as high as its certain destiny; let us not be pygmies in the case that calls for men. Never did there devolve on any generation of men higher trusts than now devolve upon us, for the preservation of this Constitution and the harmony and peace of all who are destined to live under it. Let us make our generation one of the strongest and brightest links in that golden chain which is destined, I fondly believe, to grapple the people of all the States to this Constitution for ages to come. We have a great, popular, constitutional government, guarded by law and by judicature, and defended by the affections of the whole people. No monarchical throne presses these States together, no iron chain of military power encircles them; they live and stand under a government popular in its form, representative in its character, founded upon principles of equality, and so constructed, we hope, as to last forever. In all its history it has been beneficent; it has trodden down no man's liberty; it has crushed no State. Its daily respiration is liberty and partiotism; its yet youthful veins are full of enterprise, courage, and honorable love of glory and renown. Large before, the country has now, by recent events, become vastly larger. This Republic now extends, with a vast breadth, across the whole continent. The two great seas of the world wash the one and the other shore. We realize, on a mighty scale, the beautiful description of the ornamental border of the buckler of Achilles:

> Now, the broad shield complete, the artist crowned
> With his last hand, and poured the ocean round;
> In living silver seemed the waves to roll,
> And beat the buckler's verge, and bound the whole.

Sojourner Truth

A'n't I a Woman? (1851)

It was with some trepidation that women took to the platform in America. The prejudice against women speaking grew from the deep and ingrained conviction among men that females had no role to play in public affairs, that domestic pursuits were the proper sphere of activity for the "gentler sex." Women who did speak in public, when they were able to create the opportunity, were regarded with hostility or amused curiosity. But women persisted, speaking typically on the issues of abolition and temperance. In 1840, however, an international conference on women's rights, held in London, refused even to accredit women delegates, let alone allow women to address the gathering. It was from this meeting that a furious and frustrated Elizabeth Cady Stanton returned home to join with Lucretia C. Mott in planning an American Women's Rights Convention. The resulting Seneca Falls Convention of 1848 launched in earnest the feminist movement in the United States.

Another convention was called in Akron, Ohio, in 1851. Both men and women attended to hear activists like Maria Giddings, Betsey Cowles, and Emily Robinson speak on the rights of women under the law and in the areas of labor and education. Fifteen resolutions addressing equal rights for women were debated and adopted. In the audience, however, were those who opposed these radical notions. Typically, such opposition came largely from clergymen who were, "as usual," Elizabeth Cady Stanton observed, "averse to enlarging the boundaries of freedom." Frances D. Gage, who chaired the convention, described some of the arguments presented by the "Methodist, Baptist, Episcopal, Presbyterian, and Universalist ministers [who] came in to hear and discuss the resolutions presented." These opponents of women's rights directed a barrage of attacks against the resolutions. "One claimed superior rights and privileges for man, on the ground of 'superior intellect': another because of the 'manhood of Christ,' " Mrs. Gage wrote. "Another," she went on, "gave us a theological view of the 'sin of our first mother.' " At this juncture, a black woman who had sat silently throughout the proceedings slowly took off the sunbonnet she wore and walked to the front of the room. Tall and gaunt, clad in a gray dress and white turban, she was a striking figure. She was alarming as well. Some of the women's rights' advocates were fearful that her presence would associate the meeting with abolition, and, although many of the women were in fact abolitionists, efforts were made to keep the two issues apart. Those hostile to the rights of women were doubly appalled at the prospect of listening to a black speaker. Her appearance caused a turmoil and she was greeted with a chorus of hisses. Mrs. Gage, in spite of whispered advice not to let her speak, rose and announced, "Sojourner Truth," and asked for silence.

Taking up the abolitionist cause after being freed when New York liberated its slaves in 1827, the woman who had been born as the slave Isabella adopted the name of Sojourner Truth. Although she never learned to read or write, she became widely known for her eloquence on the platform. That day in Akron she apparently turned the tide with her direct and pointed rebuttal to the arguments of the clergymen. "I have never in my life seen anything like the magical influence that subdued the mobbish spirit of the day," Mrs. Gage declared, "and turned the sneers and jeers of an excited crowd into notes of respect and admiration." The speech as it appears below is as Mrs. Gage recorded it.

"Wall, chilern, whar dar is so much racket dar must be somethin' out o' kilter. I tink dat 'twixt de niggers of de Souf and de womin at de Norf, all talkin' 'bout rights, de white men will be in a fix pretty soon. But what's all dis here talkin' 'bout?

"Dat man ober dar say dat womin needs to be helped into carriages, and lifted ober ditches, and to hab de best place everywhar. Nobody eber helps me into carriages, or ober mud-puddles, or gibs me any best place!" And raising herself to her full height, and her voice to a pitch like rolling thunder, she asked "And a'n't I a woman? Look at me! Look at my arm! (and she bared her right arm to the shoulder, showing her tremendous muscular power). I have ploughed, and planted, and gathered into barns, and no man could head me! And a'n't I a woman? I could work as much and eat as much as a man—when I could get it—and bear de lash as well! And a'n't I a woman? I have borne thirteen chilern, and seen'em mos' all sold off to slavery, and when I cried out with my mother's grief, none but Jesus heard me! And a'n't I a woman?

"Den dey talks 'bout dis ting in de head; what dis dey call it?" ("Intellect," whispered some one near.) "Dat's it, honey. What's dat got to do wid womin's rights or nigger's rights? If my cup won't hold but a pint, and yourn holds a quart, wouldn't ye be mean not to let me have my little half-measure full?" And she pointed her significant finger, and sent a keen glance at the minister who had made the argument. The cheering was long and loud.

"Den dat little man in black dar, he say women can't have as much rights as men, 'cause Christ wan't a woman! Whar did your Christ come from?" Rolling thunder couldn't have stilled that crowd, as did those deep, wonderful tones, as she stood there with outstretched arms and eyes of fire. Raising her voice still louder, she repeated, "Whar did your Christ come from? From God and a woman! Man had nothin' to do wid Him." Oh, what a rebuke that was to that little man.

Turning again to another objector, she took up the defense of Mother Eve. I can not follow her through it all. It was pointed, and witty, and solemn; eliciting at almost every sentence deafening applause; and she ended by asserting: "If de fust woman God ever made was strong enough to turn de world upside down all alone, dese women togedder (and she glanced her eye over the platform) ought to be able to turn it back, and get it right side up again! And now dey is asking to do it, de men better let'em." Long-continued cheering greeted this. "Bleeged to ye for hearin' on me, and now old Sojourner han't got nothin' more to say."

Lucy Stone

Speech to the National Woman's Rights Convention (1855)

The early nineteenth-century movement for women's rights faced a special difficulty on the public platform. Prevailing social norms, justified by a particular interpretation of the Bible, regarded public speaking as inappropriate for a woman. One of the very first female orators was the reformer Frances Wright, who began her speaking career in the late 1820's. Few women mounted the podium; those who did might attract an audience primarily for their curiosity value and found themselves the object of ridicule. The prior question of women's right to speak preempted consideration of the reforms they wished to espouse.

The antislavery movement provided the impetus for change, however gradual, in this social norm. Women who were denied the right to speak at abolitionist rallies came to realize that the plight of women was analogous to that of the slaves. Those who were allowed to speak and who articulated the evils of slavery came to realize the same analogy. Modeled on antislavery conventions, the first national women's rights convention was held in Seneca Falls, New York, in 1848, and similar conventions were held across the nation during the 1850's. At least among reformers, women's right to speak won grudging acceptance. Still there were problems, however. Some antislavery advocates believed that discussion of women's rights would divert attention from what they regarded as the primary cause. And women who appeared in unconventional dress or who otherwise departed from prevailing custom risked exposing both themselves and their cause to ridicule.

Lucy Stone frequently confronted these dilemmas. Educated at Oberlin College, she was the first woman from Massachusetts to earn a college degree. At Oberlin she organized a debating society for women, as a counter to their exclusion from the public platform. Upon graduation she became a lecturer in the antislavery cause, but soon began to espouse women's rights as well. Her friends in the abolitionist movement, fearing that feminism would taint their own effort, extracted from Stone a curious compromise: she would speak exclusively on abolition on the weekends and would be free to discuss women's rights the rest of the week. Stone developed a standard set of three lectures on women, for which she charged a nominal admission fee as a deterrent to hecklers. Not all hecklers would be deterred, though. Stone's practice of wearing Bloomer dress exposed her to ridicule, as did her decision following her marriage in 1855 to retain her own name.

If the feminist movement could be ridiculed or stigmatized, its message would be trivialized if not lost. This was the problem Stone faced at the 1855 Cincinnati convention. A previous speaker had alleged that the movement was nothing more than a few disappointed women. A standard theme in counter-movement rhetoric is to depict the movement's leaders as outside agitators, small in number, aberrant in personality, and sinister in purpose. Rather than denying the charge or going on the defensive, Stone turned the image of the "disappointed woman" to her advantage. She maintained that all women were disappointed, indeed, that "disappointment is the lot of woman." In this way she managed to transform an eccentric personality trait into socially-imposed discrimination. Her speech aimed to raise women's consciousness of their own disappointment so that growing numbers might regard the condition as intolerable. The speech is an excellent illustration of how a protest movement can be undertaken by making a disaffected group aware of its own alienation.

Stone continued during the Civil War to deliver speeches linking the rights of blacks and of women. Following the war, she became one of the major advocates of suffrage for women. When the suffrage movement split, she became one of the leaders of the American Woman Suffrage Association and espoused its platform until her death in 1893.

The last speaker alluded to this movement as being that of a few disappointed women. From the first years to which my memory stretches, I have been a disappointed woman. When, with my brothers, I reached forth after the sources of knowledge, I was reproved with "It isn't fit for you; it doesn't belong to women." Then there was but one college in the world where women were admitted, and that was in Brazil. I would have found my way there, but by the time I was prepared to go, one was opened in the young State of Ohio—the first in the United States where women and negroes could enjoy opportunities with white men. I was disappointed when I came to seek a profession worthy an immortal being—every employment was closed to me, except those of the teacher, the seamstress, and the housekeeper. In education, in marriage, in religion, in everything, disappointment is the lot of woman. It shall be the business of my life to deepen this disappointment in every woman's heart until she bows down to it no longer. I wish that women, instead of being walking show-cases, instead of begging of their fathers and brothers the latest and gayest new bonnet, would ask of them their rights.

The question of Woman's Rights is a practical one. The notion has prevailed that it was only an ephemeral idea: that it was but women claiming the right to smoke cigars in the streets, and to frequent barrooms. Others have supposed it a question of comparative intellect; others still, of sphere. Too much has already been said and written about woman's sphere. Trace all the doctrines to their source and they will be found to have no basis except in the usages and prejudices of the age. This is seen in the fact that what is tolerated in woman in one country is not tolerated in another. In this country women may hold prayer-meetings, etc., but in Mohammedan countries it is written upon their mosques, "Women and dogs, and other impure animals, are not permitted to enter." Wendell Phillips says, "The best and greatest thing one is capable of doing, that is his sphere." I have confidence in the Father to believe that when He gives us the capacity to do anything He does not make a blunder. Leave women, then, to find their sphere. And do not tell us before we are born even, that our province is to cook dinners, darn stockings, and sew on buttons. We are told woman has all the rights she wants; and even women, I am ashamed to say, tell us so. They mistake the politeness of men for rights—seats while men stand in this hall to-night, and their adulations; but these are mere courtesies. We want rights. The flour-merchant, the house-builder, and the postman charge us no less on account of our sex; but when we endeavor to earn money to pay all these, then, indeed, we find the difference. Man, if he have energy, may hew out for himself a path where no mortal has ever trod, held back by nothing but what is in himself; the world is all before him, where to choose; and we are glad for you, brothers, men, that it is so. But the same society that drives forth the young man, keeps woman at home—a dependent—working little cats on worsted, and little dogs on punctured paper; but if she goes heartily and bravely to give herself to some worthy purpose, she is out of her sphere and she loses caste. Women working in tailor-shops are paid one-third as much as men. Some one in Philadelphia has stated that women make fine shirts for twelve and a half cents apiece; that no woman can make more than nine a week, and the sum thus earned, after deducting rent, fuel, etc., leaves her just three and a half cents a day for bread. Is it a wonder that women are driven to prostitution? Female teachers in New York are paid fifty dollars a year, and for every such situation there are five hundred applicants. I know not what you believe of God, but I believe He gave yearnings and longings to be filled, and that He did not mean all our time should be devoted to feeding and clothing the body. The present condition of woman causes a horrible perversion of the marriage relation. It is asked of a lady, "Has she married well?" "Oh, yes, her husband is rich." Woman must marry for a home, and you men are the sufferers by this; for a woman who loathes you may marry you because you have the means to get money which she can not have. But when woman can enter the lists with you and make money for herself, she will marry you only for deep and earnest affection.

I am detaining you too long, many of you standing, that I ought to apologize, but women have been wronged so long that I may wrong you a little. [*Applause*]. A woman undertook in Lowell to sell shoes to ladies. Men laughed at her, but in six years she has run them out, and has a monopoly of the trade. Sarah Tyndale, whose husband was an importer of china, and died bankrupt, continued his business, paid off his debts, and has made a fortune and built the largest china warehouse in the world. [*Mrs. Mott here corrected Lucy. Mrs. Tyndale has not the largest china warehouse, but the largest assortment of china in the world*]. Mrs. Tyndale, herself, drew the plan of her warehouse, and it is the best plan ever drawn. A laborer to whom the architect showed it, said: "Don't she know e'en as much as some men?" I have seen woman at manual labor turning out chair-legs in a cabinet-shop with a dress short enough not to drag in the shavings. I wish other women would imitate her in this. It made her hands harder and broader, it is true, but I think a hand with a dollar and a quarter a day in it, better than one with a crossed ninepence. The men in the shop didn't use tobacco, nor swear—they can't do those things where there are women, and we owe it to our brothers to go wherever they work to keep them decent. The widening of woman's sphere is to improve her lot. Let us do it, and if the world scoff, let it scoff—if it sneer, let it sneer—but we will go on emulating the example of the sisters Grimke and Abby Kelly. When they first lectured against slavery they were not listened to as respectfully as you listen to us. So the first female physician meets many difficulties, but to the next the path will be made easy.

Lucretia Mott has been a preacher for years; her right to do so is not questioned among Friends. But when Antionette Brown felt that she was commanded to preach, and to arrest the progress of thousands that were on the road to hell; why, when she applied for ordination they acted as though they had rather the whole world should go to hell, than that Antionette Brown should be allowed to tell them how to keep ouit of it. She is now ordained over a parish in the state of New York, but when she meets on the Temperance platform the Rev. John Chambers, or your own Gen Carey (applause) they greet her with hisses. Theodore Parker said: "The acorn that the school-boy carries in his pocket and the squirrel stows in his cheek, has in it the possibility of an oak, able to withstand, for ages, the cold winter and the driving blast." I have seen the acorn men and women, but never the perfect oak; all are but abortions. The young mother, when first the new-born babe nestles in her bosom, and a heretofore unknown love springs up in her heart, finds herself unprepared for this new relation in life, and she sends forth the child scarred and dwarfed by her own weakness and inbecility, as no stream can rise higher than its fountain.

Frances Willard

Woman's Lesser Duties (1863)

With the Civil War at its mid-point, the issue was far from settled. The campaigns of the summer of 1862 had produced bloody clashes—at Bull Run and Antietam, at Murfreesboro and Fredricksburg—where thousands of casualties were sustained on both sides, but the results were far from conclusive. By March of 1863 the need for more troops was apparent and Congress passed the first Conscription Act.

The men at the front fighting for the Union cause were very much on the mind of Frances Willard when she travelled to Pittsburgh, Massachusetts to address the members of the Browning Association of Pittsburgh Female College on March 24, 1863. Willard was, herself, a recent graduate of Northwestern Female College in Evanston, Illinois, where she began her teaching career. She was to become President of the Evanston College for Ladies and, later, Dean of Women when the College merged with Northwestern University. But, it was primarily as a reformer that Francis Willard established a reputation as a consummate speaker.

Willard was to become the President and driving force of the Woman's Christian Temperance Union and the leading advocate of prohibition not only in America but throughout the world. A tireless traveller, she lectured extensively and established a lecture bureau to disseminate her message. She also became President of the National Council of Women and worked on behalf of woman's suffrage.

All this, however, was in her future when she addressed the subject of woman's duties in 1863. The speech given to the Browning Association, a woman's literary society, reflects the prevalent thinking of the time—among both men and women—that women had a special role in society quite distinct from the part played by men. It does not call for equality; it stresses the unique characteristics of women as they were envisioned in the mid-nineteenth century. Willard reflects the conception of the time of women: possessing "moral susceptibility," "purity of influence," and "abounding charity," and urges women to become "skilled in the arts that enrich social intercourse," and to be "true to her character in the minor matters of life." These matters are not, of course, minor in the midst of a sanguine war. A major theme of Willard's address is the need for women to stiffen the morale of the troops, to still "the cry of nature in their breasts" as they send "forth to the battle-field those . . . dearest to them." The depiction of women in this speech may seem quaint, at best, anathema, at worst to modern men and women. But the speech does show a widely-held view that influenced popular perceptions of women.

Ladies of the Browning Association: Concerning the vocation of woman a great deal has been said. Her moral susceptibility, her purity of influence, have been acknowledged since civilization's morning; her abounding charity, our own day and the exigencies of our national cause abundantly demonstrate. But of her work, æsthetically considered—of the duty that she owes to be skilled in the arts that enrich social intercourse, true to her character in the minor matters of life—less has been said. Be this our theme.

It is a principle acted upon, if not acknowledged, that process and result stand to each other in the same relation as light and darkness, sound and silence, do. For we find that processes are occult, inferior—while results are superior and luminous. An oak stands before you. What strength is in the gnarled trunk and brawny arms! What symmetry in the proportions; and

Not a prince
In all the proud old world beyond the deep
E'er wore his crown so loftily as he
Wears that green coronal of leaves with which
God's hand hath graced him.

But where are the dewy evenings, the genial showers, the yellow sun-beams, that nurtured the acorn into the tree? They are past and forgotten. Where will you find the spongioles that absorbed the nourishment? They are buried out of sight. No sound tells you of the ascending sap—the life-blood of the tree; all this pertains to process, and is hidden—result only stands before you, complete and wonderful. So is it always. The great earth, bearing her freight of bud and blossom, works silently for their growth and maintenance. The scaffolding is taken down when the obelisk is finished. A heathen imagination even, presents us with the image of Minerva leaping *full-armed* from the brain of Jove.

In the social world this principle is potent in its action. The question is not, How did you achieve it? but, What have you achieved? That inexorable *What* meets us at the threshold of the mansion—at the door of the salon. It is a peculiarity of Republican governments. At Windsor it is, Who are you? Who was your father? At Washington, Have you value? What have *you* done? True, as there are drones in every hive, so in all societies we shall find persons who are there by tolerance only. We hear them called "wall flowers," "stupid old dears," and other unflattering names.

Yet the *fact* remains, that to be admitted into really good society, one must have innate value—must have some return to make for the benefits which he receives. Into the social sunshine we bring results, processes being left to the obscurity of private life. Men grow good and great otherwhere than in society; they ponder and discover in secret places; their hard-earned spoils they lay down at the feet of the banquet's Queen, and she puts laurel wreaths upon their brows. For society is "made up of every creature's best." As the phrase has it, every one is "on his good behavior" there. So that it should seem philosophically advisable to go much into the world, that acting habitually, as well as we know how, it shall grow to be "second nature" to us after a while.

"Think of me at my best," says David Copperfield's erring friend to the gentle "Trotwood." His words are ours, said by look and tone and bearing, to every one with whom we have to do. "Think of me at my best; I will try to make your thinking only just to my acting, if you will be thus generous with me." Society cultivates the spirit of tolerance. We learn there to recognize the rights of others, to seek their happiness. In the best circles the "Golden" is also the fashionable rule, but with this difference, that in society no thought is had of the intention, the outward act alone being regarded—the retribution following instantly, no one daring to deviate from it who would win and maintain a reputation for gentility. You shall not offend my tastes; you are forbidden to put me to inconvenience, is the well understood though always *implied* "Bill of Rights," here.

To worry others—to damage them in person or estate, is to lose caste in society. Witness the discomfiture of the blundering beau who upsets his saucer of ice-cream upon his fair companion's dress, though he would fain conduct himself with Chesterfieldian elegance. His good intention cannot save him. He is marked, the chagrined man of the evening. For blunderers are not to be tolerated; they are a disfigurement—an excrescence upon the face of society. Only the graceful, the self-possessed and agreeable are in demand as members of the social commonwealth. Smiles and hand-shakings are the "small change" of its currency; good looks, good dress, good talk, its "checks" and "notes of hand," honored at sight. If one is beautiful, witty or wise, he throws this, his own peculiar gift into the general stock, receiving again that which is so sweet to every heart—the praises of his peers. There is much talk about a noble contempt for the world's opinion—but everybody's secret heart must tell him that it is a false philosophy which would lead him to be careless of a verdict so authoritative as that which society has in her power to pronounce. And what is a temperate love of praise, but a just anxiety that the verdict shall be in favor, not in disapproval of us? The enjoyment of a pleasant reputation among our companions is one of the truest delights of life.

We come, then, into society. What are the offerings that we must bring? Fortunately for us, there is choice. One need not be an Admirable Crichton in order to gain a recognition. Let each come, bringing that one preeminent gift with which his Creator has endowed him. To some, that gift is beauty; and these are always welcome. Whoever brings a lovely face or graceful form to the social assemblage, confers upon each beholder a benefit which he will be loyal enough to acknowledge in his heart, for, as one of our deepest thinkers has said: "Every man's mission is order. He is here to make what was disorderly and chaotic into a thing ruled and regular.

Disorder is dissolution, death." And we may ask: What is beauty of figure or of face but an agreement in something outside of us with conceptions of fitness and order that dwell within? Beauty is food to the eye, as music is to the ear. Our souls have been called "sweet bells jangled," but still they are "*sweet* bells." We have that within us which feels worshipful before beauty in whatever form it comes, but most when we discern it in the human face—prophetic as it is of that One ineffable Countenance which we shall one day behold. Bring on your good looks, then, and an admiring world shall thank you.

But, though we cannot stipulate (as some over-nice critics have endeavored to do,) that you shall not be conscious of your charms—knowing that your mirrors are before us in this matter—yet, let us beg, for your sakes as well as for ours who are pleased by the sight of you, Keep your own counsel on this most interesting subject, and never let a mincing air, affected tone, or a vain toss of the regal head, betray your knowledge of your dowry. You have often been told that a modest little flower, the violet, has a lesson for such as you. Do not let the advice to heed its teachings be lost upon you because you have heard it so often. As a parabola pleases the eye more than a perpendicular, so gracefulness is grateful to the æsthetic sense so often outraged by awkward angularity. It is a duty that we owe, to be as graceful as we can. We have all seen bows so awkward, attitudes and movements so full of clumsiness, that something of a moral turpitude has seemed to attach to them. Who knows that there shall not come an age when to outrage the taste—to agonize the delicate perception—to impose discord upon the sensitive ear, shall be in some way punishable as a grave offense? One of the gifts, then, which society gladly receives, is an individual of fine appearance, or grace of manner. "But I cannot bring either of those," is the plaintive cry from scores of aspiring maidens.

Well, it has been often, yet not *too* often said, that there is another kind of beauty which the soul seeks—a higher kind, because more spiritual, hence more lasting than the first, speaking of which a writer has said (describing one of the persons he met on a promenade down Broadway): "There comes the ever welcome ugly face of a beautiful soul!" All true culture at the last amounts to this. Plato's prayer we are still offering, in this Christian land, "O make me beautiful within!" or, paraphrased by Milton:

What in me is dark illume;
What is low, raise and support.

To grow pure and good is in the power of all. That is the greatest gift. But the subject is a wide one, and is made familiar to us by every sermon to which we listen, by every prayer we hear.

To be of highest value in society, a lady should have some accomplishments—should be able, in some way, to be a felt force in the entertainments of the hour. Can you sing a song for us? Can you render poetry into music by a fantasie of Thalberg, a sonata or a symphony by Beethoven? Can you give us a pathetic ballad or a humorous roundelay to the accompaniment of your harp or guitar? If so, you are welcome, says Society, and we need you hardly less than you need us. But, better than all, can you talk? Are you quick at retort—fluent, fond of badinage? Have you good descriptive powers? Are you kindly and generous in your estimates of persons and their acts? Is your language choice and free from provincial and inelegant words and phrases? Are you well read? If so, you are a prize indeed. These questions must be all affirmatively answered before one is a candidate for society's highest awards. For, though music is charming, though beauty and grace are as rich in attractions as they are rare in actualization, it remains true that conversational powers rank highest in the scale of social gifts.

It is the duty of all to do their best, even should they carry their industry so far as to prepare bon-mots beforehand, like Sheridan, or make memoranda of things suitable to be said, upon their thumb nails, like one less famous than the great wit. But all cannot talk well, though many make a feint of doing so, poising themselves over a subject like a humming-bird over a flower; dallying with ideas, playing hide-and-seek with them, the hiding being for the most part done by the ideas. But not so, your real Talker, endowed for the purpose. He can take a subject, like a flower, up by the *roots*, to look into its philosophy; or he can merely descant upon its beauties, as he would call attention to the coloring of a corolla, its size and outline—or, if botanically inclined, its species, habits and uses; or he can be so transcendental as to give you what might be termed the perfume of the subject, as he would direct your attention to the aroma of the flower. So that, as it seems, he can give to society "small talk," if the relations in which he is placed demand it (his "relations," for example, to a pouting, wordless beauty of "sweet sixteen"); or he can be descriptive, didactic, historic, polemic—what you will.

It is related to the credit of Socrates, that he said on one occasion, as his apology for leaving a social circle: "That which I know would not be suited to the occasion; and what would be suited to the occasion, of that I am ignorant." But surely these words detract from his reputation as a conversationalist, and do not add to his fame as a philosopher. Versatility may be named as the first qualification of a good talker. Practice is requisite—tact—with generosity enough to be a good listener also. Some persons wait impatiently for their *vis-a-vis* to put in a few words, and then make their next sentence tangent to his, touching it at the point of departure only. To be a good listener is not only one of the minor duties of morality, but is a *sine qua non* in polite life. Monopoly of words is intolerable. Here, then, in powers of conversation we have the highest gift that one can exercise for the benefit of the circle in which he moves. It can dispense with accessories, if need be. The nimble, eloquent, versatile tongue alone is requisite. There is no formula of invitation to the exercise of this gift, as, "May I have the honor of conducting you to the talker's chair?" "Won't you talk? Please do! Give us that imitation of Dr. Johnson, with variations; that monologue á la Coleridge. That's in your best style, I have heard." Or, "Please favor us with your new bon-mot, that original conceit which is considered so amusing." No, all is simple and direct. The machinery is not cumbrous, it can be brought into action at a moment's warning. Grammatical propriety has suggested the use of the pronoun in the third person, masculine gender, while this gift has been treated of; but its feminine correlative was all along intended. For with her quickness, her fineness of taste and delicacy of perception, woman has it in her power to be unrivaled as a conversationalist; and in Madame Roland, whose eloquence, never heard beyond her own salon, helped to kindle a revolution—Madame De Stael, whose powers were feared by even Napoleon the Great—and Margaret Fuller Ossoli, the best conversationalist of our own age and country, we have a few among the many names that might be cited to prove that woman has done much already in this department.

Another most desirable accomplishment, akin to that last mentioned, is the ability to write a good letter—one that shall be racy, genial, varied in contents—passing readily

> From grave to gay, from lively to
> severe;

though of this last quality it is possible to have too much. Gray and Charles Lamb furnish us with models of epistolary style, as faultless as our literature can boast, unless we name Lady Mary Wortley Montague or Hannah More, who, in some valuable remarks upon the subject under consideration, mentions as one cardinal virtue of a letter, that it be written as one would talk; that it furnish a fair index to the mind of the writer at the time of the writing, and that it be not too long. The vivacious Gail Hamilton, in a recent number of the "*Atlantic*," gives some hints on letter-writing to the soldiers, that are most timely. At the mention of the soldiers, our thoughts revert to the peculiar courtesies that, as American women, we owe to them. We feel deep regret, often, that we can do so little for our country, now that her need for help is sorest. Yet not at small cost have mothers, sisters and wives, stilled the cry of nature in their breasts, and sent forth to the battle-field those who were dearest to them, to encounter danger and privation, or death itself perhaps, and in its most hideous forms. Not from weak hearts come utterances like these, though the burden of them has been often on woman's lips during the last two years:

> O friend! by few is glory's wreath
> attained,
> But death or soon or late awaiteth
> all;
> To fight in Freedom's cause is
> something gained,
> And nothing lost, to fall.

Under the heroism that they evince, lies the heart-ache of a nation. By a thousand lonely hearth-stones, tonight, the kneeling figure seen in the flickering fire-light tells how well the soldier is remembered. And it is fitting that we should be mindful of the heroes to whom we owe the comfort and security, which this hour and this occasion may index to our minds. Can "fourteen dollars a month, with rations," pay the hundreds of thousands who are at this very moment making with their own brave breasts a wall between us and our foes, compared with which rampart and bastion are as vacancy itself? For cannon balls may batter down the strongest fortifications, but only through millions of loyal hearts can the enemy attack the homes and altars of the North. To the courage that faces death on the field when he comes with sickle keen, and reaps down rank after rank in his pitiless march; to the heroism that shrinks not, when he steals in like a ghost, and watches with hollow eyes the lonely couch, forsaken, save by him; to the generosity that lays life, youth, ambition, on the altar, we give but little in giving all we have—our prayers, our tears, our sympathies and toil. While the numerous Soldiers' Aid Societies all over the North attest the willing industry of the "loved ones at home"—while the store-houses of that noble organization, the Sanitary Commission, are supplied by offerings continually pouring in from town and country—while in no prayer is the soldier's name forgotten—yet may it not be true, that of the "small, sweet courtesies of life" we owe to him, we have not thought enough? We would "gather up the fragments, that nothing be lost." Is it not doubtful, then, whether we manifest enough real, personal interest in the soldiers whom we meet—who are at home on furlough, or from temporal disability—whom we see in church and drawing-room, in car and omnibus—whom we do not see, as those in the field, who were our friends at home, but who never hear from us personally, now that they have joined the army?

A soldier who had been for eighteen months in the army of the Potomac without once leaving camp, except for the march or the battle-field, brought home the report, a few days since, that in his regiment the soldiers received very few letters or messages from their friends. "A man's heart is tender when he is far from what is dearest to him, and his life is in constant peril," said the young soldier, while his eyes grew luminous. Take an incident in point. A soldier from your own State had not heard from home in months, but at first had generously apologized for his friends' neglect by saying, "Our folks were never in the habit of writing letters much, and then they don't realize how lonesome a fellow gets when he's away from what he likes best." But as weeks passed, and no tidings came, he grew moody and discontented, and at last became reckless, saying, in soldier's phrase: "Well, I don't care; I can stand it if they can." At last he ceased to inquire for letters; bad habits grew upon him. A secret mission was at this time intrusted to a favorite officer, and a certain number of men were to volunteer to go with him on a dangerous expedition. A flag, which was torn and discolored by several battles, in which it had always waved over victorious troops, was brought out, and the men who were willing to volunteer were told to gather around it. Nearly all the friends of the discontented soldier—those of his company—had offered themselves. His special friend and comrade had done so, urging him to go also. "No," he said; "he was getting tired, and wasn't going to fight, unless he was obliged to. Since nobody seemed to care about his life, he guessed he'd look after it a little himself." Soon after, a letter was handed to him, superscribed in a graceful, lady's hand. The soldier's eye kindled—he tore it open, but before he had read a page, he snatched his gun, and rushed toward the group of volunteers, singing.

> Yes, we'll rally round the flag, boys,
> rally once again,

in ringing tones, and thrusting the paper into his friend's hand, he said, "See there, Harry! what my sister says! 'We know you'll never flinch; and proudly remember, when others boast of the heroism of their friends, that our brother is a soldier, too.' "

It is observed that after letters come from home, the soldier is more thoughtful, oaths are less often on his lips, cards are laid aside—the reason often being assigned: "My mother wrote me that she knew I would be true to her and to the teachings of my home. I was growing forgetful, but her letter has reminded me."

To write often to the soldiers is as much a duty, we maintain, as to send delicacies for the hospital or books for their idle hours. I know a sweet, Christian girl, whose correspondence with the army is large enough to occupy a good deal of her time, and whose sisterly letters to her soldier friends are more highly prized by them than any other of their possessions. Aside from the racy gossip of home news—the friendly messages—the words of kind solicitude, and the quiet utterances of Christian faith, the very delicacy of the letter—the fineness of its execution—the dainty sheets of paper and corresponding envelope—the faint perfume, perhaps, discernible about it—have all a charm that will refine and elevate the soldier, and which may prove to him a shield against the temptations of his wild, abnormal life.

In the songs we sing, the soldier can not be too often named. The "Evening Song to the Virgin," "Meet me by moonlight," and "Comin thro' the Rye," make pleasant music; but for our day, the "Battle Hymn of the Republic," "Rally round the Flag" and the "Picket Guard," come nearer to men's hearts. I have in memory a scene that may be but an example of what many of you have witnessed. A group of graceful girls standing round a piano, singing, to the accompaniment played by the older sister, a touching song—an outgrowth of the crisis of our times. Their brothers—with the lover of one of them—were soldiers in the army of the Cumberland. Remembering this, it was doubly affecting to listen to the clear tones of the air, with the mournful alto running through them, in the chorus beginning:

> Brave boys are they;
> Gone at their country's call;
> And yet, and yet we cannot forget
> That many brave boys must fall.

We have read of the power of their sublime "Marseillaise" over the French soldiery. At the time of the Revolution, it was terribly shown. The principle seen there in its grander development we may trace to advantage in the life of every day. For the fires of patriotism reach white heat when music lends to glowing words her potency.

Let us think, then, of the many little things which, along with the great, we may do to show that our hearts are with those who are fighting battles, winning victories for us. "Why did you shake hands with young Dufrees at the church door, after service?" asked a fastidious friend. "Because he is a soldier," returned Arabella, with proper emphasis. The recognition more cordially given to our soldier friends than to others—the acknowledgment in frank, ingenuous manner of our great debt—the interest freely expressed for their comfort—the enthusiastic praise of their courage in trying emergencies—all these are inexpressibly grateful to a soldier's heart, and will not be misinterpreted or misapplied. "We are proud of all our army," said a beautiful girl to a young lieutenant, who had distinguished himself in a recent engagement; "but we glory in the ——Regiment, Pennsylvania Volunteers. They never fail. And then, we know so many members of that regiment; they went from our own town, and we watch their career with great interest." His comrades and himself deserved her praise. So the young soldier knew; but he answered modestly, while his eyes were bright with gratitude, "If our friends at home speak thus concerning us, we will deserve their praise in future—not to speak of the past."

Recently, on a train from the east, the passengers were leaving a car, upon arriving in this city. Lying across the tops of several seats was a soldier's cot, and upon it a white-faced boy—somebody's darling—going home to die. His look told that. The passengers all gazed at him with attention, some with sympathy, some with curiosity in their eyes. Last of all, came a lady of noble face and mien. She stopped a moment, her eyes filled with tears. "God bless you! dear boy," she said, "for helping us!" The youth's face flushed with pleasure. "Thank, you," he said; "I did not think my life too much to give, since the country needed me."

It is in our power to speak many words which shall drop like balm into hearts bruised and bleeding. Through thoughtlessness, let not one remain unsaid. Mourners are multiplying among us—the sable garments of the bereaved we may see on every hand. The end is not yet. We are passing on into the cloud. The eye of God alone can pierce its darkness. Let us weep for the "unreturning brave." Let us keep our kindliest words for those who fight our battles; remembering how grateful will be our sympathy to them, for it has been truly said:

O soldier! to thine early grave
  Thy love and valor bearing,
The bravest are the tenderest,
  The loving are the daring.

The Ordeal of the Union

Abraham Lincoln

A House Divided (1858)

Abraham Lincoln delivered this address at the conclusion of the 1858 Illinois state Republican convention. He had just been nominated as the party's choice for the U.S. Senate seat currently held by Stephen A. Douglas, an unusual act since the state legislature that would choose the senator had not yet been elected itself. Even before he was nominated, though, he had been invited to speak at the close of the convention, since some Republicans thought he would make humorous remarks so that a hard day's work would end on a light note.

He did something quite different. Studying Webster's reply to Hayne as a model, Lincoln took the Scriptural line, "A house divided against itself cannot stand," which had been widely quoted in nineteenth-century public discourse, and put it to new use: not to predict civil war or disunion—possibilities he explicitly denied—but to assert that a united nation would become either all slave or all free and that powerful conspirators were moving it in the direction of slavery.

The speech has three major parts. The oft-quoted introduction serves to exclude any middle ground between national slavery and the disappearance of the peculiar institution. The second, and by far the longest, section asserts the existence of a conspiracy to make slavery national and identifies Douglas as a conspirator. The final section discredits Doublas's position as an antislavery champion and instead links him with such odious measures as reopening the African slave trade.

Lincoln prepared this speech in response to a serious political problem. Douglas had broken with the ruling Democratic administration when President Buchanan proposed to admit Kansas to the Union with a slave-state constitution which Douglas thought fraudulent. Douglas opposed it not because it permitted slavery but because it did not reflect the wishes of the majority. Nevertheless, his opposition made him suddenly attractive to Republicans; some prominent easterners even suggested that their Illinois counterparts not oppose Douglas in his bid for reelection to the Senate. Lincoln needed, therefore, to distinguish himself sharply from Douglas and to discredit the idea that Douglas was any friend of Republicans.

Lincoln wrote the entire speech before delivering it, the first time that he had done so. He spoke, however, without manuscript or notes. When he finished, he took his manuscript to the office of the *Illinois State Journal* and supervised its preparation for printing, proofreading it and even marking the words to be italicized.

The speech was controversial from the start. To say that the only alternative to making the nation all slave was to make it all free sounded dangerously close to abolitionism—and that was far too radical a program for Illinois in the late 1850's. Especially in the central part of the state, where the contest would be decided, many people were mildly against slavery but strongly against abolition. The Democratic press seized upon the text and repeatedly drew the issue back to the radical implications of the "house-divided" doctrine. Lincoln spent much of the campaign back-pedaling, insisting that he was only offering a prediction of what would take place, not advocating a course of action. Douglas won the election by carrying most of the central counties, so one might argue that the seemingly radical "house-divided" doctrine cost him the election.

In the campaign of 1858, the "house-divided" speech was a failure. Nevertheless the text remains powerful. We can read it not only as an instance of a skillful politician responding to a difficult situation but also as a study of how a dubious conspiracy argument could be made plausible through the organization and structure of the speech, and as a prophecy of things to come.

Mr. President and Gentlemen of the Convention: If we could first know where we are, and whither we are tending, we could better judge what to do, and how to do it. We are now far into the fifth year since a policy was initiated with the avowed object and confident promise of putting an end to slavery agitation. Under the operation of that policy, that agitation has not only not ceased, but has constantly augmented. In my opinion, it will not cease until a crisis shall have been reached and passed. "A house divided against itself cannot stand." I believe this government cannot endure permanently half slave and half free. I do not expect the Union to be dissolved—I do not expect the house to fall—but I do expect it will cease to be divided. It will become all one thing, or all the other. Either the opponents of slavery will arrest the further spread of it, and place it where the public mind shall rest in the belief that it is in the course of ultimate extinction; or its advocates will push it forward till it shall become alike lawful in all the States, old as well as new, North as well as South.

Have we no tendency to the latter condition?

Let any one who doubts carefully contemplate that now almost complete legal combination—piece of machinery, so to speak—compounded of the Nebraska doctrine and the Dred Scott decision. Let him consider not only what work the machinery is adapted to do, and how well adapted; but also let him study the history of its construction, and trace, if he can, or rather fail, if he can, to trace the evidences of design and concert of action among its chief architects, from the beginning.

The new year of 1854 found slavery excluded from more than half the States by State constitutions, and from most of the national territory by congressional prohibition. Four days later commenced the struggle which ended in repealing that congressional prohibition. This opened all the national territory to slavery, and was the first point gained.

But, so far, Congress only had acted; and an indorsement by the people, real or apparent, was indispensable to save the point already gained and give chance for more.

This necessity had not been overlooked, but had been provided for, as well as might be, in the notable argument of "squatter sovereignty," otherwise called "sacred right of self-government," which latter phrase, though expressive of the only rightful basis of any government, was so perverted in this attempted use of it as to amount to just this: That if any one man choose to enslave another, no third man shall be allowed to object. That argument was incorporated into the Nebraska bill itself, in the language which follows: "It being the true intent and meaning of this act not to legislate slavery into any Territory or State, nor to exclude it therefrom; but to leave the people thereof perfectly free to form and regulate their domestic institutions in their own way, subject only to the Constitution of the United States." Then opened the roar of loose declamation in favor of "squatter sovereignty" and "sacred right of self-government." "But," said opposition members, "let us amend the bill so as to expressly declare that the people of the Territory may exclude slavery." "Not we," said the friends of the measure; and down they voted the amendment.

While the Nebraska bill was passing through Congress, a law case involving the question of a negro's freedom by reason of his owner having voluntarily taken him first into a free State and then into a Territory covered by the congressional prohibition, and held him as a slave for a long time in each, was passing through the United States Circuit Court for the District of Missouri; and both Nebraska bill and lawsuit were brought to a decision in the same month of May, 1854. The negro's name was Dred Scott, which now designates the decision finally made in the case. Before the then next presidential election, the law case came to and was argued in the Supreme Court of the United States; but the decision of it was deferred until after the election. Still, before the election, Senator Trumbull, on the floor of the Senate, requested the leading advocate of the Nebraska bill to state his opinion whether the people of a Territory can constitutionally exclude slavery from their limits; and the latter answered: "That is a question for the Supreme Court."

The election came. Mr. Buchanan was elected, and the indorsement, such as it was, secured. That was the second point gained. The indorsement, however, fell short of a clear popular majority by nearly four hundred thousand votes, and so, perhaps, was not overwhelmingly reliable and satisfactory. The outgoing President, in his last annual message, as impressively as possible echoed back upon the people the weight and authority of the indorsement. The Supreme Court met again; did not announce their decision, but ordered a reargument. The presidential inauguration came, and still no decision of the court; but the incoming President in his inaugural address fervently exhorted the people to abide by the forthcoming decision, whatever it might be. Then, in a few days, came the decision.

The reputed author of the Nebraska bill finds an early occasion to make a speech at this capital indorsing the Dred Scott decision, and vehemently denouncing all opposition to it. The new President, too, seizes the early occasion of the Silliman letter to indorse and strongly construe that decision, and to express his astonishment that any different view had ever been entertained!

At length a squabble springs up between the President and the author of the Nebraska bill, on the mere question of fact, whether the Lecompton constitution was or was not, in any just sense, made by the people of Kansas; and in that quarrel the latter declares that all he wants is a fair vote for the people, and that he cares not whether slavery be voted down or voted up. I do not understand his declaration that he cares not whether slavery be voted down or voted up to be intended by him other than as an apt definition of the policy he would impress upon the public mind—the principle for which he declares he has suffered so much, and is ready to suffer to the end. And well may he cling to that principle. If he has any parental feeling, well may he cling to it. That principle is the only shred left of his original Nebraska doctrine. Under the Dred Scott decision "squatter sovereignty" squatted out of existence, tumbled down like temporary scaffolding,—like the mold at the foundry, served through one blast and fell back into loose sand,—helped to carry an election, and then was kicked to the winds. His late joint struggle with the Republicans against the Lecompton constitution involves nothing of the original Nebraska doctrine. That struggle was made on a point—the right of a people to make their own constitution—upon which he and the Republicans have never differed.

The several points of the Dred Scott decision, in connection with Senator Douglas's "care not" policy, constitute the piece of machinery in its present state of advancement. This was the third point gained. The working points of that machinery are:

(1) That no negro slave, imported as such from Africa, and no descendant of such slave, can ever be a citizen of any State, in the sense of that term as used in the Constitution of the United States. This point is made in order to deprive the negro in every possible event of the benefit of that provision of the United States Constitution which declares that "the citizens of each State shall be entitled to all the privileges and immunities of citizens in the several States."

(2) That "subject to the Constitution of the United States," neither Congress nor a territorial legislature can exclude slavery from any United States Territory. This point is made in order that individual men may fill up the Territories with slaves, without danger of losing them as property, and thus enhance the chances of permanency to the institution through all the future.

(3) That whether the holding a negro in actual slavery in a free State makes him free as against the holder, the United States courts will not decide, but will leave to be

decided by the courts of any slave State the negro may be forced into by the master. This point is made not to be pressed immediately, but, if acquiesced in for a while, and apparently indorsed by the people at an election, then to sustain the logical conclusion that what Dred Scott's master might lawfully do with Dred Scott in the free State of Illinois, every other master may lawfully do with any other one or one thousand slaves in Illinois or in any other free State.

Auxiliary to all this, and working hand in hand with it, the Nebraska doctrine, or what is left of it, is to educate and mold public opinion, at least Northern public opinion, not to care whether slavery is voted down or voted up. This shows exactly where we now are, and partially, also, whither we are tending.

It will throw additional light on the latter, to go back and run the mind over the string of historical facts already stated. Several things will now appear less dark and mysterious than they did when they were transpiring. The people were to be left "perfectly free," "subject only to the Constitution." What the Constitution had to do with it outsiders could not then see. Plainly enough now, it was an exactly fitted niche for the Dred Scott decision to afterward come in, and declare the perfect freedom of the people to be just no freedom at all. Why was the amendment expressly declaring the right of the people voted down? Plainly enough now, the adoption of it would have spoiled the niche for the Dred Scott decision. Why was the court decision held up? Why even a senator's individual opinion withheld till after the presidential election? Plainly enough now, the speaking out then would have damaged the "perfectly free" argument upon which the election was to be carried. Why the outgoing President's felicitation on the indorsement? Why the delay of a reargument? Why the incoming President's advance exhortation in favor of the decision? These things look like the cautious patting and petting of a spirited horse preparatory to mounting him, when it is dreaded that he may give the rider a fall. And why the hasty after-indorsement of the decision by the President and others?

We cannot absolutely know that all these exact adaptations are the result of preconcert. But when we see a lot of framed timbers, different portions of which we know have been gotten out at different times and places and by different workmen,—Stephen, Franklin, Roger, and James, for instance,—and we see these timbers joined together, and see they exactly make the frame of a house or a mill, all the tenons and mortises exactly fitting, and all the lengths and proportions of the different pieces exactly adapted to their respective places, and not a piece too many or too few, not omitting even scaffolding—or, if a single piece be lacking, we see the place in the frame exactly fitted and prepared yet to bring such piece in—in such a case we find it impossible not to believe that Stephen and Franklin and Roger and James all understood one another from the beginning, and all worked upon a common plan or draft drawn up before the first blow was struck.

It should not be overlooked that, by the Nebraska bill, the people of a State as well as Territory were to be left "perfectly free," "subject only to the Constitution." Why mention a State? They were legislating for Territories, and not for or about States. Certainly the people of a State are and ought to be subject to the Constitution of the United States; but why is mention of this lugged into this merely territorial law? Why are the people of a Territory and the people of a State therein lumped together, and their relation to the Constitution therein treated as being precisely the same? While the opinion of the court, by Chief Justice Taney, in the Dred Scott case, and the separate opinions of all the concurring judges, expressly declare that the Constitution of the United States neither permits Congress nor a territorial legislature to exclude slavery from any United States Territory, they all omit to declare whether or not the same Constitution permits a State, or the people of a State, to exclude it. Possibly, this is a mere omission; but who can be quite sure, if McLean or Curtis had sought to get into the opinion a declaration of unlimited power in the people of a State to exclude slavery from their limits, just as Chase and Mace sought to get such declaration, in behalf of the people of a Territory, into the Nebraska bill—I ask, who can be quite sure that it would not have been voted down in the one case as it had been in the other? The nearest approach to the point of declaring the power of a State over slavery is made by Judge Nelson. He approaches it more than once, using the precise idea, and almost the language too, of the Nebraska act. On one occasion his exact language is: "Except in cases where the power is restrained by the Constitution of the United States, the law of the State is supreme over the subject of slavery within its jurisdiction." In what cases the power of the States is so restrained by the United States Constitution is left an open question, precisely as the same question as to the restraint on the power of the Territories was left open in the Nebraska act. Put this and that together, and we have another nice little niche, which we may, ere long, see filled with another Supreme Court decision declaring that the Constitution of the United States does not permit a State to exclude slavery from its limits. And this may especially be expected if the doctrine of "care not whether slavery be voted down or voted up" shall gain upon the public mind sufficiently to give promise that such a decision can be maintained when made.

Such a decision is all that slavery now lacks of being alike lawful in all the States. Welcome, or unwelcome, such decision is probably coming, and will soon be upon us, unless the power of the present political dynasty shall be met and overthrown. We shall lie down pleasantly dreaming that the people of Missouri are on the verge of making their State free, and we shall awake to the reality instead that the Supreme Court has made Illinois a slave State. To meet and overthrow the power of that dynasty is the work now before all those who would prevent that consummation. That is what we have to do. How can we best do it?

There are those who denounce us openly to their own friends, and yet whisper us softly that Senator Douglas is the aptest instrument there is with which to effect that object. They wish us to infer all from the fact that he now has a little quarrel with the present head of the dynasty; and that he has regularly voted with us on a single point upon which he and we have never differed. They remind us that he is a great man, and that the largest of us are very small ones. Let this be granted. But "a living dog is better than a dead lion." Judge Douglas, if not a dead lion for this work, is at least a caged and toothless one. How can he oppose the advances of slavery? He don't care anything about it. His avowed mission is impressing the "public heart" to care nothing about it. A leading Douglas Democratic newspaper thinks Douglas's superior talent will be needed to resist the revival of the African slave-trade. Does Douglas believe an effort to revive that trade is approaching? He has not said so. Does he really think so? But if it is, how can he resist it? For years he has labored to prove it a sacred right of white men to take negro slaves into the new Territories. Can he possibly show that it is less a sacred right to buy them where they can be bought cheapest? And unquestionably they can be bought cheaper in Africa than in Virginia. He has done all in his power to reduce the whole question of slavery to one of a mere right of property; and as such, how can he oppose the foreign slave-trade. How can he refuse that trade in that "property" shall be "perfectly free," unless he does it as a protection to the home production? And as the home producers will probably not ask the protection, he will be wholly without a ground of opposition.

Senator Douglas holds, we know, that a man may rightfully be wiser to-day than he was yesterday—that he may rightfully change when he finds himself wrong. But can we, for that reason, run ahead, and infer that he will make any particular change of which he, himself, has given no intimation? Can we safely base our action upon any such vague inference? Now, as ever, I wish not to misrepresent Judge Douglas's position, question his motives, or do aught that can be personally offensive to him. Whenever, if ever, he and we can come together on principle so that our great cause may have assistance from his great ability, I hope to have interposed no adventitious obstacle. But clearly, he is not now with us—he does not pretend to be—he does not promise ever to be.

Our cause, then, must be intrusted to, and conducted by, its own undoubted friends—those whose hands are free, whose hearts are in the work, who do care for the result. Two years ago the Republicans of the nation mustered over thirteen hundred thousand strong. We did this under the single impulse of resistance to a common danger, with every external circumstance against us. Of strange, discordant, and even hostile elements, we gathered from the four winds, and formed and fought the battle through, under the constant hot fire of a disciplined, proud, and pampered enemy. Did we brave all then to falter now?—now, when that same enemy is wavering, dissevered, and belligerent? The result is not doubtful. We shall not fail—if we stand firm, we shall not fail. Wise counsels may accelerate or mistakes delay it, but, sooner or later, the victory is sure to come.

Stephen A. Douglas

Popular Sovereignty (1858)

By 1858 Stephen A. Douglas was the most powerful Democrat in the nation, with the possible exception of President James Buchanan. He had been in the Senate for twelve years, serving for most of those years as chairman of the Committee on Territories. In each of the two most recent Presidential elections he had been considered as a contender, and he was the clear front-runner for the 1860 Democratic nomination. He had played a major role in 1850 in breaking the Congressional logjam that had thwarted the Compromise of 1850, and he had dominated public debate since introducing the Kansas-Nebraska bill of 1854.

The heart of Douglas's political doctrine was "popular sovereignty," the belief that decisions about slavery in a given territory should be made by the people who lived there. He viewed the territories as incipient states and entitled to the same degree of sovereignty. This principle was offered originally in 1850 as a compromise strategy; by 1854 Douglas had come to regard it as a sacred principle of territorial organization, so much so that he supported repeal of the Missouri Compromise in favor of popular sovereignty. In Douglas's view, popular sovereignty was neutral, but his opponents suspected him of having proslavery or antislavery leanings. When he broke with the Buchanan administration over its acceptance of a slave-state constitution for Kansas, Southerners denounced him as favoring popular sovereignty only when it led to freedom. Meanwhile, many Northerners, Lincoln among them, alleged that Douglas secretly was plotting to spread slavery elsewhere by acquiescing in the Supreme Court's ruling in the *Dred Scott* case in the hope that a parallel decision would be forthcoming which would deny a *state* the right to exclude slaves from its midst. The competing demands of different audiences put Douglas in a difficult position and made him vulnerable as a candidate for reelection.

Abraham Lincoln had accepted the Republican senatorial nomination in June with a speech in which he accused Douglas of conspiring to extend slavery across the land. That created a need for Douglas to defend himself, but it also opened the way for him to attack Lincoln as a dangerous radical. He could do nothing immediately, however, since he was stuck in Washington until Congress adjourned early in July. The need and opportunity came together when Douglas returned from Washington to begin his election campaign. He gave three speeches in July. On July 9 he spoke to a group of supporters in Chicago, and among his listeners was Abraham Lincoln, who was in Chicago for the opening of the U.S. District Court. On July 16, again with Lincoln present, he spoke in Bloomington Illinois, and on July 17 Senator Douglas spoke in Springfield. The speech in Bloomington, which appears below, is more fully developed than either of the other two, but, in most respects, they were very similar.

Douglas defended himself and his principles, then opened fire on Lincoln. His goal was to make Lincoln, rather than his own Senate record, the central issue in the campaign. He repeatedly contrasted his own views with those of the "house-divided" speech, which he castigated as radical abolitionism. The audience was strongly predisposed toward Douglas, to be sure, and the speech generally was well received. At the conclusion, Lincoln announced that he would return to speak the following night.

Taken together, Lincoln's and Douglas's speeches contain most of the arguments and themes that soon would figure prominently in the Lincoln-Douglas debates. Each had accused the other of being involved in secret conspiracies, and there were disputes over what the Constitution really meant and what the founding fathers would have done if they had been here. Only late in the debates, and only in an indirect fashion, was there any discussion of where the morality of the issue lay.

Mr. Chairman and fellow-citizens of McLean County: To say that I am profoundly touched by the hearty welcome you have extended me, and by the kind and complimentary sentiments you have expressed toward me, is but a feeble expression of the feelings of my heart.

I appear before you this evening for the purpose of vindicating the course which I have felt it my duty to pursue in the Senate of the United States upon the great public questions which have agitated the country since I last addressed you. I am aware that my senatorial course has been arraigned, not only by political foes, but by a few men pretending to belong to the Democratic party, and yet acting in alliance with the enemies of that party, for the purpose of electing Republicans to Congress in this State, in place of the present Democratic delegation. I desire your attention whilst I address you, and then I will ask your verdict whether I have not in all things acted in entire good faith, and honestly carried out the principles, the professions, and the avowals which I made before my constituents previous to my going to the Senate.

During the last session of Congress the great question of controversy has been the admission of Kansas into the Union under the Lecompton Constitution. I need not inform you that from the beginning to the end I took bold, determined, and unrelenting ground in opposition to that Lecompton Constitution. My reason for that course is contained in the fact that that instrument was not the act and deed of the people of Kansas, and did not embody their will. I hold it to be a fundamental principle in all free governments—a principle asserted in the Declaration of Independence, and underlying the Constitution of the United States, as well as the Constitution of every State of the Union—that every people ought to have the right to form, adopt, and ratify the constitution under which they are to live. When I introduced the Nebraska Bill in the Senate of the United States, in 1854, I incorporated in it the provision that it was the true intent and meaning of the bill not to legislate slavery into any Territory or State, or to exclude it therefrom, but to leave the people thereof perfectly free to form and regulate their own domestic institutions in their own way, subject only to the Constitution of the United States. In that bill the pledge was distinctly made that the people of Kansas should be left not only free, but perfectly free to form and regulate their own domestic institutions to suit themselves; and the question arose, when the Lecompton Constitution was sent into Congress, and the admission of Kansas not only asked, but attempted to be forced under it, whether or not that Constitution was the free act and deed of the people of Kansas. No man pretends that it embodied their will. Every man in America knows that it was rejected by the people of Kansas, by a majority of over ten thousand, before the attempt was made in Congress to force the Territory into the Union under that Constitution. I resisted, therefore, the Lecompton Constitution because it was a violation of the great principle of self-government, upon which all our institutions rest. I do not wish to mislead you, or to leave you in doubt as to the motives of my action. I did not oppose the Lecompton Constitution upon the ground of the slavery clause contained in it. I made my speech against that instrument before the vote was taken on the slavery clause. At the time I made it I did not know whether that clause would be voted in or out; whether it would be included in the Constitution, or excluded from it; and it made no difference with me what the result of the vote was, for the reason that I was contending for a principle, under which you have no more right to force a free State upon a people against their will than you have to force a slave State upon them without their consent. The error consisted in attempting to control the free action of the people of Kansas in any respect whatever. It is no argument with me to say that such and such a clause of the Constitution was not palatable, that you did not like it; it is a matter of no consequence whether you in Illinois like any clause in the Kansas Constitution or not; it is not a question for you, but it is a question for the people of Kansas. They have the right to make a constitution in accordance with their own wishes, and if you do not like it, you are not bound to go there and live under it. . . . Reasoning thus, my friends, my efforts were directed to the vindication of the great principle involving the right of the people of each State and each Territory to form and regulate their own domestic institutions to suit themselves, subject only to the Constitution of our common country. I am rejoiced to be enabled to say to you that we fought that battle until we forced the advocates of the Lecompton instrument to abandon the attempt of inflicting it upon the people of Kansas without first giving them an opportunity of rejecting it. When we compelled them to abandon that effort, they resorted to a scheme. They agreed to refer the Constitution back to the people of Kansas, thus conceding the correctness of the principle for which I had contended, and granting all I had desired, provided the mode of that reference and the mode of submission to the people had been just, fair, and equal. I did not consider the mode of submission provided in what is known as the "English" bill a fair submission, and for this simple reason, among others: It provided, in effect, that if the people of Kansas would accept the Lecompton Constitution, that they might come in with 35,000 inhabitants; but that if they rejected it, in order that they might form a constitution agreeable to their own feelings, and conformable to their own principles, that they should not be received into the Union until they had 93,420 inhabitants. In other words, it said to the people,—If you will come into the Union as a slaveholding State, you shall be admitted with 35,000 inhabitants; but if you insist on being a free State, you shall not be admitted until you have 93,420. I was not willing to discriminate between free States and slave States in this Confederacy. I will not put a restriction upon a slave State that I would not put upon a free State, and I will not permit, if I can prevent it, a restriction being put upon a free State which is not applied with the same force to the slaveholding States. Equality among the States is a cardinal and fundamental principle in our Confederacy, and cannot be violated without overturning our system of government. Hence I demanded that the free States and the slaveholding States should be kept on an exact equality, one with the other, as the Constitution of the United States had placed them. If the people of Kansas want a slaveholding State, let them have it; and if they want a free State they have a right to it; and it is not for the people of Illinois, or Missouri, or New York, or Kentucky, to complain, whatever the decision of the people of Kansas may be upon that point.

But while I was not content with the mode of submission contained in the English bill, and while I could not sanction it for the reason that, in my opinion, it violated the great principle of equality among the different States, yet when it became the law of the land, and under it the question was referred back to the people of Kansas for their decision, at an election to be held on the first Monday in August next, I bowed in deference, because whatever decision the people shall make at that election must be final, and conclusive of the whole question. If the people of Kansas accept the proposition submitted by Congress, from that moment Kansas will become a State of the Union, and there is no way of keeping her out if you should try. The act of admission would become irrepealable; Kansas would be a State, and there would be an end of the controversy. On the other hand, if at that election the people of Kansas shall reject the proposition, as is now generally thought will be the case, from that moment the Lecompton Constitution is dead, and again there is an end of the controversy. So you see that either way, on the 3d of August next, the Lecompton controversy ceases and terminates forever; and a similar question can never arise unless some man shall attempt to play the Lecompton game over again. But, my fellow-citizens, I am well convinced that that game will never be attempted again; it has been so solemnly and thoroughly rebuked during the last session of Congress that it will find but few advocates in the future. The President of the United States, in his annual message, expressly recommends that the example of the Minnesota case, wherein Congress required the Constitution to be submitted to the vote of the people for ratification or rejection, shall be followed in all future cases; and all we have to do is to sustain as one man that recommendation, and the Kansas controversy can never again arise.

. . . My friends, when I am battling for a great principle, I want aid and support from whatever quarter I can get it, in order to carry out that principle. I never hesitate in my course when I find those who on all former occasions differed from me upon the principle finally coming to its support. Nor is it for me to inquire into the motives which animated the Republican members of Congress in supporting the Crittenden-Montgomery bill. It is enough for me that in that case they came square up and indorsed the great principle of the Kansas-Nebraska Bill, which declared that Kansas should be received into the Union, with slavery or without, as its Constitution should prescribe. I was the more rejoiced at the action of the Republicans on that occasion for another reason. I could not forget, you will not soon forget, how unanimous that party was, in 1854, in declaring that never should another slave State be admitted into this Union under any circumstances whatever: and yet we find that during this last winter they came up and voted, to a man, declaring that Kansas should come in as a State with slavery under the Lecompton Constitution, if her people desired it, and that if they did not, they might form a new constitution, with slavery or without, just as they pleased. I do not question the motive when men do a good act; I give them credit for the act; and if they will stand by that principle in the future, and abandon their heresy of "no more slave States even if the people want them," I will then give them still more credit. I am afraid, though, that they will not stand by it in the future. If they do, I will freely forgive them all the abuse they heaped upon me in 1854 for having advocated and carried out that same principle in the Kansas-Nebraska Bill.

Illinois stands proudly forward as a State which early took her position in favor of the principle of popular sovereignty as applied to the Territories of the United States. When the Compromise measures of 1850 passed, predicated upon that principle, you recollect the excitement which prevailed throughout the northern portion of this State. I vindicated those measure then, and defended myself for having voted for them, upon the ground that they embodied the principle that every people ought to have the privilege of forming and regulating their own institutions to suit themselves; that each State had that right, and I saw no reason why it should not be extended to the Territories. When the people of Illinois had an opportunity of passing judgment upon those measures, they indorsed them by a vote of their representatives in the Legislature,—sixty-one in the affirmative, and only four in the negative,—in which they asserted that the principle embodied in the measures was the birthright of freemen, the gift of Heaven, a principle vindicated by our revolutionary fathers, and that no limitation should ever be placed upon it, either in the organization of a territorial government or the admission of a State into the Union. That resolution still stands unrepealed on the journals of the Legislature of Illinois. In obedience to it, and in exact conformity with the principle, I brought in the Kansas-Nebraska Bill, requiring that the people should be left perfectly free in the formation of their institutions and in the organization of their government. I now submit to you whether I have not in good faith redeemed that pledge, that the people of Kansas should be left perfectly free to form and regulate their institutions to suit themselves. And yet, while no man can arise in any crowd and deny that I have been faithful to my principles and redeemed my pledge, we find those who are struggling to crush and defeat me, for the very reason that I have been faithful in carrying out those measures. We find the Republican leaders forming an alliance with professed Lecompton men to defeat every Democratic nominee and elect Republicans in their places, and aiding and defending them in order to help them break down Anti-Lecompton men, who they acknowledge did right in their opposition to Lecompton. The only hope that Mr. Lincoln has of defeating me for Senator rests in the fact that I was faithful to my principles and that he may be able in consequence of that fact to form a coalition with Lecompton men who wish to defeat me for that fidelity. . . .

Every Republican paper takes ground with my Lecompton enemies, encouraging them, stimulating them in their opposition to me, and styling my friends bolters from the Democratic party, and their Lecompton allies the true Democratic party of the country. If they think that they can mislead and deceive the people of Illinois, or the Democracy of Illinois, by that sort of an unnatural and unholy alliance, I think they show very little sagacity, or give the people very little credit for intelligence. It must be a contest of principle. Either the radical Abolition principles of Mr. Lincoln must be maintained, or the strong, constitutional, national Democratic principles with which I am identified must be carried out.

. . . And this brings me to the consideration of the two points at issue between Mr. Lincoln and myself. The Republican Convention, when it assembled at Springfield, did me and the country the honor of indicating the man who was to be their standard-bearer, and the embodiment of their principles, in this State. I owe them my gratitude for thus making up a direct issue between Mr. Lincoln and myself. I shall have no controversies of a personal character with Mr. Lincoln. I have known him well for a quarter of a century. I have known him, as you all know him, a kind-hearted, amiable gentleman, a right good fellow, a worthy citizen, of eminent ability as a lawyer, and, I have no doubt, sufficient ability to make a good Senator. The question, then, for you to decide is whether his principles are more in accordance with the genius of our free institutions, the peace and harmony of the Republic, than those which I advocate. He tells you, in his speech made at Springfield, before the Convention which gave him his unanimous nomination, that—

"A house divided against itself cannot stand."

"I believe this government cannot endure permanently half slave and half free."

"I do not expect the Union to be dissolved, I don't expect the house to fall; but I do expect it will cease to be divided."

"It will become all one thing or all the other."

That is the fundamental principle upon which he sets out in this campaign. Well, I do not suppose you will believe one word of it when you come to examine it carefully, and see its consequences. Although the Republic has existed from 1789 to this day divided into free States and slave States, yet we are told that in the future it cannot endure unless they shall become all free or all slave. For that reason, he says, as the gentleman in the crowd says, that they must be all free. He wishes to go to the Senate of the United States in order to carry out that line of public policy, which will compel all the States in the South to become free. How is he going to do it? Has Congress any power over the subject of slavery in Kentucky, or Virginia, or any other State of this Union? How, then, is Mr. Lincoln going to carry out that principle which he says is essential to the existence of this Union, to wit, that slavery must be abolished in all the States of the Union, or must be established in them all? You convince the South that they must either establish slavery in Illinois, and in every other free State, or submit to its abolition in every Southern State, and you invite them to make a warfare upon the Northern States in order to establish slavery, for the sake of perpetuating it at home. Thus, Mr. Lincoln invites by his proposition a war of sections, a war between Illinois and Kentucky, a war between the free States and the slave States, a war between the North and the South, for the purpose of either exterminating slavery in every Southern State or planting it in every Northern State. He tells you that the safety of this Republic, that the existence of this Union, depends upon that warfare being carried on until one section or the other shall be entirely subdued. The States must all be free or slave, for a house divided against itself cannot stand. That is Mr. Lincoln's argument upon that question. My friends, is it possible to preserve peace between the North and the South if such a doctrine shall prevail in either section of the Union? Will you ever submit to a warfare waged by the Southern States to establish slavery in Illinois? What man in Illinois would not lose the last drop of his heart's blood before he would submit to the institution of slavery being forced upon us by other States, against our will? And if that be true of us, what Southern man would not shed the last drop of his heart's blood to prevent Illinois, or any other Northern State, from interfering to abolish slavery in his State? Each of these States is sovereign under the Constitution; and if we wish to preserve our liberties, the reserved rights and sovereignty of each and every State must be maintained. I have said on a former occasion, and I here repeat, that it is neither desirable nor possible to establish uniformity in the local and domestic institutions of all the States of this Confederacy. And why? Because the Constitution of the United States rests upon the right of every State to decide all its local and domestic institutions for itself. It is not possible, therefore, to make them conform to each other, unless we subvert the Constitution of the United States. No, sir, that cannot be done. God forbid that any man should ever make the attempt! Let that Constitution ever be trodden under foot and destroyed, and there will not be wisdom and patriotism enough left to make another that will work half so well. Our safety, our liberty, depends upon preserving the Constitution of the United States as our fathers made it, inviolate, at the same time maintaining the reserved rights and the sovereignty of each State over its local and domestic institutions, against Federal authority, or any outside interference.

The difference between Mr. Lincoln and myself upon this point is, that he goes for a combination of the Northern States, or the organization of a sectional political party in the free States, to make war on the domestic institutions of the Southern States, and to prosecute that war until they shall all be subdued, and made to conform to such rules as the North shall dictate to them. I am aware that Mr. Lincoln, on Saturday night last, made a speech at Chicago for the purpose, as he said, of explaining his position on this question. I have read that speech with great care, and will do him the justice to say that it is marked by eminent ability, and great success in concealing what he did mean to say in his Springfield speech. His answer to this point, which I have been arguing, is, that he never did mean, and that I ought to know that he never intended to convey the idea, that he wished the "people of the free States to *enter into* the Southern States, and interfere with slavery." Well, I never did suppose that he ever dreamed of entering into Kentucky to make war upon her institutions; nor will any Abolitionist ever enter into Kentucky to wage such war. Their mode of making war is not to enter into those States where slavery exists, and there interfere, and render themselves responsible for the consequences. Oh, no! They stand on this side of the Ohio River and shoot across. They stand in Bloomington, and shake their fists at the people of Lexington; they threaten South Carolina from Chicago. And they call that bravery! But they are very particular, as Mr. Lincoln says, not to enter into those States for the purpose of interfering with the institution of slavery there. I am not only opposed to entering into the Slave States, for the purpose of interfering with their institutions, but I am opposed to a sectional agitation to control the institutions of other States. I am opposed to organizing a sectional party, which appeals to Northern pride, and Northern passion and prejudice, against Southern institutions, thus stirring up ill-feeling and hot blood between brethren of the same Republic. I am opposed to that whole system of sectional agitation, which can produce nothing but strife, but discord, but hostility, and, finally, disunion. And yet Mr. Lincoln asks you to send him to the Senate of the United States, in order that he may carry out that great principle of his, that all the States must be slave, or all must be free. I repeat, how is he to carry it out when he gets to the Senate? Does he intend to introduce a bill to abolish slavery in Kentucky? Does he intend to introduce a bill to interfere with slavery in Virginia? How is he to accomplish what he professes must be done in order to save the Union? Mr. Lincoln is a lawyer, sagacious and able enough to tell you how he proposes to do it. I ask Mr. Lincoln how it is that he proposes ultimately to bring about this uniformity in each and all the States of the Union. There is but one possible mode which I can see, and perhaps Mr. Lincoln intends to pursue it; that is, to introduce a proposition into the Senate to change the Constitution of the United States, in order that all the State legislatures may be abolished, State sovereignty blotted out, and the power conferred upon Congress to make local laws and establish the domestic institutions and police regulations uniformly throughout the United States. Are you prepared for such a change in the institutions of your country? Whenever you shall have blotted out the State sovereignties, abolished the State legislatures, and consolidated all the power in the Federal Government, you will have established a consolidated empire as destructive to the liberties of the people and the rights of the citizen as that of Austria, or Russia, or any other despotism that rests upon the necks of the people. How is it possible for Mr. Lincoln to carry out his cherished principle of abolishing slavery everywhere or establishing it everywhere, except by the mode which I have pointed out,—by an amendment to the Constitution to the effect that I have suggested? There is no other possible mode. Mr. Lincoln intends resorting to that, or else he means nothing by the great principle upon which he desires to be elected. My friends, I trust that we will be able to get him to define what he does mean by this scriptural quotation that "A house divided against itself cannot stand"; that the government cannot endure permanently half slave and half free; that it must be all one thing, or all the other. Who among you expects to live, or have his children live, until slavery shall be established in Illinois or abolished in South Carolina? Who expects to see that occur during the lifetime of ourselves or our children?

There is but one possible way in which slavery can be abolished, and that is by leaving a State, according to the principle of the Kansas-Nebraska Bill, perfectly free to form and regulate its institutions in its own way. That was the principle upon which this Republic was founded, and it is under the operation of that principle that we have been able to preserve the Union thus far. Under its operations, slavery disappeared from New Hampshire, from Rhode Island, from Connecticut, from New York, from New Jersey, from Pennsylvania, from six of the twelve original slaveholding States; and this gradual system of emancipation went on quietly, peacefully, and steadily, so long as we in the free States minded our own business and left our neighbors alone. But the moment the abolition societies were organized throughout the North, preaching a violent crusade against slavery in the Southern States, this combination necessarily caused a counter-combination in the South, and a sectional line was drawn which was a barrier to any further emancipation. Bear in mind that emancipation has not taken place in any one State since the Free-soil party was organized as a political party in this country. Emancipation went on gradually in State after State as long as the free States were content with managing their own affairs and leaving the South perfectly free to do as they pleased; but the moment the North said, We are powerful enough to control you of the South, the moment the North proclaimed itself the determined master of the South, that moment the South combined to resist the attack, and thus sectional parties were formed, and gradual emancipation ceased in all the Northern slaveholding States. And yet Mr. Lincoln, in view of these historical facts, proposes to keep up this sectional agitation, band all the Northern States together in one political party, elect a President by Northern votes along, and then, of course, make a cabinet composed of Northern men, and administer the government by Northern men only, denying all the Southern States of this Union any participation in the administration of affairs whatsoever. I submit to you, my fellow-citizens, whether such a line of policy is consistent with the peace and harmony of the country? Can the Union endure under such a system of policy? He has taken his position in favor of sectional agitation and sectional warfare. I have taken mine in favor of securing peace, harmony, and good-will among all the States, by permitting each to mind its own business, and discountenancing any attempt at interference on the part of one State with the domestic concerns of the others.

Mr. Lincoln makes another issue with me, and he wishes to confine the contest to these two issues. I accept the other as readily as the one to which I have already referred. The other issue is a crusade against the Supreme Court of the United States, because of its decision in the Dred Scott case. My fellow-citizens, I have no issue to make with the Supreme Court. I have no crusade to preach against that august body. I have no warfare to make upon it. I receive the decision of the Judges of that Court, when pronounced, as the final adjudication upon all questions within their jurisdiction. It would be perfectly legitimate and proper for Mr. Lincoln, myself, or any other lawyer, to go before the Supreme Court and argue any question that might arise there, taking either side of it, and enforcing it with all our ability, zeal, and energy; but when the decision is pronounced, that decision becomes the law of the land, and he, and you, and myself, and every other good citizen, must bow to it, and yield obedience to it. Unless we respect and bow in deference to the final decisions of the highest judicial tribunal in our country, we are driven at once to anarchy, to violence, to mob law, and there is no security left for our property or our own civil rights. What protects your property but the law? And who expounds the law but the judicial tribunals? and if an appeal is to be taken from the decisions of the Supreme Court of the United States in all cases where a person does not like the adjudication, to whom is that appeal to be taken? Are we to appeal from the Supreme Court to a county meeting like this? And shall we here reargue the question and reverse the decision? If so, how are we to enforce our decrees after we have pronounced them? Does Mr. Lincoln intend to appeal from the Supreme Court to a Republican caucus, or a town meeting? To whom is he going to appeal?

. . . To whom is Mr. Lincoln going to appeal? Why, he says he is going to appeal to Congress. . . . He does not intend to reverse it as to Dred Scott. Oh, no! But he will reverse it so that it shall not stand as a rule in the future. How will he do it? He says that if he is elected to the Senate he will introduce and pass a law just like the Missouri Compromise, prohibiting slavery again in all the Territories. Suppose he does re-enact the same law which the Court has pronounced unconstitutional, will that make it constitutional? If the Act of 1820 was unconstitutional, in consequence of Congress having no power to pass it, will Mr. Lincoln make it constitutional by passing it again? . . .The functions of Congress are to enact the statutes, the province of the Court is to pronounce upon their validity, and the duty of the executive is to carry the decision into effect when rendered by the Court. And yet, notwithstanding the Constitution makes the decision of the Court final in regard to the validity of an Act of Congress, Mr. Lincoln is going to reverse that decision by passing another Act of Congress.

When he has become convinced of the folly of the proposition, perhaps he will resort to the same subterfuge that I have found others of his party resort to, which is to agitate and agitate until he can change the Supreme Court and put other men in the places of the present incumbents. I wonder whether Mr. Lincoln is right sure that he can accomplish that reform. He certainly will not be able to get rid of the present Judges until they die, and from present appearances I think they have as good security of life as he has himself. I am afraid that my friend Lincoln would not accomplish this task during his own lifetime, and yet he wants to go to Congress to do all this in six years. Do you think that he can persuade nine Judges, or a majority of them, to die in that six years, just to accommodate him? They are appointed Judges for life, and according to the present organization, new ones cannot be appointed during that time; but he is going to agitate until they die, and then have the President appoint good Republicans in their places. He had better be quite sure that he gets a Republican President at the same time to appoint them. He wants to have a Republican President elected by Northern votes, not a Southern man participating, and elected for the purpose of placing none but Republicans on the bench; and, consequently, if he succeeds in electing that President, and succeeds in persuading the present Judges to die, in order that their vacancies may be filled, that the President will then appoint their successors. And by what process will he appoint them? He first looks for a man who has the legal qualifications; perhaps he takes Mr. Lincoln, and says, "Mr. Lincoln, would you not like to go on the Supreme bench?" "Yes," replies Mr. Lincoln. "Well," returns the Republican President, "I cannot appoint you until you give me a pledge as to how you will decide in the event of a particular question coming before you." What would you think of Mr. Lincoln if he would consent to give that pledge? And yet he is going to prosecute a war until he gets the present Judges out, and then catechise each man and require a pledge before his appointment as to how he will decide each question that may arise upon points affecting the Republican party.

Now, my friends, suppose this scheme was practical. I ask you what confidence you would have in a court thus constituted,—a court composed of partisan judges, appointed on political grounds, selected with a view to the decision of questions in a particular way, and pledged in regard to a decision before the argument, and without reference to the peculiar state of the facts. Would such a court command the respect of the country? If the Republican party cannot trust Democratic judges, how can they expect us to trust Republican judges, when they have been selected in advance for the purpose of packing a decision in the event of a case arising? My fellow-citizens, whenever partisan politics shall be carried on to the bench; whenever the judges shall be arraigned upon the stump, and their judicial conduct reviewed in town meetings and caucuses; whenever the independence and integrity of the judiciary shall be tampered with to the extent of rendering them partial, blind, and suppliant tools, what security will you have for your rights and your liberties? I therefore take issue with Mr. Lincoln directly in regard to this warfare upon the Supreme Court of the United States. I accept the decision of that Court as it was pronounced. Whatever my individual opinions may be, I, as a good citizen, am bound by the laws of the land, as the Legislature makes them, as the Court expounds them, and as the executive officers administer them. I am bound by our Constitution as our fathers made it, and as it is our duty to support it. I am bound, as a good citizen, to sustain the constituted authorities, and to resist, discourage, and beat down, by all lawful and peaceful means, all attempts at exciting mobs, or violence, or any other revolutionary proceedings against the Constitution and the constituted authorities of the country.

Mr. Lincoln is alarmed for fear that, under the Dred Scott decision, slavery will go into all the Territories of the United States. All I have to say is that, with or without that decision, slavery will go just where the people want it, and not one inch further. You have had experience upon that subject in the case of Kansas. You have been told by the Republican party that, from 1854, when the Kansas-Nebraska Bill passed, down to last winter, that slavery was sustained and supported in Kansas by the laws of what they called a "bogus" Legislature. And how many slaves were there in the Territory at the end of last winter? Not as many at the end of that period as there were on the day the Kansas-Nebraska Bill passed. There was quite a number of slaves in Kansas, taken there under the Missouri Compromise, and in spite of it, before the Kansas-Nebraska Bill passed; and now it is asserted that there are not as many there as there were before the passage of the bill, notwithstanding that they had local laws sustaining and encouraging it, enacted, as the Republicans say, by a "bogus" Legislature, imposed upon Kansas by an invasion from Missouri. Why has not slavery obtained a foothold in Kansas under these circumstances? Simply because there was a majority of her people opposed to slavery, and every slaveholder knew that if he took his slaves there, the moment that majority got possession of the ballot-boxes, and a fair election was held, that moment slavery would be abolished, and he would lose them. For that reason, such owners as took their slaves there brought them back to Missouri, fearing that if they remained they would be emancipated. Thus you see that under the principle of popular sovereignty slavery has been kept out of Kansas, notwithstanding the fact that for the first three years they had a Legislature in that Territory favorable to it. I tell you, my friends, it is impossible under our institutions to force slavery on an unwilling people. If this principle of popular sovereignty asserted in the Nebraska Bill be fairly carried out, by letting the people decide the question for themselves, by a fair vote, at a fair election, and with honest returns, slavery will never exist one day, or one hour, in any Territory against the unfriendly legislation of an unfriendly people. . . .

Hence, if the people of a Territory want slavery, they will encourage it by passing affirmatory laws, and the necessary police regulations, patrol laws, and slave code; if they do not want it, they will withhold that legislation, and by withholding it slavery is as dead as if it was prohibited by a constitutional prohibition, especially if, in addition, their legislation is unfriendly, as it would be if they were opposed to it. They could pass such local laws and police regulations as would drive slavery out in one day, or one hour, if they were opposed to it; and therefore, so far as the question of slavery in the Territories is concerned, so far as the principle of popular sovereignty is concerned, in its practical operation, it matters not how the Dred Scott case may be decided with reference to the Territories. My own opinion on that law point is well known. It is shown by my votes and speeches in Congress. But be it as it may, the question was an abstract question, inviting no practical results; and whether slavery shall exist or shall not exist in any State or Territory will depend upon whether the people are for or against it; and whichever way they shall decide it in any Territory or in any State will be entirely satisfactory to me.

But I must now bestow a few words upon Mr. Lincoln's main objection to the Dred Scott decision. He is not going to submit to it. . . . And why? Because he says that that decision deprives the negro of the benefits of that clause of the Constitution of the United States which entitles the citizens of each State to all the privileges and immunities of citizens of the several States. Well, it is very true that the decision does have that effect. By deciding that a negro is not a citizen, of course it denies to him the rights and privileges awarded to citizens of the United States. It is this that Mr. Lincoln will not submit to. Why? For the palpable reason that he wishes to confer upon the negro all the rights, privileges, and immunities of citizens of the several States. I will not quarrel with Mr. Lincoln for his views on that subject. I have no doubt he is conscientious in them. I have not the slightest idea but that he conscientiously believes that a negro ought to enjoy and exercise all the rights and privileges given to white men; but I do not agree with him, and hence I cannot concur with him. I believe that this government of ours was founded on the white basis. I believe that it was established by white men, by men of European birth, or descended of European races, for the benefit of white men and their posterity in all time to come. I do not believe that it was the design or intention of the signers of the Declaration of Independence or the framers of the Constitution to include negroes, Indians, or other inferior races, with white men, as citizens. Our fathers had at that day seen the evil consequences of conferring civil and political rights upon the Indian and negro in the Spanish and French colonies on the American continent and the adjacent islands. In Mexico, in Central America, in South America and in the West India Islands, where the Indian, the negro, and men of all colors and all races are put on an equality by law, the effect of political amalgamation can be seen. Ask any of those gallant young men in your own county who went to Mexico to fight the battles of their country, in what friend Lincoln considers an unjust and unholy war, and hear what they will tell you in regard to the amalgamation of races in that country. Amalgamation there, first political, then social, has led to demoralization and degradation, until it has reduced that people below the point of capacity for self-government. Our fathers knew what the effect of it would be, and from the time they planted foot on the American continent, not only those who landed at Jamestown, but at Plymouth Rock and all other points on the coast, they pursued the policy of confining civil and political rights to the white race, and excluding the negro in all cases. Still, Mr. Lincoln conscientiously believes that it is his duty to advocate negro citizenship. He wants to give the negro the privilege of citizenship. He quotes Scripture again, and says: "As your Father in heaven is perfect, be ye also perfect." And he applies that Scriptural quotation to all classes; not that he expects us all to be as perfect as our Master, but as nearly perfect as possible. In other words, he is willing to give the negro an equality under the law, in order that he may approach as near perfection, or an equality with the white man, as possible. To this same end he quotes the Declaration of Independence in these words: "We hold these truths to be self-evident, that all men were created equal, and endowed by their Creator with certain inalienable rights, among which are life, liberty, and the pursuit of happiness"; and goes on to argue that the negro was included, or intended to be included, in that Declaration, by the signers of the paper. He says that, by the Declaration of Independence, therefore, all kinds of men, negroes included, were created equal and endowed by their Creator with certain inalienable rights, and, further, that the right of the negro to be on an equality with the white man is a divine right, conferred by the Almighty, and rendered inalienable according to the Declaration of Independence. Hence no human law or constitution can deprive the negro of that equality with the white man to which he is entitled by the divine law. ["Higher law."] Yes, higher law. Now, I do not question Mr. Lincoln's sincerity on this point. He believes that the negro, by the divine law, is created the equal of the white man, and that no human law can deprive him of that equality, thus secured; and he contends that the negro ought, therefore, to have all the rights and privileges of citizenship on an equality with the white man. In order to accomplish this, the first thing that would have to be done in this State would be to blot out of our State Constitution that clause which prohibits negroes from coming into this State and making it an African colony, and permit them to come and spread over these charming prairies until in midday they shall look black as night. When our friend Lincoln gets all his colored brethren around him here, he will then raise them to perfection as fast as possible, and place them on an equality with the white man, first removing all legal restrictions, because they are our equals by divine law, and there should be no such restrictions. He wants them to vote. I am opposed to it. If they had a vote, I reckon they would all vote for him in preference to me, entertaining the views I do. But that matters not. The position he has taken on this question not only presents him as claiming for them the right to vote, but their right, under the divine law and the Declaration of Independence, to be elected to office, to become members of the Legislature, to go to Congress, to become Governors, or United States Senators, or Judges of the Supreme Court; and I suppose that when they control that court they will probably reverse the Dred Scott decision. He is going to bring negroes here, and give them the right of citizenship, the right of voting, and the right of holding office and sitting on juries; and what else? Why, he would permit them to marry, would he not? And if he gives them that right, I suppose he will let them marry whom they please, provided they marry their equals. If the divine law declares that the white man is the equal of the negro woman, that they are on a perfect equality, I suppose he admits the right of the negro woman to marry the white man. In other words, his doctrine that the negro, by divine law, is placed on a perfect equality with the white man, and that that equality is recognized by the Declaration of Independence, leads him necessarily to establish negro equality under the law; but whether even then they would be so in fact would depend upon the degree of virtue and intelligence they possessed, and certain other qualities that are matters of taste rather than of law. I do not understand Mr. Lincoln as saying that he expects to make them our equals socially, or by intelligence, nor in fact as citizens, but that he wishes to make them our equals under the law, and then say to them, "As your Master in heaven is perfect, be ye also perfect."

Well, I confess to you, my fellow-citizens, that I am utterly opposed to that system of Abolition philosophy. I do not believe that the signers of the Declaration of Independence had any reference to negroes when they used the expression that all men were created equal, or that they had any reference to the Chinese or Coolies, the Indians, the Japanese, or any other inferior race. They were speaking of the white race, the European race on this continent, and their descendants, and emigrants who should come here. They were speaking only of the white race, and never dreamed that their language would be construed to include the negro. And now for the evidence of that fact: At the time the Declaration of Independence was put forth, declaring the equality of all men, every one of the thirteen colonies was a slaveholding colony, and every man who signed that Declaration represented a slaveholding constituency. Did they intend, when they put their signatures to that instrument, to declare that their own slaves were on an equality with them; that they were made their equals by divine law, and that any human law reducing them to an inferior position was void, as being in violation of divine law? Was that the meaning of the signers of the Declaration of Independence? Did Jefferson and Henry and Lee,—did any of the signers of that instrument, or all of them, on the day they signed it, give their slaves freedom? History records that they did not. Did they go further, and put the negro on an equality with the white man throughout the country? They did not. And yet if they had understood that Declaration as including the negro, which Mr. Lincoln holds they did, they would have been bound, as conscientious men, to have restored the negroes to that equality which he thinks the Almighty intended they should occupy with the white man. They did not do it. Slavery was abolished in only one State before the adoption of the Constitution in 1789, and then in others gradually, down to the time this Abolition agitation began; and it has not been abolished in one since. The history of the country shows that neither the signers of the Declaration, nor the framers of the Constitution, ever supposed it possible that their language would be used in an attempt to make this nation a mixed nation of Indians, negroes, whites, and mongrels. I repeat that our whole history confirms the proposition that, from the earliest settlement of the colonies down to the Declaration of Independence and the adoption of the Constitution of the United States, our fathers proceeded on the white basis, making the white people the governing race, but conceding to the Indian and negro, and all inferior races, all the rights and all the privileges they could enjoy consistent with the safety of the society in which they lived. That is my opinion now. I told you that humanity, philanthropy, justice, and sound policy required that we should give the negro every right, every privilege, every immunity, consistent with the safety and welfare of the State. The question then naturally arises, What are those rights and privileges, and What is the nature and extent of them? My answer is, that that is a question which each State and each Territory must decide for itself. We have decided that question. We have said that in this State the negro shall not be a slave, but that he shall enjoy no political rights; that negro equality shall not exist. I am content with that position. My friend Lincoln is not. He thinks that our policy and our laws on that subject are contrary to the Declaration of Independence. He thinks that the Almighty made the negro his equal and his brother. For my part, I do not consider the negro any kin to me, nor to any other white man; but I would still carry my humanity and my philanthropy to the extent of giving him every privilege and every immunity that he could enjoy, consistent with our own good. We in Illinois have the right to decide upon that question for ourselves, and we are bound to allow every other State to do the same. Maine allows the negro to vote on an equality with the white man. I do not quarrel with our friends in Maine for that. If they think it wise and proper in Maine to put the negro on an equality with the white man, and allow him to go to the polls and negative the vote of a white man, it is their business, and not mine. On the other hand, New York permits a negro to vote provided he owns $250 worth of property. New York thinks that a negro ought to be permitted to vote provided he is rich, but not otherwise. They allow the aristocratic negro to vote there. I never saw the wisdom, the propriety, or the justice of that decision on the part of New York, and yet it never occurred to me that I had a right to find fault with that State. It is her business; she is a sovereign State, and has a right to do as she pleases; and if she will take care of her own negroes, making such regulations concerning them as suit her, and let us alone, I will mind my business, and not interfere with her. In Kentucky they will not give a negro any political or any civil rights. I shall not argue the question whether Kentucky in so doing has decided right or wrong, wisely or unwisely. It is a question for Kentucky to decide for herself. . . . Let Kentucky mind her own business and take care of her negroes, and us attend to our own affairs and take care of our negroes, and we will be the best of friends; but if Kentucky attempts to interfere with us, or we with her, there will be strife, there will be discord, there will be relentless hatred, there will be everything but fraternal feeling and brotherly love. It is not necessary that you should enter Kentucky and interfere in that State, to use the language of Mr. Lincoln. It is just as offensive to interfere from this State, or send your missiles over there. I care not whether an enemy, if he is going to assault us, shall actually come into our State, or come along the line, and throw his bombshells over to explode in our midst. Suppose England should plant a battery on the Canadian side of the Niagara River, opposite Buffalo, and throw bombshells over, which would explode in Main Street, in that city, and destroy the buildings, and that, when we protested, she would say, in the language of Mr. Lincoln, that she never dreamed of coming into the United

States to interfere with us, and that she was just throwing her bombs over the line from her own side, which she had a right to do. Would that explanation satisfy us? So it is with Mr. Lincoln. He is not going into Kentucky, but he will plant his batteries on this side of the Ohio, where he is safe and secure for a retreat, and will throw his bombshells—his Abolition documents—over the river, and will carry on a political warfare, and get up strife between the North and the South, until he elects a sectional President, reduces the South to the condition of dependent colonies, raises the negro to an equality, and forces the South to submit to the doctrine that a house divided against itself cannot stand; that the Union divided into half slave States and half free cannot endure; that they must all be slave or they must all be free; and that as we in the North are in the majority, we will not permit them to be all slave, and therefore they in the South must consent to the States all being free. Now, fellow-citizens, I submit to you whether these doctrines are consistent with the peace and harmony of this Union? I submit to you whether they are consistent with our duties as citizens of a common confederacy; whether they are consistent with the principles which ought to govern brethren of the same family? . . . Why should this slavery agitation be kept up? Does it benefit the white man, or the slave? Whom does it benefit, except the Republican politicians, who use it as their hobby to ride into office? Why, I repeat, should it be continued? Why cannot we be content to administer this government as it was made,—a confederacy of sovereign and independent States? Let us recognize the sovereignty and independence of each State, refrain from interfering with the domestic institutions and regulations of other States, permit the Territories and new States to decide their institutions for themselves, as we did when we were in their condition; blot out these lines of North and South, and resort back to these lines of State boundaries which the Constitution has marked out and engraved upon the face of the country; have no other dividing lines but these, and we will be one united, harmonious people, with fraternal feelings, and no discord or dissension.

These are my views, and these are the principles to which I have devoted all my energies since 1850, when I acted side by side with the immortal Clay and the godlike Webster in that memorable struggle, in which Whigs and Democrats united upon a common platform of patriotism and the Constitution, throwing aside partisan feelings in order to restore peace and harmony to a distracted country. And when I stood beside the death-bed of Mr. Clay, and heard him refer, with feelings and emotions of the deepest solicitude, to the welfare of the country, and saw that he looked upon the principle embodied in the great Compromise measures of 1850, the principle of the Nebraska Bill, the doctrine of leaving each State and Territory free to decide its institutions for itself, as the only means by which the peace of the country could be preserved and the Union perpetuated,—I pledged him, on that death-bed of his, that so long as I lived, my energies should be devoted to the vindication of that principle, and of his fame as connected with it. I gave the same pledge to the great expounder of the Constitution, he who has been called the "godlike Webster." I looked up to Clay and to him as a son would to a father, and I call upon the people of Illinois, and the people of the whole Union, to bear testimony that never since the sod has been laid upon the graves of these eminent statesmen have I failed, on any occasion, to vindicate the principle with which the last great crowning acts of their lives were identified, or to vindicate their names whenever they have been assailed; and now my life and energy are devoted to this great work as the means of preserving this Union. This Union can only be preserved by maintaining the fraternal feeling between the North and the South, the East and the West. If that good feeling can be preserved, the Union will be as perpetual as the fame of its great founders. It can be maintained by preserving the sovereignty of the States, the right of each State and each Territory to settle its domestic concerns for itself, and the duty of each to refrain from interfering with the other in any of its local or domestic institutions. Let that be done, and the Union will be perpetual; let that be done, and this Republic, which began with thirteen States, and which now numbers thirty-two, which, when it began, only extended from the Atlantic to the Mississippi, but now reaches to the Pacific, may yet expand, north and south, until it covers the whole continent, and becomes one vast ocean-bound confederacy. Then, my friends, the path of duty, of honor, of patriotism, is plain. There are a few simple principles to be preserved. Bear in mind the dividing line between State rights and Federal authority; let us maintain the great principle of popular sovereignty, of State rights, and of the Federal Union as the Constitution has made it, and this Republic will endure forever.

I thank you kindly for the patience with which you have listened to me. I fear I have wearied you. I have a heavy day's work before me to-morrow. I have several speeches to make. My friends, in whose hands I am, are taxing me beyond human endurance; but I shall take the helm and control them hereafter. I am profoundly grateful to the people of McLean for the reception they have given me, and the kindness with which they have listened to me. I remember when I first came among you here, twenty-five years ago, that I was prosecuting attorney in this district, and that my earliest efforts were made here, when my deficiencies were too apparent, I am afraid, to be concealed from any one. I remember the courtesy and kindness with which I was uniformly treated by you all; and whenever I can recognize the face of one of your old citizens, it is like meeting an old and cherished friend. I come among you with a heart filled with gratitude for past favors. I have been with you but little for the past few years, on account of my official duties. I intend to visit you again before the campaign is over. I wish to speak to your whole people. I wish them to pass judgment upon the correctness of my course, and the soundness of the principles which I have proclaimed. If you do not approve my principles, I cannot ask your support. If you believe that the election of Mr. Lincoln would contribute more to preserve the harmony of the country, to perpetuate the Union, and more to the prosperity and the honor and glory of the State, then it is your duty to give him the preference. If, on the contrary, you believe that I have been faithful to my trust, and that by sustaining me you will give greater strength and efficiency to the principles which I have expounded, I shall then be grateful for your support. I renew my profound thanks for your attention.

John Brown

Speech to the Court (1859)

The war of words between the North and South broke into armed conflict in Kansas in 1856. The popular sovereignty doctrine provided that slavery would be allowed or prohibited in a territory according the the wishes of the inhabitants. This caused a scramble on both sides to settle the territory with proslavery or antislavery adherents. From May to September a virtual civil war raged in the territory as the two opposing forces struggled for control. Joined by the "Border Ruffians" from Missouri, proslavery men attacked Lawrence, pillaged the town, and destroyed the antislavery newspapers. In retaliation a small band of men captured and executed five proslavery farmers near Pottawatomie Creek. The "Pottawatomie Massacre" was carried out by a dedicated abolitionist, John Brown, who was convinced that slavery could not be eradicated except by force.

Brown was active in abolitionist causes throughout his life, supporting the underground railway in its efforts to help escaped slaves, organizing an association to promote the education of blacks, working in a black farm settlement in New York. With his sons, Brown led various small groups of antislavery forces in the fight over "Bleeding Kansas." Although the Pottawatomie Massacre was generally disavowed by most Free Soilers, Brown's spirited defense of the little town of Osawatomie against a large proslavery force captured the imagination of Northern abolitionists whose journals referred to him admiringly as "Old Brown of Osawatomie."

Money and arms supplied by the Massachusetts State Kansas Committee enabled Brown to maintain his guerilla bands and encouraged him to conceive a larger, more daring venture. He envisioned the establishment of a stronghold in the Southern mountains which would be a haven for escaped slaves and a staging area for raids on slaveholders. In 1858 he and a group of followers gathered in Canada, where they established a constitution for a free state to be carved out of Virginia and Maryland. In the summer of 1859 he led a force of about twenty men who established themselves in a farmhouse in Maryland. His plan was to seize the Federal Arsenal at Harper's Ferry, Virginia, as the first step in raising a slave insurrection.

He crossed the Potomac River on the evening of October 16 and succeeded in taking the arsenal and the town of Harper's Ferry. By the next day, however, Brown was surrounded by the militia, who were soon reinforced by a company of U.S. Marines commanded by Robert E. Lee. Refusing to surrender, Brown was captured after troops assaulted the fire station in which he had barricaded himself. Brown was wounded and Brown's two sons, along with eight other supporters, were killed.

Placed on trial on October 27, Brown was quickly found guilty and sentenced to hang. In his final speech in court, Brown asserted that what he had done "in behalf of [God's] . . . despised poor was not wrong, but right." Brown's simple defense was much admired by Northern antislavery supporters, to whom he became a hero and a martyr. In the South, however, Brown's actions intensified the fear of a slave rebellion and confirmed the conviction that Northerners would encourage such fanatical outrages. Indeed, for many Southerners Brown was seen as typical of Northern antislavery men and his raid as symbolic of Northern intentions. This episode was a key step in the polarization of Northern and Sourthern attitudes during 1860.

I have, may it please the Court, a few words to say. In the first place, I deny everything but what I have all along admitted,—the design on my part to free the slaves. I intended certainly to have made a clean thing of that matter, as I did last winter, when I went into Missouri and there took slaves without the snapping of a gun on either side, moved them through the country, and finally left them in Canada. I designed to have done the same thing again on a larger scale. That was all I intended. I never did intend murder, or treason, or the destruction of property, or to excite or incite slaves to rebellion, or to make insurrection.

I have another objection; and that is, it is unjust that I should suffer such a penalty. Had I interfered in the manner which I admit, and which I admit has been fairly proved (for I admire the truthfulness and candor of the greater portion of the witnesses who have testified in this case),—had I so interfered in behalf of the rich, the powerful, the intelligent, the so-called great, or in behalf of any of their friends,—either father, mother, brother, sister, wife, or children, or any of that class,—and suffered and sacrificed what I have in this interference, it would have been all right; and every man in this court would have deemed it an act worthy of reward rather than punishment.

This court acknowledges, as I suppose, the validity of the law of God. I see a book kissed here which I suppose to be the

Bible, or at least the New Testament. That teaches me that all things whatsoever I would that men should do to me, I should do even so to them. It teaches me, further, to "remember them that are in bonds, as bound with them." I endeavored to act up to that instruction. I say I am yet too young to understand that God is any respecter of persons. I believe that to have interfered as I have done—as I have always freely admitted I have done—in behalf of his despised poor was not wrong, but right. Now, if it is deemed necessary that I should forfeit my life for the furtherance of the ends of justice, and mingle my blood further with the blood of my children and with the blood of millions in this slave country whose rights are disregarded by wicked, cruel, and unjust enactments,—I submit; so let it be done!

Let me say one word further.

I feel entirely satisfied with the treatment I have received on my trial. Considering all the circumstances, it has been more generous than I expected. But I feel no consciousness of guilt. I have stated from the first what was my intention and what was not. I never had any design against the life of any person, nor any disposition to commit treason, or excite slaves to rebel, or make any general insurrection. I never encouraged any man to do so, but always discouraged any idea of that kind.

Let me say also a word in regard to the statements made by some of those connected with me. I hear it has been stated by some of them that I have induced them to join me. But the contrary is true. I do not say this to injure them, but as regretting their weakness. There is not one of them but joined me of his own accord, and the greater part of them at their own expense. A number of them I never saw, and never had a word of conversation with till the day they came to me; and that was for the purpose I have stated.

Now I have done.

Abraham Lincoln

Cooper Union Address (1860)

In his debates with Stephen A. Douglas, Abraham Lincoln had introduced an historical argument. The founding fathers, he said, were opposed to slavery, and, while they could do nothing about an institution already in their midst, still they hoped for its eventual demise. It was for this reason that they prohibited slavery from the Northwest Territory and omitted even the word "slavery" from the Constitution. With this argument Lincoln tried to counter Douglas's assertion that the "house-divided" doctrine was at odds with the founding fathers.

The difficulty was that the true position of the founders was ambiguous and elusive. Both men spent much of 1859 reviewing the deliberations of the Constitutional Convention and the early Congresses. Douglas published his findings in an article in *Harper's* magazine; Lincoln presented his in a speech at Cooper Institute in New York City in February 1860. The Cooper Union speech, as it is commonly called, was his fullest elaboration of the historical argument.

The invitation to speak at Cooper Union was a response to Lincoln's growing prominence as a result of the debates. Previously little known outside Illinois, he had spoken in 1859 in Ohio, Indiana, Wisconsin, Iowa, Missouri, and Kansas and had been invited to make a New England tour in the winter of 1860, including a visit to his son Robert at Harvard and culminating in the speech in New York. Lincoln had developed a lecture called "Discoveries and Inventions" but was persuaded on this occasion to make a political speech.

The speech had three major parts. The longest was historical: he outlined the views of the 39 signers of the Constitution, concluding that they believed that the federal government had the power to regulate slavery in the territories and asserting that this power should be used to exclude the institution, as the first step toward its demise. In the second section, Lincoln ostensibly appealed to Southerners, assuring them of his moderation but stressing his devotion to republican principles and his unwillingness to see the Union dissolved. It is quite possible that the Southern audience was a foil and that Lincoln's true audience was the Northern Republicans to whom he also addressed the final portion, urging them to perservere but to consider matters calmly and maturely.

The speech's message was radical—claiming the support of the fathers for the Republican cause—but the tone was conservative. The speech was presented as a lawyer's brief, without the emotional intensity or the tone of moral superiority which often characterized the abolitionists. Lincoln was pleased with the speech, writing his wife that it had given him no trouble at all. Most historians have judged it far more significant than that.

The speech, after all, was delivered in the home state of William H. Seward, then the leading candidate for the Republican Presidential nomination. The audience was composed of politically influential professional men of New York City. Many were leaning toward Seward, yet there was the fear that he could not win. They did not wish to repeat the experience of four years earlier, when John C. Fremont had lost the election because enough former Whig conservatives supported Millard Fillmore to tip the balance in favor of the Democrat, James Buchanan. Concerned with victory, they wanted a candidate who could both retain the Fremont vote and woo the Fillmore vote. When Lincoln went east he may have harbored some thought of the Vice-Presidency, but the Cooper Union speech made him a plausible candidate for President. He had held his own with Seward on the New Yorker's own ground. Availability and electability became the key arguments in Lincoln's favor when, just a few months after delivering this speech, he was nominated by the Republican Party as its candidate for the Presidency.

Mr. President and Fellow-citizens of New York: The facts with which I shall deal this evening are mainly old and familiar; nor is there anything new in the general use I shall make of them. If there shall be any novelty, it will be in the mode of presenting the facts, and the inferences and observations following that presentation. In his speech last autumn at Columbus, Ohio, as reported in the "New-York Times," Senator Douglas said:

> Our fathers, when they framed the government under which we live, understood this question just as well, and even better, than we do now.

I fully indorse this, and I adopt it as a text for this discourse. I so adopt it because it furnishes a precise and an agreed starting-point for a discussion between Republicans and that wing of the Democracy headed by Senator Douglas. It simply leaves the inquiry: What was the understanding those fathers had of the question mentioned?

What is the frame of government under which we live? The answer must be, "The Constitution of the United States." That Constitution consists of the original, framed in 1787, and under which the present government first went into operation, and twelve subsequently framed amendments, the first ten of which were framed in 1789.

Who were our fathers that framed the Constitution? I suppose the "thirty-nine" who signed the original instrument may be fairly called our fathers who framed that part of the present government. It is almost exactly true to say they framed it, and it is altogether true to say they fairly represented the opinion and sentiment of the whole nation at that time. Their names, being familiar to nearly all, and accessible to quite all, need not now be repeated.

I take these "thirty-nine," for the present, as being "our fathers who framed the government under which we live." What is the question which, according to the text, those fathers understood "just as well, and even better, than we do now"?

It is this: Does the proper division of local from Federal authority, or anything in the Constitution, forbid our Federal Government to control as to slavery in our Federal Territories?

Upon this, Senator Douglas holds the affirmative, and Republicans the negative. This affirmation and denial form an issue; and this issue—this question—is precisely what the text declares our fathers understood "better than we." Let us now inquire whether the "thirty-nine," or any of them, ever acted upon this question; and if they did, how they acted upon it—how they expressed that better understanding. In 1784, three years before the Constitution, the United States then owning the Northwestern Territory, and no other, the Congress of the Confederation had before them the question of prohibiting slavery in that Territory; and four of the "thirty-nine" who afterward framed the Constitution were in that Congress, and voted on that question. Of these, Roger Sherman, Thomas Mifflin, and Hugh Williamson voted for the prohibition, thus showing that, in their understanding, no line dividing local from Federal authority, nor anything else, properly forbade the Federal Government to control as to slavery in Federal territory. The other of the four, James McHenry, voted against the prohibition, showing that for some cause he thought it improper to vote for it.

In 1787, still before the Constitution, but while the convention was in session framing it, and while the Northwestern Territory still was the only Territory owned by the United States, the same question of prohibiting slavery in the Territory again came before the Congress of the Confederation; and two more of the "thirty-nine" who afterward signed the Constitution were in that Congress and voted on the question. They were William Blount and William Few; and they both voted for the prohibition—thus showing that in their understanding no line dividing local from Federal authority, nor anything else, properly forbade the Federal Government to control as to slavery in Federal territory. This time the prohibition became a law, being part of what is now well known as the ordinance of '87.

The question of Federal control of slavery in the Territories seems not to have been directly before the convention which framed the original Constitution; and hence it is not recorded that the "thirty-nine," or any of them, while engaged on that instrument, expressed any opinion on that precise question.

In 1789, by the first Congress which sat under the Constitution, an act was passed to enforce the ordinance of '87, including the prohibition of slavery in the Northwestern Territory. The bill for this act was reported by one of the "thirty-nine"—Thomas Fitzsimmons, then a member of the House of Representatives from Pennsylvania. It went through all its stages without a word of opposition, and finally passed both branches without ayes and nays, which is equivalent to a unanimous passage. In this Congress there were sixteen of the thirty-nine fathers who framed the original Constitution. They were John Langdon, Nicholas Gilman, Wm. S. Johnson, Roger Sherman, Robert Morris, Thos. Fitzsimmons, William Few, Abraham Baldwin, Rufus King, William Patterson, George Clymer, Richard Bassett, George Read, Pierce Butler, Daniel Carroll, and James Madison.

This shows that, in their understanding, no line dividing local from Federal authority, nor anything in the Constitution, properly forbade Congress to prohibit slavery in the Federal territory; else both their fidelity to correct principle, and their oath to support the Constitution, would have constrained them to oppose the prohibition.

Again, George Washington, another of the "thirty-nine," was then President of the United States, and as such approved and signed the bill, thus completing its validity as a law, and thus showing that, in his understanding, no line dividing local from Federal authority, nor anything in the Constitution, forbade the Federal Government to control as to slavery in Federal territory.

No great while after the adoption of the original Constitution, North Carolina ceded to the Federal Government the country now constituting the State of Tennessee; and a few years later Georgia ceded that which now constitutes the States of Mississippi and Alabama. In both deeds of cession it was made a condition by the ceding States that the Federal Government should not prohibit slavery in the ceded country. Under these circumstances, Congress, on taking charge of these countries, did not absolutely prohibit slavery within them. But they did interfere with it—take control of it—even there, to a certain extent. In 1798 Congress organized the Territory of Mississippi. In the act of organization they prohibited the bringing of slaves into the Territory from any place without the United States, by fine, and giving freedom to slaves so brought. This act passed both branches of Congress without yeas and nays. In that Congress were three of the "thirty-nine" who framed the original Constitution. They were John Langdon, George Read, and Abraham Baldwin. They all probably voted for it. Certainly they would have placed their opposition to it upon record if, in their understanding, any line dividing local from Federal authority, or anything in the Constitution, properly forbade the Federal Government to control as to slavery in Federal territory.

In 1803 the Federal Government purchased the Louisiana country. Our former territorial acquisitions came from certain of our own States; but this Louisiana country was acquired from a foreign nation. In 1804 Congress gave a territorial organization to that part of it which now constitutes the State of Louisiana. New Orleans, lying within that part, was an old and comparatively large city. There were other considerable towns and settlements, and slavery was extensively and thoroughly intermingled with the people. Congress did not, in the Territorial Act, prohibit slavery; but they did interfere with it—take control of it—in a more marked and extensive way than they did in the case of Mississippi. The substance of the provision therein made in relation to slaves was:

1st. That no slave should be imported into the Territory from foreign parts.

2d. That no slave should be carried into it who had been imported into the United States since the first day of May 1798.

3d. That no slave should be carried into it, except by the owner, and for his own use as a settler; the penalty in all the cases being a fine upon the violator of the law, and freedom to the slave.

This act also was passed without ayes or nays. In the Congress which passed it there were two of the "thirty-nine." They were Abraham Baldwin and Jonathan Dayton. As stated in the case of Mississippi, it is probable they both voted for it. They would not have allowed it to pass without recording their opposition to it if, in their understanding, it violated either the line properly dividing local from Federal authority, or any provision of the Constitution.

In 1819–20 came and passed the Missouri question. Many votes were taken, by yeas and nays, in both branches of Congress, upon the various phases of the general question. Two of the "thirty-nine"—Rufus King and Charles Pinckney—were members of that Congress. Mr. King steadily voted for slavery prohibition and against all compromises, while Mr. Pinckney as steadily voted against slavery prohibition and against all compromises. By this, Mr. King showed that, in his understanding, no line dividing local from Federal authority, nor anything in the Constitution, was violated by Congress prohibiting slavery in Federal territory; while Mr. Pinckney, by his votes, showed that, in his understanding, there was some sufficient reason for opposing such prohibition in that case.

The cases I have mentioned are the only acts of the "thirty-nine," or of any of them, upon the direct issue, which I have been able to discover.

To enumerate the persons who thus acted as being four in 1784, two in 1787, seventeen in 1789, three in 1798, two in 1804, and two in 1819–20, there would be thirty of them. But this would be counting John Langdon, Roger Sherman, William Few, Rufus King, and George Read each twice, and Abraham Baldwin three times. The true number of those of the "thirty-nine" whom I have shown to have acted upon the question which, by the text, they understood better than we, is twenty-three, leaving sixteen not shown to have acted upon it in any way.

Here, then, we have twenty-three out of our thirty-nine fathers "who framed the government under which we live," who have, upon their official responsibility and their corporal oaths, acted upon the very question which the text affirms they "understood just as well, and even better, than we do now"; and twenty-one of them—a clear majority of the whole "thirty-nine"—so acting upon it as to make them guilty of gross political impropriety and wilful perjury if, in their understanding, any proper division between local and Federal authority, or anything in the Constitution they had made themselves, and sworn to support, forbade the Federal Government to control as to slavery in the Federal Territories. Thus the twenty-one acted; and, as actions speak louder than words, so actions under such responsibility speak still louder.

Two of the twenty-three voted against congressional prohibition of slavery in the Federal Territories, in the instances in which they acted upon the question. But for what reasons they so voted is not known. They may have done so because they thought a proper division of local from Federal authority, or some provision or principle of the Constitution, stood in the way; or they may, without any such question, have voted against the prohibition on what appeared to them to be sufficient grounds of expediency. No one who has sworn to support the Constitution can conscientiously vote for what he understands to be an unconstitutional measure, however expedient he may think it; but one may and ought to vote against a measure which he deems constitutional if, at the same time, he deems it inexpedient. It, therefore, whould be unsafe to set down even the two who voted against the prohibition as having done so because, in their understanding, any proper division of local from Federal authority, or anything in the Constitution, forbade the Federal Government to control as to slavery in Federal territory.

The remaining sixteen of the "thirty-nine," so far as I have discovered, have left no record of their understanding upon the direct question of Federal control of slavery in the Federal territories. But there is much reason to believe that their understanding upon that question would not have appeared different from that of their twenty-three compeers, had it been manifested at all.

For the purpose of adhering rigidly to the text, I have purposely omitted whatever understanding may have been manifested by any person, however distinguished, other than the thirty-nine fathers who framed the original Constitution; and, for the same reason, I have also omitted whatever understanding may have been manifested by any of the "thirty-nine" even on any other phase of the general question of slavery. If we should look into their acts and declarations on those other phases, as the foreign slave-trade, and the morality and policy of slavery generally, it would appear to us that on the direct question of Federal control of slavery in Federal Territories, the sixteen, if they had acted at all, would probably have acted just as the twenty-three did. Among that sixteen were several of the most noted antislavery men of those times,—as Dr. Franklin, Alexander Hamilton, and Gouverneur Morris,—while there was not one now known to have been otherwise, unless it may be John Rutledge, of South Carolina.

The sum of the whole is that of our thirty-nine fathers who framed the original Constitution, twenty-one—a clear majority of the whole—certainly understood that no proper division of local from Federal authority, nor any part of the Constitution, forbade the Federal Government to control slavery in the Federal Territories; while all the rest had probably the same understanding. Such, unquestionably, was the understanding of our fathers who framed the original Constitution; and the text affirms that they understood the question "better than we."

But, so far, I have been considering the understanding of the question manifested by the framers of the original Constitution. In and by the original instrument, a mode was provided for amending it; and, as I have already stated, the present frame of "the government under which we live" consists of that original, and twelve amendatory articles framed and adopted since. Those who now insist that Federal control of slavery in Federal Territories violates the Constitution, point us to the provisions which they suppose it thus violates; and, as

I understand, they all fix upon provisions in these amendatory articles, and not in the original instrument. The Supreme Court, in the Dred Scott case, plant themselves upon the fifth amendment, which provides that no person shall be deprived of "life, liberty, or property without due process of law"; while Senator Douglas and his peculiar adherents plant themselves upon the tenth amendment, providing that "the powers not delegated to the United States by the Constitution" "are reserved to the States respectively, or to the people."

Now, it so happens that these amendments were framed by the first Congress which sat under the Constitution—the identical Congress which passed the act, already mentioned, enforcing the prohibition of slavery in the Northwestern Territory. Not only was it the same Congress, but they were the identical, same individual men who, at the same session, and at the same time within the session, had under consideration, and in progress toward maturity, these constitutional amendments, and this act prohibiting slavery in all the territory the nation then owned. The constitutional amendments were introduced before, and passed after, the act enforcing the ordinance of '87; so that, during the whole pendency of the act to enforce the ordinance, the constitutional amendments were also pending.

The seventy-six members of that Congress, including sixteen of the framers of the original Constitution, as before stated, were preeminently our fathers who framed that part of "the government under which we live" which is now claimed as forbidding the Federal Government to control slavery in the Federal Territories.

Is it not a little presumptuous in any one at this day to affirm that the two things which that Congress deliberately framed, and carried to maturity at the same time, are absolutely inconsistent with each other? And does not such affirmation become impudently absurd when coupled with the other affirmation, from the same mouth, that those who did the two things alleged to be inconsistent, understood whether they really were inconsistent better than we—better than he who affirms that they are inconsistent?

It is surely safe to assume that the thirty-nine framers of the original Constitution, and the seventy-six members of the Congress which framed the amendments thereto, taken together, do certainly include those who may be fairly called "our fathers who framed the government under which we live." And so assuming, I defy any man to show that any one of them ever, in his whole life, declared that, in his understanding, any proper division of local from Federal authority, or any part of the Constitution, forbade the Federal Government to control as to slavery in the Federal Territories. I go a step further. I defy any one to show that any living man in the whole world ever did, prior to the beginning of the present century (and I might almost say prior to the beginning of the last half of the present century), declare that, in his understanding, any proper division of local from Federal authority, or any part of the Constitution, forbade the Federal Government to control as to slavery in the Federal Territories. To those who now so declare I give not only "our fathers who framed the government under which we live," but with them all other living men within the century in which it was framed, among whom to search, and they shall not be able to find the evidence of a single man agreeing with them.

Now, and here, let me guard a little against being misunderstood. I do not mean to say we are bound to follow implicitly in whatever our fathers did. To do so would be to discard all the lights of current experience—to reject all progress, all improvement. What I do say is that if we would supplant the opinions and policy of our fathers in any case, we should do so upon evidence so conclusive, and argument so clear, that even their great authority, fairly considered and weighed, cannot stand; and most surely not in a case whereof we ourselves declare they understood the question better than we.

If any man at this day sincerely believes that a proper division of local from Federal authority, or any part of the Constitution, forbids the Federal Government to control as to slavery in the Federal Territories, he is right to say so, and to enforce his position by all truthful evidence and fair argument which he can. But he has no right to mislead others, who have less access to history, and less leisure to study it, into the false belief that "our fathers who framed the government under which we live" were of the same opinion—thus substituting falsehood and deception for truthful evidence and fair argument. If any man at this day sincerely believes "our fathers who framed the government under which we live" used and applied principles, in other cases, which ought to have led them to understand that a proper division of local from Federal authority, or some part of the Constitution, forbids the Federal Government to control as to slavery in the Federal Territories, he is right to say so. But he should, at the same time, brave the responsibility of declaring that, in his opinion, he understands their principles better than they did themselves; and especially should he not shirk that responsibility by asserting that they "understood the question just as well, and even better, than we do now."

But enough! Let all who believe that "our fathers who framed the government under which we live understood this question just as well, and even better, than we do now," speak as they spoke, and act as they acted upon it. This is all Republicans ask—all Republicans desire—in relation to slavery. As those fathers marked it, so let it be again marked, as an evil not to be extended, but to be tolerated and protected only because of and so far as its actual presence among us makes that toleration and protection a necessity. Let all the guaranties those fathers gave it be not grudgingly, but fully and fairly, maintained. For this Republicans contend, and with this, so far as I know or believe, they will be content.

And now, if they would listen,—as I suppose they will not,—I would address a few words to the Southern people.

I would say to them: You consider yourselves a reasonable and a just people; and I consider that in the general qualities of reason and justice you are not inferior to any other people. Still, when you speak of us Republicans, you do so only to denounce us as reptiles, or, at the best, as no better than outlaws. You will grant a hearing to pirates or murderers, but nothing like it to "Black Republicans." In all your contentions with one another, each of you deems an unconditional condemnation of "Black Republicanism" as the first thing to be attended to. Indeed, such condemnation of us seems to be an indispensable prerequisite—license, so to speak—among you to be admitted or permitted to speak at all. Now can you or not be prevailed upon to pause and to consider whether this is quite just to us, or even to yourselves? Bring forward your charges and specifications, and then be patient long enough to hear us deny or justify.

You say we are sectional. We deny it. That makes an issue; and the burden of proof is upon you. You produce your proof;

and what is it? Why, that our party has no existence in your section—gets no votes in your section. The fact is substantially true; but does it prove the issue? If it does, then in case we should, without change of principle, begin to get votes in your section, we should thereby cease to be sectional. You cannot escape this conclusion; and yet, are you willing to abide by it? If you are, you will probably soon find that we have ceased to be sectional, for we shall get votes in your section this very year. You will then begin to discover, as the truth plainly is, that your proof does not touch the issue. The fact that we get no votes in your section is a fact of your making, and not of ours. And if there be fault in that fact, that fault is primarily yours and remains so until you show that we repel you by some wrong principle or practice. If we do repel you by any wrong principle or practice, the fault is ours; but this brings you to where you ought to have started—to a discussion of the right or wrong of our principle. If our principle, put in practice, would wrong your section for the benefit of ours, or for any other object, then our principle, and we with it, are sectional, and are justly opposed and denounced as such. Meet us, then, on the question of whether our principle, put in practice, would wrong your section; and so meet us as if it were possible that something may be said on our side. Do you accept the challenge? No! Then you really believe that the principle which "our fathers who framed the government under which we live" thought so clearly right as to adopt it, and indorse it again and again, upon their official oaths, is in fact so clearly wrong as to demand your condemnation without a moment's consideration.

Some of you delight to flaunt in our faces the warning against sectional parties given by Washington in his Farewell Address. Less than eight years before Washington gave that warning, he had, as President of the United States, approved and signed an act of Congress enforcing the prohibition of slavery in the Northwestern Territory, which act embodied the policy of the government upon that subject up to and at the very moment he penned that warning; and about one year after he penned it, he wrote Lafayette that he considered that prohibition a wise measure, expressing in the same connection his hope that we should at some time have a confederacy of free States.

Bearing this in mind, and seeing that sectionalism has since arisen upon this same subject, is that warning a weapon in your hands against us, or in our hands against you? Could Washington himself speak, would he cast the blame of that sectionalism upon us, who sustain his policy, or upon you, who repudiate it? We respect that warning of Washington, and we commend it to you, together with his example pointing to the right application of it.

But you say you are conservative—eminently conservative—while we are revolutionary, destructive or something of the sort. What is conservatism? Is it not adherence to the old and tried, against the new and untried? We stick to, contend for, the identical old policy on the point in controversy which was adopted by "our fathers who framed the government under which we live"; while you with one accord reject, and scout, and spit upon that old policy, and insist upon substituting something new. True, you disagree among yourselves as to what that substitute shall be. You are divided on new propositions and plans, but you are unanimous in rejecting and denouncing the old policy of the fathers. Some of you are for reviving the foreign slave-trade; some for a congressional slave code for the Territories;

some for Congress forbidding the Territories to prohibit slavery within their limits; some for maintaining slavery in the Territories through the judiciary; some for the "gur-reat pur-rinciple" that "if one man would enslave another, no third man should object," fantastically called "popular sovereignty"; but never a man among you is in favor of Federal prohibition of slavery in Federal Territories, according to the practice of "our fathers who framed the government under which we live." Not one of all your various plans can show a precedent or an advocate in the century within which our government originated. Consider, then, whether your claim of conservatism for yourselves, and your charge of destructiveness against us, are based on the most clear and stable foundations.

Again, you say we have made the slavery question more prominent than it formerly was. We deny it. We admit that it is more prominent, but we deny that we made it so. It was not we, but you, who discarded the old policy of the fathers. We resisted, and still resist, your innovation; and thence comes the greater prominence of the question. Would you have that question reduced to its former proportions? Go back to that old policy. What has been will be again, under the same conditions. If you would have the peace of the old times, readopt the precepts and policy of the old times.

You charge that we stir up insurrections among your slaves. We deny it; and what is your proof? Harper's Ferry! John Brown!! John Brown was no Republican; and you have failed to implicate a single Republican in his Harper's Ferry enterprise. If any member of our party is guilty in that matter, you know it, or you do not know it. If you do know it, you are inexcusable for not designating the man and proving the fact. If you do not know it, you are inexcusable for asserting it, and especially for persisting in the assertion after you have tried and failed to make the proof. You need not be told that persisting in a charge which one does not know to be true, is simply malicious slander.

Some of you admit that no Republican designedly aided or encouraged the Harper's Ferry affair, but still insist that our doctrines and declarations necessarily lead to such results. We do not believe it. We know we hold no doctrine, and make no declaration, which were not held to and made by "our fathers who framed the government under which we live." You never dealt fairly by us in relation to this affair. When it occurred, some important State elections were near at hand, and you were in evident glee with the belief that, by charging the blame upon us, you could get the advantage of us in those elections. The elections came, and your expectations were not quite fulfilled. Every Republican man knew that, as to himself at least, your charge was a slander, and he was not much inclined by it to cast his vote in your favor. Republican doctrines and declarations are accompanied with a continual protest against any interference whatever with your slaves, or with you about your slaves. Surely, this does not encourage them to revolt. True, we do, in common with "our fathers who framed the government under which we live," declare our belief that slavery is wrong; but the slaves do not hear us declare even this. For anything we say or do, the slaves would scarcely know there is a Republican party. I believe they would not, in fact, generally know it but for your misrepresentations of us in their hearing. In your political contests among yourselves, each faction charges the other with sympathy with Black Republicanism; and then, to give point to the charge, defines Black Republicanism to simply be insurrection, blood, and thunder among the slaves.

Slave insurrections are no more common now than they were before the Republican party was organized. What induced the Southampton insurrection, twenty-eight years ago, in which at least three times as many lives were lost as at Harper's Ferry? You can scarcely stretch your very elastic fancy to the conclusion that Southampton was "got up by Black Republicanism." In the present state of things in the United States, I do not think a general, or even a very extensive, slave insurrection is possible. The indispensable concert of action cannot be attained. The slaves have no means of rapid communication; nor can incendiary freemen, black or white, supply it. The explosive materials are everywhere in parcels; but there neither are, nor can be supplied, the indispensable connecting trains.

Much is said by Southern people about the affection of slaves for their masters and mistresses; and a part of it, at least, is true. A plot for an uprising could scarcely be devised and communicated to twenty individuals before some one of them, to save the life of a favorite master or mistress, would divulge it. This is the rule; and the slave revolution in Hayti was not an exception to it, but a case occurring under peculiar circumstances. The gunpowder plot of British history, though not connected with slaves, was more in point. In that case, only about twenty were admitted to the secret; and yet one of them, in his anxiety to save a friend, betrayed the plot to that friend, and, by consequence, averted the calamity. Occasional poisonings from the kitchen, and open or stealthy assassinations in the field, and local revolts extending to a score or so, will continue to occur as the natural results of slavery; but no general insurrection of slaves, as I think, can happen in this country for a long time. Whoever much fears, or much hopes, for such an event, will be alike disappointed.

In the language of Mr. Jefferson, uttered many years ago, "It is still in our power to direct the process of emancipation and deportation peaceably, and in such slow degrees, as that the evil will wear off insensibly; and their places be, *pari passu*, filled up by free white laborers. If, on the contrary, it is left to force itself on, human nature must shudder at the prospect held up."

Mr. Jefferson did not mean to say, nor do I, that the power of emancipation is in the Federal Government. He spoke of Virginia; and, as to the power of emancipation, I speak of the slaveholding States only. The Federal Government, however, as we insist, has the power of restraining the extension of the institution—the power to insure that a slave insurrection shall never occur on any American soil which is now free from slavery.

John Brown's effort was peculiar. It was not a slave insurrection. It was an attempt by white men to get up a revolt among slaves, in which the slaves refused to participate. In fact, it was so absurd that the slaves, with all their ignorance, saw plainly enough it could not succeed. That affair, in its philosophy, corresponds with the many attempts, related in history, at the assassination of kings and emperors. An enthusiast broods over the oppression of a people till he fancies himself commissioned by Heaven to liberate them. He ventures the attempt, which ends in little else than his own execution. Orsini's attempt on Louis Napoleon, and John Brown's attempt at Harper's Ferry, were, in their philosophy, precisely the same. The eagerness to cast blame on old England in the one case, and on New England in the other, does not disprove the sameness of the two things.

And how much would it avail you, if you could, by the use of John Brown, Helper's Book, and the like, break up the Republican organization? Human action can be modified to some extent, but human nature cannot be changed. There is a judgment and a feeling against slavery in this nation, which cast at least a million and a half of votes. You cannot destroy that judgment and feeling—that sentiment—by breaking up the political organization which rallies around it. You can scarcely scatter and disperse an army which has been formed into order in the face of your heaviest fire; but if you could, how much would you gain by forcing the sentiment which created it out of the peaceful channel of the ballot-box into some other channel? What would that other channel probably be? Would the number of John Browns be lessened or enlarged by the operation?

But you will break up the Union rather than submit to a denial of your constitutional rights.

That has a somewhat reckless sound; but it would be palliated, if not fully justified, were we proposing, by the mere force of numbers, to deprive you of some right plainly written down in the Constitution. But we are proposing no such thing.

When you make these declarations you have a specific and well-understood allusion to an assumed constitutional right of yours to take slaves into the Federal Territories, and to hold them there as property. But no such right is specifically written in the Constitution. That instrument is literally silent about any such right. We, on the contrary, deny that such a right has any existence in the Constitution, even by implication.

Your purpose, then, plainly stated, is that you will destroy the government, unless you be allowed to construe and force the Constitution as you please, on all points in dispute between you and us. You will rule or ruin in all events.

This, plainly stated, is your language. Perhaps you will say the Supreme Court has decided the disputed constitutional question in your favor. Not quite so. But waiving the lawyer's distinction between dictum and decision, the court has decided the question for you in a sort of way. The court has substantially said, it is your constitutional right to take slaves into the Federal Territories, and to hold them there as property. When I say the decision was made in a sort of way, I mean it was made in a divided court, by a bare majority of the judges, and they not quite agreeing with one another in the reasons for making it; that it is so made as that its avowed supporters disagree with one another about its meaning, and that it was mainly based upon a mistaken statement of fact—the statement in the opinion that "the right of property in a slave is distinctly and expressly affirmed in the Constitution."

An inspection of the Constitution will show that the right of property in a slave is not "distinctly and expressly affirmed" in it. Bear in mind, the judges do not pledge their judicial opinion that such right is impliedly affirmed in the Constitution; but they pledge their veracity that it is "distinctly and expressly" affirmed there—"distinctly," that is, not mingled with anything else—"expressly," that is, in words meaning just that, without the aid of any inference, and susceptible of no other meaning.

If they had only pledged their judicial opinion that such right is affirmed in the instrument by implication, it would be open to others to show that neither the word "slave" nor "slavery" is to be found in the Constitution, nor the word "property" even, in any connection with language alluding to the things slave, or slavery; and that wherever in that instrument the slave is alluded to, he is called a "person"; and wherever his master's legal right in relation to him is alluded to, it is spoken of as "service or labor which may be due"—as a debt payable in service or labor. Also it would be open to show, by contemporaneous history, that this mode of alluding to slaves and slavery, instead of speaking of them, was employed on purpose to exclude from the Constitution the idea that there could be property in man.

To show all this is easy and certain.

When this obvious mistake of the judges shall be brought to their notice, is it not reasonable to expect that they will withdraw the mistaken statement, and reconsider the conclusion based upon it?

And then it is to be remembered that "our fathers who framed the government under which we live"—the men who made the Constitution—decided this same constitutional question in our favor long ago: decided it without division among themselves when making the decision; without division among themselves about the meaning of it after it was made, and, so far as any evidence is left, without basing it upon any mistaken statement of facts.

Under all these circumstances, do you really feel yourselves justified to break up this government unless such a court decision as yours is shall be at once submitted to as a conclusive and final rule of political action? But you will not abide the election of a Republican president! In that supposed event, you say, you will destroy the Union; and then, you say, the great crime of having destroyed it will be upon us! That is cool. A highwayman holds a pistol to my ear and mutters through his teeth, "Stand and deliver, or I shall kill you, and then you will be a murderer!"

To be sure, what the robber demanded of me—my money—was my own; and I had a clear right to keep it; but it was no more my own than my vote is my own; and the threat of death to me, to extort my money, and the threat of destruction to the Union, to extort my vote, can scarcely be distinguished in principle.

A few words now to Republicans. It is exceedingly desirable that all parts of this great Confederacy shall be at peace, and in harmony one with another. Let us Republicans do our part to have it so. Even though much provoked, let us do nothing through passion and ill temper. Even though the Southern people will not so much as listen to us, let us calmly consider their demands, and yield to them if, in our deliberate view of our duty, we possibly can. Judging by all they say and do, and by the subject and nature of their controversy with us, let us determine, if we can, what will satisfy them.

Will they be satisfied if the Territories be unconditionally surrendered to them? We know they will not. In all their present complaints against us, the Territories are scarcely mentioned. Invasions and insurrections are the rage now. Will it satisfy them if, in the future, we have nothing to do with invasions and insurrections? We know it will not. We so know, because we know we never had anything to do with invasions and insurrections; and yet this total abstaining does not exempt us from the charge and the denunciation.

The question recurs, What will satisfy them? Simply this: we must not only let them alone, but we must somehow convince them that we do let them alone. This, we know by experience, is no easy task. We have been so trying to convince them from the very beginning of our organization, but with no success. In all our platforms and speeches we have constantly protested our purpose to let them alone; but this has had no tendency to convince them. Alike unavailing to convince them is the fact that they have never detected a man of us in any attempt to disturb them.

These natural and apparently adequate means all failing, what will convince them? This, and this only: cease to call slavery wrong, and join them in calling it right. And this must be done thoroughly—done in acts as well as in words. Silence will not be tolerated—we must place ourselves avowedly with them. Senator Douglas's new sedition law must be enacted and enforced, suppressing all declarations that slavery is wrong, whether made in politics, in presses, in pulpits, or in private. We must arrest and return their fugitive slaves with greedy pleasure. We must pull down our free-State constitutions. The whole atmosphere must be disinfected from all taint of opposition to slavery, before they will cease to believe that all their troubles proceed from us.

I am quite aware they do not state their case precisely in this way. Most of them would probably say to us, "Let us alone; do nothing to us, and say what you please about slavery." But we do let them alone,—have never disturbed them,—so that, after all, it is what we say which dissatisfies them. They will continue to accuse us of doing, until we cease saying.

I am also aware they have not as yet in terms demanded the overthrow of our free-State constitutions. Yet those constitutions declare the wrong of slavery with more solemn emphasis than do all other sayings against it; and when all these other sayings shall have been silenced, the overthrow of these constitutions will be demanded, and nothing be left to resist the demand. It is nothing to the contrary that they do not demand the whole of this just now. Demanding what they do, and for the reason they do, they can voluntarily stop nowhere short of this consummation. Holding, as they do, that slavery is morally right and socially elevating, they cannot cease to demand a full national recognition of it as a legal right and a social blessing.

Nor can we justifiably withhold this on any ground save our conviction that slavery is wrong. If slavery is right, all words, acts, laws, and constitutions against it are themselves wrong, and should be silenced and swept away. If it is right, we cannot justly object to its nationality—its universality; if it is wrong, they cannot justly insist upon its extension—its enlargement. All they ask we could readily grant, if we thought slavery right; all we ask they could as readily grant, if they thought it wrong. Their thinking it right and our thinking it wrong is the precise fact upon which depends the whole controversy. Thinking it right, as they do, they are not to blame for desiring its full recognition as being right; but thinking it wrong, as we do, can we yield to them? Can we cast our votes with their view, and against our own? In view of our moral, social, and political responsibilities can we do this?

Wrong as we think slavery is, we can yet afford to let it alone where it is, because that much is due to the necessity arising from its actual presence in the nation; but can we, while our votes will prevent it, allow it to spread into the national Territories, and to overrun us here in these free States? If our sense of duty forbids this, then let us stand by our duty fearlessly and effectively. Let us be diverted by none of these sophistical contrivances wherewith we are so industriously plied and belabored—contrivances such as groping for some middle ground between the right and the wrong: vain as the search for a man who should be neither a living man nor a dead man; such as a policy of "don't care" on a question about which all true men do care; such as Union appeals beseeching true Union men to yield to Disunionists, reversing the divine rule, and calling, not the sinners, but the righteous to repentance; such as invocations to Washington, imploring men to unsay what Washington said and undo what Washington did.

Neither let us be slandered from our duty by false accusations against us, nor frightened from it by menaces of destruction to the government, nor of dungeons to ourselves. Let us have faith that right makes might, and in that faith let us to the end dare to do our duty as we understand it.

Jefferson Davis

Inaugural Address (1861)

Reaction in the South to the election of Abraham Lincoln was almost immediate. No sooner were the results of the contest known than the South Carolina legislature unanimously voted to call a state convention, which met in Columbia. On December 20, without a dissenting vote, the convention passed an ordinance dissolving the Union. By February 1, 1861, the states of the Deep South—Mississippi, Florida, Alabama, Georgia, Louisiana, and Texas—followed South Carolina. North Carolina, Virginia, Arkansas, and Tennessee hesitated to take the ultimate step, but all declared their opposition to attempts by the federal government to use force to compel the other states to stay in the Union; these states were all to join the Confederacy only after hostilities began following the firing on Fort Sumpter in April.

The seceding states moved quickly to form their own union. Meeting in Montgomery, Alabama, representatives framed a constitution which was similar to that of the United States but recognized the sovereign status of the individual states and included several provisions protecting slavery. The Montgomery convention also set up a provisional government and elected as the first President of the new Confederacy Jefferson Davis of Mississippi.

A graduate of West Point, Jefferson Davis saw service in the Black Hawk War in 1832. Resigning his commission, in 1835 he became a cotton planter and took an active role in Mississippi politics, being elected to Congress in 1844. He gave up his seat to become Colonel of the Mississippi Rifles, which he led in the Mexican War. Upon his return to Mississippi, he was appointed to the U.S. Senate, where he soon became a leading spokesman for Southern rights and a defender of slavery. He opposed the Compromise of 1850, resigned from the Senate to run for governor of Mississippi, and was narrowly defeated.

After a term as President Franklin Pierce's Secretary of War, he went once again to the Senate in 1857, where he took the lead in advocating the protection and extension of slavery. Early in 1860 he offered a series of resolutions that were to form the basis of the Southern Democrats' platform in the forthcoming election. Davis maintained that the constitution was a compact entered into by free and independent states and argued that Congress had no right to restrict the freedom of citizens to take their property into any territory held in common. After the election of Lincoln, Davis articulated secessionist views, but he was convinced that secession would lead to war and hoped for compromise. By January 1861, however, he joined other Southern senators in urging secession and the organization of a Southern Confederacy. When Mississippi seceded, Davis resigned his seat in the Senate and returned home to take command of the state militia. Before he could do so, he was chosen by the provisional government as President of the Confederacy.

Delivering his inaugural address in Montgomery a little more than two weeks before Lincoln was to give his in Washington, Davis sought to justify Southern action on the basis of the strict interpretation of the Constitution, a position that he had espoused in his years in the Senate. It was the South, he asserted, who "labored to preserve the government of our fathers in its spirit." The President of the new Confederacy strove to place the blame for the war he felt sure would come on the North; he made it clear that if the federal government was so unreasonable as not to let the South depart in peace, "a terrible responsibility will rest upon it, and the suffering of millions will bear testimony to the folly and wickedness of our aggressors."

Gentlemen of the Congress of the Confederate States of America, Friends and Fellow Citizens: Our present condition, achieved in a manner unprecedented in the history of nations, illustrates the American idea that governments rest upon the consent of the governed, and that it is the right of the people to alter and abolish governments whenever they become destructive to the ends for which they were established. The declared compact of the Union from which we have withdrawn was to establish justice, insure domestic tranquillity, provide for the common defence, promote the general welfare, and secure the blessings of liberty to ourselves and our posterity; and when in the judgment of the sovereign States now composing this Confederacy it has been perverted from the purposes for which it was ordained, and ceased to answer the ends for which it was established, a peaceful appeal to the ballot-box declared that, so far as they were concerned, the government created by that compact should cease to exist. In this they merely asserted the right which the Declaration of Independence of 1776 defined to be inalienable. Of the time and occasion of this exercise they as sovereigns were the final judges, each for himself. The impartial, enlightened verdict of mankind will vindicate the rectitude of our conduct; and He who knows the hearts of men will judge of the sincerity with which we labored to preserve the government of our fathers in its spirit.

The right solemnly proclaimed at the birth of the States, and which has been affirmed and reaffirmed in the bills of rights of the States subsequently admitted into the Union of 1789, undeniably recognizes in the people the power to resume the authority delegated for the purposes of government. Thus the sovereign States here represented proceeded to form this Confederacy; and it is by the abuse of language that their act has been denominated revolution. They formed a new alliance, but within each State its government has remained. The rights of person and property have not been disturbed. The agent through whom they communicated with foreign nations is changed, but this does not necessarily interrupt their international relations. Sustained by the consciousness that the transition from the former Union to the present Confederacy has not proceeded from a disregard on our part of our just obligations or any failure to perform every constitutional duty, moved by no interest or passion to invade the rights of others, anxious to cultivate peace and commerce with all nations, if we may not hope to avoid war, we may at least expect that posterity will acquit us of having needlessly engaged in it. Doubly justified by the absence of wrong on our part, and by wanton aggression on the part of others, there can be no use to doubt the courage and patriotism of the people of the Confederate States will be found equal to any measure of defence which soon their security may require.

An agricultural people, whose chief interest is the export of a commodity required in every manufacturing country, our true policy is peace and the freest trade which our necessities will permit. It is alike our interest and that of all those to whom we would sell and from whom we would buy, that there should be the fewest practicable restrictions upon the interchange of commodities. There can be but little rivalry between ours and any manufacturing or navigating community, such as the northeastern States of the American Union. It must follow, therefore, that mutual interest would invite good-will and kind offices. If, however, passion or lust of dominion should cloud the judgment or inflame the ambition of those States, we must prepare to meet the emergency, and maintain by the final arbitrament of the sword the position which we have assumed among the nations of the earth.

We have entered upon a career of independence, and it must be inflexibly pursued through many years of controversy with our late associates of the Northern States. We have vainly endeavored to secure tranquillity and obtain respect for the rights to which we were entitled. As a necessity, not a choice, we have resorted to the remedy of separation, and henceforth our energies must be directed to the conduct of our own affairs, and the perpetuity of the Confederacy which we have formed. If a just perception of mutual interest shall permit us peaceably to pursue our separate political career, my most earnest desire will have been fulfilled. But if this be denied us, and the integrity of our territory and jurisdiction be assailed, it will but remain for us with firm resolve to appeal to arms and invoke the blessing of Providence on a just cause. . . .

Actuated solely by a desire to preserve our own rights, and to promote our own welfare, the separation of the Confederate

States has been marked by no aggression upon others, and followed by no domestic convulsion. Our industrial pursuits have received no check, the cultivation of our fields progresses as heretofore, and even should we be involved in war, there would be no considerable diminution in the production of the staples which have constituted our exports, in which the commercial world has an interest scarcely less than our own. This common interest of producer and consumer can only be intercepted by an exterior force which should obstruct its transmission to foreign markets, a course of conduct which would be detrimental to manufacturing and commercial interests abroad.

Should reason guide the action of the government from which we have separated, a policy so detrimental to the civilized world, the Northern States included, could not be dictated by even a stronger desire to inflict injury upon us; but if it be otherwise, a terrible responsibility will rest upon it, and the suffering of millions will bear testimony to the folly and wickedness of our agressors. In the meantime there will remain to us, besides the ordinary remedies before suggested, the well-known resources for retaliation upon the commerce of an enemy. . . . We have changed the constituent parts but not the system of our government. The Constitution formed by our fathers is that of these Confederate States. In their exposition of it, and in the judicial construction it has received, we have a light which reveals its true meaning. Thus instructed as to the just interpretation of that instrument, and ever remembering that all offices are but trusts held for the people, and that delegated powers are to be strictly construed, I will hope by due diligence in the performance of my duties, though I may disappoint your expectation, yet to retain, when retiring, something of the good-will and confidence which will welcome my entrance into office.

It is joyous in the midst of perilous times to look around upon a people united in heart, when one purpose of high resolve animates and actuates the whole, where the sacrifices to be made are not weighed in the balance, against honor, right, liberty, and equality. Obstacles may retard, but they cannot long prevent, the progress of a movement sanctioned by its justice and sustained by a virtuous people. Reverently let us invoke the God of our fathers to guide and protect us in our efforts to perpetuate the principles which by his blessing they were able to vindicate, establish, and transmit to their posterity; and with a continuance of his favor, ever gratefully acknowledged, we may hopefully look forward to success, to peace, to prosperity.

Abraham Lincoln

First Inaugural Address (1861)

Probably no President has faced a more difficult rhetorical situation than did Abraham Lincoln upon assuming office in 1861. Though he had won a majority of the electoral votes, he was a minority President in a four-way race and had received almost no support in the South. He was the first Republican to be elected, and his party in some quarters had the taint of radical abolitionism. In response to his election, seven states already had seceded from the Union and established a provisional government for the Confederate States of America. There was sufficient concern for the President-elect's safety that he had arrived in Washington unannounced and in the middle of the night.

Lincoln had not campaigned in 1860, maintaining that his views were on record from the Lincoln–Douglas debates and his 1859 speaking tours and that anything he said would be misrepresented by his opponents. He maintained his policy of silence during the weeks between election and inauguration, since to do otherwise would be to accept responsibility without authority. It had been suggested that he allay Southern fears by promising not to interfere with slavery where it already existed, but the President-elect thought that he had made that statement so often that a reiteration would only suggest weakness or cowardice.

If Lincoln restrained himself, other newly elected Republicans did not. Some of the Northern governors who were far more radical than Lincoln gave the impression that his goals were the same as theirs, and they encouraged the impression that he would seek to invade and subjugate the South. The more extreme Southerners took these statements as confirmation of their worst fears, and therefore eyed Lincoln with distrust.

Matters reached a head when South Carolina adopted an ordinance of secession on December 20, 1860. By February 1 other states of the Deep South had followed suit. Secession talk had been in the air for two generations; the threat had been made and retracted so many times that it was seen as a bluff and not taken seriously. This time, however, it was real. Still many politicians assumed that it was a temporary, attention-getting device and tried to fashion a compromise that, like the famous Compromise of 1850, would have adjusted the outstanding issues and defused the situation. A variety of measures were proposed, such as extension of the old Missouri Compromise line to the Pacific Ocean, or the immediate admission of New Mexico as a slave state. These Lincoln opposed. While he was a moderate within his party and was committed to saving the Union, he was not willing to violate the fundamental Republican principle of opposition to the spread of slavery into new territory. Compromises such as those mentioned would require the Republican Party, having fairly won an election, to abandon the very principles that brought it to power. The one measure Lincoln *would* support was a proposed amendment to the Constitution which would have been an unrepealable guarantee of the survival of slavery in the states where it then existed. Lincoln had no wish to do otherwise, and he thought that this amendment only restated what already was implicit in the Constitution itself.

This situation shaped Lincoln's approach to the inaugural address. He wanted to reassure people of his own moderation and to display his eagerness to conciliate while not abandoning his principles. In outlining his policy and asserting the prerogatives of the federal government, he nevertheless promised that the federal government would undertake no provocative act such as insisting on delivery of mail through hostile areas. The government would maintain and resupply federal forts, however, but would not use them as a basis for aggressive action. The onus for hostilities would rest with the disaffected Southerners.

In the light of history, the speech is seen as conciliatory, but it was not so viewed by much of the influential Southern press. Barely a month later, a federal attempt to resupply Fort Sumter (which was running out of food) led to an attack on the fort by South Carolinians, "and the war came."

Fellow-Citizens of the United States: In compliance with a custom as old as the Government itself, I appear before you to address you briefly and to take in your presence the oath prescribed by the Constitution of the United States to be taken by the President "before he enters on the execution of this office."

I do not consider it necessary at present for me to discuss those matters of administration about which there is no special anxiety or excitement.

Apprehension seems to exist among the people of the Southern States that by the accession of a Republican Administration their property and their peace and personal security are to be endangered. There has never been any reasonable cause for such apprehension. Indeed, the most ample evidence to the contrary has all the while existed and been open to their inspection. It is found in nearly all the published speeches of him who now addresses you. I do but quote from one of those speeches when I declare that—

I have no purpose, directly or indirectly, to interfere with the institution of slavery in the States where it exists. I believe I have no lawful right to do so, and I have no inclination to do so.

Those who nominated and elected me did so with full knowledge that I had made this and many similar declarations and had never recanted them; and more than this, they placed in the platform for my acceptance, and as a law to themselves and to me, the clear and emphatic resolution which I now read:

Resolved, That the maintenance inviolate of the rights of the States, and especially the right of each State to order and control its own domestic institutions according to its own judgment exclusively, is essential to that balance of power on which the perfection and endurance of our political fabric depend; and we denounce the lawless invasion by armed force of the soil of any State or Territory, no matter what pretext, as among the gravest of crimes.

I now reiterate these sentiments, and in doing so I only press upon the public attention the most conclusive evidence of which the case is susceptible that the property, peace, and security of no section are to be in any wise endangered by the now incoming Administration. I add, too, that all the protection which, consistently with the Constitution and the laws, can be given will be cheerfully given to all the States when lawfully demanded, for whatever cause—as cheerfully to one section as to another.

There is much controversy about the delivering up of fugitives from service or labor. The clause I now read is as plainly written in the Constitution as any other of its provisions:

> No person held to service or labor in one State, under the laws thereof, escaping into another, shall in consequence of any law or regulation therein be discharged from such service or labor, but shall be delivered up on claim of the party to whom such service or labor may be due.

It is scarcely questioned that this provision was intended by those who made it for the reclaiming of what we call fugitive slaves; and the intention of the lawgiver is the law. All members of Congress swear their support to the whole Constitution—to this provision as much as to any other. To the proposition, then, that slaves whose cases come within the terms of this clause "shall be delivered up" their oaths are unanimous. Now, if they would make the effort in good temper, could they not with equal unanimity frame and pass a law by means of which to keep good that unanimous oath?

There is some difference of opinion whether this clause should be enforced by national or by State authority, but surely that difference is not a very material one. If the slave is to be surrendered, it can be of but little consequence to him or to others by which authority it is done. And should anyone in any case be content that his oath shall go unkept on a merely unsubstantial controversy as to *how* it shall be kept?

Again: In any law upon this subject ought not all the safeguards of liberty known in civilized and humane jurisprudence to be introduced, so that a free man be not in any case surrendered as a slave? And might it not be well at the same time to provide by law for the enforcement of that clause in the Constitution which guarantees that "the citizens of each State shall be entitled to all privileges and immunities of citizens in the several States"?

I take the official oath to-day with no mental reservations and with no purpose to construe the Constitution or laws by any hypercritical rules; and while I do not choose now to specify particular acts of Congress as proper to be enforced, I do suggest that it will be much safer for all, both in official and private stations, to conform to and abide by all those acts which stand unrepealed than to violate any of them trusting to find impunity in having them held to be unconstitutional.

It is seventy-two years since the first inauguration of a President under our National Constitution. During that period fifteen different and greatly distinguished citizens have in succession administered the executive branch of the Government. They have conducted it through many perils, and generally with great success. Yet, with all this scope of precedent, I now enter upon the same task for the brief constitutional term of four years under great and peculiar difficulty. A disruption of the Federal Union, heretofore only menaced, is now formidably attempted.

I hold that in contemplation of universal law and of the Constitution the Union of these States is perpetual. Perpetuity is implied, if not expressed, in the fundamental law of all national governments. It is safe to assert that no government proper ever had a provision in its organic law for its own termination. Continue to execute all the express provisions of our National Constitution, and the Union will endure forever, it being impossible to destroy it except by some action not provided for in the instrument itself.

Again: If the United States be not a government proper, but an association of States in the nature of contract merely, can it, as a contract, be peaceably unmade by less than all the parties who made it? One party to a contract may violate it—break it, so to speak—but does it not require all to lawfully rescind it?

Descending from these general principles, we find the proposition that in legal contemplation the Union is perpetual confirmed by the history of the Union itself. The Union is much older than the Constitution. It was formed, in fact, by the Articles of Association in 1774. It was matured and continued by the Declaration of Independence in 1776. It was further matured, and the faith of all the then thirteen States expressly plighted and engaged that it should be perpetual, by the Articles of Confederation in 1778. And finally, in 1787, one of the declared objects for ordaining and establishing the Constitution was "*to form a more perfect Union.*"

But if destruction of the Union by one or by a part only of the States be lawfully possible, the Union is *less* perfect than before the Constitution, having lost the vital element of perpetuity.

It follows from these views that no State upon its own mere motion can lawfully get out of the Union; that *resolves* and *ordinances* to that effect are legally void, and that acts of violence within any State or States against the authority of the United States are insurrectionary or revolutionary, according to circumstances.

I therefore consider that in view of the Constitution and the laws of the Union is unbroken, and to the extent of my ability, I shall take care, as the Constitution itself expressly enjoins upon me, that the laws of the Union be faithfully executed in all the

States. Doing this I deem to be only a simple duty on my part, and I shall perform it so far as practicable unless my rightful masters, the American people, shall withhold the requisite means or in some authoritative manner direct the contrary. I trust this will not be regarded as a menace, but only as the declared purpose of the Union that it *will* constitutionally defend and maintain itself.

In doing this there needs to be no bloodshed or violence, and there shall be none unless it be forced upon the national authority. The power confided to me will be used to hold, occupy, and possess the property and places belonging to the Government and to collect the duties and imposts; but beyond what may be necessary for these objects, there will be no invasion, no using of force against or among the people anywhere. Where hostility to the United States in any interior locality shall be so great and universal as to prevent competent resident citizens from holding the Federal offices, there will be no attempt to force obnoxious strangers among the people for that object. While the strict legal right may exist in the Government to enforce the exercise of these offices, the attempt to do so would be so irritating and so nearly impracticable withal that I deem it better to forego for the time the uses of such offices.

The mails, unless repelled, will continue to be furnished in all parts of the Union. So far as possible the people everywhere shall have that sense of perfect security which is most favorable to calm thought and reflection. The course here indicated will be followed unless current events and experience shall show a modification or change to be proper, and in every case and exigency my best descretion will be exercised, according to circumstances actually existing and with a view and a hope of a peaceful solution of the national troubles and the restoration of fraternal sympathies and affections.

That there are persons in one section or another who seek to destroy the Union at all events and are glad of any pretext to do it I will neither affirm or deny; but if there be such, I need address no word to them. To those, however, who really love the Union may I not speak?

Before entering upon so grave a matter as the destruction of our national fabric, with all its benefits, its memories, and its hopes, would it not be wise to ascertain precisely why we do it? Will you hazard so desperate a step while there is any possibility that any portion of the ills you fly from have no real existence? Will you, while the certain ills you fly to are greater than all the real ones you fly from, will you risk the commission of so fearful a mistake?

All profess to be content in the Union if all constitutional rights can be maintained. Is it true, then, that any right plainly written in the Constitution has been denied? I think not. Happily, the human mind is so constituted that no party can reach to the audacity of doing this. Think, if you can, of a single instance in which a plainly written provision of the Constitution has ever been denied. If by the mere force of numbers a majority should deprive a minority of any clearly written constitutional right, it might in a moral point of view justify revolution; certainly would if such right were a vital one. But such is not our case. All the vital rights of minorities and of individuals are so plainly assured to them by affirmations and negations, guaranties and prohibitions, in the Constitution that controversies never arise concerning them. But no organic law can ever be framed with a provision specifically applicable to every question which may occur in practical administration. No foresight can anticipate nor any document of reasonable length contain express provisions for all possible questions. Shall fugitives from labor be surrendered by national or by State authority? The Constitution does not expressly say. *May* Congress prohibit slavery in the Territories? The Constitution does not expressly say. *Must* Congress protect slavery in the Territories? The Constitution does not expressly say.

From questions of this class spring all our constitutional controversies, and we divide upon them into majorities and minorities. If the minority will not acquiesce, the majority must, or the Government must cease. There is no other alternative, for continuing the Government is acquiescence on one side or the other. If a minority in such case will secede rather than acquiesce, they make a precedent which in turn will divide and ruin them, for a minority of their own will secede from them whenever a majority refuses to be controlled by such minority. For instance, why may not any portion of a new confederacy a year or two hence arbitrarily secede again, precisely as portions of the present Union now claim to secede from it? All who cherish disunion sentiments are now being educated to the exact temper of doing this.

Is there such perfect identity of interests among the States to compose a new union as to produce harmony only and prevent renewed secession?

Plainly the central idea of secession is the essence of anarchy. A majority held in restraint by constitutional checks and limitations, and always changing easily with deliberate changes of popular opinions and sentiments, is the only true sovereign of a free people. Whoever rejects it does of necessity fly to anarchy or to despotism. Unanimity is impossible. The rule of a minority, as a permanent arrangement, is wholly inadmissible; so that, rejecting the majority principle, anarchy or despotism in some form is all that is left.

I do not forget the position assumed by some that constitutional questions are to be decided by the Supreme Court, nor do I deny that such decisions must be binding in any case upon the parties to a suit as to the object of that suit, while they are also entitled to very high respect and consideration in all parallel cases by all other departments of the Government. And while it is obviously possible that such decision may be erroneous in any given case, still the evil effect following it, being limited to that particular case, with the chance that it may be overruled and never become a precedent for other cases, can better be borne than could the evils of a different practice. At the same time, the candid citizen must confess that if the policy of the Government upon vital questions affecting the whole people is to be irrevocably fixed by decisions of the Supreme Court, the instant they are made in ordinary litigation between parties in personal actions the people will have ceased to be their own rulers, having to that extent practically resigned their Government into the hands of that eminent tribunal. Nor is there in this view any assault upon the court or the judges. It is a duty from which they may not shrink to decide cases properly brought before them, and it is no fault of theirs if others seek to turn their decisions to political purposes.

One section of our country believes slavery is *right* and ought to be extended, while the other believes it is *wrong* and ought not to be extended. This is the only substantial dispute. The fugitive-slave clause of the Constitution and the law for the suppression of the foreign slave trade are each as well enforced, perhaps, as any law can ever be in a community where the moral sense of the people imperfectly supports the law itself. The great body of the people abide by the dry legal obligation in both cases, and a few break over in each. This, I think, can not be perfectly cured, and it would be worse in both cases *after* the separation of the sections than before. The foreign slave trade, now imperfectly suppressed, would be ultimately revived without restriction in one section, while fugitive slaves, now only partially surrendered, would not be surrendered at all by the other.

Physically speaking, we can not separate. We can not remove our respective sections from each other nor build an impassable wall between them. A husband and wife may be divorced and go out of the presence and beyond the reach of each other, but the different parts of our country can not do this. They can not but remain face to face, and intercourse, either amicable or hostile, must continue between them. Is it possible, then, to make that intercourse more advantageous or more satisfactory *after* separation than *before?* Can aliens make treaties easier than friends can make laws? Can treaties be more faithfully enforced between aliens than laws can among friends? Suppose you go to war, you can not fight always; and when, after much loss on both sides and no gain on either, you cease fighting, the identical old questions, as to terms of intercourse, are again upon you.

This country, with its institutions, belongs to the people who inhabit it. Whenever they shall grow weary of the existing Government, they can exercise their *constitutional* right of amending it or their *revolutionary* right to dismember or overthrow it. I can not be ignorant of the fact that many worthy and patriotic citizens are desirous of having the National Constitution amended. While I make no recommendation of amendments, I fully recognize the rightful authority of the people over the whole subject, to be exercised in either of the modes prescribed in the instrument itself; and I should, under existing circumstances, favor rather than oppose a fair opportunity being afforded the people to act upon it. I will venture to add that to me the convention mode seems preferable, in that it allows amendments to originate with the people themselves, instead of only permitting them to take or reject propositions originated by others, not especially chosen for the purpose, and which might not be precisely such as they would wish to either accept or refuse. I understand a proposed amendment to the Constitution—which amendment, however, I have not seen—has passed Congress, to the effect that the Federal Government shall never interfere with the domestic institutions of the States, including that of persons held to service. To avoid misconstruction of what I have said, I depart from my purpose not to speak of particular amendments so far as to say that, holding such a provision to now be implied constitutional law, I have no objection to its being made express and irrevocable.

The Chief Magistrate derives all his authority from the people, and they have referred none upon him to fix terms for the separation of the States. The people themselves can do this if also they choose, but the Executive as such has nothing to do with it. His duty is to administer the present Government as it came to his hands and to transmit it unimpaired by him to his successor.

Why should there not be a patient confidence in the ultimate justice of the people? Is there any better or equal hope in the world? In our present differences, is either party without faith of being in the right? If the Almighty Ruler of Nations, with His eternal truth and justice, be on your side of the North, or on yours of the South, that truth and that justice will surely prevail by the judgment of this great tribunal of the American people.

By the frame of the Government under which we live this same people have wisely given their public servants but little power for mischief, and have with equal wisdom provided for the return of that little to their own hands at very short intervals. While the people retain their virtue and vigilance no Administration by any extreme wickedness or folly can very seriously injure the Government in the short space of four years.

My countrymen, one and all, think calmly and *well* upon this whole subject. Nothing valuable can be lost by taking time. If there be an object to *hurry* any of you in hot haste to a step which you would never take *deliberately*, that object will be frustrated by taking time; but no good object can be frustrated by it. Such of you as are now dissatisfied still have the old Constitution unimpaired, and, on the sensitive point, the laws of your own framing under it; while the new Administration will have no immediate power, if it would, to change either. If it were admitted that you who are dissatisfied hold the right side in the dispute, there still is no single good reason for precipitate action. Intelligence, patriotism, Christianity, and a firm reliance on Him who has never yet forsaken his favored land are still competent to adjust in the best way all our present difficulty.

In *your* hands, my dissatisfied fellow-countrymen, and not in *mine*, is the momentous issue of civil war. The Government will not assail *you*. You can have no conflict without being yourselves the aggressors. *You* have no oath registered in heaven to destroy the Government, while *I* shall have the most solemn one to "preserve, protect, and defend it."

I am loath to close. We are not enemies, but friends. We must not be enemies. Though passion may have strained it must not break our bonds of affection. The mystic chords of memory, stretching from every battlefield and patriot grave to every living heart and hearthstone all over this broad land, will yet swell the chorus of the Union, when again touched, as surely they will be, by the better angels of our nature.

Abraham Lincoln

Gettysburg Address (1863)

The two most decisive battles of the Civil War took place in the first week of July 1863. At Vicksburg, Union General Ulysses S. Grant successfully completed the siege of the town, securing a position which effectively assured Northern control of the Mississippi River and cut Texas, Arkansas, and Louisiana off from the remaining Confederate States. New supplies of cotton and new sources of manpower became available to the North, and morale especially in the Northwest received a great boost. Almost simultaneously at Gettysburg, newly promoted General George Gordon Meade repulsed the Confederate advance into the North, led by General Robert E. Lee, thereby ensuring that the South would fight purely on the defensive and encouraging the belief that war's end was at hand.

The outcome of the Gettysburg contest had been uncertain, and the momentum of the war hung in the balance. In deciding to mount an offensive there, Lee had been unaware of the size or placement of Union forces. On the other hand, the North had failed to put into the field a decidedly larger army than Lee's. The Confederates initially gained the advantageous position but then faltered when General George Pickett's forces were rebuffed in their effort to charge and hold Cemetery Ridge, one of the peaks just outside the town. Unsure of the remaining Confederate forces, Meade did not order his own exhausted army to pursue and destroy Lee's after the failure of Pickett's charge. Lee's army was able to retreat to Virginia rather than face its likely destruction. The battle, in short, was a bundle of errors on both sides, but it added up to a decisive Northern victory and the beginning of the end of the war.

The battle of Gettysburg took a heavy toll. Over 3,000 Union troops were killed, and total casualties for both sides exceeded 43,000.

A national cemetery was to be established there, and the dedication was scheduled for November 19, 1863. The local planner of the event had invited the President to speak, probably anticipating a refusal. The main speaker would be Edward Everett of Massachusetts, one of the most renowned orators in the nation. Lincoln, however, felt indebted to all who had died in battle, felt the need to speak to the grief felt by their kin, and felt the importance of reminding his countrymen of the higher purposes of the war. He would go to Gettysburg.

Legend has it that Lincoln composed his remarks on scraps of paper while riding on the train from Washington. In fact, he began work on the speech at the White House and completed it in the home of his Gettysburg host the night before its delivery. He worked on the speech carefully and intensively, but his remarks were to be only the formal dedication of the cemetery and not the major address of the day. That role would be filled by Everett. Everett's two-hour oration included a narrative of the campaign and the battle. Then, drawing from historical examples, he predicted that American unity would survive and be strengthened by the experience of civil war. Lincoln listened approvingly; he then spoke for little more than two minutes and seemed disappointed with the seeming lack of impact of his speech.

Yet it was Lincoln's address, not Everett's, which not only has survived but is commonly regarded as one of the masterpieces of American public discourse. The speech was an elegant yet simple statement of the nation's war aims, and it placed American aspirations in a universal context. Partisanship or sectionalism were altogether absent. The words were spoken from the heart and the eloquence was almost poetic in its starkness. In describing the nation as dedicated to a proposition, Lincoln challenged his hearers to bring about the day when the proposition of human equality would be commonly regarded as true. That challenge reverberates through the years and helps to explain the inclusion of the Gettysburg address in virtually any collection of significant American speeches.

Fourscore and seven years ago our fathers brought forth upon this continent a new nation, conceived in liberty, and dedicated to the proposition that all men are created equal. Now we are engaged in a great civil war, testing whether that nation, or any nation so conceived and so dedicated, can long endure. We are met on a great battlefield of that war. We have come to dedicate a portion of that field as a final resting-place for those who here gave their lives that that nation might live. It is altogether fitting and proper that we should do this. But in a larger sense we cannot dedicate, we cannot consecrate, we cannot hallow this ground. The brave men, living and dead, who struggled here, have consecrated it far above our power to add or detract. The world will little note, nor long remember, what we say here, but it can never forget what they did here. It is for us, the living, rather to be dedicated here to the unfinished work which they who fought here have thus far so nobly advanced. It is rather for us to be here dedicated to the great task remaining before us, that from these honored dead we take increased devotion to that cause for which they gave the last full measure of devotion; that we here highly resolve that these dead shall not have died in vain; that this nation, under God, shall have a new birth of freedom, and that government of the people, by the people, and for the people, shall not perish from the earth.

Abraham Lincoln

Second Inaugural Address (1865)

By the time Lincoln rose on March 4, 1865, to take the Presidential oath of office a second time, the outcome of the Civil War was certain. It was only a matter of time before the North would prevail. For some time, however, neither the result of the war nor Lincoln's reelection was a foregone conclusion. The South had won many of the early battles. Not until the Union victories at Gettysburg and Vicksburg did the tide turn, and not until the success of General William Tecumseh Sherman's Southern campaign of 1864 was the outcome decisive.

As for the political situation, Democrats had made impressive gains after the debacle of 1860. In the 1862 midterm elections they had reduced the Republican Congressional majority by half, even without the votes of the seceded states. Many opposed emancipation and wished to abandon the war as futile; certainly they did not support broadening war goals to include abolition of slavery. In early 1864 the Administration was beset by eroding public confidence in its prosecution of the war, and even Republicans expressed doubts about whether Lincoln should be renominated or could be reelected. He prevailed at the convention through astute management of the platform and his selection of Tennessee War Democrat Andrew Johnson as his running mate.

Sensing victory in the face of Republican division, Democrats nominated the deposed but popular Union General George B. McClellan and ran on a peace platform. It was an attractive combination. The fear that it might succeed, together with the fortune of good news about the war, led Republicans to close ranks. Even so, the election was expected to be very close. That Lincoln won 55 percent of the popular vote and scored a landslide in the Electoral College was a surprise probably even to him.

The disagreement in 1865 was not about the outcome of the war but about the nature of the postwar Union. Lincoln needed to articulate his planned course of action, knowing that it would be highly controversial. Essential to his proposal was an explanation or account for the war, and Lincoln used the Second Inaugural Address to accomplish this task. This speech completes a slow but steady evolution of Lincoln's thought, both reaffirming the original cause of the war (preservation of the Union) and acknowledging slavery as the underlying root cause.

Lincoln's explanation fuses secular and sacred. He sees the war as Divine punishment for human sins. By implication, changing attitudes about slavery was necessary to atone for sin, and only when that was done would the "scourge of war" pass away. In this respect the speech falls within the genre of the jeremiad, a form of address in which the speaker laments the present calamity, warns of even worse evil to come, and urges repentance in order to evert even greater tragedy. But if it is a jeremiad, it is also an inaugural address, and it partakes of the features of that form as well. It reconstitutes an audience by recalling a similar scene four years earlier, recalls values drawn from the past, puts forward the broad political principles of reconstruction policy, and acknowledges Executive limitations by placing the ultimate outcome of the war in the hands of God. The speech is noteworthy as a fusion of these two quite different rhetorical forms.

Six weeks after delivering this speech, Abraham Lincoln lay dead, the first President to fall victim to assassination. In retrospect the Second Inaugural Address takes on added significance as a kind of valedictory or farewell message and, with respect to reconstruction policy, a poignant reminder of the road not taken.

Fellow-Countrymen: At this second appearing to take the oath of the Presidential office there is less occasion for an extended address than there was at the first. Then a statement somewhat in detail of a course to be pursued seemed fitting and proper. Now, at the expiration of four years, during which public declarations have been constantly called forth on every point and phase of the great contest which still absorbs the attention and engrosses the energies of the nation, little that is new could be presented. The progress of our arms, upon which all else chiefly depends, is as well known to the public as to myself, and it is, I trust, reasonably satisfactory and encouraging to all. With high hope for the future, no prediction in regard to it is ventured.

On the occasion corresponding to this four years ago all thoughts were anxiously directed to an impending civil war. All dreaded it, all sought to avert it. While the inaugural address was being delivered from this place, devoted altogether to *saving* the

Union without war, insurgent agents were in the city seeking to *destroy* it without war—seeking to dissolve the Union and divide effects by negotiation. Both parties deprecated war, but one of them would *make* war rather than let the nation survive, and the other would *accept* war rather than let it perish, and the war came.

One-eighth of the whole population were colored slaves, not distributed generally over the Union, but localized in the southern part of it. These slaves constituted a peculiar and powerful interest. All knew that this interest was somehow the cause of the war. To strengthen, perpetuate, and extend this interest was the object for which the insurgents would rend the Union even by war, while the Government claimed no right to do more than to restrict the territorial enlargement of it. Neither party expected for the war the magnitude or the duration which it has already attained. Neither anticipated that the *cause* of the conflict might cease with or even before the conflict itself should cease. Each looked for an easier triumph, and a result less fundamental and astounding. Both read the same Bible and pray to the same God, and each invokes His aid against the other. It may seem strange that any men should dare to ask a just God's assistance in wringing their bread from the sweat of other men's faces, but let us judge not, that we be not judged. The prayers of both could not be answered. That of neither has been answered fully. The Almighty has His own purposes. "Woe unto the world because of offenses; for it must needs be that offenses come, but woe to that man by whom the offense cometh." If we shall suppose that American slavery is one of those offenses which, in the providence of God, must needs come, but which having continued through His appointed time, He now wills to remove, and that He gives to both North and South this terrible war as the woe due to those by whom the offense came, shall we discern therein any departure from those divine attributes which the believers in a living God always ascribe to Him? Fondly do we hope, fervently do we pray, that this mighty scourge of war may speedily pass away. Yet, if God wills that it continue until all the wealth piled by the bondsman's two hundred and fifty years of unrequited toil shall be sunk, and until every drop of blood drawn with the lash shall be paid by another drawn with the sword, as was three thousand years ago, so still it must be said "the judgments of the Lord are true and righteous altogether."

With malice toward none, with charity for all, with firmness in the right as God gives us to see the right, let us strive on to finish the work we are in, to bind up the nation's wounds, to care for him who shall have borne the battle and for his widow and his orphan, to do all which may achieve and cherish a just and lasting peace among ourselves and with all nations.

Challenges at Home and Abroad

Susan B. Anthony

Women's Right to the Suffrage (1873) and On Behalf of the Woman Suffrage Amendment (1884)

The ratification of the Fourteenth Amendment in 1868 established the rights of blacks as citizens of the United States. But, not all blacks, of course. The Amendment gave the right to vote to "male inhabitants," maintaining the exclusion of women from the right of suffrage. One ardent abolitionist who campaigned for black suffrage made strenuous efforts to have women included in the provisions of the Fourteenth Amendment. Susan B. Anthony failed in that attempt, but devoted the rest of her life to the fight for women's rights.

Susan B. Anthony was brought up in Western New York, the daughter of Quaker parents who were themselves reformers and who encouraged her own zeal for change and her dedication to social and moral causes. She became a teacher, heading the Female Department of the Canajoharie Academy in New York. When her initial efforts to work for temperance were rebuffed by the men who directed the temperance movement, she formed, in 1852, the Woman's State Temperance Society of New York. It is was this time that she met the redoubtable Elizabeth Cady Stanton, the woman who had been one of the chief organizers of the Seneca Falls Convention of 1848, the first woman's Rights Convention held in America. Anthony was to work closely with Stanton throughout her life.

Campaigning in New York, and then throughout the country, Susan Anthony urged legislatures to pass laws that would protect women's property rights, that would give them the right to an education, and that would establish their rights of child custody in the case of divorce. After the failure to secure a stipulation insuring woman's rights in the Fourteenth Amendment, Anthony focused her energies on the struggle for woman's suffrage. She created a sensation when, in 1872, she registered and voted in Rochester. She was arrested and tried for violating the election laws. In the first speech by Susan Anthony that follows, she questioned the legal and moral validity of the law and refused to pay the fine that was imposed on her.

With her friend and mentor, Elizabeth Stanton, Susan B. Anthony came to believe that the way to obtain suffrage was through an admendment to the United States Constitution. This strategy was opposed by others in the movement who argued that change could best be brought about by changes in state laws, and the suffrage movement split into two groups. When the movement finally reunited in 1892, Anthony served as President of the National Woman Suffrage Association until her retirement from the office, at age 80, in 1900. She died in 1906, fourteen years before the Nineteenth Amendment to the Constitution gave women the right to vote.

In 1884 Susan B. Anthony and some of her supporters appeared to testify before a Senate Select Committee on Woman Suffrage. Anthony, who told the committee that she did not propose to argue the fundamental issue since she took "it for granted that the members of this committee understand that we have all the argument on our side," even so made a strong case for the right to vote as inseparable from the other obligations and rights of citizens. Her most direct and forceful plea, however, was for the strategy that she and her colleagues thought most likely to succeed: the granting of woman suffrage through constitutional amendment. She urged the legislators not to "drive us back to the States any more," but, rather, to support a constitutional amendment, "a method of procedure which has been practiced from the beginning of the Government."

Women's Right to the Suffrage (1873)

Friends and fellow citizens: I stand before you to-night under indictment for the alleged crime of having voted at the last presidential election, without having a lawful right to vote. It shall be my work this evening to prove to you that in thus voting, I not only committed no crime, but, instead, simply exercised my *citizen's rights*, guaranteed to me and all United States citizens by the National Constitution, beyond the power of any State to deny. . . . The preamble of the Federal Constitution says:

> We, the people of the United States, in order to form a more perfect union, establish justice, insure *domestic* tranquillity, provide for the common defense, promote the general welfare, and secure the blessings of liberty to ourselves and our posterity, do ordain and establish this Constitution for the United States of America.

It was we, the people; not we, the white male citizens; nor yet we, the male citizens; but we, the whole people, who formed the Union. And we formed it, not to give the blessings of liberty, but to secure them; not to the half of ourselves and the half of our posterity, but to the whole people—women as well as men. And it is a downright mockery to talk to women of their enjoyment of the blessings of liberty while they are denied the use of the only means of securing them provided by this democratic-republican government—the ballot.

For any State to make sex a qualification that must ever result in the disfranchisement of one entire half of the people is to pass a bill of attainder, or an *ex post facto* law, and is therefore a violation of the supreme law of the land. By it the blessings of liberty are for ever withheld from women and their female posterity. To them this government has no just powers derived from the consent of the governed. To them this government is not a democracy. It is not a republic. It is an odious aristocracy; a hateful oligarchy of sex; the most hateful aristocracy ever established on the face of the globe; an oligarchy of wealth, where the rich govern the poor. An oligarchy of learning, where the educated govern the ignorant, or even an oligarchy of race, where the Saxon rules the African, might be endured; but this oligarchy of sex, which makes father, brothers, husband, sons, the oligarchs over the mother and sisters, the wife and daughters of every household—which ordains all men sovereigns, all women subjects, carries dissension, discord and rebellion into every home of the nation.

Webster, Worcester and Bouvier all define a citizen to be a person in the United States, entitled to vote and hold office.

The only question left to be settled now is: Are women persons? And I hardly believe any of our opponents will have the hardihood to say they are not. Being persons, then, women are citizens; and no State has a right to make any law, or to enforce any old law, that shall abridge their privileges or immunities. Hence, every discrimination against women in the constitutions and laws of the several States is to-day null and void, precisely as in every one against negroes.

On Behalf of the Woman Suffrage Amendment (1884)

Mr. Chairman and Gentlemen: Mrs. Spencer said that I would make an argument. I do not propose to do so, because I take it for granted that the members of this committee understand that we have all the argument on our side, and such an argument would be simply a series of platitudes and maxims of government. The theory of this Government from the beginning has been perfect equality to all the people. That is shown by every one of the fundamental principles, which I need not stop to repeat. Such being the theory, the application would be, of course, that all persons not having forfeited their right to representation in the Government should be possessed of it at the age of twenty-one. But instead of adopting a practice in conformity with the theory of our Government, we began first by saying that all men of property were the people of the nation upon whom the Constitution conferred equality of rights. The next step was that all white men were the people to whom should be practically applied the fundamental theories. There we halt to-day and stand at a deadlock, so far as the application of our theory may go. We women have been standing before the American republic for thirty years, asking the men to take yet one step further and extend the practical application of the theory of equality of rights to all the people to the other half of the people—the women. That is all that I stand here to-day to attempt to demand.

Of course, I take it for granted that the committee are in sympathy at least with the reports of the Judiciary Committees presented both in the Senate and the House. I remember that after the adoption of the fourteenth and fifteenth amendments Senator Edmunds reported on the petition of the ten thousand foreign-born citizens of Rhode Island who were denied equality of rights in Rhode Island simply because of their foreign birth; and in that report held that the amendments were enacted and attached to the Constitution simply for men of color, and therefore that their provisions could not be so construed as to bring within their purview the men of foreign birth in Rhode Island. Then the House Committee on the Judiciary, with Judge Bingham, of Ohio, at its head, made a similar report upon our petitions, holding that because those amendments were made essentially with the black men in view, therefore their provisions could not be extended to the women citizens of this country or to any class except men citizens of color.

I voted in the State of New York in 1872 under the construction of those amendments, which we felt to be the true one, that all persons born in the United States, or any State thereof, and under the jurisdiction of the United States, were citizens, and entitled to equality of rights, and that no State could deprive them of their equality of rights. I found three young men, inspectors of election, who were simple enough to read the Constitution and understand it in accordance with what was the letter and what should have been its spirit. Then, as you will remember, I was prosecuted by the officers of the Federal court, and the cause was carried through the different courts in the State of New York, in the northern district, and at last I was brought to trial at Canandaigua.

When Mr. Justice Hunt was brought from the supreme bench to sit upon that trial, he wrested my case from the hands of the jury altogether, after having listened three days to testimony, and brought in a verdict himself of guilty, denying to my counsel even the poor privilege of having the jury polled. Through all that trial when I, as a citizen of the United States, as a citizen of the State of New York and city of Rochester, as a person who had done something at least that might have entitled her to a voice in speaking for herself and for her class, in all that trial I not only was denied my right to testify as to whether I voted or not, but there was not one single woman's voice to be heard nor to be considered, except as witnesses, save when it came to the judge asking, "Has the prisoner anything to say why sentence shall not be pronounced?" Neither as judge, nor as attorney, nor as jury was I allowed any person who could be legitimately called my peer to speak for me.

Then, as you will remember, Mr. Justice Hunt not only pronounced the verdict of guilty, but a sentence of $100 fine and costs of prosecution. I said to him, "May it please your honor, I do not propose to pay it"; and I never have paid it, and I never shall. I asked your honorable bodies of Congress the next year—in 1874—to pass a resolution to remit that fine. Both Houses refused it; the committees reported against it; though through Benjamin F. Butler, in the House, and a member of your committee, and Matthew H. Carpenter, in the Senate, there were plenty of precedents brought forward to show that in cases of multitudes of men fines had been remitted. I state this merely to show the need of woman to speak for herself, to be as judge, to be as juror.

Mr. Justice Hunt in his opinion stated that suffrage was a fundamental right, and therefore a right that belonged to the State. It seemed to me that was just as much of a retroversion of the theory of what is right in our Government as there could possibly be. Then, after the decision in my case came that of Mrs. Minor, of Missouri. She prosecuted the officers there for denying her the right to vote. She carried her case up to your Supreme Court, and the Supreme Court answered her the same way; that the amendments were made for black men; that their provisions could not protect women; that the Constitution of the United States has no voters of its own.

MRS. SPENCER: And you remember Judge Cartter's decision in my case.

MISS ANTHONY: Mr. Cartter said that women are citizens and may be qualified, &c., but that it requires some sort of legislation to give them the right to vote.

The Congress of the United States notwithstanding, and the Supreme Court of the United States notwithstanding, with all deference and respect, I differ with them all, and know that I am right and that they are wrong. The Constitution of the United States as it is protects me. If I could get a practical application of the Constitution it would protect me and all women in the enjoyment of perfect equality of rights everywhere under the shadow of the American flag.

I do not come to you to petition for special legislation, or for any more amendments to the Constitution, because I think they are unnecessary, but because you say there is not in the Constitution enough to protect me. Therefore I ask that you, true to your own theory and assertion, should go forward to make more constitution.

Let me remind you that in the case of all other classes of citizens under the shadow of our flag you have been true to the theory that taxation and representation are inseparable. Indians not taxed are not counted in the basis of representation, and are not allowed to vote; but the minute that your Indians are counted in the basis of representation and are allowed to vote they are taxed; never before. In my State of New York, and in nearly all the States, the members of the State militia, hundreds and thousands of men, are exempted from taxation on property; in my State to the value of $800, and in most of the States to a value in that neighborhood. While such a member of the militia lives, receives his salary, and is able to earn money, he is exempted; but when he dies the assessor puts his widow's name down upon the assessor's list, and the tax-collector never fails to call upon the widow and make her pay the full tax upon her property. In most of the States clergymen are exempted. In my State of New York they are exempted on property to the value of $1,500. As long as the clergyman lives and receives his fat salary, or his lean one, as the case may be, he is exempted on that amount of property; but when the breath leaves the body of the clergyman, and the widow is left without any income, or without any means of support, the State comes in and taxes the widow.

So it is with regard to all black men. In the State of New York up to the day of the passage of the fifteenth amendment, black men who were willing to remain without reporting themselves worth as much as $250, and thereby to remain without exercising the right to vote, never had their names put on the assessor's list; they were passed by, while, if the poorest colored woman owned 50 feet of real estate, a little cabin anywhere, that colored woman's name was always on the assessor's list, and she was compelled to pay her tax. While Frederick Douglass lived in my State he was never allowed to vote until he could show himself worth the requisite $250; and when he did vote in New York, he voted not because he was a man, not because he was a citizen of the United States, nor yet because he was a citizen of the State, but simply because he was worth the requisite amount of money. In Connecticut both black men and black women were exempted from taxation prior to the adoption of the fifteenth amendment.

The law was amended in 1848, by which black men were thus exempted, and black women followed the same rule in that State. That, I believe, is the only State where black women were exempted from taxation under the law. When the fourteenth and fifteenth amendments were attached to the Constitution they carried to the black man of Connecticut the boon of the ballot as well as the burden of taxation, whereas they carried to the black woman of Connecticut the burden of taxation, but no ballot by which to protect her property. I know a colored woman in New Haven, Conn., worth $50,000, and she never paid a penny of taxation until the ratification of the fifteenth amendment. From that day on she is compelled to pay a heavy tax on that amount of property.

MRS. SPENCER: Is it because she is a citizen? Please explain.

MISS ANTHONY: Because she is black.

MRS. SPENCER: Is it because the fourteenth and fifteenth amendments made women citizens?

MISS ANTHONY: Certainly; because it declared the black people citizens.

Gentlemen, you have before you various propositions of amendment to the Federal Constitution. One is for the election of President by the vote of the people direct. Of course women are not people.

SENATOR EDMUNDS: Angels.

MISS ANTHONY: Yes; angels up in heaven or else devils down there.

SENATOR EDMUNDS: I have never known any of that kind.

MISS ANTHONY: I wish you, gentlemen, would look down there and see the myriads that are there. We want to help them and lift them up. That is exactly the trouble with you, gentlemen; you are forever looking at your own wives, your own mothers, your own sisters, and your own daughters, and they are well cared for and protected; but only look down to the struggling masses of women who have no one to protect them, neither husband, father, brother, son, with no mortal in all the land to protect them. If you would look down there the question would be solved; but the difficulty is that you think only of those who are doing well. We are not speaking for ourselves, but for those who can not speak for themselves. We are speaking for the doomed as much as you, Senator Edmunds, used to speak for the doomed on the plantations in the South.

Amendments have been proposed to put God in the Constitution and to keep God out of the Constitution. All sorts of propositions to amend the Constitution have been made; but I ask that you allow no other amendment to be called the sixteenth but that which shall put into the hands of one-half of the entire people of the nation the right to express their opinions as to how the Constitution shall be amended henceforth. Women have the right to say whether we shall have God in the Constitution as well as men. Women have a right to say whether we shall have a national law or an amendment to the Constitution prohibiting the importation or manufacture of alcoholic liquors. We have a right to have our opinions counted on every possible question concerning the public welfare.

You ask us why we do not get this right to vote first in the school districts, and on school questions, or the questions of liquor license. It has been shown very clearly why we need something more than that. You have good enough laws to-day in every State in this Union for the suppression of what are termed the social vices; for the suppression of the grog-shops, the gambling houses, the brothels, the obscene shows. There is plenty of legislation in every State in this Union for their suppression if it could be executed. Why is the Government, why are the States and the cities, unable to execute these laws? Simply because there is a large balance of power in every city that does not want those laws executed. Consequently both parties must alike cater to that balance of political power. The party that puts a plank in its platform that the laws against the grog-shops and all the other sinks of iniquity must be executed, is the party that will not get this balance of power to vote for it, and, consequently, the party that can not get into power.

What we ask of you is that you will make of the women of the cities a balance of political power, so that when a mayor, a member of the common council, a supervisor, a justice of the peace, a district attorney, a judge on the bench even, shall go before the people of that city as a candidate for the suffrages of the people he shall not only be compelled to look to the men who frequent the grog-shops, the brothels, and the gambling houses, who will vote for him if he is not in favor of executing the law, but that he shall have to look to the mothers, the sisters, the wives, the daughters of those deluded men to see what they will do if he does not execute the law.

We want to make of ourselves a balance of political power. What we need is the power to execute the laws. We have got laws enough. Let me give you one little fact in regard to my own city of Rochester. You all know how that wonderful whip called the temperance crusade roused the whisky ring. It caused the whisky force to concentrate itself more strongly at the ballot-box than ever before, so that when the report of the elections in the spring of 1874 went over the country the result was that the whisky ring was triumphant, and that the whisky ticket was elected more largely than ever before. Senator Thurman will remember how it was in his own State of Ohio. Everybody knows that if my friends, Mrs. ex-Governor Wallace, Mrs. Allen, and all the women of the great West could have gone to the ballot-box at those municipal elections and voted for candidates, no such result would have occurred; while you refused by the laws of the State to the women the right to have their opinions counted, every rum-seller, every drunkard, every pauper even from the poor-house, and every criminal outside of the State's prison came out on election day to express his opinion and have it counted.

The next result of that political event was that the ring demanded new legislation to protect the whisky traffic everywhere. In my city the women did not crusade the streets, but they said they would help the men to execute the law. They held meetings, sent out committees, and had testimony secured against every man who had violated the law, and when the board of excise held its meeting those women assembled, three or four hundred, in the church one morning, and marched in a solid body to the common council chamber where the board of excise was sitting. As one rum-seller after another brought in his petition for a renewal of license, who had violated the law, those women presented the testimony against him. The law of the State of New York is that no man shall have a renewal who has violated the law. But in not one case did that board refuse to grant a renewal license because of the testimony which those women presented, and at the close of the sitting it was found that twelve hundred more licenses had been granted than ever before in the history of the State. Then the defeated women said they would have those men punished according to law.

Again they retained an attorney and appointed committees to investigate all over the city. They got the proper officer to prosecute every rum-seller. I was at their meeting. One woman reported that the officer in every city refused to prosecute the liquor dealer who had violated the law. Why? Because if he should do so he would lose the votes of all the employes of certain shops on that street, if another he would lose the votes of the railroad employes, and if another he would lose the German vote, if another the Irish vote, and so on. I said to those women what I say to you, and what I know to be true to-day, that if the women of the city of Rochester had held the power of the ballot in their hands they would have been a great political balance of power.

The last report was from District Attorney Raines. The women complained of a lager-beer-garden keeper. Said the district attorney, "Ladies, you are right, this man is violating the law, everybody knows it, but if I should prosecute him I would lose the entire German vote." Said I, "Ladies, do you not see that if the women of the city of Rochester had the right to vote District Attorney Raines would have been compelled to have stopped and counted, weighed and measured? He would have said, 'If I prosecute that lager-beer German I shall lose the 5,000 German votes in this city, but if I fail to prosecute him and execute the laws I shall lose the votes of 20,000 women.' "

Do you not see, gentlemen, that so long as you put this power of the ballot in the hands of every possible man, rich, poor, drunk, sober, educated, ignorant, outside of the State's prison, to make or unmake, not only every law and lawmaker, but every office-holder who has to do with the executing of the law, and take the power from the hands of the women of the nation, the mothers, you put the long arm of the lever, as we call it in mechanics, in the hands of the whisky power and make it utterly impossible for regulation of sobriety to be maintained in our community? The first step towards social regulation and good society in towns, cities, and villages is the ballot in the hands of the mothers of those places. I appeal to you especially in this matter.

I do not know what you think about the proper sphere of women. It matters little what any of us think about it. We shall each and every individual find our own proper sphere if we are left to act in freedom; but my opinion is that when the whole arena of politics and government is thrown open to women they will endeavor to do very much as they do in their homes; that the men will look after the greenback theory or the hard-money theory, that you will look after free-trade or tariff, and the women will do the home house-keeping of the government, which is to take care of the moral government and the social regulation of our home department.

It seems to me that we have the power of government outside to shape and control circumstances, but that the inside power, the government house-keeping, is powerless, and is compelled to accept whatever conditions or circumstances shall be granted.

Therefore I do not ask for liquor suffrage alone, nor for school suffrage alone, because that would amount to nothing. We must be able to have a voice in the election not only of every law-maker, but of every one who has to do either with the making or the executing of the laws.

Then you ask why we do not get suffrage by the popular-vote method, State by State? I answer, because there is no reason why I, for instance, should desire the women of one State of this nation to vote any more than the women of another State. I have no more interest as regards the women of New York than I have as regards the women of Indiana, Iowa, or any of the States represented by the women who have come up here. The reason why I do not wish to get this right by what you call the popular-vote method, the State vote, is because I believe there is a United States citizenship. I believe that this is a nation, and to be a citizen of this nation should be a guaranty to every citizen of the right to a voice in the Government, and should give to me my right to express my opinion. You deny to me my liberty, my freedom, if you say that I shall have no voice whatever in making, shaping, or controlling the conditions of society in which I live. I differ from Judge Hunt, and I hope I am respectful when I say that I think he made a very funny mistake when he said that fundamental rights belong to the States and only surface rights to the National Government. I hope you will agree with me that the fundamental right of citizenship, the right to voice in the Government, is a national right.

The National Government may concede to the States the right to decide by a majority as to what banks they shall have, what laws they shall enact with regard to insurance, with regard to property, and any other question; but I insist upon it that the National Government should not leave it a question with the States that a majority in any State may disfranchise the minority under any circumstances whatsoever. The franchise to you men is not secure. You hold it to-day, to be sure, by the common consent of white men, but if at any time, on your principle of government, the majority of any of the States should choose to amend the State constitution so as to disfranchise this or that portion of the white men by making this or that condition, by all the decisions of the Supreme Court and by the legislation thus far there is nothing to hinder them.

Therefore the women demand a sixteenth amendment to bring to women the right to vote, or if you please to confer upon women their right to vote, to protect them in it, and to secure men in their right, because you are not secure.

I would let the States act upon almost every other question by majorities, except the power to say whether my opinion shall be counted. I insist upon it that no State shall decide that question.

Then the popular-vote method is an impracticable thing. We tried to get negro suffrage by the popular vote, as you will remember. Senator Thurman will remember that in Ohio the Republicans submitted the question in 1867, and with all the prestige of the national Republican party and of the State party, when every influence that could be brought by the power and the patronage of the party in power was brought to bear, yet negro suffrage ran behind the regular Republican ticket 40,000.

It was tried in Kansas, it was tried in New York, and everywhere that it was submitted the question was voted down overwhelmingly. Just so we tried to get women suffrage by the popular-vote method in Kansas in 1867, in Michigan in 1874, in Colorado in 1877, and in each case the result was precisely the same, the ratio of the vote standing one-third for women suffrage and two-thirds against women suffrage. If we were to canvass State after State we should get no better vote than that. Why? Because the question of the enfranchisement of women is a question of government, a question of philosophy, of understanding, of great fundamental principle, and the masses of the hard-working people of this nation, men and women, do not think upon principles. They can only think on the one eternal struggle wherewithal to be fed, to be clothed, and to be sheltered. Therefore I ask you not to compel us to have this question settled by what you term the popular-vote method.

Let me illustrate by Colorado, the most recent State, in the election of 1877. I am happy to say to you that I have canvassed three States for this question. If Senator Chandler were alive, or if Senator Ferry were in this room, they would remember that I followed in their train in Michigan, with larger audiences than either of those Senators throughout the whole canvass. I want to say, too, that although those Senators may have believed in woman suffrage, they did not say much about it. They did not help us much. The Greenback movement was quite popular in Michigan at that time. The Republicans and Greenbackers made a most humble bow to the grangers, but women suffrage did not get much help. In Colorado, at the close of the canvass, 6,666 men voted "Yes." Now I am going to describe the men who voted "Yes." They were native-born white men, temperance men, cultivated, broad, generous, just men, men who think. On the other hand, 16,007 voted "No."

Now I am going to describe that class of voters. In the southern part of that State there are Mexicans, who speak the Spanish language. They put their wheat in circles on the ground with the heads out, and drive a mule around to thrash it. The vast population of Colorado is made up of that class of people. I was sent out to speak in a voting precinct having 200 voters; 150 of those voters were Mexican greasers, 40 of them foreign-born citizens, and just 10 of them were born in this country; and I was supposed to be competent to convert those men to let me have as much right in this Government as they had, when, unfortunately, the great majority of them could not understand a word that I said. Fifty or sixty Mexican greasers stood against the wall with their hats down over their faces. The Germans put seats in a lager-beer saloon, and would not attend unless I made a speech there; so I had a small audience.

MRS. ARCHIBALD: There is one circumstance that I should like to relate. In the county of Las Animas, a county where there is a large population of Mexicans, and where they always have a large majority over the native population, they do not know our language at all. Consequently a number of tickets must be printed for those people in Spanish. The gentleman in our little town of Trinidad who had the charge of the printing of those tickets, being adverse to us, had every ticket printed against woman suffrage. The samples that were sent to us from Denver were "for" or "against," but the tickets that were printed only had the word "against" on them, so that our friends had to scratch their tickets, and all those Mexican people who could not understand this trick and did not know the facts of the case, voted against woman suffrage; so that we lost a great many votes. This was man's generosity.

MISS ANTHONY: Special legislation for the benefit of woman! I will admit you that on the floor of the constitutional convention was a representative Mexican, intelligent, cultivated, chairman of the committee on suffrage, who signed the petition, and was the first to speak in favor of woman suffrage. Then they have in Denver about four hundred negroes. Governor Routt said to me, "The four hundred Denver negroes are going to vote solid for woman suffrage." I said, "I do not know much about the Denver negroes, but I know certainly what all negroes were educated in, and slavery never educated master or negro into a comprehension of the great principles of human freedom of our nation; it is not possible, and I do not believe they are going to vote for us." Just ten of those Denver negroes voted for woman suffrage. Then, in all the mines of Colorado the vast majority of wage laborers, as you know, are foreigners.

There may be intelligent foreigners in this country, and I know there are, who are in favor of the enfranchisement of woman, but that one does not happen to be Carl Schurz, I am ashamed to say. And I want to say to you of Carl Schurz, that side by side with that man on the battlefield of Germany was Madame Anneke, as noble a woman as ever trod the American soil. She rode by the side of her husband, who was an officer, on the battlefield; she slept in battlefield tents, and she fled from Germany to this country, for her life and property, side by side with Carl Schurz. Now, what is it for Carl Schurz, stepping up to the very door of the Presidency and looking back to Madame Anneke, who fought for liberty as well as he, to say, "You be subject in this Republic; I will be sovereign." If it is an insult for Carl Schurz to say that to a foreign-born woman, what is it for him to say it to Mrs. ex-Governor Wallace, Elizabeth Cady Stanton, Lucretia Mott—to the native-born, educated, tax-paying women in this Republic? I can forgive an ignorant foreigner; I can forgive an ignorant negro; but I can not forgive Carl Schurz.

Right in the file of the foreigners opposed to woman suffrage, educated under monarchical governments that do not comprehend our principles, whom I have seen traveling through the prairies of Iowa or the prairies of Minnesota, are the Bohemians, Swedes, Norweigians, Germans, Irishmen, Mennonites; I have seen them riding on those magnificent loads of wheat with those magnificent Saxon horses, shining like glass on a sunny morning, every one of them going to vote "no" against woman suffrage. You can not convert them; it is impossible. Now and then there is a whisky manufacturer, drunkard, inebriate, libertine, and what we call a fast man, and a colored man, broad and generous enough to be willing to let women vote, to let his mother have her opinion counted as to whether there shall be license or no license, but the rank and file of all classes who wish to enjoy full license in what are termed the petty vices of men are pitted solid against the enfranchisement of women.

Then, in addition to all these, there are, as you know, a few religious bigots left in the world who really believe that somehow or other if women are allowed to vote St. Paul would feel badly about it. I do not know but that some of the gentlemen present belong to that class. So, when you put those best men of the nation, having religion about everything except on this one question, whose prejudices control them, with all this vast mass of ignorant, uneducated, degraded population in this country, you make an overwhelming and insurmountable majority against the enfranchisement of women.

It is because of this fact that I ask you

not to remand us back to the States, but submit to the States the proposition of a sixteenth amendment. The popular-vote method is not only of itself an impossibility, but it is too humiliating a process to compel the women of this nation to submit to any longer.

I am going to give you an illustration, not because I have any disrespect for the person, because on many other questions he was really a good deal better than a good many other men who had not so bad a name in this nation. When, under the old *régime*, John Morrissey, of my State, the king of gamblers, was a Representative on the floor of Congress, it was humiliating enough for Lucretia Mott, for Elizabeth Cady Stanton, for all of us to come down here to Washington to beg at the feet of John Morrissey that he would let intelligent, native-born women vote, and let us have as much right in this Government and in the government of the city of New York as he had. When John Morrissey was a member of the New York State Legislature it would have been humiliating enough for us to go to the New York State Legislature and pray of John Morrissey to vote to ratify the sixteenth amendment, giving us the right to vote; but if instead of a sixteenth amendment you tell us to go back to the popular-vote method, the old-time method, and go down into John Morrissey's seventh Congressional district in the city of New York, and there, in the sloughs and slums of that great Sodom, in the grog-shops, the gambling-houses, and the brothels, beg at the feet of each individual fisticuff of his constituency to give the noble, educated, native-born, tax-paying women of the State of New York as much right as he has, that would be too bitter a pill for a native-born woman to swallow any longer.

I beg you, gentlemen, to save us from the mortification and the humiliation of appealing to the rabble. We already have on our side the vast majority of the better educated—the best classes of men. You will remember that Senator Christiancy, of Michigan, two years ago, said on the floor of the Senate that of the 40,000 men who voted for woman suffrage in Michigan it was said that there was not a drunkard, not a libertine, not a gambler, not a depraved, low man among them. Is not that something that tells for us, and for our right? It is the fact, in every State of the Union, that we have the intelligent lawyers and the most liberal ministers of all the sects, not excepting the Roman Catholics. A Roman Catholic priest preached a sermon the other day, in which he said, "God grant that there were a thousand Susan B. Anthonys in this city to vote and work for temperance." When a Catholic priest says that there is a great moral necessity pressing down upon this nation demanding the enfranchisement of women, I ask you that you shall not drive us back to beg our rights at the feet of the most ignorant and depraved men of the nation, but that you, the representative men of the nation, will hold the question in the hollow of your hands. We ask you to lift this question out of the hands of the rabble.

You who are here upon the floor of Congress in both Houses are the picked men of the nation. You may say what you please about John Morrissey, the gambler, &c.: he was head and shoulders above the rank and file of his constituency. The world may gabble ever so much about members of Congress being corrupt and being bought and sold; they are as a rule head and shoulders above the great majority who compose their State governments. There is no doubt about it. Therefore I ask of you, as representative men, as men who think, as men who study, as men who philosophize, as men who know, that you will not drive us back to the States any more, but that you will carry out this method of procedure which has been practiced from the beginning of the Government; that is, that you will put a prohibitory amendment in the Constitution and submit the proposition to the several State legislatures. The amendment which has been presented before you reads:

> ARTICLE XVI
>
> SECTION 1. The right of suffrage in the United States shall be based on citizenship, and the right of citizens in the United States to vote shall not be denied or abridged by the United States, or by any State, on account of sex, or for any reason not equally applicable to all citizens of the United States.
>
> SECTION 2. Congress shall have power to enforce this article by appropriate legislation.

In this way we would get the right of suffrage just as much by what you call the consent of the States, or the States' rights method, as by any other method. The only point is that it is a decision by the representative men of the States instead of by the rank and file of the ignorant men of the States. If you would submit this proposition for a sixteenth amendment, by a two-thirds vote of the two Houses to the several legislatures, and the several legislatures ratify it, that would be just as much by the consent of the States as if Tom, Dick, and Harry voted "yes" or "no." Is it not, Senator? I want to talk to Democrats as well as Republicans, to show that it is a States' rights method.

SENATOR EDMUNDS: Does anybody propose any other, in case it is done at all by the nation?

MISS ANTHONY: Not by the nation, but they are continually driving us back to get it from the States, State by State. That is the point I want to make. We do not want you to drive us back to the States. We want you men to take the question out of the hands of the rabble of the State.

THE CHAIRMAN: May I interrupt you?

MISS ANTHONY: Yes, sir, I wish you would.

THE CHAIRMAN: You have reflected on this subject a great deal. You think there is a majority, as I understand, even in the State of New York, against women suffrage?

MISS ANTHONY: Yes, sir; overwhelmingly.

THE CHAIRMAN: How, then, would you get Legislatures elected to ratify such a constitutional amendment?

MISS ANTHONY: That brings me exactly to the point.

THE CHAIRMAN: That is the point I wish to hear you upon.

MISS ANTHONY: Because the members of the State Legislatures are intelligent men and can vote and enact laws embodying great principles of the government without in anywise endangering their positions with their constituencies. A constituency composed of ignorant men would vote solid against us because they have never thought on the question. Every man or woman who believes in the enfranchisement of women is educated out of every idea that he or she was born into. We were all born into the idea that the proper sphere of women is subjection, and it takes education and thought and culture to lift us out of it. Therefore when men go to the ballot-box they all vote "no," unless they have actual argument on it. I will illustrate. We have six Legislatures in the nation, for instance, that have extended the right to vote on school questions to the women, and not a single member of the State Legislature has ever lost his office or forfeited the respect or confidence of his constituents as a representative because he voted to give women the right to vote on school questions. It is a question that the unthinking masses never have thought upon. They do not care about it one way or the other, only they have an instinctive feeling that because women never did vote therefore it is wrong that they ever should vote.

MRS. SPENCER: Do make the point that the Congress of the United States leads the Legislatures of the States and educates them.

MISS ANTHONY: When you, representative men, carry this matter to Legislatures, State by State, they will ratify it. My point is that you can safely do this. Senator Thurman, of Ohio, would not lose a single vote in Ohio in voting in favor of the enfranchisement of women. Senator Edmunds would not lose a single Republican vote in the State of Vermont if he puts himself on our side, which, I think, he will do. It is not a political question. We are no political power that can make or break either party to-day. Consequently each man is left independent to express his own moral and intellectual convictions on the matter without endangering himself politically.

SENATOR EDMUNDS: I think, Miss Anthony, you ought to put it on rather higher, I will not say stronger, ground. If you can convince us that it is right we would not stop to see how it affected us politically.

MISS ANTHONY: I was coming to that. I was going to say to all of you men in office here to-day that if you can not go forward and carry out either your Democratic or your Republican or your Greenback theories, for instance, on the finance, there is no great political power that is going to take you away from these halls and prevent you from doing all those other things which you want to do, and you can act out your own moral and intellectual convictions on this without let or hindrance.

SENATOR EDMUNDS: Without any danger to the public interests, you mean.

MISS ANTHONY: Without any danger to the public interests. I did not mean to make a bad insinuation, Senator.

I want to give you another reason why we appeal to you. In these three States where the question has been submitted and voted down we can not get another Legislature to resubmit it, because they say the people have expressed their opinion and decided no, and therefore nobody with any political sense would resubmit the question. It is therefore impossible in any one of those States. We have tried hard in Kansas for ten years to get the question resubmitted; the vote of that State seems to be taken as a finality. We ask you to lift the sixteenth Amendment out of the arena of the public mass into the arena of thinking legislative brains, the brains of the nation, under the law and the Constitution. Not only do we ask it for that purpose, but when you will have by a two-thirds vote submitted the proposition to the several Legislatures, you have put the pin down and it never can go back. No subsequent Congress can revoke that submission of the proposition; there will be so much gained; it can not slide back. Then we will go to New York or to Pennsylvania, and urge upon the Legislatures the ratification of that amendment. They may refuse; they may vote it down the first time. Then we will go to the next Legislature, and the next Legislature, and plead and plead, from year to year, if it takes ten years. It is an open question to every Legislature until we can get one that will ratify it, and when that Legislature has once voted and ratified it no subsequent legislation can revoke their ratification.

Thus, you perceive, Senators, that every step we would gain by this sixteenth amendment process is fast and not to be done over again. . . . I appeal to you, therefore, to adopt the course that we suggest. . . .

Henry George

The Crime of Poverty (1885)

Following the Civil War, workers began their long struggle to organize against the power of manufacturers, businessmen, and financiers who were beginning to reap the benefits of American industrialization. A depression in 1873 brought in its wake a rise in unemployment and intensified labor unrest. In 1874, for example, a radical labor meeting was broken up by police in what came to be known as the Tompkins Square riot. A general strike against the railroads in 1877 led to rioting in Baltimore, Pittsburgh, Chicago, and St. Louis and was finally broken only after President Hayes sent federal troops to quell disturbances by angry workers who had burned down or destroyed railroad property and fought off the militia.

Most businessmen reflected the popular wisdom of the day that accepted as natural and appropriate the intervention of the government in ways that would protect business, such as the imposition of tariffs to shelter American industry. At the same time, they dismissed as radical the notion that the government could interpose itself in any fashion to protect the interests of employees; the relationship between an employer and his workers was, in the prevailing opinion, one that only the parties involved could determine. Individual workers, of course, were no match for the large commercial concerns, and they began serious efforts to combine through the formation of unions.

The Knights of Labor began in 1869 as a secret society, and it wasn't until ten years later that it began to grow into prominence as a labor organization. When Henry George traveled to Burlington, Iowa, to address the Knights of Labor Assembly there, the organization was approaching 700,000 members. The mid-1880's were hard times for many workers and prompted a series of strikes, especially those against the Union Pacific and Wabash railroads, whose success boosted the prestige of the Knights of Labor. The organization was to suffer devastating reverses toward the end of the century and was eventually overshadowed and then overwhelmed by the new American Federation of Labor, but in 1885, when George spoke on the "Crime of Poverty," the Knights were at their peak and were able to publish and distribute 50,000 copies of the speech.

Henry George was a journalist and economist who, in 1879 in his book *Progress and Poverty*, advocated a policy of land value taxation. The "single tax" theory called for the abolition of "all taxation save that upon land values." George argued that poverty existed amidst plenty and that the cycle of good times followed by depression occurred because the land was owned by relatively few people. Put simply, George held that landowners did not have produce to make profits; they collected rents in good times and such profits encouraged others to speculate in land. When rents exceeded what labor and capital could pay, depression occurred. George maintained that a policy of taxing land would have far-reaching social effects, establishing equal rights in land for all persons and leading ultimately to higher wages.

Aside from the particular fiscal reform that George offered, his message was one that was to be expressed in many ways and one that fostered a myriad of solutions as America grappled with the paradox of poverty existing side by side with plenty. His firm belief that "poverty is unnecessary" and is "a crime for which society is responsible" was a humane counter to the hard conviction that every man was personally responsible for his fate; George's underlying notion sparked debate and forwarded action as others were also to embrace the idea of collective social responsibility.

Ladies and Gentlemen: I propose to talk to you to-night of the Crime of Poverty. I cannot, in a short time, hope to convince you of much; but the thing of things I should like to show you is that poverty is a crime. I do not mean that it is a crime to be poor. Murder is a crime; but it is not a crime to be murdered; and a man who is in poverty, I look upon, not as a criminal in himself, so much as a victim of a crime for which others, as well perhaps as himself, are responsible. That poverty is a curse, the bitterest of curses, we all know. Carlyle was right when he said that the hell of which Englishmen are most afraid is the hell of poverty; and this is true, not of Englishmen alone, but of people all over the civilised world, no matter what their nationality. It is to escape this hell that we strive and strain and struggle; and work on oftentimes in blind habit long after the necessity for work is gone.

The curse born of poverty is not confined to the poor alone; it runs through all classes, even to the very rich. They, too, suffer; they must suffer; for there cannot be suffering in a community from which any class can totally escape. The vice, the crime, the ignorance, the meanness born of poverty, poison, so to speak, the very air which rich and poor alike must breathe.

Poverty is the mother of ignorance, the breeder of crime. I walked down one of your streets this morning, and I saw three men going along with their hands chained together. I knew for certain that those men were not rich men; and, although I do not know the offence for which they were carried in chains through your streets, this I think I can safely say, that, if you trace it up you will find it in some way to spring from poverty. Nine tenths of human misery, I think you will find, if you look, to be due to poverty. If a man chooses to be poor, he commits no crime in being poor, provided his poverty hurts no one but himself. If a man has others dependent upon him; if there are a wife and children whom it is his duty to support, then, if he voluntarily chooses poverty, it is a crime—aye, and I think that, in most cases, the men who have no one to support but themselves are men that are shirking their duty. A woman comes into the world for every man; and for every man who lives a single life, caring only for himself, there is some woman who is deprived of her natural supporter. But while a man who chooses to be poor cannot be charged with crime, it is certainly a crime to force poverty on others. And it seems to me clear that the great majority of those who suffer from poverty are poor not from their own particular faults, but because of conditions imposed by society at large. Therefore I hold that poverty is a crime—not an individual crime, but a social crime, a crime for which we all, poor as well as rich, are responsible.

Two or three weeks ago I went one Sunday evening to the church of a famous Brooklyn preacher. Mr. Sankey was singing and something like a revival was going on there. The clergyman told some anecdotes connected with the revival, and recounted some of the reasons why men failed to become Christians. One case he mentioned struck me. He said that he had noticed on the outskirts of the congregation, night after night, a man who listened intently and who gradually moved forward. One night, the clergyman said, he went to him, saying: "My brother, are you not ready to become a Christian?" The man said, no, he was not. He said it, not in a defiant tone, but in a sorrowful tone; the clergyman asked him why, whether he did not believe in the truths he had been hearing? Yes, he believed them all. Why, then, wouldn't he become a Christian? "Well," he said, "I can't join the church without giving up my business; and it is necessary for the support of my wife and children. If I give that up, I don't know how in the world I can get along. I had a hard time before I found my present business, and I cannot afford to give it up. Yet I can't become a Christian without giving it up." The clergyman asked, "are you a rum-seller?" No, he was not a rum-seller. Well, the clergyman said, he didn't know what in the world the man could be; it seemed to him that a rum-seller was the only man who does a business that would prevent his becoming a Christian; and he finally said: "What is your business?" The man said, "I sell soap." "Soap!" exclaimed the clergyman, "you sell soap?" How in the world does that prevent your becoming a Christian?" "Well," the man said, "it is this way; the soap I sell is one of those patent soaps that are extensively advertised as enabling you to clean clothes very quickly, as containing no deleterious compound whatever. Every cake of the soap that I sell is wrapped in a paper on which is printed a statement that it contains no injurious chemicals, whereas the truth of the matter is that it does, and that though it will take the dirt out of clothes pretty quickly, it will, in a little while, rot them completely. I have to make my living in this way; and I cannot feel that I can become a Christian if I sell that soap." The minister went on, describing how he laboured unsuccessfully with that man, and finally wound up by saying: "He stuck to his soap and lost his soul."

But, if that man lost his soul, was it his fault alone? Whose fault is it that social conditions are such that men have to make that terrible choice between what conscience tells them is right, and the necessity of earning a living? I hold that it is the fault of society; that it is the fault of us all. Pestilence is a curse. The man who would bring cholera to this country, or the man who, having the power to prevent its coming here, would make no effort to do so, would be guilty of a crime. Poverty is worse than cholera; poverty kills more people than pestilence, even in the best of times. Look at the death statistics of our cities; see where the deaths come quickest; see where it is that the little children die like flies—it is in the poorer quarters. And the man who looks with careless eyes upon the ravages of this pestilence, the man who does not set himself to stay and eradicate it, he, I say, is guilty of a crime.

If poverty is appointed by the power which is above us all, then it is no crime; but if poverty is unnecessary, then it is a crime for which society is responsible and for which society must suffer.

I hold, and I think no one who looks at the facts can fail to see, that poverty is utterly unnecessary. It is not by the decree of the Almighty, but it is because of our own injustice, our own selfishness, our own ignorance, that this scourge, worse than any pestilence, ravages our civilisation, bringing want and suffering and degradation, destroying souls as well as bodies. Look over the world, in this heyday of nineteenth century civilisation. In every civilised country under the sun you will find men and women whose condition is worse than that of the savage: men and women and little children with whom the veriest savage could not afford to exchange. Even in this new city of yours with virgin soil around you, you have had this winter to institute a relief society. Your roads have been filled with tramps, fifteen, I am told, at one time taking shelter in a round-house here. As here, so everywhere; and poverty is deepest where wealth most abounds.

What more unnatural than this? There is nothing in nature like this poverty which to-day curses us. We see rapine in nature; we see one species destroying another; but as a general thing animals do not feed on their own kind; and, wherever we see one kind enjoying plenty, all creatures of that kind share it. No man, I think, ever saw a herd of buffalo, of which a few were fat and the great majority lean. No man ever saw a flock of birds, of which two or three were swimming in grease and the others all skin and bone. Nor in savage life is there anything like the poverty that festers in our civilisation.

In a rude state of society there are seasons of want, seasons when people starve; but they are seasons when the earth has refused to yield her increase, when the rain has not fallen from the heavens, or when the land has been swept by some foe—not when there is plenty. And yet the peculiar characteristic of this modern poverty of ours is that it is deepest where wealth most abounds.

Why, to-day, while over the civilised world there is so much distress, so much want, what is the cry that goes up? What is the current explanation of the hard times? Over-production! There are so many clothes that men must go ragged, so much coal that in the bitter winters people have to shiver, such over-filled granaries that people actually die by starvation! Want due to over-production! Was a greater absurdity ever uttered? How can there be over-production till all have enough? It is not over-production; it is unjust distribution.

Poverty necessary! Why, think of the enormous powers that are latent in the human brain! Think how invention enables us to do with the power of one man what not long ago could not be done by the power of a thousand. Think that in England alone the steam machinery in operation is said to exert a productive force greater than the physical force of the population of the world, were they all adults. And yet we have only begun to invent and discover. We have not yet utilised all that has already been invented and discovered. And look at the powers of the earth. They have hardly been touched. In every direction as we look new resources seem to open. Man's ability to produce wealth seems almost infinite—we can set no bounds to it. Look at the power that is flowing by your city in the current of the Mississippi that might be set at work for you. So in every direction energy that we might utilise goes to waste; resources that we might draw upon are untouched. Yet men are delving and straining to satisfy mere animal wants; women are working, working, working their lives away, and too frequently turning in despair from that hard struggle to cast away all that makes the charm of woman.

If the animals can reason what must they think of us? Look at one of those great ocean steamers ploughing her way across the Atlantic, against wind, against wave, absolutely setting at defiance the utmost power of the elements. If the gulls that hover over her were thinking beings could they imagine that the animal that could create such a structure as that could actually want for enough to eat? Yet, so it is. How many even of those of us who find life easiest are there who really live a rational life? Think of it, you who believe that there is only one life for man—what a fool at the very best is a man to pass his life in this struggle to merely live? And you who believe, as I believe, that this is not the last of man, that this is a life that opens but another life, think how nine tenths, aye, I do not know but ninety-nine-hundredths of all our vital powers are spent in a mere effort to get a living; or to heap together that which we cannot by any possibility take away. Take the life of the average workingman. Is that the life for which the human brain was intended and the human heart was made? Look at the factories scattered through our country. They are little better than penitentiaries.

I read in the New York papers a while ago that the girls at the Yonkers factories had struck. The papers said that the girls did not seem to know why they had struck, and intimated that it must be just for the fun of striking. Then came out the girls' side of the story and it appeared that they had struck against the rules in force. They were fined if they spoke to one another, and they were fined still more heavily if they laughed. There was a heavy fine for being a minute late. I visited a lady in Philadelphia who had been a forewoman in various factories, and I asked her, "Is it possible that such rules are enforced?" She said it was so in Philadelphia. There is a fine for speaking to your next neighbor, a fine for laughing; and she told me that the girls in one place where she was employed were fined ten cents a minute for being late, though many of them had to come for miles in winter storms. She told me of one poor girl who really worked hard one week and made $3.50; but the fines against her were $5.25. That seems ridiculous; it is ridiculous, but it is pathetic and it is shameful.

But take the cases of those even who are comparatively independent and well off. Here is a man working hour after hour, day after day, week after week, in doing one thing over and over again, and for what? Just to live. He is working ten hours a day in order that he may sleep eight and may have two or three hours for himself when he is tired out and all his faculties are exhausted. That is not a reasonable life; that is not a life for a being possessed of the powers that are in man, and I think every man must have felt it for himself. I know that when I first went to my trade I thought to myself that it was incredible that a man was created to work all day long just to live. I used to read the "Scientific American," and as invention after invention was heralded in that paper I used to think to myself that when I became a man it would not be necessary to work so hard. But on the contrary, the struggle for existence has become more and more intense. People who want to prove the contrary get up masses of statistics to show that the condition of the working classes is improving. Improvement that you have to take a statistical microscope to discover does not amount to anything. But there is not improvement.

Improvement! Why according to the last report of the Michigan Bureau of Labour Statistics, as I read yesterday in a Detroit paper, taking all the trades, including some of the very high priced ones, where the wages are from $6 to $7 a day, the average earnings amount to $1.77, and, taking out waste time, to $1.40. Now, when you consider how a man can live and bring up a family on $1.40 a day, even in Michigan, I do not think you will conclude that the condition of the working classes can have very much improved.

Here is a broad general fact that is asserted by all who have investigated the question, by such men as Hallam, the historian, and Professor Thorold Rogers, who has made a study of the history of prices as they were five centuries ago. When all the productive arts were in the most primitive state, when the most prolific of our modern vegetables had not been introduced, when the breeds of cattle were small and poor, when there were hardly any roads and transportation was exceedingly difficult, when all manufacturing was done by hand—in that rude time the condition of the labourers of England was far better than it is to-day. In those rude times no man need fear want save when actual famine came, and owing to the difficulties of transportation the plenty of one district could not relieve the scarcity of another. Save in such times, no man need fear want. Pauperism, such as exists in modern times, was absolutely unknown. Everyone, save the physically disabled, could make a living, and the poorest lived in rude plenty. But perhaps the most astonishing fact brought to light by this investigation is that at that time, under those conditions in those "dark ages," as we call them, the working day was only eight hours. While with all our modern inventions and improvements, our working classes have been agitating and struggling in vain to get the working day reduced to eight hours.

Do these facts show improvement? Why, in the rudest state of society in the most primitive state of the arts the labour of the natural bread-winner will suffice to provide a living for himself and for those who are dependent upon him. Amid all our inventions there are large bodies of men who cannot do this. What is the most astonishing thing in our civilisation? Why, the most astonishing thing to those Sioux chiefs who were recently brought from the Far West and taken through our manufacturing cities in the East, was not the marvelous inventions that enabled machinery to act almost as if it had intellect; it was not the growth of our cities; it was not the speed with which the railway car whirled along; it was not the telegraph or the telephone that most astonished them; but the fact that amid this marvelous development of productive power they found little children at work. And astonishing that ought to be to us; a most astounding thing!

Talk about improvement in the condition of the working classes, when the facts are that a larger and larger proportion of women and children are forced to toil. Why, I am told that, even here in your own city, there are children of thirteen and fourteen working in factories. In Detroit, according to the report of the Michigan Bureau of Labour Statistics, one half of the children of school age do not go to school. In New Jersey, the report made to the legislature discloses an amount of misery and ignorance that is appalling. Children are growing up there, compelled to monotonous toil when they ought to be at play, children who do not know how to play; children who have been so long accustomed to work that they have become used to it; children growing up in such ignorance that they do not know what country New Jersey is in, that they never heard of George Washington, that some of them think Europe is in New York. Such facts are appalling; they mean that the very foundations of the Republic are being sapped. The dangerous man is not the man who tries to excite discontent; the dangerous man is the man who says that all is as it ought to be. Such a state of things cannot continue; such tendencies as we see at work here cannot go on without bringing at last an overwhelming crash.

I say that all this poverty and the ignorance that flows from it is unnecessary; I say that there is no natural reason why we should not all be rich, in the sense, not of having more than each other, but in the sense of all having enough to completely satisfy all physical wants; of all having enough to get such an easy living that we could develop the better part of humanity. There is no reason why wealth should not be so abundant, that no one should think of such a thing as little children at work, or a woman compelled to a toil that nature never intended her to perform; wealth so abundant that there would be no cause for that harassing fear that sometimes paralyses even those who are not considered "the poor," the fear that every man of us has probably felt, that if sickness should smite him, or if he should be taken away, those whom he loves better than his life would become charges upon charity. "Consider the lilies of the field, how they grow; they toil not, neither do they spin." I believe that in a really Christian community, in a society that honoured not with the lips but with the act, the doctrines of Jesus, no one would have occasion to worry about physical needs any more than do the lilies of the field. There is enough and to spare. The trouble is that, in this made struggle, we trample in the mire what has been provided in sufficiency for us all; trample it in the mire while we tear and rend each other.

There is a cause for this poverty; and, if you trace it down, you will find its root in a primary injustice. Look over the world to-day—poverty everywhere. The cause must be a common one. You cannot attribute it to the tariff, or to the form of government, or to this thing or to that in which nations differ; because, as deep poverty is common to them all the cause that produces it must be a common cause. What is that common cause? There is one sufficient cause that is common to all nations; and that is the appropriation as the property of some of that natural element on which and from which all must live.

Take that fact I have spoken of, that appalling fact that, even now, it is harder to live than it was in the ages dark and rude five centuries ago—how do you explain it? There is no difficulty in finding the cause. Whoever reads the history of England, or the history of any other civilised nation (but I speak of the history of England because that is the history with which we are best acquainted) will see the reason. For century after century a parliament composed of aristocrats and employers passed laws endeavouring to reduce wages, but in vain. Men could not be crowded down to wages that gave a mere living because the bounty of nature was not wholly shut up from them; because some remains of the recognition of the truth that all men have equal rights on the earth still existed; because the land of that country, that which was held in private possession, was only held on a tenure derived from the nation, and for a rent payable back to the nation. The church lands supported the expenses of public worship, of the maintenance of seminaries and the care of the poor; the crown lands defrayed the expenses of the civil list; and from a third portion of the lands, those held under the military tenures, the army was provided for. There was no national debt in England at that time. They carried on wars for hundreds of years, but at the charge of the landowners. And more important still, there remained everywhere, and you can see in every old English town their traces to this day, the common lands to which any of the neighborhood was free. It was as those lands were inclosed; it was as the commons were gradually monopolised, as the church lands were made the prey of greedy courtiers, as the crown lands were given away as absolute property to the favourites of the king, as the military tenants shirked their rents and laid the expenses they had agree to defray, upon the nation, in taxation that bore upon industry and upon thrift—it was then that poverty began to deepen, and the tramp appeared in England; just as to-day he is appearing in our new States.

Now, think of it—is not land monopolisation a sufficient reason for poverty? What is man? In the first place, he is an animal, a land animal who cannot live without land. All that man produces comes from land; all productive labour, in the final analysis, consists in working up land; or materials drawn from land, into such forms as fit them for the satisfaction of human wants and desires. Why, man's very body is drawn from the land. Children of the soil, we come from the land, and to the land we must return. Take away from man all that belongs to the land, and what have you but a disembodied spirit? Therefore he who holds the land on which and from which another man must live, is that man's master; and the man is his slave. The man who holds the land on which I must live can command me to life or to death just as absolutely as though I were his chattel. Talk about abolishing slavery—we have not abolished slavery; we have only abolished one rude form of it, chattel slavery. There is a deeper and a more insidious form, a more cursed form yet before us to abolish, in this industrial slavery that makes a man a virtual slave, while taunting him and mocking him with the name of freedom. Poverty! want! they will sting as much as the lash. Slavery! God knows there are horrors enough in slavery; but there are deeper horrors in our civilised society to-day. Bad as chattel slavery was, it did not drive slave mothers to kill their children, yet you may read in official reports that the system of child insurance which has taken root so strongly in England, and which is now spreading over our Eastern States, has perceptibly and largely increased the rate of child mortality!—What does that mean?

Robinson Crusoe, as you know, when he rescued Friday from the cannibals, made him his slave. Friday had to serve Crusoe. But, supposing Crusoe had said, "O man and brother, I am very glad to see you, and I welcome you to this island, and you shall be a free and independent citizen, with just as much to say as I have—except that this island is mine, and of course, as I can do as I please with my own property, you must not use it save upon my terms" Friday would have been just as much Crusoe's slave as though he had called him one. Friday was not a fish, he could not swim off through the sea; he was not a bird, and could not fly off through the air; if he lived at all, he had to live on that island. And if that island was Crusoe's, Crusoe was his master through life to death.

A friend of mine, who believes as I do upon this question, was talking a while ago with another friend of mine who is a greenbacker, but who had not paid much attention to the land question. Our greenback friend said, "Yes, yes, the land question is a very important question; oh, I admit the land question is an important question; but then there are other important questions. There is this question and that question, and the other question; and there is the money question. The money question is a very important question; it is a more important question than the land question. You give me all the money, and you can take all the land." My friend said, "Well, suppose you had all the money in the world and I had all the land in the world. What would you do if I were to give you notice to quit?"

Do you know that I do not think that the average man realises what land is? I know a little girl who has been going to school for some time, studying geography, and all that sort of thing; and one day she said to me: "Here is something about the surface of the earth. I wonder what the surface of the earth looks like?" "Well," I said, "look out into the yard there. That is the surface of the earth." She said, "That the surface of the earth? Our yard the surface of the earth? Why, I never thought of it!" That is very much the case not only with grown men, but with such wise beings as newspaper editors. They seem to think, when you talk of land, that you always refer to farms; to think that the land question is a question that relates entirely to farmers, as though land had no other use than growing crops. Now, I should like to know how a man could even edit a newspaper without having the use of some land. He might swing himself by straps and go up in a balloon, but he could not even then get along without land. What supports the balloon in the air? Land; the surface of the earth. Let the earth drop, and what would become of the balloon? The air that supports the balloon is supported in turn by land. So it is with everything else men can do. Whether a man is working away three thousand feet under the surface of the earth, or whether he is working up in the top of one of those immense buildings that they have in New York; whether he is ploughing the soil or sailing across the ocean, he is still using land.

Land! Why, in owning a piece of ground, what do you own? The lawyers will tell you that you own from the centre of the earth right up to heaven; and, so far as all human purposes go, you do. In New York they are building houses thirteen and fourteen stories high. What are men, living in those upper stories, paying for? There is a friend of mine who has an office in one of them, and he estimates that he pays by the cubic foot for air. Well, the man who owns the surface of the land has the renting of the air up there, and would have if the buildings were carried up for miles.

This land question is the bottom question. Man is a land animal. Suppose you want to build a house; can you build it without a place to put it? What is it built of? Stone, or mortar, or wood, or iron—they all come from the earth. Think of any article of wealth you choose, any of those things which men struggle for, where do they come from? From the land. It is the bottom question. The land question is simply the labour question; and when some men own that element from which all wealth must be drawn, and upon which all must live, then they have the power of living without work, and, therefore, those who do work get less of the products of work.

Did you ever think of the utter absurdity and strangeness of the fact that, all over the civilised world, the working classes are the poor classes? Go into any city in the world, and get into a cab and ask the man to drive you where the working people live. He won't take you to where the fine houses are. He will take you, on the contrary, into the squalid quarters, the poorer quarters. Did you ever think how curious that is? Think for a moment how it would strike a rational being who had never been on the earth before, if such an intelligence could come down, and you were to explain to him how we live on earth, how houses and food and clothing, and all the many things we need were all produced by work, would he not think that the working people would be the people who lived in the finest houses and had most of everything that work produces? Yet, whether you took him to London or Paris or New York, or even to Burlington, he would find that those called the working people were the people who live in the poorest houses.

All this is strange—just think of it. We naturally despise poverty; and it is reasonable that we should. I do not say—I distinctly repudiate it—that the people who are poor are poor always from their own fault, or even in most cases; but it ought to be so. If any good man or woman could create a world, it would be a sort of a world in which no one would be poor unless he was lazy or vicious. But that is just precisely the kind of a world this is; that is just precisely the kind of a world the Creator has made. Nature gives to labour, and to labour alone; there must be human work before any article of wealth can be produced; and in the natural state of things the man who toiled honestly and well would be the rich man, and he who did not work would be poor. We have so reversed the order of nature that we are accustomed to think of the workingman as a poor man.

And if you trace it out I believe you will see that the primary cause of this is that we compel those who work to pay others for permission to do so. You may buy a coat, a horse, a house; there you are paying the seller for labour exerted, for something that he has produced, or that he has got from the man who did produce it; but when you pay a man for land, what are you paying him for? You are paying for something that no man has produced; you pay him for something that was here before man was, or for a value that was created, not by him individually, but by the community of which you are a part. What is the reason that the land here, where we stand to-night, is worth more than it was twenty-five years ago? What is the reason that land in the centre of New York, that once could be bought by the mile for a jug of whiskey, is now worth so much that, though you were to cover it with gold, you would not have its value? Is it not because of the increase of population? Take away that population, and where would the value of the land be? Look at it in any way you please.

We talk about over-production. How can there be such a thing as over-production while people want? All these things that are said to be over-produced are desired by many people. Why do they not get them? They do not get them because they have not the means to buy them; not that they do not want them. Why have not they the means to buy them? They earn too little. When the great masses of men have to work for an average of $1.40 a day, it is no wonder that great quantities of goods cannot be sold.

Now why is it that men have to work for such low wages? Because if they were to demand higher wages there are plenty of unemployed men ready to step into their places. It is this mass of unemployed men who compel that fierce competition that drives wages down to the point of bare subsistence. Why is it that there are men who cannot get employment? Did you ever think what a strange thing it is that men cannot find employment? Adam had no difficulty in finding employment; neither had Robinson Crusoe; the finding of employment was the last thing that troubled them.

If men cannot find an employer, why cannot they employ themselves? Simply because they are shut out from the element on which human labour can alone be exerted. Men are compelled to compete with each other for the wages of an employer, because they have been robbed of the natural opportunities of employing themselves; because they cannot find a piece of God's world on which to work without paying some other human creature for the privilege.

I do not mean to say that even after you had set right this fundamental injustice, there would not be many things to do; but this I do mean to say, that our treatment of land lies at the bottom of all social questions. This I do mean to say, that, do what you please, reform as you may, you never can get rid of wide-spread poverty so long as the element on which and from which all men must live is made the private property of some men. It is utterly impossible. Reform government—get taxes down to the minimum—build railroads, institute co-operative stores; divide profits, if you choose, between employers and employed—and what will be the result? The result will be that the land will increase in value—that will be the result—that and nothing else. Experience shows this. Do not all improvements simply increase the value of land—the price that some must pay others for the privilege of living?

Consider the matter, I say it with all reverence, and I merely say it because I wish to impress a truth upon your minds—it is utterly impossible, so long as His laws are what they are, that God himself could relieve poverty—utterly impossible. Think of it and you will see. Men pray to the Almighty to relieve poverty. But poverty comes not from God's laws—it is blasphemy of the worst kind to say that; it comes from man's injustice to his fellows. Supposing the Almighty were to hear the prayer, how could He carry out the request so long as His laws are what they are? Consider—the Almighty gives us nothing of the things that constitute wealth; He merely gives us the raw material, which must be utilised by man to produce wealth. Does He not give us enough of that now? How could He relieve poverty even if He were to give us more? Supposing in answer to these prayers He were to increase the power of the sun; or the virtue of the soil? Supposing He were to make plants more prolific, or animals to produce after their kind more abundantly? Who would get the benefit of it? Take a country where land is completely monopolized, as it is in most of the civilised countries—who would get the benefit of it? Simply the landowners. And even if God in answer to prayer were to send down out of the heavens those things that men require, who would get the benefit?

In the Old Testament we are told that when the Israelites journeyed through the desert, they were hungered, and that God sent manna down out of the heavens. There was enough for all of them, and they all took it and were relieved. But supposing that desert had been held as private property, as the soil of Great Britain is held, as the soil even of our new States is being held; suppose that one of the Israelites had a square mile, and another one had twenty square miles, and another one had a hundred square miles, and the great majority of the Israelites did not have enough to set the soles of their feet upon, which they could call their own—what would become of the manna? What good would it have done to the majority? Not a whit. Though God had sent down manna enough for all, that manna would have been the property of the landholders; they would have employed some of the others perhaps, to gather it up into heaps for them, and would have sold it to their hungry brethren. Consider it; this purchase and sale of manna might have gone on until the majority of Israelites had given all they had, even to the clothes off their backs. What then? Then they would not have had anything left to buy manna with, and the consequences would have been that while they went hungry, the manna would have lain in great heaps, and the landowners would have been complaining of the over-production of manna. There would have been a great harvest of manna and hungry people, just precisely the phenomenon that we see to-day.

I cannot go over all the points I would like to try, but I wish to call your attention to the utter absurdity of private property in land! Why, consider it, the idea of a man's selling the earth—the earth, our common mother. A man selling that which no man produced—a man passing title from one generation to another. Why, it is the most absurd thing in the world. Why, did you ever think of it? What right has a dead man to land? For whom was this earth created? It was created for the living, certainly, not for the dead. Well, now we treat it as though it was created for the dead. Where do our land titles come from? They come from men who for the most part are past and gone. Here in this new country you get a little nearer to original source; but go to the Eastern States and go back over the Atlantic. There you may clearly see the power that comes from landownership.

As I say, the man that owns the land is the master of those who must live on it. Here is a modern instance: you who are familiar with the history of the Scottish Church know that in the forties there was a disruption in the church. You who have read Hugh Miller's work on "The Cruise of the *Betsey*" know something about it; how a great body, led by Dr. Chalmers, came out from the Established Church and said they would set up a Free Church. In the Established Church were a great many of the landowners. Some of them, like the Duke of Buccleugh, owning miles and miles of land on which no common Scotsman had a right to put his foot, save by the Duke of Buccleugh's permission. These landowners refused not only to allow these Free Churchmen to have ground upon which to erect a church, but they would not let them stand on their land and worship God. You who have read "The Cruise of the *Betsey*" know that it is the story of a clergyman who was obliged to make his home in a boat on that wild sea because he was not allowed to have land enough to live on. In many places the people had to take the sacrament with the tide coming to their knees—many a man lost his life worshipping on the roads in rain and snow. They were not permitted to go on Mr. Landlord's land and worship God, and had to take to the roads. The Duke of Buccleugh stood out for seven years compelling people to worship in the roads, until finally relenting a little, he allowed them to worship God in a gravel pit; whereupon they passed a resolution of thanks to His Grace.

But that is not what I wanted to tell you. The thing that struck me was this significant fact: As soon as the disruption occurred, the Free Church, composed of a great many able men, at once sent a delegation to the landlords to ask permission for Scotsmen to worship God in Scotland in their own way. This delegation set out for London—they had to go to London, England, to get permission for Scotsmen to worship God in Scotland, and in their own native home!

But that is not the most absurd thing. In one place where they were refused land upon which to stand and worship God, the late landowner had died and his estate was in the hands of the trustees, and the answer of the trustees was, that so far as they were concerned they would exceedingly like to allow them to have a place to put up a church to worship God, but they could not conscientiously do it because they knew that such a course would be very displeasing to the late Mr. Monaltie! Now this dead man had gone to heaven, let us hope; at any rate he had gone away from this world, but lest it might displease him men yet living could not worship God. Is it possible for absurdity to go any further?

You may say that those Scotch people are very absurd people, but they are not a whit more so than we are. I read only a little while ago of some Long Island fishermen who had been paying as rent for the privilege of fishing there, a certain part of the catch. They paid it because they believed that James II., a dead man centuries ago, a man who never put his foot in America, a king who was kicked off the English throne, had said they had to pay it, and they got up a committee, went to the county town and searched the records. They could not find anything in the records to show that James II. had ever ordered that they should give any of their fish to anybody, and so they refused to pay any longer. But if they had found that James II. had really said they should they would have gone on paying. Can anything be more absurd?

There is a square in New York—Stuyvesant Square—that is locked up at six o'clock every evening, even on the long summer evenings. Why is it locked up? Why are the children not allowed to play there? Why because old Mr. Stuyvesant, dead and gone I don't know how many years ago, so willed it. Now can anything be more absurd?

Yet that is not any more absurd than our land titles. From whom do they come? Dead man after dead man. Suppose you get on the cars here going to Council Bluffs or Chicago. You find a passenger with his baggage strewn over the seats. You say: "Will you give me a seat, if you please, sir?"

He replies: "No; I bought this seat." "Bought this seat? From whom did you buy it?" "I bought it from the man who got out at the last station." That is the way we manage this earth of ours.

Is it not a self-evident truth, as Thomas Jefferson said, that "the land belongs in usufruct to the living," and that they who have died have left it, and have no power to say how it shall be disposed of? Title to land! Where can a man get any title which makes the earth his property? There is a sacred right to property—sacred because ordained by the laws of nature, that is to say, by the laws of God, and necessary to social order and civilisation. That is the right of property in things produced by labour; it rests on the right of a man to himself. That which a man produces, that is his against all the world, to give or to keep, to lend, to sell or to bequeath; but how can he get such a right to land when it was here before he came? Individual claims to land rest only on appropriation. I read in a recent number of the "Nineteenth Century," possibly some of you may have read it, an article by an ex-prime minister of Australia in which there was a little story that attracted my attention. It was of a man named Galahard, who in the early days got up to the top of a high hill in one of the finest parts of western Australia. He got up there, looked all around, and made this proclamation: "All the land that is in my sight from the top of this hill I claim for myself; and all the land that is out of sight I claim for my son John."

That story is of universal application. Land titles everywhere come from just such appropriations. Now, under certain circumstances, appropriation can give a right. You invite a company of gentlemen to dinner and you say to them: "Be seated gentlemen," and I get into this chair. Well, that seat for the time being is mine by the right of appropriation. It would be very ungentlemanly, it would be very wrong for any one of the other guests to come up and say: "Get out of that chair; I want to sit there!" But that right of possession, which is good so far as the chair is concerned, for the time, does not give me a right to appropriate all there is on the table before me. Grant that a man has a right to appropriate such natural elements as he can use, has he any right to appropriate more than he can use? Has a guest in such a case as I have supposed a right to appropriate more than he needs and make other people stand up? That is what is done.

Why, look all over this country—look at this town or any other town. If men only took what they wanted to use we should all have enough; but they take what they do not want to use at all. Here are a lot of Englishmen coming over here and getting titles to our land in vast tracts; what do they want with our land? They do not want it at all; it is not the land they want; they have no use for American land. What they want is the income that they know they can in a little while get from it. Where does that income come from? It comes from labour, from the labour of American citizens. What we are selling to these people is our children, not land.

Poverty! Can there be any doubt of its cause? Go into the old countries—go into western Ireland, into the highlands of Scotland—these are purely primitive communities. There you will find people as poor as poor can be—living year after year on oatmeal or on potatoes, and often going hungry. I could tell you many a pathetic story. Speaking to a Scottish physician who was telling me how this diet was inducing among these people a disease similar to that which from the same cause is ravaging Italy (the Pellagra), I said to him: "There is plenty of fish; why don't they catch fish?

There is plenty of game; I know the laws are against it, but cannot they take it on the sly?" "That," he said, "never enters their heads. Why, if a man was even suspected of having a taste for trout or grouse he would have to leave at once." There is no difficulty in discovering what makes those people poor. They have no right to anything that nature gives them. All they can make above a living they must pay to the landlord. They not only have to pay for the land that they use, but they have to pay for the seaweed that comes ashore and for the turf they dig from the bogs. They dare not improve, for any improvements they make are an excuse for putting up the rent. These people who work hard live in hovels, and the landlords, who do not work at all—oh! they live in luxury in London or Paris. If they have hunting boxes there, why they are magnificent castles as compared with the hovels in which the men live who do the work. Is there any question as to the cause of poverty there?

Now go into the cities and what do you see! Why, you see even a lower depth of poverty; aye, if I would point out the worst of the evils of land monopoly I would not take you to Connemara; I would not take you to Skye or Kintire—I would take you to Dublin or Glasgow or London. There is something worse than physical deprivation, something worse than starvation; and that is the degradation of the mind, the death of the soul. That is what you will find in those cities.

Now, what is the cause of that? Why, it is plainly to be seen; the people driven off the land in the country are driven into the slums of the cities. For every man that is driven off the land the demand for the produce of the workmen of the cities is lessened; and the man himself with his wife and children, is forced among those workmen to compete upon any terms for a bare living and force wages down. Get work he must or starve—get work he must or do that which these people, so long as they maintain their manly feelings, dread more than death, go to the alms-houses. That is the reason, here as in Great Britain, that the cities are overcrowded. Open the land that is locked up, that is held by dogs in the manger, who will not use it themselves and will not allow anybody else to use it, and you would see no more of tramps and hear no more of over-production.

The utter absurdity of this thing of private property in land! I defy any one to show me any good from it, look where you please. Go out in the new lands, where my attention was first called to it, or go to the heart of the capital of the world—London. Everywhere, when your eyes are once opened, you will see its inequality and you will see its absurdity. You do not have to go farther than Burlington. You have here a most beautiful site for a city, but the city itself as compared to what it might be is a miserable, straggling town. A gentleman showed me to-day a big hole alongside one of your streets. The place has been filled up all around it and this hole is left. It is neither pretty nor useful. Why does that hole stay there? Well, it stays there because somebody claims it as his private property. There is a man, this gentleman told me, who wished to grade another lot and wanted somewhere to put the dirt he took off it, and he offered to buy this hole so that he might fill it up. Now it would have been a good thing for Burlington to have it filled up, a good thing for you all—your town would look better, and you yourself would be in no danger of tumbling into it some dark night. Why, my friend pointed out to me another similar hole in which water had collected and told me that two children had been drowned there. And he likewise told me that a drunken man some years ago had fallen into such a hole and had brought suit against the city which cost you taxpayers some $11,000. Clearly it is to the interest of you all to have that particular hole I am talking of filled up. The man who wanted to fill it up offered the hole owner $300. But the hole owner refused the offer and declared that he would hold out until he could get $1000; and in the meanwhile that unsightly and dangerous hole must remain. This is but an illustration of private property in land.

You may see the same thing all over this country. See how injuriously in the agricultural districts this thing of private property in land affects the roads and the distances between people. A man does not take what land he wants, what he can use, but he takes all he can get, and the consequence is that his next neighbour has to go further along, people are separated from each other further than they ought to be, to the increased difficulty of production, to the loss of neighbourhood and companionship. They have more roads to maintain than they can decently maintain; they must do more work to get the same result, and life is in every way harder and drearier.

When you come to the cities it is just the other way. In the country the people are too much scattered; in the great cities they are too crowded. Go to a city like New York and there they are jammed together like sardines in a box, living family upon family, one above the other. It is an unnatural and unwholesome life. How can you have anything like a home in a tenement room, or two or three rooms? How can children be brought up healthily with no place to play? Two or three weeks ago I read of a New York judge who fined two little boys five dollars for playing hopscotch in the street—where else could they play? Private property in land had robbed them of all place to play. Even a temperance man, who had investigated the subject, said that in his opinion the gin palaces of London were a positive good in this, that they enabled the people whose abodes were dark and squalid rooms to see a little brightness and thus prevent them from going wholly mad.

What is the reason for this overcrowding of cities? There is no natural reason. Take New York, one half its area is not built upon. Why, then, must people crowd together as they do there? Simply because of private ownership of land. There is plenty of room to build houses and plenty of people who want to build houses, but before anybody can build a house a blackmail price must be paid to some dog in the manger. It costs in many cases more to get vacant ground upon which to build a house than it does to build the house. And then what happens to the man who pays this blackmail and builds a house? Down comes the tax-gatherer and fines him for building the house.

It is so all over the United States—the men who improve, the men who turn the prairie into farms and the desert into gardens, the men who beautify your cities, are taxed and fined for having done these things. Now, nothing is clearer than that the people of New York want more houses; and I think that even here in Burlington you could get along with more houses. Why, then, should you fine a man who builds one? Look all over this country—the bulk of the taxation rests upon the improver; the man who puts up a building, or establishes a factory, or cultivates a farm, he is taxed for it; and not merely taxed for it, but I think in nine cases out of ten the land which he uses, the bare land, is taxed more than the adjoining lot or the adjoining 160 acres that some speculator is holding as a mere dog in the manger, not using it himself and not allowing anybody else to use it.

I am talking too long; but let me in a

few words point out the way of getting rid of land monopoly, securing the right of all to the elements which are necessary for life. We could not divide the land. In a rude state of society, as among the ancient Hebrews, giving each family its lot and making it inalienable we might secure something like equality. But in a complex civilization that will not suffice. It is not, however, necessary to divide up the land. All that is necessary is to divide up the income that comes from the land. In that way we can secure absolute equality; nor could the adoption of this principle involve any rude shock or violent change. It can be brought about gradually and easily by abolishing taxes that now rest upon capital, labour and improvements, and raising all our public revenues by the taxation of land values; and the longer you think of it the clearer you will see that in every possible way will it be a benefit.

Now, supposing we should abolish all other taxes direct and indirect, substituting for them a tax upon land values, what would be the effect? In the first place it would be to kill speculative values. It would be to remove from the newer parts of the country the bulk of the taxation and put it on the richer parts. It would be to exempt the pioneer from taxation and make the larger cities pay more of it. It would be to relieve energy and enterprise, capital and labour, from all those burdens that now bear upon them. What a start that would give to production! In the second place we could, from the value of the land, not merely pay all the present expenses of the government, but we could do infinitely more. In the city of San Francisco James Lick left a few blocks of ground to be used for public purposes there, and the rent amounts to so much, that out of it will be built the largest telescope in the world, large public baths and other public buildings, and various costly works. If, instead of these few blocks, the whole value of the land upon which the city is built had accrued to San Francisco what could she not do?

So in this little town, where land values are very low as compared with such cities as Chicago and San Francisco, you could do many things for mutual benefit and public improvement did you appropriate to public purposes the land values that now go to individuals. You could have a great free library; you could have an art gallery; you could get yourselves a public park, a magnificent public park, too. You have here one of the finest natural sites for a beautiful town I know of, and I have travelled much. You might make on this site a city that it would be a pleasure to live in. You will not as you go now—oh, no! Why, the very fact that you have a magnificent view here will cause somebody to hold on all the more tightly to the land that commands this view and charge higher prices for it. The State of New York wants to buy a strip of land so as to enable the people to see Niagara, but what a price she must pay for it? Look at all the great cities; in Philadelphia, for instance, in order to build their great city hall they had to block up the only two wide streets they had in the city. Everywhere you go you may see how private property in land prevents public as well as private improvement.

But I have not time to enter into further details. I can only ask you to think upon this thing, and the more you will see its desirability. As an English friend of mine puts it: "No taxes and a pension for everybody," and why should it not be? To take land values for public purposes is not really to impose a tax, but to take for public purposes a value created by the community. And out of the fund which would thus accrue from the common property, we might, without degradation to anybody, provide enough to actually secure from want all who were deprived of their natural protectors or met with accident, or any man who should grow so old that he could not work. All prating that is heard from some quarters about its hurting the common people to give them what they do not work for is humbug. The truth is, that anything that injures self-respect, degrades, does harm; but if you give it as a right, as something to which every citizen is entitled to, it does not degrade. Charity schools do degrade children that are sent to them, but public schools do not.

But all such benefits as these, while great, would be incidental. The great thing would be that the reform I propose would tend to open opportunities to labour and enable men to provide employment for themselves. That is the great advantage. We should gain the enormous productive power that is going to waste all over the country, the power of idle hands that would gladly be at work. And that removed, then you would see wages begin to mount. It is not that everyone would turn farmer, or everyone would build himself a house if he had an opportunity for doing so, but so many could and would, as to relieve the pressure on the labour market and provide employment for all others. And as wages mounted to the higher levels, then you would see the productive power increased. The country where wages are high is the country of greatest productive powers. Where wages are highest, there will invention be most active; there will labour be most intelligent; there will be the greatest yield for the expenditure of exertion. The more you think of it the more clearly you will see that what I say is true. I cannot hope to convince you in an hour or two, but I shall be content if I shall put you upon inquiry. Think for yourselves; ask yourselves whether this wide-spread fact of poverty is not a crime, and a crime for which every one of us, man and woman, who does not do what he or she can do to call attention to it and do away with it, is responsible.

Russell Conwell

Acres of Diamonds (1870's–1924)

America at the end of the nineteenth century was fast growing into a major industrial power. The growing wealth of the business and commercial community was accomplished at the same time that the labor movement began its long struggle for recognition and power. Ideas and interests were in conflict as the Sherman Antitrust Act was passed to combat large industrial combinations, the Populist party sought to redress the grievances of the agricultural sections while joining in an alliance with labor, and the free silver men pitted themselves against the financial interests of the East. The writings of the English philosopher Herbert Spencer, particularly *Social Statics*, in which he argued strenuously against government interference in the commercial and social sphere, established the *laissez-faire* doctrine firmly in the minds of American businessmen, and his *Principles of Biology*, translating Darwinian concepts into the social sphere, offered a strong rationale for the "survival of the fittest."

In this bumptious period, poverty and exploitation were clearly in evidence while, at the same time, there were fortunes to be made and great wealth to be obtained. One of those whose rhetoric aimed at resolving the paradoxes and conflicts in American society was Russell Conwell, probably one of the most successful and popular public lecturers American has ever known.

Conwell served in the Union army during the Civil War and later became a newspaper correspondent and a lawyer. After a conversion experience he was ordained a Baptist minister in 1879 and became pastor of Grace Baptist Church in Philadelphia in 1881. He founded Temple University, largely to help those who could least afford it to get a university education. He was a notable preacher and accomplished Herculean feats in promoting the growth and development of his church. But it was as a popular lecturer that Conwell excelled.

Having traveled extensively, Conwell became a favorite lecturer of the famous Redpath agency with his interesting and entertaining travel lectures. But his "Acres of Diamonds" speech, given, incredibly, five or six thousand times over a long span of time, was his crowning rhetorical achievement.

In this speech Conwell demonstrated his exceptional skill as a storyteller, weaving together anecdotes that reinforce his message: America is a land of great opportunity, a "nation stepping upward more certainly toward all that is grand and beautiful and true." Such a land offers the chance for all who would take it to gather wealth; indeed, it is everyone's "duty to be rich." With wealth comes the power, also, to do good, to help "those in need," to reach "down to those below and lift them up." The message that it was good and right to be rich was of course comforting and encouraging to those who were able to become so—even if they forgot the injunction to do good with the power that money brought them—and of cold cheer to those who had no bootstraps by which to pull themselves up. As a statement of the limitless opportunities the country afforded and as a justification for accumulating wealth, it struck a chord in the late nineteenth and early twentieth centuries. As a popular expression of what Andrew Carnegie called the "Gospel of Wealth," Conwell's "Acres of Diamonds" was unsurpassed.

The title of this lecture originated away back in 1869. When going down the Tigris River, we hired a guide from Bagdad to show us down to the Arabian Gulf. That guide whom we employed resembled the barbers we find in America. That is, he resembled the barbers in certain mental characteristics. He thought it was not only his duty to guide us down the river, but also to entertain us with stories; curious and weird, ancient and modern, strange and familiar; many of them I have forgotten, and I am glad I have. But there was one which I recall tonight. The guide grew irritable over my lack of appreciation, and as he led my camel by the halter he introduced his story by saying: "This is a tale I reserve for my *particular friends*." So I then gave him my close attention. He told me that there once lived near the shore of the River Indus, toward which we were then traveling, an ancient Persian by the name of Al Hafed. He said that Al Hafed owned a large farm, with orchards, grain fields and gardens; that he had money at interest, had a beautiful wife and lovely children, and was a wealthy and contented man. Contented because he was wealthy, and wealthy because he was contented.

One day there visited this old Persian farmer one of those ancient Buddhist priests, one of the wise men of the East, who sat down by Al Hafed's fireside and told the old farmer how this world was made. He told him that this world was once a great bank of fog, and that the Almighty thrust His finger into this bank of fog, and began slowly to move his finger around, and then increased the speed of his finger until he whirled this bank of fog into a solid ball of fire; and as it went rolling through the universe, burning its way through other banks of fog, it condensed the moisture, until it fell in floods of rain upon the heated surface of the world, and cooled the outward crust; then the internal fires, bursting the cooling crust, threw up the mountains, and the hills, and the valleys of this wonderful world of ours.

"And" said the old priest, "if this internal melted mass burst forth and cooled very quickly it became granite, if it cooled more slowly, it became copper; if it cooled less quickly, silver; less quickly, gold; and after gold, diamonds were made." Said the old priest, "A diamond is a congealed drop of sunlight." That statement is literally true.

And the old priest said another very curious thing. He said that a diamond was the last and the highest of God's mineral creations, as a woman is the last and highest of God's animal creations. That is the reason, I suppose, why the two have such a liking for each other.

The old priest told Al Hafed if he had a diamond the size of his thumb, he could purchase a dozen farms like his. "And," said the priest, "if you had a handful of diamonds, you could purchase the county, and if you had a mine of diamonds you could purchase kingdoms, and place your children upon thrones, through the influence of your great wealth."

Al Hafed heard all about the diamonds that night, and went to bed a poor man. He wanted a whole mine of diamonds. Early in the morning he sought the priest and awoke him. Well, I know, by experience, that a priest is very cross when awakened early in the morning.

Al Hafed said: "Will you tell me where I can find diamonds?"

The priest said: "Diamonds? What do you want of diamonds?"

Said Al Hafed: "I want to be immensely rich."

"Well," said the priest, "if you want diamonds, all you have to do is to go and find them, and then you will have them."

"But," said Al Hafed, "I don't know where to go."

"If you will find a river that runs over white sands, between high mountains, in those white sands you will always find diamonds," answered the priest.

"But," asked Al Hafed, "do you believe there is such a river?"

"Plenty of them; all you have to do is just go where they are."

"Well," said Al Hafed, "I will go."

So he sold his farm; collected his money that was at interest; left his family in charge of a neighbor, and away he went in search of diamonds.

He began his search, very properly to my mind, at the Mountains of the Moon. Afterwards he came around into Palestine, and then wandered on into Europe. At last, when his money was all gone and he was in rags, poverty and wretchedness, he stood on the shore at Barcelona, in Spain, when a great tidal wave swept through the pillars of Hercules; and the poor, starving, afflicted stranger could not resist the awful temptation to cast himself into that incoming tide; and he sank beneath its foaming crest, never to rise in this life again.

When the old guide had told me that story, he stopped the camel I was riding upon and went back to arrange the baggage on another camel, and I had an opportunity to muse over his story. And I asked myself this question: "Why did this old guide reserve this story for his *particular friends*?" But when he came back and took up the camel's halter once more, I found that was the first story I ever heard wherein the hero was killed in the first chapter. For he went on into the second chapter, just as though there had been no break.

Said he: "The man who purchased Al Hafed's farm, led his camel out into the garden to drink, and as the animal put his nose into the shallow waters of the garden brook, Al Hafed's successor noticed a curious flash of light from the white sands of the stream. Reaching in he pulled out a black stone containing a strange eye of light. He took it into the house as a curious pebble and, putting it on the mantel that covered the central fire, went his way and forgot all about it.

"But not long after that that same old priest came to visit Al Hafed's successor. The moment he opened the door he noticed the flash of light. He rushed to the mantel and said:

"'Here is a diamond! Here is a diamond! Has Al Hafed returned?'

"'Oh no, Al Hafed has not returned and we have not heard from him since he went away, and that is not a diamond. It is nothing but a stone we found out in our garden.'

"'But,' said the priest, 'I know a diamond when I see it. I tell you that is a diamond.'

"Then together they rushed out into the garden. They stirred up the white sands with their fingers, and there came up other more beautiful, more valuable gems than the first.

"Thus," said the guide,—and friends, it is historically true,—"was discovered the diamond minds of Golconda, the most valuable diamond mines in the history of the ancient world."

Well, when the guide had added the second chapter to his story, he then took off his Turkish red cap, and swung it in the air to call my special attention to the moral; those Arab guides always have morals to their stores, though the stories are not always moral.

He said to me: "Had Al Hafed remained at home, and dug in his own cellar, or underneath his own wheat field, instead of wretchedness, starvation, poverty and death in a strange land, he would have had *acres of diamonds*."

Acres of diamonds! For every acre of that old farm, yes, every shovelful, afterwards revealed the gems which since have decorated the crowns of monarchs.

When the guide had added the moral to this story, I saw why he reserved it for his *particular friends*. But I didn't tell him that I could see it. It was that mean, old Arab's way of going around a thing, like a lawyer, and saying indirectly what he didn't dare say directly; that in his private opinion "there was a certain young man traveling down the Tigris River, who might better be at home, in America."

I told him his story reminded me of one. You all know it. I told him that a man in California, in 1847, owned a ranch there. He heard that they had discovered gold in Southern California, though they had not. And he sold his farm to Colonel Sutter, who put a mill on the little stream below the house. One day his little girl gathered some of the sand in her hands from the raceway, and brought it into the house. And while she was sifting it through her fingers, a visitor there noticed the first shining scales of real gold that were ever discovered in California. Acres and acres of gold. I was introduced, a few years ago, while in California, to the one-third owner of the farm, and he was then receiving one hundred and twenty dollars in gold for every fifteen minutes of his life, sleeping or waking. You and I would enjoy an income like that, now that we have no income tax.

Professor Agassiz, the great geologist

of Harvard University, that magnificent scholar, told us, at the Summer School of Mineralogy, that there once lived in Pennsylvania a man who owned a farm,—and he did with his farm just what I should do if I had a farm in Pennsylvania. He sold it. But, before he sold it, he decided to secure employment, collecting coal oil. He wrote to his cousin in Canada that he would like to go into that business. His cousin wrote back to him: "I cannot engage you, because you don't understand the oil business." "Then," said he, "I will understand it," and with commendable zeal, he set himself at the study of the whole theory of the coal-oil subject. He began away back at the second day of God's creation. He found that there was once another sun that shone on this world, and that then there were immense forests of vegetation. He found that the other sun was put out, and that this world after a time fell into the wake of the present sun. It was then locked in blocks of ice. Then there rose mighty icebergs that human imagination cannot grasp, and as those mountains of ice did ride those stormy seas, they beat down this original vegetation, they planed down the hills, toppled over the mountains, and everywhere buried this original vegetation which has since been turned by chemical action to the primitive beds of coal, and in connection with which only is found coal oil in paying quantities.

So he found out where oil originated. He studied it until he knew what it looked like, what it smelled like, how to refine it, and where to sell it.

"Now," said he to his cousin in a letter, "I know all about the oil business, from the second day of God's creation to the present time."

His cousin replied to him to "come on." So he sold his farm in Pennsylvania for $833—even money, no cents.

After he had gone from the farm, the farmer who had purchased his place, went out to arrange for watering the cattle; and he found that the previous owner had already arranged for that matter. There was a stream running down the hillside back of the barn; and across that stream from bank to bank, the previous owner had put in a plank edgewise at a slight angle, for the purpose of throwing over to one side of the brook a dreadful looking scum through which the cattle would not put their noses, although they would drink on this side below the plank. Thus that man, who had gone to Canada, and who had studied all about the oil business, had been himself damming back for twenty-three years a flood of coal oil, which the state geologist said in 1870 was worth to our state a hundred millions of dollars. A hundred millions! The city of Titusville stands bodily on that farm now. And yet, though he knew all about the theory, he sold the farm for $833—again I say "no *sense*."

I need another illustration. I find it in Massachusetts. The young man went down to Yale College and studied mines and mining, and became such an adept at mineralogy, that during his senior year in the Sheffield School, they paid him as a tutor fifteen dollars a week for the spare time in which he taught. When he graduated they raised his pay to forty-five dollars a week and offered him a professorship. As soon as they did that he went home to his mother! If they had raised his salary to fifteen dollars and sixty cents, then he would have stayed. But when they made it forty-five dollars a week he said: "I won't work for forty-five dollars a week! The idea of a man with a brain like mine, working for forty-five dollars a week! Let us go out to California and stake out gold and silver and copper claims, and be rich!"

Said his mother: "Now Charley, it is

just as well to be happy as it is to be rich."

"Yes," said he. "It is just as well to be rich and happy too."

They were both right about it. And as he was the only son, and she was a widow, of course he had his way. They always do. So they sold out in Massachusetts and went, not to California, but to Wisconsin, and there he entered the employ of the Superior Copper Mining Company, at fifteen dollars a week again. But with the proviso that he should have an interest in any mines he should discover for the company. I don't believe he ever discovered a mine there. Still I have often felt when I mentioned this fact in Northern Wisconsin, that he might be in the audience and feel mad at the way I speak about it. Still here is the fact, and it seems unfortunate to be in the way of a good illustration. But I don't believe he ever found any other mine. Yet I don't know anything about that end of the line. I know that he had scarcely gone for Massachusetts, before the farmer who had purchased his farm was bringing a large basket of potatoes in through the gateway. You know in Massachusetts our farms are almost entirely stone wall. Hence the basket hugged very close in the gate, and he dragged it on one side and then on the other. And as he was pulling that basket through the gateway, the farmer noticed in the upper and outer corner of that stone wall next to the gate, a block of native silver eight inches square. And this professor of mines and mining and mineralogy, who would not work for forty-five dollars a week, because he knew so much about the subject, when he sold that homestead, sat on that very stone to make the bargain. He was born on that very farm, and they told me that he had gone by that piece of silver and rubbed it with his sleeve, until it reflected his countenance and seemed to say to him, "Here, take me! Here is a hundred thousand dollars right down here in the rocks just for the taking." But he wouldn't take it. This was near Newburyport, Massachusetts. He wouldn't believe in silver at home. He said: "There is no silver in Newburyport. It is all away off,—well, I don't know where,"—and he didn't. But somewhere else. And he was a professor of mineralogy. I don't know of anything I would better enjoy in taking the whole time, than telling of the blunders like this which I have heard that "professors" have made.

I say that I would enjoy it. But after all there is another side of the question. For the more I think about it, the more I would like to know what he is doing in Wisconsin tonight. I don't believe he has found any mines, but I can tell you what I do believe is the case. I think he sits out there by his fireside tonight, and his friends are gathered around him and he is saying to them something like this:

"Do you know that man Conwell who lives in Philadelphia?"

"Oh, yes, I have heard of him."

"Well you know that man Jones who live in———"

"Yes, I have also heard of him," say they.

Then he begins to shake his sides with laughter, and he says:

"They have both done the same thing I did precisely!" And that spoils the whole joke.

Because you and I have done it. Yet nearly every person here will say: "Oh no, I never had any acres of diamonds or any gold mines or any silver mines."

But I say to you that you did have silver mines, and gold mines, and acres of diamonds, and you have them now.

Now let me speak with the greatest care lest my eccentricity of manner should mislead my listeners, and make you think I am here to entertain more than to help. I want to hold your attention on this oppressive night, with sufficient interest to leave my lesson with you.

You had an opportunity to be rich; and to some of you it has been a hardship to purchase a ticket for this lecture. Yet you have no right to be poor. It is all wrong. You have no right to be poor. It is your duty to be rich.

Oh, I know well that there are some things higher, sublimer than money! Ah, yes, there are some things sweeter, holier than gold! Yet I also know that there is not one of those things but is greatly enhanced by the use of money.

"Oh," you will say, "Mr. Conwell, can you, as a Christian teacher, tell the young people to spend their lives making money?"

Yes, I do. Three times I say, I do, I do, I do. You ought to make money. Money is power. Think how much good you could do if you had money now. Money is power and it ought to be in the hands of good men. It would be in the hands of good men if we comply with the Scripture teachings, where God promises prosperity to the righteous man. That means more than being goody-good—it means the all-around righteous man. You should be a righteous man, and if you were, you would be rich.

I need to guard myself right here. Because one of my theological students came to me once to labor with me, for heresy, inasmuch as I had said that money was power.

He said: "Mr. Conwell, I feel it my duty to tell you that the Scriptures say that money 'is the root of all evil.' "

I asked him: "Have you been spending your time making a new Bible when you should have been studying theology." He said: "That is in the old Bible."

I said "I would like to have you find it for me. I have never seen it."

He triumphantly brought a Bible, and with all the bigoted pride of a narrow sectarian, who founds his creed on some misinterpretation of Scripture, threw it down before me and said: "There it is! You can read it for yourself"!

I said to him: "Young man, you will learn before you get much older, that you can't trust another denomination to read the Bible for you. Please read it yourself, and remember that 'emphasis is exegesis.' "

So he read: "The *love* of money is the root of all evil."

Indeed it is. The *love* of money is the root of all evil. The love of the money, rather than the love of the good it secures, is a dangerous evil in the community. The desire to get hold of money, and to hold on to it, "hugging the dollar until the eagle squeals," is the root of all evil. But it is a grand ambition for men to have the desire to gain money, that they may use it for the benefit of their fellowmen.

Young man! you may never have the opportunity to charge at the head of your nation's troops on some Santiago's heights; young woman, you may never be called on to go out in the seas like Grace Darling to save suffering humanity. But every one of you can earn money honestly, and with that money you can fight the battles of peace; and the victories of peace are always grander than those of war!

I say then to you, that you ought to be rich.

"Well," you say, "I would like to be rich, but I have never had an opportunity. I never had any diamonds about me!"

My friends, you did have an opportunity. And let us see where your mistake was.

What business have you been in?

"Oh," some man or woman will say, "I keep a store upon one of these side streets, and I am so far from the great commercial center that I cannot make any money."

"Are you poor? How long have you kept that store?"

"Twenty years."

"Twenty years, and not worth five hundred thousand dollars now? There is something the matter with you. Nothing the matter with the side street. It is with you."

"Oh now," you will say, "any person knows that you must be in the center of trade if you are going to make money."

The man of common sense will not admit that that is necessarily true at all. If you are keeping that store and you are not making money, it would have been better for the community if they had kicked you out of that store, nineteen years ago.

No man has a right to go into business and not make money. It is a crime to go into business and lose money, because it is a curse to the rest of the community. No man has a moral right to transact business unless he makes something out of it. He has also no right to transact business unless the man he deals with has an opportunity also to make something. Unless he lives and lets live, he is not an honest man in business. There are no exceptions to this great rule.

You ought to have been rich. You have no right to keep a store for twenty years and still be poor. You will say to me:

"Now Mr. Conwell, I know the mercantile business better than you do."

My friend, let us consider it a minute.

When I was young, my father kept a country store, and once in a while he left me in charge of that store. Fortunately for him it was not often. When I had it in my charge a man came in the store door and said:

"Do you keep jackknives?"

"No, we don't keep jackknives." I went off and whistled a tune, and what did I care for that man? Then another man would come in and say:

"Do you keep jackknives?" "No, we don't keep jackknives." Then I went off and whistled another tune, and what did I can for that man?

Then another man would come in the same door and say: "Do you keep jackknives?"

"No, we don't keep jackknives. Do you suppose we are keeping this store just for the purpose of supplying the whole neighborhood with jackknives?"

Do you carry on your business like that? Do you ask what was the difficulty with it? The difficulty was that I had not then learned that the foundation principles of business success and the foundation principles of Christianity, itself, are both the same. It is the whole of every man's life to be doing for his fellowmen. And he who can do the most to help his fellowmen, is entitled to the greatest reward himself. No only so saith God's holy book, but also saith every man's business common sense. If I had been carrying on my father's store on a Christian plan, or on a plan that leads to success, I would have had a jackknife for the third man when he called for it.

But you say: "I don't carry on my store like that." If you have not made any money you are carrying on your business like that, and I can tell you what you will say to me tomorrow morning when I go into your store.

I come to you and inquire: "Do you know neighbor A?"

"Oh yes. He lives up in the next block. He trades here at my little store."

"Well, where did he come from when he came to———?"

"I don't know."

"Does he own his own house?"

"I don't know."

"What business is he in?"

"I don't know."

"Do his children go to school?"

"I don't know."

"What ticket does he vote?"

"I don't know."

"What church does he go to?"

"I don't know, and I don't care."

Do you answer me like that tomorrow morning, in your store? Then you are carrying on your business just as I carried on my father's business in Worthington, Massachusetts.

You don't know where neighbor A came from and you *don't care.* You don't care whether he has a happy home or not. You don't know what church he goes to, and you don't care! If you had cared, you would have been a rich man now.

You never thought it was any part of your duty to help him make money. So you cannot succeed! It is against every law of business and every rule of political economy, and I would give five dollars myself, to see your failure in the *Ledger* tomorrow morning. What right have you to be in business taking no interest in your fellowmen, and not endeavoring to supply them with what they need? You cannot succeed.

That merchant, who, in the City of Boston, made his fifteen millions of dollars, began his enterprises out in the suburbs where there were not a dozen houses on the street; although there were other stores scattered about. He became such a necessity to the neighborhood that when he wished to move into the city to start a wholesale house, they came to him with a great petition, signed by all the people, begging that he would not close that store, but keep it open for the benefit of that community. He had always looked after their interests. He had always carefully studied what they wanted and advised them rightly. He was a necessity; and they must make him wealthy; for in proportion as you are of use to your fellowmen in that proportion can they afford to pay you.

Oh my friend, going through this world and thinking you are unjustly dealth with! You are poor because you are not wanted. You should have made yourself a necessity to the world, and then the world would have paid you your own price. Friends, learn that lesson. I would speak tenderly and kindly to the poor; but I sometimes need to speak decidedly.

Young man, remember if you are going to invest your life or talent or money, you must look around and see what people need and then invest yourself, or your money, in that which they need most. Then will your fortune be made, for they must take care of you. It is a difficult lesson to learn.

Some young man will say to me:

"I cannot go into that mercantile business."

"Why not?"

"Because I have no capital."

Capital! Capital! Capital! Capital! is the cry of a dudish generation which cannot see over its collar.

Who are the rich men now? The poor boys of fifty years ago. You know it. The rich men of your town, in whatever profession or calling they are, as a rule were the poor boys of forty or fifty years ago. If they had not been poor then they wouldn't be rich now.

The statistics of Massachusetts say, and I presume it holds good in your state, that not one rich man's son in seventeen ever dies rich. I pity the rich man's son. He is not to be praised for his magnificent, palatial home, not to be congratulated on having plenty of money, or his yachts, carriages, and diamonds. Oh no, but rather to be commiserated. It is often a misfortune to be born the son of a rich man. There are many things a rich man's son cannot know, because he is not passing through the school of actual experience.

A young man in our college asked me: "What is the happiest hour in the history of a man's life?" The definition I gave him was this: The happiest hour in the history of a man's life is when he takes his bride for the first time over the threshold of his own door, into a house which he has earned by his own hands; and as he enters the nest he has built he says to her, with an eloquence of feeling no words of mine can ever touch: "Wife, I earned this home myself!" Oh, that is the grandest moment a man may ever know. "Wife, I earned this home. It is all mine, and I divide it with thee!" It is a magnificent moment!

But the rich man's son cannot know that. He may go into a house that is more beautiful; but as he takes his wife into his mansion he will go all through it and say to her: "My mother gave me that! My mother gave me that. My mother gave me that!"—until his wife wishes he had married his mother.

I pity such a young man as that.

It is said that the elder Vanderbilt, when a boy, went to his father and said:

"Father, did you earn all your money?"

And the old Commodore said: "I did, I earned every penny of it."

And he did. It is cruel to slander the rich because they have been successful. It is a shame to "look down" upon the rich the way we do. They are not scoundrels because they have gotten money. They have blessed the world. They have gone into great enterprises that have enriched the nation and the nation has enriched them. It is all wrong for us to accuse a rich man of dishonesty simply because he secured money. Go through this city and your very best people are among your richest people. Owners of property are always the best citizens. It is all wrong to say they are not good.

The elder Vanderbilt went to his father and said: "Did you earn all your money?"

And when the Commodore said that he did, the boy said: "Then I will earn mine."

And he insisted on going to work for three dollars a week. If a rich man's son will go to work like that he will be able to take care of his father's money when the father is gone. If he has the bravery to fight the battle of poverty like the poor boy, then of course he has a double advantage. But as a rule the rich father won't allow his son to work; and the boy's mother!—oh, she would think it a social disgrace for her poor, weak, little, lily-fingered, sissy sort of a boy to earn his living with honest toil. And so I say it is not capital you want. It is not copper cents, but common sense.

Let me illustrate it again. A. T. Stewart had a dollar and fifty cents to begin life on. That was of course before he was a schoolteacher. He lost eight-seven and a half cents on his very first venture. How did he come to lose it? He lost it because he purchased some needles, thread, and buttons to sell, which people did not want. And he said: "I will never do that again." Then he went around first to the doors of the houses and asked the people what they did want; then when he found out what they wanted he invested his sixty-two and a half cents and supplied a "known demand."

Why does one merchant go beyond another? Why does one manufacturer outsell any other? It is simply because that one has found out what people want, and does not waste his money buying things they do not need. That is the whole of it. And A. T. Stewart said: "I am not going to buy things people do not want. I will take an interest in people and study their needs." And he pursued that until he was worth forty millions of dollars.

"But," you will say, "I cannot do that here." Yes, you can. It is being done in smaller places now, and you can do it as well as others.

But a better illustration was John Jacob Astor, the elder. They say that he had a mortgage on a millinery store. I never reach this point without thinking that the ladies will say that "Fools rush in where angels fear to tread." But John Jacob Astor had a mortgage on a millinery store, and foreclosed the mortgage and went into business with the same people who had failed on his hands. After he entered into partnership, he went out and sat down on a bench in the park. What was the successful merchant doing out there, in partnership with people who had just failed on his own hands? Ah, he had the most important, and to my mind, the pleasantest part of that partnership. He was out there watching the ladies as they went by:—and where is the man who would not get rich at that business? As he sat upon that bench if a lady passed him with her shoulders thrown back and her head up, and looking straight to the front, as though she didn't care if all the world did gaze on her, then John Jacob Astor studied the bonnet she wore; and before it was out of sight, he knew the shape of the frame, and the curl of the lace, and crimp of the feathers, and lots of intricate things that go into a bonnet which I cannot describe. Then he went to his millinery store and said: "Now put in the show window just such a bonnet as I describe to you, because I have just seen a real lady who likes just such a bonnet." Then he went and sat down again. Another lady, with another form and complexion came, and, of course, she wore another style of bonnet. He then went back and described that and had that put into the window. He didn't fill his show window full of hats and bonnets to drive the people away, and then sit down in the back of the store and bawl because people went somewhere else to trade. He didn't have a hat or a bonnet that some lady didn't like. That has since been the wealthiest millinery firm on the face of the earth. There has been taken out of the business seventeen millions of dollars and over, by partners who have retired. Yet not a dollar of capital have they ever put into that business, except what they turned in from their profits,—to use as capital. Now John Jacob Astor made the fortune of that millinery firm not by lending them money, but by finding out what the ladies liked for bonnets, before they wasted any material in making them up. And if a man can foresee the millinery business, he can foresee anything under Heaven!

But perhaps a better illustration may strike closer home. You ought to go into the manufacturing business. But you will say there is no room here. Great corporations which have gotten possession of the field make it impossible to make a success of a small manufacturing business now. I say to you, young man, that there was never a time in your history and never will be in your history again when the opportunity for a poor man to make money in the manufacturing business is so clearly apparent as it is at this very hour.

"But," says some young man to me, "I have no capital."

Oh, capital, capital! Do you know of any manufacturer around here who was not born poor? Capital! you don't want capital now. I want to illustrate again, for the best way to teach is always by illustration.

There was a man in Hingham, Massachusetts, who was a carpenter and out of work. He sat around the stove until his wife told him to "go out of doors"; and he did,—what every man in Massachusetts is compelled to do by law,—he obeyed his wife. He went out and sat down on the shore of the bay and he whittled out an oak shingle into a wooden chain. His children that evening quarrelled over it. So he whittled another to keep peace in the family. While he was whittling the second toy a neighbor came in and said to him: "Why don't you whittle toys and sell them? You can make money." The carpenter said "I could not whittle toys, and if I could do it, I would not know what to make!" There is the whole thing. It is to know what to make. It is the secret of life everywhere. You may take it in the ministry. You may take it in law. You may take it in mechanics or in labor. You may take it in professional life, or anywhere on earth—the whole question is what to make of yourself for other people. "What to make" is the great difficulty.

He said he would "not know what to make." His neighbor said to him, with good New England common sense: "Why don't you ask your own children what to make?"

"Oh," said he, "my children are different from other people's children."

I used to see people like that when I taught school.

But he consulted his children later, and whittled toys to please them and found that other people's children wanted the same things. He called his children right around his feet and whittled out of firewood those "Hingham tops"; the wooden shovels; the wooden buckets and such things, and when his children were especially pleased, he then made copies to sell. He began to get a little capital of his own earning, and secured a footlathe, and then secured a room, then hired a factory, and then hired power; and so he went on. The last law case I ever tried in my life was in the United States Courtroom at Boston, and this very Hingham man who had whittled those toys stood upon the stand. He was the last man I ever cross-examined. Then I left the law, and went into the minsitry,—left practicing entirely and went to preaching exclusively. But I said to this man as he stood upon the stand:

"When did you begin to whittle those toys?"

He said: "1870."

Said I: "In these seven years how much have those toys become worth?"

He answered: "Do you mean the taxable value or the estimated value?"

I said: "Tell his Honor the taxable value, that there may be no question about it." He answered me from the witness stand, under oath:

"Seventy-eight thousand dollars."

Seventy-eight thousand dollars in only seven years, and beginning with nothing but a jackknife (and a few hundred dollars of debts he owed other people), and so he was worth at least $100,000. His fortune was made by consulting his own children, in his own house, and deciding that other people's children would like the same thing. You can do the same thing if you will. You don't need to go out of your house to find out where the diamonds are. You don't need to go out of your own room.

But your wealth is too near. I was speaking in New Britain, Connecticut, on this very subject. There sat five or six rows from me a lady. I noticed the lady at the time, from the color of her bonnet. I said to them, what I say to you now, "Your wealth is too near to you! You are looking right over it!" She went home after the lecture and tried to take off her collar. The button stuck in the buttonhole. She twisted and tugged and pulled and finally broke it out of the buttonhole and threw it away. She said: "I wonder why they don't make decent collar buttons?"

Her husband said to her: "After what Conwell said tonight, why don't you get up a collar button yourself? Did he not say that if you need anything other people need it; so if you need a collar button there are millions of people needing it. Get up a collar button and get rich. *'Wherever there is a need there is a fortune.'* "

Then she made up her mind to do it; and when a woman makes up her mind, and don't say anything about it, she does it! And she invented this "snap button," a kind of a button that snaps together from two pieces, through the buttonhole. That very woman can now go over the sea every summer in her own yacht and take her husband with her. And if he were dead she would have enough money left to buy a foreign count or duke, or some such thing.

What is my lesson in it? I said to her what I say to you, "Your fortune is too near to you! So near that you are looking over it." She had to look over it. It was right under her chin. And it is just as near to you.

In East Brookfield, Massachusetts, there was a shoemaker out of work. His wife drove him out of doors with the mopstick, because she wanted to mop around the stove. He went out and sat down on the ash barrel in the back yard. Close by that ash barrel ran a little mountain stream. I have sometimes wondered if, as he sat there on that ash barrel, he thought of Tennyson's beautiful poem:

> Chatter, chatter, as I flow,
> To join the brimming river,
> Men may come, and men may go,
> But I go on forever.

I don't believe he thought of it, because it was not a poetical situation, on an ash barrel in the back yard. But as he sat on that ash barrel he looked down into the stream, and he saw a trout go flashing up the stream and hiding under the bank. He leaped down and caught the fish in his hands and took it into the house. His wife sent it a friend in Worcester. The friend wrote back that they would give five dollars for another such trout. And the shoemaker and his wife immediately started out to find one. They went up and down the stream, but not another trout to be found. Then they went to the preacher. But that is not half as foolish as some other things young people go to a preacher for. That preacher could not explain why they could not find another trout. But he was true to his profession; he "pointed the way." He said: "Secure Seth Green's book on the *Culture of Trout*, and it will give you the information you need." They got the book and found that if they started with a pair of trout, a trout would lay thirty-six hundred eggs every year, and that every trout would grow an ounce the first year, and a quarter of a pound every succeeding year, so that in four years a man could secure from two trout four tons per annum to sell. They said: "Oh, we don't believe such a great story as that. But if we could raise a few and sell them for five dollars apiece, we might make money." So they purchased two little trout and put them in the stream, with a coal sifter down the stream and a window screen upstream to keep the trout in. Afterwards, they moved to the banks of the Connecticut River, and afterwards to the Hudson, and one of them has been on the United States Fish Commission, and had a large share in the preparation for the World's Fair in 1900 at Paris. But he sat that day, on that ash barrel in the back yard, right by his acres of diamonds. But he didn't see them. He had not seen his fortune although he had lived there for twenty-three years, until his wife drove him out there with a mopstick. It may be you will not find your wealth until your wife assumes the sceptre of power! But nevertheless, your wealth is there.

But the people who make the greatest mistakes are the farmers. When I could not keep my father's store he set me to work on the farm, knowing that as the ground was nearly all rock I could not do much harm there.

I know by experience that a very ordinary man can be a lawyer. I also know that it does not take a man with a gigantic intellect to be a preacher. It takes a greater man than either, to make a successful farmer today. The farmer will be more successful when he gives more attention to what people want and not so much to what will grow, though he needs them both. But now the whole time of most of our farmers is taken up with the finding out of "what will grow."

I was going up through Iowa a while ago and saw the wheat decaying in mud, and I said to a farmer:

"Why is it that all this grain here is decaying?"

"Oh," he said, "it is the 'awful' monopoly of the railroads." He didn't use the word "awful," but he used a word that he thought was more emphatic.

I got into the train and I sympathized with the poor downtrodden farmer. The conductor came along and I asked him:

"How much dividend does this railroad pay on its stock?"

He looked at me and said: "It has not paid any for nine years and it has been in the hands of the receiver the most of the time."

Then I changed my mind. If that farmer had raised what the people wanted, not only would he have been rich, but the railroad would have paid interest on its stock.

I was at Evansville, Indiana, and a man drove up in his beautiful carriage and told me: "Eighteen years ago I borrowed two hundred dollars and I went into farming. I began the first year to raise wheat, rye, and hogs. But the second year I decided to raise what the people wanted, so I ploughed the ground over and put in small fruits. Now, I own this farm and a great deal more." They told me at the hotel that he owned two-thirds of the stock in the bank of which he was president. He had made his money all because he planted what people wanted.

Let me go down through the audience now, and ask you to show me the great inventors here. You will say: "That doesn't mean me." But it does mean you. Great inventors that hear me now! Oh, you will say, we don't have any inventors here. They all live away off somewhere else. But who are the great inventors? Always the men who are the simplest and plainest. They are the great inventors. The great inventor has the simple mind, and invents the simplest machine.

Did you ever think how simple the telephone and the telegraph were? Now the simplest mind is always the greatest. Did you ever see a great man? Great in every noble and true sense? If so, you could walk right up to him and say: "How are you, Jim?" Just think of the great men you have met and you find this is true.

I went out to write the biography of General Garfield and found him crowded with other people. I went to a neighbor's to wait until they were gone. But the neighbor told me that if I wanted to get a chance to see him I had better go over at once, and he offered to introduce me. He took his old hat and stuck it on the back of his head, and climbed over the fence and went to the back-door of the house, and shouted:

"Jim! Jim! Jim!"

Very soon "Jim" came to the door; and the neighbor said: "Here is a man who wants to see you."

I went into the home of one of the grandest men that America ever raised. To his neighbors he was "Jim," a plain man, a simple man.

I went to see President Lincoln one time when I was an officer in the War of 1861. I had never seen him before, and his secretary sent me in to see him as one would enter a neighbor's office. Simple, plain "old Abe."

The simple men are the greatest always. Did you ever see a man strut proudly along, puffed up in his individual pride, not willing to notice an ordinary mechanic? Do you think he is great? Do you really think that man is great? He is nothing but a puffed-up balloon, held down by his big feet. There may be greatness in self-respect, but there is no greatness in feeling above one's fellowmen.

I asked a class in Minnesota once who were the great inventors, and a girl hopped up and said, "Columbus." Columbus was a great inventor. Columbus married a wife who owned a farm, and he carried it on just as I carried on my father's farm. We took the hoe and went out and sat down on a rock. But as Columbus sat on that rock on the Island of Porto Santo, Spain, he was thinking. I was not. That was a great difference. Columbus as he sat on that rock held in his hand a hoe handle. He looked out on the ocean and saw the departing ships apparently sink into the sea, and the tops of the masts went down, out of sight. Since that time some "other Spanish ships have sunk into the sea!" Said Columbus: "This world is like a hoe handle, the further off the further down, the further off the further down,—just like a hoe handle. I can sail around to the East Indies." How clear it all was. Yet how simple the mind. It is the simplest minds that observe the very simplest things, which accomplish the greatest marvels.

I went up into New Hampshire and when I came back I said I would never go to New Hampshire to lecutre again. And I said to a relative of mine, who was a professor at Harvard:

"I was cold all the time I was there and I shivered so that my teeth shook."

Said he: "Why did you shiver?"

"Because it was cold."

"No, that is not the reason you shivered."

Then I said: "I shivered because I had not bedclothes enough."

"No, that is not the reason."

"Well," said I, "Professor, you are a scientific man, I am not, I would like to have an expert, scientific opinion now, why I shivered."

He arose in his facetious way and said to me: "Young man, you shivered because you did not know any better! Didn't you have in your pocket a two-cent paper?"

"Oh, yes, I had a *Herald* and a *Journal*."

"That is it. You had them in your pocket, and if you had spread one newspaper over your sheet when you went to bed, you would have been as warm as you lay there as the richest man in America under all his silk coverlids. But you shivered because you didn't know enough to put a two-center newspaper on your bed, and you had it in your pocket."

It is the power to appreciate the little things that brings success. How many women want divorces, and ought to have them too; but how many divorces originate like this? A man will hurry home from the factory, and his wife rushes in from the kitchen with the potatoes that have been taken out before they seem to be done, and she puts them on the table for her husband to eat. He chops them up and eats them in a hurry. They go down in hard lumps; he doesn't feel good, and he is all full of crankiness. He frets and scolds, and perhaps swears, and there is a row in the family right there. And these hearts that were almost divinely united will separate to satanic hatred. What is the difficulty? The difficulty is that that lady didn't know what all these ladies do know, that if with potatoes raised in lime soil she had put in a pinch of salt when she put them in the kettle, she could have brought them forth at the right time, and they would have been ready to laugh themselves to pieces with edible joy. He would have digested them readily, and there would have been love in that family, just for a little pinch of salt.

Now, I say, it is the appreciation of these things that makes the great inventors of the world. I read in a newspaper the other day that no woman ever invented anything. Of course this didn't refer to gossip, but machines and improvements. If it had referred to gossip, it would have applied better to that newspaper than to women. Who invented the Jacquard loom? Mrs. [Joseph] Jacquard. Who invented the printer's roller? A woman. Who invented the cottin gin? Mrs. Greene; although a patent was taken out on an improvement in Mr. [Eli] Whitney's name. Who invented the sewing machine? A woman. Mrs. Howe, the wife of Elias Howe. If a woman can invent a sewing machine, if a woman can invent a printing roller, if a woman can invent a cotton gin, we men can invent anything under Heaven! I say that to encourage the men. Anyhow, our civilization would roll back if we should cross out the great inventions of women, though the patents were taken out often in the names of men.

The greatest inventors are those who see what the people need, and then invent something to supply that need. Let me illustrate only once more. Suppose I were to go through this house and shake hands with each of you and say: 'Please introduce me to the great men and women in this hall tonight."

You would say: "Great men! We don't have any here. There are none in this audience. If you want to find great men you must go to some other part of the world! Great men always come from somewhere else."

How many of your men with vast power to help your city, how many with great genius, or great social power, who might enrich and beautify and elevate this their own city, are now taking their money and talents and spending them in some foreign place, instead of benefiting their own people here? Yet here is the place for them to be great. There are as great men here as in any other place of its size. But it is so natural for us to say that great men come from afar. They come from London, from Rome, from San Francisco, from New York, from Manayunk, or anywhere else. But there are just as great men hearing me speak tonight as there are elsewhere, and yet, who, because of their simplicity, are not now appreciated. But "the world knows nothing of its greatest men," says the great philosopher; and it is true. Your neighbor is a great man and it is time you appreciated it, and if you do not appreciate it now, you never will. The only way to be a true patriot is to be a true patriot at home. A man who cannot benefit his own city should never be sent to Washington. Towns and cities are cursed because their own people talk them down. A man who cannot bless his own community, the place in which he lives, should not be called a patriot anywhere else. To these young men I want to utter this cry with all my force. Here is the place for you to be great, and here are your great men.

But we teach our young people to believe that all the great people are away off. I heard a professor in an Illinois college say that "nearly all the great men are dead." We don't want him in Philadelphia. They don't want him anywhere. The greatest men are living now, and will only be exceeded by the generations to come; and he who appreciates that fact will look around him and will respect his neighbor, and will respect his environment. I have to say tonight that the great men of the world are those who appreciate that which is next to them, and the danger now to our nation is that we belittle everything that is at home.

Have you heard the campaign speeches this year? I heard a man at the Academy of Music say that our nation is going to ruin; that the Ship of State is drifting upon the rocks and will soon be shattered into ten thousand fragments, and this republic will be no more; that there will be founded an empire, and upon the empire we will put a throne, and upon the throne will be placed a tyrant, and he with his iron heel will grind the people into dust! It is a lie! Never in the history of God's government of mankind was there a nation stepping upward more certainly toward all that is grand and beautiful and true than is the nation of America today! Let the politicians say what they will for personal greed, let them declaim with all their powers, and try to burden the people, you and I know that whichever way the elections may go, the American people are not dead, and the nation will not be destroyed. It is a living body, this mighty republic, and it cannot be killed by a single election. And they that will belittle our nation are not patriots. Let the land be filled with hope. Some young men will say: "Oh well, the nation is having a hard time." But it is not. The Bible says: "It is good for me that I was afflicted." We are getting down to where we can consider and take account of stock. In the next five years from now you will see the most flourishing institutions; all through this land will be united a prosperity such as this nation never knew before. Whatever the result of the election, don't belittle your own nation.

Some young man is saying: "There is going to be a great man here, although I don't know of any now."

"Young man when are you going to be great?"

"When I am elected to some political office, then I will be great."

"Oh young man, learn right now, in these exciting times, that to hold a political office under our form of government is no evidence of greatness. Why, my friends, what would become of this nation if our great men should take office? Suppose you select the greatest men of your city right now, and ask them to leave their great enterprises and go into some political office. My friends, what a ruin would be left if the great men were to take political offices. The great men cannot afford to take political office, and you and I cannot afford to put them there. To hold a political office is to be a servant of the people. And the Bible says, "He that is sent cannot be greater than he who sends him," and "the servant cannot be greater than his master." The officeholder is the servant of others. He is sent by the people, he cannot be greater than the people. You think you are going to be a great man by being elected to some political office! Young man, greatness is intrinsic, it is in the personality, not in the office. If you are not great as an individual before you go into the office, you may rattle around in it after you get in, like "shot in a tin pan." There will be no greatness there. You will hold the office for a year or more and never be heard of again. There are greater things than political office. Many a young man's fortune has been made by being defeated when he was up for political office. You never saw a really great man in office who did not take the office at a sacrifice to himself.

Another young man says: "There is going to be a great man here."

"When?"

"When there comes a war! When we get into another conflict with Spain over Cuba; with England over the Monroe Doctrine, or over the Russian boundary, or with New Jersey, or some distant country of the world, then I will sweep up among the glittering bayonets, then I will tear down their flag from the staff, bear it away in triumph, and come home with stars on my shoulders, and hold every office in the gift of the nation; then I will be great!"

Young man, remember greatness does not consist in holding office, even in war. The office does not make the great man. But, alas, we mislead the young in teaching history. If you ask a scholar in school who sank the *Merrimac*, he will answer "Hobson," and tell seven-eighths of a lie. For eight men sank the *Merrimac* at Santiago. Yet where are the women here tonight who have kissed the other seven men?

A young man says: "I was studying the history of the [Civil] War the other day and read about Generals Grant, Meade, Beauregard, Hood, and these great leaders, and they were great."

Did you read anything about their predecessors? There is very little in history about them. If the office had made their predecessors great, you would not have heard of Grant, or Sherman, or McClellan. But they were great men intrinsically, not made so by the office. The way we teach history leads the young to think that when people get into office then they become great men. But it is terribly misleading.

Every great general of the war is credited with many victories he never knew anything about, simply because they were won by his subordinates. But it is unfair to give the credit to a general who did not know anything about it. I tell you if the lightning of heaven had struck out of existence every man who wore shoulder straps in our wars, there would have arisen out of the ranks of our private soldiers just as great men to lead the nation on to victory.

I will give one more illustration. I don't like to give it. I don't know how I ever fell into the habit. Indeed, it was first given off-hand to a Grand Army post of which I was a member. I hesitate to give it now.

I close my eyes and I can see my own native hills once more. I can see my mountain town and plateau, the Congregational Church, and the Town Hall. They are there spread before me with increasing detail as my years fly by. I close my eyes and I can see the crowd again that was there in that wartime, 1864, dressed in red, white and blue; the flags flying, the band playing. I see a platoon of soldiers who have returned from one term of service and reenlisted for the second, and are now to be received by the mountain town. Oh, well do I remember the day. I was captain of the company. Although in my teens, I was marching at the head of that company and puffed out with pride. A cambric needle would have burst me all to pieces! I am sincerely ashamed of the whole thing now.

But what august pride, then in my youth, marching at the head of my troops, being received by the country town authorities! We marched into the Town Hall. They seated my soldiers in the middle of the hall, and the crowds came in on the right and on the left. Then the town officers filed upon the stand and took up their position in a half-circle. The good old mayor of the town, and the chairman of the Selectmen (his family gave me permission to use this without offense to them), he sat there in his dignity, with his powerful spectacles. He had never held an office in his life before. He may have thought that if he could get into office that would give him power to do almost anything. He never held an office before, and never made a speech before. When he had taken his place he saw me on the front seat, and he came right forward and invited me up on the platform with the "Selectmen." Invited me, me! up on the stand with the town officers! Why, no town officer ever took any notice of me before I went to war; yet perhaps I ought not to say that, because one of them, I remember, did advise a teacher to "whale" me: but I mean no "honorable mention." Now I am invited on the stand with the Selectmen. They gave me a chair in just about this relation to the table. [*Indicating the position.*] I sat down, let my sword fall to the floor and waited to be received—Napoleon the Vth!—"Pride goeth before destruction," and it ought. When the Selectmen and the mayor had taken seats the mayor waited for quite a while, and then came forward to the table. Oh, that speech! We had supposed he would simply introduce the Congregational minister, who usually gave such public addresses. But you should have seen the surprise when this old man arose to deliver the address, on this august occasion. He had never delivered an address before. He thought the office would make him an orator. But he forgot that a man must speak his piece as a boy if he wishes to become an orator as a man. Yet he made a most common mistake. So he had written out his speech and learned it by heart. But he brought his manuscript with him, very wisely, and took it out, opened it, and spread it on the table, and then adjusted his spectacles that he might see it. Then he walked back and came forward again to deliver that address. He must have studied the idea a great deal, because he assumed an "elocutionary attitude." He "rested heavily on his left heel, slightly advanced his right foot, threw back his shoulders, and advanced his right hand at an angle of forty-five." As he stood in that elocutionary attitude, this is just the way he delivered that speech. Friends often ask me if I do not exaggerate it. You couldn't exaggerate it. I haven't the power to exaggerate it.

"Fellow citizens!"—and then he paused until his fingers and knees shook, and began to swallow, then turned aside to look at his manuscript.

"Fellow citizens: We are—we are—we are—we are very happy. We are very happy—we are very happy—we are very happy. We are very happy—to welcome back to their native town—to their native town—these soldiers—these soldiers—who have fought and bled, and are back again in their native town. We are especially,—we are especially pleased to see with us tonight this young hero,—(that meant me)—who in imagination—friends, remember he said that; if he hadn't said that I wouldn't have been egotistic enough to refer to it today, I assure you)—who, in imagination,—we have seen leading his troops on to the deadly breach. We have seen his shining—we have his shining—his shining sword—we have seen his shining sword, flashing in the sunlight, as he shouted to his troops, 'Come on!' "

Oh, dear, dear, dear! He was a good old man, but how little he knew about the War. If he had known anything about war at all, he ought to have known that it is next to a crime for an officer of infantry ever, in time of danger, to go ahead of his men. I, with "my shining sword flashing in the sunlight," and calling to my troops, "Come on!" I never did it. Do you suppose I would go in front of my men to be shot in front by the enemy, and in the back by my own men? It is no place for an officer. The place for an officer in time of danger is behind the private soldier. It is the private soldier who faces the enemy. Often, as a staff officer, I have ridden down the line, before the battle, and as I rode I have given the general's order, shouting, "Officers to the rear!" And then every officer goes behind the line of private soldiers, and the higher the officer's rank, the further behind he goes. It is the place for him; for, if your officers and your generals were killed on the first discharge, where would the plan of the battle be? How ashamed I was of the whole affair. In actual battle such an officer has no right to go ahead of his men. Some of those men had carried that boy across the Carolina rivers. Some of them had given him their last draught of coffee. One of them had leaped in front of him and had his cheek bone shot away; he had leaped in front of the boy to save his life. Some were not there at all, and the tears flowing from the eyes of the widows and orphans showed that they had gone down for their country. Yet in the good man's speech he scarcely noticed those who had died; the hero of the hour was that boy. We do not know even now where many of those comrades do sleep. They went down to death. Sometimes in my dreams I call, "Answer me, ye sighing pines of the Carolinas; answer me, ye shining sands of Florida; answer me, ye crags and rocks of Kentucky and Tennessee,—where sleep my dead?" But to my call no answer comes. I know not where many of those men now sleep. But I do know this, they were brave men. I know they went down before a brave foe, fighting for a cause both believed to be right. Yet the hero of this hour was this boy. He was an officer, and they were only private soldiers.

I learned a lesson then I will never forget, until the bell of time ceases to swing for me,—that greatness consists not in holding an office. Greatness really consists in doing great deeds with little means,—in the accomplishment of vast purposes; from the private ranks of life—in benefiting one's own neighborhood, in blessing one's own city, the community in which he dwells. There, and there only, is the great test of human goodness and human ability. He who waits for an office before he does great and noble deeds must fail altogether.

I learned that lesson then, that henceforth in life I will call no man great simply because he holds an office. Greatness! It is something more than office, something more than fame, more than genius! It is the great-heartedness that encloses those in need, reaches down to those below, and lifts them up. May this thought come to every one of these young men and women who hear me speak tonight and abide through future years.

I close with the words of [Rufus] Bailey. He was not one of our greatest writers, but, after all, in this he was one of our best:

> We live in deeds, not years,
> In feelings, not in figures on a dial,
> In thoughts, not breaths;
> We should count time by heart
> throbs; (in the cause of right.)
> He most lives who *thinks most.*

Oh, friends, if you forget everything

else I say, don't forget these two lines for, if you think *two* thoughts where I think *one*, you live twice as much as I do in the same length of time.

He most lives who thinks most
Who feels the noblest,
And who acts the best.

Henry Grady

The New South (1886)

In April 1877, when the last federal troops left South Carolina and Louisiana, the Reconstruction period technically ended. Actual reconstruction—of the South following the devastation of the Civil War and of Northern attitudes toward their old slaveholding enemies—took longer than the decade following the close of the war.

Healing the psychological wounds caused by the civil conflict proved to be just as difficult as restoring economic stability. It was not uncommon for Northern politicians of the 1800's to capitalize on the hostile feelings that had been unleashed by the war and that the passage of years had not erased. By "waving the bloody shirt," some sought once again to arouse sectional antagonisms and gain political advantage in the process. Also, apart from these efforts to exploit old tensions, there existed the patriotic pride felt by the victors who honored the glorious memory of the triumphant Union forces.

In the South there were progressive forces who, while cherishing the memory of their own Confederate heroes, were willing to accept the judgment against slavery and lay the bitterness of the war to rest, to move on toward reforging ties of unity among the sections of the country. The publisher and part-owner of the *Atlanta Constitution*, Henry Grady, was among this group.

Grady's own father was killed while serving in the Confederate Army and Grady himself paid tribute to traditional Southern virtues. But the Georgia newspaperman was convinced, and set out to convince audiences in both North and South, that reconciliation was the surest path to recovery and prosperity for all sections of the country.

Grady attained national prominence as a speaker as a result of a speech given to the New England Society of New York in December

1886, "The New South." In his address, Grady referred to the speeches that preceded his, speeches that would not, on the face of it, have seemed likely to promote his message. Dr. Thomas Dewitt Talmage, a popular Presbyterian preacher, described in vivid detail the return of the victorious Union armies at the end of the Civil War. He was followed by General William T. Sherman, who had achieved fame as the commander of the federal troops who cut a fiery path through Georgia in the famous march to the sea.

Grady, however, used Talmage's description as a contrast to his own account of the returning Confederate veterans and assured Sherman that from the ashes of 1864 had arisen "a brave and beautiful city," in which is enshrined "not one ignoble prejudice or memory." Grady's message that the South had grown stronger and better and was ready to take its place in the new economic life of the nation was coupled with a plea to the North to recognize the achievements of this new South and to let the old wounds heal; this was a message that incorporated Grady's belief in the "imperishable brotherhood of the American people," in spite of "difficulties, contentions, and controversies."

"There was a South of slavery and secession—that South is dead. There is a South of union and freedom—that South, thank God, is living, breathing, growing every hour." These words, delivered from the immortal lips of Benjamin H. Hill, at Tammany Hall, in 1866, true then and truer now, I shall make my text to-night.

Mr. President and Gentlemen: Let me express to you my appreciation of the kindness by which I am permitted to address you. I make this abrupt acknowledgment advisedly, for I feel that if, when I raise my provincial voice in this ancient and august presence, I could find courage for no more than the opening sentence, it would be well if in that sentence I had met in a rough sense my obligation as a guest, and had perished, so to speak, with courtesy on my lips and grace in my heart. Permitted, through your kindness, to catch my second wind, let me say that I appreciate the significance of being the first Southerner to speak at this board, which bears the substance, if it surpasses the semblance, of original New England hospitality—and honors the sentiment that in turn honors you, but in which my personality is lost, and the compliment to my people made plain.

I bespeak the utmost stretch of your courtesy to-night. I am not troubled about those from whom I come. You remember the man whose wife sent him to a neighbor with a pitcher of milk, and who, tripping on the top step, fell with such casual interruptions as the landings afforded into the basement, and, while picking himself up, had the pleasure of hearing his wife call out: "John, did you break the pitcher?"

"No, I didn't," said John, "but I'll be dinged if I don't."

So, while those who call me from behind may inspire me with energy, if not with courage, I ask an indulgent hearing from you. I beg that you will bring your full faith in American fairness and frankness to judgment upon what I shall say. There was an old preacher once who told some boys of the Bible lesson he was going to read in the morning. The boys, finding the place, glued together the connecting pages. The next morning he read on the bottom of one page, "When Noah was one hundred and twenty years old he took unto himself a wife, who was"—then turning the page—"140 cubits long—40 cubits wide, built of gopher wood—and covered with pitch inside and out." He was naturally puzzled at this. He read it again, verified it, and then said: "My friends, this is the first time I ever met this in the Bible, but I accept this as an evidence of the assertion that we are fearfully and wonderfully made." If I could get you to hold such faith to-night I could proceed cheerfully to the task I otherwise approach with a sense of consecration.

Pardon me one word, Mr. President, spoken for the sole purpose of getting into the volumes that go out annually freighted with the rich eloquence of your speakers—the fact that the Cavalier as well as the Puritan was on the continent in its early days, and that he was "up and able to be about." I have read your books carefully and I find no mention of that fact, which seems to me an important one for preserving a sort of historical equilibrium if for nothing else.

Let me remind you that the Virginia Cavalier first challenged France on the continent—that Cavalier, John Smith, gave New England its very name, and was so pleased with the job that he has been handing his own name around ever since—and that while Myles Standish was cutting off men's ears for courting a girl without her parents' consent, and forbade men to kiss their wives on Sunday, the Cavalier was courting everything in sight, and that the Almighty had vouchsafed great increase to the Cavalier colonies, the huts in the wilderness being as full as the nests in the woods.

But having incorporated the Cavalier as a fact in your charming little books, I shall let him work out his own salvation, as he has always done, with engaging gallantry, and we will hold no controversy as to his merits. Why should we? Neither Puritan nor Cavalier long survived as such. The virtues and good traditions of both happily still live for the inspiration of their sons and the saving of the old fashion. But both Puritan and Cavalier were lost in the storm of the first Revolution, and the American citizen, supplanting both and stronger than either, took possession of the republic bought by their common blood and fashioned to wisdom, and charged himself with teaching men government and establishing the voice of the people as the voice of God.

My friends, Dr. Talmage has told you that the typical American has yet to come. Let me tell you that he has already come. Great types, like valuable plants, are slow to flower and fruit. But from the union of these colonists, Puritans and Cavaliers, from the straightening of their purposes and the crossing of their blood, slow perfecting through a century, came he who stands as the first typical American, the first who comprehended within himself all the strength and gentleness, all the majesty and grace of this republic—Abraham Lincoln. He was the sum of Puritan and Cavalier, for in his ardent nature were fused the virtues of both, and in the depths of his great soul the faults of both were lost. He was greater than Puritan, greater than Cavalier, in that he was American, and that in his honest form were first gathered the vast and thrilling forces of his ideal government—charging it with such tremendous meaning and elevating it above human suffering that martyrdom, though infamously aimed, came as a fitting crown to a life consecrated from the cradle to human liberty. Let us, each cherishing the traditions and honoring his fathers, build with reverent hands to the type of this simple but sublime life, in which all types are honored, and in our common glory as Americans there will be plenty and to spare for your forefathers and for mine.

Dr. Talmage has drawn for you, with a master's hand, the picture of your returning armies. He has told you how, in the pomp and circumstance of war, they came back to you, marching with proud and victorious tread, reading their glory in a nation's eyes! Will you bear with me while I tell you of another army that sought its home at the close of the late war—an army that marched home in defeat and not in victory—in pathos and not in splendor, but in glory that equaled yours, and to hearts as loving as ever welcomed heroes home! Let me picture to you the footsore Confederate soldier, as buttoning up in his faded gray jacket the parole which was to bear testimony to his children of his fidelity and faith, he turned his face southward from Appomatox in April, 1865. Think of him as ragged, half-starved, heavy-hearted, enfeebled by want and wounds, having fought to exhaustion, he surrenders his gun, wrings the hands of his comrades in silence, and lifting his tear-stained and pallid face for the last time to the graves that dot, old Virginia hills, pulls his gray cap over his brow and begins the slow and painful journey. What does he find—let me ask you who went to your homes eager to find, in the welcome you had justly earned, full payment for four years' sacrifice—what does he find when, having followed the battle-stained cross against overwhelming odds, dreading death not half so much as surrender, he reaches the home he left so prosperous and beautiful? He finds his house in ruins, his farm devastated, his slaves free, his stock killed, his barns empty, his trade destroyed, his money worthless, his social system, feudal in its magnificence, swept away; his people without law or legal status; his comrades slain, and the burdens of others heavy on his shoulders. Crushed by defeat, his very traditions are gone. Without money, credit, employment, material, or training; and beside all this, confronted with the gravest problem that ever met human intelligence—the establishing of a status for the vast body of his liberaved slaves.

What does he do—this hero in gray with a heart of gold? Does he sit down in sullenness and despair? Not for a day. Surely God, who had stripped him of his prosperity, inspired him in his adversity. As ruin was never before so overwhelming, never was restoration swifter. The soldier stepped from the trenches into the furrow; horses that had charged Federal guns marched before the plow, and fields that ran red with human blood in April were green with the harvest in June; women reared in luxury cut up their dresses and made breeches for their husbands, and, with a patience and heroism that fit women always as a garment, gave their hands to work. There was little bitterness in all this. Cheerfulness and frankness prevailed. "Bill Arp" struck the key-note when he said: "Well, I killed as many of them as they did of me, and now I'm going to work." Of the soldier returning home after defeat and roasting some corn on the roadside, who made the remark to his comrades: "You may leave the South if you want to, but I am going to Sandersville, kiss my wife and raise a crop, and if the Yankees fool with me any more, I'll whip 'em again." I want to say to General Sherman, who is considered an able man in our parts, though some people think he is a kind of careless man about fire, that from the ashes he left us in 1864 we have raised a brave and beautiful city; that somehow or other we have caught the sunshine in the bricks and mortar of our homes, and have builded therein not one ignoble prejudice or memory.

But what is the sum of our work? We have found out that in the summing up the free negro counts more than he did as a slave. We have planted the schoolhouse on the hilltop and made it free to white and black. We have sowed towns and cities in the place of theories, and put business above politics. We have challenged your spinners in Massachusetts and your ironmakers in Pennsylvania. We have learned that the $400,000,000 annually received from our cotton crop will make us rich when the supplies that make it are home-raised. We have reduced the commercial rate of interest from 24 to 6 per cent., and are floating 4 per cent. bonds. We have learned that one northern immigrant is worth fifty foreigners; and have smoothed the path to southward, wiped out the place where Mason and Dixon's line used to be, and hung out latchstring to you and yours. We have reached the point that marks perfect harmony in every household, when the husband confesses that the pies which his wife cooks are as good as those his mother used to bake; and we admit that the sun shines as brightly and the moon as softly as it did before the war. We have established thrift in city and country. We have fallen in love with work. We have restored comfort to homes from which culture and elegance never departed. We have let economy take root and spread among us as rank as the crabgrass which sprung from Sherman's cavalry camps, until we are ready to lay odds on the Georgia Yankee as he manufactures relics of the battlefield in a one-story shanty and squeezes pure olive oil out of his cotton seed, against any down-easter that ever swapped wooden nutmegs for flannel sausage in the valleys of Vermont. Above all, we know that we have achieved in these "piping times of peace" a fuller independence for the South than that which our fathers sought to win in the forum by their eloquence or compel in the field by their swords.

It is a rare privilege, sir, to have had part, however humble, in this work. Never was nobler duty confided to human hands than the uplifting and upbuilding of the prostrate and bleeding South—misguided, perhaps, but beautiful in her suffering, and honest, brave and generous always. In the record of her social, industrial and political illustration we await with confidence the verdict of the world.

But what of the negro? Have we solved the problem he presents or progressed in honor and equity toward solution? Let the record speak to the point. No section shows a more prosperous laboring population than the negroes of the South, none in fuller sympathy with the employing and land-owning class. He shares our school fund, has the fullest protection of our laws and the friendship of our people. Self-interest, as well as honor, demand that he should have this. Our future, our very existence depend upon our working out this problem in full and exact justice. We understand that when Lincoln signed the emancipation proclamation, your victory was assured, for he then committed you to the cause of human liberty, against which the arms of man cannot prevail—while those of our statesmen who trusted to make slavery the corner-stone of the Confederacy doomed us to defeat as far as they could, committing us to a cause that reason could not defend or the sword maintain in sight of advancing civilization.

Had Mr. Toombs said, which he did not say, "that he would call the roll of his slaves at the foot of Bunker Hill," he would have been foolish, for he might have known that whenever slavery became entangled in war it mush perish, and that the chattel in human flesh ended forever in New England when your fathers—not to be blamed for parting with what didn't pay—sold their slaves to our fathers—not to be praised for knowing a paying thing when they saw it. The relations of the southern people with the negro are close and cordial. We remember with what fidelity for four years he guarded our defenseless women and children, whose husbands and fathers were fighting against his freedom. To his eternal credit be it said that whenever he struck a blow for his own liberty he fought in open battle, and when at last he raised his black and humble hands that the shackles might be struck off, those hands were innocent of wrong against his helpless charges, and worthy to be taken in loving grasp by every man who honors loyalty and devotion. Ruffians have maltreated him, rascals have misled him, philanthropists established a bank for him, but the South, with the North, protests against injustice to this simple and sincere people. To liberty and enfranchisement is as far as law can carry the negro. The rest must be left to conscience and common sense. It must be left to those among whom his lot is cast, with whom he is indissolubly connected and whose prosperity depends upon their possessing his intelligent sympathy and confidence. Faith has been kept with him, in spite of caluminous assertions to the contrary by those who assume to speak for us or by frank opponents. Faith will be kept with him in the future, if the South holds her reason and integrity.

But have we kept faith with you? In the fullest sense, yes. When Lee surrendered—I don't say when Johnson surrendered, because I understand he still alludes to the time when he met General Sherman last as the time when he determined to abandon any further prosecution of the struggle—when Lee surrendered, I say, and Johnson quit, the South became, and has since been, loyal to this Union. We fought hard enough to know that we were whipped, and in perfect frankness accept as final the arbitrament of the sword to which we had appealed. The South found her jewel in the toad's head of defeat. The shackles that had held her in narrow limitations fell forever when the shackles of the negro slave were broken. Under the old régime the negroes were slaves to the South; the South was a slave to the system. The old plantation, with its simple police regulations and feudal habit, was the only type possible under slavery. Thus was gathered in the hands of a splendid and chivalric oligarchy the substance that should have been diffused among the people, as the rich blood, under certain artificial conditions, is gathered at the heart, filling that with affluent rapture but leaving the body chill and colorless.

The old South rested everything on slavery and agriculture, unconscious that these could neither give nor maintain healthy growth. The new South presents a perfect democracy, the oligarchs leading in the popular movement—a social system compact and closely knitted, less splendid on the surface, but stronger at the core—a hundred farms for every plantation, fifty homes for every palace—and a diversified industry that meets the complex need of this complex age.

The new South is enamored of her new work. Her soul is stirred with the breath of a new life. The light of a grander day is falling fair on her face. She is thrilling with the consciousness of growing power and prosperity. As she stands upright, full-statured and equal among the people of the earth, breathing the keen air and looking out upon the expanded horizon, she understands that her emancipation came because through the inscrutable wisdom of God her honest purpose was crossed, and her brave armies were beaten.

This is said in no spirit of time-serving or apology. The South has nothing for which to apologize. She believes that the late struggle between the States was war and not rebellion; revolution and not conspiracy, and that her convictions were as honest as yours. I should be unjust to the dauntless spirit of the South and to my own convictions if I did not make this plain in this presence. The South has nothing to take back. In my native town of Athens is a monument that crowns its central hill—a plain, white shaft. Deep cut into its shining side is a name dear to me above the names of men—that of a brave and simple man who died in brave and simple faith. Not for all the glories of New England, from Plymouth Rock all the way, would I exchange the heritage he left me in his soldier's death. To the foot of that I shall send my children's children to reverence him who ennobled their name with his heroic blood. But, sir, speaking from the shadow of that memory which I honor as I do nothing else on earth, I say that the cause in which he suffered and for which he gave his life was adjudged by higher and fuller wisdom than his or mine, and I am glad that the omniscient God held the balance of battle in His Almighty hand and that human slavery was swept forever from American soil, the American Union was saved from the wreck of war.

This message, Mr. President, comes to you from consecrated ground. Every foot of soil about the city in which I live is as sacred as a battle-ground of the republic. Every hill that invests it is hallowed to you by the blood of your brothers who died for your victory, and doubly hallowed to us by the blow of those who died hopeless, but undaunted, in defeat—sacred soil to all of us—rich with memories that make us purer and stronger and better—silent but staunch witnesses in its red desolation of the matchless valor of American hearts and the deathless glory of American arms—speaking an eloquent witness in its white peace and prosperity to the indissoluble union of American States and the imperishable brotherhood of the American people.

Now, what answer has New England to this message? Will she permit the prejudice of war to remain in the hearts of the conquerors, when it has died in the hearts of the conquered? Will she transmit this prejudice to the next generation, that in their hearts which never felt the generous ardor of conflict it may perpetuate itself? Will she withhold, save in strained courtesy, the hand which straight from his soldier's heart Grant offered to Lee at Appomatox? Will she make the vision of a restored and happy people, which gathered above the couch of your dying captain, filling his heart with grace; touching his lips with praise, and glorifying his path to the grave—will she make this vision on which the last sigh of his expiring soul breathed a benediction, a cheat and delusion? If she does, the South, never abject in asking for comradeship, must accept with dignity its refusal; but if she does not refuse to accept in frankness and sincerity this message of good will and friendship, then will the prophecy of Webster, delivered in this very society forty years ago amid tremendous applause, become true, be verified in its fullest sense, when he said: "Standing hand to hand and clasping hands, we should remain united as we have been for sixty years, citizens of the same country, members of the same government, united, all united now and united forever." There have been difficulties, contentions, and controversies, but I tell you that in my judgment,

Those opened eyes,
Which like the meteors of a troubled heaven,
All of one nature, of one substance bred,
Did lately meet in th' intestine shock,
Shall now, in mutual well beseeming ranks,
March all one way.

Elizabeth Cady Stanton

Solitude of Self (1892)

In 1840 a group of Americans traveled to London for an antislavery convention. The London Antislavery Society, sponsors of the event, were willing to allow women to observe the proceedings, but were scandalized at the prospect of accrediting women as delegates. Two of the American visitors, Elizabeth Cady Stanton and Lucretia C. Mott, outraged at being denied official recognition, returned home with the idea of holding a convention that would focus attention on women's rights. In 1848, in Seneca Falls, New York, the first women's rights convention was held in the Wesleyan Methodist Church. Under the leadership of women, principally Stanton, the convention passed a series of resolutions calling for rights for women and advocating the radical step of woman suffrage.

Elizabeth Stanton was an interested advocate of temperance and the abolition of slavery, but it was woman's rights—and particularly the right to vote—that absorbed most of her energy and attention. Together with Susan B. Anthony, she founded the magazine, *The Revolution* in 1868. As the first President of the National Woman Suffrage Association she was instrumental in organizing the International Council of Women which met in Washington in 1888.

When the NWSA merged with the American Woman Suffrage Association in 1890 to form the united National American Woman Suffrage Association, Elizabeth Cady Stanton became it first president and redoubled her efforts to have a woman's suffrage amendment adopted. In testifying before the Judiciary Committee in 1892, Stanton explained the principles upon which women's rights were based. Arguing for the "solitude of self," Elizabeth Cady Stanton decried "the need of courage, judgment, and the exercise of every faculty of mind and body, strengthened and developed by use, in women as well as men."

Mr. Chairman and gentlemen of the committee: We have been speaking before Committees of the Judiciary for the last twenty years, and we have gone over all the arguments in favor of a sixteenth amendment which are familiar to all you gentlemen; therefore, it will not be necessary that I should repeat them.

The point I wish plainly to bring before you on this occasion is the individuality of each human soul; our Protestant idea, the right of individual conscience and judgment—our republican idea, individual citizenship. In discussing the rights of woman, we are to consider, first, what belongs to her as an individual, in a world of her own, the arbiter of her own destiny, an imaginary Robinson Crusoe with her woman Friday on a solitary island. Her rights under such circumstances are to use all her faculties for her own safety and happiness.

Secondly, if we consider her as a citizen, as a member of a great nation, she must have the same rights as all other members, according to the fundamental principles of our Government.

Thirdly, viewed as a woman, an equal factor in civilization, her rights and duties are still the same—individual happiness and development.

Fourthly, it is only the incidental relations of life, such as mother, wife, sister, daughter, that may involve some special duties and training. In the usual discussion in regard to woman's sphere, such men as Herbert Spencer, Frederic Harrison, and Grant Allen uniformly subordinate her rights and duties as an individual, as a citizen, as a woman, to the necessities of these incidental relations, some of which a large class of women may never assume. In discussing the sphere of man we do not decide his rights as an individual, as a citizen, as a man by his duties as a father, a husband, a brother, or a son, relations some of which he may never fill. Moreover, he would be better fitted for these very relations, and whatever special work he might choose to do to earn his bread, by the complete development of all his faculties as an individual.

Just so with woman. The education that will fit her to discharge the duties in the largest sphere of human usefulness, will best fit her for whatever special work she may be compelled to do.

The isolation of every human soul and the necessity of self-dependence must give each individual the right to choose his own surroundings. The strongest reason for giving woman all the opportunities for higher education, for the full development of her faculties, forces of mind and body; for giving her the most enlarged freedom of thought and action; a complete emancipation from all forms of bondage, of custom, dependence, superstition; from all the crippling influences of fear, is the solitude and personal responsibility of her own individual life. The strongest reason why we ask for woman a voice in the government under which she lives; in the religion she is asked to believe; equality in social life, where she is the chief factor; a place in the trades and professions, where she may earn her bread, is because of her birthright to self-sovereignty; because, as an individual, she must rely on herself. No matter how much women prefer to lean, to be protected and supported, nor how much men desire to have them do so, they must make the voyage of life alone, and for safety in an emergency they must know something of the laws of navigation. To guide our own craft, we must be captain, pilot, engineer; with chart and compass stand at the wheel; watch the wind and waves and know when to take in the sail, and read the signs in the firmament over all. It matters not whether the solitary voyager is man or woman.

Nature having endowed them equally, leaves them to their own skill and judgment in the hour of danger, and, if not equal to the occasion, alike they perish.

To appreciate the importance of fitting every human soul for independent action, think for a moment of the immeasurable solitude of self. We come into the world alone, unlike all who have gone before us; we leave it alone under circumstances peculiar to ourselves. No mortal ever has been, nor mortal ever will be like the soul just launched on the sea of life. There can never again be just such environments as make up the infancy, youth and manhood of this one. Nature never repeats herself, and the possibilities of one human soul will never be found in another. No one has ever found two blades of grass alike, and no one will ever find two human beings alike. Seeing, then, what must be the infinite diversity in human character, we can in a measure appreciate the loss to a nation when any large class of the people is uneducated and unrepresented in the government. We ask for the complete development of every individual, first, for his own benefit and happiness. In fitting out an army we give each soldier his own knapsack, arms, powder, his blanket, cup, knife, fork and spoon. We provide alike for all their individual necessities, then each man bears his own burden.

Again we ask complete individual development for the general good; for the consensus of the competent on the whole round of human interests; on all questions of national life, and here each man must bear his share of the general burden. It is sad to see how soon friendless children are left to bear their own burdens before they can analyze their feelings; before they can even tell their joys and sorrows, they are thrown on their own resources. The great lesson that nature seems to teach us at all ages is self-dependence, self-protection, self-support. What a touching instance of a child's solitude, of that hunger of the heart for love and recognition, in the case of the little girl who helped to dress a Christmas tree for the children of the family in which she served. On finding there was no present for herself, she slipped away in the darkness and spent the night in an open field sitting on a stone, and when found in the morning, was weeping as if her heart would break. No mortal will ever know the thoughts that passed through the mind of that friendless child in the long hours of that cold night, with only the silent stars to keep her company. The mention of her case in the daily papers moved many generous hearts to send her presents; but in the hours of her keenest suffering, she was thrown wholly on herself for consolation.

In youth our most bitter disappointments, our brightest hopes and ambitions are known only to ourselves; even our friendship and love we never fully share with another; there is something of every passion, in every situation we conceal. Even so in our triumphs and our defeats. The successful candidate for the Presidency and his opponent each have a solitude peculiarly his own, and good form forbids either to speak of his pleasure or regret. The solitude of the king on his throne and the prisoner in his cell differs in character and degree, but it is solitude nevertheless.

We ask no sympathy from others in the anxiety and agony of a broken friendship or shattered love. When death sunders our nearest ties, alone we sit in the shadow of our affliction. Alike mid the greatest triumphs and darkest tragedies of life we walk alone. On the divine heights of human attainments, eulogized and worshiped as a hero or saint, we stand alone. In ignorance, poverty, and vice, as a pauper or criminal, alone we starve or steal; alone we suffer the sneers and rebuffs of our fellows; alone we are hunted and hounded through dark courts and alleys, in by-ways and highways; alone we stand before the judgment seat; alone in the prison cell we lament our crimes and misfortunes; alone we expiate them on the gallows. In hours like these we realize the awful solitude of individual life, its pains, its penalties, its responsibilities; hours in which the youngest and most helpless are thrown on their own resources for guidance and consolation. Seeing then that life must ever be a march and a battle, that each soldier must be equipped for his own protection, it is the height of cruelty to rob the individual of a single natural right.

To throw obstacles in the way of a complete education is like putting out the eyes; to deny the rights of property, like cutting off the hands. To deny political equality is to rob the ostracised of all self-respect; of credit in the market place; of recompense in the world of work; of a voice among those who make and administer the law; a choice in the jury before whom they are tried, and in the judge who decides their punishment. Shakespeare's play of Titus and Andronicus contains a terrible satire on woman's position in the nineteenth century—"Rude men" (the play tell us) "seized the king's daughter, cut out her tongue, cut off her hands, and then bade her go call for water and wash her hands." What a picture of woman's position. Robbed of her natural rights, handicapped by law and custom at every turn, yet compelled to fight her own battles, and in the emergencies of life to fall back on herself for protections.

The girl of sixteen, thrown on the world to support herself, to make her own place in society, to resist the temptations that surround her and maintain a spotless integrity, must do all this by native force or superior education. She does not acquire this power by being trained to trust others and distrust herself. If she wearies of the struggle, finding it hard work to swim upstream, and allows herself to drift with the current, she will find plenty of company, but not one to share her misery in the hour of her deepest humiliation. If she tries to retrieve her position, to conceal the past, her life is hedged about with fears lest willing hands should tear the veil from what she fain would hide. Young and friendless, *she* knows the bitter solitude of self.

How the little courtesies of life on the surface of society, deemed so important from man towards woman, fade into utter insignificance in view of the deeper tragedies in which she must play her part alone, where no human aid is possible.

The young wife and mother, at the head of some establishment with a kind husband to shield her from the adverse winds of life, with wealth, fortune and position, has a certain harbor of safety, secure against the ordinary ills of life. But to manage a household, have a desirable influence in society, keep her friends and the affections of her husband, train her children and servants well, she must have rare common sense, wisdom, diplomacy, and a knowledge of human nature. To do all this she needs the cardinal virtues and the strong points of character that the most successful statesman possesses.

An uneducated woman, trained to dependence, with no resources in herself must make a failure of any position in life. But society says women do not need a knowledge of the world, the liberal training that experience in public life must give, all the advantages of collegiate education; but when for the lack of all these, the woman's happiness is wrecked, alone she bears her humiliation. The solitude of the weak and the ignorant is indeed pitiable; in the wild chase for the prizes of life they are ground to powder.

In age, when the pleasures of youth are passed, children grown up, married and gone, the hurry and bustle of life in a measure over, when the hands are weary of active service, when the old arm chair and the fireside are the chosen resorts, then men and women alike must fall back on their own resources. If they cannot find companionship in books, if they have no interest in the vital questions of the hour, no interest in watching the consummation of reforms, with which they might have been identified, they soon pass into their dotage. The more fully the faculties of the mind are developed and kept in use, the longer the period of vigor and active interest in all around us continues. If from a lifelong participation in public affairs a woman feels responsible for the laws regulating our system of education, the discipline of our jails and prisons, the sanitary condition of our private homes, public buildings, and thoroughfares, an interest in commerce, finance, our foreign relations, in any or all of these questions, her solitude will at least be respectable, and she will not be driven to gossip or scandal for entertainment.

The chief reason for opening to every soul the doors to the whole round of human duties and pleasures, is the individual development thus attained, the resources thus provided under all circumstances to mitigate the solitude that at times must come to everyone. I once asked Prince Krapotkin, the Russian nihilist, how he endured his long years in prison, deprived of books, pen, ink, and paper. "Ah," he said, "I thought out many questions in which I had a deep interest. In the pursuit of an idea I took no note of time. When tired of solving knotty problems, I recited all the beautiful passages in prose or verse I had ever learned. I became acquainted with myself and my own resources. I had a world of my own, a vast empire, that no Russian jailor or Czar could invade." Such is the value of liberal thought and broad culture when shut off from all human companionship, bringing comfort and sunshine within even the four walls of a prison cell.

As women ofttimes share a similar fate, should they not have all the consolation that the most liberal education can give? Their suffering in the prisons of St. Petersburg, in the long, weary marches to Siberia, and in the mines, working side by side with men, surely call for all the self-support that the most exalted sentiments of heroism can give. When suddenly roused at midnight, with the startling cry of "fire! fire!" to find the house over their heads in flames, do women wait for men to point the way to safety? And are the men, equally bewildered and half suffocated with smoke, in a position to more than try to save themselves? At such times the most timid women have shown a courage and heroism in saving their husbands and children that has surprised everybody. Inasmuch, then, as woman shares equally the joys and sorrows of time and eternity, is it not the height of presumption in man to propose to represent her at the ballot box and the throne of grace, to do her voting in the state, her praying in the church, and to assume the position of high priest at the family altar?

Nothing strengthens the judgment and quickens the conscience like individual responsibility. Nothing adds such dignity to character as the recognition of one's self-sovereignty; the right to an equal place, everywhere conceded; a place earned by personal merit, not an artificial attainment, by inheritance, wealth, family, and position. Seeing, then, that the responsibilities of life rest equally on man and woman, that their destiny is the same, they need the same preparation for time and eternity. The talk of sheltering woman from the fierce storms of life is the sheerest mockery, for they beat on her from every point of the compass, just as they do on man, and with more fatal results, for he has been trained to protect himself, to resist, to conquer. Such are the facts in human experience, the responsibilities of individual sovereignty. Rich and poor, intelligent and ignorant, wise and foolish, virtuous and vicious, man and woman, it is ever the same, each soul must depend wholly on itself.

Whatever the theories may be of woman's dependence on man, in the supreme moments of her life he cannot bear her burdens. Alone she goes to the gates of death to give life to every man that is born into the world. No one can share her fears, no one can mitigate her pangs; and if her sorrow is greater than she can bear, alone she passes beyond the gates into the vast unknown. From the mountain tops of Judea, long ago, a heavenly voice bade his disciples, "Bear ye one another's burdens," but humanity has not yet risen to that point of self-sacrifice, and if ever so willing, how few the burdens are that one soul can bear for another. In the highways of Palestine; in prayer and fasting on the solitary mountain top; in the Garden of Gethsemane; before the judgment seat of Pilate; betrayed by one of his trusted disciples at his last supper; in his agonies on the cross, even Jesus of Nazareth, in these last sad days on earth, felt the awful solitude of self. Deserted by man, in agony he cries, "My God! My God! why hast Thou forsaken me?" And so it ever must be in the conflicting scenes of life, in the long, weary march, each one walks alone. We may have many friends, love, kindness, sympathy and charity to smooth our pathway in everyday life, but in the tragedies and triumphs of human experience each mortal stands alone.

But when all artificial trammels are removed, and women are recognized as individuals, responsible for their own environments, thoroughly educated for all positions in life they may be called to fill; with all the resources in themselves that liberal thought and broad culture can give; guided by their own conscience and judgment; trained to self-protection by a healthy development of the muscular system and skill in the use of weapons of defense, and stimulated to self-support by a knowledge of the business world and the pleasure that pecuniary independence must ever give; when women are trained in this way they will, in a measure, be fitted for those hours of solitude that come alike to all, whether prepared or otherwise. As in our extremity we must depend on ourselves, the dictates of wisdom point to complete individual development.

In talking of education how shallow the argument that each class must be educated for the special work it proposes to do, and all those faculties not needed in this special walk must lie dormant and utterly wither for want of use, when, perhaps, these will be the very faculties needed in life's greatest emergencies. Some say, "Where is the use of drilling girls in the languages, the sciences, in law, medicine, theology? As wives, mothers, housekeepers, cooks, they need a different curriculum from boys who are to fill all positions." The chief cooks in our great hotels and ocean steamers are men. In our large cities men run the bakeries, they make our bread, cake and pies, they manage the laundries, they are now considered our best milliners and dressmakers. Because some men fill these departments of usefulness, shall we regulate the curriculum in Harvard and Yale to their present necessities? If not, why this talk in our best colleges of a curriculum for girls who are crowding into the trades and professions, teachers in all our public schools, rapidly filling many lucrative and honorable positions in life?

They are showing, too, their calmness and courage in the most trying hours of human experience. You have probably all read in the daily papers of the terrible storm in the Bay of Biscay when a tidal wave made such havoc on the shore, wrecking vessels, unroofing houses, and carrying destruction everywhere. Among other buildings the woman's prison was demolished. Those who escaped saw men struggling to reach the shore. They promptly by clasping hands made a chain of themselves and pushed out into the sea, again and again, at the risk of their lives until they had brought six men to shore, carried them to a shelter, and did all in their power for their comfort and protection.

What special school of training could have prepared these women for this sublime moment in their lives? In times like this humanity rises above all college curriculums and recognizes Nature as the greatest of all teachers in the hour of danger and death. Women are already the equals of men in the whole realm of thought, in art, science, literature, and government. With telescopic vision they explore the starry firmament and bring back the history of the planetary world. With chart and compass they pilot ships across the mighty deep, and with skillful finger send electric messages around the globe. In galleries of art the beauties of nature and the virtues of humanity are immortalized by them on canvas, and by their inspired touch dull blocks of marble are transformed into angels of light.

In music they speak again the language of Mendelssohn, Beethoven, Chopin, Schumann, and are worthy interpreters of their great thoughts. The poetry and novels of the century are theirs, and they have touched the keynote of reform in religion, politics, and social life. They fill the editor's and professor's chair, and plead at the bar of justice, walk the wards of the hospital, and speak from the pulpit and the platform; such is the type of womanhood that an enlightened public sentiment welcomes to-day, and such the triumph of the facts of life over the false theories of the past.

Is it, then, consistent to hold the developed woman of this day within the same narrow political limits as the dame with the spinning wheel and knitting needle occupied in the past? No! no! Machinery has taken the labors of woman as well as man on its tireless shoulders; the loom and the spinning wheel are but dreams of the past; the pen, the brush, the easel, the chisel, have taken their places, while the hopes and ambitions of women are essentially changed.

We see reason sufficient in the outer conditions of human beings for individual liberty and development, but when we consider the self-dependence of every human soul we see the need of courage, judgment, and the exercise of every faculty of mind and body, strengthened and developed by use, in woman as well as man.

Whatever may be said of man's protecting power in ordinary conditions, mid all the terrible disasters by land and sea, in the supreme moments of danger, alone, woman must ever meet the horrors of the situation, the Angel of Death even makes no royal pathway for her. Man's love and sympathy enter only into the sunshine of our lives. In that solemn solitude of self, that links us with the immeasurable and the eternal, each soul lives alone forever. A recent writer says:

> I remember once, in crossing the Atlantic, to have gone upon the deck of the ship at midnight, when a dense black cloud enveloped the sky, and the great deep was roaring madely under the lashes of demoniac winds. My feeling was not of danger or fear (which is a base surrender of the immortal soul), but of utter desolation and loneliness; a little speck of life shut in by a tremendous darkness. Again I remember to have climbed the slopes of the Swiss Alps, up beyond the point where vegetation ceases, and the stunted conifers no longer struggle against the unfeeling blasts. Around me lay a huge confusion of rocks, out of which the gigantic ice peaks shot into the measureless blue of the heavens, and again my only feeling was the awful solitude.
>
> And yet, there is a solitude, which each and every one of us has always carried with him, more inaccessible than the ice-cold mountains, more profound than the midnight sea; the solitude of self. Our inner being, which we call ourself, no eye nor touch of man or angel has ever pierced. It is more hidden than the caves of the gnome; the sacred adytum of the oracle; the hidden chamber of eleusinian mystery, for to it only omniscience is permitted to enter.

Such is individual life. Who, I ask you, can take, dare take, on himself the rights, the duties, the responsibilities of another human soul?

Booker T. Washington

Atlanta Exposition Address (1895)

In 1895, in an effort to attract investment to the South, a Cotton States Exposition was organized to display to the world the economic gains made there. Planners of the exposition, which was to be held in Atlanta, made what some considered the bold move of inviting a black educator, Booker T. Washington, president of Tuskegee Institute, to speak at the opening ceremonies to a racially mixed audience.

Washington, born a slave, moved from Virginia to West Virginia after the Civil War. He worked as a miner while gaining a rudimentary education and then attended Hampton Institute, a school established by a former Union general, Samuel C. Armstrong, to educate freed blacks. After teaching school in West Virginia for two years, he returned to Hampton as a member of the faculty. He stayed there from 1879 to 1881, leaving to head a newly founded Normal School for blacks, the Tuskegee Institute in Alabama. The new school had only one teacher and about fifty students and was housed in an old church. Under Washington's leadership, the Institute grew in size and reputation, becoming one of the leading centers for black education in the country.

The Atlanta Exposition speech was typical in its message of Washington's stance on racial questions. He urged cooperation between the races but recognized the harsh realities of segregation. Instead of urging blacks to strive for political or social advancement, Washington emphasized the need for blacks to acquire education and technical skills and argued that black improvement would benefit whites as well. Washington's assertion that "agitation of questions of social equality is the extremest folly," and that blacks would make "progress in the enjoyment of all the privileges that will come to us" only through hard work, made him acceptable to white leaders. His lack of militancy in the area of civil rights, however, was bitterly resented by more radical blacks, such as W. E. B. DuBois, who criticized Washington for his failure to speak against the prevailing white view of the inequality of the races.

His speech in Atlanta was well received by the Exposition audience and was widely reported throughout the country. From the President of the United States, Grover Cleveland, came a note to Washington praising the speech and offering the opinion that it "cannot fail to delight and encourage all who wish well for your race."

Mr. President and Gentlemen of the Board of Directors and Citizens.

One-third of the population of the South is of the Negro race. No enterprise seeking the material, civil, or moral welfare of this section can disregard this element of our population and reach the highest success. I but convey to you, Mr. President and Directors, the sentiment of the masses of my race when I say that in no way have the value and manhood of the American Negro been more fittingly and generously recognized than by the managers of this magnificent Exposition at every stage of its progress. It is a recognition that will do more to cement the friendship of the two races than any occurrence since the dawn of our freedom.

Not only this, but the opportunity here afforded will awaken among us a new era of industrial progress. Ignorant and inexperienced, it is not strange that in the first years of our new life we began at the top instead of at the bottom; that a seat in Congress or the state legislature was more sought than real estate or industrial skill; that the political convention of stump speaking had more attractions than starting a dairy farm or truck garden.

A ship lost at sea for many days suddenly sighted a friendly vessel. From the mast of the unfortunate vessel was seen a signal, "Water, water; we die of thirst!" The answer from the friendly vessel at once came back, "Cast down your bucket where you are." A second time the signal, "Water, water; send us water!" ran up from the distressed vessel, and was answered, "Cast down your bucket where you are." And a third and fourth signal for water was answered, "Cast down your bucket where you are." The captain of the distressed vessel, at last heeding the injunction, cast down his bucket, and it came up full of fresh, sparkling water from the mouth of the Amazon River. To those of my race who depend on bettering their condition in a foreign land or who underestimate the importance of cultivating friendly relations with the Southern white man, who is their next-door neighbour, I would say: "Cast down your bucket where you are"—cast it down in making friends in every manly way of the people of all races by whom we are surrounded.

Cast it down in agriculture, mechanics, in commerce, in domestic service, and in the professions. And in this connection it is well to bear in mind that whatever other sins the South may be called to bear, when it comes to business, pure and simple, it is in the South that the Negro is given a man's chance in the commercial world, and in nothing is this Exposition more eloquent than in emphasizing this chance. Our greatest danger is that in the great leap from slavery to freedom we may overlook the fact that the masses of us are to live by the productions of our hands, and fail to keep in mind that we shall prosper in proportion as we learn to dignify and glorify common labour and put brains and skill into the common occupations of life; shall prosper in proportion as we learn to draw the line between the superficial and the substantial, the ornamental gewgaws of life and the useful. No race can prosper till it learns that there is as much dignity in tilling a field as in writing a poem. It is at the bottom of life we must begin, and not at the top. Nor should we permit our grievances to overshadow our opportunities.

To those of the white race who look to the incoming of those of foreign birth and strange tongue and habits for the prosperity of the South, were I permitted I would repeat what I say to my own race, "Cast down your bucket where you are." Cast it down among the eight millions of Negroes whose habits you know, whose fidelity and love you have tested in days when to have proved treacherous meant the ruin of your firesides. Cast down your bucket among these people who have, without strikes and labour wars, tilled your fields, cleared your forests, builded your railroads and cities, and brought forth treasures from the bowels of the earth, and helped make possible this magnificent representation of the progress of the South. Casting down your bucket among my people, helping and encouraging them as you are doing on these grounds, and to education of head, hand, and heart, you will find that they will buy your surplus land, make blossom the waste places in your fields, and run your factories. While doing this, you can be sure in the future, as in the past, that you and your families will be surrounded by the most patient, faithful, law-abiding, and unresentful people that the world has seen. As we have proved our loyalty to you in the past, in nursing your children, watching by the sick-bed of your mothers and fathers, and often following them with tear-dimmed eyes to their graves, so in the future, in our humble way, we shall stand by you with a devotion that no foreigner can approach, ready to lay down our lives, if need be, in defence of yours, interlacing our industrial, commercial, civil, and religious life with yours in a way that shall make the interests of both races one. In all things that are purely social we can be as separate as the fingers, yet one as the hand in all things essential to mutual progress.

There is no defence or security for any of us except in the highest intelligence and development of all. If anywhere there are efforts tending to curtail the fullest growth of the Negro, let these efforts be turned into stimulating, encouraging, and making him the most useful and intelligent citizen. Effort or means so invested will pay a thousand per cent interest. These efforts will be twice blessed—"blessing him that gives and him that takes."

There is no escape through law of man or God from the inevitable:—

> The laws of changeless justice bind
>   Oppressor with oppressed;
> And close as sin and suffering joined
>   We march to fate abreast.

Nearly sixteen millions of hands will aid you in pulling the load upward, or they will pull against you the load downward. We shall constitute one-third and more of the ignorance and crime of the South, or one-third its intelligence and progress; we shall contribute one-third to the business and industrial prosperity of the South, or we shall prove a veritable body of death, stagnating, depressing, retarding every effort to advance the body politic.

Gentlemen of the Exposition, as we present to you our humble effort at an exhibition of our progress, you must not expect overmuch. Starting thirty years ago with ownership here and there in a few quilts and pumpkins and chickens (gathered from miscellaneous sources), remember the path that has led from these to the inventions and production of agricultural implements, buggies, steam-engines, newspapers, books, statuary, carving, paintings, the management of drug-stores and banks, has not been trodden without contact with thorns and thistles. While we take pride in what we exhibit as a result of our independent efforts, we do not for a moment forget that our part in this exhibition would fall far short of your expectations but for the constant help that has come to our educational life, not only from the Southern states, but especially from Northern philanthropists, who have made their gifts a constant stream of blessing and encouragement.

The wisest among my race understand that the agitation of questions of social equality is the extremest folly, and that progress in the enjoyment of all the privileges that will come to us must be the result of severe and constant struggle rather than of artificial forcing. No race that has anything to contribute to the markets of the world is long in any degree ostracized. It is important and right that all privileges of the law be ours, but it is vastly more important that we be prepared for the exercises of these privileges. The opportunity to earn a dollar in a factory just now is worth infinitely more than the opportunity to spend a dollar in an opera-house.

In conclusion, may I repeat that nothing in thirty years has given us more hope and encouragement, and drawn us so near to you of the white race, as this opportunity offered by the Exposition; and here bending, as it were, over the altar that represents the results of the struggles of your race and mine, both starting practically empty-handed three decades ago, I pledge that in your effort to work out the great and intricate problem which God has laid at the doors of the South, you shall have at all times the patient, sympathetic help of my race; only let this be constantly in mind, that, while from representations in these buildings of the product of field, of forest, of mine, of factory, letters, and art, much good will come, yet far above and beyond material benefits will be that higher good, that, let us pray God, will come, in a blotting out of sectional differences and racial animosities and suspicions, in a determination to administer absolute justice, in a willing obedience among all classes to the mandates of law. This, this, coupled with our material prosperity, will bring into our beloved South a new heaven and a new earth.

Albert Beveridge

The March of the Flag (1898)

After the Civil War, America, now virtually consolidated within its continental boundaries, began the process of reaching out to extend its influence and control in other parts of the globe. In the Pacific, the Midway Islands, over 1,000 miles west of Hawaii, had been occupied by the United States since their discovery in 1859, but it was in Hawaii itself that American interest grew. A commercial treaty with Hawaii was signed in 1875, and in 1887 a treaty gave the United States the exclusive right to a fortified naval base at Pearl Harbor. A coup led primarily by American sugar planters, abetted by a contingent of Marines called in by the pro-annexationist United States minister to Hawaii, overthrew Queen Liliuokalani, in 1893. The Republic of Hawaii was recognized by the United States in 1894, but the Democratic President, Grover Cleveland, condemned the means by which power had been seized and refused to submit an annexation treaty to Congress. His Republican successor, President McKinley, however, succeeded in annexing Hawaii in 1898 during the Spanish-American War, when its strategic importance as a naval base became clear. Congress granted the islands territorial status in 1900.

The Spanish-American War brought to the forefront America's imperial ambitions. The United States had long taken a proprietary interest in the Caribbean. As early as 1870, President Grant attempted unsuccessfully to annex Santo Domingo. In was in Cuba, however, that matters reached a crisis that eventually called forth American action.

The last quarter of the century had seen continuous unrest as the Cubans resisted Spanish rule. The insurrection that broke out in 1897 was marked by widespread destruction of the sugar plantations—largely controlled by American investors—by the revolutionaries, and severe repression by the Spanish authorities. The American public learned of the concentration camps established by General Valeriano Weyler through the lurid reports published in Hearst's *New York Journal* and Pulitzer's *New York World*, and American opinion clearly favored the rebels. In February 1898 the U.S. battleship *Maine* was sunk in Havana Harbor. Even though a naval court of inquiry could not determine responsibility, the Spanish were widely believed to be at fault, and by April the United States was at war with Spain.

The Assistant Secretary of the Navy, Theodore Roosevelt, had previously ordered the commander of the Asiatic squadron, Commodore Dewey, to be prepared to attack the Spanish fleet in the Philippines should war break out. The squadron was, accordingly, ready for immediate action; it sailed from Hong Kong and caught and destroyed the Spanish fleet at Manila Bay on May 1. This victory was followed by the arrival of American troops, who, with Filipino guerrillas, took Manila. The Spanish capitulated on August 14 and a military occupation of the Philippines by the United States was proclaimed. Meanwhile, American forces had landed in June in Cuba, and by July they had seized the high ground outside Santiago. Attempting to break through the American blockade, the Spanish fleet left Santiago harbor and was decimated in an engagement with Admiral Sampson's naval force. On July 17 the Spanish garrison at Santiago surrendered and the war was virtually over.

At the close of the nineteenth century, then, like it or not, the United States was on the verge of joining England, Germany, and France as an imperial power.

Some liked it very much, indeed. Although the imperialist/anti-imperialist division was not strictly along party lines, Republicans tended to favor the idea of extending American hegemony throughout the globe while Democrats were hostile to such pretensions. Among those who relished the dominating role America was to play in the world was a Republican candidate for the U.S. Senate, Albert Beveridge of Indiana.

An Indianapolis lawyer, Beveridge launched his Senate campaign with a speech at Tomlinson Hall in Indianapolis in September 1898; this speech was widely distributed throughout the Midwest as an important campaign document. In it, Beveridge proudly proclaimed the rights and ablities of Americans to rule those not capable of self-government; his arguments were based firmly on the assumption of nationalistic and racial superiority. He saw the expansion of America as divinely inspired and the acquisition of new territory as but an extension of the westward and southern spread of liberty that had distinguished all of American history. The current challenges and opportunities afforded in the Pacific and the Caribbean were at one with the past, a continuation of "the march of the flag."

It is a noble land that God has given us; a land that can feed and clothe the world; a land whose coastlines would inclose half the countries of Europe; a land set like a sentinel between the two imperial oceans of the globe, a greater England with a nobler destiny.

It is a mighty people that He has planted on this soil; a people sprung from the most masterful blood of history; a people perpetually revitalized by the virile, man-producing working-folk of all the earth; a people imperial by virtue of their power, by right of their institutions, by authority of their Heaven-directed purposes—the propagandists and not the misers of liberty.

It is a glorious history our God has bestowed upon His chosen people; a history heroic with faith in our mission and our future; a history of statesmen who flung the boundaries of the Republic out into unexplored lands and savage wilderness; a history of soldiers who carried the flag across blazing deserts and through the ranks of hostile mountains, even to the gates of sunset; a history of a multiplying people who overran a continent in half a century; a history of prophets who saw the consequences of evils inherited from the past and of martyrs who died to save us from them; a history divinely logical, in the process of whose tremendous reasoning we find ourselves to-day.

Therefore, in this campaign, the question is larger than a party question. It is an American question. It is a world question. Shall the American people continue their march toward the commercial supermacy of the world? Shall free institutions broaden their blessed reign as the children of liberty wax in strength, until the empire of our principles is established over the hearts of all mankind?

Have we no mission to perform, no duty to discharge to our fellow-man? Has God endowed us with gifts beyond our deserts and marked us as the people of His peculiar favor, merely to rot in our own selfishness, as men and nations must, who take cowardice for their companion and self for their deity—as China has, as India has, as Egypt has?

Shall we be as the man who had one talent and hid it, or as he who had ten talents and used them until they grew to riches? And shall we reap the reward that waits on our discharge of our high duty; shall we occupy new markets for what our farmers raise, our factories make, our merchants sell—aye, and, please God, new markets for what our ships shall carry?

Hawaii is ours; Porto Rico is to be ours; at the prayer of her people Cuba finally will be ours; in the islands of the East, even to the gates of Asia, coaling stations are to be ours at the very least; the flag of a liberal government is to float over the Philippines, and may it be the banner that Taylor unfurled in Texas and Fremont carried to the coast.

The Opposition tells us that we ought not to govern a people without their consent. I answer, The rule of liberty that all just government derives its authority from the consent of the governed, applies only to those who are capable of self-government. We govern the Indians without their consent, we govern our territories without their consent, we govern our children without their consent. How do they know that our government would be without their consent? Would not the people of the Philippines prefer the just, humane, civilizing government of this Republic to the savage, bloody rule of pillage and extortion from which we have rescued them?

And, regardless of this formula of words made only for enlightened, self-governing people, do we owe no duty to the world? Shall we turn these peoples back to the reeking hands from which we have taken them? Shall we abandon them, with Germany, England, Japan, hungering for them? Shall we save them from those nations, to give them a self-rule of tragedy?

They ask us how we shall govern these new possessions. I answer: Out of local conditions and the necessities of the case methods of government will grow. If England can govern foreign lands, so can America. If Germany can govern foreign lands, so can America. If they can supervise protectorates, so can America. Why is it more difficult to administer Hawaii than New Mexico or California? Both had a savage and an alien population; both were more remote from the seat of government when they came under our dominion than the Philippines are to-day.

Will you say by your vote that American ability to govern has decayed; that a century's experience in self-rule has failed of a result? Will you affirm by your vote that you are an infidel to American power and practical sense? Or will you say that ours is the blood of government; ours the heart of dominion; ours the brain and genius of administration? Will you remember that we do but what our fathers did—we but pitch the tents of liberty farther westward, farther southward—we only continue the march of the flag?

The march of the flag! In 1789 the flag of the Republic waved over 4,000,000 souls in thirteen states, and their savage territory which stretched to the Mississippi, to Canada, to the Floridas. The timid minds of that day said that no new territory was needed, and, for the hour, they were right. But Jefferson, through whose intellect the centuries marched; Jefferson, who dreamed of Cuba as an American state; Jefferson, the first Imperialist of the Republic—Jefferson acquired that imperial territory which swept from the Mississippi to the mountains, from Texas to the British possessions, and the march of the flag began!

The infidels to the gospel of liberty raved, but the flag swept on! The title to that noble land out of which Oregon, Washington, Idaho and Montana have been carved was uncertain; Jefferson, strict constructionist of constitutional power though he was, obeyed the Anglo-Saxon impulse within him, whose watchword then and whose watchword throughout the world to-day is, "Forward!": another empire was added to the Republic, and the march of the flag went on!

Those who deny the power of free institutions to expand urged every argument, and more, that we hear, to-day; but the people's judgment approved the command of their blood, and the march of the flag went on!

A screen of land from New Orleans to Florida shut us from the Gulf, and over this and the Everglade Peninsula waved the saffron flag of Spain; Andrew Jackson seized both, the American people stood at his back, and, under Monroe, the Floridas came under the dominion of the Republic, and the march of the flag went on! The Cassandras prophesied every prophecy of despair we hear, to-day, but the march of the flag went on!

Then Texas responded to the bugle calls of liberty, and the march of the flag went on! And, at last, we waged war with Mexico, and the flag swept over the southwest, over peerless California, past the Gate of Gold to Oregon on the north, and from ocean to ocean its folds of glory blazed.

And, now, obeying the same voice that Jefferson heard and obeyed, that Jackson heard and obeyed, that Monroe heard and obeyed, that Seward heard and obeyed, that Grant heard and obeyed, that Harrison heard and obeyed, our President to-day plants the flag over the islands of the seas, outposts of commerce, citadels of national security, and the march of the flag goes on!

Distance and oceans are no arguments. The fact that all the territory our fathers bought and seized is contiguous, is no argument. In 1819 Florida was farther from New York than Porto Rico is from Chicago to-day; Texas, farther from Washington in 1845 than Hawaii is from Boston in 1898; California, more inaccessible in 1847 than the Philippines are now. Gibraltar is farther from London than Havana is from Washington; Melbourne is farther from Liverpool than Manila is from San Francisco.

The ocean does not separate us from lands of our duty and desire—the oceans join us, rivers never to be dredged, canals never to be repaired. Steam joins us; electricity joins us—the very elements are in league with our destiny. Cuba not contiguous! Porto Rico not contiguous! Hawaii and the Philippines not contiguous! The oceans make them contiguous. And our navy will make them contiguous.

But the Opposition is right—there is a difference. We did not need the western Mississippi Valley when we acquired it, nor Florida, no Texas, nor California, nor the royal provinces of the far northwest. We had no emigrants to people this imperial wilderness, no money to develop it, even no highways to cover it. No trade awaited us in its savage fastnesses. Our productions were not greater than our trade. There was not one reason for the land-lust of our statesmen from Jefferson to Grant, other than the prophet and the Saxon within them. But, to-day, we are raising more than we can consume, making more than we can use. Therefore we must find new markets for our produce.

And so, while we did not need the territory taken during the past century at the time it was acquired, we do need what we have taken in 1898, and we need it now. The resources and the commerce of these immensely rich dominions will be increased as much as American energy is greater than Spanish sloth. In Cuba, alone, there are 15,000,000 acres of forest unacquainted with the ax, exhaustless mines of iron, priceless deposits of manganese, millions of dollars' worth of which we must buy, to-day, from the Black Sea districts. There are millions of acres yet unexplored.

The resources of Porto Rico have only been trifled with. The riches of the Philippines have hardly been touched by the finger-tips of modern methods. And they produce what we consume, and consume what we produce—the very predestination of reciprocity—a reciprocity "not made with hands, eternal in the heavens." They sell hemp, sugar, cocoanuts, fruits of the tropics, timber of price like mahogany; they buy flour, clothing, tools, implements, machinery and all that we can raise and make. Their trade will be ours in time. Do you indorse that policy with your vote?

Cuba is as large as Pennsylvania, and is the richest spot on the globe. Hawaii is as large as New Jersey; Porto Rico half as large as Hawaii; the Philippines larger than all New England, New York, New Jersey, and Delaware combined. Together they are larger than the British Isles, larger than France, larger than Germany, larger than Japan.

If any man tells you that trade depends on cheapness and not on government influence, ask him why England does not abandon South Africa, Egypt, India. Why does France seize South China, Germany the vast region whose port is Kaouchou?

Our trade with Porto Rico, Hawaii and the Philippines must be as free as between the states of the Union, because they are

American territory, while every other nation on earth must pay our tariff before they can compete with us. Until Cuba shall ask for annexation, our trade with her will, at the very least, be like the preferential trade of Canada with England. That, and the excellence of our goods and products; that, and the convenience of traffic; that, and the kinship of interests and destiny, will give the monopoly of these markets to the American people.

The commercial supremacy of the Republic means that this nation is to be the sovereign factor in the peace of the world. For the conflicts of the future are to be conflicts of trade—struggles for markets—commercial wars for existence. And the golden rule of peace is impregnability of position and invincibility of prepardness. So, we see England, the greatest strategist of history, plant her flag and her cannon on Gibraltar, at Quebec, in the Bermudas, at Vancouver, everywhere.

So Hawaii furnishes us a naval base in the heart of the Pacific; the Ladrones another, a voyage further on; Manila another, at the gates of Asia—Asia, to the trade of whose hundreds of millions American merchants, manufacturers, farmers, have as good right as those of Germany or France or Russia or England; Asia, whose commerce with the United Kingdom alone amounts to hundreds of millions of dollars every year; Asia, to whom Germany looks to take her surplus products; Asia, whose doors must not be shut against American trade. Within five decades the bulk of Oriential commerce will be ours.

No wonder that, in the shadows of coming events so great, free-silver is already a memory. The current of history has swept past that episode. Men understand, to-day, that the greatest commerce of the world must be conducted with the steadiest standard of value and most convenient medium of exchange human ingenuity can devise. Time, that unerring reasoner, has settled the silver question. The American people are tired of talking about money—they want to make it. Why should the farmer get a half-measure dollar of money any more than he should give a half-measure bushel of grain?

Why should not the proposition for the free coinage of silver be as dead as the proposition of irredeemable paper money? It is the same proposition in a different form. If the Government stamp can make a piece of silver, which you can buy for 45 cents, pass for 100 cents, the Government stamp can make a piece of pewter, worth one cent, pass for 100 cents, and a piece of paper, worth a fraction of a cent, pass for 100 cents. Free-silver is the principle of fiat money applied to metal. If you favor fiat silver, you necessarily favor fiat paper.

If the Government can make money with a stamp, why does the Government borrow money? If the Government can create value out of nothing, why not abolish all taxation?

And if it is not the stamp of the Government that raises the value, but the demand which free coinage creates, why has the value of silver gone down at a time when more silver was bought and coined by the Government than ever before? Again, if the people want more silver, why do they refuse what we already have? And if free silver makes money more plentiful, how will *you* get any of it? Will the silver-mine owner give it to you? Will he loan it to you? Will the Government give or loan it to you? Where do you or I come in on this free-silver proposition?

The American people want this money question settled for ever. They want a uniform currency, a convenient currency, a currency that grows as business grows, a currency based on science and not on chance.

And now, on the threshold of our new

and great career, is the time permanently to adjust our system of finance. The American people have the mightiest commerce of the world to conduct. They can not halt to unsettle their money system every time some ardent imagination sees a vision and dreams a dream. Think of Great Britain becoming the commercial monarch of the world with her financial system periodically assailed! Think of Holland or Germany or France bearing their burdens, and, yet, sending their flag to every sea, with their money at the mercy of politicians-out-of-an-issue. Let us settle the whole financial system on principles so sound that no agitation can shake it. And then, like men and not like children, let us on to our tasks, our mission and our destiny.

There are so many real things to be done—canals to be dug, railways to be laid, forests to be felled, cities to be builded, fields to be tilled, markets to be won, ships to be launched, peoples to be saved, civilization to be proclaimed and the flag of liberty flung to the eager air of every sea. Is this an hour to waste upon triflers with nature's laws? Is this a season to give our destiny over to word-mongers and prosperity-wreckers? No! It is an hour to remember our duty to our homes. It is a moment to realize the opportunities fate has opened to us. And so it is an hour for us to stand by the Government.

Wonderfully has God guided us. Yonder at Bunker Hill and Yorktown His Providence was above us. At New Orleans and on ensanguined seas His hand sustained us. Abraham Lincoln was His minister and His was the altar of freedom the Nation's soldiers set up on a hundred battle-fields. His power directed Dewey in the East and delivered the Spanish fleet into our hands, as He delivered the elder Armada into the hands of our English sires two centuries ago. The American people can not use a dishonest medium of exchange; it is ours to set the world its example of right and honor. We can not fly from our world duties; it is ours to execute the purpose of a fate that has driven us to be greater than our small intentions. We can not retreat from any soil where Providence has unfurled our banner; it is ours to save that soil for liberty and civilization.

Theodore Roosevelt

The Strenuous Life (1899)

Having easily defeated its enemy in the brief Spanish-American War, the United States found itself divided over the question of what to do with the spoils of victory. The Treaty of Paris, concluded with Spain in December of 1898, stipulated that Spain cede the Philippines to the United States in exchange for a payment of $20 million; Puerto Rico and Guam were also ceded as a war indemnity. Further, Spain relinquished all claim to sovereignty over Cuba while assuming liability for the Cuban debt.

Differences over what to do with this newly acquired territory were sharp. The imperialists saw the hand of God at work in furthering America's mission as harbinger of civilization; they also were aware of the economic and strategic advantages of the Philippines and feared that other nations would establish their own influence in the islands if America withdrew. For their part, the anti-imperialists were alarmed by the prospect of acquiring land that was not contiguous to the United States and that was inhabited by those whose culture would not permit easy assimilation. They also argued that the right of self-government was a fundamental American principle that imperialism would destroy.

These disagreements came to a head in the debate in the Senate over the ratification of the Treaty of Paris. It seemed unlikely that the necessary two-thirds majority in favor of the treaty would be obtained until William Jennings Bryan, the leader of the Democratic Party, decided that the treaty should pass simply to bring the war to an end and that the issue of what to do with the conquered territories be resolved in the coming election campaign. He was successful in convincing enough of the opponents of the treaty to vote for it to secure ratification by a scant two votes in February 1899. The matter was not thereby settled, however, and an uprising of Filipino nationalists against the United States further complicated the issue.

When the war broke out, orders sent to Commodore Dewey by the young Assistant Secretary of the Navy, Theodore Roosevelt, put the Asiatic squadron on the alert. These orders were not authorized by Secretary of the Navy John Long, who, with President McKinley, hoped to avoid a war. Long had taken the afternoon of February 25 off; he opined that "the very devil had seemed to possess" the Assistant Secretary when the Secretary was gone and Roosevelt had the temporary power to send his dispatch to Dewey. Theodore Roosevelt often seemed possessed of a frantic energy and reckless determination. Secretary Long was not alone in comparing him to a bull in a china shop.

Roosevelt had been eagerly anticipating the war; once it broke out, he immediately left his Washington post to serve as second in command to Leonard Wood, colonel of a volunteer cavalry unit that came to be known as the "Rough Riders." Lieutenant Colonel Roosevelt was in the van in the charge up Kettle Hill—later referred to popularly by the name of an adjacent hill, San Juan Hill—that earned instant fame for him and the Rough Riders. He returned home a hero and, despite the opposition of some party leaders in New York, became the Republican nominee for governor. Roosevelt's patriotic campaign, coupled with a maladroit attack by the leader of Tammany Hall on the independence of the judiciary, led him to a narrow victory.

The frail child with poor eyesight and a passion for collecting insects would not have seemed a likely candidate to assume the role played by Roosevelt in his adult years. He consciously and tenaciously developed his physical strength, taking up boxing at Harvard and throwing himself vigorously into athletic pursuits. As a young man in his late twenties he managed a cattle ranch in the Dakota Territory. If Theodore Roosevelt was anything he was energetic (Henry Adams called it "abnormal energy" and wrote that Roosevelt was "pure act") and he approached politics and life with strenuous enthusiasm.

The newly inaugurated governor of New York traveled to Chicago in April 1899 to lay out his view of America's place in the world before a meeting of the Hamilton Club. Disdaining "ignoble ease," Roosevelt preached his doctrine of "toil and effort; of labor and strife," the doctrine of "the strenuous life" that applied to nations as much as to individuals. This is a doctrine that contrasts the "timid," the "lazy," the "overcivilized," with the "manly and adventurous qualities" apparent in the "great fighting, masterful virtues" that had characterized and should continue to characterize Americans and America. To Roosevelt, the anti-imperialists' concern for liberty and self-government was so much cant, an excuse for their "unwillingness to play the part of men." For him, America's imperial mission—to safeguard national honor, to accept international responsibility, to uplift mankind—could be carried out only through "hard and dangerous endeavor" which would lead ultimately to "true national greatness."

In speaking to you, men of the greatest city of the West, men of the State which gave to the country Lincoln and Grant, men who preëminently and distinctly embody all that is most American in the American character, I wish to preach, not the doctrine of ignoble ease, but the doctrine of the strenuous life, the life of toil and effort, of labor and strife; to preach that highest form of success which comes, not to the man who desires mere easy peace, but to the man who does not shrink from danger, from hardship, or from bitter toil, and who out of these wins the splendid ultimate triumph.

A life of slothful ease, a life of that peace which springs merely from lack either of desire or of power to strive after great things, is as little worthy of a nation as of an individual. I ask only that what every self-respecting American demands from himself and from his sons shall be demanded of the American nation as a whole. Who among you would teach your boys that ease, that peace, is to be the first consideration in their eyes—to be the ultimate goal after which they strive? You men of Chicago have made this city great, you men of Illinois have done your share, and more than your share, in making America great, because you neither preach nor practise such a doctrine. You work yourselves, and you bring up your sons to work. If you are rich and are worth your salt, you will teach your sons that though they may have leisure, it is not to be spent in idleness; for wisely used leisure merely means that those who possess it, being free from the necessity of working for their livelihood, are all the more bound to carry on some kind of non-remunerative work in science, in letters, in art, in exploration, in historical research—work of the type we most need in this country, the successful carrying out of which reflects most honor upon the nation. We do not admire the man of timid peace. We admire the man who embodies victorious effort; the man who never wrongs his neighbor, who is prompt to help a friend, but who has those virile qualities necessary to win in the stern strife of actual life. It is hard to fail, but it is worse never to have tried to succeed. In this life we get nothing save by effort. Freedom from effort in the present merely means that there has been stored up effort in the past. A man can be freed from the necessity of work only by the fact that he or his fathers before him have worked to good purpose. If the freedom thus purchased is used aright, and the man still does actual work, though of a different kind, whether as a writer or a general, whether in the field of politics or in the field of exploration and adventure, he shows he deserves his good fortune. But if he treats this period of freedom from the need of actual labor as a period, not of preparation, but of mere enjoyment, even though perhaps not of vicious enjoyment, he shows that he is simply a cumberer of the earth's surface, and he surely unfits himself to hold his own with his fellows if the need to do so should again arise. A mere life of ease is not in the end a very satisfactory life, and, above all, it is a life which ultimately unfits those who follow it for serious work in the world.

In the last analysis a healthy state can exist only when the men and women who make it up lead clean, vigorous, healthy lives; when the children are so trained that they shall endeavor, not to shirk difficulties, but to overcome them; not to seek ease, but to know how to wrest triumph from toil and risk. The man must be glad to do a man's work, to dare and endure and to labor; to keep himself, and to keep those dependent upon him. The woman must be the housewife, the helpmeet of the homemaker, the wise and fearless mother of many healthy children. In one of Daudet's powerful and melancholy books he speaks of "the fear of maternity, the haunting terror of the young wife of the present day." When such words can be truthfully written of a nation, that nation is rotten to the heart's core. When men fear work or fear righteous war, when women fear motherhood, they tremble on the brink of doom; and well it is that they should vanish from the earth, where they are fit subjects for the scorn of all men and women who are themselves strong and brave and high-minded.

As it is with the individual, so it is with the nation. It is a base untruth to say that happy is the nation that has no history. Thrice happy is the nation that has a glorious history. Far better it is to dare mighty things, to win glorious triumphs, even though checkered by failure, than to take rank with those poor spirits who neither enjoy much nor suffer much, because they live in the gray twilight that knows not victory nor defeat. If in 1861 the men who loved the Union had believed that peace was the end of all things, and war and strife the worst of all things, and had acted up to their belief, we would have saved hundreds of thousands of lives, we would have saved hundreds of millions of dollars. Moreover, besides saving all the blood and treasure we then lavished, we would have prevented the heartbreak of many women, the dissolution of many homes, and we would have spared the country those months of gloom and shame when it seemed as if our armies marched only to defeat. We could have avoided all this suffering simply by shrinking from strife. And if we had thus avoided it, we would have shown that we were weaklings, and that we were unfit to stand among the great nations of the earth. Thank God for the iron in the blood of our fathers, the men who upheld the wisdom of Lincoln, and bore sword or rifle in the armies of Grant! Let us, the children of the men who proved themselves equal to the mighty days, let us, the children of the men who carried the great Civil War to a triumphant conclusion, praise the God of our fathers that the ignoble counsels of peace were rejected; that the suffering and loss, the blackness of sorrow and despair, were unflinchingly faced, and the years of strife endured; for in the end the slave was freed, the Union restored, and the mighty American republic placed once more as a helmeted queen among nations.

We of this generation do not have to face a task such as that our fathers faced, but we have our tasks, and woe to us if we fail to perform them! We cannot, if we would, play the part of China, and be content to rot by inches in ignoble ease within our borders, taking no interest in what goes on beyond them, sunk in a scrambling commercialism; heedless of the higher life, the life of aspiration, of toil and risk, busying ourselves only with the wants of our bodies for the day, until suddenly we should find, beyond a shadow of question, what China has already found, that in this world the nation that has trained itself to a career of unwarlike and isolated ease is bound, in the end, to go down before other nations which have not lost the manly and adventurous qualities. If we are to be a really great people, we must strive in good faith to play a great part in the world. We cannot avoid meeting great issues. All that we can determine for ourselves is whether we shall meet them well or ill. In 1898 we could not help being brought face to face with the problem of war with Spain. All we could decide was whether we should shrink like cowards from the contest, or enter into it as beseemed a brave and high-spirited people; and, once in, whether failure or success should crown our banners. So it is now. We cannot avoid the responsibilities that confront us in Hawaii, Cuba, Porto Rico, and the Philippines. All we can decide is whether we shall meet them in a way that will redound to the national credit, or whether we shall make of our dealings with these new problems a dark and shameful page in our history. To refuse to deal with them at all merely amounts to dealing with them badly. We have a given problem to solve. If we undertake the solution, there is, of course, always danger that we may not solve it aright; but to refuse to undertake the solution simply renders it certain that we cannot possibly solve it aright. The timid man, the lazy man, the man who distrusts his country, the over-civilized man, who has lost the great fighting, masterful virtues, the ignorant man, and the man of dull mind, whose soul is incapable of feeling the mighty lift that thrills "stern men with empires in their brains"—all these, of course, shrink from seeing the nation undertake its new duties; shrink from seeing us build a navy and an army adequate to our needs; shrink from seeing us do our share of the world's work, by bringing order out of chaos in the great, fair tropic islands from which the valor of our soldiers and sailors has driven the Spanish flag. These are the men who fear the strenuous life, who fear the only national life which is really worth leading. They believe in that cloistered life which saps the hardy virtues in a nation, as it saps them in the individual; or else they are wedded to that base spirit of gain and greed which recognizes in commercialism the be-all and end-all of national life, instead of realizing that, though an indispensable element, it is, after all, but one of the many elements that go to make up true national greatness. No country can long endure if its foundations are not laid deep in the material prosperity which comes from thrift, from business energy and enterprise, from hard, unsparing effort in the fields of industrial activity; but neither was any nation ever yet truly great if it relied upon material prosperity alone. All honor must be paid to the architects of our material prosperity, to the great captains of industry who have built our factories and our railroads, to the strong men who toil for wealth with brain or hand; for great is the debt of the nation to these and their kind. But our debt is yet greater to the men whose highest type is to be found in a statesman like Lincoln, a soldier like Grant. They showed by their lives that they recognized the law of work, the law of strife; they toiled to win a competence for themselves and those dependent upon them; but they recognized that there were yet other and even loftier duties—duties to the nation and duties to the race.

We cannot sit huddled within our own borders and avow ourselves merely an assemblage of well-to-do hucksters who care nothing for what happens beyond. Such a policy would defeat even its own end; for as the nations grow to have ever wider and wider interests, and are brought into closer and closer contact, if we are to hold our own in the struggle for naval and commercial supremacy, we must build up our power without our own borders. We must build the isthmian canal, and we must grasp the points of vantage which will enable us to have our say in deciding the destiny of the oceans of the East and the West.

So much for the commercial side. From the standpoint of international honor the argument is even stronger. The guns that thundered off Manila and Santiago left us echoes of glory, but they also left us a legacy of duty. If we drove out a medieval tyranny only to make room for savage anarchy, we had better not have begun the task at all. It is worse than idle to say that we have no duty to perform, and can leave to their fates the islands we have conquered. Such a course would be the course of infamy. It would be followed at once by utter chaos in the wretched islands themselves. Some stronger, manlier power would have to step in and do the work, and we would have shown ourselves weaklings, unable to carry to successful completion the labors that great and high-spirited nations are eager to undertake.

The work must be done; we cannot escape our responsibility; and if we are worth our salt, we shall be glad of the chance to do the work—glad of the chance to show ourselves equal to one of the great tasks set modern civilization. But let us not deceive ourselves as to the importance of the task. Let us not be misled by vainglory into underestimating the strain it will put on our powers. Above all, let us, as we value our own self-respect, face the responsibilities with proper seriousness, courage, and high resolve. We must demand the highest order of integrity and ability in our public men who are to grapple with these new problems. We must hold to a rigid accountability those public servants who show unfaithfulness to the interests of the nation or inability to rise to the high level of the new demands upon our strength and our resources.

Of course we must remember not to judge any public servant by any one act, and especially should we beware of attacking the men who are merely the occasions and not the causes of disaster. Let me illustrate what I mean by the army and the navy. If twenty years ago we had gone to war, we should have found the navy as absolutely unprepared as the army. At that time our ships could not have encountered with success the fleets of Spain any more than nowadays we can put untrained soldiers, no matter how brave, who are armed with archaic black-powder weapons, against well-drilled regulars armed with the highest type of modern repeating rifle. But in the early eighties the attention of the nation became directed to our naval needs. Congress most wisely made a series of appropriations to build up a new navy, and under a succession of able and patriotic secretaries, of both political parties, the navy was gradually built up, until its material became equal to its splendid personnel, with the result that in the summer of 1898 it leaped to its proper place as one of the most brilliant and formidable fighting navies in the entire world. We rightly pay all honor to the men controlling the navy at the time it won these great deeds, honor to Secretary Long and Admiral Dewey, to the captains who handled the ships in action, to the daring lieutenants who braved death in the smaller craft, and to the heads of bureaus at Washington who saw that the ships were so commanded, so armed, so equipped, so well engined, as to insure the best results. But let us also keep ever in mind that all of this would not have availed if it had not been for the wisdom of the men who during the preceding fifteen years had built up the navy. Keep in mind the secretaries of the navy during those years; keep in mind the senators and congressmen who by their votes gave the money necessary to build and to armor the ships, to construct the great guns, and to train the crews; remember also those who actually did build the ships, the armor, and the guns; and remember the admirals and captains who handled battle-ship, cruiser, and torpedo-boat on the high seas, alone and in squadrons, developing the seamanship, the gunnery, and the power of acting together, which their successors utilized so gloriously at Manila and off Santiago. And, gentlemen, remember the converse, too. Remember that justice has two sides. Be just to those who built up the navy, and, for the sake of the future of the country, keep in mind those who opposed its building up. Read the "Congressional Record." Find out the senators and congressmen who opposed the grants for building the new ships; who opposed the purchase of armor, without which the ships were worthless; who opposed any adequate maintenance for the Navy Department, and strove to cut down the number of men necessary to man our fleets. The men who did these things were one and all working to bring disaster on the country. They have no share in the glory of Manila, in the honor of Santiago. They have no cause to feel proud of the valor of our sea-captains, of the renown of our flag. Their motives may or may not have been good, but their acts were heavily fraught with evil. They did ill for the national honor, and we won in spite of their sinister opposition.

Now, apply all this to our public men of to-day. Our army has never been built up as it should be built up. I shall not discuss with an audience like this the puerile suggestion that a nation of seventy millions of freemen is in danger of losing its liberties from the existence of an army of one hundred thousand men, three fourths of whom will be employed in certain foreign islands, in certain coast fortresses, and on Indian reservations. No man of good sense and stout heart can take such a proposition seriously. If we are such weaklings as the proposition implies, then we are unworthy of freedom in any event. To no body of men in the United States is the country so much indebted as to the splendid officers and enlisted men of the regular army and navy. There is no body from which the country has less to fear, and none of which it should be prouder, none which it should be more anxious to upbuild.

Our army needs complete reorganization,—not merely enlarging,—and the reorganization can only come as the result of legislation. A proper general staff should be established, and the positions of ordnance, commissary, and quartermaster officers should be filled by detail from the line. Above all, the army must be given the chance to exercise in large bodies. Never again should we see, as we saw in the Spanish war, major-generals in command of divisions who had never before commanded three companies together in the field. Yet, incredible to relate, Congress has shown a queer inability to learn some of the lessons of the war. There were large bodies of men in both branches who opposed the declaration of war, who opposed the ratification of peace, who opposed the upbuilding of the army, and who even opposed the purchase of armor at a reasonable price for the battle-ships and cruisers, thereby putting an absolute stop to the building of any new fighting-ships for the navy. If, during the years to come, any disaster should befall our arms, afloat or ashore, and thereby any shame come to the United States, remember that the blame will lie upon the men whose names appear upon the roll-calls of Congress on the wrong side of these great questions. On them will lie the burden of any loss of our soldiers and sailors, of any dishonor to the flag; and upon you and the people of this country will lie the blame if you do not repudiate, in no unmistakable way, what these men have done. The blame will not rest upon the untrained commander of untried troops, upon the civil officers of a department the organization of which has been left utterly inadequate, or upon the admiral with an insufficient number of ships; but upon the public men who have so lamentably failed in forethought as to refuse to remedy these evils long in advance, and upon the nation that stands behind those public men.

So, at the present hour, no small share of the responsibility for the blood shed in the Philippines, the blood of our brothers, and the blood of their wild and ignorant foes, lies at the thresholds of those who so long delayed the adoption of the treaty of peace, and of those who by their worse than foolish words deliberately invited a savage people to plunge into a war fraught with sure disaster for them—a war, too, in which our own brave men who follow the flag must pay with their blood for the silly, mock humanitarianism of the prattlers who sit at home in peace.

The army and the navy are the sword and the shield which this nation must carry if she is to do her duty among the nations of the earth—if she is not to stand merely as the China of the western hemisphere. Our proper conduct toward the tropic islands we have wrested from Spain is merely the form which our duty has taken at the moment. Of course we are bound to handle the affairs of our own household well. We must see that there is civic honesty, civic cleanliness, civic good sense in our home administration of city, State, and nation. We must strive for honesty in office, for honesty toward the creditors of the nation and of the individual; for the widest freedom of individual initiative where possible, and for the wisest control of individual initiative where it is hostile to the welfare of the many. But because we set our own household in order we are not thereby excused from playing our part in the great affairs of the world. A man's first duty is to his own home, but he is not thereby excused from doing his duty to the State; for if he fails in this second duty it is under the penalty of ceasing to be a freeman. In the same way, while a nation's first duty is within its own borders, it is not thereby absolved from facing its duties in the world as a whole; and if it refuses to do so, it merely forfeits its right to struggle for a place among the peoples that shape the destiny of mankind.

In the West Indies and the Philippines alike we are confronted by most difficult problems. It is cowardly to shrink from solving them in the proper way; for solved they must be, if not by us, then by some stronger and more manful race. If we are too weak, too selfish, or too foolish to solve them, some bolder and abler people must undertake the solution. Personally, I am far too firm a believer in the greatness of my country and the power of my countrymen to admit for one moment that we shall ever be driven to the ignoble alternative.

The problems are different for the different islands. Porto Rico is not large enough to stand alone. We must govern it wisely and well, primarily in the interest of its own people. Cuba is, in my judgment, entitled ultimately to settle for itself whether it shall be an independent state or an integral portion of the mightiest of republics. But until order and stable liberty are secured, we must remain in the island to insure them, and infinite tact, judgment, moderation, and courage must be shown by our military and civil representatives in keeping the island pacified, in relentlessly stamping out brigandage, in protecting all alike, and yet in showing proper recognition to the men who have fought for Cuban liberty. The Philippines offer a yet graver problem. Their population includes half-caste and native Christians, warlike Moslems, and wild pagans. Many of their people are utterly unfit for self-government, and show no signs of becoming fit. Others may in time become fit but at present can only take part in self-government under a wise supervision, at once firm and beneficent. We have driven Spanish tyranny from the islands. If we now let it be replaced by savage anarchy, our work has been for harm and not for good. I have scant patience with those who fear to undertake the task of governing the Philippines, and who openly avow that they do fear to undertake it, or that they shrink from it because of the expense and trouble; but I have even scanter patience with those who make a pretense of humanitarianism to hide and cover their timidity, and who cant about "liberty" and the "consent of the governed," in order to excuse themselves for their unwillingness to play the part of men. Their doctrines, if carried out, would make it incumbent upon us to leave the Apaches of Arizona to work out their own salvation, and to decline to interfere in a single Indian reservation. Their doctrines condemn your forefathers and mine for ever having settled in these United States.

England's rule in India and Egypt has been of great benefit to England, for it has trained up generations of men accustomed to look at the larger and loftier side of public life. It has been of even greater benefit to India and Egypt. And finally, and most of all, it has advanced the cause of civilization. So, if we do our duty aright in the Philippines, we will add to that national renown which is the highest and finest part of national life, will greatly benefit the people of the Philippine Islands, and, above all, we will play our part well in the great work of uplifting mankind. But to do this work, keep ever in mind that we must show in a very high degree the qualities of courage, of honesty, and of good judgment. Resistance must be stamped out. The first and all-important work to be done is to establish the supremacy of our flag. We must put down armed resistance before we can accomplish anything else, and there should be no parleying, no faltering, in dealing with our foe. As for those in our own country who encourage the foe, we can afford contemptuously to disregard them; but it must be remembered that their utterances are not saved from being treasonable merely by the fact that they are despicable.

When once we have put down armed resistance, when once our rule is acknowledged, then an even more difficult task will begin, for then we must see to it that the islands are administered with absolute honesty and with good judgment. If we let the public service of the islands be turned into the prey of the spoils politician, we shall have begun to tread the path which Spain trod to her own destruction. We must send out there only good and able men, chosen for their fitness, and not because of their partizan service, and these men must not only administer impartial justice to the natives and serve their own government with honesty and fidelity, but must show the utmost tact and firmness, remembering that, with such people as those with whom we are to deal, weakness is the greatest of crimes, and that next to weakness comes lack of consideration for their principles and prejudices.

I preach to you, then, my countrymen, that our country calls not for the life of ease but for the life of strenuous endeavor. The twentieth century looms before us big with the fate of many nations. If we stand idly by, if we seek merely swollen, slothful ease and ignoble peace, if we shrink from the hard contests where men must win at hazard of their lives and at the risk of all they hold dear, then the bolder and stronger peoples will pass us by, and will win for themselves the domination of the world. Let us therefore boldly face the life of strife, resolute to do our duty well and manfully; resolute to uphold righteousness by deed and by word; resolute to be both honest and brave, to serve high ideals, yet to use practical methods. Above all, let us shrink from no strife, moral or physical, within or without the nation, provided we are certain that the strife is justified, for it is only through strife, through hard and dangerous endeavor, that we shall ultimately win the goal of true national greatness.

William Jennings Bryan

Imperialism (1900)

In 1896 the Democratic party met in Chicago and constructed a platform calling for free and unlimited coining of silver and attacking trusts and monopolies. The assembled Democracy also condemned high protective tariffs and the use of the injunction to prevent strikes. The Convention was most moved by a passionate speech by a young newspaper editor and former Congressman from Nebraska, who, in attacking advocates of the gold standard, pledged, "You shall not press down upon the brow of labor this crown of thorns, you shall not crucify mankind upon a cross of gold." These lines from the "Cross of Gold" speech were perhaps the most famous that William Jennings Bryan was to utter in a long career as a politician and orator. They no doubt played a role in securing him the nomination of his party at that Chicago convention.

In the campaign that followed, much was made of the "money question," but this issue seemed to translate into a clash between creditors and debtors as the agrarian West and South, led by Bryan, fought against the financial establishment of the East, symbolized by the Republican party and its candidate, William McKinley of Ohio. Bryan carried his message via a grueling campaign through 29 states while McKinley stayed at his home in Canton, speaking to delegations and reporters from his front porch. Bryan lost the election but increased his reputation as one of the most popular orators of his day.

By the time the Democrats met four years later, once again nominating Bryan to run against McKinley, much had happened to change the focus of campaign issues. President McKinley had, reluctantly, yielded to the popular pressure generated by the "yellow" tabloids and the political pressure exerted by Congress, and he had called for a declaration of war against Spain. The Spanish forces were no match against American military might and succumbed to the overwhelming odds. Two Spanish fleets were destroyed, one in Manila Bay and one in Santiago Bay, and in a matter of months the United States found itself in possession of Puerto Rico, the Philippines, and, temporarily, Cuba. The fate of Cuba was settled when the United States guaranteed independence and withdrew from there after a Cuban constitution that ensured that a virtual American protectorate was adopted. The matter of the Philippines was another matter.

Republican imperialists saw in the Philippines a heaven-sent opportunity for America to compete with the European imperial powers for trade, for prestige, and for glory—and all this could be accomplished while spreading civilization and Christianity. Democrats, for the most part, saw the matter in a quite different light.

The Democrats meeting in Kansas City in 1900 were still concerned with what they viewed as the contest between the rights of man, for which they stood, and the forces of wealth and privilege, supported by their Republican opponents. However, the fate of the Philippines and the proper role that America was to play in the world had been the subject of intense debate for almost two years. Bryan was partly responsible for the ratification of the peace treaty; he had urged anti-imperialist opponents to vote for it on the grounds that the war would thereby be brought to a close. But, he had argued, the whole question would be a theme of the 1900 campaign.

In accepting the nomination, Byran acknowledged other Democratic concerns, but the major emphasis of his speech, given in Indianapolis on his receiving official word that he had been nominated a month before, was on imperialism.

Bryan's speech is a detailed refutation of the major imperialist arguments and an assertion that imperialism is inimical to all the ideals of the Republic and contrary to its historic mission. Contrary also to the precepts of Christian civilization is the imperialist penchant to "civilize with dynamite and proselyte with the sword." Rather than point with pride at the march of the flag, as Senator Beveridge and the Republican imperialists would do, Bryan thought it "Better a thousand times that our flag in the Orient give way to a flag representing the idea of self-government than that the flag of this Republic should become the flag of an empire."

Mr. Chairman and Members of the Notification Committee: I shall, at an early day, and in a more formal manner, accept the nomination which you tender, and shall at that time discuss the various questions covered by the Democratic platform. It may not be out of place, however, to submit a few observations at this time upon the general character of the contest before us and upon the question which is declared to be of paramount importance in this campaign.

When I say that the contest of 1900 is a contest between Democracy on the one hand and plutocracy on the other I do not mean to say that all our opponents have deliberately chosen to give to organized wealth a predominating influence in the affairs of the Government, but I do assert that on the important issues of the day the Republican party is dominated by those influences which constantly tend to substitute the worship of mammon for the protection of the rights of man.

In 1859 Lincoln said that the Republican party believed in the man and the dollar, but that in case of conflict it believed in the man before the dollar. This is the proper relation which should exist between the two. Man, the handiwork of God, comes first; money, the handiwork of man, is of inferior importance. Man is the master, money the servant, but upon all important questions to-day Republican legislation tends to make money the master and man the servant.

The maxim of Jefferson, "Equal rights to all and special privileges to none," and the doctrine of Lincoln, that this should be a government "of the people, by the people and for the people," are being disregarded and the instrumentalities of government are being used to advance the interests of those who are in a position to secure favors from the Government.

The Democratic party is not making war upon the honest acquisition of wealth; it has no desire to discourage industry, economy and thrift. On the contrary, it gives to every citizen the greatest possible stimulus to honest toil when it promises him protection in the enjoyment of the proceeds of his labor. Property rights are most secure when human rights are most respected. Democracy strives for a civilization in which every member of society will share according to his merits.

No one has a right to expect from society more than a fair compensation for the services which he renders to society, if he secures more it is at the expense of some one else. It is no injustice to him to prevent his doing injustice to another. To him who would, either through class legislation or in the absence of necessary legislation, trespass upon the rights of another the Democratic party says, "Thou shalt not."

Against us are arrayed a comparatively small but politically and financially powerful number who really profit by Republican policies; but with them are associated a large number who, because of their attachment to their party name, are giving their support to doctrines antagonistic to the former teachings of their own party.

Republicans who used to advocate bimetalism now try to convince themselves that the gold standard is good; Republicans who were formerly attached to the greenback are now seeking an excuse for giving national banks control of the Nation's paper money; Republicans who used to boast that the Republican party was paying off the national debt are now looking for reasons to support a perpetual and increasing debt; Republicans who formerly abhorred a trust now beguile themselves with the delusion that there are good trusts and bad trusts, while, in their minds, the line between the two is becoming more and more obscure; Republicans who, in times past, congratulated the country upon the small expense of our standing army, are now making light of the objections which are urged against a large increase in the permanent military establishment; Republicans who gloried in our independence when the Nation was less powerful now look with favor upon a foreign alliance; Republicans who three years ago condemned "forcible annexation" as immoral and even criminal are now sure that it is both immoral and criminal to oppose forcible annexation. That partizanship has already blinded many to present dangers is certain; how large a portion of the Republican party can be drawn over to the new policies remains to be seen.

For a time Republican leaders were inclined to deny to opponents the right to criticize the Philippine policy of the administration, but upon investigation they found that both Lincoln and Clay asserted and exercised the right to critize a President during the progress of the Mexican war.

Instead of meeting the issue boldly and submitting a clear and positive plan for dealing with the Philippine question, the Republican convention adopted a platform the larger part of which was devoted to boasting and self-congratulation.

In attempting to press economic questions upon the country to the exclusion of those which involve the very structure of our government, the Republican leaders give new evidence of their abandonment of the earlier ideals of the party and of their complete subserviency to pecuinary considerations.

But they shall not be permitted to evade the stupendous and far-reaching issue which they have deliberately brought into the arena of politics. When the President, supported by a practically unanimous vote of the House and Senate, entered upon a war with Spain for the purpose of aiding the struggling patriots of Cuba, the country, without regard to party, applauded.

Altho the Democrats realized that the administration would necessarily gain a political advantage from the conduct of a war which in the very nature of the case must soon end in a complete victory, they vied with the Republicans in the support which they gave to the President. When the war was over and the Republican leaders began to suggest the propriety of a colonial policy opposition at once manifested itself.

When the President finally laid before the Senate a treaty which recognized the independence of Cuba, but provided for the cession of the Philippine Islands to the United States, the menace of imperialism became so apparent that many preferred to reject the treaty and risk the ills that might follow rather than take the chance of correcting the errors of the treaty by the independent action of this country.

I was among the number of those who believed it better to ratify the treaty and end the war, release the volunteers, remove the excuse for war expenditures and then give the Filipinos the independence which might be forced from Spain by a new treaty.

In view of the criticism which my action aroused in some quarters, I take this occasion to restate the reasons given at that time. I thought it safer to trust the American people to give independence to the Filipinos than to trust the accomplishment of that purpose to diplomacy with an unfriendly nation.

Lincoln embodied an argument in the question when he asked, "Can aliens make treaties easier than friends can make laws?" I believe that we are now in a better position to wage a successful contest against imperialism than we would have been had the treaty been rejected. With the treaty ratified a clean-cut issue is presented between a government by consent and a government by force, and imperialists must bear the responsibility for all that happens until the question is settled.

If the treaty had been rejected the opponents of imperialism would have been held responsible for any international complications which might have arisen before the ratification of another treaty. But whatever difference of opinion may have existed as to the best method of opposing a colonial policy, there never was any difference as to the great importance of the question and there is no difference now as to the course to be pursued.

The title of Spain being extinguished we were at liberty to deal with the Filipinos according to American principles. The Bacon resolution, introduced a month before hostilities broke out at Manila, promised independence to the Filipinos on the same terms that it was promised to the Cubans. I supported this resolution and believe that its adoption prior to the breaking out of hostilities would have prevented bloodshed, and that its adoption at any subsequent time would have ended hostilities.

If the treaty had been rejected considerable time would have necessarily elapsed before a new treaty could have been agreed upon and ratified, and during that time the question would have been agitating the public mind. If the Bacon resolution had been adopted by the Senate and carried out by the President, either at the time of the ratification of the treaty or at any time afterwards, it would have taken the question of imperialism out of politics, and left the American people free to deal with their domestic problems. But the resolution was defeated by the vote of the Republican Vice-President, and from that time to this a Republican Congress has refused to take any action whatever in the matter.

When hostilities broke out at Manila Republican speakers and Republican editors at once sought to lay the blame upon those who had delayed the ratification of the treaty, and, during the progress of the war, the same Republicans have accused the opponents of imperialism of giving encouragement to the Filipinos. This is a cowardly evasion of responsibility.

If it is right for the United States to hold the Philippine Islands permanently and imitate European empires in the government of colonies, the Republican party ought to state its position and defend it, but it must expect the subject races to protest against such a policy and to resist to the extent of their ability.

The Filipinos do not need any encouragement from Americans now living. Our whole history has been an encouragement, not only to the Filipinos, but to all who are denied a voice in their own government. If the Republicans are prepared to censure all who have used language calculated to make the Filipinos hate foreign domination, let them condemn the speech of Patrick Henry. When he uttered that passionate appeal, "Give me liberty or give me death," he exprest a sentiment which still echoes in the hearts of men.

Let them censure Jefferson; of all the statesmen of history none have used words so offensive to those who would hold their fellows in political bondage. Let them censure Washington, who declared that the colonists must choose between liberty and slavery. Or, if the statute of limitations has run against the sins of Henry and Jefferson and Washington, let them censure Lincoln, whose Gettysburg speech will be quoted in defense of popular government when the present advocates of force and conquest are forgotten.

Some one has said that a truth once spoken can never be recalled. It goes on and on, and no one can set a limit to its ever-widening influence. But if it were possible to obliterate every word written or spoken in defense of the principles set forth in the Declaration of Independence, a war of conquest would still leave its legacy of perpetual hatred, for it was God himself who placed in every human heart the love of liberty. He never made a race of people so low in the scale of civilization or intelligence that it would welcome a foreign master.

Those who would have this Nation enter upon a career of empire must consider, not only the effect of imperialism on the Filipinos, but they must also calculate its effects upon our own nation. We cannot repudiate the principle of self-government in the Philippines without weakening that principle here.

Lincoln said that the safety of this Nation was not in its fleets, its armies, or its forts, but in the spirit which prizes liberty as the heritage of all men, in all lands, everywhere, and he warned his countrymen that they could not destroy this spirit without planting the seeds of despotism at their own doors.

Even now we are beginning to see the paralyzing influence of imperialism. Heretofore this Nation has been prompt to express its sympathy with those who were fighting for civil liberty. While our sphere of activity has been limited to the Western Hemisphere, our sympathies have not been bounded by the seas. We have felt it due to ourselves and to the world, as well as to those who were struggling for the right to govern themselves, to proclaim the interest which our people have, from the date of their own independence, felt in every contest between human rights and arbitrary power.

Three-quarters of a century ago, when our nation was small, the struggles of Greece aroused our people, and Webster and Clay gave eloquent expression to the universal desire for Grecian independence. In 1898 all parties manifested a lively interest in the success of the Cubans, but now when a war is in progress in South Africa, which must result in the extension of the monarchical idea, or in the triumph of a republic, the advocates of imperialism in this country dare not say a word in behalf of the Boers.

Sympathy for the Boers does not arise from any unfriendliness towards England; the American people are not unfriendly toward the people of any nation. This sympathy is due to the fact that, as stated in our platform, we believe in the principles of self-government and reject, as did our forefathers, the claims of monarchy. If this nation surrenders its belief in the universal application of the principles set forth in the Declaration of Independence, it will lose the prestige and influence which it has enjoyed among the nations as an exponent of popular government.

Our opponents, conscious of the weakness of their cause, seek to confuse imperialism with expansion, and have even dared to claim Jefferson as a supporter of their policy. Jefferson spoke so freely and used language with such precision that no one can be ignorant of his views. On one occasion he declared: "If there be one principle more deeply rooted than any other in the mind of every American, it is that we should have nothing to do with conquest." And again he said: "Conquest is not in our principles; it is inconsistent with our government."

The forcible annexation of territory to be governed by arbitrary power differs as much from the acquisition of territory to be built up into States as a monarchy differs from a democracy. The Democratic party does not oppose expansion when expansion enlarges the area of the Republic and incorporates land which can be settled by American citizens, or adds to our population people who are willing to become citizens and are capable of discharging their duties as such.

The acquisition of the Louisiana territory, Florida, Texas and other tracts which have been secured from time to time enlarged the Republic and the Constitution followed the flag into the new territory. It is now proposed to seize upon distant territory already more densely populated than our own country and to force upon the people a government for which there is no warrant in our Constitution or our laws.

Even the argument that this earth belongs to those who desire to cultivate it and who have the physical power to acquire it cannot be invoked to justify the appropriation of the Philippine Islands by the United States. If the islands were uninhabited American citizens would not be willing to go there and till the soil. The white race will not live so near the equator. Other nations have tried to colonize in the same latitude. The Netherlands have controlled Java for three hundred years and yet today there are less than sixty thousand people of European birth scattered among the twenty-five million natives.

After a century and a half of English domination in India, less than one-twentieth of one per cent. of the people of India are of English birth, and it requires an army of seventy thousand British soldiers to take care of the tax collectors. Spain had asserted title to the Philippine Islands for three centuries and yet when our fleet entered Manila bay there were less than ten thousand Spaniards residing in the Philippines.

A colonial policy means that we shall send to the Philippine Islands a few traders, a few taskmasters and a few office-holders and an army large enough to support the authority of a small fraction of the people while they rule the natives.

If we have an imperial policy we must have a great standing army as its natural and necessary complement. The spirit which will justify the forcible annexation of the Philippine Islands will justify the seizure of other islands and the domination of other people, and with wars of conquest we can expect a certain, if not rapid, growth of our military establishment.

That a large permanent increase in our regular army is intended by Republican leaders is not a matter of conjecture, but a matter of fact. In his message of December 5, 1898, the President asked for authority to increase the standing army to 100,000. In 1896 the army contained about 25,000. Within two years the President asked for four times that many, and a Republican House of Representatives complied with the request after the Spanish treaty had been signed, and when no country was at war with the United States.

If such an army is demanded when an imperial policy is contemplated, but not openly avowed, what may be expected if the people encourage the Republican party by indorsing its policy at the polls?

A large standing army is not only a pecuniary burden to the people and, if accompanied by compulsory service, a constant source of irritation, but it is ever a menace to a republican form of government.

The army is the personification of force and militarism will inevitably change the ideals of the people and turn the thoughts of our young men from the arts of peace to the science of war. The government which relies for its defense upon its citizens is more likely to be just than one which has at call a large body of professional soldiers.

A small standing army and a well-equipped and well-disciplined State militia are sufficient at ordinary times, and in an emergency the nation should in the future as in the past place its dependence upon the volunteers who come from all occupations at their country's call and return to productive labor when their services are no longer required—men who fight when the country needs fighters and work when the country needs workers.

The Republican platform assumes that the Philippine Islands will be retained under American sovereignty, and we have a right to demand of the Republican leaders a discussion of the future status of the Filipino. Is he to be a citizen or a subject? Are we to bring into the body politic eight or ten million Asiatics, so different from us in race and history that amalgamation is impossible? Are they to share with us in making the laws and shaping the destiny of this nation? No Republican of prominence has been bold enough to advocate such a proposition.

The McEnery resolution, adopted by the Senate immediately after the ratification of the treaty, expressly negatives this idea. The Democratic platform describes the situation when it says that the Filipinos cannot be citizens without endangering our civilization. Who will dispute it? And what is the alternative? If the Filipino is not to be a citizen, shall we make him a subject? On that question the Democratic platform speaks with equal emphasis. It declares that the Filipino cannot be a subject without endangering our form of government. A republic can have no subjects. A subject is possible only in a government resting upon force; he is unknown in a government deriving its just powers from the consent of the governed.

The Republican platform says that "the largest measure of self-government consistent with their welfare and our duties shall be secured to them (the Filipinos) by law." This is a strange doctrine for a government which owes its very existence to the men who offered their lives as a protest against government without consent and taxation without representation.

In what respect does the position of the Republican party differ from the position taken by the English government in 1776? Did not the English government promise a good government to the colonists? What king ever promised a bad government to his people? Did not the English government promise that the colonists should have the largest measure of self-government consistent with their welfare and English duties? Did not the Spanish government promise to give to the Cubans the largest measure of self-government consistent with their welfare and Spanish duties? The whole difference between a monarchy and a republic may be summed up in one sentence. In a monarchy the king gives to the people what he believes to be a good government; in a republic the people secure for themselves what they believe to be a good government.

The Republican party has accepted the European idea and planted itself upon the ground taken by George III., and by every ruler who distrusts the capacity of the people for self-government or denies them a voice in their own affairs.

The Republican platform promises that some measure of self-government is to be given the Filipinos by law; but even this pledge is not fulfilled. Nearly sixteen months elapsed after the ratification of the treaty before the adjournment of Congress last June and yet no law was passed dealing with the Philippine situation. The will of the President has been the only law in the Philippine Islands wherever the American authority extends.

Why does the Republican party hesitate to legislate upon the Philippine question? Because a law would disclose the radical departure from history and precedent contemplated by those who control the Republican party. The storm of protest which greeted the Porto Rican bill was an indication of what may be expected when the American people are brought face to face with legislation upon this subject.

If the Porto Ricans, who welcomed annexation, are to be denied the guarantees of our Constitution, what is to be the lot of the Filipinos, who resisted our authority? If secret influences could compel a disregard of our plain duty toward friendly people, living near our shores, what treatment will those same influences provide for unfriendly people 7,000 miles away? If, in this country where the people have a right to vote, Republican leaders dare not take the side of the people against the great monopolies which have grown up within the last few years, how can they be trusted to protect the Filipinos from the corporations which are waiting to exploit the islands?

Is the sunlight of full citizenship to be enjoyed by the people of the United States, and the twilight of semi-citizenship endured by the people of Porto Rico, while the thick darkness of perpetual vassalage covers the Philippines? The Porto Rico tariff law asserts the doctrine that the operation of the Constitution is confined to the forty-five States.

The Democratic party disputes this doctrine and denounces it as repugnant to both the letter and spirit of our organic law. There is no place in our system of government for the deposit of arbitrary and irresponsible power. That the leaders of a great party should claim for any President or Congress the right to treat millions of people as mere "possessions" and deal with them unrestrained by the Constitution or the bill of rights shows how far we have already departed from the ancient landmarks and indicates what may be expected if this nation deliberately enters upon a career of empire.

The territorial form of government is temporary and preparatory, and the chief security a citizen of a territory has is found in the fact that he enjoys the same constitutional guarantees and is subject to the same general laws as the citizen of a State. Take away this security and his rights will be violated and his interests sacrificed at the demand of those who have political influence. This is the evil of the colonial system, no matter by what nation it is applied.

What is our title to the Philippine Islands? Do we hold them by treaty or by conquest? Did we buy them or did we take them? Did we purchase the people? If not, how did we secure title to them? Were they thrown in with the land? Will the Republicans say that inanimate earth has value but that when that earth is molded by the divine hand and stamped with the likeness of the Creator it becomes a fixture and passes with the soil? If governments derive their just powers from the consent of the governed, it is impossible to secure title to people, either by force or by purchase.

We could extinguish Spain's title by treaty, but if we hold title we must hold it by some method consistent with our ideas of government. When we made allies of the Filipinos and armed them to fight against Spain, we disputed Spain's title. If we buy Spain's title we are not innocent purchasers.

There can be no doubt that we accepted and utilized the services of the Filipinos, and that when we did so we had full knowledge that they were fighting for their own independence, and I submit that history furnishes no example of turpitude baser than ours if we now substitute our yoke for the Spanish yoke.

Let us consider briefly the reasons which have been given in support of an imperialistic policy. Some say that it is our duty to hold the Philippine Islands. But duty is not an argument; it is a conclusion. To ascertain what our duty is, in any emergency, we must apply well-settled and generally accepted principles. It is our duty to avoid stealing, no matter whether the thing to be stolen is of great or little value. It is our duty to avoid killing a human being, no matter where the human being lives or to what race or class he belongs.

Every one recognizes the obligation imposed upon individuals to observe both the human and the moral law, but as some deny the application of those laws to nations, it may not be out of place to quote the opinions of others. Jefferson, than whom there is no higher political authority, said:

> I know of but one code of morality for men, whether acting singly or collectively.

Franklin, whose learning, wisdom and virtue are a part of the priceless legacy bequeathed to us from the revolutionary days, exprest the same idea in even stronger language when he said:

> Justice is strictly due between neighbor nations as between neighbor citizens. A highwayman is as much a robber when he plunders in a gang as when single; and the nation that makes an unjust war is only a great gang.

Many may dare to do in crowds what they would not dare to do as individuals, but the moral character of an act is not determined by the number of those who join it. Force can defend a right, but force has never yet created a right. If it was true, as declared in the resolutions of intervention, that the Cubans "are and of right ought to be free and independent" (language taken from the Declaration of Independence), it is equally true that the Filipinos "are and of right ought to be free and independent."

The right of the Cubans to freedom was not based upon their proximity to the United States, nor upon the language which they spoke, nor yet upon the race or races to which they belonged. Congress by a practically unanimous vote declared that the principles enunciated at Philadelphia in 1776 were still alive and applicable to the Cubans. Who will draw a line between the natural rights of the Cubans and the Filipinos? Who will say that the former has a right to liberty and that the latter has no rights which we are bound to respect? And, if the Filipinos "are and of right ought to be free and independent," what right have we to force our government upon them without their consent? Before our duty can be ascertained their rights must be determined, and when their rights are once determined it is as much our duty to respect those rights as it was the duty of Spain to respect the rights of the people of Cuba or the duty of England to respect the rights of the American colonists. Rights never conflict; duties never clash. Can it be our duty to usurp political rights which belong to others? Can it be our duty to kill those who, following the example of our forefathers, love liberty well enough to fight for it?

Some poet has described the terror which overcame a soldier who in the midst of the battle discovered that he had slain his brother. It is written "All yet are brethren." Let us hope for the coming of the day when human life—which when once destroyed cannot be restored—will be so sacred that it will never be taken except when necessary to punish a crime already committed, or to prevent a crime about to be committed.

It is said that we have assumed before the world obligations which make it necessary for us to permanently maintain a government in the Philippine Islands. I reply first, that the highest obligation of this nation is to be true to itself. No obligation to any particular nations, or to all the nations combined, can require the abandonment of our theory of government, and the substitution of doctrines against which our whole national life has been a protest. And, second, that our obligation to the Filipinos, who inhabit the islands, is greater than any obligation which we can owe to foreigners who have a temporary residence in the Philippines or desire to trade there.

It is argued by some that the Filipinos are incapable of self-government and that, therefore, we owe it to the world to take control of them. Admiral Dewey, in an official report to the Navy Department, declared the Filipinos more capable of self-government than the Cubans and said that he based his opinion upon a knowledge of both races. But I will not rest the case upon the relative advancement of the Filipinos. Henry Clay, in defending the right of the people of South America to self-government, said:

> It is the doctrine of thrones that man is too ignorant to govern himself. Their partizans assert his incapacity in reference to all nations; if they cannot command universal assent to the proposition, it is then demanded to particular nations; and our pride and our presumption too often make converts of us. I contend that it is to arraign the disposition of Providence himself to suppose that he has created beings incapable of governing themselves, and to be trampled on by kings. Self-government is the natural government of man.

Clay was right. There are degrees of proficiency in the art of self-government, but it is a reflection upon the Creator to say that he denied to any people the capacity for self-government. Once admit that some people are capable of self-government and that others are not and that the capable people have a right to seize upon and govern the incapable, and you make force—brute force—the only foundation of government and invite the reign of a despot. I am not willing to believe that an all-wise and an all-loving God created the Filipinos and then left them thousands of years helpless until the islands attracted the attention of European nations.

Republicans ask, "Shall we haul down the flag that floats over our dead in the Philippines?" The same question might have been asked, when the American flag floated over Chapultepec and waved over the dead who fell there; but the tourist who visits the City of Mexico finds there a national cemetery owned by the United States and cared for by an American citizen.

Our flag still floats over our dead, but when the treaty with Mexico was signed American authority withdrew to the Rio Grande, and I venture the opinion that during the last fifty years the people of Mexico have made more progress under the stimulus of independence and self-government than they would have made under a carpet-bag government held in place by bayonets. The United States and Mexico, friendly republics, are each stronger and happier than they would have been had the former been cursed and the latter crushed by an imperialistic policy disguised as "benevolent assimilation."

"Can we not govern colonies?" we are asked. The question is not what we can do, but what we ought to do. This nation can do whatever it desires to do, but it must accept responsibility for what it does. If the Constitution stands in the way, the people can amend the Cosntitution. I repeat, the nation can do whatever it desires to do, but it cannot avoid the natural and legitimate results of its own conduct.

The young man upon reaching his majority can do what he pleases. He can disregard the teachings of his parents; he can trample upon all that he has been taught to consider sacred; he can disobey the laws of the State, the laws of society and the laws of God. He can stamp failure upon his life and make his very existence a curse to his fellow men, and he can bring his father and mother in sorrow to the grave; but he cannot annul the sentence, "The wages of sin is death."

And so with the nation. It is of age and it can do what it pleases; it can spurn the traditions of the past; it can repudiate the principles upon which the nation rests; it can employ force instead of reason; it can substitute might for right; it can conquer weaker people; it can exploit their lands, appropriate their property and kill their people; but it cannot repeal the moral law or escape the punishment decreed for the violation of human rights.

> Would we tread in the paths of
> tyranny,
> Nor reckon the tyrant's cost?
> Who taketh another's liberty
> His freedom is also lost.
> Would we win as the strong have
> ever won,
> Make ready to pay the debt,
> For the God who reigned over
> Babylon
> Is the God who is reigning yet.

Some argue that American rule in the Philippine Islands will result in the better education of the Filipinos. Be not deceived. If we expect to maintain a colonial policy, we shall not find it to our advantage to educate the people. The educated Filipinos are now in revolt against us, and the most ignorant ones have made the least resistance to our domination. If we are to govern them without their consent and give them no voice in determining the taxes which they must pay, we dare not educate them, lest they learn to read the Declaration of Independence and Constitution of the United States and mock us for our inconsistency.

The principal arguments, however, advanced by those who enter upon a defense of imperialism are:

First—That we must improve the present opportunity to become a world power and enter into international politics.

Second—That our commercial interests in the Philippine Islands and in the Orient make it necessary for us to hold the islands permanently.

Third—That the spread of the Christian religion will be facilitated by a colonial policy.

Fourth—That there is no honorable retreat from the position which the nation has taken.

The first argument is addrest to the nation's pride and the second to the nation's pocket-book. The third is intended for the church member and the fourth for the partizan.

It is sufficient answer to the first argument to say that for more than a century this nation has been a world power. For ten decades it has been the most potent influence in the world. Not only has it been a world power, but it has done more to shape the politics of the human race than all the other nations of the world combined. Because our Declaration of Independence was promulgated others have been promulgated. Because the patriots of 1776 fought for liberty others have fought for it. Because our Constitution was adopted other constitutions have been adopted.

The growth of the principle of self-government, planted on American soil, has been the overshadowing political fact of the nineteenth century. It has made this nation conspicuous among the nations and given it a place in history such as no other nation has ever enjoyed. Nothing has been able to check the onward march of this idea. I am not willing that this nation shall cast aside the omnipotent weapon of truth to seize again the weapons of physical warfare. I would not exchange the glory of this Republic for the glory of all the empires that have risen and fallen since time began.

The permanent chairman of the last Republican National Convention presented the pecuniary argument in all its baldness when he said:

> We make no hypocritical pretense of being interested in the Philippines solely on account of others. While we regard the welfare of those people as a sacred trust, we regard the welfare of the American people first. We see our duty to ourselves as well as to others. We believe in trade expansion. By every legitimate means within the province of government and constitution we mean to stimulate the expansion of our trade and open new markets.

This is the commercial argument. It is based upon the theory that war can be rightly waged for pecuniary advantage, and that it is profitable to purchase trade by force and violence. Franklin denied both of these propositions. When Lord Howe asserted that the acts of Parliament which brought on the revolution were necessary to prevent American trade from passing into foreign channels, Franklin replied:

> To me it seems that neither the obtaining nor retaining of any trade, howsoever valuable, is an object for which men may justly spill each other's blood; that the true and sure means of extending and securing commerce are the goodness and cheapness of commodities, and that the profits of no trade can ever be equal to the expense of compelling it and holding it by fleets and armies. I consider this war against us, therefore, as both unjust and unwise.

I place the philosophy of Franklin against the sordid doctrine of those who would put a price upon the head of an American soldier and justify a war of conquest upon the ground that it will pay. The Democratic party is in favor of the expansion of trade. It would extend our trade by every legitimate and peaceful means; but it is not willing to make merchandise of human blood.

But a war of conquest is as unwise as it is unrighteous. A harbor and coaling station in the Philippines would answer every trade and military necessity and such a concession could have been secured at any time without difficulty.

It is not necessary to own people in order to trade with them. We carry on trade today with every part of the world, and our commerce has expanded more rapidly than the commerce of any European empire. We do not own Japan or China, but we trade with their people. We have not absorbed the republics of Central and South America, but we trade with them. It has not been necessary to have any political connection with Canada or the nations of Europe in order to trade with them. Trade cannot be permanently profitable unless it is voluntary.

When trade is secured by force, the cost of securing it and retaining it must be taken out of the profits, and the profits are never large enough to cover the expense. Such a system would never be defended but for the fact that the expense is borne by all the people, while the profits are enjoyed by a few.

Imperialism would be profitable to the army contractors; it would be profitable to the ship owners, who would carry live soldiers to the Philippines and bring dead soldiers back; it would be profitable to those who would seize upon the franchises, and it would be profitable to the officials whose salaries would be fixt here and paid over there; but to the farmer, to the laboring man and to the vast majority of those engaged in other occupations it would bring expenditure without return and risk without reward.

Farmers and laboring men have, as a rule, small incomes and under systems which place the tax upon consumption pay much more than their fair share of the expenses of government. Thus the very people who receive least benefit from imperialism will be injured most by the military burdens which accompany it.

In addition the evils which he and the farmer share in common, the laboring man will be the first to suffer if oriental subjects seek work in the United States; the first to suffer if American capital leaves our shores to employ oriental labor in the Philippines to supply the trade of China and Japan; the first to suffer from the violence which the military spirit arouses and the first to suffer when the methods of imperialism are applied to our own Government.

It is not strange, therefore, that the labor organizations have been quick to note the approach of these dangers and prompt to protest against both militarism and imperialism.

The pecuniary argument, tho more effective with certain classes, is not likely to be used so often or presented with so much enthusiasm as the religious argument. If what has been termed the "gunpowder gospel" were urged against the Filipinos only it would be a sufficient answer to say that a majority of the Filipinos are now members of one branch of the Christian church; but the principle involved is one of much wider application and challenges serious consideration.

The religious argument varies in positiveness from a passive belief that Providence delivered the Filipinos into our hands, for their good and our glory, to the exultation of the minister who said that we ought to "thrash the natives (Filipinos) until they understand who we are," and that "every bullet sent, every cannon shot and every flag waved means righteousness."

We cannot approve of this doctrine in one place unless we are willing to apply it everywhere. If there is poison in the blood of the hand it will ultimately reach the heart. It is equally true that forcible Christianity, if planted under the American flag in the far-away Orient, will sooner or later be transplanted upon American soil.

If true Christianity consists in carrying out in our daily lives the teachings of Christ, who will say that we are commanded to civilize with dynamite and proselyte with the sword? He who would declare the divine will must prove his authority either by Holy Writ or by evidence of a special dispensation.

Imperialism finds no warrant in the Bible. The command, "Go ye into all the world and preach the gospel to every creature," has no Gatling gun attachment. When Jesus visited a village of Samaria and the people refused to receive him, some of the disciples suggested that fire should be called down from heaven to avenge the insult; but the Master rebuked them and said: "Ye know not what manner of spirit ye are of; for the Son of Man is not come to destroy men's lives, but to save them." Suppose he had said: "We will thrash them until they understand who we are," how different would have been the history of Christianity! Compare, if you will, the swaggering, bullying, brutal doctrine of imperialism with the golden rule and the commandment, "Thou shalt love thy neighbor as thyself."

Love, not force, was the weapon of the Nazarene; sacrifice for others, not the exploitation of them, was His method of reaching the human heart. A missionary recently told me that the Stars and Stripes once saved his life because his assailant recognized our flag as a flag that had no blood upon it.

Let it be known that our missionaries are seeking souls instead of sovereignty; let it be known that instead of being the advance guard of conquering armies, they are going forth to help and uplift, having their loins girt about with truth and their feet shod with the preparation of the gospel of peace, wearing the breastplate of righteousness and carrying the sword of the spirit; let it be known that they are citizens of a nation which respects the rights of the citizens of other nations as carefully as it protects the rights of its own citizens, and the welcome given to our missionaries will be more cordial than the welcome extended to the missionaries of any other nation.

The argument made by some that it was unfortunate for the nation that it had anything to do with the Philippine Islands, but that the naval victory at Manila made the permanent acquisition of those islands necessary, is also unsound. We won a naval victory at Santiago, but that did not compel us to hold Cuba.

The shedding of American blood in the Philippine Islands does not make it imperative that we should retain possession forever; American blood was shed at San Juan Hill and El Caney, and yet the President has promised the Cubans independence. The fact that the American flag floats over Manila does not compel us to exercise perpetual sovereignty over the islands; the American flag waves over Havana to-day, but the President has promised to haul it down when the flag of the Cuban Republic is ready to rise in its place. Better a thousand times that our flag in the Orient give way to a flag representing the idea of self-government than that the flag of this Republic should become the flag of an empire.

There is an easy, honest, honorable solution of the Philippine question. It is set forth in the Democratic platform and it is submitted with confidence to the American people. This plan I unreservedly indorse. If elected, I will convene Congress in extraordinary session as soon as inaugurated and recommend an immediate declaration of the nation's purpose, first, to establish a stable form of government in the Philippine Islands, just as we are now establishing a stable form of government in Cuba; second, to give independence to the Filipinos as we have promised to give independence to the Cubans; third, to protect the Filipinos from outside interference while they work out their destiny, just as we have protected the republics of Central and South America, and are, by the Monroe doctrine, pledged to protect Cuba.

A European protectorate often results in the plundering of the ward by the guardian. An American protectorate gives to the nation protected the advantage of our strength, without making it the victim of our greed. For three-quarters of a century the Monroe doctrine has been a shield to neighboring republics and yet it has imposed no pecuniary burden upon us. After the Filipinos had aided us in the war against Spain, we could not honorably turn them over to their former masters; we could not leave them to be the victims of the ambitious designs of European nations, and since we do not desire to make them a part of us or to hold them as subjects, we propose the only alternative, namely, to give them independence and guard them against molestation from without.

When our opponents are unable to defend their position by argument they fall back upon the assertion that it is destiny, and insist that we must submit to it, no matter how much it violates our moral precepts and our principles of government. This is a complacent philosophy. It obliterates the distinction between right and wrong and makes individuals and nations the helpless victims of circumstance.

Destiny is the subterfuge of the invertebrate, who, lacking the courage to oppose error, seeks some plausible excuse for supporting it. Washington said that the destiny of the republican form of government was deeply, if not finally, staked on the experiment entrusted to the American people. How different Washington's definition of destiny from the Republican definition!

The Republicans say that this nation is in the hands of destiny; Washington believed that not only the destiny of our own nation but the destiny of the republican form of government throughout the world was entrusted to American hands. Immeasurable responsibility! The destiny of this republic is in the hands of its own people, and upon the success of the experiment here rests the hope of humanity. No exterior force can disturb this republic, and no foreign influence should be permitted to change its course. What the future has in store for this nation no one has authority to declare, but each individual has his own idea of the nation's mission, and he owes it to his country as well as to himself to contribute as best he may to the fulfilment of that mission.

Mr. Chairman and Gentlemen of the Committee: I can never fully discharge the debt of gratitude which I owe to my countrymen for the honors which they have so generously bestowed upon me; but, sirs, whether it be my lot to occupy the high office for which the convention has named me, or to spend the remainder of my days in private life, it shall be my constant ambition and my controlling purpose to aid in realizing the high ideals of those whose wisdom and courage and sacrifices brought this republic into existence.

I can conceive of a national destiny surpassing the glories of the present and the past—a destiny which meets the responsibilities of to-day and measures up to the possibilities of the future. Behold a republic, resting securely upon the foundation stones quarried by revolutionary patriots from the mountain of eternal truth—a republic applying in practise and proclaiming to the world the self-evident propositions that all men are created equal; that they are endowed by their Creator with inalienable rights; that governments are instituted among men to secure these rights, and that governments derive their just powers from the consent of the governed. Behold a republic in which civil and religious liberty stimulate all to earnest endeavor and in which the law restrains every hand uplifted for a neighbor's injury—a republic in which every citizen is a sovereign, but in which no one cares or dares to wear a crown. Behold a republic standing erect while empires all around are bowed beneath the weight of their own armaments—a republic whose flag is loved while other flags are only feared. Behold a republic increasing in population, in wealth, in strength and in influence, solving the problems of civilization and hastening the coming of an universal brotherhood—a republic which shakes thrones and dissolves aristocracies by its silent example and gives light and inspiration to those who sit in darkness. Behold a republic gradually but surely becoming the supreme moral factor in the world's progress and the accepted arbiter of the world's disputes—a republic whose history, like the path of the just, "is as the shining light that shineth more and more unto the perfect day."

Woodrow Wilson

War Message (1917)

In 1914 the heir to the Austrian throne, the Archduke Francis Ferdinand, made a state visit to Serbia, a Balkan state whose relations with the Austro-Hungarian Empire were tense. In Sarajevo, the Archduke and his wife were assassinated by a Serbian student, initiating a series of events that plunged the European powers into war. A dizzying sequence of diplomatic maneuvers, ultimatums, and declarations ensued that summer. In July Austria-Hungary declared war on Serbia, bringing about general mobilization by Serbia's ally, Russia. On the August 1 Austria's ally, Germany, mobilized and declared war on Russia, followed within days by a declaration against France, partner of Russia and Britain in the Triple Entente. German forces then invaded Belgium. In defense of Belgian neutrality, to which they were pledged by treaty, France and Britain declared war on Germany. They soon followed with declarations of war on Austria-Hungary as well. Turkey concluded a treaty with Germany directed against Russia and, within a few months, was at war with Great Britain, France, and Russia. By the time Americans went to the polls for the Congressional elections in November, the lines in Europe were drawn. On one side were the Entente Powers (the Allies) of Great Britain, France, and Russia (they would be joined in 1915 by Italy); on the other, the Central Powers: Germany, Austria-Hungary, and Turkey.

The intricate network of treaties and alliances, the clear desire for territorial aggrandizement, and the array of kings, emperors, and generals sending massive armies into battle over the checkerboard of Europe baffled and disgusted most Americans, whose only wish was to stay out of it. On August 19, 1914, President Woodrow Wilson issued the Neutrality Proclamation and urged Americans to remain impartial.

In May of the following year the President declared in a speech in Philadelphia that "There is such a thing as a man being too proud to fight. There is such a thing as a nation being so right that it does not need to convince others that it is right," and he bent every effort in continuance of his policy of unarmed neutrality.

There were those, however, who argued that the nation should be prepared to fight if the need arose. Their insistence on military preparedness sparked a debate with those who maintained that America's vital interests were not involved in the European war. It soon became apparent that neutrality was not an easy path as both the Allies and the Central Powers took actions that disrupted American trade with Europe. However, it was German submarine attacks that most angered Americans and caused the President to join the preparedness movement himself. The sinking of the British liner *Lusitania* in May 1915, with the loss of 124 American lives, and of the *Arabic* a few months later, brought the United States and Germany close to war. Germany agreed to suspend its policy of unrestricted submarine warfare, and Americans believed that they had gained a diplomatic triumph. The Administration, however, was alarmed, and the President, despite his resolve to maintain peace, supported efforts to prepare for war. The National Defense Act of 1916 enlarged the Army and National Guard and provided for steps to be taken for industrial preparedness. A few months later a Council of National Defense was organized to make plans for preparing the country for war in nonmilitary areas such as industry, transportation, and medicine.

In 1916 the President was reelected under the campaign slogan, "He kept us out of war," in an extremely close race against the Republican nominee, Charles Evans Hughes. Wilson had, just barely, kept the United States out of war, and it became increasingly difficult for him to continue to do so. His "Peace Note" to both sides, sent after the election, met with no success, and Wilson called for the establishment of an international organization as a means to a stable world peace.

Meanwhile, the murderous losses on both sides and the effective stalemate in the trenches were causing domestic political problems for all the belligerent governments, and pressures for an end to war mounted on both sides. The German High Command determined that the only way to break the stalemate was to starve out the Allies. To do so, they determined to resume unrestricted submarine warfare with the hope that Britain could be brought to her knees before American intervention, which such a move would surely bring, could have any effect on the war. The resumption of unrestricted submarine warfare in February 1917 prompted Wilson to break diplomatic relations with Germany, a move supported by a resolution in the Senate. The following month, with the publication of an intercepted German diplomatic message to Mexico (the Zimmermann Note) suggesting an alliance against the United States in the event of war, American public opinion against Germany was further inflamed.

The President, in spite of opposition from a small group of antiwar senators, took steps to arm merchant ships and authorized them to take action against submarines. As American ships were sunk in February and March, the President's hesitation in taking the final step was eroded. On April 2, 1917, Wilson appeared before a joint session of Congress to condemn German policy and argue that the United States join in the war with the goal of ultimately establishing a stable peace that would "make the world safe for democracy."

Gentlemen of the Congress: I have called the Congress into extraordinary session because there are serious, very serious, choices of policy to be made, and made immediately, which it was neither right nor constitutionally permissible that I should assume the responsibility of making.

On the third of February last I officially laid before you the extraordinary announcement of the Imperial German Government that on and after the first day of February it was its purpose to put aside all restraints of law or of humanity and use its submarines to sink every vessel that sought to approach either the ports of Great Britain and Ireland or the western coasts of Europe or any of the ports controlled by the enemies of Germany within the Mediterranean. That had seemed to be the object of the German submarine warfare earlier in the war, but since April of last year the Imperial Government had somewhat restrained the commanders of its undersea craft in conformity with its promise then given to us that passenger boats should not be sunk and that due warning would be given to all other vessels which its submarines might seek to destroy, when no resistance was offered or escape attempted, and care taken that their crews were given at least a fair chance to save their lives in their open boats. The precautions taken were meagre and haphazard enough, as was proved in distressing instance after instance in the progress of the cruel and unmanly business, but a certain degree of restraint was observed. The new policy has swept every restriction aside. Vessels of every kind, whatever their flag, their character, their cargo, their destination, their errand, have been ruthlessly sent to the bottom without warning and without thought of help or mercy for those on board, the vessels of friendly neutrals along with those of belligerents. Even hospital ships and ships carrying relief to the sorely bereaved and stricken people of Belgium, though the latter were provided with safe conduct through the proscribed areas by the German Government itself and were distinguished by unmistakable marks of identity, have been sunk with the same reckless lack of compassion or of principle.

I was for a little while unable to believe that such things would in fact be done by any government that had hitherto subscribed to the humane practices of civilized nations. International law had its origin in the attempt to set up some law which would be respected and observed upon the seas, where no nation had right of dominion and where lay the free highways of the world. By painful stage after stage has that law been built up, with meagre enough results, indeed, after all was accomplished that could be accomplished, but always with a clear view, at least, of what the heart and conscience of mankind demanded. This minimum of right the German Government has swept aside under the plea of retaliation and necessity and because it had no weapons which it could use at sea except these which it is impossible to employ as it is employing them without throwing to the winds all scruples of humanity or of respect for the understandings that were supposed to underlie the intercourse of the world. I am not now thinking of the loss of property involved, immense and serious as that is, but only of the wanton and wholesale destruction of the lives of noncombatants, men, women, and children, engaged in pursuits which have always, even in the darkest periods of modern history, been deemed innocent and legitimate. Property can be paid for; the lives of peaceful and innocent people cannot be. The present German submarine warfare against commerce is a warfare against mankind.

It is a war against all nations. American ships have been sunk, American lives taken, in ways which it has stirred us very deeply to learn of, but the ships and people of other neutral and friendly nations have been sunk and overwhelmed in the waters in the same way. There has been no discrimination. The challenge is to all mankind. Each nation must decide for itself how it will meet it. The choice we make for ourselves must be made with a moderation of counsel and a temperateness of judgment befitting our character and our motives as a nation. We must put excited feeling away. Our motive will not be revenge or the victorious assertion of the physical might of the nation, but only the vindication of right, of human right, of which we are only a single champion.

When I addressed the Congress on the twenty-sixth of February last I thought that it would suffice to assert our neutral rights with arms, our right to use the seas against unlawful interference, our right to keep our people safe against unlawful violence. But armed neutrality, it now appears, is impracticable. Because submarines are in effect outlaws when used as the German submarines have been used against merchant shipping, it is impossible to defend ships against their attacks as the law of nations has assumed that merchantmen would defend themselves against privateers or cruisers, visible craft giving chase upon the open sea. It is common prudence in such circumstances, grim necessity indeed, to endeavour to destroy them before they have shown their own intention. They must be dealt with upon sight, if dealt with at all. The German Government denies the right of neutrals to use arms at all within the areas of the sea which it has proscribed, even in the defense of rights which no modern publicist has ever before questioned their right to defend. The intimation is conveyed that the armed guards which we have placed on our merchant ships will be treated as beyond the pale of law and subject to be dealt with as pirates would be. Armed neutrality is ineffectual enough at best; in such circumstances and in the face of such pretensions it is worse than ineffectual: it is likely only to produce what it was meant to prevent; it is practically certain to draw us into the war without either the rights or the effectiveness of belligerents. There is one choice we cannot make, we are incapable of making: we will not choose the path of submission and suffer the most sacred rights of our nation and our people to be ignored or violated. The wrongs against which we now array ourselves are no common wrongs; they cut to the very roots of human life.

With a profound sense of the solemn

and even tragical character of the step I am taking and of the grave responsibilities which it involves, but in unhesitating obedience to what I deem my constitutional duty, I advise that the Congress declare the recent course of the Imperial German Government to be in fact nothing less than war against the government and people of the United States; that it formally accept the status of belligerent which has thus been thrust upon it; and that it take immediate steps not only to put the country in a more thorough state of defense but also to exert all its power and employ all its resources to bring the Government of the German Empire to terms and end the war.

What this will involve is clear. It will involve the utmost practicable cooperation in counsel and action with the governments now at war with Germany, and, as incident to that, the extension to those governments of the most liberal financial credits, in order that our resources may so far as possible be added to theirs. It will involve the organization and mobilization of all the material resources of the country to supply the materials of war and serve the incidental needs of the nation in the most abundant and yet the most economical and efficient way possible. It will involve the immediate full equipment of the navy in all respects but particularly in supplying it with the best means of dealing with the enemy's submarines. It will involve the immediate addition to the armed forces of the United States already provided for by law in case of war at least five hundred thousand men, who should, in my opinion, be chosen upon the principle of universal liability to service, and also the authorization of subsequent additional increments of equal force so soon as they may be needed and can be handled in training. It will involve also, of course, the granting of adequate credits to the Government, sustained, I hope, so far as they can equitably be sustained by the present generation, by well conceived taxation.

I say sustained so far as may be equitable by taxation because it seems to me that it would be most unwise to base the credits which will now be necessary entirely on money borrowed. It is our duty, I most respectfully urge, to protect our people so far as we may against the very serious hardships and evils which would be likely to arise out of the inflation which would be produced by vast loans.

In carrying out the measures by which these things are to be accomplished we should keep constantly in mind the wisdom of interfering as little as possible in our own preparation and in the equipment of our own military forces with the duty,—for it will be a very practical duty,—of supplying the nations already at war with Germany with the materials which they can obtain only from us or by our assistance. They are in the field and we should help them in every way to be effective there.

I shall take the liberty of suggesting, through the several executive departments of the Government, for the consideration of your committees, measures for the accomplishment of the several objects I have mentioned. I hope that it will be your pleasure to deal with them as having been framed after very careful thought by the branch of the Government upon which the responsibility of conducting the war and safeguarding the nation will most directly fall.

While we do these things, these deeply momentous things, let us be very clear, and make very clear to all the world what our motives and our objects are. My own thought has not been driven from its habitual and normal course by the unhappy events of the last two months, and I do ot believe that the thought of the nation has been altered or clouded by them. I have exactly the same things in mind now that I had in mind when I addressed the Senate on the twenty-second of January last; the same that I had in mind when I addressed the Congress on the third of February and on the twenty-sixth of February. Our object now, as then, is to vindicate the principles of peace and justice in the life of the world as against selfish and autocratic power and to set up amongst the really free and self-governed peoples of the world such a concert of purpose and of action as will henceforth ensure the observance of those principles. Neutrality is no longer feasible or desirable where the peace of the world is involved and the freedom of its peoples, and the menace to that peace and freedom lies in the existence of autocratic governments backed by organized force which is controlled wholly by their will, not by the will of their people. We have seen the last of neutrality in such circumstances. We are at the beginning of an age in which it will be insisted that the same standards of conduct and of responsibility for wrong done shall be observed among nations and their governments that are observed among the individual citizens of civilized states.

We have no quarrel with the German people. We have no feeling towards them but one of sympathy and friendship. It was not upon their impulse that their government acted in entering this war. It was not with their previous knowledge or approval. It was a war determined upon as wars used to be determined upon in the old, unhappy days when peoples were nowhere consulted by their rulers and wars were provoked and waged in the interest of dynasties or of little groups of ambitious men who were accustomed to use their fellow men as pawns and tools. Self-governed nations do not fill their neighbour states with spies or set the course of intrigue to bring about some critical posture of affairs which will give them an opportunity to strike and make conquest. Such designs can be successfully worked out only under cover and where no one has the right to ask questions. Cunningly contrived plans of deception or aggression, carried, it may be, from generation to generation, can be worked out and kept from the light only within the privacy of courts or behind the carefully guarded confidences of a narrow and privileged class. They are happily impossible where public opinion commands and insists upon full information concerning all the nation's affairs.

A steadfast concert for peace can never be maintained except by a partnership of democratic nations. No autocratic government could be trusted to keep faith within it or observe its covenants. It must be a league of honour, a partnership of opinion. Intrigue would eat its vitals away; the plottings of inner circles who could plan what they would and render account to no one would be a corruption seated at its very heart. Only free peoples can hold their purpose and their honour steady to a common end and prefer the interests of mankind to any narrow interest of their own.

Does not every American feel that assurance has been added to our hope for the future peace of the world by the wonderful and heartening things that have been happening within the last few weeks in Russia? Russia was known by those who knew it best to have been always in fact democratic at heart, in all the vital habits of her thought, in all the intimate relationships of her people that spoke their natural instinct, their habitual attitude towards life. The autocracy that crowned the summit of her political structure, long as it had stood and terrible as was the reality of its power, was not in fact Russian in origin, character, or purpose; and now it has been shaken off and the great, generous Russian people have been added in all their naive majesty and might to the forces that are fighting for freedom in the world, for justice, and for peace. Here is a fit partner for a League of Honour.

One of the things that has served to convince us that the Prussian autocracy was not and could never be our friend is that from the very outset of the present war it has filled our unsuspecting communities and even our offices of government with spies and set criminal intrigues everywhere afoot against our national unity of counsel, our peace within and without, our industries and our commerce. Indeed it is now evident that its spies were here even before the war began; and it is unhappily not a matter of conjecture but a fact proved in our courts of justice that the intrigues which have more than once come perilously near to disturbing the peace and dislocating the industries of the country have been carried on at the instigation, with the support, and even under the personal direction of official agents of the Imperial Government accredited to the Government of the United States. Even in checking these things and trying to extirpate them we have sought to put the most generous interpretation possible upon them because we knew that their source lay, not in any hostile feeling or purpose of the German people towards us (who were, no doubt as ignorant of them as we ourselves were), but only in the selfish designs of a Government that did what it pleased and told its people nothing. But they have played their part in serving to convince us at last that that Government entertains no real friendship for us and means to act against our peace and security at its convenience. That it means to stir up enemies against us at our very doors the intercepted note to the German Minister at Mexico City is eloquent evidence.

We are accepting this challenge of hostile purpose because we know that in such a government, following such methods, we can never have a friend; and that in the presence of its organized power, always lying in wait to accomplish we know not what purpose, there can be no assured security for the democratic governments of the world. We are now about to accept gauge of battle with this natural foe to liberty and shall, if necessary, spend the whole force of the nation to check and nullify its pretensions and its power. We are glad, now that we see the facts with no veil of false pretence about them, to fight thus for the ultimate peace of the world and for the liberation of its peoples, the German peoples included: for the rights of nations great and small and the privilege of men everywhere to choose their way of life and of obedience. The world must be made safe for democracy. Its peace must be planted upon the tested foundations of political liberty. We have no selfish ends to serve. We desire no conquest, no dominion. We seek no indemnities for ourselves, no material compensation for the sacrifices we shall freely make. We are but one of the champions of the rights of mankind. We shall be satisfied when those rights have been made as secure as the faith and the freedom of nations can make them.

Just because we fight without rancour and without selfish object, seeking nothing for ourselves but what we shall wish to share with all free peoples, we shall, I feel confident, conduct our operations as belligerents without passion and ourselves observe with proud punctilio the principles of right and of fair play we profess to be fighting for.

I have said nothing of the governments

allied with the Imperial Government of Germany because they have not made war upon us or challenged us to defend our right and our honour. The Austro-Hungarian Government has, indeed, avowed its unqualified endorsement and acceptance of the reckless and lawless submarine warfare adopted now without disguise by the Imperial German Government, and it has therefore not been possible for this Government to receive Count Tarnowski, the Ambassador recently accredited to this Government by the Imperial and Royal Government of Austria-Hungary; but that Government has not actually engaged in warfare against citizens of the United States on the seas, and I take the liberty, for the present at least, of postponing a discussion of our relations with the authorities at Vienna. We enter this war only where we are clearly forced into it because there are no other means of defending our rights.

It will be all the easier for us to conduct ourselves as belligerents in a high spirit of right and fairness because we act without animus, not in enmity towards a people or with the desire to bring any injury or disadvantage upon them, but only in armed opposition to an irresponsible government which has thrown aside all considerations of humanity and of right and is running amuck. We are, let me say again, the sincere friends of the German people, and shall desire nothing so much as the early re-establishment of intimate relations of mutual advantage between us,—however hard it may be for them, for the time being, to believe that this is spoken from our hearts. We have borne with their present government through all these bitter months because of that friendship,—exercising a patience and forbearance which would otherwise have been impossible. We shall, happily, still have an opportunity to prove that friendship in our daily attitude and actions towards the millions of men and women of German birth and native sympathy who live amongst us and share our life, and we shall be proud to prove it towards all who are in fact loyal to their neighbours and to the Government in the hour of test. They are, most of them, as true and loyal Americans as if they had never known any other fealty or allegiance. They will be prompt to stand with us in rebuking and restraining the few who may be a different mind and purpose. If there should be disloyalty, it will be dealt with with a firm hand of stern repression; but, if it lifts its head at all, it will lift it only here and there and without countenance except from a lawless and malignant few.

It is a distressing and oppressive duty, Gentlemen of the Congress, which I have performed in thus addressing you. There are, it may be, many months of fiery trial and sacrifice ahead of us. It is a fearful thing to lead this great peaceful people into war, into the most terrible and disastrous of all wars, civilization itself seeming to be in the balance. But the right is more precious than peace, and we shall fight for the things which we have always carried nearest our hearts,—for democracy, for the right of those who submit to authority to have a voice in their own governments, for the rights and liberties of small nations, for a universal dominion of right by such a concert of free peoples as shall bring peace and safety to all nations and make the world itself at last free. To such a task we can deidcate our lives and our fortunes, everything that we are and everything that we have, with the pride of those who know that the day has come when America is privileged to spend her blood and her might for the principles that gave her birth and happiness and the peace which she has treasured. God helping her, she can do no other.

Eugene Debs

Statement to the Court (1918)

When war broke out in Europe in 1914, Americans held themselves aloof from the conflict, most hoping that the United States could remain neutral. Although President Woodrow Wilson initially stood opposed to an increase in the standing army and supported unarmed neutrality, the growing tensions between the United States and Germany led him to join with those calling for preparedness. The President attempted to maintain an impartial stance toward the belligerents, and his supporters proudly proclaimed during his campaign for election to a second term in 1916 that "he kept us out of war." Events, however, caught up with the country and its President, and Congress heeded Wilson's call for a Declaration of War against Germany in April 1917.

Within weeks of the commencement of hostilities, a flurry of legislation designed to promote the prosecution of the war was passed by Congress. On May 18, 1917, it passed the Selective Service Act, establishing a system of registration and inaugurating the draft. Less than a month later, Congress passed the Espionage Act, which imposed severe penalties for aiding the enemy, for attempting to obstruct the draft, and for refusing to serve in the armed forces. A provision of the Act empowered the Postmaster General to prevent periodicals deemed to be treasonable from being sent through the mails. Almost a year later, in May 1918, the Act was amended by the passage of the Sedition Act. This legislation imposed strict limitations on freedom of speech during wartime; it provided penalties for making false statements that interfered with the prosecution of the war, for employing disloyal language about the Constitution, the government, the flag, or the military, and for urging anyone else to do such things.

A clear target of this legislation were the Socialists, who had steadfastly opposed American participation in the war. Socialist publications were denied use of the U.S. mail and over 1,500 persons were arrested, many of whom were prosecuted and sent to jail. Perhaps the most prominent Socialist to be tried and convicted under the Sedition Act was Eugene V. Debs of Indiana. Debs went to work at age 14 in Terre Haute, first in the railroad repair shops and then as a locomotive fireman. He began his long career as a labor leader with the Brotherhood of Locomotive Firemen. He founded the American Railway Union and was sent to jail for contempt of court in 1894 when the ARU strike against Pullman was broken with the help of federal troops and the legal device of an injunction against the union. Debs became leader of the Socialist Party and was its candidate for President in the elections of 1900, 1904, 1908, and 1912, when he received 6 percent of the total vote. From a federal penitentiary in Atlanta, where he was imprisoned after his conviction under the Sedition Act, he ran for President for the last time in 1920.

Debs's critics assailed him variously as unpatriotic or naive; they attacked the lack of sophistication of his economic theory and the radicalism of his politics. Yet few could doubt the sincerity of his concern for the underprivileged, his unselfish devotion to the betterment of living conditions for all classes and conditions of people, or his genuine humanity. Debs held deeply the belief that war was in itself evil, especially war waged by the upper classes against each other while the lower classes furnished the cannon foder.

Debs was concerned that so many Socialists had been jailed under the Sedition Act and resolved to test the law himself. In Canton, Ohio, in June 1918 he launched a stinging attack on American capitalism and the war, arguing that Allied aims were no more pure or high-minded that those of Germany. He lashed out as the American "Junkers" of Wall Street who were no better than their Prussian counterparts. Debs was subsequently arrested and tried in Federal Court in Cleveland. In his own defense, Debs made an impassioned plea to the jury for freedom of speech, but he was found guilty and faced sentencing before Judge Westonhaver on September 18, 1918.

His short speech to the court before sentence was passed pulled together in a concise and moving fashion all that Debs had been saying for years. It was a statement of his conviction that the social order was flawed and of his faith that "the order of things cannot always endure," as well as of his personal commitment that "while there is a lower class, I am in it, while there is a criminal element, I am of it, and while there is a soul in prison, I am not free."

Your Honor, years ago I recognized my kinship with all living beings, and I made up my mind that I was not one bit better than the meanest on earth. I said then, and I say now, that while there is a lower class, I am in it, while there is a criminal element I am of it, and while there is a soul in prison, I am not free.

I listened to all that was said in this court in support and justification of this prosecution, but my mind remains unchanged. I look upon the Espionage Law as a despotic enactment in flagrant conflict with democratic principles and with the spirit of free institutions. . . .

Your Honor, I have stated in this court that I am opposed to the social system in which we live; that I believe in a fundamental change—but if possible by peaceable and orderly means. . . .

Standing here this morning, I recall my boyhood. At fourteen I went to work in a railroad shop; at sixteen I was firing a freight engine on a railroad. I remember all the hardships and privations of that earlier day, and from that time until now my heart has been with the working class. I could have been in Congress long ago. I have preferred to go to prison. . . .

I am thinking this morning of the men in the mills and factories; of the men in the mines and on the railroads. I am thinking of the women who for a paltry wage are compelled to work out their barren lives; of the little children who in this sytem are robbed of their childhood and in their tender years are seized in the remorseless grasp of Mammon and forced into the industrial dungeons, there to feed the monster machines while they themselves are being starved and stunted, body and soul. I see them dwarfed and diseased and their little lives broken and blasted because in this high noon of our twentieth-century Christian civilization money is still so much more important than the flesh and blood of childhood. In very truth gold is god today and rules with pitiless sway in the affairs of men.

In this country—the most favored beneath the bending skies—we have vast areas of the richest and most fertile soil, material resources in inexhaustible abundance, the most marvelous productive machinery on earth, and millions of eager workers ready to apply their labor to that machinery to produce in abundance for every man, woman, and child—and if there are still vast numbers of our people who are the victims of poverty and whose lives are an unceasing struggle all the way from youth to old age, until at last death comes to their rescue and stills their aching hearts and lulls these hapless victims to dreamless sleep, it is not the fault of the Almighty: it cannot be charged to nature, but it is due entirely to the outgrown social system in which we live that ought to be abolished not only in the interest of the toiling masses but in the higher interest of all humanity. . . .

I believe, Your Honor, in common with all Socialists, that this nation ought to own and control its own industries. I believe, as all Socialists do, that all things that are jointly needed and used ought to be jointly owned—that industry, the basis of our social life, instead of being the private property of the few and operated for their encirhment, ought to be the common property of all, democratically administered in the interest of all. . . .

I am opposing a social order in which it is possible for one man who does absolutely nothing that is useful to amass a fortune of hundreds of millions of dollars, while millions of men and women who work all the days of their lives secure barely enough for a wretched existence.

This order of things cannot always endure. I have registered my protest against it. I recognize the feebleness of my effort, but, fortunately, I am not alone. There are multiplied thousands of others who, like myself, have come to realize that before we may truly enjoy the blessings of civilized life, we must reorganize society upon a mutual and cooperative basis; and to this end we have organized a great economic and political movement that spreads over the face of all the earth.

There are today upwards of sixty millions of Socialists, loyal, devoted adherents to this cause, regardless of nationality, race, creed, color, or sex. They are all making common cause. They are spreading with tireless energy the propaganda of the new social order. They are waiting, watching, and working hopefully through all the hours of the day and the night. They are still in a minority. But they have learned how to be patient and to bide their time. They feel—they know, indeed—that the time is coming, in spite of all opposition, all persecution, when this emancipating gospel will spread among all the peoples, and when this minority will become the triumphant majority and, sweeping into power, inaugurate the greatest social and economic change in history.

In that day we shall have the universal commonwealth—the harmonious cooperation of every nation with every other nation on earth. . . .

Your Honor, I ask no mercy and I plead for no immunity. I realize that finally the right must prevail. I never so clearly comprehended as now the great struggle between the powers of greed and exploitation on the one hand and upon the other the rising hosts of industrial freedom and social justice.

I can see the dawn of the better day for humanity. The people are awakening. In due time they will and must come to their own.

"When the mariner, sailing over tropic seas, looks for relief from his weary watch, he turns his eyes toward the southern cross, burning luridly above the tempest-vexed ocean. As the midnight approaches, the southern cross begins to bend, the whirling worlds change their places, and with starry finger-points the Almighty marks the passage of time upon the dial of the universe, and though no bell may beat the glad tidings, the lookout knows that the midnight is passing and that relief and rest are close at hand. Let the people everywhere take heart of hope, for the cross is bending, the midnight is passing, and joy cometh with the morning.

I am now prepared to receive your sentence.

Woodrow Wilson

The League of Nations (1919)

In October 1916, six months before the United States entered World War I, President Woodrow Wilson told an audience in Indianapolis that "when the great present war is over it will be the duty of America to join with the other nations of the world in some kind of league for the maintenance of peace." Wilson firmly believed that a stable peace could be secured only through international cooperation and, in stating the "Fourteen Points" that made up American war aims in January 1918, the President called for "a general association of nations" to be "formed under specific covenants for the purpose of affording mutual guarantees of political independence and territorial integrity to great and small states alike."

The Armistice that brought the Great War to a close was signed on November 11, 1918, and on December 4 President Wilson embarked aboard the *George Washington* for France to attend the Peace Conference. Wilson's demand that the League be made a part of the peace settlement was accepted at a Plenary Session of the Conference, and he returned to the United States, docking in Boston on February 24, 1919. Back home, the President found mounting opposition to the League. The Republican-controlled Senate Foreign Relations Committee included members who were opposed to the League in the form proposed and others who were hostile to it in any form. Thirty-seven Republican senators expressed their reservations to the League in a statement read in the Senate. It was becoming clear that ratification of a peace treaty containing the League Covenant would in no wise be easy.

It was probable that the treaty and the League would have passed the Senate if the President had been willing to make concessions that would have allayed American fears of becoming entangled in

European affairs. However, the President was adamant that the League should be accepted as he had negotiated it—without any advice from the Senate, his critics pointed out—and he would not budge. He went so far as to urge his supporters to vote with the most extreme enemies of the League, the "irreconcilables," to defeat the resolutions proposed by Senator Lodge of Massachusetts providing for acceptance of the Treaty with reservations. This move, he thought, would prompt acceptance of the treaty in a straight up-or-down vote.

In the battle over ratification, the "irreconcilables" launched a nationwide campaign for the League's defeat, Senators Johnson of California, Borah of Idaho, and LaFollette of Wisconsin leading the attack. Wilson countered with a speaking tour of his own, convinced that he could win public support for the League. The President set for himself a grueling task, traveling to 29 cities and delivering 37 speeches between the commencement of the tour on September 4 and its abrupt end on September 25, 1919, when the President broke down after a speech in Pueblo, Colorado, and was rushed back to Washington, where he suffered a stroke. In the Pueblo speech, which follows, Wilson insisted that "nothing less than the liberation and salvation of the world" depended on the establishment of the League. He recognized that the League was not "an absolute insurance against war" but argued that it was better than nothing at all. Wilson believed that the opponents of the League had distorted the facts and confused the issue. This speech—indeed, the entire speaking tour—was designed, in Wilson's view, to clear away the mists so that "men will see the truth, eye to eye and face to face."

Mr. Chairman and fellow countrymen: It is with a great deal of genuine pleasure that I find myself in Pueblo, and I feel it a compliment in this beautiful hall. One of the advantages of this hall, as I look about, is that you are not too far away from me, because there is nothing so reassuring to men who are trying to express the public sentiment as getting into real personal contact with their fellow citizens. I have gained a renewed impression as I have crossed the continent this time of the homogeneity of this great people to whom we belong. They come from many stocks, but they are all of one kind. They come from many origins, but they are all shot through with the same principles and desire the same righteous and honest things. I have received a more inspiring impression this time of the public opinion of the United States than it was ever my privilege to receive before.

The chief pleasure of my trip has been that it has nothing to do with my personal fortunes, that it has nothing to do with my personal reputation, that it has nothing to do with anything except great principles uttered by Americans of all sorts and of all parties which we are now trying to realize at this crisis of the affairs of the world. But there have been unpleasant impressions as well as pleasant impressions, my fellow citizens, as I have crossed the continent. I have perceived more and more that men have been busy creating an absolutely false impression of what the treaty of peace and the Covenant of the League of Nations contain and mean. I find, moreover, that there is an organized propaganda against the League of Nations and against the treaty proceeding from exactly the same sources that the organized propaganda proceeded from which threatened this country here and there with disloyalty, and I want to say—I cannot say too often—any man who carries a hyphen about with him carries a dagger that he is ready to plunge into the vitals of this Republic whenever he gets ready. If I can catch any man with a hyphen in this great contest I will know that I have got an enemy of the Republic. My fellow citizens, it is only certain bodies of foreign sympathies, certain bodies of sympathy with foreign nations that are organized against this great document which the American representatives have brought back from Paris. Therefore, in order to clear away the mists, in order to remove the impressions, in order to check the falsehoods that have clustered around this great subject, I want to tell you a few very simple things about the treaty and the covenant.

Do not think of this treaty of peace as merely a settlement with Germany. It is that. It is a very severe settlement with Germany, but there is not anything in it that she did not earn. Indeed, she earned more than she can ever be able to pay for, and the punishment exacted of her is not a punishment greater than she can bear, and it is absolutely necessary in order that no other nation may ever plot such a thing against humanity and civilization. But the treaty is so much more than that. It is not merely a settlement with Germany; it is a readjustment of those great injustices which underlie the whole structure of European and Asiatic society. This is only the first of several treaties. They are all constructed upon the same plan. The Austrian treaty follows the same lines. The treaty with Hungary follows the same lines. The treaty with Bulgaria follows the same lines. The treaty with Turkey, when it is formulated, will follow the same lines. What are those lines? They are based upon the purpose to see that every government dealt with in this great settlement is put in the hands of the people and taken out of the hands of coteries and of sovereigns who had no right to rule over the people. It is a people's treaty, that accomplishes by a great sweep of practical justice the liberation of men who never could have liberated themselves, and the power of the most powerful nations has been devoted not to their aggrandizement but to the liberation of people whom they could have put under their control if they had chosen to do so. Not one foot of territory is demanded by the conquerors, not one single item of submission to their authority is demanded by them. The men who sat around that table in Paris knew that the time had come when the people were no longer going to consent to live under masters, but were going to live the lives that they chose themselves, to live under such governments as they chose themselves to erect. That is the fundamental principle of this great settlement.

And we did not stop with that. We added a great international charter for the rights of labor. Reject this treaty, impair it, and this is the consequence of the laboring men of the world, that there is no international tribunal which can bring the moral judgments of the world to bear upon the great labor questions of the day. What we need to do with regard to the labor questions of the day, my fellow countrymen, is to lift them into the light, is to lift them out of the haze and distraction of passion, of hostility, out into the calm spaces where men look at things without passion. The more men you get into a great discussion the more you exclude passion. Just as soon as the calm judgment of the world is directed upon the question of justice to labor, labor is going to have to forum such as it never was supplied with before, and men everywhere are going to see that the problem of labor is nothing more nor less than the problem of the elevation of humanity. We must see that all the questions which have disturbed the world, all the questions which have eaten into the confidence of men toward their governments, all the questions which have disturbed the processes of industry, shall be brought out where men of all points of view, men of all attitudes of mind, men of all kinds of experience, may contribute their part of the settlement of the great questions which we must settle and cannot ignore.

At the front of this great treaty is put the Covenant of the League of Nations. It will also be at the front of the Austrian treaty and the Hungarian treaty and the Bulgarian treaty and the treaty with Turkey. Every one of them will contain the Covenant of the League of Nations, because you cannot work any of them without the Covenant of the League of Nations. Unless you get the united, concerted purpose and power of the great Governments of the world behind this settlement, it will fall down like a house of cards. There is only one power to put behind the liberation of mankind, and that is the power of mankind. It is the power of the united moral forces of the world, and in the Covenant of the League of Nations the moral forces of the world are mobilized. For what purpose? Reflect, my fellow citizens, that the membership of this great League is going to include all the great fighting nations of the world, as well as the weak ones. It is not for the present going to include Germany, but for the time being Germany is not a great fighting country. All the nations that have power that can be mobilized are going to be members of this League, including the United States. And what do they unite for? They enter into a solemn promise to one another that they will never use their power against one another for aggression; that they never will impair the territorial integrity of a neighbor; that they never will interfere with the political independence of a neighbor; that they will abide by the principle that great populations are entitled to determine their own destiny and that they will not interfere with that destiny; and that no matter what differences arise amongst them they will never resort to war without first having done one or other of two things—either submitted the matter of controversy to arbitration, in which case they agree to abide by the result without question, or submitted it to the consideration of the council of the League of Nations, laying before that council all the documents, all the facts, agreeing that the council can publish the documents and the facts to the whole world, agreeing that there shall be six months allowed for the mature consideration of those facts by the council, and agreeing that at the expiration of the six months, even if they are not then ready to accept the advice of the council with regard to the settlement of the dispute, they will still not go to war for another three months. In other words, they consent, no matter what happens, to submit every matter of difference between them to the judgment of mankind, and just so certainly as they do that, my fellow citizens, war will be in the far background, war will be pushed out of that foreground of terror in which it has kept the world for generation after generation, and men will know that there will be a calm time of deliberate counsel. The most dangerous thing for a bad cause is to expose it to the opinion of the world. The most certain way that you can prove that a man is mistaken is by letting all his neighbors know what he thinks, by letting all his neighbors discuss what he thinks, and if he is in the wrong you will notice that he will stay at home, he will not walk on the street. He will be afraid of the eyes of his neighbors. He will be afraid of their judgment of his character. He will know that his cause is lost unless he can sustain it by the arguments of right and of justice. The same law that applies to individuals applies to nations.

But, you say, "We have heard that we might be at a disadvantage in the League of Nations." Well, whoever told you that either was deliberately falsifying or he had not read the Covenant of the League of Nations. I leave him the choice. I want to give you a very simple account of the organization of the League of Nations and let you judge for yourselves. It is a very simple organization. The power of the League, or rather the activities of the league, lie in two bodies. There is the council, which consists of one representative from each of the principal allied and associated powers—that is to say, the United States, Great Britain, France, Italy, and Japan, along with four other representatives of smaller powers chosen out of the general body of the membership of the League. The council is the source of every active policy of the League, and no active policy of the League can be adopted without a unanimous vote of the council. That is explicitly stated in the Covenant itself. Does it not evidently follow that the League of Nations can adopt no policy whatever without the consent of the United States? The affirmative vote of the representative of the United States is necessary in every case. Now, you have heard of six votes belonging to the British Empire. Those six votes are not in the council. They are in the assembly, and the interesting thing is that the assembly does not vote. I must qualify that statement a little, but essentially it is absolutely true. In every matter in which the assembly is given a voice, and there are only four or five, its vote does not count unless concurred in by the representatives of all the nations represented on the council, so that there is no validity to any vote of the assembly unless in that vote also the representative of the United States concurs. That one vote of the United States is as big as the six votes of the British Empire. I am not jealous for advantage, my fellow citizens, but I think that is a perfectly safe situation. There is no validity in a vote, either by the council or the assembly, in which we do not concur. So much for the statements about the six votes of the British Empire.

Look at it in another aspect. The assembly is the talking body. The assembly was created in order that anybody that purposed anything wrong should be subjected to the awkward circumstance that everybody could talk about it. This is the great assembly in which all the things that are likely to disturb the peace of the world or the good understanding between nations are to be exposed to the general view, and I want to ask you if you think it was unjust, unjust to the United States, that speaking parts should be assigned to the several portions of the British Empire? Do you think it unjust that there should be some spokesman in debate for that fine little stout Republic down in the Pacific, New Zealand? Do you think it was unjust that Australia should be allowed to stand up and take part in the debate—Australia, from which we have learned some of the most useful progressive policies of modern time, a little nation only five million in a great continent, but counting for several times five in its activities and in its interest in liberal reform? Do you think it unjust that that little Republic down in South Africa, whose gallant resistance to being subjected to any outside authority at all we admired for so many months and whose fortunes we followed with such interest, should have a speaking part? Great Britain obliged South Africa to submit to her sovereignty, but she immediately after that felt that it was convenient and right to hand the whole self-government of that colony over to the very men whom she had beaten. The representatives of South Africa in Paris were two of the most distinguished generals of the Boer Army, two of the realest men I ever met, two men that could talk sober counsel and wise advice, along with the best statesmen in Europe. To exclude Gen. Botha and Gen. Smuts from the right to stand up in the parliament of the world and say something concerning the affairs of mankind would be absurd. And what about Canada? Is not Canada a good neighbor? I ask you, Is not Canada more likely to agree with the United States than with Great Britain? Canada has a speaking part. And then, for the first time in the history of the world, that great voiceless multitude, that throng hundreds of millions strong in India, has a voice, and I want to testify that some of the wisest and most dignified figures in the peace conference at Paris came from India, men who seemed to carry in their minds an older wisdom than the rest of us had, whose traditions ran back into so many of the unhappy fortunes of mankind that they seemed very useful counselors as to how some ray of hope and some prospect of happiness could be opened to its people. I for my part have no jealousy whatever of those five speaking parts in the assembly. Those speaking parts cannot translate themselves into five votes that can in any matter override the voice and purpose of the United States.

Let us sweep aside all this language of jealousy. Let us be big enough to know the facts and to welcome the facts, because the facts are based upon the principle that America has always fought for, namely, the equality of self-governing peoples, whether they were big or little—not counting men, but counting rights, not counting representation, but counting the purpose of that representation. When you hear an opinion quoted you do not count the number of persons who hold it; you ask, "Who said that?" You weigh opinions, you do not count them, and the beauty of all democracies is that every voice can be heard, every voice can have its effect, every voice can contribute to the general judgment that is finally arrived at. That is the object of democracy. Let us accept what America has always fought for, and accept it with pride that America showed the way and made the proposal. I do not mean that America made the proposal in this particular instance; I mean that the principle was an American principle, proposed by America.

When you come to the heart of the Covenant, my fellow citizens, you will find it in article ten, and I am very much interested to know that the other things have been blown away like bubbles. There is nothing in the other contentions with regard to the league of nations, but there is something in article ten that you ought to realize and ought to accept or reject. Article ten is the heart of the whole matter. What is article ten? I never am certain that I can from memory give a literal repetition of its language, but I am sure that I can give an exact interpretation of its meaning. Article ten provides that every member of the league covenants to respect and preserve the territorial integrity and existing political independence of every other member of the league as against external aggression. Not against internal disturbance. There was not a man at that table who did not admit the sacredness of the right of self-determination, the sacredness of the right of any body of people to say that they would not continue to live under the Government they were then living under, and under article eleven of the Covenant they are given a place to say whether they will live under it or not. For following article ten is article eleven, which makes it the right of any member of the League at any time to call attention to anything, anywhere, that is likely to disturb the peace of the world or the good understanding between nations upon which the peace of the world depends. I want to give you an illustration of what that would mean.

You have heard a great deal—something that was true and a great deal that was false—about that provision of the treaty which hands over to Japan the rights which Germany enjoyed in the Province of Shantung in China. In the first place, Germany did not enjoy any rights there that other nations had not already claimed. For my part, my judgment, my moral judgment, is against the whole set of concessions. They were all of them unjust to China, they ought never to have been exacted, they were all exacted by duress, from a great body of thoughtful and ancient and helpless people. There never was any right in any of them. Thank God, America never asked for any, never dreamed of asking for any. But when Germany got this concession in 1898, the Government of the United States made no protest whatever. That was not because the Government of the United States was not in the hands of high-minded and conscientious men. It was. William McKinley was President and John Hay was Secretary of State—as safe hands to leave the honor of the United States in as any that you can cite. They made no protest because the state of international law at that time was that it was none of their business unless they could show that the interests of the United States were affected, and the only thing that they could show with regard to the interests of the United States was that Germany might close the doors of Shantung Province against the trade of the United States. They, therefore, demanded and obtained promises that we could continue to sell merchandise in Shantung. Immediately following that concession to Germany there was a concession to Russia of the same sort, of Port Arthur, and Port Arthur was handed over subsequently to Japan on the very territory of the United States. Don't you remember that when Russia and Japan got into war with one another the war was brought to a conclusion by a treaty written at Portsmouth, N.H., and in that treaty without the slightest intimation from any authoritative sources in America that the Government of the United States had any objection, Port Arthur, Chinese territory, was turned over to Japan? I want you distinctly to understand that there is no thought of criticism in my mind. I am expounding to you a state of international law. Now, read articles ten and eleven. You will see that international law is revolutionized by putting morals into it. Article ten says that no member of the League, and that includes all these nations that have demanded these things unjustly of China, shall impair the territorial integrity or the political independence of any other member of the League. China is going to be a member of the League. Article eleven says that any member of the League can call attention to anything that is likely to disturb the peace of the world or the good understanding between nations, and China is for the first time in the history of mankind afforded a standing before the jury of the world. I, for my part, have a profound sympathy for China, and I am proud to have taken part in an arrangement which promises the protection of the world to the rights of China. The whole atmosphere of the world is changed by a thing like that, my fellow citizens. The whole international practice of the world is revolutionized.

But you will say, "What is the second sentence of article ten? That is what gives very disturbing thoughts." The second sentence is that the council of the League shall advise what steps, if any, are necessary to carry out the guaranty of the first sentence, namely, that the members will respect and preserve the territorial integrity and political independence of the other members. I do not know any other meaning for the word "advise" except "advise." The council advises, and it cannot advise without the vote of the United States. Why gentlemen should fear that the Congress of the United States would be advised to do something that it did not want to do I frankly cannot imagine, because they cannot even be advised to do anything unless their own representative has participated in the advice. It may be that that will impair somewhat the vigor of the League, but, nevertheless, the fact is so, that we are not obliged to take any advice except our own, which to any man who wants to go his own course is a very satisfactory state of affairs. Every man regards his own advice as best, and I dare say every man mixes his own advice with some thought of his own interest. Whether we use it wisely or unwisely, we can use the vote of the United States to make impossible drawing the United States into any enterprise that she does not care to be drawn into.

Yet article ten strikes at the taproot of war. Article ten is a statement that the very things that have always been sought in imperialistic wars are henceforth foregone by every ambitious nation in the world. I would have felt very much disturbed if, sitting at the peace table in Paris, I had supposed that I was expounding my own ideas. Whether you believe it or not, I know the relative size of my own ideas; I know how they stand related in bulk and proportion to the moral judgments of my fellow countrymen, and I proposed nothing whatever at the peace table at Paris that I had not sufficiently certain knowledge embodied the moral judgment of the citizens of the United States. I had gone over there with, so to say, explicit instructions. Don't you remember that we laid down fourteen points which should contain the principles of the settlement? They were not my points. In every one of them I was conscientiously trying to read the thought of the people of the United States, and after I uttered those points I had every assurance given me that could be given me that they did speak the moral judgment of the United States and not my single judgment. Then when it came to that critical period just a little less than a year ago, when it was evident that the war was coming to its critical end, all the nations engaged in the war accepted those fourteen principles explicitly as the basis of the armistice and the basis of the peace. In those circumstances I crossed the ocean under bond to my own people and to the other governments with which I was dealing. The whole specification of the method of settlement was written down and accepted before hand, and we were architects building on those specifications. It reassures me and fortifies my position to find how before I went over men whose judgment the United States has often trusted were of exactly the same opinion that I went abroad to express.

Here is something I want to read from Theodore Roosevelt:

"The one effective move for obtaining peace is by an agreement among all the great powers in which each should pledge itself not only to abide by the decisions of a common tribunal but to back its decisions by force. The great civilized nations should combine by solemn agreement in a great world league for the peace of righteousness; a court should be established. A changed and amplified Hague court would meet the requirements, composed of representatives from each nation, whose representatives are sworn to act as judges in each case and not in a representative capacity." Now there is article ten. He goes on and says this: "The nations should agree on certain rights that should not be questioned, such as territorial integrity, their right to deal with their domestic affairs, and with such matters as whom they should admit to citizenship. All such guarantee each of their number in possession of these rights."

Now, the other specification is in the Covenant. The Covenant in another portion guarantees to the members the independent control of their domestic questions. There is not a leg for these gentlemen to stand on when they say that the interests of the United States are not safeguarded in the very points where we are most sensitive. You do not need to be told again that the Covenant expressly says that nothing in this covenant shall be construed as affecting the validity of the Monroe doctrine, for example. You could not be more explicit than that. And every point of interest is covered, partly for one very interesting reason. This is not the first time that the Foreign Relations Committee of the Senate of the United States has read and considered this covenant. I brought it to this country in March last in a tentative, provisional form, in practically the form that it now has, with the exception of certain additions which I shall mention immediately. I asked the Foreign Relations Committees of both Houses to come to the White House and we spent a long evening in the frankest discussion of every portion that they wished to discuss. They made certain specific suggestions as to what should be contained in this document when it was to be revised. I carried those suggestions to Paris, and every one of them was adopted. What more could I have done? What more could have been obtained? The very matters upon which these gentlemen were most concerned were, the right of withdrawal, which is now expressly stated; the safeguarding of the Monroe doctrine, which is now accomplished; the exclusion from action by the League of domestic questions, which is now accomplished. All along the line, every suggestion of the United States was adopted after the Covenant had been drawn up in its first form and had been published for the criticism of the world. There is a very true sense in which I can say this is a tested American document.

I am dwelling upon these points, my fellow citizens, in spite of the fact that I dare say to most of you they are perfectly well known, because in order to meet the present situation we have got to know what we are dealing with. We are not dealing with the kind of document which this is represented by some gentlemen to be; and inasmuch as we are dealing with a document simon-pure in respect of the very principles we have professed and lived up to, we have got to do one or other of two things—we have got to adopt it or reject it. There is no middle course. You cannot go in on a special-privilege basis of your own. I take it that you are too proud to ask to be exempted from responsibilities which the other members of the League will carry. We go in upon equal terms or we do not go in at all; and if we do not go in, my fellow citizens, think of the tragedy of that result—the only sufficient guaranty to the peace of the world withheld! Ourselves drawn apart with that dangerous pride which means that we shall be ready to take care of ourselves, and that means that we shall maintain great standing armies and an irresistible navy; that means we shall have the organization of a military nation; that means we shall have a general staff, with the kind of power that the general staff of Germany had; to mobilize this great manhood of the Nation when it pleases, all the energy of our young men drawn into the thought and preparation for war. What of our pledges to the men that lie dead in France? We said that they went over there not to prove the prowess of America or her readiness for another war but to see to it that there never was such a war again. It always seems to make it difficult for me to say anything, my fellow citizens, when I think of my clients in this case. My clients are the children; my clients are the next generation. They do not know what promises and bonds I undertook when I ordered the armies of the United States to the soil of France, but I know, and I intend to redeem my pledges to the children; they shall not be sent upon a similar errand.

Again and again, my fellow citizens, mothers who lost their sons in France have come to me and, taking my hand, have shed tears upon it not only, but they have added, "God bless you, Mr. President!" Why, my fellow citizens, should they pray God to bless me? I advised the Congress of the United States to create the situation that led to the death of their sons. I ordered their sons overseas. I consented to their sons being put in the most difficult parts of the battle line, where death was certain, as in the impenetrable difficulties of the forest of Argonne. Why should they weep upon my hand and call down the blessings of God upon me? Because they believe that their boys died for something that vastly transcends any of the immediate and palpable objects of the war. They believe, and they rightly believe, that their sons saved the liberty of the world. They believe that wrapped up with the liberty of the world is the continuous protection of that liberty by the concerted powers of all civilized people. They believe that this sacrifice was made in order that other sons should not be called upon for a similar gift—the gift of life, the gift of all that died—and if we did not see this thing through, if we fulfilled the dearest present wish of Germany and now dissociated ourselves from those alongside whom we fought in the world, would not something of the halo go away from the gun over the mantelpiece, or the sword? Would not the old uniform lose something of its significance? These men were crusaders. They were not going forth to prove the might of the United States. They were going forth to prove the might of justice and right, and all the world accepted them as crusaders, and their transcendent achievement has made all the world believe in America as it believes in no other nation organized in the modern world. There seem to me to stand between us and the rejection or qualification of this treaty the serried ranks of those boys in khaki, not only these boys who came home, but those dear ghosts that still deploy upon the fields of France.

My friends, on last Decoration day I went to a beautiful hillside near Paris, where was located the cemetery of Suresnes, a cemetery given over to the burial of the American dead. Behind me on the slopes was rank upon rank of living American soldiers, and lying before me upon the levels of the plain was rank upon rank of departed American soldiers. Right by the side of the stand where I spoke there was a little group of French women who had adopted those graves, had made themselves mothers of those dear ghosts by putting flowers every day upon those graves, taking them as their own sons, their own beloved, because they had died in the same cause—France was free and the world was free because America had come! I wish some men in public life who are now opposing the settlement for which these men died could visit such a spot as that. I wish that the thought that comes out of those graves could penetrate their consciousness. I wish that they could feel the moral obligation that rests upon us not to go back on those boys, but to see the thing through, to see it through to the end and make good their redemption of the world. For nothing less depends upon this decision, nothing less than liberation and salvation of the world.

You will say, "Is the League an absolute guaranty against war?" No; I do not know any absolute guaranty against the errors of human judgment or the violence of human passion, but I tell you this: With a cooling space of nine months for human passion, not much of it will keep hot. I had a couple of friends who were in the habit of losing their tempers, and when they lost their tempers they were in the habit of using very unparliamentary language. Some of their friends induced them to make a promise that they never would swear inside the town limits. When the impulse next came upon them, they took a street car to go out of town to swear, and by the time they got out of town they did not want to swear. They came back convinced that they were just what they were, a couple of unspeakable fools, and the habit of getting angry and of swearing suffered great inroads upon it by that experience. Now, illustrating the great by the small, that is true of the passions of nations. It is true of the passions of men however you combine them. Give them space to cool off. I ask you this: If it is not an absolute insurance against war, do you want no insurance at all? Do you want nothing? Do you want not only no probability that war will not recur, but the probability that it will recur? The arrangements of justice do not stand of themselves, my fellow citizens. The arrangements of this treaty are just, but they need the support of the combined power of the great nations of the world. And they will have that support. Now that the mists of this great question have cleared away, I believe that men will see the truth, eye to eye and face to face. There is one thing that the American people always rise to and extend their hand to, and that is the truth of justice and of liberty and of peace. We have accepted that truth and we are going to be led by it, and it is going to lead us, and through us the world, out into pastures of quietness and peace such as the world never dreamed of before.

Margaret Sanger

The Children's Era (1926)

At the end of the nineteenth century, certain Victorian sexual values were firmly entrenched in American moral and legal codes. The League for the Suppression of Vice had successfully lobbied for a law, passed by Congress in 1873, that defined as obscene all material that described or advocated birth control and prohibited such information from being disseminated through the mail. Further, a variety of laws had been enacted by state governments that effectively prohibited anyone from providing information about artificial means of controlling contraception. The prevailing belief in the early years of the twentieth century, furthered by such physical culturalists as Bernarr MacFadden, was that marriage without children was a perverse abnormality.

A young nurse in New York, Margaret Sanger, was particularly frustrated by her inability to help poor women to control the size of their families. She was horrified by the results of unplanned pregnancies among poverty-stricken women in New York City, and the death of one of her patients who attempted a self abortion roused Margaret Sanger to action. For her, this was a serious social problem, one that affected most dramatically the lower classes. She resolved to "strike out—I would scream from the housetops. I would tell the world what was going on in the lives of poor women."

In 1914 Margaret Sanger and a few likeminded friends founded the National Birth Control League; the next year she started a magazine, the *Woman Rebel*, followed soon by the *Birth Control Review*. Such activity outraged the sensibilities of many and led to strong reaction by the authorities. In 1916 the New York police arrested Sanger for maintaining a "public nuisance," namely, the first birth control clinic in the United States, set up to provide information primarily to poor immigrant women. Prosecution did not deter her, however, and Margaret Sanger toured the country speaking on behalf of birth control. Her several arrests and trials led to judicial decisions that paved the way for physicians to provide birth control information and put the issue of birth control before the public.

Margaret Sanger persisted in her struggle to disseminate information and to advocate birth control; she set up clinics throughout the country and organized conferences such as the Sixth International Birth Control Conference in 1926 at which she addressed the delegates on "The Children's Era." In this speech Mrs. Sanger articulated the principal goal of her efforts: "We want to free women from enslaved and unwilling motherhood. We are fighting for the emancipation of the mothers of the world, of the children of the world, and the children to be."

Mr. Chairman, Ladies and Gentlemen: My subject is "The Children's Era." The Children's Era! This makes me think of Ellen Key's book—The Century of the Child. Ellen Key hoped that this twentieth century was to be the century of the child. The twentieth century, she said, would see this old world of ours converted into a beautiful garden of children. Well, we have already lived through a quarter of this twentieth century. What steps have we taken toward making it the century of the child? So far, very, very few.

Why does the Children's Era still remain a dream of the dim and the distant future? Why has so little been accomplished?—in spite of all our acknowledged love of children, all our generosity, all our good-will, all the enormous spending of millions on philanthrophy and charities, all our warm-hearted sentiment, all our incessant activity and social consciousness? Why?

Before you can cultivate a garden, you must know something about gardening. You have got to give your seeds a proper soil in which to grow. You have got to give them sunlight and fresh air. You have got to give them space and the opportunity (if they are to lift their flowers to the sun), to strike their roots deep into that soil. And always—do not forget this—you have got to fight weeds. You cannot have a garden, if you let weeds overrun it. So, if we want to make this world a garden for children, we must first of all learn the lesson of the gardener.

So far we have not been gardeners. We have only been a sort of silly reception committee. A reception committee at the Grand Central Station of life. Trainload after trainload of children are coming in, day and night—nameless refugees arriving out of the Nowhere into the Here. Trainload after trainload—many unwelcome, unwanted, unprepared for, unknown, without baggage, without passports, most of them without pedigrees. These unlimited hordes of refugees arrive in such numbers that the reception committee is thrown into a panic—a panic of activity. The reception committee arouses itself heroically, establishes emergency measures: milk stations, maternity centers, settlement houses, playgrounds, orphanages, welfare leagues and every conceivable kind of charitable effort. But still trainloads of children keep on coming—human weeds crop up that spread so fast in this sinister struggle for existence, that the overworked committee becomes exhausted, inefficient and can think of no way out.

When we protest against this immeasurable, meaningless waste of motherhood and child-life; when we protest against the ever-mounting cost to the world of asylums, prisons, homes for the feeble-minded and such institutions for the unfit, when we protest against the disorder and chaos and tragedy of modern life, when we point out the biological corruption that is destroying the very heart of American life, we are told that we are making merely an "emotional" appeal. When we point the one immediate practical way toward order and beauty in society, the only way to lay the fundations of a society composed of happy children, happy women and happy men, they call this idea indecent and immoral.

It is not enough to clean up the filth and disorder of our overcrowded cities. It is not enough to stop the evil of Child Labor—even if we could! It is not enough to decrease the rate of infantile mortality. It is not enough to open playgrounds, and build more public schools in which we can standardize the minds of the young. It is not enough, to throw millions upon millions of dollars into charities and philanthropies. Don't deceive ourselves that by so doing we are making the world "Safe for Children."

Those of you who have followed the sessions of this Conference must, I am sure, agree with me that the first real step toward the creation of a Children's Era must lie in providing the conditions of healthy life for children not only before birth but even more imperatively before conception. Human society must protect its children—yes, but prenatal care is most essential! The child-to-be, as yet not called into being, has rights no less imperative.

We have learned in the preceding sessions of this Conference that, if we wish to produce strong and sturdy children, the embryo must grow in a chemically healthy medium. The blood stream of the mother must be chemically normal. Worry, strain, shock, unhappiness, enforced maternity, may all poison the blood of the enslaved mother. This chemically poisoned blood may produce a defective baby—a child foredoomed to idiocy, or feeblemindedness, crime, or failure.

Do I exaggerate? Am I taking a rare exception and making it a general rule? Our opponents declare that children are conceived in love, and that every new-born baby converts its parents to love and unselfishness. My answer is to point to the asylums, the hospitals, the ever-growing institutions for the unfit. Look into the family history of those who are feebleminded; or behind the bars of jails and prisons. Trace the family histories; find out the conditions under which they were conceived and born, before you attempt to persuade us that reckless breeding has nothing to do with these grave questions.

There is only one way out. We have got to fight for the health and happiness of the Unborn Child. And to do that in a practical, tangible way, we have got to free women from enforced, enslaved maternity. There can be no hope for the future of civilization, no certainty of racial salvation, until every woman can decide for herself whether she will or will not become a mother and when and how many children she cares to bring into the world. That is the first step.

I would like to suggest Civil Service examinations for parenthood! Prospective parents after such an examination would be given a parenthood license, proving that they are physically and mentally fit to be the fathers and mothers of the next generation.

This is an interesting idea—but then arises the questions "Who is to decide?" "Would there be a jury, like a play jury?" Would a Republican administration give parenthood permits only to Republicans—or perhaps only to Democrats? The more you think of governmental interference, the less it works out. Take this plan of civil service examination for parenthood. It suggests Prohibition: there might even be bootlegging in babies!

No, I doubt the advisability of governmental sanction. The problem of bringing children into the world ought to be decided by those most seriously involved—those who run the greatest risks; in the last analysis—by the mother and the child. If there is going to be any Civil Service examination, let it be conducted by the Unborn Child, the Child-to-be.

Just try for a moment to picture the possibilities of such an examination.

When you want a cook or housemaid, you go to an employment bureau. You have to answer questions. You have to exchange references. You have to persuade the talented cook that you conduct a proper well-run household. Children ought to have at least the same privilege as cooks.

Sometimes in idle moments I like to think it would be a very good scheme to have a bureau of the Child-to-be.

At such a bureau of the unborn, the wise child might be able to find out a few things about its father—and its mother. Just think for a moment of this bureau where prospective parents might apply for a baby. Think of the questions they would be asked by the agent of the unborn or by the baby itself.

First: "Mr. Father, a baby is an expensive luxury. Can you really afford one?"

"Have you paid for your last baby yet?"

"How many children have you already? Six? You must have your hands full. Can you take care of so many?"

"Do you look upon children as a reward—or a penalty?"

"How are your ductless glands—well balanced?"

"Can you provide a happy home for one! A sunny nursery? Proper food?"

"What's that you say? Ten children already? Two dark rooms in the slums?"

"No, thank you! I don't care to be born at all if I cannot be well-born. Good-bye!"

And if we could organize a society for the prevention of cruelty to unborn children, we would make it a law that children should be brought into the world only when they were welcome, invited and wanted; that they would arrive with a clean bill of health and heritage; that they would possess healthy, happy, well-mated and mature parents.

And there would be certain conditions of circumstances which would preclude parenthood. These conditions, the presence of which would make parenthood a crime, are the following:

1 Transmissible disease
2 Temporary disease
3 Subnormal children already in the family
4 Space out between births
5 Twenty-three years as a minimum age for parents
6 Economic circumstances adequate
7 Spiritual harmony between parents.

In conclusion, let me repeat:

We are not trying to establish a dictatorship over parents. We want to free women from enslavery and unwilling motherhood. We are fighting for the emancipation of the mothers of the world, of the children of the world, and the children to be. We want to create a real Century of the Child—usher in a Children's Era. We can do this by handing the terrific gift of life in bodies fit and perfect as can be fashioned. Help us to make this Conference which has aroused so much interest the turning point toward this era. Only so can you help in the creation of the future.

The Troubled Decade

Franklin Delano Roosevelt

First Inaugural Address (1933)

The decade of the 1920's heralded what seemed like unlimited prosperity and unchallenged Republican rule. Campaigning for the Presidency in 1928, Herbert Hoover foresaw the day when poverty would be eliminated from the nation. The economy grew rapidly, stock prices soared, and "a chicken in every pot" was not an altogether fanciful political slogan.

By 1932, after the stock market crash and the ensuing Depression, those optimistic expectations seemed so remote as to be otherworldly. During Hoover's Presidency, industrial production had been cut by more than half and more than 13 million people became unemployed. Many were without homes; more were without hope. Worst of all, nobody seemed to know how to deal with the problem. Hoover proposed the Reconstruction Finance Corporation to lend money to banks but was reluctant to do more because he believed that relief measures were not the responsibility of the federal government. For their part, Democrats condemned the President for being a big spender, and Franklin D. Roosevelt accepted his party's 1932 nomination on the promise of a balanced budget. Where Roosevelt stood on most issues was not clear, and he had the reputation as a vacillating politician who would temper his principles to the requirements of the situation. During the campaign he sounded inconsistent themes, pledging both to expand and to restrict federal power, to aid the farmer yet not spend money, to provide aid for the unemployed but to cut government spending. These inconsistencies did not loom large in a campaign in which the repeal of prohibition was a key issue, in which the Democrats seemed certain of victory in any case, and in which Roosevelt's mellow voice and constant smile conveyed a message of optimism and hope.

Four months separated Election Day from the inauguration of the new President, and during the interregnum both Roosevelt and the nation remained uncertain as to his course. His relations with the outgoing President, whom he defeated for reelection, were strained to say the least. Some of his advisers were urging higher taxes; some were arguing for income redistribution; still others favored deficit spending as an economic stimulus. Similar disparities characterized the advice he received on foreign affairs. While others presumed to speak in his behalf, the President-elect generally kept his own counsel. Meanwhile, economic conditions worsened even further. A brief recovery in the summer of 1932 had been followed by further deflation. Five thousand banks had failed; 9 million savings accounts were lost. Unemployment reached 15 million. In the face of these developments the lame-duck Congress had failed to pass any important economic legislation. Crisis was in the air. Many said it was the end of an era, and some even predicted imminent revolution.

Even Roosevelt's pre-inauguration courtesy call on Hoover had been sour, and the two rode to the inauguration on March 4, 1933, with a somberness that matched the gray skies and heavy clouds of the day, which in turn matched the mood of the nation. Nearly 100,000 gathered for the ceremonies at the Capitol, where Roosevelt would have the first opportunity to articulate his goals and priorities. The mix of uncertainty, curiosity, and hope among the Washington crowd was paralleled all over the country as millions listened to the inauguration on their radio sets.

The new President's first task was to reignite confidence, and he spoke to the need early in the speech, with his oft-quoted line that "the only thing we have to fear is fear itself." He promised action, called for sacrifice, promised to seek whatever powers would be required, and asked for the help of God. The applause was thunderous. No matter that the advisers were divided, the leaders of the professions bereft of new ideas. The President had promised to take charge, and from that moment the restoration of national confidence began.

I am certain that my fellow Americans expect that on my induction into the Presidency I will address them with a candor and a decision which the present situation of our Nation impels. This is preeminently the time to speak the truth, the whole truth, frankly and boldly. Nor need we shrink from honestly facing conditions in our country to-day. This great Nation will endure as it has endured, will revive and will prosper. So, first of all, let me assert my firm belief that the only thing we have to fear is fear itself—nameless, unreasoning, unjustified terror which paralyzes needed efforts to convert retreat into advance. In every dark hour of our national life a leadership of frankness and vigor has met with that understanding and support of the people themselves which is essential to victory. I am convinced that you will again give that support to leadership in these critical days.

In such a spirit on my part and on yours we face our common difficulties. They concern, thank God, only material things. Values have shrunken to fantastic levels; taxes have risen; our ability to pay has fallen; government of all kinds is faced by serious curtailment of income; the means of exchange are frozen in the currents of trade; the withered leaves of industrial enterprise lie on every side; farmers find no markets for their produce; the savings of many years in thousands of families are gone.

More important, a host of unemployed citizens face the grim problem of existence, and an equally great number toil with little return. Only a foolish optimist can deny the dark realities of the moment.

Yet our distress comes from no failure of substance. We are stricken by no plague of locusts. Compared with the perils which our forefathers conquered because they believed and were not afraid, we have still much to be thankful for. Nature still offers her bounty and human efforts have multiplied it. Plenty is at our doorstep, but a generous use of it languishes in the very sight of the supply. Primarily this is because the rulers of the exchange of mankind's goods have failed, through their own stubbornness and their own incompetence, have admitted their failure, and abdicated. Practices of the unscrupulous money changers stand indicted in the court of public opinion, rejected by the hearts and minds of men.

True they have tried, but their efforts have been cast in the pattern of an outworn tradition. Faced by failure of credit they have proposed only the lending of more money. Stripped of the lure of profit by which to induce our people to follow their false leadership, they have resorted to exhortations, pleading tearfully for restored confidence. They know only the rules of a generation of self-seekers. They have no vision, and when there is no vision the people perish.

The money changers have fled from their high seats in the temple of our civilization. We may now restore that temple to the ancient truths. The measure of the restoration lies in the extent to which we apply social values more noble than mere monetary profit.

Happiness lies not in the mere possession of money; it lies in the joy of achievement, in the thrill of creative effort. The joy and moral stimulation of work no longer must be forgotten in the mad chase of evanescent profits. These dark days will be worth all they cost us if they teach us that our true destiny is not to be ministered unto but to minister to ourselves and to our fellow men.

Recognition of the falsity of material wealth as the standard of success goes hand in hand with the abandonment of the false belief that public office and high political position are to be valued only by the standards of pride of place and personal profit; and there must be an end to a conduct in banking and in business which too often has given to a sacred trust the likeness of callous and selfish wrongdoing. Small wonder that confidence languishes, for it thrives only on honesty, on honor, on the sacredness of obligations, on faithful protection, on unselfish performance; without them it can not live.

Restoration calls, however, not for changes in ethics alone. This Nation asks for action, and action now.

Our greatest primary task is to put people to work. This is no unsolvable problem if we face it wisely and courageously. It can be accomplished in part by direct recruiting by the Government itself, treating the task as we would treat the emergency of a war, but at the same time, through this employment, accomplishing greatly needed projects to stimulate and reorganize the use of our natural resources.

Hand in hand with this we must frankly recognize the overbalance of population in our industrial centers and, by engaging on a national scale in a redistribution, endeavor to provide a better use of the land for those best fitted for the land. The task can be helped by definite efforts to raise the values of agricultural products and with this the power to purchase the output of our cities. It can be helped by preventing realistically the tragedy of the growing loss through foreclosure of our small homes and our farms. It can be helped by insistence that the Federal, State, and local governments act forthwith on the demand that their cost be drastically reduced. It can be helped by the unifying of relief activities which to-day are often scattered, uneconomical, and unequal. It can be helped by national planning for and supervision of all forms of transportation and of communications and other utilities which have a definitely public character. There are many ways in which it can be helped, but it can never be helped merely by talking about it. We must act and act quickly.

Finally, in our progress toward a resumption of work we require two safeguards against a return of the evils of the old order; there must be a strict supervision of all banking and credits and investments; there must be an end to speculation with other people's money, and there must be provision for an adequate but sound currency.

There are the lines of attack. I shall presently urge upon a new Congress in special session detailed measures for their fulfillment, and I shall seek the immediate assistance of the several States.

Through this program of action we address ourselves to putting our own national house in order and making income balance outgo. Our international trade relations, though vastly important, are in point of time and necessity secondary to the establishment of a sound national economy. I favor as a practical policy the putting of first things first. I shall spare no effort to restore world trade by international economic readjustment, but the emergency at home can not wait on that accomplishment.

The basic thought that guides these specific means of national recovery is not narrowly nationalistic. It is the insistence, as a first consideration, upon the interdependence of the various elements in all parts of the United States—a recognition of the old and permanently important manifestation of the American spirit of the pioneer. It is the way to recovery. It is the immediate way. It is the strongest assurance that the recovery will endure.

In the field of world policy I would dedicate this Nation to the policy of the good neighbor—the neighbor who resolutely respects himself and, because he does so, respects the rights of others—the neighbor who respects his obligations and respects the sanctity of his agreements in and with a world of neighbors.

If I read the temper of our people correctly, we now realize as we have never realized before our interdependence on each other; that we can not merely take but we must give as well; that if we are to go forward, we must move as a trained and loyal army willing to sacrifice for the good of a common discipline, because without such discipline no progress is made, no leadership becomes effective. We are, I know, ready and willing to submit our lives and property to such discipline, because it makes possible a leadership which aims at a larger good. This I propose to offer, pledging that the larger purposes will bind upon us all as a sacred obligation with a unity of duty hitherto evoked only in time of armed strife.

With this pledge taken, I assume unhesitatingly the leadership of this great army of our people dedicated to a disciplined attack upon our common problems.

Action in this image and to this end is feasible under the form of government which we have inherited from our ancestors. Our Constitution is so simple and practical that it is possible always to meet extraordinary needs by changes in emphasis and arrangement without loss of essential form. That is why our constitutional system has proved itself the most superbly enduring political mechanism the modern world has produced. It has met every stress of vast expansion of territory, of foreign wars, of bitter internal strife, of world relations.

It is to be hoped that the normal balance of executive and legislative authority may be wholly adequate to meet the unprecedented task before us. But it may be that an unprecedented demand and need for undelayed action may call for temporary departure from that normal balance of public procedure.

I am prepared under my constitutional duty to recommend the measures that a stricken nation in the midst of a stricken world may require. These measures, or such other measures as the Congress may build out of its experience and wisdom, I shall seek, within my constitutional authority, to bring to speedy adoption.

But in the event that the Congress shall fail to take one of these two courses, and in the event that the national emergency is still critical, I shall not evade the clear course of duty that will then confront me. I shall ask the Congress for the one remaining instrument to meet the crisis—broad Executive power to wage a war against the emergency, as great as the power that would be given to me if we were in fact invaded by a foreign foe.

For the trust reposed in me I will return the courage and the devotion that befit the time. I can do no less.

We face the arduous days that lie before us in the warm courage of the national uity; with the clear consciousness of seeking old and precious moral values; with the clean satisfaction that comes from the stern performance of duty by old and young alike. We aim at the assurance of a rounded and permanent national life.

We do not distrust the future of essential democracy. The people of the United States have not failed. In their need they have registered a mandate that they want direct, vigorous action. They have asked for discipline and direction under leadership. They have made me the present instrument of their wishes. In the spirit of the gift I take it.

In this dedication of a Nation we humbly ask the blessing of God. May He protect each and every one of us. May He guide me in the days to come.

Franklin Delano Roosevelt

First Fireside Chat (1933)

Roosevelt's most pressing need was to resolve the crisis in the banking system. When a bank failed, depositors stood to lose their entire life's savings. Rumor or fear that a failure was imminent would prompt a run by the depositors to withdraw their money, bringing about the very collapse they feared. Worse, as money was taken out of the banks and hoarded at home, the funds were not available for investment in economic renewal. They were effectively withdrawn from the economy. As this process was repeated on a larger scale, the Depression became worse. It was a downward and seemingly unstoppable spiral.

The new President was ready to act. The old Congress had just adjourned, and the newly elected Congress was not scheduled to convene until December 1933. Roosevelt issued a proclamation calling them back into session on March 9, just five days after his inauguration, in order to address the banking crisis. Meanwhile, involving little-known provisions of legislation passed during World War I, he issued a proclamation closing all banks in the United States—declaring a "bank holiday," as he said at the time. Closing the banks served two basic purposes. First, it gave the President a few days' time to prepare his proposals for Congress without further deterioration in the condition of the banks. Second, though temporarily preventing withdrawals from the banks, the action also gave citizens a message of hope: if all the banks are closed, then the Depression must have bottomed out; there now is no way to go but up.

After closing the banks, Roosevelt put his aides to the task of devising a program he could present to Congress. The group worked long hours amid great tension; there were many disagreements which had to be resolved in a very short time. Proposals to nationalize or otherwise radically reform banking were not seriously considered, if only because Roosevelt's greatest need was to restore confidence and dispel fear. The plan as finally developed contained provisions to prevent hoarding of gold and to increase the supply of money in circulation. The House received the proposed bill at noon on March 9; only one copy was available. Nevertheless, the House limited debate to 40 minutes and passed the measure unanimously by midafternoon; by 7:30 in the evening the Senate followed suit by a vote of 73 to 7. The President signed the bill into law that very night, barely eight hours after it had been introduced in Congress. That the Senate and House were willing to grant the President such broad authority with so little understanding of the bill's contents is a sign of how deeply they felt a sense of crisis.

Once the bill was signed, banks began to reopen, but Roosevelt still had to explain to the American people what he had done, since the public's confidence was essential for the banks to survive. He planned a radio address for Sunday, March 12. Discarding the text that had been prepared for him, the President tried to imagine individual citizens and spoke simply and directly to them. The speech was the first of what came to be known as "fireside chats," informal radio remarks delivered as if the President were a guest in the listener's living room, chatting by the fire. The March 12 fireside chat is instructive in at least two respects. First, it illustrates the skill with which Roosevelt was able to translate the complexities of the banking issue into terms the general public could both understand and trust. Also, it reflects the skill with which the new President used a new medium to break down the gap between leaders and led. Ironically, Roosevelt relied on the new mass media to reestablish a sense of informal interpersonal communication.

I want to talk for a few minutes with the people of the United States about banking—with the comparatively few who understand the mechanics of banking but more particularly with the overwhelming majority who use banks for the making of deposits and the drawing of checks. I want to tell you what has been done in the last few days, why it was done, and what the next steps are going to be. I recognize that the many proclamations from State capitols and from Washington, the legislation, the Treasury regulations, etc., couched for the most part in banking and legal terms, should be explained for the benefit of the average citizen. I owe this in particular because of the fortitude and good temper with which everybody has accepted the inconvenience and hardships of the banking holiday. I know that when you understand what we in Washington have been about I shall continue to have your cooperation as fully as I have had your sympathy and help during the past week.

First of all, let me state the simple fact that when you deposit money in a bank the bank does not put the money into a safe deposit vault. It invests your money in many different forms of credit—bonds, commercial paper, mortgages and many other kinds of loans. In other words, the bank puts your money to work to keep the wheels of industry and of agriculture turning around. A comparatively small part of the money you put into the bank is kept in currency—an amount which in normal times is wholly sufficient to cover the cash needs of the average citizen. In other words, the total amount of all the currency in the country is only a small fraction of the total deposits in all of the banks.

What, then, happened during the last few days of February and the first few days of March? Because of undermined confidence on the part of the public, there was a general rush by a large portion of our population to turn bank deposits into currency or gold—a rush so great that the soundest banks could not get enough currency to meet the demand. The reason for this was that on the spur of the moment it was, of course, impossible to sell perfectly sound assets of a bank and convert them into cash except at panic prices far below their real value.

By the afternoon of March 3d scarcely a bank in the country was open to do business. Proclamations temporarily closing them in whole or in part had been issued by the Governors in almost all the States.

It was then that I issued the proclamation providing for the nationwide bank holiday, and this was the first step in the Government's reconstruction of our financial and economic fabric.

The second step was the legislation promptly and patriotically passed by the Congress confirming my proclamation and broadening my powers so that it became possible in view of the requirement of time to extend the holiday and lift the ban of that holiday gradually. This law also gave authority to develop a program of rehabilitation of our banking facilities. I want to tell our citizens in every part of the Nation that the national Congress—Republicans and Democrats alike—showed by this action a devotion to public welfare and a realization of the emergency and the necessity for speed that it is difficult to match in our history.

The third stage has been the series of regulations permitting the banks to continue their functions to take care of the distribution of food and household necessities and the payment of payrolls.

This bank holiday, while resulting in many cases in great inconvenience, is affording us the opportunity to supply the currency necessary to meet the situation. No sound bank is a dollar worse off than it was when it closed its doors last Monday. Neither is any bank which may turn out not to be in a position for immediate opening. The new law allows the twelve Federal Reserve Banks to issue additional currency on good assets and thus the banks which reopen will be able to meet every legitimate call. The new currency is being sent out by the Bureau of Engraving and Printing in large volume to every part of the country. It is sound currency because it is backed by actual, good assets.

A question you will ask is this: why are all the banks not to be reopened at the same time? The answer is simple. Your Government does not intend that the history of the past few years shall be repeated. We do not want and will not have another epidemic of bank failures.

As a result, we start tomorrow, Monday, with the opening of banks in the twelve Federal Reserve Bank cities—those banks which on first examination by the Treasury have already been found to be all right. This will be followed on Tuesday by the resumption of all their functions by banks already found to be sound in cities where there are recognized clearing houses. That means about 250 cities of the United States.

On Wednesday and succeeding days banks in smaller places all through the country will resume business, subject, of course, to the Government's physical ability to complete its survey. It is necessary that the reopening of banks be extended over a period in order to permit the banks to make applications for necessary loans, to obtain currency needed to meet their requirements and to enable the Government to make common sense checkups.

Let me make it clear to you that if your bank does not open the first day you are by no means justified in believing that it will not open. A bank that opens on one of the subsequent days is in exactly the same status as the bank that opens tomorrow.

I know that many people are worrying about State banks not members of the Federal Reserve System. These banks can and will receive assistance from member banks and from the Reconstruction Finance Corporation. These State banks are following the same course as the National banks except that they get their licenses to resume business from the State authorities, and these authorities have been asked by the Secretary of the Treasury to permit their good banks to open up on the same schedule as the national banks. I am confident that the State Banking Departments will be as careful as the national Government in the policy relating to the opening of banks and will follow the same broad policy.

It is possible that when the banks resume a very few people who have not recovered from their fear may again begin withdrawals. Let me make it clear that the banks will take care of all needs—and it is my belief that hoarding during the past week has become an exceedingly unfashionable pastime. It needs no prophet to tell you that when the people find that they can get their money—that they can get it when they want it for all legitimate purposes—the phantom of fear will soon be laid. People will again be glad to have their money where it will be safely taken care of and where they can use it conveniently at any time. I can assure you that it is safer to keep your money in a reopened bank than under the mattress.

The success of our whole great national program depends, of course, upon the cooperation of the public—on its intelligent support and use of a reliable system.

Remember that the essential accomplishment of the new legislation is that it makes it possible for banks more readily to convert their assets into cash than was the case before. More liberal provision has been made for banks to borrow on these assets at the Reserve Banks and more liberal provision has also been made for issuing currency on the security of these good assets. This currency is not fiat currency. It is issued only on adequate security, and every good bank has an abundance of such security.

One more point before I close. There will be, of course, some banks unable to reopen without being reorganized. The new law allows the Government to assist in making these reorganizations quickly and effectively and even allows the Government to subscribe to at least a part of new capital which may be required.

I hope you can see from this elemental recital of what your Government is doing that there is nothing complex, or radical, in the process.

We had a bad banking situation. Some of our bankers had shown themselves either incompetent or dishonest in their handling of the people's funds. They had used the money entrusted to them in speculations and unwise loans. This was, of course, not true in the vast majority of our banks, but it was true in enough of them to shock the people for a time into a sense of insecurity and to put them into a frame of mind where they did not differentiate, but seemed to assume that the acts of a comparative few had tainted them all. It was the Government's job to straighten out this situation and do it as quickly as possible. And the job is being performed.

I do not promise you that every bank will be reopened or that individual losses will not be suffered, but there will be no losses that possibly could be avoided; and there would have been more and greater losses had we continued to drift. I can even promise you salvation for some at least of the sorely pressed banks. We shall be engaged not merely in reopening sound banks but in the creation of sound banks through reorganization.

It has been wonderful to me to catch the note of confidence from all over the country. I can never be sufficiently grateful to the people for the loyal support they have given me in their acceptance of the judgment that has dictated our course, even though all our processes may not have seemed clear to them.

After all, there is an element in the readjustment of our financial system more important than currency, more important than gold, and that is the confidence of the people. Confidence and courage are the essentials of success in carrying out our plan. You people must have faith; you must not be stampeded by rumors or guesses. Let us unite in banishing fear. We have provided the machinery to restore our financial system; it is up to you to support and make it work.

It is your problem no less than it is mine. Together we cannot fail.

Huey P. Long

Sharing Our Wealth (1935)

The New Deal that President Franklin Roosevelt promised the American people was launched with a flurry of legislative activity designed to stem the tide of the Great Depression by putting people back to work and restoring the nation's self-confidence. The welter of agencies and programs that sprang up evidenced the desire to take vigorous action. While popular support for the New Deal was substantial, there were enemies on the right who were profoundly alarmed by what they saw as the "socialist" drift in government which was undermining the capitalist system. The Liberty League, with the backing of business leaders from such companies as DuPont and General Motors, and with support from conservative politicians and big city newspapers, orchestrated a well-financed attack on the New Deal; Hearst papers, for example, on orders from the chief himself, always made reference to the "Raw Deal" and routinely labeled the President's tax programs as "Soak the Successful" plans. These assaults, however, had little political impact on Rooseveltian policy. No more successful in eroding popular support for the President were the Fascist and Communist political groups that sprung up.

More worrisome to the White House were those whose impatience with the New Deal's progress toward solving some of the most pressing problems of the poor and elderly spawned simplistic, but appealing, schemes for social welfare. Dr. Francis E. Townsend proposed an old-age pension plan providing payments of $200 a month to anyone over the age of 60. Father Charles E. Coughlin, who formed the National Union for Social Justice, savaged Communists, organized labor, international bankers, and the Roosevelt Administration in his popular, nationally broadcast radio addresses. But it was the "Share-Our-Wealth" Movement that the President and his advisers found most threatening.

Franklin Roosevelt was elected to the Presidency in 1932 with the support of the senator from Louisiana, Huey P. Long. Even so, Senator Long had called the candidate during the campaign to warn him against moving too far to the right. Roosevelt was in office for less than two years when Senator Long was urging the President to do something to correct the uneven distribution of wealth in the country. FDR explained the great difficulty in distinguishing between fortunes gained through "the abuse of social ethics" and those earned by "ingenuity . . . honest toil," and "good management." Senator Long was not impressed; such distinctions did not concern him. He had a simple, straightforward plan for redistribution of wealth, a plan that he seemed to believe would ultimately carry him to the White House in President Roosevelt's place.

Huey Pierce Long was born in Winnfield, Louisiana, in 1893. With little formal education, but a powerful and flamboyant personality and speaking style, he was a notable success as a politician who attacked the established interests. He was defeated in his first attempt to capture the governorship in 1924 but was elected four years later and quickly built one of the most powerful political machines in American history, assuming almost dictatorial powers in Louisiana. In 1930 he was elected to the U.S. Senate. Breaking with Roosevelt, who considered Long one of the most dangerous men in America, Long promoted his scheme to cure the ills of what he began to call the "Roosevelt depression." Washington was well aware of the potential political threat that Long represented, and the President retaliated by depriving Senator Long of any federal patronage in Louisiana. There may well have been some measure of relief in the White House when, in September 1935, Senator Long was assassinated in the Rotunda of the Louisiana State House in Baton Rouge. Jim Farley, the President's chief political operative, was confident that Long would have polled 5 million votes at the next election had he lived.

Huey Long's plan, as he outlined in the radio address that follows, was simple enough and, to many, attractive in its apparent simple fairness. The scheme might not have been taken seriously by lawmakers and economists, but the idea that everyone could have a home, a car, a radio, and a guaranteed income just by limiting the fortunes of the rich had its appeal. The President's graduated tax program, introduced in 1935, was believed by many to be an effort to undercut Long, and it likely did have that effect. Long's "Share-Our-Wealth" movement was carried on after his death and an attempt to merge it with the Coughlin and Townsend forces was made. This group failed to present a viable third-party alternative to the major parties, however, and Long's scheme did not long outlive him.

President Roosevelt was elected on November 8, 1932. People look upon an elected President as the President. This is January 1935. We are in our third year of the Roosevelt depression, with the conditions growing worse. . . .

We must now become awakened! We must know the truth and speak the truth. There is no use to wait three more years. It is not Roosevelt or ruin; it is Roosevelt's ruin.

Now, my friends, it makes no difference who is President or who is senator. America is for 125 million people and the unborn to come. We ran Mr. Roosevelt for the presidency of the United States because he promised to us by word of mouth and in writing:

1 That the size of the big man's fortune would be reduced so as to give the masses at the bottom enough to wipe out all poverty; and

2 That the hours of labor would be so reduced that all would share in the work to be done and in consuming the abundance mankind produced.

Hundreds of words were used by Mr. Roosevelt to make these promises to the people, but they were made over and over again. He reiterated these pledges even after he took his oath as President. Summed up, what these promises meant was: "Share our wealth."

When I saw him spending all his time of ease and recreation with the business partners of Mr. John D. Rockefeller, Jr., with such men as the Astors, etc., maybe I ought to have had better sense than to have believed he would ever break down their big fortunes to give enough to the masses to end poverty—maybe some will think me weak for ever believing it all, but millions of other people were fooled the same as myself. I was like a drowning man grabbing at a straw, I guess. The face and eyes, the hungry forms of mothers and children, the aching hearts of students denied education were before our eyes, and when Roosevelt promised, we jumped for that ray of hope.

So therefore I call upon the men and women of America to immediately join in our work and movement to share our wealth.

There are thousands of share-our-wealth societies organized in the United States now. We want 100,000 such societies formed for every nook and corner of this country—societies that will meet, talk, and work, all for the purpose that the great wealth and abundance of this great land that belongs to us may be shared and enjoyed by all of us.

We have nothing more for which we should ask the Lord. He has allowed this land to have too much of everything that humanity needs.

So in this land of God's abundance we propose laws, viz.:

1 The fortunes of the multimillionaires and billionaires shall be reduced so that no one person shall own more than a few million dollars to the person. We would do this by a capital levy tax. On the first million that a man was worth, we would not impose any tax. We would say, "All right for your first million dollars, but after you get that rich you will have to start helping the balance of us." So we would not levy any capital levy tax on the first million one owned. But on the second million a man owns, we would tax that 1 percent, so that every year the man owned the second million dollars he would be taxed $10,000. On the third million we would impose a tax of 2 percent. On the fourth million we would impose a tax of 4

percent. On the fifth million we would impose a tax of 8 percent. On the sixth million we would impose a tax of 16 percent. On the seventh million we would impose a tax of 32 percent. On the eighth million we would impose a tax of 64 percent; and on all over the eighth million we would impose a tax of 100 percent.

What this would mean is that the annual tax would bring the biggest fortune down to $3 or $4 million to the person because no one could pay taxes very long in the higher brackets. But $3 to $4 million is enough for any one person and his children and his children's children. We cannot allow one to have more than that because it would not leave enough for the balance to have something.

2 We propose to limit the amount any one man can earn in one year or inherit to $1 million to the person.

3 Now, by limiting the size of the fortunes and incomes of the big men, we will throw into the government Treasury the money and property from which we will care for the millions of people who have nothing; and with this money we will provide a home and the comforts of home, with such common conveniences as radio and automobile, for every family in America, free of debt.

4 We guarantee food and clothing and employment for everyone who should work by shortening the hours of labor to thirty hours per week, maybe less, and to eleven months per year, maybe less. We would have the hours shortened just so much as would give work to everybody to produce enough for everybody; and if we were to get them down to where they were too short, then we would lengthen them again. As long as all the people working can produce enough of automobiles, radios, homes, schools, and theaters for everyone to have that kind of comfort and convenience, then let us all have work to do and have that much of heaven on earth.

5 We would provide education at the expense of the states and the United States for every child, not only through grammar school and high school but through to a college and vocational education. We would simply extend the Louisiana plan to apply to colleges and all people. Yes, we would have to build thousands of more colleges and employ 100,000 more teachers; but we have materials, men, and women who are ready and available for the work. Why have the right to a college education depend upon whether the father or mother is so well-to-do as to send a boy or girl to college? We would give every child the right to education and a living at birth.

6 We would give a pension to all persons above sixty years of age in an amount sufficient to support them in comfortable circumstances, excepting those who earn $1,000 per year or who are worth $10,000.

7 Until we could straighten things out—and we can straighten things out in two months under our program—we would grant a moratorium on all debts which people owe that they cannot pay.

And now you have our program, none too big, none too little, but every man a king.

We owe debts in America today, public and private, amounting to $252 billion. That means that every child is born with a $2,000 debt tied around his neck to hold him down before he gets started. Then, on top of that, the wealth is locked in a vise owned by a few people. We propose that children shall be born in a land of opportunity, guaranteed a home, food, clothes, and the other things that make for living, including the right to education.

Our plan would injure no one. It

would not stop us from having millionaires—it would increase them tenfold, because so many more people could make $1 million if they had the chance our plan gives them. Our plan would not break up big concerns. The only difference would be that maybe 10,000 people would own a concern instead of 10 people owning it.

But, my friends, unless we do share our wealth, unless we limit the size of the big man so as to give something to the little man, we can never have a happy or free people. God said so! He ordered it.

We have everything our people need. Too much of food, clothes, and houses—why not let all have their fill and lie down in the ease and comfort God has given us? Why not? Because a few own everything—the masses own nothing.

I wonder if any of you people who are listening to me were ever at a barbecue! We used to go there—sometimes 1,000 people or more. If there were 1,000 people, we would put enough meat and bread and everything else on the table for 1,000 people. Then everybody would be called and everyone would eat all they wanted. But suppose at one of these barbecues for 1,000 people that one man took 90 percent of the food and ran off with it and ate until he got sick and let the balance rot. Then 999 people would have only enough for 100 to eat and there would be many to starve because of the greed of just one person for something he couldn't eat himself.

Well, ladies and gentlemen, America, all the people of America, have been invited to a barbecue. God invited us all to come and eat and drink all we wanted. He smiled on our land and we grew crops of plenty to eat and wear. He showed us in the earth the iron and other things to make everything we wanted. He unfolded to us the secrets of science so that our work might be easy. God called: "Come to my feast."

Then what happened? Rockefeller, Morgan, and their crowd stepped up and took enough for 120 million people and left only enough for 5 million for all the other 125 million to eat. And so many millions must go hungry and without these good things God gave us unless we call on them to put some of it back.

John L. Lewis

Rights of Labor (1937)

New Deal legislation of the 1930's did much to strengthen the hand of organized labor. The Wagner Act of 1935, for example, established the National Labor Relations Board, ensured labor's right to collective bargaining, and outlawed unfair labor practices on the part of employers. Union membership grew dramatically, with the American Federation of Labor claiming over 3 million members by 1935. The AF of L had traditionally concentrated its organizing efforts on skilled workers and favored the craft union concept. In 1935 the Committee of Industrial Organizations (the CIO), made up of eight large AF of L unions, was established on the theory that unions should be organized accordig to mass-production industries. Leaders of the CIO were soon expelled from the AF of L and formed their own rival organization, renamed the Congress of Industrial Unions.

The president of this new union organization was the head of the United Mine Workers, John L. Lewis. The son of an immigrant Welsh coal miner, Lewis was born in Iowa, worked at times as a miner, and rose through the ranks of the UMW to become its president in 1920. As leader of the CIO, Lewis worked tirelessly to increase the unions' membership and political power. Lewis and the CIO were dramatically successful, particularly in organizing the steel and automobile industries.

In 1936 and 1937 Lewis and the CIO made news as a wave of strikes swept the auto and steel industries. At General Motors plants in Flint, Michigan strikers employed a new tactic. They not only struck, they stayed in the plants and refused to leave. These "sit-down" strikes were eventually outlawed in a 1939 Supreme Court decision, but they were highly effective when first employed.

President Roosevelt refused to use federal troops to dislodge the strikers, reasoning that bloodshed and bitterness would result. Governor Murphy of Michigan was equally reluctant to use the militia, and the company finally gave in and recognized the United Auto Workers as bargaining agent. Lewis, flushed with success, pushed on. In June 1937 the CIO sponsored strikes against those steel companies that were still holding out against the union. President Roosevelt, exasperated by the continuing strife between labor and business, was moved to express his frustration in a famous statement which invoked "a plague on both your houses." Even though the President later tried to explain the remark to Lewis as one directed against the holdout companies and the strikers who employed violence, the CIO chief saw it as aimed at him and retaliated in his Labor Day speech in 1937.

Lewis's speech was an insistence on "the acceptance of collective bargaining as a recognized American institution," an attempt to strengthen union resolve and enlist popular support against the agents of big business. It was also a demand for support from its political allies and a clear threat directed against inaction by those whom Lewis believed owed their political successes to organized labor. Lewis was convinced in his own mind that his, and labor's, support was instrumental in FDR's election—and unions were, indeed, contributing large amounts to the Democratic coffers. He took offense at those who had "supped at labor's table" and had "been sheltered in labor's house" now appearing to "curse with equal fervor and fine impartiality both labor and its adversaries." Lewis's speech was a call to heed "the voice of labor" and an insistence that labor's struggle to attain its rights was consistent with justice and the American conscience.

The United States Chamber of Commerce, the National Association of Manufacturers and similar groups representing industry and financial interests are rendering a disservice to the American people in their attempts to frustrate the organization of labor and in their refusal to accept collective bargaining as one of our economic institutions.

These groups are encouraging a systematic organization under the sham pretext of local interests. They equip these vigilantes with tin hats, wooden clubs, gas masks and lethal weapons and train them in the arts of brutality and oppression.

No tin hat brigade of goose-stepping vigilantes or bibble-babbling mob of blackguarding and corporation-paid scoundrels will prevent the onward march of labor, or divert its purpose to play its natural and rational part in the development of the economic, political and social life of our nation.

Unionization, as opposed to communism, presupposes the relation of employment; it is based upon the wage system and it recognizes fully and unreservedly the institution of private property and the right to investment profit. It is upon the fuller development of collective bargaining, the wider expansion of the labor movement, the increased influence of labor in our national councils, that the perpetuity of our democratic institutions must largely depend.

The organized workers of America, free in their industrial life, conscious partners in production, secure in their homes and enjoying a decent standard of living, will prove the finest bulwark against the intrusion of alien doctrines of government.

Do those who have hatched this foolish cry of communism in the C.I.O. fear the increased influence of labor in our democracy? Do they fear its influence will be cast on the side of shorter hours, a better system of distributed employment, better homes for the underprivileged, social security for the aged, a fairer distribution of the national income?

Certainly the workers that are being organized want a voice in the determination of these objectives of social justice.

Certainly labor wants a fairer share in the national income. Assuredly labor wants a larger participation in increased productive efficiency. Obviously the population is entitled to participate in the fruits of the genius of our men of achievement in the field of the material sciences.

Labor has suffered just as our farm population has suffered from a viciously unequal distribution of the national income. In the exploitation of both classes of workers has been the source of panic and depression, and upon the economic welfare of both rests the best assurance of a sound and permanent prosperity.

Under the banner of the Committee for Industrial Organization American labor is on the march. Its objectives today are those it had in the beginning: to strive for the unionization of our unorganized millions of workers and for the acceptance of collective bargaining as a recognized American institution.

It seeks peace with the industrial world. It seeks cooperation and mutuality of effort with the agricultural population. It would avoid strikes. It would have its rights determined under the law by the peaceful negotiations and contract relationships that are supposed to characterize American commercial life.

Until an aroused public opinion demands that employers accept that rule, labor has no recourse but to surrender its rights or struggle for their realization with its own economic power.

The objectives of this movement are not political in a partisan sense. Yet it is true that a political party which seeks the support of labor and makes pledges of good faith to labor must, in equity and good conscience, keep that faith and redeem those pledges.

The spectacle of august and dignified members of Congress, servants of the people and agents of the Republic, skulking in hallways and closets, hiding their faces in a party caucus to prevent a quorum from acting upon a larger measure, is one that emphasizes the perfidy of politicians and blasts the confidence of labor's millions in politicians' promises and statesmen's vows.

Labor next year cannot avoid the necessity of a political assay of the work and deeds of its so-called friends and its political beneficiaries. It must determine who are its friends in the arena of politics as elsewhere. It feels that its cause is just and that its friends should not view its struggle with neutral detachment or intone constant criticism of its activities.

Those who chant their praises of democracy, but who lose no chance to drive their knives into labor's defenseless back, must feel the weight of labor's woe, even as its open adversaries must ever feel the thrust of labor's power.

Labor, like Israel, has many sorrows. Its women weep for their fallen and they lament for the future of the children of the race. It ill behooves one who has supped at labor's table and who has been sheltered in labor's house to curse with equal fervor and fine impartiality both labor and its adversaries when they become locked in deadly embrace.

I repeat that labor seeks peace and guarantees its own loyalty, but the voice of labor, insistent upon its rights, should not be annoying to the ears of justice nor offensive to the conscience of the American people.

William Allen White

For the Consumer (1937)

In 1936 the American people validated the New Deal by handing President Franklin D. Roosevelt a stunning electoral victory over the Republican challenger, Governor Alfred M. Landon of Kansas. In building the New Deal coalition, Roosevelt had enlisted the support of organized labor, and unions began to flourish after so many years of discouragement and setback. These gains, however, were not made without bitter opposition from large corporations and employers.

The National Industrial Recovery Act of 1933 established the right of unions to collective bargaining and outlawed infamous "yellow dog" contracts, a means whereby employers extracted a pledge from workers that they would not join a union. The constitutionality of this legislation was doubted by many employers, who refused to abide by its provisions, and strikes were frequent. In 1934, for example, the textile industry and the auto industry were racked with strikes; the use of strikebreakers, private armies, and even militia to end the strikes often resulted in violence.

After the Supreme Court found the National Industrial Recovery Act unconstitutional, Congress passed new legislation, the Wagner Act, which was designed to meet constitutional objections while reenacting the major provisions of the old legisalation. This Act, passed in 1935, was sustained by the Supreme Court in 1937, and the rights of labor seemed more assured.

With the formation of a new labor organization, the Committee (later Congress) of Industrial Organizations, led by the flamboyant head of the Mine Workers, John L. Lewis, the country witnessed a new wave of strikes. These strikes were largely organizational in nature; that is, the CIO fought management, not over the traditional issues of wages and hours, but for the right to become the exclusive bargaining agents for workers. The "sit-down" tactic—workers took possession of the work place and refused to leave until the strike was settled—was of doubtful legality, but it was successful in several important cases. In others, further violence resulted: the Goodyear Tire strike of May 1937 in Chicago, for example, culminated in a battle between strikers and police that resulted in ten deaths. Franklin Roosevelt's disgusted comment, "a plague on both your houses," mirrored public opinion.

In September 1937 the International Management Congress met in Washington. Among the speakers addressing the conference was William Allen White, editor and publisher of the Emporia (Kansas) *Gazette*, winner of the Pulitzer Prize, and probably the most well-known and admired journalist of his time. White was a Republican, but also a liberal, who was deeply respected across the political spectrum. White was seen as the exemplar of the middle-class, Midwestern American; he was a logical choice to speak on behalf of the average consumers who found themselves caught in the middle of the struggle between labor and management.

In this speech White relates the failings both of the capitalists, whose lack of "social sense" brought on the woes from which they now suffered, and of labor, whose leaders had "become more interested in their party welfare than in the fundamental objectives of labor unions." White, clearly and directly, gave voice to what many Americans wanted as the country struggled out of the Depression: an "equitable compromise between the contending forces—capital and labor—known as justice."

In this discussion I am supposed to represent the public—the American consumer. He is a mythical character who never lived on land or sea, but for that matter, the capitalist is a myth and the worker's status is an economic hypothesis. It is trite to say that in America we are all more or less owners, all workers of high or low degrees, and certainly we are all consumers. We are all the children of John Q. Public, and our interests as members of the consuming public are after all our chief end and objective as citizens of our democracy.

Let me begin by telling you both, laborer and capitalist, that you have got us citizen consumers in a pretty sad mess. Every time we consumers think of what one of you has done we are dead sore at each of you until we begin to think of what the other has done. Let me start on capital, the employer. Not that he is more to blame than labor. But he is more responsible. He enjoys more freedom. He could have done better. You employers have wasted twenty years since the end of the World War. In those twenty years, a little intelligent self-interest, a little foresight—not much—would have solved equitably the problems that are now pressing upon us, problems that have been adjusted in haste and in the emergency of calamity. Take the eight-hour day. You knew that it was coming. Why didn't you men willingly, sensibly grant it? But no. You had to fight it, every inch, and make the consuming public think you were greedy—when you were not. You were just dumb—dumb to give labor a sense of deep antagonism. Take the old age pension and job insurance to cover seasonal and technological unemployment. A thousand voices rose across the land, telling you of the trouble ahead. What did you do? You put cotton in your ears, and if you could hear through the cotton you began yelling "Communism!" at the academician and the liberal politician and spokesmen of the consuming public. Everyone realized 20 years ago and more that sooner or later, with the pensions of the Civil War gone which took care of the aged until the World War, we should have old age pensions as a federal problem. Yet you employers let a generation of old people, unprovided for, begin to clamor for old age pensions and begin to listen to demagogues with silly panaceas. Then, having squandered your substance, you turned your men on the street in the days of the locust, and put into the hands of the most adroit politician America ever has seen the votes of ten million men whom your slipshod social viewpoint rendered jobless. If a dozen or twenty years ago you, Mr. Capitalist, had used the social sense of the average man in the street, this problem of unemployment and old age pensions would not be handing to your arch-enemies an organized subsidized class-conscious proletariat which can be voted to your destruction. By your sloth you created the particular head devil who is mocking you. He is your baby. You begot him two decades ago in the days of your youth when you were going to handle your business in your own way and no man could come into your shop and tell you how to run it!

But labor has been no Solomon. The proper business of a labor union is to get higher wages, better hours and good shop conditions for the workmen. But when labor en masse plunks its vote for its own party, then the spirit of party loyalty begins to obscure labor's objectives—high wages, short hours, decent shop conditions. Thus class-conscious labor leaders become more interested in their party welfare than in the fundamental objectives of labor unions. So we shall have the class-conscious political worker trading his vote not for the immediate objective of wages, hours and shop conditions, but for power for his political labor boss. The political labor boss will ask the workers to swallow a whole ticket in order to dominate a whole government. He would turn a democracy into a contest between two class-conscious parties, a class-conscious proletariat and a class-conscious plutocracy. In that setup where is the Consumer; where indeed is the compromise between labor and capital under the supervision of a middle class? In short with only two class-conscious political parties what becomes of democracy? The labor union militant and undefiled—yes; the vertical union and the closed shop? Yes. But a class-conscious labor party in a democracy—no! If labor insists upon maintaining its class lines of bitter intransigent hostility to all capital, the American middle class—old John Q. Public and his heirs and assigns will not support labor.

This is a middle-class country and the middle class will have its will and way. For the middle class is the real owner of American industry. The middle class is also 80 percent worker and the consumer of 80 percent of American industrial production in the home market. The middle class thinks and feels chiefly as The Consumer. And before the middle class demands an increase in either interest for investors or higher wages for the worker, the middle class will demand fair prices and a stable industry. That means industrial peace. No peace is lasting until it is founded upon that essential equitable compromise between the contending forces—capital and labor—known as justice.

America and the Global Conflict

Franklin Delano Roosevelt

Quarantine the Aggressor (1937)

World War I was supposed to have made the world safe for democracy, but it did not work out that way. For Americans, euphoria at the war's end was followed by disillusionment stemming from the realization that balance-of-power politics continued in Europe as before and that some Americans actually had reaped considerable financial benefit from the war. Ambitious proposals such as the League of Nations, the World Court, and even the ill-fated Briand-Kellogg Pact to outlaw war were followed by a determination that Americans must remain absolutely uninvolved in the affairs of Europe. This sentiment, which has been labeled "new isolationism," was at its peak during the mid-1930's.

Congress passed Neutrality Acts in 1935, 1936, and again in 1937, to ensure that the United States would not be drawn into a future European quarrel. In the Senate, a committee chaired by Gerald P. Nye of South Dakota held hearings in support of the thesis that the United States had entered the First World War at the behest of munitions makers and because of having been duped by British propaganda. In November 1936 a public opinion poll found that 95 percent of its sample believed that the United States should not take part if there were another world war. Similar sentiments were held by large majorities throughout the next year. By the autumn of 1937 three-quarters of the poll sample thought that a declaration of war should require approval of the people in a national referendum.

American "new isolationism," however, coincided with threats to democracy in Europe and Asia. Japan had attacked Manchuria in 1931; Hitler came to power in 1933. In 1935 Mussolini attacked Ethiopia; in 1936 Hitler annexed the Saar. President Franklin D. Roosevelt saw these developments as threats to the peace, but he also was constrained by American public opinion. He had accepted the various Neutrality Acts, perhaps fearing that to do otherwise would jeopardize his domestic program in Congress, but he did not agree that an impartial arms embargo would insure Americans against involvement in future wars, and he groped for some way to avert war between the dictatorships and democracies. Twice he had sought discussions of this topic with British Prime Minister Neville Chamberlain but each time he had been rebuffed.

Roosevelt went to Chicago to speak at the dedication of the new S-curve bridge across the Chicago River. He reportedly faced west, fixing his gaze on Tribune Tower, which was the home of the isolationist *Chicago Tribune*, and delivered a warning against ignoring aggressors. As for what the free nations might do, the President suggested the analogy of a quarantine to stop the spread of disease.

Of Roosevelt's motives for giving this speech, much has been written. Many contemporaries viewed it as signaling a new departure in foreign policy, and in retrospect it appears to be the first in a series of efforts to mobilize American public opinion prior to World War II. Others viewed it as nothing more than a trial balloon sent by a President who was groping for a foreign-policy stance and hoping at best to develop public awareness and understanding of the complexities of the world scene. The speech illustrates the almost studied ambiguity for which Roosevelt was well-known.

Immediate response to the speech was generally favorable, but there was hostile reaction as well; some isolationist Congressmen threatened Roosevelt with impeachment. There was no follow-up to the speech. The President neglected to amplify the details of any plans he might have had in mind, perhaps because administration officials did not embrace the plan and perhaps because the world situation was complex and he did not know what to do. The "quarantine" speech illustrates an attempt to redirect an unfavorable audience attitude, but Roosevelt did not again try to mobilize public opinion to support aid to the democracies until much closer to the outbreak of the Second World War.

I am glad to come once again to Chicago and especially to have the opportunity of taking part in the dedication of this important project of civic betterment.

On my trip across the continent and back I have been shown many evidences of the result of common sense cooperation between municipalities and the federal government, and I have been greeted by tens of thousands of Americans who have told me in every look and word that their material and spiritual well-being has made great strides forward in the past few years.

And yet, as I have seen with my own eyes, the prosperous farms, the thriving factories and the busy railroads—as I have ssen the happiness and security and peace which covers our wide land, almost inevitably I have been compelled to contrast our peace with very different scenes being enacted in other parts of the world.

It is because the people of the United States under modern conditions must, for the sake of their own future, give thought to the rest of the world, that I, as the responsible executive head of the nation, have chosen this great inland city and this gala occasion to speak to you on a subject of definite national importance.

The political situation in the world, which of late has been growing progressively worse, is such as to cause grave concern and anxiety to all the peoples and nations who wish to live in peace and amity with their neighbors.

Some fifteen years ago the hopes of mankind for a continuing era of international peace were raised to great heights when more than sixty nations solemnly pledged themselves not to resort to arms in furtherance of their national aims and policies. The high aspirations expressed in the Briand-Kellogg Peace Pact and the hopes for peace thus raised have of late given way to a haunting fear of calamity. The present reign of terror and international lawlessness began a few years ago.

It began through unjustified interference in the internal affairs of other nations or the invasion of alien territory in violation of treaties and has now reached a stage where the very foundations of civilization are seriously threatened. The landmarks and traditions which have marked the progress of civilization toward a condition of law, order, and justice are being wiped away.

Without a declaration of war and without warning or justification of any kind, civilians, including women and children, are being ruthlessly murdered with bombs from the air. In times of so-called peace, ships are being attacked and sunk by submarines without cause or notice. Nations are fomenting and taking sides in civil warfare in nations that have never done them any harm. Nations claiming freedom for themselves deny it to others. Innocent peoples and nations are being cruelly sacrificed to a greed for power and supremacy which is devoid of all sense of justice and humane consideration.

To paraphrase a recent author, "perhaps we foresee a time when men, exultant in the technique of homicide, will rage so hotly over the world that every precious thing will be in danger, every book and picture and harmony, every treasure garnered through two milleniums, the small, the delicate, the defenseless—all will be lost or wrecked or utterly destroyed."

If those things come to pass in other parts of the world, let no one imagine that America will escape, that it may expect mercy, that this Western Hemisphere will not be attacked, and that it will continue tranquilly and peacefully to carry on the ethics and the arts of civilization. If those days come, "there will be no safety by arms, no help from authority, no answer in science. The storm will rage till every flower of culture is trampled and all human beings are leveled in a vast chaos."

If those days are not to come to pass—if we are to have a world in which we can breathe freely and live in amity without fear—the peace-loving nations must make a concerted effort to uphold laws and principles on which alone peace can rest secure. The peace-loving nations must make a concerted effort in opposition to those violations of treaties and those ignorings of humane instincts which today are creating a state of international anarchy and instability from which there is no escape through mere isolation or neutrality.

Those who cherish their freedom and recognize and respect the equal right of their neighbors to be free and live in peace must work together for the triumph of law and moral principles in order that peace, justice, and confidence may prevail in the world. There must be a return to a belief in the pledged word, in the value of a signed treaty. There must be recognition of the fact that national morality is as vital as private morality.

A bishop wrote me the other day:

> It seems to me that something greatly needs to be said in behalf of ordinary humanity against the present practice of carrying the horrors of war to helpless civilians, especially women and children. It may be that such a protest might be regarded by many, who claim to be realists, as futile, but may it not be that the heart of mankind is so filled with horror at the present needless suffering that that force could be mobilized in sufficient volume to lessen such cruelty in the days ahead. Even though it may take twenty years, which God forbid, for civilization to make effective its corporate protest against this barbarism, surely strong voices may hasten the day.

There is a solidarity and interdependence about the modern world, both technically and morally, which makes it impossible for any nation completely to isolate itself from economic and political upheavals in the rest of the world, especially when such upheavals appear to be spreading and not declining. There can be no stability or peace either within nations or between nations except under laws and moral standards adhered to by all. International anarchy destroys every foundation for peace. It jeopardizes either the immediate or the future security of every nation, large or small. It is, therefore, a matter of vital interest and concern to the people of the United States that the sanctity of international treaties and the maintenance of international morality be restored.

The overwhelming majority of the peoples and nations of the world today want to live in peace. They seek the removal of barriers against trade. They want to exert themselves in industry, in agriculture, and in business that they may increase their wealth through the production of wealth-producing goods rather than striving to produce military planes and bombs and machine guns and cannon for the destruction of human lives and useful property.

In those nations of the world which seem to be piling armament on armament for purposes of aggression, and those other nations which fear acts of aggression against them and their security, a very high proportion of their national income is being spent directly for armaments. It runs from 30 to as high as 50 percent. The proportion that we in the United States spend is far less—11 or 12 percent.

How happy we are that the circumstances of the moment permit us to put our money into bridges and boulevards, dams and reforestation, the conservation of our soil, and many other kinds of useful works rather than into huge standing armies and vast supplies of implements of war.

I am compelled and you are compelled, nevertheless, to look ahead. The peace, the freedom, and the security of 90 percent of the population of the world is being jeopardized by the remaining 10 percent who are threatening a break-down of all international order and law. Surely the 90 percent who want to live in peace under law and in accordance with moral standards that have received almost universal acceptance through the centuries can and must find some way to make their will prevail.

The situation is definitely of universal concern. The questions involved relate not merely to violations of specific provisions of particular treaties; they are questions of war and of peace, of international law, and especially of principles of humanity. It is true that they involve definite violations of agreements, and especially of the Covenant of the League of Nations, the Briand-Kellogg Pact, and the Nine Power Treaty. But they also involve problems of world economy, world security, and world humanity.

It is true that the moral consciousness of the world must recognize the importance of removing injustices and well-founded grievances; but at the same time it must be aroused to the cardinal necessity of honoring sanctity of treaties, of respecting the rights and liberties of others, and of putting an end to acts of international aggression.

It seems to be unfortunately true that the epidemic of world lawlessness is spreading. When an epidemic of physical disease starts to spread, the community approves and joins in a quarantine of the patients in order to protect the health of the community against the spread of the disease.

It is my determination to pursue a policy of peace and to adopt every practicable measure to avoid involvement in war. It ought to be inconceivable that in this modern era, and in the face of experience, any nation could be so foolish and ruthless as to run the risk of plunging the whole world into war by invading and violating, in contravention of solemn treaties, the territory of other nations that have done them no real harm and which are too weak to protect themselves adequately. Yet the peace of the world and the welfare and security of every nation is today being threatened by that very thing.

No nation which refuses to exercise forebearance and to respect the freedom and rights of others can long remain strong and retain the confidence and respect of other nations. No nation ever loses its dignity or good standing by conciliating its differences and by exercising great patience with, and consideration for, the rights of other nations.

War is a contagion, whether it be declared or undeclared. It can engulf states and peoples remote from the original scene of hostilities. We are determined to keep out of war, yet we cannot insure ourselves against the disastrous effects of war and the dangers of involvement. We are adopting such measures as will minimize our risk of involvement, but we cannot have complete protection in a world of disorder in which confidence and security have broken down.

If civilization is to survive, the principles of the Prince of Peace must be restored. Shattered trust between nations must be revived. Most important of all, the will for peace on the part of peace-loving nations must express itself to the end that nations that may be tempted to violate their agreements and the rights of others will desist from such a cause. There must be positive endeavors to preserve peace.

America hates war. America hopes for peace. Therefore, America actively engages in the search for peace.

Charles A. Lindbergh

An Independent Policy (1941)

When the German army smashed into Poland in September 1939, Europe was, for the second time in the twentieth century, plunged into a general war. In America, as in 1914, public sentiment strongly favored nonintervention. President Roosevelt immediately declared that the United States "would remain a neutral nation." He did not, however, assume the strict impartiality that Woodrow Wilson had called for in the early days of World War I; Roosevelt acknowledged that he could not ask that "every American remain neutral in thought as well."

Certainly the President was not neutral in his sympathies. He called Congress into special session to pass a new Neutrality Act to replace the Act of 1937, which had embargoed the sale of arms and munitions to belligerents. The new Act allowed for the sale of arms on a "cash and carry" basis, which helped the British, but the legislation was not carried without dissent. In 1940 and 1941 Roosevelt consistently pursued a policy designed to aid the British against Germany, but he was careful not to move too quickly ahead of public opinion. At the same time, he instigated measures to begin to prepare the country for war, although these were cautious and most action was met with some measure of opposition and suspicion by isolationists both in and out of Congress.

Isolationism drew its support from disparate elements in America, many of whom would be hardly likely to agree on other issues. Senators LaFollette and Wheeler were old-fashioned progressives who had opposed foreign involvement for virtually their entire careers. Senator Nye had built a career on attacking munitions manufacture as the the root cause of war; in the House of Representatives Martin Dies saw a Communist conspiracy behind all international efforts, while

Representative Vito Marcantonio, with Communist support, opposed American intervention in Europe. Aside from the politicians, isolationists were to be found among some of America's most distinguished citizens: intellectuals like Robert Hutchins, Charles Beard, and Kingman Brewster; United Mine Workers President John L. Lewis, and the legendary industrialist Henry Ford; novelist Kathleen Norris and actress Lillian Gish; the Socialist Norman Thomas and the Chairman of Sears, Roebuck, Robert E. Wood.

Wood was instrumental in founding and financing an isolationist organization, the America First Committee, whose most spectacular recruit was the popular American hero, Charles Lindbergh. Lindbergh was the son of a Minnesota Congressman whose own political career had been damaged by his opposition to American entry into World War I. Young Lindbergh gained international fame in 1927 when he piloted the *Spirit of St. Louis* on the first nonstop flight from New York to Paris in just over 33 hours. He was feted throughout Europe; back in America, the young aviator was awarded the Congressional Medal of Honor and accorded wild demonstrations and parades in New York and other cities throughout the country. After the sensational kidnapping and murder of his infant son, Lindbergh lived in England for a time and then in France, returning to the United States in 1939. While in Europe, Lindbergh studied the air power of several European countries and was impressed by German superiority in aircraft production. He was sincerely convinced that no other European power could stand up to Germany and was keenly aware that the United States was not prepared for a major war. Speaking on the radio and at rallies, Lindbergh argued that American interests did not call for participation in a European war and that American military superiority could be ensured only by a defensive posture. This, Lindbergh argued, was in keeping with both historic American traditions and practical military wisdom.

President Roosevelt came close to branding Lindbergh as a traitor, and Lindbergh, insulted, resigned his commission in the Air Corps Reserve. The America First Committee, however, was damaged as much by its endorsement as "patriotic" in a Nazi shortwave broadcast as by the President's attacks. And Lindbergh himself did not help his cause when he attacked the "British and Jewish races" for attempting to involve the United States in war "for reasons which are not American." The odor of anti-Semitism clung to the movement with its implication that America First supported Nazi policy, and eroded confidence in the "independent policy" that Lindbergh was trying to promote. Lindbergh's speech, however, is an example of isolationist thinking prior to the war and represents the nature of the principal opposition faced by President Roosevelt in pursuing pro-British policies.

There are many viewpoints from which the issues of this war can be argued. Some are primarily idealistic. Some are primarily practical. One should, I believe, strive for a balance of both. But, since the subjects that can be covered in a single address are limited, tonight I shall discuss the war from a viewpoint which is primarily practical. It is not that I believe ideals are unimportant, even among the realities of war; but if a nation is to survive in a hostile world its ideals must be backed by the hard logic of military practicability. If the outcome of war depended upon ideals alone, this would be a different world than it is today.

I know I will be severely criticized by the interventionists in America when I say we should not enter a war unless we have a reasonable chance of winning. That, they will claim, is far too materialistic a viewpoint. They will advance again the same arguments that were used to persuade France to declare war against Germany in 1939. But I do not believe that our American ideals and our way of life will gain through an unsuccessful war. And I know that the United States is not prepared to wage war in Europe successfully at this time. We are no better prepared today than France was when the interventionists in Europe persuaded her to attack the Siegfried Line.

I have said before, and I will say again, that I believe it will be a tragedy to the entire world if the British empire collapses. That is one of the main reasons why I opposed this war before it was declared, and why I have constantly advocated a negotiated peace. I did not feel that England and France had a reasonable chance of winning. France has now been defeated and despite the propaganda and confusion of recent months it is now obvious that England is losing the war. I believe this is realized even by the British government. But they have one last desperate plan remaining. They hope that they may be able to persuade us to send another American Expeditionary Force to Europe and to share with England militarily, as well as financially, the fiasco of this war.

I do not blame England for this hope, or for asking for our assistance. But we now know that she declared a war under circumstances which led to the defeat of every nation that sided with her from Poland to Greece. We know that in the desperation of war England promised to all these nations armed assistance that she could not send. We know that she misinformed them, as she has misinformed us, concerning her state of preparation, her military strength and the progress of the war.

In time of war, truth is always replaced by propaganda. I do not believe we should be too quick to criticize the actions of a belligerent nation. There is always the question whether we, ourselves, would do better under similar circumstances. But we in this country have a right to think of the welfare of America first, just as the people in England thought first of their own country when they encouraged the smaller nations of Europe to fight against hopeless odds. When England asks us to enter this war she is considering her own future and that of her empire. In making our reply, I believe we should consider the future of the United States and that of the Western Hemisphere.

It is not only our right, but it is our obligation as American citizens to look at this war objectively, and to weigh our chances for success if we should enter it. I have attempted to do this, especially from the standpoint of aviation, and I have been forced to the conclusion that we cannot win this war for England, regardless of how much assistance we extend.

I ask you to look at the map of Europe

today and see if you can suggest any way in which we could win this war if we entered it. Suppose we had a large army in America, trained and equipped. Where would we send it to fight? The campaigns of the war show only too clearly how difficult it is to force a landing, or to maintain an army, on a hostile coast. Suppose we took our Navy from the Pacific and used it to convoy British shipping. That would not win the war for England. It would, at best, permit her to exist under the constant bombing of the German air fleet. Suppose we had an air force that we could send to Europe. Where could it operate? Some of our squadrons might be based in the British Isles, but it is physically impossible to base enough aircraft in the British Isles alone to equal in strength the aircraft that can be based on the continent of Europe.

I have asked these questions on the supposition that we had in existence an army and an air force large enough and well enough equipped to send to Europe; and that we would dare to remove our Navy from the Pacific. Even on the basis, I do not see how we could invade the continent of Europe successfully as long as all of that continent and most of Asia is under Axis domination. But the fact is that none of these suppositions are correct. We have only a one-ocean Navy. Our Army is still untrained and inadequately equipped for foreign war. Our air force is deplorably lacking in modern fighting planes because most of them have already been sent to Europe.

When these facts are cited, the interventionists shout that we are defeatists, that we are undermining the principles of democracy, and that we are giving comfort to Germany by talking about our military weakness. But every thing I mention here has been published in our newspapers, and in the reports of Congressional hearings in Washington. Our military position is well known to the governments of Europe and Asia. Why, then, should it not be brought to the attention of our own people?

I say it is the interventionist in America, as it was in England and in France, who gives comfort to the enemy. I say it is they who are undermining the principles of democracy when they demand that we take a course to which more than 80 per cent of our citizens are opposed. I charge them with being the real defeatists, for their policy has led to the defeat of every country that followed their advice since this war began. There is no better way to give comfort to an enemy than to divide the people of a nation over the issue of foreign war. There is no shorter road to defeat than by entering a war with inadequate preparation. Every nation that has adopted the interventionist policy of depending on some one else for its own defense has met with nothing but defeat and failure.

When history is written, the responsibility for the downfall of the democracies of Europe will rest squarely upon the shoulders of the interventionists who led their nations into war uninformed and unprepared. With their shouts of defeatism, and their disdain of reality, they have already sent countless thousands of young men to death in Europe. From the campaign of Poland to that of Greece, their prophecies have been false and their policies have failed. Yet these are the people who are calling us defeatists in America today. And they have led this country, too, to the verge of war.

There are many such interventionists in America, but there are more people among us of a different type. That is why you and I are assembled here tonight. There is a policy open to this nation that will lead to success—a policy that will leave us free to follow our own way of life, and to develop our own civilization. It is not a new and untried idea. It was advocated by Washington. It was incorporated in the Monroe Doctrine. Under its guidance, the United States became the greatest nation in the world. It is based upon the belief that the security of a nation lies in the strength and character of its own people. It recommends the maintenance of armed forces sufficient to defend this hemisphere from attack by any combination of foreign powers. It demands faith in an independent American destiny. This is a policy of the America First Committee today. It is a policy not of isolation, but of independence; not of defeat, but of courage. It is a policy that led this nation to success during the most trying years of our history, and it is a policy that will lead us to success again.

We have weakened ourselves for many months, and still worse, we have divided our own people by this dabbling in Europe's wars. While we should have been concentrating on American defense, we have been forced to argue over foreign quarrels. We must turn our eyes and our faith back to our own country before it is too late. And when we do this, a different vista opens before us. Practically every difficulty we would face in invading Europe becomes an asset to us in defending America. Our enemy, and not we, would then have the problem of transporting millions of troops across the ocean and landing them on a hostile shore. They, and not we, would have to furnish the convoys to transport guns and trucks and munitions and fuel across 3,000 miles of water. Our battleships and submarines would then be fighting close to their home bases. We would then do the bombing from the air, and the torpedoing at sea. And if any part of an enemy convoy should ever pass our Navy and air force, they would still be faced with the guns of our Coast Artillery, and behind them, the divisions of our Army.

The United States is better situated from a military standpoint than any other nation in the world. Even in our present condition of unpreparedness, no foreign power is in a position to invade us today. If we concentrate on our own defenses, and build the strength that this nation should maintain, no foreign army will ever attempt to land on American shores.

War is not inevitable for this country. Such a claim is defeatism in the true sense. No one can make us fight abroad unless we ourselves are willing to do so. No one will attempt to fight us here if we arm ourselves as a great nation should be armed. Over 100,000,000 people in this nation are opposed to entering the war. If the principles of democracy mean anything at all, that is reason enough for us to stay out. If we are forced into a war against the wishes of an overwhelming majority of our people, we will have proved democracy such a failure at home that there will be little use fighting for it abroad.

The time has come when those of us who believe in an independent American destiny must band together and organize for strength. We have been led toward war by a minority of our people. This minority has power. It has influence. It has a loud voice. But it does not represent the American people. During the last several years I have traveled over this country, from one end to the other. I have talked to many hundreds of men and women, and I have had letters from tens of thousands more, who feel the same way as you and I. These people—the majority of hard-working American citizens—are with us. They are the true strength of our country. And they are beginning to realize, as you and I, that there are times when we must sacrifice our normal interests in life in order to insure the safety and the welfare of our nation.

Such a time has come. Such a crisis is here. That is why the America First Committee has been formed—to give voice to the people who have no newspaper, or news reel, or radio station at their command; to the people who must do the paying and the fighting and the dying, if this country enters the war.

Whether or not we do enter the war rests upon the shoulders of you in this audience, upon us here on this platform, upon meetings of this kind that are being held by Americans in every section of the United States today. It depends upon the action we take and the courage we show at this time. If you believe in an independent destiny for America, if you believe that this country should not enter the war in Europe, we ask you to join the America First Committee in its stand. We ask you to share our faith in the ability of this nation to defend itself, to develop its own civilization, and to contribute to the progress of mankind in a more constructive and intelligent way than has yet been found by the warring nations of Europe. We need your support, and we need it now. The time to act is here.

Wendell L. Willkie

American Liberty (1941)

In 1940 the Republican Party, somewhat surprisingly, passed over its more prominent political leaders to nominate a Wall Street lawyer and former Democrat, Wendell Willkie, to run for President. Willkie, a native of Indiana, practiced law for an industrial firm in Akron, Ohio, after returning from World War I and, as an active Democrat, he attended the national convention in 1924. In 1929 Willkie joined a law firm in New York that represented a utility holding company, the Commonwealth and Southern Corporation, and he became its president in 1933. Willkie had already established a reputation as an effective speaker; as chief executive of a major utilities company opposed to government competition in the form of the Tennessee Valley Authority, he soon became a determined enemy of the New Deal and the leading spokesman among business critics of the Roosevelt Administration.

In the area of foreign policy, however, Willkie's views were not markedly different from the President's. He had always spoken in behalf of international cooperation, and he was clearly not in the isolationist camp. Popular sentiment against the possibility of American involvement in the war, however, was strong enough to induce Willkie in the closing weeks of the campaign to attack the President's sale of aged destroyers to Britain and to insist that "We do not want to send our boys over there again and we do not intend to." This attack prompted the President to reaffirm the Democratic Party's pledge not to participate in foreign wars. Despite the lack of any real difference between the two on international issues, sloganeers in both parties tried to contrast Willkie and Roosevelt on foreign policy, the Republicans equating a vote for the President to a vote for war and the Democrats castigating Willkie's "pro Hitler" backing.

Willkie ran a vigorous campaign. In a little over eight weeks the Republican nominee gave 500 speeches, his special campaign train traveling to thirty states. In the end, Willkie got over 22 million votes to FDR's 27 million, but he carried only 10 states with 82 electoral votes against the President's 449 electoral votes gleaned from 38 states.

After the election, Willkie articulated his conception of a "loyal opposition," one that was free to offer justifiable criticism on domestic matters while supporting the President in the areas of national defense and foreign policy. In contrast to the strong isolationist position held by conservatives in his own party, Willkie was clearly sympathetic to the Allied cause and approved of the President's cautious but sustained support of Nazi Germany's enemies.

By the summer of 1941 American ties with Britain were growing stronger and the threat of war intensified. The Lend-Lease Act, passed in the spring, enabled the President to provide direct assistance to Britain; a little over two months later the President declared a national emergency and ordered all German and Italian consulates closed. In the Pacific, Japan's expansionist policy caused growing alarm in Washington. On July 4 Wendell Willkie delivered a radio address on "American Liberty." In this speech the titular head of the Republican Party made it clear that his views coincided with the Administration's. "Despite the occasional hesitations and doubts," Willkie asserted, Americans would not let liberty "disappear from the world, either in Europe or in Asia or in America." Willkie unequivocally described the war in ideological terms as a fight against "totalitarianism," and he repudiated "isolationism and defeatism" at home. Americans were still not ready to plunge into the war, however; many hoped that the Allies could win with American financial and industrial support, support that stopped short of the commitment of American military forces. Willkie's voice nevertheless encouraged the development of the overwhelmingly pro-Allied sentiment that was growing in the United States.

After America's entry into the war, Willkie undertook private diplomatic missions on behalf of President Roosevelt and became the leading internationalist spokesman for the Republican Party.

Men and women, I want to talk to you today very simply and very sincerely about the things that are in my heart and in my mind. All over America people are gathered in city, in village and in town, celebrating the Fourth of July, which is America's patriotic holiday. Speakers are telling of our heroic past, reciting the deeds, the gallant deeds, of our soldiers, recalling to our people our long struggle for liberty and the developments of our free system.

Songs are being sung, songs that move the hearts of men. Prayers are being offered all over America. Men are rededicating themselves to the principles of human freedom. But there is not a thoughtful person in all our broad land but understands that this Fourth of July celebration is in many ways more significant than any one of the celebrations we have had in the last one hundred and fifty years.

We understand, we appreciate and try to realize that as we celebrate liberty in America we must also celebrate the hope that liberty will return to many peoples who have been deprived of it in other countries.

Since the last celebration of this holiday in America millions of people, just like us, who lived peaceful, contented lives, lived free lives, with the right to go about their way of life as they pleased, have been deprived of their liberty. And we also know that unless their liberty is restored liberty cannot remain a permanent possession of America.

Liberty, like all doctrines, must be an expanding doctrine. It must be constantly searching out for new areas, or else it will die. We understand that if we permit the last stronghold of liberty in Europe to fall before the onslaught of totalitarianism the opportunity to save liberty in America will be lessened and, therefore, the overwhelming percentage of the American people are resolved that at whatever hazard or cost we will sustain the fighting men of Britain.

Every minute more and more people in America are coming to realize that the hope of Britain standing up depends upon our seeing to it that the products of our factories and our farms are delivered to her, and I am quite sure that before long now the great force of the American Navy will be brought into play to insure the delivery of those products to the fighting men of Britain.

American liberty means, of course, certain governmental processes. It means the right of men to vote in free election for public officials of their own choice, responsive to their will; it means, of course, the right of men to have their differences determined in courts undominated by government and the powerful.

It means, of course, the right of freedom of religion and freedom of speech and freedom from another thing that has come into the world with the cruelty of totalitarianism—the freedom from espionage, the freedom from interference with one's private life and one's daily doings and one's daily habits.

But American liberty means much more than that. American liberty is a religion. It is a thing of the spirit. It is an aspiration on the part of people for not alone a free life but a better life; and so I say to you people of the world, I think I know the heart of the American people. I have lived among them; I know them well. And despite the occasional hesitation and doubts, the American people will reach out, will give their utmost to see that this precious thing we call liberty shall not disappear from the world, either in Europe or in Asia or in America.

Yet none of us underestimates either the cost or the effort that will be required to do this. The forces of totalitarianism have harnessed and directed this mechanical age for the creation of the greatest military machine that the world has ever seen. It has directed the energies of 80,000,000 people toward one end—toward aggression, toward the destruction of other people; and we with our free way of life, with our individual desires and opinions, did not learn until lately how to meet such a menace.

But I am proud to say of my fellow-citizens in the United States that they are beginning to realize it now and that the vast industrial and agricultural resources of our nation are being brought into a firm and cohesive force. The spirit of our people is arising to direct that force so that totalitarianism will disappear from this world.

I was talking recently to some of my fellow-soldiers of the World War of 1917 to 1919, and I told them how proud I was that it is the soldiers of that war who are the leaders in the movement in America today against isolationism and defeatism. It is the soldiers of 1917 to 1919 that are calling America to a rededication to the spirit of liberty.

Many people preached for many years to those soldiers that all they did in the last war was futile and to no avail. As I told them, they did not make a mistake in fighting that first World War—as a matter of fact, if they had not, perhaps today there would be no liberty to fight for. Their mistake was in not fighting after the war as citizens to see that the kind of world was brought into being in which there could exist no such force as totalitarianism today.

When we have triumphed in this war, all men who fought in the last war must see to it that there is a peace drawn not in bitterness and in hatred, not of unpayable indemnities, not of the kind that produces inevitably another war, but that we must draw a peace in which the defeated people have the same right to the aspiration of liberty and of a full life as the conquered.

We must see to it that the trade areas of the world are enlarged, that artificial barriers between men are removed, so that there will be a constantly rising standard of living for all men who work, in which men of all races and creeds and religions and nations can live in peace and harmony, in which the just fruits of enterprise will find their just fulfillment, in which children may look forward to a constantly better world, free of hatred and bitterness and narrow isolationism and of economic degradation.

I speak tonight not alone to my fellow-citizens of America: I speak to the citizens of the remaining free country of Europe. I speak to the people of the enslaved countries of Europe. I speak to the people of Germany, where my forebears came from, and I say to all of you, American liberty is a generous thing. We reach out to all of you and only hope and pray that every one of you may have liberty.

We want to share it with you all. All we seek to do is to remove from the world the menace of a doctrine of government and a system of economics that lives by the enslavement of men, lives by the enslavement of men under its own rule, lives by the enslavement of men that it conquers.

Surely before another Fourth of July celebration comes about all the world will join with America in celebrating the principles of human freedom.

Franklin Delano Roosevelt

War Message (1941)

When war broke out in Europe in 1939, the United States remained neutral—at least diplomatically and economically. Although they wished to avoid war, most Americans nevertheless sympathized with the Allies. Hoping that the Axis powers (Germany, Italy, and Japan) could be defeated without American involvement, the public moved only slowly from the strongest provisions of the 1937 Neutrality Act, which had embargoed arms and banned loans to belligerents while prohibiting Americans from traveling on belligerent ships. Confidence that America could avoid the war eroded as the Axis powers conquered much of Europe. By June 1941 they had defeated Poland, Norway, the Netherlands, Belgium, France, Yugoslavia, Romania, and Greece. They had invaded the Soviet Union and threatened to attack Great Britain.

Congress moved gradually in response to these developments. In 1939 it repealed the arms embargo and authorized cash-and-carry sales. In 1940 it approved the country's first peacetime draft in history. In early 1941 it passed the Lend-Lease Act, which permitted Britain to receive arms and supplies by sale, transfer, exchange, or lease. Nevertheless, when the draft was due to expire in the fall of 1941, it was renewed by a single vote.

Less attention was paid to developments in Asia. Japan invaded China in 1937. Three years later Japan, Germany, and Italy signed a ten-year military and economic alliance. When Japan assumed air bases in Indochina under agreement with the occupation government in France, President Roosevelt responded with an embargo on exports of scrap iron and steel. When Japan later occupied French Indochina, Roosevelt froze all Japanese credits in the United States, virtually halting the flow of trade, and he nationalized the armed forces of the Philippines.

Americans divided in their attitudes toward the war. Some thought the United States should intervene on behalf of the Allies. They were represented by the Committee to Defend America by Aiding the Allies, which was organized by Kansas newspaper editor William Allen White and quickly numbered 700 local chapters. In response to this effort, citizens opposed to entering the war in any way formed the America First Committee, which had over 400 local chapters. The activities of these two rival groups kept the issues of peace and war on the public agenda.

Relations between Japan and the United States deteriorated during 1941, and discussions which began in late November were almost doomed to be unproductive. Japan demanded that the United States abandon China, lift the freeze on Japanese credits, and resume trade. American negotiators countered with the demands that Japan withdraw troops from China and Indochina and sign a multilateral nonaggression pact. Japan publicly rejected these terms on December 1, while secretly planning for an attack on U.S. territory.

In response to intelligence reports of an impending Japanese attack somewhere in the West, the military stepped up security in American posts in the Western Pacific. Still, the attack on Pearl Harbor in the morning of December 7 came as a surprise. In less than two hours, 19 ships were sunk or disabled, 150 planes were destroyed, and more than 2,000 people were killed. There was little doubt what the American response would be. Those who wanted to enter the war now had clear justification; those who wanted to stay out concluded reluctantly that the matter was now beyond their control.

President Roosevelt addressed a joint session of Congress the next day to request a declaration of war. His speech, however, was not addressed solely to the immediate situation. He needed to justify American entry for a larger world audience and to provide the premises that would sustain the commitment of the American people in the event of a long war in which the Allies might suffer many reversals. He needed, therefore, to provide both a moral and a practical justification for war. To these ends, he sought to establish that the Japanese attack was unprovoked, that morality was on the American side, that the war was necessary for American security, and that the timing was right. The speech reveals many characteristic features of the rhetoric of war, including the stark contrast of moral positions, the distinction between the enemy government and its own people, the portrayal of Americans as reluctant but fervent warriors, the prediction of ultimate triumph, and the appeal for Divine sanction.

By near-unanimous votes in both houses, Congress approved a declaration of war against Japan. Since that nation, as a member of the Axis, was formally aligned with Germany and Italy, three days later the declaration was extended to those nations as well. It was now truly a *world* war, and the course of the war would be the single most important concern of the American people until Japan surrendered in August 1945.

Mr. Vice President, Mr. Speaker, members of the Senate and the House of Representatives: Yesterday, Dec. 7, 1941—a date which will live in infamy—the United States of America was suddenly and deliberately attacked by naval and air forces of the empire of Japan.

The United States was at peace with that nation, and, at the solicitation of Japan, was still in conversation with its government and its Emperor looking toward the maintenance of peace in the Pacific.

Indeed, one hour after Japanese air squadrons had commenced bombing in the American island of Oahu the Japanese Ambassador to the United States and his colleague delivered to our Secretary of State a formal reply to a recent American message. And, while this reply stated that it seemed useless to continue the existing diplomatic negotiations, it contained no threat or hint of war or of armed attack.

It will be recorded that the distance of Hawaii from Japan makes it obvious that the attack was deliberately planned many days or even weeks ago. During the intervening time the Japanese Government has deliberately sought to deceive the United States by false statements and expressions of hope for continued peace.

The attack yesterday on the Hawaiian Islands has caused severe damage to American naval and military forces. I regret to tell you that very many American lives have been lost. In addition, American ships have been reported torpedoed on the high seas between San Francisco and Honolulu.

Yesterday the Japanese Government also launched an attack against Malaya.

Last night Japanese forces attacked Hong Kong.

Last night Japanese forces attacked Guam.

Last night Japanese forces attacked the Philippine Islands.

Last night the Japanese attacked Wake Island.

And this morning the Japanese attacked Midway Island.

Japan has therefore undertaken a surprise offensive extending throughout the Pacific area. The facts of yesterday and today speak for themselves. The people of the United States have already formed their opinions and well understand the implications to the very life and safety of our nation.

As Commander in Chief of the Army and Navy I have directed that all measures be taken for our defense, that always will our whole nation remember the character of the onslaught against us.

No matter how long it may take us to overcome this premeditated invasion, the American people, in their righteous might, will win through to absolute victory.

I believe that I interpret the will of the Congress and of the people when I assert that we will not only defend ourselves to the uttermost but will make it very certain that this form of treachery shall never again endanger us.

Hostilities exist. There is no blinking at the fact that our people, our territory and our interests are in grave danger.

With confidence, in our armed forces, with the unbounding determination of our people, we will gain the inevitable triumph. So help us God.

I ask that the Congress declare that since the unprovoked and dastardly attack by Japan on Sunday, Dec. 7, 1941, a state of war has existed between the United States and the Japanese Empire.

Appendix: Biographical Notes and Bibliography

Following are biographical notes on the speakers included in this volume, listed alphabetically. The suggestions for additional reading that follow each note are not intended as comprehensive bibliographies; rather they should serve as starting points for interested students who wish to explore in more depth topics related to the speakers.

SAMUEL ADAMS was born in Boston in 1722. An active and adroit political agitator and propagandist, Adams was a leading force in anti-British agitation for more than a decade preceding the Revolution. He served in the Continental Congress, was lieutenant governor of Massachusetts from 1789 to 1794, and was governor of the state in 1797. He died in 1803.

Stewart Beach, *Samuel Adams: The Fateful Years, 1764–1776*. New York: Dodd Mead, 1966.

Donald B. Chidsey, *The World of Samuel Adams*. Nashville: T. Nelson, 1974.

P. Maier, "Coming to Terms with Sam Adams." *American Historical Review* 81 (1976): 12–37.

John C. Miller, *Sam Adams: Pioneer in Propaganda*. Stanford, CA: Stanford UP, 1960.

SUSAN B. ANTHONY was born in Massachusetts in 1820, the daughter of Quaker parents who soon moved to Rochester, New York. She was an early supporter of temperance reform and an abolitionist. A friend and associate of Elizabeth Cady Stanton, Anthony directed her greatest effort toward woman suffrage. When the woman's movement split in 1869, Susan Anthony joined Stanton in leading the group dedicated to establishing women's right to vote through a constitutional amendment. From 1892 until 1900 Anthony led the reunited wings of the movement as president of the National American Woman Suffrage Association. She retired from the presidency when she was 80 years old and died in Rochester in 1906.

Katherine S. Anthony, *Susan B. Anthony:*

Her Personal History and Her Era. Garden City, NY: Doubleday, 1954.

Ellen Carol Dubois, "Outgrowing the Compact of the Fathers: Equal Rights, Woman Suffrage, and the United States Constitution, 1820–1878." *Journal of American History* 74 (December 1987): 836–862.

Alma Lutz, *Susan B. Anthony: Rebel, Crusader, Humanitarian*. Boston: Beacon Press, 1959.

Elaine E. McDavitt, "Susan B. Anthony, Reformer and Speaker." *Quarterly Journal of Speech* 30 (1944): 173–180.

ALBERT BEVERIDGE was born in 1862 and, after graduating from DePauw University, was admitted to the bar in Indianapolis. He was elected as a Republican to the United States Senate in 1899 and 1905 but was defeated for reelection in 1910. Beveridge supported Theodore Roosevelt's bid for President on the Progressive (Bull Moose) Party ticket in 1912, and he was the unsuccessful Progressive Party candidate for governor of Indiana. A historian and biographer, Beveridge won the Pulitzer Prize in 1920 for *The Life of John Marshall*.

Claude G. Bowers, *Beveridge and the Progressive Era*. Boston: Houghton Mifflin, 1932.

John Braeman, *Albert J. Beveridge: American Nationalist*. Chicago: U of Chicago Press, 1971.

John A. Coffin, "The Senatorial Career of Albert J. Beveridge." *Indiana Magazine of History* 24 (1928): 242–294.

Harold T. Ross, "The Education of an Orator." *Quarterly Journal of Speech* 18 (1932): 70–82.

J. A. Thompson, "An Imperialist and the First World War: The Case of Albert J. Beveridge." *Journal of American Studies* 5 (1971): 133–150.

JONATHAN BOUCHER was born in England in 1738. In 1759 he traveled to Virginia, where he was a tutor for three years. He returned to Britain, was subsequently ordained in the Church of England, and became rector of a church in Hanover, Virginia. From there he moved to Caroline County, Virginia, and then to Maryland. He served as a tutor for the children of prominent colonial families, including among his pupils George Washington's stepson. He was also chaplain to the Maryland House of Delegates. His strong Tory principles made him unpopular with his parishioners; he resigned his parish in 1775 and went back to England, where in 1797, he published several of his American sermons as *A View of the Causes and Consequences of the American Revolution*.

Jonathan Boucher, ed., *Reminiscences of an American Loyalist, 1738–1789*. Boston and New York: Houghton Mifflin, 1925.

Philip Evanson, "Jonathan Boucher: The Mind of an American Loyalist." *Maryland Historical Magazine* 58 (1963): 123–136.

J. C. Spalding, "Loyalist as Royalist, Patriot as Puritan: The American Revolution as a Repetition of the English Civil Wars." *Church History* 45 (1976): 329–340.

Robert G. Walker, "Jonathan Boucher: Champion of the Minority." *William and Mary Quarterly* 2 (1945): 3–14.

Anne Y. Zimmer, *Jonathan Boucher, Loyalist in Exile*. Detroit: Wayne State UP, 1978.

JOHN BROWN was born in Connecticut in 1800. An ardent abolitionist, he was involved in antislavery activities throughout the country. In 1854 he moved to Kansas, where he and five of his sons fought in the guerilla war between the proslavery and antislavery forces. In 1859 he led a small band of men in an attack on the federal arsenal at Harper's Ferry, Virginia, where he was captured after being severely wounded. He was tried and found guilty of insurrection, treason, and murder and was hanged in 1859.

Richard O. Boyer, *The Legend of John Brown: A Biography and a History*. New York: Knopf, 1973.

Herbert L. Carson, "An Eccentric Kinship: Henry David Thoreau's 'A Plea for Captain John Brown.'" *Southern Speech Communication Journal* 27 (1961): 151–156.

John W. Monsma, Jr., "John Brown: The Two-Edged Sword of Abolition." *Central States Speech Journal* 13 (1961): 22–29.

Stephen B. Oates, *To Purge This Land with Blood: A Biography of John Brown*. New York: Harper and Row, 1970.

Benjamin Quarles, *Allies for Freedom: Blacks and John Brown*. New York: Oxford UP, 1974.

Gordon L. Thomas, "John Brown's Courtroom Speech." *Quarterly Journal of Speech* 48 (1962): 291–296.

WILLIAM JENNINGS BRYAN was born in Illinois in 1860. He practiced law in Nebraska and was elected a United States congressman in 1890. He was three times the Democratic candidate for President—in 1896 and 1900, when he was defeated by William McKinley; and in 1908, when William Howard Taft was elected. He served as Woodrow Wilson's secretary of state from 1913 to 1915, when he resigned over the strongly worded note sent by Wilson to Germany after the sinking of the liner *Lusitania*. Throughout his life he was a popular lecturer on the Chautauqua circuit. In his later years Bryan attacked Darwinism and appeared for the prosecution in the famous Scopes trial in Tennessee just before his death in 1925.

William Jennings Bryan, *The Memoirs of William Jennings Bryan*. New York: Haskell House, 1971. Originally published, 1925.

Louis W. Koenig, *Bryan: A Political Biography of William Jennings Bryan*. New York: Putnam, 1971.

Lawrence W. Levine, *Defender of the Faith: William Jennings Bryan*. New York: Oxford UP, 1968.

John H. Sloan, "'I Have Kept the Faith': William Jennings Bryan and the Democratic National Convention of 1904." *Southern Speech Communication Journal* 31 (1965): 114–123.

John H. Sloan, "Bryan Versus 'Bosses' at Baltimore." *Southern Speech Communication Journal* 32 (1967): 260–272.

JOHN C. CALHOUN was born in 1782 in South Carolina and studied law at Yale. As a young Congressman he supported the War of 1812 against Britain and was appointed by President Monroe as secretary of war in 1817. He was vice-president under John Quincy Adams from 1825 to 1829. Calhoun argued that a state had the right to nullify federal laws deemed unconstitutional and he published his theory of states' rights in his *Address to the People of South Carolina* in 1830. He was serving as Andrew Jackson's vice-president in 1832 when South Carolina passed the nullification ordinance; he resigned to enter the United States Senate, where he became the leading Southern spokesman. He was secretary of state when the treaty of annexation of Texas was signed, but he returned to the Senate to lead the states' rights forces. He opposed the Compromise of 1850 but died before the legislation was enacted.

Bert E. Bradley and Jerry L. Tarver, "John C. Calhoun, Argumentation in Defence of Slavery." *Southern Speech Communication Journal* 35 (1969): 163–175.

Margaret L. Coit, ed., *John C. Calhoun.* Englewood Cliffs, NJ: Prentice-Hall, 1970.

Robert A. Garson, "Proslavery as Political Theory: The Examples of John C. Calhoun and George Fitzhugh." *South Atlantic Quarterly* 84 (1985): 197–212.

J. William Harris, "Last of the Classical Republicans: An Interpretation of John C. Calhoun." *Civil War History* 30 (1984): 255–267.

John L. Thomas, ed., *John C. Calhoun: A Profile.* New York: Hill and Wang, 1968.

Michael Volpe, "The Logic of Calhoun's Constitutional Theory." *Southern Speech Communication Journal* 39 (1973): 161–172.

HENRY CLAY was born in Virginia in 1777. In 1797 he moved to Lexington, Kentucky, where he became a successful lawyer. Elected to Congress in 1811, he became a leader of the "War Hawks," who pressed for war with Britain, and he was chosen Speaker of the House. As a United States senator, he was instrumental in bringing about the Missouri Compromise in 1821. Three times he was unsuccessful in his bid for the presidency. In 1850 he came out of retirement to return to the Senate, where he was the chief architect of the "Great Compromise," whereby he hoped to end the sectional controversy that divided the North and South. He died in Washington in 1852.

Clement Eaton, *Henry Clay and the Art of American Politics.* Boston: Little, Brown, 1957.

Robert G. Gunderson, "The Magnanimous Mr. Clay." *Southern Speech Communication Journal* 16 (1950): 133–140.

Bernard Mayo, *Henry Clay, Spokesman of the New West.* Hamden, CT: Archon, 1966.

Robert T. Oliver, "Behind the Word: III. Clay." *Quarterly Journal of Speech* 23 (1937): 409–426.

Glynson G. VanDeusen, *The Life of Henry Clay.* Boston: Little, Brown, 1963.

RUSSELL CONWELL was born in Massachusetts in 1843 and was an officer in the Northern army during the Civil War. As a journalist, he served as a foreign correspondent for papers in New York and Boston; he then practiced law from 1870 to 1879. In that year he was ordained as a Baptist minister, and in 1881 he moved from Boston to Philadelphia, where he was pastor first of the Grace Baptist Church and then of the Baptist Temple. In 1888 he founded Temple University, and he served as its president for the rest of his life. He died in Philadelphia in 1925.

Daniel W. Bjork, *The Victorian Flight: Russell Conwell and the Crisis of American Individualism.* Washington, DC: UP of America, 1979.

Agnes R. Burr, *Russell H. Conwell and His Work.* Philadelphia: The John C. Winston Co., 1917.

Albert H. Smith, *The Life of Russell H. Conwell, Preacher, Lecturer, Philanthropist.* New York: Silver, Burdett, 1899.

JEFFERSON DAVIS was born in 1808 in Kentucky. Pursuing a military career, he graduated from West Point and served on active duty on the frontier. He was elected to Congress from Mississippi in 1845 and then returned to military service as a colonel of volunteers during the Mexican War in 1846–1847. After a short term in the United States Senate, he became secretary of war from 1853 to 1857. Back in the Senate, Davis soon became a leader of the Southern bloc and secured the passage of resolutions proclaiming that Congress had no right to interfere with slavery. When the government of the Confederate States of America was formed in 1861, Davis was selected as President. With the collapse of the Confederacy in 1865, Davis was captured and imprisoned for two years but was granted amnesty in 1868. He lived on in Mississippi, an "unreconstructed rebel," until his death in 1889.

Michael B. Ballard, *A Long Shadow: Jefferson Davis and the Final Days of the Confederacy*. Jackson, MS: UP of Mississippi, 1986.

Cass Canfield, *The Iron Will of Jefferson Davis*. New York: Harcourt, Brace, Jovanovich, 1978.

Bruce Collins, "The Making of Jefferson Davis." *Journal of American Studies* 18 (1984): 437–442.

Eric Langhein, *Jefferson Davis, Patriot: A Biography, 1808–1865*. New York: Vantage Press, 1962.

Walter E. Simonson and Bennett Strange, "Foote versus Davis: The Mississippi Election of 1851." *Southern Speech Communication Journal* 27 (1961): 126–134.

F. E. Vandiver, "Jefferson Davis—Leader Without a Legend." *Journal of Southern History* 43 (1977): 3–18.

EUGENE DEBS was born in Terre Haute, Indiana, in 1855. As a boy he began working for the railroad and eventually he became a locomotive fireman. A tireless and dedicated union organizer, in 1880 Debs became secretary-treasurer of the national Brotherhood of Locomotive Firemen as well as editor of that organization's magazine. He briefly entered politics as a Democrat, serving for four years as city clerk of Terre Haute and then, from 1885 to 1887, as a member of the state legislature. He formed the American Railway Union in 1893 and led the Pullman Strike in 1894. Debs went to jail for refusing to obey a court injunction that helped break the strike and, during this time, he embraced Socialism. He ran for President as a Socialist in 1900, 1904, 1908, and 1912, when he received 6 percent of the total vote. His opposition to World War I led to his prosecution and conviction for violating the Espionage Act, and it was while he was in prison that he ran for President for the last time in 1920. President Harding commuted his sentence in 1921; Debs died in 1926.

Bernard J. Brommel, "Eugene V. Debs: The Agitator as Speaker." *Central States Speech Journal* 20 (1969): 202–214.

Bernard J. Brommel, "The Pacifist Speechmaking of Eugene V. Debs." *Quarterly Journal of Speech* 52 (1966): 146–154.

D. A. Corbin, "Betrayal in the West Virginia Coalfields: Eugene V. Debs and the Socialist Party of America, 1912–1914." *Journal of American History* 64 (1978): 987–1009.

Ray Ginger, *The Bending Cross: A Biography of Eugene Victor Debs*. New York: Russell and Russell, 1969.

Nick Salvatore, *Eugene V. Debs: Citizen and Socialist*. Urbana, IL: U of Illinois Press, 1982.

JOHN DICKINSON was born in Maryland in 1732 and moved to Delaware with his family in 1740. After studying law in Philadelphia and in the Middle Temple, London, he began practicing in Philadelphia in 1757. He served in the Pennsylvania Assembly from 1762 until 1765 and from 1770 to 1776. In the period preceding the American Revolution, Dickinson became famous as the writer of political pamphlets upholding the rights of the colonies, most notably the *Letters from a Pennsylvania Farmer to the Inhabitants of the Colonies*, which was published in 1767 and widely read both in the colonies and in England. A member of the Continental Congress from 1774 to 1776, Dickinson was allied with conservatives who opposed independence from Great Britain. Although he refused to sign the Declaration of Independence, he ultimately supported the American cause, serving in the Revolutionary army and then as governor of Pennsylvania from 1782 to 1785. He was also a delegate to the Constitutional Convention of 1787. He died in 1808.

H. Trevor Colbourn, "John Dickinson, Historical Revolutionary." *Pennsylvania Magazine of History and Biography* 83 (1959): 271–292.

Milton E. Flower, *John Dickinson, Conservative Revolutionary*. Charlottesville, VA: U of Virginia Press, 1983.

Lionel E. Fredman, *John Dickinson, American Revolutionary*. Charlottesville, VA: SamHar Press, 1974.

David L. Jacobson, *John Dickinson and the Revolution in Pennsylvania*, 1764–1776. Berkeley: U of California Press, 1965.

STEPHEN A. DOUGLAS was born in 1813. He trained in law, and became attorney-general of Illinois in 1834. After serving in various state offices, he was named judge of the Illinois Supreme Court in 1841. First a member of the House of Representatives for four years, he was elected to the United States Senate in 1847. He supported the Compromise of 1850 and was the most famous proponent of the "popular sovereignty" doctrine, which held that the people of the territories should decide for themselves whether or not to be slave or free states. His famous debates with Abraham Lincoln in 1858 helped propel Lincoln into national prominence. Although Douglas defeated Lincoln for the Senate seat, Douglas's position on slavery in the territories was compromised in the eyes of Southerners who refused to support him in his 1860 bid for the presidency. Douglas pledged his support for President Lincoln but did not live long enough after the inauguration to exercise that support. He died in Chicago in 1861.

Gerald M. Capers, *Stephen A. Douglas, Defender of the Union*. Boston: Little, Brown, 1959.

Bruce Collins, "The Lincoln–Douglas Contest of 1858 and Illinois Electorate." *Journal of American Studies* 20 (1986): 391–420.

Richard A. Heckman, *Lincoln vs. Douglas: The Great Debates Campaign*. Washington, DC: Public Affairs Press, 1967.

Robert W. Johannsen, *Stephen A. Douglas*. New York: Oxford UP, 1973.

George Fort Milton, *The Eve of Conflict: Stephen A. Douglas and the Needless War*. Boston: Houghton Mifflin, 1934.

David Zarefsky, "The Lincoln–Douglas Debates Revisited: The Evolution of Public Argument." *Quarterly Journal of Speech* 72 (1986): 162–184.

FREDERICK DOUGLASS was born a slave in Maryland in 1817. He escaped in 1838 and fled north. He was a powerful speaker for the abolitionist cause both in the United States and in Great Britain, where he conducted a highly successful speaking tour from 1845 to 1847. It was while he was in England that funds were raised to buy his freedom. Back in America he started an abolitionist newspaper in Rochester, New York, and continued to lecture on the evils of slavery. After the Civil War Douglass held various government posts and served as the United States ambassador to Haiti. He died in 1895.

Anna W. Bontemps, *Free At Last: The Life of Frederick Douglass*. New York: Dodd Mead, 1971.

Frederick Douglass, *The Life and Writings of Frederick Douglass*. Phillip S. Foner, ed. New York: International Publishers, 1950–1975.

Frederick Douglass, *My Bondage and My Freedom*. New York: Arno Press, 1968. Originally published, 1855.

Gerald Fulkerson, "Frederick Douglass and the Kansas-Nebraska Act: A Case Study in Agitational Versatility." *Central States Speech Journal* 23 (1972): 261–269.

L. F. Goldstein, "Violence as an Instrument for Social Change: The Views of Frederick Douglass." *Journal of Negro History* 61 (1976): 61–72.

JONATHAN EDWARDS was born in Connecticut in 1703 and graduated from Yale University in 1720. After his ordination in 1727 he joined his grandfather, Solomon Stoddard, in Northampton, Massachusetts, and remained there for seventeen years, succeeding Stoddard as pastor. In these years he achieved fame as an evangelical preacher during the "Great Awakening." In addition to being a preacher, Edwards was a prolific writer, producing such theological works as *Freedom of the Will, Original Sin, and Christian Virtue*, in which he expounded a strict Calvinist doctrine. He quarreled with his congregation over his demand that only those who were consciously converted be admitted to church membership, and he resigned as pastor in 1750. For the next eight years he served as a missionary to the Housatonnuck Indians. In 1758 he became president of Princeton College but died a little over a month after taking office.

Alfred O. Aldridge, *Jonathan Edwards*. New York: Washington Square Press, 1964.

Edward H. Davidson, *Jonathan Edwards: The Narrative of a Puritan Mind*. Cambridge, MA: Harvard UP, 1968.

P. F. Gura, "Seasonable Thought: Reading Edwards in the 1980s." *New England Quarterly* 53 (1980): 388–394.

Rosemary Hearn, "Form as Argument in Edwards' Sinners in the Hands of an Angry God." *CLA Journal* 28 (1985): 452–459.

Perry Miller, *Jonathan Edwards*. New York: Meridian Books, 1959.

William J. Scheick, *The Writings of Jonathan Edwards: Theme, Motif, and Style*. College Station: Texas A & M UP, 1975.

Stephen R. Yarbrough, "Jonathan Edwards on Rhetorical Authority." *Journal of the History of Ideas* 47 (1986): 395–408.

RALPH WALDO EMERSON was born in Boston in 1803. After graduating from Harvard in 1820, he taught for several years and then, in 1829, became pastor of a Unitarian church in Boston. Leaving the church in 1832, Emerson devoted the rest of his life to writing and lecturing. He visited Europe in 1833 and began a lifelong friendship with Thomas Carlyle. When he returned in 1834, he moved to Concord, where he formed friendships with such literary figures as Thoreau and Hawthorne and wrote the essays and poems for which he is known. With the publication of *Nature* in 1836 and the presentation of the "The American Scholar" the following year, Emerson's career was launched. His 1838 "Address before the Divinity Class," at Harvard, in which Emerson argued for individual conscience over established religious creeds and institutions, caused a sensation. His conviction that human beings had a spiritual nature that enabled them to seek beauty and truth intuitively, and not through the senses alone, nor through the reasoning of authority, was at the heart of the transcendentalist movement that flourished in New England in the nineteenth century. Emerson died in 1882.

Barnet Baskerville, "Emerson as a Critic of Oratory." *Southern Speech Communication Journal* 18 (1953): 150–162.

Anthony Hillbruner, "Emerson: Democratic Egalitarian" *Central States Speech Journal* 10 (1959): 25–31.

B. Packer, "Uriel's Cloud: Emerson's Rhetoric." *Georgia Review* 31 (1977): 322–344.

Joel Porte, *Representative Man: Ralph Waldo Emerson in His Time.* New York: Oxford UP, 1979.

M. M. Sealts, Jr., "American Scholar and Public Issues: The Case of Emerson." *Ariel* 7 (1976): 109–121.

John A. Sloan, "'The Miraculous Uplifting': Emerson's Relationship with His Audience." *Quarterly Journal of Speech* 52 (1966): 10–15.

Edward C. Wagenknecht, *Ralph Waldo Emerson: Portrait of a Balanced Soul.* New York: Oxford UP, 1974.

BENJAMIN FRANKLIN was born in Boston in 1703, apprenticed in 1718 to his elder brother, a printer, and then, in 1723, set out on his own. Franklin's career as a journalist began with the publication of the *Pennsylvania Gazette* in 1729; *Poor Richard's Almanac,* begun in 1732, was circulated in the colonies and abroad and brought Franklin wide recognition. Active in political affairs, Franklin was clerk of the Pennsylvania Assembly in 1736, postmaster of Philadelphia in 1737, and an almost constant member of the Assembly. In 1754 Franklin urged a plan of colonial union to meet the French threat. Franklin had been acquiring a reputation as a scientist through his experiments with electricity, and he was elected a Fellow of the Royal Society. From 1757 to 1762, and again in 1764 until 1775, Franklin represented various colonial interests in London. Returning home in time to serve in the Continental Congress, Franklin was a signer of the Declaration of Independence. He resumed a diplomatic career, traveling to Paris, where he successfully cemented the alliance with France. Back in Philadelphia in 1785, Franklin was elected president of the Pennsylvania Assembly and was then chosen as a delegate to the Constitutional Convention in 1787. In 1790 he died in Philadelphia.

Alfred O. Aldridge, *Benjamin Franklin,*

Philosopher and Man. Philadelphia: Lippincott, 1965.

James R. Andrews, "The Rhetoric of a Lobbyist: Benjamin Franklin in England, 1765–1775." *Central States Speech Journal* 18 (1967): 261–267.

Paul W. Conner, *Poor Richard's Politicks: Benjamin Franklin and His New American Order*. New York: Oxford UP, 1965.

Thomas J. Fleming, *The Man Who Dared the Lightning: A New Look at Benjamin Franklin*. New York: Morrow, 1971.

David F. Hawke, *Franklin*. New York: Harper and Row, 1976.

Sandra Lewis, "Franklin's Advice to Speakers." *Communication Quarterly* 7 (1959): 18–21.

Lester C. Olson, "Benjamin Franklin's Pictorial Representations of the British Colonies in America: A Study in Rhetorical Iconology." *Quarterly Journal of Speech* 73 (1987): 18–42.

Gerald Stourzh, *Benjamin Franklin and American Foreign Policy*. Chicago: U of Chicago Press, 1969.

HENRY GEORGE was born in Philadelphia in 1839. He became a printer, and then editor of the San Francisco *Times* in 1867. As a journalist, George developed a serious interest in economic questions, writing *Our Land and Land Policy* in 1871 and *Progress and Poverty* in 1879. In these works, George proposed a policy of land value tax, or the single tax, as it was known, and argued that the wages a laborer earns come, in reality, from the value created by the laborer him or herself and not from a fund of capital. His work first gained attention in England and later became popular in the United States. From 1880 onward, George lived in New York and devoted his energy to promoting the land tax idea through lecturing and writing. His lecture tours frequently took him across America, as well as to England and Ireland. With the nomination of the United Labor Party, George ran unsuccessfully for mayor of New York in 1886; he was again a candidate for mayor in 1897, but he died before the election.

Charles A. Barker, *Henry George*. Westport, CT: Greenwood Press, 1974. Originally published, 1955.

Steven B. Cord, *Henry George: Dreamer or Realist?* Philadelphia: U of Pennsylvania Press, 1965.

Anna A. G. DeMille, *Henry George, Citizen of the World*. Chapel Hill, NC: U of North Carolina Press, 1950.

George R. Geiger, *The Philosophy of Henry George*. New York: Macmillan, 1933.

B. Peebles-Lawson, "Henry George the Prophet." *Journal of American Studies* 10 (1976): 37–51.

Charles W. Lomas, "Kearney and George: The Demagogue and the Prophet." *Communication Monographs* 28 (1961): 50–59.

Edward J. Rose, *Henry George*. New York: Twayne Publishers, 1968.

HENRY W. GRADY was born in 1850 in Athens, Georgia, where he eventually attended the University of Georgia. After a year in law school at the University of Virginia, Grady became the editor of the Rome, Georgia, *Courier* in 1870. He tried his hand at being both publisher and editor of another Rome paper, the *Daily Commercial*. This paper, however, was not successful and Grady moved to Atlanta to join others in founding the *Herald*, which also failed. For a little over a year, in 1876–1877, Grady worked for the New

York *Herald* as its Georgia correspondent. Then, in 1879, he bought an interest in the Atlanta *Constitution* and remained with that paper until his death. Grady became a popular public speaker who presented the views of the more progressive Southerners to Northern audiences.

Harold Barrett, "The Lamp of Henry Grady." *Communication Quarterly* 11 (1963): 19–21.

J. Louis Campbell, "In Search of the New South." *Southern Speech Communication Journal* 47 (1982): 361–388.

Charles F. Lindsley, "Henry Woodfin Grady, Orator." *Quarterly Journal of Speech* 6 (1920): 27–42.

David L. Matheny, "The New South: Grady's Use of Hegelian Dialectic." *Southern Speech Communication Journal* 31 (1965): 34–41.

Raymond B. Nixon, *Henry W. Grady, Spokesman for the New South*. New York: Russell and Russell, 1969. Originally published, 1943.

ANDREW HAMILTON was born in England in 1676 and emigrated to Virginia in 1700. He later returned to London, where he was admitted to the bar. He then settled in Philadelphia, and not long after that he became attorney general of Pennsylvania. From 1727 to 1739 Hamilton sat in the Pennsylvania Assembly representing Bucks County. During most of his years in the Assembly, Hamilton served as its speaker. In 1732 he designed Province House in Philadelphia, a historic building that is now known as Independence Hall. Hamilton was a distinguished and highly respected lawyer in his day; his most historically important case was his defense of Peter Zenger when the New York printer was tried for seditious libel in 1735. Hamilton died in 1741 in Philadelphia.

Joshua F. Fisher, "Andrew Hamilton, Esq., of Pennsylvania." *Pennsylvania Magazine of History and Biography* 16 (1892): 1–27.

Burton A. Konkle, *The Life of Andrew Hamilton, 1676–1741*. Freeport, NY: Books for Libraries Press, 1972. Originally published, 1941.

Foster C. Nix, "Andrew Hamilton's Early Years in the American Colonies." *William and Mary Quarterly* 21 (1964): 390–407.

Bernard C. Steiner, "Andrew Hamilton and John Peter Zenger." *Pennsylvania Magazine of History and Biography* 20 (1896): 405–408.

Henry Weinberger, *The Liberty of the Press*. Berkeley Heights, NJ: The Oriole Press, 1934.

JOHN HANCOCK was born in Braintree, Massachusetts, in 1737. He graduated from Harvard and went into business with an uncle from whom he subsequently inherited a large fortune. Between 1766 and 1772 he served several terms in the colonial assembly (the Massachusetts General Court), where he was a close associate of Samuel Adams. Active in the patriot party, Hancock was serving as president of the Provincial Congress in 1775 when British troops marched to Concord to seize the colonial stores and also to arrest Hancock and Adams. In that same year Hancock was elected president of the continental congress and was the first signer of the Declaration of Independence. He remained in Congress until 1780, and during that time he also held the rank of major general and led Massachusetts forces in action in Rhode Island. Hancock was a member of the Massachusetts Constitutional Convention of 1780 and was elected the first governor under that constitution. With the exception of the time he spent as a member of Congress (1785–1786), Hancock was reelected governor of Massachusetts each year until his death in 1793.

Herbert S. Allan, *John Hancock, Patriot in Purple.* New York: Macmillan, 1948.

William M. Fowler, *The Baron of Beacon Hill: A Biography of John Hancock.* Boston: Houghton Mifflin, 1980.

D. J. Proctor, "John Hancock: New Soundings on an Old Barrel." *Journal of American History* 64 (1977) 652–677.

Kenneth B. Umbreit, *Founding Fathers: Men Who Shaped Our Tradition.* New York: Kennikat Press, 1969. Originally published, 1941.

Frederick Wagner, *Patriot's Choice: The Story of John Hancock.* New York: Dodd Mead, 1964.

Michael Weatherly, "Propaganda and the Rhetoric of the American Revolution." *Southern Speech Communication Journal* 36 (1971): 352–363.

PATRICK HENRY was born in Hanover County, Virginia, in 1736. After a series of unsuccessful business ventures, the 24-year-old Henry read law by himself and managed to pass the examinations necessary to be admitted to the bar. A popular country lawyer, Henry achieved fame in a famous case, the Parsons Cause, wherein he argued that the King, in disallowing a popular law passed by the Virginia Assembly, had acted unjustly; Henry went on to censure British actions that undermined colonial rights. This radical doctrine was highly acceptable in western Virginia, and in 1765 Henry was elected to the General Assembly. He arrived in time to propose a set of resolutions condemning the Stamp Act; while the more radical provisions were not ultimately passed, the Virginia Resolves were widely distributed throughout the colonies and Henry acquired a substantial reputation. Henry soon became allied with the patriots in the Virginia House of Burgesses and was sent as a delegate to the First Continental Congress in 1774. He returned to Virginia to urge the arming of the Virginia militia, in a speech given in 1775 and known for the line, "Give me liberty or give me death." Henry was elected governor of the newly formed Commonwealth of Virginia in 1776 and served until 1779. He was chosen governor again from 1784 to 1786 and sat in the legislature from 1786 to 1790. An outspoken opponent of the new federal Constitution, Henry led the unsuccessful fight against ratification in Virginia. He practiced law after leaving the legislature and retired in 1794. Washington coaxed him out of retirement to run for the legislature in 1799. He was elected but died before he could take his seat.

Richard R. Beeman, *Patrick Henry: A Biography.* New York: McGraw-Hill, 1974.

Lois J. Einhorn, "Basic Assumptions in the Virginia Ratification Debates: Patrick Henry vs. James Madison on the Nature of Man and Reason." *Southern Speech Communication Journal* 46 (1981): 327–340.

Mabel Frantz, *The Voice: Patrick Henry of Virginia.* Philadelphia: Dorrance, 1954.

Judy Hample, "The Textual and Cultural Authenticity of Patrick Henry's 'Liberty or Death' Speech." *Quarterly Journal of Speech* 63 (1977): 298–310.

David A. McCants, "The Role of Patrick Henry in the Stamp Act Debates." *Southern Speech Communication Journal* 46 (1981): 205–227.

Michael Weatherly, "Propaganda and the Rhetoric of the American Revolution." *Southern Speech Communication Journal* 36 (1971): 352–363.

George F. Willison, *Patrick Henry and His World*. Garden City, NY: Doubleday, 1969.

THOMAS JEFFERSON was born in Virginia in 1743. A diligent and bright student of law, Jefferson was admitted to the bar in 1767 and two years later was elected to the House of Burgesses, where he quickly became identified with the patriot cause. He was sent as a delegate from Virginia to the First Continental Congress in 1774, and it was Jefferson who prepared the draft of the Declaration of Independence. Jefferson played a prominent role in the writing of the Virginia constitution, and he followed Patrick Henry as governor of the state from 1779 to 1781. Sent to France to serve with Benjamin Franklin and John Adams as plenipotentiaries to negotiate the peace treaty with Great Britain, Jefferson stayed on as American ambassador to France when Franklin returned to the United States in 1785. President Washington appointed Jefferson as the first secretary of state in 1789. He resigned from the cabinet in 1794; in 1796 he was defeated for the presidency by John Adams. In accordance with constitutional practice at that time, he became vice-president. In 1800 he defeated Adams and was inaugurated as the third President of the United States in 1801; he was reelected in 1804. During his presidency the Louisiana Territory was purchased, adding a vast expanse of land to the new United States. After his retirement, Jefferson continued his many scientific and intellectual pursuits and helped to found the University of Virginia. He died on July 4, 1826.

Lance Banning, "Jeffersonian Ideology Revisited: Liberal and Classical Ideas in the New American Republic." *William and Mary Quarterly* 43 (1986): 3–34.

Noble E. Cunningham, Jr., *In Pursuit of Reason: The Life of Thomas Jefferson*. Baton Rouge: LSU Press, 1987.

Eleanor Davidsen and E. C. McClintock, Jr. "Thomas Jefferson and Rhetoric." *Quarterly Journal of Speech* 33 (1947): 1–8.

Thomas J. Fleming, *The Man from Monticello: An Intimate Life of Thomas Jefferson*. New York: Morrow, 1969.

Henry F. Graff, *Thomas Jefferson*. Morristown, NJ: Silver Burdett, 1968.

Dumas Malone, *Jefferson and His Time*. Boston: Little, Brown, 1951–1968.

Dumas Malone, *Thomas Jefferson as Political Leader*. Berkeley: U of California Press, 1963.

Forrest McDonald, *The Presidency of Thomas Jefferson*. Lawrence: UP of Kansas, 1976.

John C. Miller, *The Wolf by the Ears: Thomas Jefferson and Slavery*. New York Free Press, 1977.

Merrill D. Peterson, *Thomas Jefferson and the New Nation: A Biography*. New York: Oxford UP, 1970.

JOHN L. LEWIS was born in Iowa in 1880. The son of a Welsh immigrant coal miner, Lewis held various jobs as a young man, but his principal occupation was that of a miner. He began his career as a union official in 1909 as a legislative representative of the United Mine Workers, and by 1920 he was president of that union. Lewis believed that unions should be organized according to industry rather than crafts. He was the first president of the Committee for Industrial Organization (CIO) in 1935 and continued to lead that organization after it was expelled from the American Federation of Labor (AF of L) in 1936. He was highly successful in organizing the automobile and the steel industries. Lewis at first supported Franklin Roosevelt but opposed his reelection in 1940. Two years later Lewis quarreled with the new CIO president, took the United Mine Workers out of the CIO, and was successful in getting the UMW readmitted to the AF of L. Lewis's leadership of the mine workers was marked by frequent and bitter strikes, but the lot of the miners was significantly improved, and miners were fiercely loyal to him. Lewis disaffiliated from the AF of L in 1947, and the UMW remained an independent union even after the AFL and CIO were merged in 1955. Lewis retired as UMW president in 1960 and died in 1969.

Saul D. Alinsky, *John L. Lewis*. New York: Putnam, 1949.

Melvyn Dubofsky and Warren Van Tine, *John L. Lewis: A Biography*. New York: Quadrangle/New York Times Books, 1977.

Mary B. Gallagher, "John L. Lewis: The Oratory of Pity and Indignation." *Communication Quarterly* 9 (1961): 15–16.

J. Hutchinson, "John L. Lewis: To the Presidency of the UMWA." *Labor History* 19 (1978): 185–203.

Richard M. Rothman, "On the Speaking of John L. Lewis." *Central States Speech Journal* 14 (1963): 177–185.

ABRAHAM LINCOLN was born in Kentucky in 1809. His family settled in southern Indiana in 1816, and there young Lincoln worked on his father's farm and, for a short time, on a flatboat on the nearby Ohio River. In 1830, when the Lincolns moved to New Salem, Illinois, Abraham worked as a clerk in a store and then opened his own store, which failed. He volunteered for the militia in the Black Hawk War, ran unsuccessfully for the legislature, and educated himself by reading as widely as he could. He also studied law and obtained his license in 1836. Lincoln began his political career as a Whig admirer of Henry Clay. From 1834 until 1842 he served in the Illinois legislature and was elected for one term, 1846–1848, in the United States House of Representatives. He gradually became a very successful lawyer and devoted much of his time and energy to riding the judicial circuit in Illinois. Lincoln's opposition to the Kansas-Nebraska Act led to his election to the legislature in 1854; he soon became a recognized leader of the new Republican Party. As the Republican nominee for the Senate in 1858, he traveled throughout the state debating the author of the Kansas-Nebraska Act and leading proponent of popular sovereignty, Stephen A. Douglas. Even though Lincoln lost the election, the debates established him as a major force in the Republican Party, and he became its presidential nominee in 1860. Following Lincoln's election as the sixteenth President of the United States, the Southern states began to secede. When the Confederates fired on Fort Sumter in Charleston harbor in April 1861, Lincoln called up the militia, ordered the enlistment of additional soldiers for the regular army, and proclaimed a blockade of the southern ports. Lincoln was reelected in 1864 after leading the country through four bitter and difficult years of war. He favored a plan of reconciliation between the sections, but just over a month after his second inauguration, on Good Friday, April 14, 1865, he was shot while attending a play at Ford's Theatre and died the next day.

Roy P. Baler, *Lincoln*. Gloucester, MA: Peter Smith, 1963.

Mildred F. Berry, "Lincoln—The Speaker (Part I)." *Quarterly Journal of Speech* 17 (1931): 25–40.

Mildred F. Berry, "Lincoln—The Speaker (Part II)." *Quarterly Journal of Speech* 17 (1931): 177–190.

W. A. Dahlberg, "Lincoln, The Wit." *Quarterly Journal of Speech* 31 (1945): 424–427.

Lee Devin, "Lincoln's Ethos: Viewed and Practiced." *Central States Speech Journal* 16 (1965): 99–105.

Don E. Fehrenbacher, *The Leadership of Abraham Lincoln*. New York. Wiley, 1970.

Don E. Fehrenbacher, *Prelude to Greatness: Lincoln in the 1850s*. New York: McGraw-Hill, 1964.

Don E. Fehrenbacher, *Lincoln in Text and Context*. Stanford, CA: Stanford UP, 1987.

Robert G. Gunderson, "Lincoln and the Policy of Eloquent Silence: November 1860 to March 1861." *Quarterly Journal of Speech* 47 (1961): 1–9.

Robert L. Kincaid, "Abraham Lincoln: The Speaker." *Central States Speech Journal* 16 (1951): 241–250.

Michael C. Leff and G. P. Mohrmann, "Lincoln at Cooper Union: A Rhetorical Analysis of the Text." *Quarterly Journal of Speech* 60 (1974): 346–358.

Wil A. Linkugel, "Lincoln, Kansas, and Cooper Union." *Communication Monographs* 37 (1970): 172–179.

Marie Hochmuth Nichols, "Lincoln's First Inaugural." In *American Speeches*, Wayland M. Parrish and Marie Hochmuth Nichols, eds. London: Longman, Green, 1954.

Stephen B. Oates, *With Malice Toward None: The Life of Abraham Lincoln*. New York: Harper and Row, 1977.

James G. Randall, *Mr. Lincoln*. New York: Dodd Mead, 1957.

Carl Sandburg, *Abraham Lincoln: The Prairie Years and the War Years*. New York: Dell, 1925–1954.

Charles J. Stewart, "The Pulpit and the Assassination of Lincoln." *Quarterly Journal of Speech* 50 (1964): 299–307.

Benjamin Thomas, *Abraham Lincoln*. New York: Knopf, 1952.

David Zarefsky, "The Lincoln-Douglas Debates Revisited: The Evolution of Public Argument." *Quarterly Journal of Speech* 72 (1986): 162–224.

CHARLES A. LINDBERGH was born in Detroit in 1902. After studying mechanical engineering at the University of Wisconsin for two years, Lindbergh enrolled in a flying school in Lincoln, Nebraska. He joined the United States Air Reserve and graduated as a second lieutenant in 1925. The next year he flew from Chicago to St. Louis as an airmail pilot. On May 20, 1927, he left Roosevelt Field in Long Island and flew nonstop to Le Bourget Airport near Paris in thirty-three and one half hours. This first nonstop flight across the Atlantic won him instant international fame. President Coolidge presented him with the Congressional Medal of Honor and he was feted at parades and celebrations across the country. After Lindbergh's infant son was kidnapped and murdered in 1932, Lindbergh and his wife, Anne Morrow Lindbergh, lived in France. In the late 1930's Lindbergh studied aircraft production in various European countries and reported his findings to the United States army. He returned to the United States in 1939 and became an outspoken isolationist, arguing against American involvement in the Second World War.

Wayne S. Cole, *Charles A. Lindbergh and the Battle Against American Intervention in World War II*. New York: Harcourt, Brace, Jovanovich, 1974.

Brendan Gill, *Lindbergh Alone*. New York: Harcourt, Brace, Jovanovich, 1977.

Charles A. Lindbergh, *The Wartime Journals of Charles A. Lindbergh*. New York: Harcourt, Brace, Jovanovich, 1970.

Charles A. Lindbergh, *Autobiography of Values*. New York: Harcourt, Brace, Jovanovich, 1978.

Leonard Mosley, *Lindbergh: A Biography*. Garden City, NY: Doubleday, 1976.

Walter S. Ross, *The Last Hero: Charles A. Lindbergh*. New York: Harper and Row, 1976.

HUEY P. LONG was born in Winnfield, Louisiana, in 1893. Long grew up on a poor Louisiana farm, had a public school education, and spent less than a year at the University of Oklahoma. He studied law at Tulane and was admitted to the bar in 1915. A spellbinding orator, Long entered politics. He was defeated for governor of Louisiana in 1924 but won the post four years later. Once chosen governor, Long built one of the most powerful and long-lived political machines in the country, installing his supporters in all important government posts and maintaining a strong popular following. He was elected to the United States Senate in 1930 but didn't take his seat until his hand-picked successor was sworn in as Louisiana's governor. His flamboyant characteristics—in dress, in speaking, in personal style—gained him national attention. His "Share Our Welath" scheme provided him with a springboard from which he was catapulted into political prominence. Long sought to maintain his grip on Louisiana politics and was attending a special session of the state legislature when he was shot in the rotunda of the state capitol building. He died in Baton Rouge two days later, on September 10, 1935.

Elton Abernathy, "Huey Long: Oratorical 'Wealth Sharing.'" *Southern Speech Communication Journal* 21 (1955): 87–102.

Ernest G. Bormann, "Huey Long: Analysis of a Demagogue." *Communication Quarterly* 2 (1954): 16–19.

Ernest G. Bormann, "A Rhetorical Analysis of the National Radio Broadcasts of Senator Huey Pierce Long." *Communication Monographs* 24 (1957): 244–257.

Henry C. Dethloff, ed., *Huey P. Long: Southern Demagogue or American Democrat?* Boston: Heath, 1967.

Hugh D. Graham, ed., *Huey Long*. Englewood Cliffs, NJ: Prentice-Hall, 1970.

T. Harry Williams, *Huey Long*. New York: Knopf, 1969.

JAMES MADISON was born in Virginia in 1751. He was educated at the College of New Jersey (now Princeton University) and in 1774 was elected to the Orange County Revolutionary Committee. Two years later he was a member of the Virginia Convention that urged the Continental Congress to declare independence. In 1779 he was the youngest member of the Continental Congress. Concerned about the weak state of the federal government, he attended the Annapolis Convention in 1786 and played a prominent part as a delegate to the Constitutional Convention in 1787; Madison's notes on the Convention proceedings have provided us with most of what is known about the framing of the Constitution. Madison joined with Alexander Hamilton and John Jay in writing the *Federalist Papers* in support of the new Constitution and led the battle in Virginia for ratification. Beginning in 1789 Madison served for eight years in the House of Representatives. In 1801 President Jefferson appointed Madison secretary of state, and, with Jefferson's support, Madison was elected President in 1808. War between England and France meant serious disruption in American trade, and the United States was on the brink of war with first one and then the other of these powers. When the British failed to repeal Orders-in-Council that banned American trade with France, war was declared against Britain in June 1812. Madison was reelected President in that year, but he soon suffered the indignity of fleeing from his capital when British troops attacked Washington, D.C. The war ended in 1814, and Madison retired from public life at the conclusion of his second term in 1817. In retirement he served as co-chairman of the Virginia Constitutional Convention of 1829–1830, supported the Monroe Doctrine, and argued for the supremacy of the federal judiciary and against the doctrine of nullification. He died at his Virginia estate, Montpelier, in 1836.

Edward M. Burns, *James Madison: Philosopher of the Constitution*. New York: Octagon Books, 1968.

Frank R. Donovan, *Mr. Madison's Constitution: The Story Behind the Constitutional Convention*. New York: Dodd Mead, 1965.

Lois J. Einhorn, "Basic Assumptions in the Virginia Ratification Debates: Patrick Henry vs. James Madison on the Nature of Man and Reason." *Southern Speech Communication Journal* 46 (1981): 327–340.

Robert L. Ivie, "Presidential Motives for War." *Quarterly Journal of Speech* 60 (1974): 337–345.

Ralph L. Ketcham, *James Madison: A Biography*. New York: Macmillan, 1971.

Ralph L. Ketcham, "James Madison: The Unimperial President." *Virginia Quarterly Review* 54 (1978): 116–136.

Wilbur E. Moore, "James Madison, the Speaker." *Quarterly Journal of Speech* 31 (1945): 155–162.

Neal Riemer, *James Madison*. New York: Washington Square Press, 1968.

JAMES OTIS was born in Massachusetts in 1725, graduated from Harvard, and practiced law in Boston. He resigned as King's Advocate General of the Vice-Admiralty Court in 1761 in order to argue against the Writs of Assistance. Otis was active in the Patriot Party as a member of the Massachusetts legislature and wrote a series of pamphlets arguing the colonial position against Great Britain: *A Vindication of the Conduct of the House of Representatives of the Province of Massachusetts Bay* in 1762, *The Rights of the British Colonists Asserted and Proved* in 1764, and *Considerations on Behalf of the Colonies* in 1765. Otis went to New York in 1765 as a delegate to the Stamp Act Congress and continued to serve in the Massachusetts legislature. Always an impetuous and somewhat unstable person, Otis became increasingly unbalanced and unpredictable in his behavior, although he continued as a member of the Massachusetts legislature until 1771. He wandered onto the battlefield and into the line of fire during the battle of Bunker Hill, but escaped unhurt. Out of touch with reality, Otis spent his last years on a farm in Andover, Massachusetts, where he was struck by lightning and killed in 1783.

Jerald L. Banninga, "James Otis on the Writs of Assistance: A Textual Investigation." *Communication Monographs* 27 (1960): 351–352.

Ellen E. Brennan, "James Otis: Recreant and Patriot." *New England Quarterly* 12 (1939): 691–725.

J. R. Ferguson, "Reason in Madness: The Political Thought of James Otis." *William and Mary Quarterly* 36 (1979): 194–214.

John R. Galvin, *Three Men of Boston*. New York: Crowell, 1976.

John C. Ridpath, *James Otis, the Prerevolutionist*. Milwaukee: H. G. Campbell Publishing, 1898.

WENDELL PHILLIPS was born in Boston in 1811. He graduated from Harvard, studied at Harvard Law School, and began his practice in Boston in 1834. Phillips soon became an abolitionist in association with William Lloyd Garrison and gained attention following his 1837 speech in Faneuil Hall condemning the murder of Elijah Lovejoy. Phillips quickly became one of the most notable, if usually controversial, orators of his era. He argued that the abolition of slavery was more important than the preservation of the union and initially urged that the Southern states be allowed to secede. He did not think highly of Lincoln and disagreed with Garrison, who supported the President's reelection in 1864. Phillips also differed with Garrison when the great abolitionist leader urged that the Abolitionist Society be disbanded after the Civil War. Phillips continued to work for the rights of blacks and black education as well as to champion such reforms as woman suffrage, prison reform, and temperance. Phillips, in addition to speaking on behalf of social reform, was also a popular and highly regarded lecturer on a variety of topics. He died in Boston in 1884.

Raymond H. Barnard, "An Objective Study of the Speeches of Wendell Phillips." *Quarterly Journal of Speech* 18 (1932): 571–584.

Raymond H. Barnard, "Wendell Phillips' Adaptability as a Speaker." *Western Journal of Speech Communication* 5 (1941): 6–10.

Irving H. Bartlett, *Wendell Phillips, Brahmin Radical*. Boston: Beacon Press, 1961.

Ralph Korngold, *Two Friends of Man: William Lloyd Garrison and Wendell Phillips*. Boston: Little, Brown, 1950.

Robert D. Marcus, "Wendell Phillips and American Institutions." *Journal of American History* 56 (1969): 41–58.

Oscar Sherwin, *Prophet of Liberty: The Life and Times of Wendell Phillips*. New York: Bookman Associates, 1958.

RED JACKET, whose Indian name was **SAGOYEWATHA,** was born in northern New York about 1758. As chief of the Seneca, he led them against the colonists and in support of the British during the Revolutionary War. It was at this time that a British officer gave him the red army tunic from which his English name was taken. Red Jacket finally made peace with the new United States. In 1792 he visited George Washington and received a silver medal from the President. When war with Great Britain broke out in 1812, Red Jacket supported the United States, but his relations with the American government were not entirely cordial; Red Jacket was strenuously opposed to efforts to Christianize the Indians and to introduce the white culture among the Senecas. He was deposed by his own people but became chief again before his death in 1830.

John L. Hubbard, *An Account of Sagoyewatha: Or, Red Jacket and His People, 1750–1830*. New York: B. Franklin, 1971. Originally published, 1886.

Arthur C. Parker, *Red Jacket, Last of the Seneca*. New York; McGraw-Hill, 1952.

William L. Stone, *The Life and Times of Red Jacket, or Sagoyewatha*. St. Clair Shores, MI: Scholarly Press, 1970. Originally published, 1841.

Benjamin B. Thatcher, *Indian Biography*. Glorieta, NM: Rio Grande Press, 1973. Originally published, 1832.

Norman B. Wood, *Lives of Famous Indian Chiefs*. Aurora, IL: American Indian Historical Publishing Co., 1906.

FRANKLIN DELANO ROOSEVELT was born in Hyde Park, New York, in 1882, the son of a wealthy old New York family. After graduating from Harvard and being admitted to the bar in 1907, Roosevelt entered New York politics as a Democrat. He was a state senator from 1910 until 1913, when he was appointed assistant secretary of the navy in the Wilson administration. He served in this post until 1920, when Wilson left office and Roosevelt was selected as the Democratic candidate for vice-president of the United States. He was defeated in the election. Roosevelt was stricken with polio the next year and it appeared that his political career was over. In 1928, however, he was nominated for the governorship of New York and appeared at the Democratic national convention to give the nominating speech for the convention's subsequent choice for President, Governor Alfred E. Smith of New York, whom FDR called, "the happy warrior." Smith was defeated, but Roosevelt was elected to the governorship. Four years later Roosevelt was nominated for President and easily defeated incumbent Republican Herbert Hoover. Roosevelt launched his "New Deal" to combat the great Depression and was reelected by a landslide in 1936. The first President to seek a third term, Roosevelt beat off a serious challenge from Wendell Wilkie in 1940. FDR was sympathetic to the allied cause in World War II but was unable to bring America into the war until after the Japanese surprise attack on Pearl Harbor on December 7, 1941. Roosevelt was elected for a fourth term in 1944, as the war was nearing its end. He died in 1945, however, just a few weeks before Germany surrendered.

Thomas W. Benson, "Inaugurating Peace: Franklin D. Roosevelt's Last Speech." *Communication Monographs* 36 (1969): 138–147.

Waldo W. Braden and Earnest Bradenburg, "Roosevelt's Fireside Chats." *Communication Monographs* 22 (1955): 290–302.

Earnest Bradenburg, "The Preparation of Franklin D. Roosevelt's Speeches." *Quarterly Journal of Speech* 35 (1949): 214–221.

James M. Burns, *Roosevelt: The Lion and the Fox*. New York: Harcourt, 1963.

James M. Burns, *Roosevelt: The Soldier of Freedom*. New York: Harcourt, 1973.

Laura Crowell, "Franklin D. Roosevelt's Audience Persuasion in the 1936 Campaign." *Communication Monographs* 17 (1950): 48–64.

Kenneth Davis, *FDR: The Beckoning of Destiny, 1882–1928*. New York: Putnam, 1972.

Jack G. Gravlee, "Franklin D. Roosevelt's Speech Preparation During His First National Campaign." *Communication Monographs* 31 (1964): 437–460.

Robert D. King, "Franklin D. Roosevelt's Second Inaugural Address." *Quarterly Journal of Speech* 23 (1937): 439–444.

Joseph P. Lash, *Roosevelt and Churchill, 1939–1941*. Franklin Center, PA: Franklin Library, 1976.

Robert T. Oliver, "The Speech that Established Roosevelt's Reputation." *Quarterly Journal of Speech* 31 (1945): 274–282.

Frances Perkins, *The Roosevelt I Knew*. Gloucester, MA: P. Smith, 1965.

James E. Pollard, "Franklin D. Roosevelt and the Press." *Journalism Quarterly* 22 (1945): 197–206.

Samuel I. Rosenman, *Working with Roosevelt*. New York: Da Capo Press, 1972.

Halford Ryan Ross, "Roosevelt's First Inaugural: A Study of Technique." *Quarterly Journal of Speech* 65 (1979): 137–149.

Halford Ryan Ross, "Roosevelt's Fourth Inaugural Address: A Study of Its Composition." *Quarterly Journal of Speech* 67 (1981): 157–166.

Joseph Schiffman, "Observations on Roosevelt's Literary Style." *Quarterly Journal of Speech* 35 (1949): 222–226.

Richard W. Steele, "The Great Debate: Roosevelt, the Media, and the Coming of the War, 1940–1941." *Journal of American History* 71 (1984): 69–92.

Hermann G. Stelzner, " 'War Message,' December 8, 1941: An Approach to Language." *Communication Monographs* 33 (1966): 419–437.

Rexford G. Tugwell, *In Search of Roosevelt*. Cambridge, MA: Harvard UP, 1972.

THEODORE ROOSEVELT was born in New York in 1858. Having poor vision and being not very strong as a child, Roosevelt sought to improve his physical condition and throughout his life was given to vigorous outdoor activities, from managing a ranch in the west, to big game hunting in Africa, to exploring in the Brazilian wilds. He began his political career as a Republican member of the New York legislature. From 1895 to 1897 he served as police commissioner in New York City. From New York, TR went to Washington to serve as assistant secretary of the navy in the McKinley administration, and he was in that post when the Spanish-American War broke out in 1898. Roosevelt became famous for his exploits in Cuba with the "Roughriders," and he returned from the war to be elected governor of New York. Elected as vice-president with McKinley in 1900, Roosevelt became President when McKinley was assassinated the next year; TR was elected in his own right in 1904. Known as a "trust-buster" and a proponent of a strong navy, TR was a popular President. He ended his term in 1908 and was succeeded by William Howard Taft. Roosevelt became dissatisfied with Taft, however, and broke from the Republican Party—which had nominated Taft for reelection—to form his own Progressive Party in 1912. Woodrow Wilson was elected that year and TR set off for an exploring trip to Brazil. He returned to support American preparedness prior to our entry into World War I. He was generally critical of Wilson and joined with other Republicans in opposing the treaty that would have established the League of Nations. Roosevelt died in 1919.

William A. Behl, "Theodore Roosevelt's Principles of Invention." *Communication Monographs* 14 (1947): 93–110.

William A. Behl, "Theodore Roosevelt's Principles of Speech Preparation and Delivery." *Communication Monographs* 12 (1945): 112–122.

John M. Blum, *The Republican Roosevelt*. Cambridge, MA: Harvard UP, 1954.

David H. Burton, *Theodore Roosevelt: Confident Imperialist*. Philadelphia: U of Pennsylvania Press, 1969.

G. Wallace Chessman, *Theodore Roosevelt and the Politics of Power*. Boston: Little Brown, 1969.

Willard B. Gatewood, *Theodore Roosevelt and the Art of Controversy*. Baton Rouge: Louisiana State UP, 1970.

William H. Harbaugh, *Power and Responsibility: The Life and Times of Theodore Roosevelt*. New York: Farrar, Straus, and Cudahy, 1961.

Stefan Lorant, The Life and Times of Theodore Roosevelt. Garden City, NY: Doubleday, 1959.

Stephen E. Lucas, "The Man with the Muck Rake: A Reinterpretation." *Quarterly Journal of Speech* 59 (1973): 452–462.

Henry F. Pringle, *Theodore Roosevelt: A Biography*. New York: Harcourt, Brace, 1956.

Vito N. Silvestri, "Theodore Roosevelt's Preparedness Oratory: The Minority Voice of an Ex-President." *Central States Speech Journal* 20 (1969): 178–186.

Harold Zyskind, "A Case Study in Philosophic Rhetoric: Theodore Roosevelt." *Philosophy and Rhetoric* (1968): 228–254.

JOHN RUTLEDGE was born in Charleston, South Carolina, in 1739. He studied law in England, was called to the bar in 1760, and returned to Charleston to practice. Although a supporter of the Patriot Party and the brother of Edward Rutledge, who signed the Declaration of Independence, John Rutledge was of an aristocratic family and never supported the idea of democracy. He was elected governor of South Carolina in 1779 but had to flee to North Carolina to avoid capture by the British. After the Revolutionary War, Rutledge served a term in Congress and then, from 1784 to 1790, was a member of the state legislature. He attended the Constitutional Convention in 1787 and generally expressed the views of conservatives. He became an associate justice of the supreme court in 1790 and chief justice of South Carolina the following year. He was nominated to be chief justice of the United States in 1795, but the Senate did not confirm the appointment. Rutledge died in 1800.

Richard H. Barry, *Mr. Rutledge of South Carolina*. New York: Duell, Sloan and Pearce, 1942.

Henry Flanders, *The Lives and Times of the Chief Justices of the Supreme Court of the United States*. Philadelphia: Lippincott, Grambo, and Co., 1855–1858.

K. R. Middleton, "Partisan Press and the Rejection of a Chief Justice." *Journalism Quarterly* 53 (1976): 106–110.

Michael Weatherly, "Propaganda and the Rhetoric of the American Revolution." *Southern Speech Communication Journal* 36 (1971): 352–363.

MARGARET SANGER was born in Corning, New York, in 1879 and became a public health nurse in New York City. Her experiences as a midwife and nurse among poor immigrants convinced her that women needed information on birth control. She traveled in Europe, learning about birth control techniques there, and returned to the United States to publish *The Woman Rebel*. In 1916 she opened the first birth control clinic in America and in 1921 founded the American Birth Control League. A tireless lecturer, writer, and organizer, Sanger promoted the cause of women's rights generally and their right to determine their maternity, specifically. Her efforts brought her arrest several times, but she refused to be intimidated and carried on her efforts worldwide. She died in 1966.

Emily Douglas, *Margaret Sanger: Pioneer of the Future*. New York: Holt, Rinehart and Winston, 1969.

Madeline Gray, *Margaret Sanger: A Biography of the Champion of Birth Control*. New York: R. Marek, 1979.

David M. Kennedy, *Birth Control in America: The Career of Margaret Sanger*. New Haven, CT: Yale UP, 1970.

Lawrence Lader, *The Margaret Sanger Story and the Fight for Birth Control*. Garden City, NY: Doubleday, 1955.

Margaret Sanger, *Margaret Sanger: An Autobiography*. New York: Maxwell Reprints, 1970. Originally published, 1938.

ELIZABETH CADY STANTON was born in Johnstown, New York, in 1815 and graduated from Troy Female Seminary in 1832. An active abolitionist, Stanton attended an antislavery convention in London, where women were excluded from participating in the conference. She and another delegate, Lucretia Mott, returned to America to plan for a Women's Rights Convention, which was held in Seneca Falls, New York, in 1848. Working with Susan B. Anthony, Stanton helped found the New York Temperance Society and, in 1869, the National Woman Suffrage Association, which attempted to gain the vote for women through a constitutional amendment. As a Lyceum lecturer she traveled throughout the country speaking on behalf of women's rights. As a writer she, with Anthony, produced the *History of Woman Suffrage*. She served as president of the National American Women Suffrage Association from 1890 to 1892 and published her autobiography, *Eighty*

Years and More, in 1898. She died in New York in 1902.

Lois W. Brunner, *Elizabeth Cady Stanton: A Radical for Women's Rights*. Boston: Little, Brown, 1980.

Karlyn Khors Campbell, "Stanton's 'The Solitude of Self': A Rationale for Feminism," *Quarterly Journal of Speech* 66 (1980): 304–312.

Elizabeth Griffith, *In Her Own Right: The Life of Elizabeth Cady Stanton*. New York: Oxford UP, 1984.

Elizabeth Cady Stanton, *Eighty Years and More: Reminiscences, 1815–1897*. New York: Schocken Books, 1971. Originally published, 1898.

Winifred E. Wise, *Rebel in Petticoats: The Life of Elizabeth Cady Stanton*. Philadelphia: Chilton, 1960.

LUCY STONE was born in Brookfield, Massachusetts, in 1818. In 1847 she became the first woman from Massachusetts to receive a college degree when she graduated from Oberlin College. In 1850 she organized a Women's Rights Convention in Worcester, and from then until the end of her life she devoted herself to the cause of women's rights as a lecturer, writer, and organizational leader. Stone's belief that suffrage should be gained through state laws and not by constitutional amendment precipitated a break with Stanton and Anthony. Stone's group, founded by her in 1869, became the American Woman's Suffrage Association. In 1872 Stone started the *Woman's Journal*, and she served as its editor for over twenty years. In 1890 the two woman suffrage groups merged and Lucy Stone chaired the new executive committee. She died in Dorchester, Massachusetts, in 1893.

Alice Stone Blackwell, *Lucy Stone: Pioneer of Women's Rights*. Boston: Little, Brown, 1930.

Elinor Rice Hays, *Morning Star: A Biography of Lucy Stone, 1818–1893*. New York: Octagon Books, 1978.

SOJOURNER TRUTH was born in Ulster County in upstate New York about 1790. After being freed in 1827, she and her family moved to New York City. A deeply religious woman, she believed that she was divinely instructed to travel and preach. In 1843 she gave up the name Isabella Hardenburgh, took instead Sojourner Truth, and began her travels. She met the leading spokesmen of the antislavery movement in Northampton, Massachusetts, and soon became an abolitionist speaker. She preached about abolition throughout the Midwest, speaking in Ohio, Indiana, and Michigan. Sojourner Truth was also an advocate of women's rights and spoke at suffrage meetings. In her later years she worked in Washington, D.C., where she sought to improve the living conditions of poor blacks. She died in Battle Creek, Michigan, in 1883.

Jacqueline Bernard, *Journey Toward Freedom: The Story of Sojourner Truth*. New York: Norton, 1967.

Karlyn K. Campbell, "Style and Content in the Rhetoric of Early Afro-American Feminists." *Quarterly Journal of Speech* 72 (1986): 434–445.

Arthur H. Fauset, *Sojourner Truth: God's Faithful Pilgrim*. New York: Russell and Russell, 1971. Originally published, 1938.

J. Lebedun, "Harriet Beecher Stowe's Interest in Sojourner Truth, Black Feminist." *American Literature* 46 (1974): 359–363.

Hertha E. Pauli, *Her Name Was Sojourner Truth.* New York: Appleton-Century-Crofts, 1962.

Gerard A. Wagner, "Sojourner Truth: God's Appointed Apostle of Reform." *Southern Speech Communication Journal* 28 (1962): 123–130.

BOOKER T. WASHINGTON was born in Virginia in 1856, the son of a plantation slave. After the Civil War was over, he worked at various jobs in West Virginia and obtained a rudimentary education. In 1872 he returned to Virginia to attend a school for freed blacks, the Hampton Institute. Washington left Hampton in 1875, taught school for two years, and attended Wayland Seminary in Washington, D.C. He went back to Hampton Institute to teach in 1879; two years later Washington was selected to head a new normal school for blacks in Alabama, the Tuskegee Normal and Industrial Institute. Washington approached the challenge vigorously and built Tuskegee into one of the most important and respected centers of black education in the world. Washington urged blacks to concentrate on acquiring skills and education before pressing for their rights as citizens and he accepted segregation as inevitable, at least until blacks had gained more economic security. His emphasis on the need for the development of economic enterprise among blacks led Washington to found the National Negro Business League in 1900. Washington died in Tuskegee in 1915.

L. J. Friedman, "Life in the Lion's Mouth: Another Look at Booker T. Washington." *Journal of Negro History* 59 (1974): 337–351.

Louis R. Harlan, *Booker T. Washington: The Making of a Black Leader, 1856–1901.* New York: Oxford UP, 1975.

Thomas E. Harris and Patrick C. Kennicott, "Booker T. Washington: A Study of Conciliatory Rhetoric." *Southern States Speech Journal* 37 (1971): 47–59.

Hugh Hawkins, ed., *Booker T. Washington and His Critics: The Problem of Negro Leadership.* Boston: Heath, 1962.

Robert L. Heath, "A Time for Silence: Booker T. Washington in Atlanta." *Quarterly Journal of Speech* 64 (1978): 385–399.

Emma Thornbrough, ed., *Booker T. Washington.* Englewood Cliffs, NJ: Prentice-Hall, 1969.

Booker T. Washington, *Up from Slavery: An Autobiography.* New York: Dodd Mead, 1965. Originally published, 1900.

DANIEL WEBSTER was born in New Hampshire in 1782. He graduated Phi Beta Kappa from Dartmouth College in 1801, studied law, and opened a practice in 1805. An opponent of Jefferson and of the war with Great Britain, Webster was elected as a Federalist to Congress in 1812. At the end of his second term he moved to Boston and launched a highly successful career as a lawyer. He argued several constitutional cases and became known as a defender of a strong national government. He also developed a reputation as a commemorative orator, chiefly through his speeches given at Plymouth in 1820 and at the laying of the Bunker Hill Monument cornerstone in 1825, and through his famous eulogy of Adams and Jefferson in 1826. After having served in the House of Representatives, Webster was elected to the Senate in 1827 and soon became leader of the newly emerging Whig Party that formed in opposition to President Jackson. In 1830 he defended the Union in a famous rebuttal of the sectionalist views of Senator Robert Hayne of South Carolina. He was unsuccessful in his bid for the presidency in 1836; in 1840 Webster supported William Henry Harrison for President and afterwards became Harrison's secretary of state. Back in the Senate in 1845, Webster opposed the Mexican War and the annexation of Texas. In 1848 Webster again aspired to the presidency, but the military hero Zachary Taylor was nominated instead by the Whigs. Webster's support for Clay's compromise was crucial to its passage in 1850, but New Englanders denounced Webster for his acceptance of the harsher measures for returning fugitive slaves enacted as a part of the compromise. Webster was once more appointed secretary of state, this time by Millard Fillmore in 1850. Webster died at Green Harbor, his estate in Marshfield, Massachusetts, in 1852.

Paul Arntson and Craig R. Smith, "The Seventh of March Address: A Mediating Influence." *Southern Speech Communication Journal* 40 (1975): 288–301.

Irving H. Bartlett, *Daniel Webster*. New York: Norton, 1978.

Maurice G. Baxter, *Daniel Webster and the Supreme Court*. Amherst, MA: U of Massachusetts Press, 1966.

John W. Black, "Webster's Peroration in the Dartmouth College Case." *Quarterly Journal of Speech* 23 (1937): 636–642.

Richard N. Current, *Daniel Webster and the Rise of National Conservatism*. Boston: Little, Brown, 1955.

Arthur A. Eisenstadt, "Daniel Webster and the Seventh of March." *Southern Speech Communication Journal* 20 (1954): 136–147.

Robert G. Gunderson, "Webster in Linsey-Woolsey." *Quarterly Journal of Speech* 37 (1951): 23–30.

Glen E. Mills, "Daniel Webster's Principles of Rhetoric." *Communication Monographs* 9 (1942): 124–140.

James E. Sayer, "Webster v. Hayne: A Reanalysis of Motive." *Central States Speech Journal* 30 (1979): 241–249.

Craig R. Smith, "Daniel Webster's July 17th Address: A Mediating Influence in the 1850 Compromise." *Quarterly Journal of Speech* 71 (1985): 349–361.

Alfred Steinberg, *Daniel Webster*. New York: Putnam, 1959.

WILLIAM ALLEN WHITE was born in Emporia, Kansas, in 1868. He attended the University of Kansas but left school to become business manager of the El Dorado (Kansas) *Republican*. He moved to Kansas City and was editorial writer for the *Star* from 1892 to 1895. In that year he bought the Emporia *Gazette* and he was editor and publisher of this newspaper until his death. White's writings gained him national attention. A Republican, White attacked the populists in 1896 and was credited with helping McKinley carry the presidency. Known as "the sage of Emporia." White was considered an authentic voice of the Midwest, and he won a Pulitzer Prize for his editorials in 1923. Published collections of his editorials, stories, and sketches were highly popular, and his autobiography, first published in 1946, was widely read and admired. White died in Emporia in 1944.

Frank C. Clough, *William Allen White of Emporia*. New York: McGraw-Hill, 1941.

David Hinshaw, *A Man from Kansas: The Story of William Allen White*. New York: G. P. Putnam's Sons, 1945.

Walter Johnson, *William Allen White's America*. New York: Holt, 1947.

William Allen White, *Selected Letters of William Allen White, 1899–1943*, Walter Johnson, ed. New York: Greenwood Press, 1968.

FRANCES WILLARD was born in Churchville, New York, in 1839. She graduated from North Western Female College in Evanston, Illinois, in 1859 and began a career as an educator. She was president of Evanston College for Ladies from 1871 to 1873 and became Dean of Women when that institution merged with Northwestern University in 1873. When she resigned as dean the following year, Willard turned her full attention to social reform. An advocate of women's rights and the suffrage, she was most closely identified with the temperance movement. She held various offices in the Women's Christian Temperance Union before becoming president of the National W.C.T.U. in 1879, a post that she held for almost twenty years. She also served, from 1891 onward, as president of the World W.C.T.U. A captivating speaker, Willard visited several states recruiting new members for the W.C.T.U. She organized the Home-Protection Party, which later merged with the Prohibition Party, in an effort to exert direct political influence. Willard died in 1898.

Ruth B.A. Bordin, *Frances Willard: A Biography*. Chapel Hill, NC: U of North Carolina Press, 1986.

Mary E. Earhart, *Frances Willard: From Prayers to Politics*. Chicago: U of Chicago Press, 1944.

Lydia Trowbridge, *Frances Willard of Evanston*. Chicago: Willett, Clark and Co., 1938.

Frances Willard, *Glimpses of Fifty Years: The Autobiography of an American Woman*. Boston: G. M. Smith, 1889.

ROGER WILLIAMS was born in England in 1603. He studied at Cambridge and in 1628 became chaplain to a wealthy family in Essex. Attracted to the Puritan wing of the Church, Williams in 1629 attended a meeting of Puritan leaders, including John Cotton and Thomas Hooker, to consider emigration to America. Williams arrived in Massachusetts in 1631 and declined an appointment to the Salem church since he believed that it was not appropriately separated from the Church of England. Williams' views brought him constantly into friction with both church and civil authorities, and he was banished from the colony in 1635. The next year he and a few followers founded Providence and established the principle of religious liberty in the new Rhode Island colony. In 1642 Williams sailed for England to secure a charter for his new colony. While he was there he entered into several church-state controversies, publishing works that defended separatism in the church and attacking Parliamentary authority in influencing church policy. He also published his indictment of religious persecution, *The Bloudy Tenent of Persecution* at this time. Back in Rhode Island in 1644 as leader of this unique, democratic colony, Williams continued to write against the contention that the government should sustain the church. Williams was forced to make yet another trip to England in 1651 to have his charter confirmed. In his later years Williams, who had some sympathy for the Quakers, entered into extended theological debates with them in an effort to correct what he thought of as their errors; he defended the Quakers' right to practice their religion, however, at a time when they were uniformly persecuted. Williams died in Providence in 1683.

Leon R. Camp, "Roger Williams: Rhetoric or Ranting?" *Communication Quarterly* 12 (1964): 21–22.

Jeanette Eaton, *Lone Journey: The Life of Roger Williams*. New York: Harcourt, 1966.

John Garrett, *Roger Williams, Witness Beyond Christiendom*. New York: Macmillan, 1970.

S. D. Goulding, "Roger Williams of Rhode Island." *History Today* 25 (1975): 741–748.

Perry Miller, *Roger Williams: His Contribution to the American Tradition*. Indianapolis: Bobbs-Merrill, 1953.

Oscar S. Straus, *Roger Williams: The Pioneer of Religious Liberty*. Freeport, NY: Books for Libraries Press, 1970.

WENDELL WILLKIE was born in Elwood, Indiana, in 1892, graduated from Indiana University and Indiana University Law School, and practiced for a short time with his father. After a tour of duty in the army during World War I, Willkie became a corporation lawyer in Akron, Ohio, and then joined a firm specializing in utility law. In the 1920's Willkie was a Democrat and, although he did not hold any elective office, was a highly regarded speaker and a delegate to the 1924 Democratic National Convention. A member of a New York law firm that represented a utility holding company—the Commonwealth and Southern Corporation—Willkie impressed its president, Bernard Cobb, who selected Willkie as his successor when Cobb retired in 1933. As president of Commonwealth and Southern, Willkie was an outspoken opponent of New Deal domestic policies, particularly the government's rural electrification plans. He soon attained national prominence as a leading spokesman for those business interests opposed to President Roosevelt. Willkie was nominated for President by the Republican Party at its 1940 Philadelphia convention, and he went on to mount a vigorous campaign against FDR. After his defeat, Willkie espoused a doctrine of "loyal opposition," in which the President could expect support on international issues and criticism on domestic matters. Roosevelt sent Willkie abroad on various missions during the war and Willkie became known for his strong internationalist views. He called for international cooperation in his popular book, *One World*, published in 1943. Willkie died of a heart attack in New York in 1944.

Mary E. Dillon, *Wendell Willkie, 1892–1944*. Philadelphia: Lippincott, 1952.

Edward N. Doan, "Willkie Received Unparalleled Newspaper Circulation Support." *Journalism Quarterly* 18 (1941): 137–145.

Will D. Howe, "Wendell Willkie: The 'Man Thinking.'" *American Scholar* 14 (1944): 7–8.

Carl Allen Pitt, "An Analysis and Criticism of the 1940 Campaign Speeches of

Wendell L. Willkie." *Communication Monographs* 21 (1954): 64–72.

Muriel Rukeyser, *One Life.* New York: Simon and Schuster, 1957.

Henry Z. Scheele, "The Nomination of Wendell Willkie." *Communication Quarterly* 16 (1968): 45–50.

William Severn, *Toward One World: The Life of Wendell Willkie.* New York: I. Washburn, 1967.

WOODROW WILSON was born in Staunton, Virginia, in 1856. The son of a Presbyterian minister who had been a chaplain in the Confederate army, Wilson moved with his family to various places in the South. He graduated from Princeton University, was admitted to the bar, but left law to study history at Johns Hopkins University, where he obtained his Ph.D. After a career as teacher and historian, Wilson joined the faculty of Princeton and became president of the University in 1902. Nominated by the Democrats for the governorship of New Jersey in 1910, Wilson went on to win the election. He quickly won a reputation as a reformer and became a contender for the Democratic presidential nomination, which he secured in 1912. Wilson defeated the incumbent President, William Howard Taft, when the Bull Moose candidacy of Theodore Roosevelt split the Republican vote. Wilson hoped to keep America neutral when war broke out in Europe, and he attempted on several occasions to mediate that dispute. He was reelected in 1916 on a campaign slogan that proclaimed: "He kept us out of war." America was, however, drawn into the war and on April 2, 1917, President Wilson asked Congress for a declaration of war against Germany. In establishing America's war aims, Wilson called for an ultimate settlement of the war based on the right of European peoples to self-determination and on democratic principles. The Peace Conference in which Wilson took an active part called for the formulation of a League of Nations and, although Wilson campaigned vigorously for ratification of the treaty, the anti-League forces in the Senate defeated the treaty. Wilson broke down on a speaking tour and returned to Washington, where he suffered a stroke in October 1919. In 1920, with the election of the Republican President Warren Harding, hopes for the League were extinguished, and America soon concluded a separate peace with Germany. Wilson left office in 1920 and died in 1924.

John Braeman, *Wilson.* Englewood Cliffs, NJ: Prentice-Hall, 1972.

Henry W. Bragdon, *Woodrow Wilson: The Academic Years.* Cambridge, MA: Belknap Press, 1967.

Herbert L. Carson, "War Requested: Wilson-Roosevelt." *Central States Speech Journal* 10 (1958): 28–32.

Elmer E. Cornwell, "The Press Conferences of Woodrow Wilson." *Journalism Quarterly* 39 (1962): 292–300.

Hardin Craig, "Woodrow Wilson as an Orator." *Quarterly Journal of Speech* 38 (1952): 145–148.

Patrick D. Devlin, *Too Proud to Fight: Woodrow Wilson's Neutrality.* New York: Oxford UP, 1974.

Clari R. Henderlider, "Woodrow Wilson's Speeches on the League of Nations, September 4–25, 1919." *Communication Monographs* 13 (1946): 23–34.

Arthur S. Link, *Wilson.* Princeton, NJ: Princeton UP, 1960.

Dayton D. McKeon, "Notes on Woodrow Wilson's Speeches." *Quarterly Journal of Speech* 16 (1930): 176–184.

Silas B. McKinley, *Woodrow Wilson, A Biography*. New York: Praeger, 1957.

Robert T. Oliver, "Wilson's Rapport with His Audience." *Quarterly Journal of Speech* 27 (1941): 79–90.

George C. Osborn, "Woodrow Wilson as a Speaker." *Southern Speech Communication Journal* 22 (1956): 61–72.

Ronald F. Reid, "The Young Woodrow Wilson's Political Laboratories." *Southern Speech Communication Journal* 28 (1963): 227–235.

Alfred Steinberg, *Woodrow Wilson*. New York: Putnam, 1961.

J. A. Thompson, "Woodrow Wilson and World War I: A Reappraisal." *Journal of American Studies* 19 (1985): 325–348.

Joseph P. Tumulty, *Woodrow Wilson as I Know Him*. New York: AMS Press, 1970. Originally published, 1921.

JOHN WINTHROP was born in Suffolk, England, in 1588. While a student at Cambridge University, Winthrop experienced a religious conversion that led him eventually to Puritanism. He was a successful attorney and justice of the peace when, in 1629, Charles I and Bishop Laud attempted to rid the church of Puritanism and enforce conformity. Winthrop had been dissatisfied with his life in England for some time, and he agreed to a proposal made by a group of wealthy Puritans that he lead a band of settlers to the newly chartered Massachusetts Bay colony. In 1630 Winthrop, as first governor of the colony, arrived in Massachusetts. He was not inclined to democracy and only grudgingly allowed settlers other than the original ones to acquire the right to vote, and he insisted that they be members of the church. Dedicated to rule by magistrates who could be relied upon to carry out the will of God, Winthrop often found himself in disputes over the extension of popular rights. Winthrop was a dedicated public official whose personal fortune was often turned to public purposes. He was not tolerant of dissent, however, and was instrumental in the banishment of both Anne Hutchinson and Roger Williams. He died in Boston in 1649.

Charles E. Banks, *The Winthrop Fleet of 1630*. Baltimore: Genealogical Publishing Co., 1968. Originally published, 1930.

Richard S. Dunn, "John Winthrop Writes His Journal." *William and Mary Quarterly* 41 (1984): 185–212.

R. L. Ferm, "John Winthrop, the Infidel and the Bicentennial." *Religion in Life* 45 (1976): 146–151.

Edmund S. Morgan, *The Puritan Dilemma: The Story of John Winthrop*. Boston: Little, Brown, 1958.

Robert G. Raymer, *John Winthrop, Governor of the Company of Massachusetts Bay of New England*. New York: Vantage Press, 1963.